The Social Psychology *of* Health

To the turtle.

She only makes progress when she sticks her neck out.

The Social Psychology *of* Health

Essays and Readings

EDITORS

WILLIAM D. MARELICH
California State University, Fullerton

JEFF S. ERGER
University of Wisconsin–Eau Claire

SAGE Publications
International Educational and Professional Publisher
Thousand Oaks ▪ London ▪ New Delhi

For information:

Sage Publications, Inc.
2455 Teller Road
Thousand Oaks, California 91320
E-mail: order@sagepub.com

Sage Publications Ltd.
1 Oliver's Yard
55 City Road
London EC1Y 1SP
United Kingdom

Sage Publications India Pvt. Ltd.
B-42, Panchsheel Enclave
Post Box 4109
New Delhi 110 017 India

Printed in the United States of America

Library of Congress Cataloging-in-Publication data

The social psychology of health : essays and readings / edited by William D. Marelich, Jeff S. Erger.
p. cm.
Includes bibliographical references and index.
ISBN 0-7619-2821-9 (pbk.)
1. Clinical health psychology. 2. Social medicine. 3. Medicine and psychology. I. Marelich, William D. II. Erger, Jeff S. R726.7 .S697 2004 616.89—dc22
2003024761

03 04 05 06 07 10 9 8 7 6 5 4 3 2 1

Acquiring Editor: Jim Brace-Thompson
Editorial Assistant: Karen Ehrmann
Production Editor: Sanford Robinson
Typesetter: C&M Digitals (P) Ltd.
Copy Editor: Carla Freeman
Indexer: Karen McKenzie
Cover Designer: Michelle Lee Kenny

Brief Contents

Detailed Contents

PREFACE

SARS.

Sudden Acute Respiratory Syndrome.

When we began writing this book, SARS did not exist. Now, a year later, it does. This emergence afforded us an ideal testing ground for the premise of this book. While SARS was breaking, we were teaching classes on Health Psychology and Medical Sociology. Our students were reading the readings included in this book, and applying those readings to what they were hearing on the news daily.

Our goals in teaching are many, but always included is the goal of encouraging "critical thinking" from our students. This is a wonderful goal, but one that is hard to produce and very difficult to measure. Of course we like it when people learn about specific issues such as HIV/AIDS or heart disease. However, we love it when students learn to apply general ideas from social psychology to emerging health issues. The readings in this volume are designed to do that—to draw on past research in such a way as to be valuable today and in the future. There are no articles on SARS in this volume, but the concepts, theories, and research findings included should be useful in understanding SARS and future disease outbreaks common within societies.

Our students started with a basic question about SARS, one common when dealing with health issues. They asked, "Will I get it?" This led to discussions about disease etiology, transmission vectors, and basic epidemiological concepts. The question of "Will I get sick?" developed into "Why are people getting SARS, and how big of a problem will it be?"

Soon, students began to wonder what can and should be done about SARS. What public health measures were being taken to combat the spread of the disease, and would those measures be effective? How did the measures being taken compare with past public health "emergencies"? Were lessons learned from the past, or were old mistakes being repeated? Was China's reaction in the early stages of SARS problematic in the same ways (and for the same reasons) as Western reactions to the initial stages of the spread of AIDS?

Student trips overseas were canceled. A travel warning was issued to Toronto, Canada. Were these appropriate decisions? Were they based on medical science, or other issues such as legal liability for sponsoring such trips? How was government policy being implemented and changed by SARS? What was the economic impact on the world economy of SARS and the decreased travel that came from the *fear* of SARS? What policy actors were bringing political pressures to bear in fighting for their interests?

Our students asked all of these questions and more. They took the concepts in this book and applied them by digging under the headlines on the nightly news. They found current sources daily, reading government statements and medical reports, and checked the Centers for Disease Control Web site (http://www.cdc.gov). More important, they were critical consumers of this information. They looked at individual, group, and institutional behaviors and how those behaviors together created what they were seeing happening with SARS. This made us very happy.

This book is not a textbook per se. It does not cover all the vast and varied areas of the social psychology of health in a linear way. Instead, it roams far and wide, touching some areas lightly and exploring others in great detail—a winding path through the many issues that are the *social psychology of health.* After making the journey down this winding path, you the reader should be better able to traverse the wilds of "health" issues that you encounter every day of your life. And we wish you a healthful journey.

Introduction

Jeff S. Erger and William D. Marelich

Be careful about reading health books. You may die of a misprint.

Mark Twain

We would like you to do a simple thought experiment to start your exploration into the social psychology of health.

Both of us have picked a student from our introductory level classes. Both students are 19-year-old male sophomores, sitting in the back row of a lecture hall. Both are Caucasian, 6 feet tall, and of average build. Both are dressed in blue jeans and a T-shirt with the university name on it (one of the universities is based in an urban setting in southern California, the other in a small town in western Wisconsin). Which is more likely to be an alcoholic by the time he is 25 years old?

Does that sound like an impossible question to answer? There seems to be little to go on in making a judgment, and without more information, you might as well flip a coin to decide which one to choose. However, with more information, you might be able to improve your odds to better than 50%. What information would you want to know?

Perhaps you would like there to be a genetic marker for alcoholism, then test the genome of both young men to see whether one has the marker. Does either have a family history of alcoholism? How do they react to stress, and does one use alcohol as a "coping" mechanism? Does one currently abstain from alcohol entirely? What are their attitudes about alcohol use in particular and health in general? Those all seem like good questions to ask and should improve your odds of a correct prediction. Seeking differences between the two students is a very scientific approach.

Keep in mind that you already hold in your hands information that shows one difference between the two students, that of their locations. One is in an urban setting in southern California, and the other is in a small town in western Wisconsin. Are there any differences between these two situations that are relevant to the consumption of alcohol? What if you found out that Wisconsin has 7 of the top 10 cities in terms of "taverns per capita?" What if you learned that small towns in Wisconsin have a tavern-friendly culture and many families go to taverns for a few hours on the weekend, sending their children to the back room to play games while they have a few drinks and watch a football game? What if you learned that Wisconsin has one of the lowest beer taxes in the nation?

Now you might be thinking that the best choice is the student in Wisconsin, but is that really the case? Alcoholism is a diagnosis, a medical condition, and a label that means a person is having problems with alcohol. How is this label applied? Medical professionals will apply the label, but so do friends and family, coworkers, and neighbors. In an environment where many people are drinking and drinking is seen as normal behavior, is a person more or less likely to be seen as having problems due to drinking? Don't forget that even in a situation where drinking is normal, many people do not use alcohol at all.

So, which student is more likely to become an alcoholic? The answer is "It depends." It depends on a variety of factors, including biological, psychological, and sociological. Individuals vary, their backgrounds vary, their interpersonal networks vary, their environments vary, and their reactions to those environments vary. To focus completely on one aspect of the human condition and ignore others can lead to missing the reality of a situation. To focus on individual factors ignores the huge influence of social groups and institutions. To focus on society ignores variation in individuals. To focus on both society and the individual and how they interact is the approach of social psychology. We are social psychologists, and this is our approach.

What Is Health?

If you look at the table of contents of this book, you will notice that most of the articles have very little to do with "health" and being healthy, but rather look at illness and how we treat illness. This is partially because illness is easy to identify, whereas health is difficult to measure, except as the absence of illness. However, many have been critical of the "absence of illness" definition of health and have attempted to conceptualize health independent of illness.

One such conceptualization of health might include the notion of "metabolic efficiency." Our levels of health can be considered higher as our metabolisms work better. This provides a clear, quantifiable measure of health that has a certain attraction. We could come up with tests for metabolic efficiency, go to a testing center, then have a number that would track our health, much as cholesterol screenings give us numbers to track our "good" and "bad" cholesterol numbers. Unfortunately, such a definition cannot cover many of the issues involved with mental health, so we need to seek a broader definition than simply "metabolic efficiency."

Consider the definition of health used by the World Health Organization (WHO): "a state of complete physical, mental and social well-being and not merely the absence of disease or infirmity." But what is "well-being"? Isn't that just another term for health, and so isn't the WHO definition circular? Also, doesn't the inclusion of "social well-being" make for a definition that can cover every aspect of life? This potentially would make levels of economic inequality, political participation, or the quality of a community's schools a health issue. Such a broad definition leads to a concept of health little different from the concept of humanity itself. So, is there a way to define health that is neither too narrow nor too broad, that will encompass both health and illness?

We like to think of health as "the overall physical and mental condition of a human being at a given time." Note that this definition does not include notions of illness or well-being, but merely of condition. That would make the social psychology of health an area of study that looks at psychological and social processes that affect the physical and mental condition of human beings. The readings in each of the sections of this book are designed to give some insight into this process.

The Structure of the Book

Why did we decide to write this book? We both love to teach about the issues of health, and we both do research on issues that revolve around health. We began working together on a research project a few years ago and quickly found that we saw the world through very different eyes. While we are both social psychologists, one of us was trained by psychologists and the other by sociologists. This made for some very interesting conversations, where each of us would throw out concepts and research findings that the other was not very familiar with. Combine this with the fact that we were also working with medical doctors, epidemiologists, and others who had very different training and perspectives from us, and you can imagine that there was a lot of positive debate going on. Take one empirical situation, in our case HIV medication treatments, and attack the issue and problem from a variety of perspectives, and you quickly strengthen your own ideas or they get shot down. After a while, we realized that by listening to a variety of voices, we learned a great deal about what we were interested in, and we did so very quickly indeed.

We tried to take this experience into our classes, and to some extent succeeded. We wanted a book that would be as wide ranging as our own social psychological perspectives had become, but we simply could not find one out there. Books tend to hug academic boundaries, being either psychological or sociological in focus. So, we provided readings for our students with an eye toward teaching important information and spurring classroom discussion. We like to be able to challenge our psychology majors with sociological readings, and our sociology majors with psychological readings, much in the same way as we challenged each other when doing our research. We also included readings that explore social psychological issues from areas typically not associated with psychology and sociology, namely, medicine and public health.

As you read these articles, you will be ranging far and wide. Some of the readings are many years old, but they can be considered classic in the sense that they still have important things to say about health processes. Many of these older articles are still referred to in contemporary research, and some of them chart the beginning of ongoing research traditions. Other readings are very recent and deal with issues as current as those in the morning news. Some readings are theoretical and focus on issues and perspectives involved in the study of health, while others are research projects. The research papers included here have a mix of qualitative, descriptive research as well as strict quantitative approaches. With such a wide field of study, we feel it is important that you get a taste for the type of information that is available. However, the readings in this book do not cover every area in the study of health, nor was that our intent. Instead, we tried to pick broad areas and give you a sampling of readings within each of those areas. After reading this book, you should have a good understanding of the field and be ready to delve into areas we have not been able to include given the limited size of a single book of readings. To this end, we have chosen to group the readings into five sections.

The first section of readings, "Foundations," gives an overview of the various perspectives used to study health, including overviews from psychology, sociology, public health, and epidemiology. The various areas are often intertwined, and presenting overviews from each of these areas "back-to-back" allows us to see how the disciplines differ, how they overlap, and how each area informs the others. As you read these articles, keep in mind that you will be encountering the ideas in them throughout the rest of the readings. Sometimes articles will explicitly spell out their perspectives, but often the perspective or perspectives employed will be buried deep in the assumptions underlying the research. Following these overviews, the cause-effect of health is addressed. The *biopsychosocial* model is presented, followed by a reading that explores how deviant behaviors sometimes undergo a transformation and become medicalized and treated as disease. The last article rounds out the section by addressing health outcomes as the ultimate end point for health.

"Health Attitude Change" is the title of Part II, which presents health attitude change models and perspectives. Think about all the activities in our society that are oriented around changing our way of thinking about health and illness, and more important, our way of acting. Every television infomercial for a new diet or exercise machine tries to change our attitudes and behaviors. Every trip to the doctor, every health class in school, every magazine article on how to change our lives and shapes in 30 days, and every news story about a new medical study combine in a constant bombardment to influence our thoughts and actions regarding health. The first reading in this section is a broad overview paper that summarizes individual and group behavioral change issues. Next, detailed articles on some of the more popular behavior change strategies are presented. As you read these articles, focus on how the strategies were implemented, as well as the pros and cons of the various intervention model strategies. The last article looks at the construction of health messages in an effort to make them more effective. After you read this section, ask yourself the following questions. If you wanted to change your friend's behavior, which model would you employ? If you wanted to change the behavior of the population in your city, which model would you employ? How would you shape your message(s) to have the maximum impact on the maximum number of people?

Part III, "The Health Care Setting," looks at patients and health care providers in the health care setting. Consider that you behave one way when sitting in class, but another way when walking across campus between classes, and a totally different way at 11 p.m. on a Saturday night at a party. You are the same person, but the place you find yourself affects how you act to a great extent. School is different from a party. Also, think about your different classes. In a large lecture hall, you will act one way, and professors will tend to act in a certain way. If you are in a class of 20 students, sitting in a circle, you will probably act differently, as will your professors. Both large lecture halls and small classrooms are in a college setting, but the actions and interactions in the two situations are very different. Changes in setting and changes in interactions are intertwined, both at college and in the health care setting.

The first three articles in this section address the patient-provider interaction, incorporating social construction issues, nonverbal cues, and an observational study of interactions. They illustrate how the patient-provider interaction is negotiated and the influencing cues that can drive such interactions. The section closes with the classic article by Rosenthal, showing how simply being in a hospital setting can lead to each action a patient takes contributing to and strengthening an illness diagnosis. We have all been to the doctor and have been or will be in the hospital. As you read the (sometimes extreme) examples of behavior and interpretation of behavior in this section, keep in mind that you have been subject to the same forces that you are reading about. You may not have noticed them, and the content of labels may have been different, but the forces were in play. They will be in play the next time you go to the doctor as well.

The readings in Part IV, "Stress, Coping, and Social Relationships" focus on the identification of potential stressors and the coping strategies and resources available to handle stress. If you get sick with a bad cold or influenza, does anyone take care of you? Perhaps you have a spouse who will or a roommate who will at least run to the store to get you some orange juice and cold-and-flu medicine. Maybe even the knowledge that someone is available to help you is comforting—although you may not require their assistance if you get sick, just knowing they are available may act to increase your well-being. How lucky you are compared with someone who has no one to help them! Now, think about how much more important it would be to have people to help if you were wheelchair bound, or had suffered a stroke, or were recovering from a heart attack. Being ill does not stop the world from turning, much as we would like it to at times. Our social responsibilities continue, even if they are temporarily deferred, and this is a great source of stress. How we cope with our illness affects our level of stress, and how we cope with our stress affects our recovery and/or overall health.

Although these areas are typically broad (stressful events, coping with various illnesses, social support, social networks, etc.), the articles included underscore the main concepts. First, we present two articles looking at stressful life events, appraisal of stressors, and coping resources and strategies. Next, we turn to a basic overview of the effects of social relationships on health. The final readings in this section on responsibility and empowerment are meant to further the stress/coping/relationship area by looking at how individuals, by taking control of their health-related issues, can actually improve health status and health care.

"Health Policy and Future Paths," the final section of readings, considers what we should do as a society about health issues. Historically, governments have responded to health issues in more or less effective ways, and new health issues will arise in coming years that will challenge our health care system. Will we make the mistakes of the past, or will we learn from them? This section begins with health policy issues and the successes of social activism on health. These are followed by the article that brings to the forefront arguments for/against behavior change technologies and their ethics in wide application. The subsection "Looking to the Future of Health" argues for focusing on primary prevention strategies (instead of the typical secondary prevention approach). To close this last section, we have included an article addressing bioterrorism and the inherent social fear associated with it, where fear is itself a very real threat.

Final Note

Your journey through this book will take you on a path that leads you to look at things in a specific order. You will look at the field, the individual, the interaction of individuals, the social networks of relationships and their effects on health, and, finally, consider the level of society and public policy. Keep in mind that these processes can be theoretically separated, but empirically they are intertwined. This should become clear as you read the selections in the first section of this book.

PART I

SOCIAL PSYCHOLOGY OF HEALTH: FOUNDATIONS

Essay: Health and Illness Seen Through Different Lenses

William D. Marelich and Jeff S. Erger

Overviews From Various Fields

Part I begins as an overview of how different scientific disciplines (i.e., psychology, sociology, public health, epidemiology) approach health and illness. As you read, note the similarities across these disciplines, and the differences. What we find fascinating is that many of the similarities across disciplines actually reflect the social psychological perspective.

The health and illness of individuals are affected by many different factors, including factors inherent to individuals' personal dispositions or personalities, the social forces surrounding individuals (e.g., social groups/networks, family, peers), the individuals' physical surroundings (e.g., dwellings, places of work), cultural norms, and the broader social/political environment (e.g., health care availability). No single discipline can fully account for all of these factors within their operating frameworks, nor do they attempt such an undertaking. Some of these disciplines focus more on individual and small-group factors, while others focus more on the broader societal influences. As we noted earlier, both of our disciplines (sociology and psychology) are complementary in understanding the interaction between health and social factors. Here, we provide you perspectives from health psychology, medical sociology, public health, and epidemiology, which together help explain these factors.

Shelley Taylor's article on health psychology starts the section and provides a general overview of the field. The field of health psychology primarily focuses on the effects of personal dispositions (e.g., individuals' optimistic/pessimistic, negative emotional states) on health and illness, and secondarily includes social-environmental factors (e.g., social support and social interactions, ways of coping with stress, broader health system constraints). Both personal dispositions and social-environmental factors are seen as moderating health diagnoses, treatment, and outcomes. Although published almost 15 years ago, Taylor's conclusions are as relevant today as they were back in 1990. Of interest regarding this article is that it may be viewed as a definitive turning point in the firm establishment of Health Psychology within the broader field of psychology and also the formal acceptance of psychologists into the study of health and illness.

Brown's article follows next, providing an overview of medical sociology. In his article, Brown notes that medical sociology is concerned with the social structures and the social construction of health and illness. Unlike health psychology, which includes a focus on personal dispositions, medical sociology is concerned with broader structural issues that affect health, including social order, rules, institutions, and policy. The constructionists or interactionists focus on *interaction* between human beings in a given *situation or context* and the meaning they evoke through this interaction as being the prime focus of sociological inquiry, and take as one of their primary assumptions about social life the maxim by W.I. Thomas, "That which is seen as real will be real in its consequences." In general, medical sociology attempts to explain health at three levels: micro, meso, and macro. The *microlevel* focuses on individual actions and communications with others and how these communications create ordered patterns, the *mesolevel* looks at issues related to medical education and settings in which health care occurs, while the *macrolevel* is concerned with the structure of the health care system and health policy. The occurrence of disease is viewed through a "social lens," with the suggestion that resulting biomedical problems can be influenced by social forces.

We next go on to the public health perspective, which is an area that many health psychology texts underemphasize. We feel Mullan's article is an excellent overview regarding the intent of public health and what professionals in the public health field have to do to ensure that the greater public health is maintained. He illustrates the many roles that public health professionals must adopt to carry out their goals, which include balancing politics and science in an effort to maintain and improve the greater public health. As *Don Quixote,* the public health official is an idealist striving for the greater good against odds and surrounded by naysayers. As *Machiavelli,* the public health official must be crafty and cunning regarding implementation of public health rules and regulations in an effort to balance the concerns of the many stakeholders who are affected (e.g., the public, organizations, businesses, community groups, etc.). Finally, as *Robin Hood,* the public health official has to have the political savvy and professional stamina to address health issues where they are most widely needed. Typically, these are areas associated with lower socioeconomic populations or populations associated with negative public stigma (e.g., those with HIV/AIDS, drug users). Thus, funds must be constantly obtained to ensure that proper public health programs are in place to serve these populations.

The last field we address in the first section is epidemiology. *Epidemiology* is the study of disease patterns, their occurrence, and the disease-influencing factors that occur in populations. Epidemiology may be viewed as a broad "reasoning process" in which disease etiology and spread begin as puzzlelike problems that may be solved through logical reasoning (implemented via epidemiological observations and biostatistics). We included an article on an epidemiology investigation to illustrate how disease outbreaks can start simply with a microbe introduced into a population and how it is subsequently spread across that population. And how is this related to social psychology? Typically, disease spread is spirited by social activities that subsequently place individuals in situations where disease exposure is heightened. In other words, individuals' social behaviors can put them "at risk" for contracting and spreading diseases. Hence, it is understanding these social activities and their association with the spread of microbes that concerns social psychologists.

The article by MacDonald, Spengler, Hatheway, Hargrett, and Cohen is a formal disease investigation of an outbreak of *Type A botulism,* applying epidemiological methods. This article clearly illustrates the use of science and problem solving to discern the patterns of disease within this population. As you read this disease outbreak investigation, realize that such rigorous epidemiologic investigations go on constantly within your area health department.

Cause-Effect and Health Status

What causes an illness? Simple question, right? You feel rather ill, and at some point you go see a health care provider, who will take your temperature, look at your throat (they always do, don't they?), listen to your chest and make you cough, and maybe draw some blood for testing. And from all of this, what do they find? Germs, viruses, and bacteria: the microbes that cause illness.

Yet what about social psychological causes of illness? You might be surprised to know that psychological and social forces can lead to serious illness, even death, without any microbe being part of the etiology. For example, say you have a friend who experiences a death of a close family member. During the month following this event, you notice your friend is exhibiting lackluster behavior, appears somewhat depressed, can't concentrate on his tasks, and generally is nonsocial. Is your friend suffering from an illness? Well, his behaviors do appear to be affected, and an etiology of the illness can be surmised (i.e., the death of the family member). One can even argue there may be a cure for such an illness (you should have guessed by now, the illness we are referring to is *grief*), namely, some type of interpersonal counseling or even doing nothing (e.g., "time heals all wounds"). Yet if your friend were to go to a physician, would the physician "diagnose" your friend with some type of ailment? Would the physician prescribe any type of medication to help your friend "get through the tough times?"

Today, such an experience would probably be treated as a form of illness, and the health care provider might even prescribe an antidepressant to help your friend. However, 30 years ago, a person presenting to a physician for such an ailment might have been tested for various biomedical causes, and finding none, the physician might have simply dismissed the patient. The "change" that has taken place over the past 30 years has been the general adoption of the *biopsychosocial model* in the medical sciences, which incorporates both psychological and social influences as affecting health and illness. In presenting the "grief" example, we have borrowed from the first reading in this section by Engel, who makes a call for the medical sciences to replace the biomedical model with the biopsychosocial model. Engel shares his frustration with the existing biomedical model and provides background on its historic origins and limitations. Next, he outlines the advantages of the biopsychosocial model, with an application to "grief." It is interesting to look back on this early argument for integrating psychological and social issues into the treatment of general health and illness, for it allows us to see how far the medical sciences have come in accepting the social causes of illness. Next time you go to your health care provider, take special care in what your provider asks you: If he or she inquires about stresses in your life, family situations, or work pressures, then indeed your provider is attempting to discern any social influences of your presenting ailment.

While Engel focuses on the individual and how the social context affects individuals, the next article by Peter Conrad (who takes a decidedly constructionist stand) suggests that some diseases are in fact a product of social forces. He illustrates this idea using *hyperkinesis,* also known as attention deficit/hyperactive disorder. ADHD affects anywhere from 3% to 5% of all children in the United States, or about 2 million children, and individuals with this disorder exhibit hyperactive and impulsive behaviors and show an inability to concentrate on tasks. This, in turn, can negatively affect their interactions with others (e.g., peers, parents, teachers) and performance (e.g., education, employment).

According to Conrad, the "discovery" and treatment of hyperkinesis may have actually been driven by pressures to provide individualistic reasons for hyperactive/impulsive behaviors that have been labeled as deviant by our society. Furthermore, government action helped solidify the disorder *as a disorder,* and the pharmaceutical industry is also implicated in establishing the disorder. Given these factors, the etiology of hyperkinesis is *social psychological,* driven by social and political factors. Unlike the grief example presented by Engel, with the etiology of loss of a loved one, the underlying biomedical cause of hyperkinesis is not available. Therefore, this grouping of deviant behaviors has been "made real" or reified into the disorder called "hyperkinesis" by our society. And now that it has been made real, it may be treated.

The article by Conrad may be viewed as controversial and may even be upsetting to those of you who may be diagnosed with ADHD ("How can Conrad say that my ADHD is a socially constructed illness? What I have is a real illness!"). Yet—and this is one of the points of understanding health from a social psychological perspective—hyperkinesis/ADHD is a real disorder *with an etiology that is socially derived.*

Health Outcomes

Earlier, we asked, "What is health?" and offered a very broad definition, that of "the overall physical and mental condition of a human being at a given time." Part of the attraction of this definition is that it can accommodate both biomedical and biopsychosocial issues in regard to health. Furthermore, the definition is inclusive of issues related to health outcomes such as behavioral functioning, quality of life, and mortality.

The importance of health outcomes as they are applied to health-related interventions and their assessments are addressed by the last article in this section. Kaplan argues that the biostatus of an individual is used much of the time as the "sole" indicator of health, while outcomes related to behavioral functioning, quality of life, and mortality are underassessed. For example, prescribed medications can have severe side effects, and even though the biostatus of the individual has been restored, the side effects may actually be creating more problems than the original ailment, thus affecting the quality of life of the individual. Regarding disease-related mortality (i.e., deaths), Kaplan notes that seemingly helpful medical interventions may actually "open the door" for other causes of mortality. To illustrate, he uses research on the effects of aspirin on the reduction of heart attacks (i.e., *myocardial infarctions*). You may even recall news headlines a number of years ago touting the effects: Study participants who took 325 mg of aspirin per day experienced fewer myocardial infarctions compared with a control group receiving a placebo. However, if one looks at overall mortality due to any causes across groups, one finds that the overall death rates did not vary. In fact, there is even some evidence to suggest that those in the "aspirin" group died of other cardiovascular problems such as hemorrhagic stroke that may be associated with the blood-thinning qualities associated with aspirin. Yes, aspirin use did result in a decline in deaths associated with myocardial infarctions, but overall mortality was not affected. According to Kaplan, these are the types of results that should be focused upon—the ultimate health outcomes of general well-being and mortality—not just tissue pathology.

A. Overviews From Various Fields

1

HEALTH PSYCHOLOGY: THE SCIENCE AND THE FIELD

SHELLEY E. TAYLOR

Health psychology is defined as the "educational, scientific, and professional contributions of the discipline of psychology to the promotion and maintenance of health, the prevention and treatment of illness, the identification of etiologic and diagnostic correlates of health, illness, and related dysfunction, and the improvement of the health care system and health policy formation" (Matarazzo, 1980, p. 815). As such, its mission is broad, involving all branches of psychology in virtually every aspect of the health enterprise.

As a field, health psychology has made substantial contributions to the understanding of healthy behaviors and to the comprehension of the myriad factors that undermine health and often lead to illness. Much of the strongest work has involved providing theoretical and conceptual frameworks that elucidate the (non)practice of health behaviors, the role of stress in affecting illness and illness behavior, the representations that people hold regarding their health and illness, and the ways in which people cope with illness and the determinants of their adjustment to it.

These theoretical conceptualizations constitute major contributions inasmuch as they are often lacking in traditional medicine and medical practice. They provide a basis for making sense of otherwise isolated and confusing bits of data. For example, it is difficult for physicians to understand why 93% of patients fail to adhere to certain aspects of their treatment regimens; social psychological models not only make sense of these data but suggest ways of ameliorating them. Theoretical models also suggest new directions for research

EDITOR'S NOTE: From *American Psychologist, 45*, pp. 40-50.

that might otherwise remain elusive and left as isolated observations. Finally, such models often point directly to interventions that can improve the practice of health behavior and adjustment to stress or illness. As such, these interventions constitute both tests and applications of the theories.

Research in behavioral medicine and, correspondingly, in health psychology has taken the position that biological, psychological, and social factors are implicated in all stages of health and illness, ranging from those behaviors and states that keep people healthy to those that produce severe, long-term, and debilitating disease. This position is termed the biopsychosocial model and is a guiding framework for both research and practice (Engel, 1977; Schwartz, 1982). This article will emphasize its guiding role for basic research.

Recent Scientific Developments in Health Psychology

If one asks where the field of health psychology is going, there would be no simple answer. As a microcosm of both psychology and the interdisciplinary endeavor of behavioral medicine, the field is pulled and pushed in many directions simultaneously. In this article, I first attempt to characterize some of the recent scientific developments that illustrate the trends in the field generally. I then focus on some of the major directions and forces affecting the future of the field as a whole. Although an exhaustive analysis of health psychology's contributions is precluded here, a focus on some of the more recent and exciting research developments is instructive in illustrating the progress of the field. For more comprehensive reviews, the reader is referred to overviews of the field (e.g., H.S. Friedman & DiMatteo, 1989; Taylor, 1986) and to the *Annual Review of Psychology,* chapter by Rodin and Salovey (1989).

Health Promotion and Health Habit Modification

Health promotion and primary prevention have been of increasing concern to researchers and practitioners because of changing patterns of illness. In the past 80 years in the United States, the prevalence of acute infectious disorders such as influenza, tuberculosis, measles, and polio has declined while what have been termed the "preventable" disorders have increased, including lung cancer, cardiovascular disease, drug and alcohol abuse, and vehicular accidents (Matarazzo, 1982).

The role of behavioral factors in the development of these diseases and disorders is increasingly clear. For example, 25% of all cancer deaths and approximately 350,000 premature deaths from heart attack could be avoided each year by modifying just one risk factor: smoking (American Heart Association, 1988). A 10% weight reduction in men aged 35 to 55 through dietary modifications and exercise would produce an estimated 20% decrease in coronary artery disease (American Heart Association, 1984a, 1984b; Ashley & Kannel, 1974); it would also lower the degree of degenerative arthritis, gastrointestinal cancer, diabetes, stroke, and heart attack. The percentage of the gross national product that goes for health care has been climbing steadily, in part because the diseases that are currently most prevalent are chronic in nature and thus require continual treatment and monitoring. Successful modification of health behaviors may help to reduce both the numbers of deaths and the incidence of preventable disease as well as make a dent in the more than $400 billion spent yearly on health and illness (cf. Matarazzo, 1982).

The desire to keep people healthy rather than wait to treat them after they become ill has been the impetus for much work on the development of the healthy lifestyle and the modification of faulty health habits. Although a number of conceptual models have been developed both to explain existing health practices and as impetus for changing faulty ones, there is now considerable convergence on the beliefs that contribute to a given health practice. Specifically, we now know that people are most likely to practice a good health measure or to change a faulty one when (a) the threat to health is severe; (b) the perceived personal vulnerability and/or the likelihood of developing the disorder is high; (c) the person believes that he or she is able to perform the response that will reduce the threat (self-efficacy); and (d) the response is effective in overcoming the threat (response efficacy) (Bandura,

1986; Janz & Becker, 1984; Rogers, 1984). These four elements borrow heavily from distinct theoretical models—specifically, Bandura's self-efficacy framework, Roger's protection/motivation theory, and the health belief model—but in practice, most researchers now make efforts to conceptualize and measure all four components.

Conceptual convergence has helped to clarify the difficulty and complexity of actually modifying health behaviors. Health habits predict each other only modestly, and their interrelations may decline with age (see Mechanic, 1979). One of the reasons for this is the fact that each health habit has a complex pattern of etiology, maintenance, change, and relapse (see Jessor & Jessor, 1982, and Leventhal & Cleary, 1980, for discussions of smoking). For example, although peer group influence and issues of personal identity may be bound up in the practice of faulty health habits in adolescence, these factors are less important in considering health habits in adulthood (Botvin & Eng, 1982; Evans et al., 1978). Consequently, it is often difficult to develop intervention programs that will appeal to a broad segment of the population to change some targeted health habit. Whereas individualized appeals often have the greatest impact on behavior, such methods are intensive and expensive and affect only a limited portion of the population at a time. Mass-media appeals, however, sometimes change attitudes about health problems but may produce only modest behavior change (Lau, Kane, Berry, Ware, & Roy, 1980; Leventhal, Meyer, & Nerenz, 1980). How best to combine the advantages of the two methods is a problem on which much recent attention has been focused, and efforts to tailor interventions to designated communities have been one method used (Multiple Risk Factor Intervention Trial Research Group; see Matarazzo, Weiss, Herd, Miller, & Weiss, 1984, for a review).

Perhaps the most important problem for future research is that of preventing relapse (Marlatt & Gordon, 1985), the often-observed phenomenon that, after successfully altering a health practice on their own for weeks or even months, many individuals revert to their former behaviors (Brownell, Marlatt, Lichtenstein, & Wilson, 1986). In this context, it becomes essential to consider not only the short-term effects of interventions designed to modify health habits but also their long-range effectiveness, focusing especially on factors that undermine long-term maintenance of short-term change.

Do Psychological States Cause Illness?

For centuries, philosophers and scientists have speculated about the role that personality factors and coping styles may play in the development of illness. In the 1930s and the 1940s, Flanders Dunbar (1943), Franz Alexander (1950), and their associates developed specific personality profiles of those prone to hypertension, coronary artery disease, cancer, ulcers, rheumatoid arthritis, and other specific disease states. Until recently, however, theory outstripped methodology, so that convincing evidence regarding such relationships was lacking (e.g., Fox, 1978). Several recent research developments have improved this situation.

Early research relating personality factors to disease states focused on whether personality states were related to a host of diseases (the general model) or whether particular personality traits could be related to specific diseases (the specificity model). Research continues to investigate both kinds of links. Recent research using meta-analysis suggests that a general negative affective style marked by depression, anxiety, and, to a lesser extent, hostility may be associated with the development of a broad range of diseases, including coronary artery disease, asthma, headache, ulcers, and arthritis (H.S. Friedman & Booth-Kewley, 1987). Repression, as a coping style, may also be implicated in this cluster (Weinberger, in press). These findings suggest the possibility of a general disease-prone personality, although at present the exact causal nature of the relationship is uncertain. Although negative emotional states certainly result from illness, longitudinal studies also suggest the validity of the reverse direction of causality. The links through which such relationships occur have drawn considerable attention (Matthews, 1988). A negative emotional state may produce pathogenic physiological changes; it may lead people to practice faulty health behaviors; it may produce illness behavior (such as visiting a physician) but no underlying pathology; or it may be associated with illness via other factors in some as-yet-undetermined manner.

These developments have been paralleled by increasing attention to specific models of personality-disease relationships. Chief among these have been the exploration of the Type A behavior syndrome, characterized by competitive drive, impatience, hostility, and rapid speech and motor movements, in the development of coronary heart disease (CHD). Compared to earlier work, recent research has reported weaker links between Type A behavior and CHD (Matthews, 1988), although researchers concur that the structured interview assessment technique shows a stronger relationship to CHD than other measures (H.S. Friedman & Booth-Kewley, 1988; Matthews, 1988). The emphasis on negative emotional states has prompted researchers investigating the role of Type A behavior in the etiology of CHD to focus most closely on hostility as the potential culprit (Dembroski & Costa, 1987; H.S. Friedman & Booth-Kewley, 1987). Other components of the Type A behavior syndrome, such as competitiveness and time urgency, do not seem to be as lethal. Such discoveries lay the groundwork for more sophisticated interventions to modify the Type A behavior syndrome in the hope that those susceptible to it may avoid the development of disease (e.g., Suinn, 1982; Thoresen, Friedman, Gill, & Ulmer, 1982). Research to date suggests that interventions to reduce Type A behavior can be successful (M. Friedman et al., 1986).

For many years, researchers have suspected links between a passive, acquiescent, or repressed personality style and the development or progression of cancer. Although research relating personality variables to the development of cancer is lacking, in large part because such studies are difficult to design (Fox, 1978), some evidence for the role of an acquiescent, repressed personality style in the rapid progression of cancer has accumulated (e.g., Derogatis, Abeloff, & Melasaratos, 1979; Levy, Herberman, Lippman, & d'Angelo, 1987; Levy, Herberman, Maluish, Schlien, & Lippman, 1985). The increasingly sophisticated efforts to relate personality variables to the onset or progression of cancer have been plagued by methodological difficulties: Inasmuch as cancers grow over a long period, it is difficult to establish causality unambiguously (Fox, 1978).

Research on the health significance of negative emotional states is fueled by related discoveries in other fields. Research in psychoimmunology using quasi-experimental studies of samples exposed to stress documents declines in certain indicators of immune activity, such as natural killer cell activity and lymphocyte proliferation in response to mitogenic stimulation (see Kiecolt-Glaser & Glaser, in press, and Stein, Keller, & Schleifer, 1985, for reviews). Although direct links to disease have usually not been established, such results are useful in identifying potential biobehavioral mechanisms whereby psychologic states may exert adverse effects on health. The psychologic factors implicated to date in immunocompromise are the stressful event of bereavement, the state of depression, and stressful events involving the lack or loss of perceived control (see Kiecolt-Glaser & Glaser, in press; Stein et al., 1985). For example, animal studies have suggested a causal chain linking uncontrollable stress to cancer in susceptible animals (Laudenslager, Ryan, Drugan, Hyson, & Maier, 1983), although the relationship appears to be moderated by the temporal course of the stressor in as yet unpredictable ways. This knowledge is now being applied to the effort to understand the role of psychosocial factors in the development of the acquired immunodeficiency syndrome (AIDS) following exposure to the human immunodeficiency virus (HIV) (Kemeny et al., 1989).

Increasingly, researchers are focusing on the potentially protective role of positive emotional states and coping styles in the development of illness. Chief among these are optimism (e.g., Scheier & Carver, 1985) and perceived control. Optimists appear to experience fewer physical symptoms (Scheier & Carver, 1985), and they may show faster or better recoveries from certain illnesses (Scheier et al., in press; see also Peterson, Seligman, & Vaillant, 1988). The importance of self-efficacy beliefs in the practice of health behaviors (Bandura, 1986) and the health benefits of control (e.g., Langer & Rodin, 1976; Rodin, 1986) are well established.

Of the many issues meriting further exploration, a chief concern is whether these psychological variables represent predisposing (or protective) personality states or whether they exert their impacts on health in interaction with situational variables such as stress. For example, whereas some researchers have regarded the Type A constellation as a predisposing personality factor for CHD, others have considered it to be a behavioral syndrome elicited by certain circumstances and not others (see Matthews, 1982). Good cases for particular causal paths have not yet been made. This issue is part of the larger question regarding the pathways by which psychologic factors are involved in the etiology of health and illness, a concern that will guide research in the coming years.

The additional question arises as to whether the literature linking psychosocial factors to the etiology of illness provides any basis for intervention studies. Should we be intervening with people who show pronounced negative affect (H.S. Friedman & Booth-Kewley, 1988) or a pessimistic explanatory style (Peterson et al., 1988) with the goal of improving their health farther down the line? The effect sizes in these relationships are typically small, and it is not yet clear whether such interventions would have an identifiable impact on health. The possibility of using such relationships to develop interventions, however, remains a prospect for future research.

Cognitive Factors in Health and Illness

Just as emotional factors are involved in the experience of health and illness, cognitive factors influence how people appraise their health and cope with the threat of illness. Several researchers (e.g., Jemmott, Croyle, & Ditto, 1988; Lau, Bernard, & Hartman, 1989; Leventhal et al., 1980; Millstein & Irwin, 1987; Turk, Rudy, & Salovey, 1985) have argued that people hold articulated general conceptions of illness against which particular symptoms or disorders may be evaluated. These so-called commonsense representations of illness include several dimensions: identity (the label of the illness and its symptoms), cause, consequences, time frame, and cure (e.g., Leventhal et al., 1980). When people make appropriate matches of symptoms to their preexisting representations of illness, they may show appropriate illness behavior such as seeking treatment promptly and demonstrating effective follow-through; however, the improper match of symptoms to illness conceptions may account for delay behavior, the faulty practice of certain health behaviors, poor adherence to health recommendations, and other adverse effects on health (Baumann & Leventhal, 1985; Turk, Rudy, & Salovey, 1984).

Cognitions have also been examined in the context of coping with chronic disease and disability. In particular, researchers have focused on the causal attributions that people make for their chronic conditions and on the perceptions of control that they generate regarding the current course of their disorder and/or its daily symptoms, treatments, and side effects. Attributions for the cause of a chronic illness appear to be commonly made (e.g., Taylor, Lichtman, & Wood, 1984a), and a relatively high percentage are made to the self. Some have regarded self-attribution as potentially destructive, whereas others have considered it indicative of efforts to assert control over the illness (see Bulman & Wortman, 1977). Results concerning self-blame or self-responsibility for illness have been inconclusive (Miller & Porter, 1983), perhaps because causality, blame, and responsibility have been used somewhat interchangeably in this literature (Shaver & Drown, 1986). Attributions for an illness made to another person (such as an ex-spouse for causing stress), however, have been uniformly associated with poor psychological adjustment to chronic conditions (e.g., Bulman & Wortman, 1977; Taylor et al., 1984a). A factor that appears to promote positive adjustment is perceived control. Those who believe they can control either the course of their illness or their day-to-day symptoms appear to be better adjusted to their disorders (Affleck, Tennen, Pfeiffer, & Fifield, 1987; Taylor et al., 1984a).

Stress and Illness

Conceptual work on stress began with the fight-flight reaction described by Cannon (1932). Early work on stress largely ignored psychological factors, perhaps because much of it was conducted with animals. Human research spearheaded by Lazarus and his associates (e.g., Lazarus, 1966;

Lazarus & Folkman, 1984), however, identified psychological appraisal as a crucial mediating process in the experience of stress. Events are judged to be positive, negative, or neutral in their implications, and if judged negative, they are further evaluated as to whether they are harmful, threatening, or challenging.

Early efforts to identify stressful events in humans focused on the amount of change that was required to deal with these events, that is, the life events approach. The measurement of stress involved checking off whether particular stressful events (e.g., death of a spouse, arguments with family members) had occurred within a given time period (e.g., 6 months) and then relating them to disease at later points in time. Such studies established modest but reliable relationships to illness.

More recent and sophisticated work has enabled researchers to identify the dimensions of events that are most likely to produce stress. Events appraised as negative, uncontrollable, unpredictable, or ambiguous are typically experienced as more stressful than those not so appraised. Research identifying the significance of these dimensions has come both from well-controlled laboratory studies (e.g., Glass, 1977) and from opportunistic studies of people undergoing major stressful events such as unemployment (I. Fleming, Baum, Davidson, Rectanus, & McArdle, 1987) or crises such as the Three Mile Island catastrophe (R. Fleming, Baum, Gisriel, & Gatchel, 1982). Of the factors implicated in stress, controllability may be especially important. In studies involving stressful events, when those events were under the control of the organisms studied, those organisms showed physiological profiles similar to those of organisms undergoing no stress at all, whereas organisms experiencing the event without the experience of control showed physiological reactions indicative of anxiety and arousal (Hanson, Larson, & Snowden, 1976; Laudenslager et al., 1983).

In this context, it is useful to distinguish explicitly between illness behavior and illness inasmuch as the two only partially overlap. Illness behavior refers to the steps people take when they believe they are experiencing symptoms of illness (such as going to the doctor, taking days off from work). Illness itself involves documented pathology. The distinction is important because illness behaviors do not necessarily implicate underlying pathology, and the psychologic and biologic pathways responsible for the two types of outcomes are often totally different (cf. Cohen, 1988). Much of the research implicating psychosocial factors in illness looks primarily at illness behaviors as the outcome points, rather than at pathology verified through such sources as physician records (see Kasl, 1983). Extensions of these relationships to documented illness are needed.

Until relatively recently, research examining the role of stress in illness behavior and the development of illness focused on major stressful events and the impact these often extreme and dramatic conditions can have on health. More recently, research has investigated the day-to-day process of coping with minor stressful events such as daily hassles (Kanner, Coyne, Schaeffer, & Lazarus, 1981). Unfortunately, the measurement of day-to-day stress sometimes confounds stress with psychological and physical symptoms, and it has been difficult to disentangle cause and effect (Dohrenwend, Dohrenwend, Dodson, & Shrout, 1984). Whether minor stressors will ultimately prove to be important predictors of psychological distress and illness remains to be seen.

Just as recent efforts to relate personality variables to illness have focused on potential pathways, so research relating stress to illness has focused on the pathways by which such developments may occur. Of particular concern have been the patterns of physiological reactivity produced by stressful events. Initially, work was guided by Selye's (1956) general adaptation syndrome, which maintained that people develop patterned physiological reactions to stress which they then exhibit across a wide variety of stressful situations. More recent evidence, however, suggests that there is some physiological specificity in response to particular kinds of stressful events (e.g., Mason, 1974) and emotional reactions (Smith, 1989). Other pathways explored include the likelihood that stressful events erode health habits, such as smoking, drinking, and appropriate eating and sleeping patterns (see Krantz, Grunberg, & Baum, 1985), or change illness behaviors without necessarily affecting health.

Understanding Coping

Coping has been defined as the process of managing external or internal demands that are perceived as taxing or exceeding a person's resources (Lazarus & Folkman, 1984). Coping may consist of behaviors and intrapsychic responses designed to overcome, reduce, or tolerate these demands (Lazarus & Launier, 1978). Until recently, research on coping was in disarray, characterized in one report as a "three-car garage filled to the rafters with junk" (Taylor, 1984, p. 2313). The reason was that researchers studied the same phenomena in different ways using idiosyncratic concepts, measures, and methods. The rise of health psychology as a field has ameliorated this situation in one important way by providing avenues and forums for communication. This has moved researchers toward greater awareness of the need for commonality in the definition of concepts and issues in the study of coping. Other important developments include advances in the conceptualization and measurement of coping (e.g., Folkman, Lazarus, Dunkel-Schetter, DeLongis, & Gruen, 1986; Holahan & Moos, 1987; Stone & Neale, 1984). For example, as conceptualized by Lazarus and his associates, coping is initiated by an appraisal process secondary to the assessment of circumstances as harmful, threatening, or challenging. In this view, a person judges his or her resources, such as time or money, assesses his or her coping skills and abilities, and then determines whether or not they will be sufficient to overcome the threat or challenge posed by a stressful event. Several measures of coping now exist. They include the Ways of Coping instrument, which is based on the Lazarus group's work and which identifies the specific actions, thoughts, and reactions that people have to stressful events; Stone and Neale's (1984) measure of daily coping, specifically designed for use in longitudinal studies; and the COPE measure (Carver, Scheier, & Weintraub, 1989). Increasingly, too, researchers have found that coping measures targeted to particular populations experiencing particular stressors may be more useful than more general coping measures. For example, in this context, Wills (1986) has designed a coping measure for use with adolescents.

There are many ways in which coping responses can be grouped (Billings & Moos, 1982). Two general categories of coping strategies are problem-solving efforts and strategies aimed at the regulation of emotions (Lazarus & Folkman, 1984). Although both sets of strategies are brought to bear on most stressful events, problem-solving efforts are especially useful for managing controllable stressors, and emotional-regulation efforts are well-suited to managing the impact of uncontrollable stressors. A distinction among coping strategies that overlaps with but does not perfectly correspond to the problem-solving/emotional-regulation distinction is that between active coping (behavioral or cognitive efforts to manage a stressful event directly) and avoidance (attempts to avoid dealing with the problem or reduce tension through escapist behaviors). Although most negative life events appear to elicit both types of coping strategies, people with more personal and environmental resources may rely more on active coping and less on avoidance coping (Holahan & Moos, 1987). A long-standing issue in the individual-differences perspective is whether avoidant/repressive responses to stressful events are more adaptive or whether more vigilant/confrontational coping methods are superior. Avoidant responses may be more effective for managing short-term threats, but for long-term threats vigilant coping may manage stress more effectively (Suls & Fletcher, 1985). These findings, too, will no doubt prove to be contingent on the nature of the stressful event (see Taylor & Clark, 1986, for a review).

This emphasis on individual differences has shifted somewhat with the findings that most people appear to use a variety of coping strategies to deal with any given stressor (e.g., Folkman et al., 1986). Successful coping may depend more on a match of coping strategies to the features of the stressful event than on the relative efficacy of one strategy over another (Folkman et al., 1986). This may explain the observation that the use of multiple coping styles may be most adaptive in managing at least some stressful events (e.g., Collins, Taylor, & Skokan, 1989).

Many issues in coping remain to be investigated. In particular, the relationship between ongoing self-regulatory activities (such as mentally simulating potential stressful events; Taylor & Schneider, 1989) and the initiation of specific coping activities to deal with specific stressors has received relatively little attention. Coping researchers are also investigating some of the costs of coping, such as the energy expenditure and physiologic arousal that may be required when people must be vigilant in response to threatening events (Cohen, Evans, Stokols, & Krantz, 1986).

Social Support

Coping research has also focused on coping resources, most particularly on social support. A substantial amount of research documents the psychological and physical benefits of social support and shows how those with social support adjust better psychologically to stressful events, recover more quickly from already-diagnosed illness, and reduce their risk of mortality from specific diseases (House, Landis, & Umberson, 1988). Findings concerning the impact of social support on the likelihood of developing illness have been mixed (Holahan & Moos, 1986; Sarason & Sarason, 1984; Wallston, Alagna, DeVellis, & DeVellis, 1983). Certain of the positive effects of social support appear to occur whether an organism is under stress or not (direct effects), whereas other salutary effects of social support appear largely to exert a buffering effect such that they are protective primarily when people are under high degrees of stress (Cohen & McKay, 1984). In particular, studies that have measured social support in terms of social integration or social networks have tended to report direct effects, whereas studies that have focused on aid, resources, and emotional support from specific network members have tended to uncover buffering effects (Cohen & Wills, 1985).

Time and additional data have produced a more differentiated view of support. For example, research now examines different kinds of social support, such as emotional support, information and advice, tangible assistance, and appraisal support, identifying which types of support are perceived to be helpful for which types of events (Cohen, 1988; Dunkel-Schetter, Folkman, & Lazarus, 1987). A question that arises in this context is whether social support may actually be an individual-difference resource such that some people have better skills for making effective use of potential social support than others (Dunkel-Schetter et al., 1987).

Research also addresses the fact that social support is sometimes not forthcoming to those under stress (Wortman & Dunkel-Schetter, 1979) and that some efforts to provide social support misfire and aggravate stressful circumstances (Coyne, Wortman, & Lehman, 1988). Social support researchers are also increasingly turning their attention to the problems that providers experience in their attempts to provide social support, as in trying to care for an ill family member (see, e.g., Coyne et al., 1988; Kiecolt-Glaser et al., 1987; Schulz, Tompkins, Wood, & Decker, 1987). Other outstanding issues in the field include how best to measure social support (e.g., Heitzmann & Kaplan, 1988) and the need to identify the psychologic and biologic pathways by which different aspects of social support affect health (Cohen, 1988).

Interventions to Improve Coping With Stressful Events

Health Psychology became Division 38 of the American Psychological Association in 1978; the division has approximately 3,000 members, roughly 65% of whom are involved in clinical practice, 55% in research activities, and 50% in teaching and supervision (Houston, 1988).

Reflecting the composition of the division, intervention has been a major concern of health psychology since the inception of the field. Indeed, successful interventions with patients undergoing noxious medical procedures such as surgery actually predated sophisticated models of stress and coping (see Janis, 1958). Psychological control has been the conceptual focus of much of this intervention work. Those who believe that they can exert some controlling behavior in response to a stressful event, whether behavioral or cognitive, appear to adjust better to those stressful events than those without such feelings of control. Research documents the coping benefits of being told in advance what sensations to expect and why, being alerted to the specific procedures to be undertaken, and being given cognitive or behavioral coping strategies to use during the noxious procedure (Taylor & Clark, 1986; Thompson, 1981). More recently, similar interventions have been undertaken successfully with children awaiting noxious medical procedures (e.g., Melamed, 1986).

This is not to suggest that control is a panacea for stressful events, whether naturally occurring or induced during treatment. Manipulations designed to enhance feelings of psychological control may produce feelings of responsibility or blame instead (Krantz & Schulz, 1980; Rodin, 1986), and in many circumstances, they may aggravate negative consequences and lead to increased stress and worry (Burger, 1989; Rodin, 1986). Thus the potential benefits of the concept of psychological control and interventions based on it must be tempered by knowledge of its potential psychological costs as well.

Some interventions have focused on the regulation of emotional and physiologic states through relaxation and guided imagery (Burish & Lyles, 1979), whereas others have encouraged more confrontational coping methods, such as training in swallowing to ease the passage of a tube in an endoscopic examination (Johnson & Leventhal, 1974). Some intervention procedures use avoidant techniques such as cognitive distraction, whereas others enlist vigilant coping, as in inducing a person to reinterpret a stressful experience as a positive one. Although all of these types of interventions appear to be successful in reducing stress, those involving relaxation, avoidance, and cognitive restructuring have been the most commonly used, perhaps because many noxious medical procedures are typically only minimally conducive to direct patient intervention. Indeed, the psychological technology of relaxation has proven to have wide applicability to a variety of issues relating to health and illness, including its use as an accompanying intervention in efforts to modify health habits such as obesity or smoking (see Rodin & Salovey, 1989); its application to stress management (Suinn, 1982); its widespread use in the management of pain (Turner & Chapman, 1982a); and its impact on coping with chronic disease and its treatments (Taylor, Lichtman, & Wood, 1984b).

Aided self-help is another low-cost effective intervention technique that psychologists and health practitioners have implemented across a broad array of health problems. Programs designed to help smokers quit on their own using manuals provided by the American Cancer Society and other organizations are a reasonably effective and cost-effective way of inducing people to quit (e.g., Cummings, Emont, Jaen, & Sciandra, 1988). Self-help telephone lines (Ossip-Klein, Shapiro, & Stiggins, 1984) also provide support for those who are attempting with difficulty to maintain behavior change over time, such as not smoking.

Conclusion

This brief overview of the health psychology field may be significant less for what it has included than for what it has left out. The field is now so diverse and productive that no one article can easily cover all of the significant trends. For example, the review touched only briefly on the enormous and important areas of health promotion and health behavior modification, areas in which health psychologists have made consistent and exceptional contributions. Research on substance abuse is not addressed at all, nor the complex question of ethnic, socioeconomic, gender, and racial patterns in health and illness (see Rodin & Salovey, 1989, for a discussion of these issues). Only a passing nod was given to the huge problem of nonadherence to medical treatment regimens (Meichenbaum & Turk, 1987), which can be as high as 95% for some health care recommendations. Pain mechanisms and pain management received little mention. There is also little coverage of the problems and issues associated with particular chronic diseases, including the most common ones of coronary artery disease, cancer, stroke, and diabetes (Burish & Bradley, 1983). And finally, research investigations on biobehavioral pathways to disease was alluded to only briefly (for examples of this work in the areas of CHD and hypertension, see Cinciripini, 1986a, 1986b; Krantz & Manuck, 1984).

Despite the gaps in this review, certain commonalities in the field may be highlighted. Research that examines whether or not psychological and social factors are involved in health and illness has largely made its point. More recent investigations have gone beyond the demonstration of such simple relationships to an attempt to specify the models and pathways whereby psychological and social factors can be integrated into the biology of health and illness in multifactorial causal chains. This trend is evidenced in research on health promotion, stress and illness, personality and disease, coping, social support, and the factors affecting recovery. These investigations have addressed the direct impact of stress and other psychological states on physiological processes, the impact of psychological and social factors on risky health practices, and the impact of psychological and social factors on how people respond to potential illness states, such as whether or not they engage in appropriate illness behavior. As such, the field has advanced to an unprecedented level of complexity in research investigations.

Yet simultaneously the field has also succeeded in identifying certain broad principles of behavior that seem to cut across specific diseases and specific issues of health and illness. For example, the importance of feelings of personal control emerges in whether people practice particular health behaviors, whether they experience stress, whether their pain control efforts are successful, and how they adapt to chronic disease and disability. Relaxation training, a psychological intervention that requires little training and expense, can be applied in a wealth of settings, as noted earlier. Thus, unlike medicine, which is highly specialized and organized around particular diseases, health psychology affords the opportunity to look beyond particular disorders to the broad principles of thought and behavior that cut across specializations of diseases or problems studied to elucidate more fundamental psychosocial mechanisms.

Trends Affecting Health Psychology

In the past 10 years, I have had the opportunity to comment on the developing field of health psychology on four prior occasions. What seems to distinguish the present occasion from prior ones is an increasing sense that health psychologists are now better integrated into the health enterprise. No longer acting primarily as consultants, statistical advisors, or peripheral members of research teams, health psychologists now number heavily among the chief architects framing the research questions, providing the conceptual structure, developing the research designs, and carrying the projects to fruition. In the early days of research in this field, we often worked alone or with a few students, seeking each other's counsel concerning how best to reach practitioners, obtain samples, and convince medical establishments of the value of our enterprise. That has changed. We seem no longer to need each other so much, as many of us are well integrated into the collaborative arrangements we have engineered with other health professionals. In so doing, we have come face to face with some of the major issues facing the health enterprise.

One of the major forces facing health psychology, as well as every other disciplinary contributor to behavioral medicine, is the growing cost of health care services and the accompanying mounting pressures to contain costs. Fueled by the spiraling expense of high-tech medicine and the increasing costs of malpractice cases and insurance, health care now costs roughly $400 billion a year in the United States alone. The growing spectre of the AIDS crisis threatens to push costs even further, simultaneously putting affordable health care and insurance out of reach of increasing numbers of people.

This unhappy reality is relevant to health psychologists in several respects. It nudges us to keep an eye on the bottom line in research and intervention. Although effective health care interventions are an important goal of the field, the likelihood of their being integrated into medical practice will be influenced by their cost-effectiveness. Subtly, the pressures of cost containment push us in the direction of research questions designed to keep people out of the health care system altogether. On the clinical practice side, interventions increasingly examine the benefits and liabilities of self-help groups, peer counseling, self-management programs such as those for hemodialysis (Kirschenbaum, Sherman, & Penrod, 1987), and other inexpensive ways to provide service delivery to those who might otherwise not receive care. Research suggesting that the stress-reduction and pain-amelioration benefits of expensive biofeedback equipment and training can be achieved by simple, less expensive techniques of relaxation (e.g., Blanchard et al., 1988; Turner & Chapman, 1982a, 1982b) is consistent with this viewpoint. On the research side, the emphasis on cost containment draws researchers heavily into primary prevention activities designed to keep people healthy with the goal of reducing the use of health care services. By identifying the risks of smoking and drinking and the health benefits of exercise, stress management, and a proper diet and by developing programs that best help people to achieve a healthy life-style, psychology contributes to the larger endeavor that attempts to keep people healthy with the ultimate goal of containing health care costs. Whether this implicit goal is a pipe dream remains to be seen. Research examining the efficacy of health behavior interventions in reducing disease and lowering health costs has so far not been very encouraging (Kaplan, 1984). To date, however, the evidence has only slightly tempered the idealistic goal.

There are benefits and risks attached to the formidable role that economic exigencies play in the field. On the one hand, health psychology cannot afford to pursue its scientific and clinical mission without at least some regard to cost. To do so would produce an ivory-tower isolation that would render its results of limited use. On the other hand, cost-containment issues can compromise the scientific and practical mission of the field by choking off prematurely areas of inquiry that do not immediately appear to be cost-effective. The relative lack of attention to issues of rehabilitation, in contrast to the heavy preponderance of research in primary prevention activities, can be regarded as one casualty of these pressures. Just as we must keep an intermittent eye on the bottom line to avoid putting our science and practice out of financial reach, we must also watch the bottom line to be sure that it does not come to dictate the nature of the field as a basic scientific enterprise.

The emphasis on primary prevention, both in medicine and in health psychology, will likely increase, especially as medicine itself becomes more oriented toward preventive health activities. Although the incidence of heart disease, stroke, and infectious disease is decreasing, the incidence of cirrhosis, lung cancer, and automobile deaths is still increasing. Our high-frequency illnesses and growing health problems continue to be tied directly to behavioral pathogens or life-style factors (Matarazzo, 1983). Consequently, there will be a continuing role for health psychologists in this endeavor. As medicine and health psychology pay increasing attention to risky health behaviors, the at-risk role may become a more important construct (e.g., Alien et al., 1987). Individuals who are identified early as at risk for particular disorders need to be trained in how to change any modifiable risk-relevant behaviors as well as in how to cope psychologically with their risk status.

Health psychologists may serve the effort toward primary prevention even further by refocusing health efforts on ways to keep people from developing problematic health habits initially. This trend represents part of an increasing emphasis within health psychology on optimizing health rather than on preventing illness (Evans, 1988). At present, the concept of a healthy life-style has clear media appeal but less applicability to the general population. Because health habits are only modestly intercorrelated, bringing about integrated life-style change essential in the prevention of certain disorders, such as coronary artery disease, is difficult. At least some of the emphasis on health habit change should go to developing methods designed to modify more than one health habit simultaneously, such as smoking, diet control, and exercise among individuals at risk for CHD.

Because there is an applied component to the field, health psychology is necessarily responsive to social problems and issues, including those within medicine. One need not be clairvoyant to appreciate certain developments that can be expected as a result. Increasingly, the field will be called on to address concerns of aging, including the problems of living with chronic disability and disease, the problems of adjustment to bereavement and geographic relocation (Rowe & Kahn, 1987), and psychological changes associated with aging.

This point illustrates a larger concern of health psychology—namely, the need to monitor changing patterns of illness and disease and their implications. To the extent that we can successfully anticipate health- and illness-related problems of the future, we can begin to anticipate now how we must prepare for them. With respect to the elderly, for example, we need to identify the kinds of living situations these increasing numbers of people will have and what kinds of economic resources will be available to them. These factors in turn will influence their health habits, their levels of health, and their need to seek treatment, all of which will require advance planning.

Foretelling the future is never an easy task. Some trends are obvious and have relatively clear implications for the field; others are not so easily anticipated, and thus their implications for health psychology are still elusive. The foregoing set of issues represents a mere fraction of the ways in which health psychology will be shaped and molded by the changing dimensions of medicine and medical practice.

Only one prediction regarding the future of health psychology can be generated with confidence—namely, that articles like this one will gradually disappear from the literature. The diversity of issues studied and the complexity and sophistication of the models and designs used to explore them will preclude simple statements about the major empirical directions and developments of the field. Asking "What's new in health psychology?" will be like asking "What's new in psychology or in medicine?," queries that can be answered in only the most general and superficial ways. Those of us who have regularly taken the temperature and pulse of the field and confidently offered diagnoses and prognoses will be out of business, for whatever trends could be culled from the myriad and diverse directions in the field will be dwarfed in significance by the divergences.

References

Affleck, G., Tennen, H., Pfeiffer, C, & Fifield, J. (1987). Appraisals of control and predictability in adapting to a chronic disease. *Journal of Personality and Social Psychology, 53,* 273-279.

Alexander, F. (1950). *Psychosomatic medicine.* New York: Norton.

Alien, M. T., Lawler, K. A., Mitchell, V. P., Matthews, K. A., Rakaczky, C. J., & Jamison, W. (1987). Type A behavior pattern, parental history of hypertension, and cardiovascular reactivity in college males. *Health Psychology, 6,* 113-130.

American Heart Association. (1984a). *Exercise and your heart.* Dallas, TX: American Heart Association.

American Heart Association. (1984b). *Nutritional counseling for cardiovascular health.* Dallas, TX: American Heart Association.

American Heart Association. (1988). *Cigarette smoking and cardiovascular disease: Special report for the public.* Dallas, TX: American Heart Association.

Ashley, F., Jr., & Kannel, W. (1974). Relation of weight change to changes in atherogenic traits: The Framingham Study. *Journal of Chronic Diseases, 27,* 103-114.

Bandura, A. (1986). *Social foundations of thought and action: A social cognitive theory.* Englewood Cliffs, NJ: Prentice-Hall.

Baumann, L. J., & Leventhal, H. (1985). I can tell when my blood pressure is up, can't I? *Health Psychology, 4,* 203-218.

Billings, A. G., & Moos, R. H. (1982). Family environments and adaptation: A clinically applicable typology. *American Journal of Family Therapy, 10,* 26-38.

Blanchard, E. B., McCoy, G. C, Wittrock, D., Musso, A., Gerardi, R. J., & Pangburn, L. (1988). A controlled comparison of thermal biofeedback and relaxation training in the treatment of essential hypertension: II. Effects on cardiovascular reactivity. *Health Psychology, 7,* 19-33.

Botvin, G. J., & Eng, A. (1982). The efficacy of a multicomponent approach to the prevention of cigarette smoking. *Preventive Medicine, 11,* 199-211.

Brownell, K. D., Marlatt, G. A., Lichtenstein, E., & Wilson, G. T. (1986). Understanding and preventing relapse. *American Psychologist, 41,* 765-782.

Bulman, J. R., & Wortman, C. B. (1977). Attributions of blame and coping in the "real world": Severe accident victims react to their lot. *Journal of Personality and Social Psychology, 35,* 351-363.

Burger, J. M. (1989). Negative reactions to increases in perceived personal control. *Journal of Personality and Social Psychology, 56,* 246-256.

Burish, T. G., & Bradley, L. A. (1983). *Coping with chronic disease: Research and applications.* New York: Academic Press.

Burish, T. G., & Lyles, J. N. (1979). Effectiveness of relaxation training in reducing the aversiveness of chemotherapy in the treatment of cancer. *Journal of Behavior Therapy and Experimental Psychology, 10,* 357-361.

Cannon, W. B. (1932). *The wisdom of the body.* New York: Norton.

Carver, C. S., Scheier, M. F, & Weintraub, J. K. (1989). Assessing coping strategies: A theoretically based approach. *Journal of Personality and Social Psychology, 56,* 267-283.

Cinciripini, P. M. (1986a). Cognitive stress and cardiovascular reactivity. I. Relationship to hypertension. *American Heart Journal, 112,* 1044-1050.

Cinciripini, P. M. (1986b). Cognitive stress and cardiovascular reactivity. II. Relationship to atherosclerosis, arrhythmias, and cognitive control. *American Heart Journal, 112,* 1051-1065.

Cohen, S. (1988). Psychosocial models of the role of social support in the etiology of physical disease. *Health Psychology, 7,* 269-297.

Cohen, S., Evans, G. W., Stokols, D., & Krantz, D. S. (1986). *Behavior, health, and environmental stress.* New York: Plenum.

Cohen, S., & McKay, G. (1984). Social support, stress and the buffering hypothesis: A theoretical analysis. In A. Baum, J. E. Singer, & S. E. Taylor (Eds.), *Handbook of psychology and health* (Vol. 4, pp. 253-267). Hillsdale, NJ: Erlbaum.

Cohen, S., & Wills, T. A. (1985). Stress, social support, and the buffering hypothesis. *Psychological Bulletin, 98,* 310-357.

Collins, R. L., Taylor, S. E., & Skokan, L. A. (1989). *A better world or a shattered vision? Positive and negative assumptions about the world following victimization.* Manuscript submitted for publication.

Coyne, J. C, Wortman, C. B., & Lehman, D. R. (1988). The other side of support: Emotional overinvolvement and miscarried helping. In B. Gottlieb (Ed.), *Marshalling social support* (pp. 305-330). Newbury Park, CA: Sage Publications.

Cummings, K. M., Emont, S. L., Jaen, C., & Sciandra, R. (1988). Format and quitting instructions as factors influencing the impact of a self-administered quit smoking program. *Health Education Quarterly, 15,* 199-216.

Dembroski, T. M., & Costa, P. T. Jr. (1987). Coronary prone behavior: Components of the Type A pattern and hostility. *Journal of Personality, 55,* 211-235.

Derogatis, L. R., Abeloff, M., & Melasaratos, N. (1979). Psychological coping mechanisms and survival time in metastatic breast cancer. *Journal of the American Medical Association, 242,* 1504-1508.

Dohrenwend, B. S., Dohrenwend, B. P., Dodson, M., & Shrout, P. E. (1984). Symptoms, hassles, social supports, and life events: Problem of confounded measures. *Journal of Abnormal Psychology, 93,* 222-230.

Dunbar, F. (1943). *Psychosomatic diagnosis.* New York: Hoeber.

Dunkel-Schetter, C., Folkman, S., & Lazarus, R. S. (1987). Correlates of social support receipt. *Journal of Personality and Social Psychology, 53,* 71-80.

Engel, G. L. (1977). The need for a new medical model: A challenge for biomedicine. *Science, 196,* 126-129.

Evans, R. I. (1988). Health promotion—science or ideology? *Health Psychology, 7,* 203-219.

Evans, R. L., Rozelle, R. M., Mittelmark, M. B., Hansen, W. B., Bane, A. L., & Havis, J. (1978). Deterring the onset of smoking in children: Knowledge of immediate physiological effects and coping with peer pressure, media pressure, and parent modeling. *Journal of Applied Social Psychology, 8,* 126-135.

Fleming, I., Baum, A., Davidson, L. M., Rectanus, E., & McArdle, S. (1987). Chronic stress as a factor in physiologic reactivity to challenge. *Health Psychology, 6,* 221-237.

Fleming, R., Baum, A., Gisriel, M. M., & Gatchel, R. J. (1982, September). Mediating influences of social support on stress at Three Mile Island. *Journal of Human Stress,* 14-22.

Folkman, S., Lazarus, R. S., Dunkel-Schetter, C., DeLongis, A., & Gruen, R. J. (1986). Dynamics of a stressful encounter: Cognitive appraisal, coping, and encounter outcomes. *Journal of Personality and Social Psychology, 50,* 992-1003.

Fox, B. H. (1978). Premorbid psychological factors as related to cancer incidence. *Journal of Behavioral Medicine, 1,* 45-134.

Friedman, H. S., & Booth-Kewley, S. (1987). The "disease-prone personality": A meta-analytic view of the construct. *American Psychologist, 42,* 539-555.

Friedman, H. S., & Booth-Kewley, S. (1988). Validity of the Type A construct: A reprise. *Psychological Bulletin, 104,* 381-384.

Friedman, H. S., & DiMatteo, M. R. (1989). *Health psychology.* Englewood Cliffs, NJ: Prentice Hall.

Friedman, M., Thoresen, C. E., Gill, J. J., Ulmer, D., Powell, L. H., Price, V. A., Brown, B., Thompson, L., Rabin, D. D., Breall, W. S., Bourg, E., Levy, R., & Dixon, T. (1986). Alteration of Type A behavior and its effect on cardiac recurrences in post myocardial infarction patients: Summary results of the recurrent coronary prevention project. *American Heart Journal, 112,* 653-665.

Glass, D. C. (1977). *Behavior patterns, stress, and coronary disease.* Hillsdale, NJ: Erlbaum.

Hanson, J. D., Larson, M. E., & Snowden, C. T. (1976). The effects of control over high intensity noise on plasma cortisol levels in rhesus monkeys. *Behavioral Biology, 16,* 333-334.

Heitzmann, C. A., & Kaplan, R. M. (1988). Assessment of methods for measuring social support. *Health Psychology, 7,* 75-109.

Holahan, C. J., & Moos, R. H. (1986). Personality, coping, and family resources in stress resistance: A longitudinal analysis. *Journal of Personality and Social Psychology, 51,* 389-395.

Holahan, C. J., & Moos, R. H. (1987). Personal and contextual determinants of coping strategies. *Journal of Personality and Social Psychology, 52,* 946-955.

House, J. S., Landis, K. R., & Umberson, D. (1988). Social relationships and health. *Science, 241,* 540-545.

Houston, B. K. (1988). Division 38 survey: Synopsis of results. *The Health Psychologist, 10,* 2-3.

Janis, I. L. (1958). *Psychological stress.* New York: Wiley.

Janz, N. K., & Becker, M. H. (1984). The health belief model: A decade later. *Health Education Quarterly, 11,* 1-47.

Jemmott, J. B. III., Croyle, R. T., & Ditto, P. H. (1988). Commonsense epidemiology: Self-based judgments from laypersons and physicians. *Health Psychology, 7,* 55-73.

Jessor, R., & Jessor, S. L. (1982). Adolescence to young adulthood: A twelve year prospective study of problem behavior and psychosocial development. In A. A. Mednick & M. Harway (Eds.), *Longitudinal research in the United States* (pp. 34-61). Boston: Martinus Nijhoff.

Johnson, J. E., & Leventhal, H. (1974). Effects of accurate expectations and behavioral instructions on reactions during a noxious medical examination. *Journal of Personality and Social Psychology, 29,* 710-718.

Kanner, A. D., Coyne, J. C., Schaeffer, C., & Lazarus, R. S. (1981). Comparison of two modes of stress measurement: Daily hassles and uplifts versus major life events. *Journal of Behavioral Medicine, 4,* 1-39.

Kaplan, R. M. (1984). The connection between clinical health promotion and health status: A critical overview. *American Psychologist, 39,* 755-765.

Kasl, S. V. (1983). Pursuing the link between stressful life experiences and disease: A time for reappraisal. In C. L. Cooper (Ed.), *Stress research* (pp. 79-102). New York: Wiley.

Kemeny, M. E., Weiner, H., Taylor, S. E., Schneider, S., Visscher, B., & Fahey, J. L. (1989). *Repeated bereavement, depressed mood, and immune parameters in HIV seropositive and seronegative homosexual men.* Manuscript submitted for publication.

Kiecolt-Glaser, J. K., & Glaser, R. (in press). Behavioral influences on immune function: Evidence for the interplay between stress and health. In T. Field, P. McCabe, & N. Schneiderman (Eds.), *Stress and coping* (Vol. 2). Hillsdale, NJ: Erlbaum.

Kiecolt-Glaser, J. K., Glaser, R., Shuttleworth, E. C., Dyer, C. S., Ogrocki, P., & Speicher, C. E. (1987). Chronic stress and immunity in family caregivers of Alzheimer's disease victims. *Psychosomatic Medicine, 49,* 523-535.

Kirschenbaum, D. S., Sherman, J., & Penrod, J. D. (1987). Promoting self-directed hemodialysis: Measurement and cognitive-behavioral intervention. *Health Psychology, 6,* 373-385.

Krantz, D. S., Grunberg, N. E., & Baum, A. (1985). Health psychology. *Annual Review of Psychology, 36,* 349-383.

Krantz, D. S., & Manuck, S. B. (1984). Acute psychophysiologic reactivity and risk of cardiovascular disease: A review and methodologic critique. *Psychological Bulletin, 96,* 435-464.

Krantz, D. S., & Schulz, R. (1980). A model of life crisis, control, and health outcomes: Cardiac rehabilitation and relocation of the elderly. In A. Baum & J. E. Singer (Eds.), *Advances in environmental psychology.* Volume 2: Applications of personal control (pp. 25-60). Hillsdale, NJ: Erlbaum.

Langer, E. J., & Rodin, J. (1976). The effects of choice and enhanced personal responsibility for the aged: A field experiment in an institutional setting. *Journal of Personality and Social Psychology, 34,* 191-198.

Lau, R. R., Bernard, T. M., & Hartman, K. A. (1989). Further explorations of common sense representations of common illnesses. *Health Psychology, 8,* 195-219.

Lau, R. R., Kane, R., Berry, S., Ware, J., & Roy, D. (1980). Channeling health: A review of televised health campaigns. *Health Education Quarterly, 7,* 56-89.

Laudenslager, M. L., Ryan, S. M., Drugan, R. C., Hyson, R. L., & Maier, S. F. (1983). Coping and immunosuppression: Inescapable but not escapable shock suppresses lymphocyte proliferation. *Science, 231,* 568-570.

Lazarus, R. S. (1966). *Psychological stress and the coping process.* New York: McGraw-Hill.

Lazarus, R. S., & Folkman, S. (1984). *Stress, appraisal, and coping.* New York: Springer.

Lazarus, R. S., & Launier, R. (1978). Stress-related transactions between person and environment. In L. A. Pervin & M. Lewis (Eds.), *Internal and external determinants of behavior* (pp. 287-327). New York: Plenum.

Leventhal, H., & Cleary, P. D. (1980). The smoking problem: A review of the research and theory in behavioral risk modification. *Psychological Bulletin, 88,* 370-405.

Leventhal, H., Meyer, D., & Nerenz, D. (1980). The commonsense representation of illness danger. In S. Rachman (Ed.), *Contributions to medical psychology* (pp. 7-30). Oxford, England: Pergamon Press.

Levy, S., Herberman, R., Lippman, M., & d'Angelo, T. (1987). Correlation of stress factors with sustained depression of natural killer cell activity and predicted prognosis in patients with breast cancer. *Journal of Clinical Oncology, 5,* 348-353.

Levy, S., Herberman, R., Maluish, A., Schlien, B., & Lippman, M. (1985). Prognostic risk assessment in primary breast cancer by behavioral and immunological parameters. *Health Psychology, 4,* 99-113.

Marlatt, G. A., & Gordon, J. R. (Eds.). (1985). *Relapse prevention: Maintenance strategies in the treatment of addictive behaviors.* New York: Guilford.

Mason, J. W. (1974). Specificity in the organization of neuro-endocrine response profiles. In P. Seeman & G. M. Brown (Eds.), *Frontiers in neurology and neuroscience research.* First International Symposium of the Neuroscience Institute. Toronto, Ontario, Canada: University of Toronto.

Matarazzo, J. D. (1980). Behavioral health and behavioral medicine: Frontiers for a new health psychology. *American Psychologist, 35,* 807-817.

Matarazzo, J. D. (1982). Behavioral health's challenge to academic, scientific, and professional psychology. *American Psychologist, 37,* 1-14.

Matarazzo, J. D. (1983). Behavioral health: A 1990 challenge for the health sciences professions. In J. D. Matarazzo, N. E. Miller, S. M. Weiss, J. A. Herd, & S. M. Weiss (Eds.), *Behavioral health: A handbook of health enhancement and disease prevention* (pp. 3-40). New York: Wiley.

Matarazzo, J. D., Weiss, S. M., Herd, J. A., Miller, N. E., & Weiss, S. M. (Eds.). (1984). *Behavioral health: A handbook of health enhancement and disease prevention.* New York: Wiley. Matthews, K. A. (1982). Psychological perspectives on the Type A behavior pattern. *Psychological Bulletin, 91,* 293-323.

Matthews, K. A. (1988). Coronary heart disease and Type A behavior: Update on and alternative to the Booth-Kewley and Friedman (1987) quantitative review. *Psychological Bulletin, 104,* 373-380.

Mechanic, D. (1979). The stability of health and illness behavior: Results from a 16-year followup. *American Journal of Public Health, 69,* 1142-1145.

Meichenbaum, D., & Turk, D. C. (1987). *Facilitating treatment adherence.* New York: Plenum.

Melamed, B. G. (1986). Special issue on child health psychology. *Health Psychology, 5*(3).

Miller, D. T., & Porter, C. A. (1983). Self-blame in victims of violence. *Journal of Social Issues, 39,* 139-152.

Millstein, S. G., & Irwin, C. E. Jr. (1987). Concepts of health and illness: Different constructs of variations on a theme? *Health Psychology, 6,* 515-524.

Multiple Risk Factor Intervention Trial Research Group (MRFIT). (1982). Multiple risk factor intervention trial: Risk factor changes and mortality results. *Journal of the American Medical Association, 248,* 1465-1477.

Ossip-Klein, D. J., Shapiro, R. M., & Stiggins, J. (1984). Brief report: Freedom line: Increasing utilization of a telephone support service for ex-smokers. *Addictive Behaviors, 9,* 227-230.

Peterson, C., Seligman, M. E. P., & Vaillant, G. E. (1988). Pessimistic explanatory style is a risk factor for physical illness: A thirty-five-year longitudinal study. *Journal of Personality and Social Psychology, 55,* 23-27.

Rodin, J. (1986). Aging and health: Effects of the sense of control. *Science, 233,* 1271-1276.

Rodin, J., & Salovey, P. (1989). Health psychology. *Annual Review of Psychology, 40,* 533-579.

Rogers, R. W. (1984). Changing health-related attitudes and behavior: The role of preventive health psychology. In J. H. Harvey, J. E. Maddux, R. P. McGlynn, & C. D. Stoltenberg (Eds.), *Social perception in clinical and consulting psychology* (Vol. 2, pp. 91-112). Lubbock: Texas Tech University Press.

Rowe, J. W., & Kahn, R. L. (1987). Human aging: Usual and successful. *Science, 237,* 143-149.

Sarason, I. G., & Sarason, B. R. (Eds.). (1984). *Social support: Theory, research and applications.* The Hague, The Netherlands: Martinus Nijhoff.

Scheier, M. F., & Carver, C. S. (1985). Optimism, coping, and health: Assessment and implications of generalized outcome expectancies. *Health Psychology, 4,* 219-247.

Scheier, M. F., Matthews, K. A., Owens, J., Magovern, G. J. Sr., Lefebvre, R. C., Abbott, R. A., & Carver, C. S. (in press). Dispositional optimism and recovery from coronary artery bypass surgery: The beneficial effects on physical and psychological well-being. *Journal of Personality and Social Psychology.*

Schulz, R., Tompkins, C., Wood, D., & Decker, S. (1987). The social psychology of caregiving: The physical and psychological costs of providing support to the disabled. *Journal of Applied Social Psychology, 77,* 401-428.

Schwartz, G. E. (1982). Testing the biopsychosocial model: The ultimate challenge facing behavioral medicine? *Journal of Consulting and Clinical Psychology, 50,* 1040-1052.

Selye, H. (1956). *The stress of life.* New York: McGraw-Hill.

Shaver, K. G., & Drown, D. (1986). On causality, responsibility, and self-blame: A theoretical note. *Journal of Personality and Social Psychology, 50,* 697-702.

Smith, C. A. (1989). Dimensions of appraisal and physiological response in emotion. *Journal of Personality and Social Psychology, 56,* 339-353.

Stein, M., Keller, S. E., & Schleifer, S. J. (1985). Stress and immunomodulation: The role of depression and neuroendocrine function. *Journal of Immunology, 135,* 827s-833s.

Stone, A. A., & Neale, J. M. (1984). New measure of daily coping: Development and preliminary results. *Journal of Personality and Social Psychology, 46,* 892-906.

Suinn, R. M. (1982). Intervention with Type A behaviors. *Journal of Consulting and Clinical Psychology, 50,* 797-803.

Suls, J., & Fletcher, B. (1985). The relative efficacy of avoidant and nonavoidant coping strategies: A meta-analysis. *Health Psychology, 4,* 249-288.

Taylor, S. E. (1984). Issues in the study of coping: A commentary. *Cancer, 53,* 2313-2315.

Taylor, S. E. (1986). *Health psychology.* New York: Random House.

Taylor, S. E., & Clark, L. F. (1986). Does information improve adjustment to noxious events? In M. J. Saks & L. Saxe (Eds.), *Advances in applied social psychology* (Vol. 3, pp. 1-28). Hillsdale, NJ: Erlbaum.

Taylor, S. E., Lichtman, R. R., & Wood, J. V. (1984a). Attributions, beliefs about control, and adjustment to breast cancer. *Journal of Personality and Social Psychology, 46,* 489-502.

Taylor, S. E., Lichtman, R. R., & Wood, J. V. (1984b). Compliance with chemotherapy among breast cancer patients. *Health Psychology, 3,* 553-562.

Taylor, S. E., & Schneider, S. K. (1989). Coping and the simulation of events. *Social Cognition, 7,* 176-196.

Thompson, S. C. (1981). Will it hurt less if I can control it? A complex answer to a simple question. *Psychological Bulletin, 90,* 89-101.

Thoresen, C. E., Friedman, M., Gill, J. K., & Ulmer, D. (1982). Recurrent coronary prevention project: Some preliminary findings. *Ada Medica Scandinavica Supplement, 660,* 172-192.

Turk, D. C., Rudy, T. E., & Salovey, P. (1984). Health protection: Attitudes and behaviors of LPNs, teachers, and college students. *Health Psychology, 3,* 189-210.

Turk, D. C., Rudy, T. E., & Salovey, P. (1985). Implicit models of illness. *Journal of Behavioral Medicine, 9,* 453-474.

Turner, J. A., & Chapman, C. R. (1982a). Psychological interventions for chronic pain: A critical review. I. Relaxation training and biofeedback. *Pain, 12,* 1-21.

Turner, J. A., & Chapman, C. R. (1982b). Psychological interventions for chronic pain: A critical review. II. Operant conditioning, hypnosis, and cognitive-behavioral therapy. *Pain, 12,* 23-46.

Wallston, B. S., Alagna, S. W., DeVellis, B. McE., & DeVellis, R. F. (1983). Social support and physical health. *Health Psychology, 2,* 367-391.

Weinberger, D. A. (in press). The construct validity of the repressive coping style, In J. L. Singer (Ed.), *Repression and association: Defense mechanisms and personality style.* Chicago: University of Chicago Press.

Wills, T. A. (1986). Stress and coping in early adolescence: Relationships to substance use in urban school samples. *Health Psychology, 5,* 503-529.

Wortman, C. B., & Dunkel-Schetter, C. (1979). Interpersonal relationships and cancer: A theoretical analysis. *Journal of Social Issues, 35,* 120-155.

2

Themes in Medical Sociology

Phil Brown

The largest section of the American Sociological Association (ASA) for at least two decades has been Medical Sociology. Approximately 1,100 medical sociologists, making up 11 percent of the ASA membership, work in sociology departments, public health schools, medical schools, hospitals, state and federal health agencies, and population and family planning programs. What kinds of work do they do? What theoretical foundations do they share? What is the nature of their discipline?

I present here a sketch of the field of medical sociology (frequently called the sociology of health and illness) for those who study health from the standpoint of other disciplines. It is not meant to be a thorough survey but a selective discussion of key elements, issues, and debates that represents my own orientation to the field.[1] I deal almost exclusively with American medical sociology even though by doing so we lose sight of, for instance, the vibrant British medical sociology. British sociologists are largely qualitative, concentrating on doctor-patient interaction, the experience of illness, and, increasingly, the narrative approach to illness experience.

Scope of the Field

Medical sociology centers on the social construction of health and illness—that is a construction shaped by the many elements of the social order and often independent from biomedical phenomena. In this perspective, medical sociology links together and makes sense of the varied manifestations of health and illness: biomedical data, professional practice, institutional structures, social policy, economics and financing, the social epidemiology of disease and death, and the individual experience of health, illness, and medical care. The discipline links the micro-level (self-awareness, individual action, and interpersonal communication), meso-level (hospitals, medical education), and macro-level (the nation's health status, the structure and political economy of the health care system, national health policy). This linkage ensures that individual entities are not studied in

EDITOR'S NOTE: Previously published in *Journal of Health, Politics, and Law, 16,* pp. 595-601.

isolation from their surroundings. For example, an ethnic group's particular set of attitudes to health is related to the ways the members understand health-related processes, seek medical care, and interact with providers. At the same time, we must understand the ethnic group as a whole, in light of its history of immigration and acculturation, its standing in the hierarchies of status, power, and wealth, and the attitudes of the professions and the public toward the group.

For another example, if we want to understand what goes on in the interaction between client and health provider, we cannot simply analyze the language, information exchange, and power relationships in that encounter. After all, the encounter is influenced by the larger context—including professional, institutional, sociocultural, political, and economic factors. Likewise, if we want to examine the effects of diagnosis-related groups (DRGs), we cannot look only at aggregate data on a patient's length of stay in hospital. We must also explore the impacts of DRGs on particular interchanges between providers and consumers, such as discussions between doctor and patient about a hospital discharge that may be premature.

In studying health and illness in the social context, medical sociology is concerned with the distinction between disease and illness. *Disease* is a more biomedical phenomenon, though strongly affected by social forces. The distribution of disease and death differs on the basis of class, race, sex, ethnicity, education, and other social factors. The key issue here is how social position or social factors affect the production of disease. *Illness* reflects a more subjective phenomenon. The same social forces which affect disease—such as race, class, gender, and ethnicity—also lead to varying perceptions, conceptions, and experiences of disease and illness. This explains why people differ in making their way to various providers and institutions to seek care—some people with the same symptoms or conditions as others choose widely disparate ways of dealing with those symptoms or conditions.

In viewing illness as a social construction, we also examine how people interact with health providers and institutions, paying special attention to conceptual differences based on conflicts between lay and professional beliefs. For instance, many people treat themselves when they are sick, sometimes using additional formal care and sometimes not. Our field looks at how they decide and carry out that regimen.

On a larger scale, the viewpoint of the field leads to an examination of the backgrounds, structures, and functions of health care providers and institutions. From here, it is a logical next step to the examination of health policy and its interaction with major components of the state and political economy. Medical sociology increasingly emphasizes the interactions between health and social change, seeing as paramount the societal determinants of health and illness.

Early Issues and Concerns

The growth of early medical sociology was tied to the expansion of the health care system and the attempts by medical schools, medical foundations, and institutions to incorporate social science perspectives in the study and practice of medicine. This was in part fueled by federal funding through the National Institute of Mental Health and the Public Health Service, which provided substantial research and graduate training funds.

In the 1950s and 1960s, the young field of medical sociology focused on a narrow range of topics. Talcott Parsons's (1951) notion of the "sick role" drove much of this work. Parsons argued that illness allows people to be temporarily exempted from normal social responsibilities, but, in exchange, they must accept that they cannot get well on their own, that they have a duty to get well, and that they need to seek professional help to do so. Parsons viewed doctors as objective and largely altruistic scientists who are universally committed to helping their patients. For Parsons, illness was a form of social deviance, and medical care was the appropriate mechanism of social control for restoring social equilibrium.

Other scholars, working on more specifically applied models, focused on people's actions in preventive health and health care utilization. Irwin Rosenstock's (1966) "health belief model" viewed people as rational actors. Faced with potential illness, people considered their susceptibility to the illness and its seriousness, as they perceived it. They then evaluated how serious a problem it was for them and how much it would help to seek treatment, making a decision on the basis of this evaluation. The whole process of information gathering and decision making was modified by sociodemographic factors. Edward Suchman (1965), David Mechanic (1962), and others examined the processes of help seeking, developing a conceptualization of "illness behavior." People evaluated not only their own illnesses, but also the available resources, alternative courses of action, and the probability of the treatment succeeding.

Early research in medical sociology also used intensive field studies to examine the training and socialization of doctors. Two major approaches have dominated the field. The first, exemplified by the work of Renee Fox (1957) and Robert K. Merton et al. (1957), sees medical education as a process of socialization in the values of a profession. An alternate perspective, developed by Howard Becker and his colleagues (1961), suggests that becoming professional is much more of an interactional and negotiated process where learning is mediated by the situation and where students selectively interpret medical knowledge and values. What the two perspectives have in common is their belief that medical education is not a value-free or idealistic phenomenon. For Fox, for instance, medical students learn to be emotionally detached from patients and to tolerate the great uncertainties of medical work. For Becker, students make the transformation from idealism to cynicism, largely with regard to how much knowledge they can actually learn. These two approaches have tended to merge in recent years, but the distinctive perspectives can still be discerned.

The epidemiology of mental illness and the nature of the mental hospital were other areas of early attention in medical sociology. As a result of massive federal involvement in mental health policy, sociologists worked on their own or alongside psychiatrists to measure the incidence and prevalence of mental illness, including in their studies social factors such as class and race, which modified those rates (August Hollingshead, for example, working with Frederick Redlich [Hollingshead and Redlich, 1958]). Other sociologists, also often working with psychiatrists, focused on the life of the mental hospital (Morris Schwartz with Alfred Stanton, for example [Stanton and Schwartz 1954]). Perhaps Erving Goffman (1961), more than any other individual, brought this research into the academic limelight with his classic study of inpatient culture. These studies of psychiatric sociology made significant contributions to social constructivist views by showing how health institutions themselves shaped the nature of diseases, often making them worse through institutionalization. This research also provided understanding of and respect for the individuals, subcultures, and underlives of mental hospitals.

Talcott Parsons's sick role theory and other early approaches to illness behavior were largely descriptive, not unexpected for a new field trying to describe and categorize the elements of people's health status and the health care system. While there was some theoretical basis, it was largely the conservative, consensus functionalism of the period that defined other social sciences. This work held a positivist view of both health and society, a viewpoint that all the features of the social world were knowable, measurable, and largely invariant across people and communities. Overall, there was a narrow emphasis on the medical world, a general acceptance of medical definitions and outlooks, and an undue preoccupation with doctors. Indeed, many medical sociologists conducted research aimed at helping doctors and health institutions to achieve patient compliance. There was little concern for challenging existing medical authority. The social structure was bracketed, with the assumption that social roles and institutions just fit together.

Yet challenge was developing to this view of a harmonious society, apparently free of major conflicts. Studies of mental hospital life and psychiatric epidemiology mentioned above were notable advances—the former often derived from the more critical symbolic interactionist school,[2] and the latter tending to focus on social causation of mental illness, making them the earliest developments of conflict theory in the field. Fred Davis (1963), Julius Roth (1963), Anselm Strauss et al. (1964), Elliot Freidson (1970), and Irving Zola (1966) used an interactionist perspective to pioneer the study of the subjective experience of illness and the negotiation between patients, practitioners, and institutions. Freidson also provided valuable insights into the differences and conflicts between lay and professional worldviews, and how these inherent conflicts were played out in medical institutions.

Recent Developments

In the 1970s, the public's use of health care continued to be a significant focus of research. Ronald Anderson (1968) and his colleagues developed an approach that was widely adopted, in which utilization was seen as a function of predisposing factors (sociodemographic variables, health attitudes), enabling characteristics (access to financial, insurance, and medical resources), and need (actual health status). Not surprisingly, the factor that always explained the most variation in the use of care was need. Research also continued on the early areas of interest: medical education, nursing and other professions, and hospital structure. Discussions of health policy began to be more prevalent, as a result of government health programs starting in the mid-1960s.

But the 1970s also brought significant change to medical sociology. Conflict and interactionist perspectives grew during the 1960s and provided more cohesive challenges to earlier studies marked by conservative, functionalist approaches. This development was nourished by critical and radical viewpoints stemming from the 1960s social movements, which carried over into the social sciences and indeed to all academic disciplines. The social structure was no longer taken for granted but was actively questioned. Indeed, the social structure was held accountable for much of the sickness in society and for the society's inability to address poor health successfully.

Elliot Freidson (1970) ushered in the critical medical sociology of the 1970s. He provided a trenchant critique of Parsons's sick role and of other contemporary approaches to utilization. Freidson argued that patient and provider perspectives were vastly divergent, based on their positions in the social order. Thus, one could expect difficulty in their interaction and a continual conflict over the significance of symptoms, the accuracy of diagnoses, and the efficacy of treatments. Unequal power relations therefore became a central feature of much work in the field. Race, class, and sex were no longer seen merely as sociodemographic variables that modified help seeking and utilization. Instead, they became key social determinants. Freidson's *Profession of Medicine* (1970), strikingly as fresh today as when it appeared two decades ago, was at the forefront of a spate of studies that took a more critical stance on the organization and operation of the medical system. Freidson's treatment of the medical profession as but one profession among others enabled sociology to escape the moralistic and normative approaches which earlier scholars had employed.

Starting in the mid-1970s, an emerging feminist sociology and the women's health movement began to have an impact on medical sociology. The women's health movement discovered many sexist biases, as well as factually incorrect knowledge (e.g., the myth of the vaginal orgasm) and improper practices (e.g., unnecessary hysterectomies) in obstetrics and gynecology. They linked reproductive rights to both medical power and political power. They pointed to the gender basis of the medical division of labor. Further, the women's health movement organized alternative health clinics designed to bypass such problems and to empower women as medical consumers. Medical sociologists took up these concerns in several ways. First, they analyzed the consequences of these biases and the poor medical practices that affected over half the population. Second, they used this example as a model for assessing medical ideology and practice in general, with particular attention to power relations. Third, they examined the significance of this and other social movements in altering the production of medical knowledge. Finally, they examined the impact of alternative types of practitioner and facility, such as those found in the women's health movement.

The 1970s also brought a sharp focus on the political economy of health. The Health Policy Advisory Committee (Health-PAC) provided an early impetus in their *Bulletin* and two subsequent books (Ehrenreich and Ehrenreich 1971; Kotelchuck 1976). Indeed, Health-PAC coined the term "medical-industrial complex," later widely used by many health policy analysts. Vicente

Navarro (1976), Howard Waitzkin (1983), and other Marxist-oriented scholars provided a further boost in situating health and health care in the context of social class relations and the perpetuation of an inegalitarian society. They emphasized the international linkages of health status, the health labor force, and the provision of services, and generally pointed to the social control functions of health and health services. Not only did the capitalist system produce ill health but existing social inequalities were perpetuated by that illness and the health care system designed to treat it. This line of analysis became an important, though still underdeveloped, strain in medical sociology. In addition, few medical sociologists have adopted the international orientations that these approaches emphasize.

In extending this conflict approach, some within medical sociology took up issues of occupational safety and environmental impacts on health, though this emphasis is even more underdeveloped than the general political-economic approach. Occupational health was clearly linked to underlying economic and political arrangements, whereby people's safety was compromised for increased efficiency and profit. Not only did government fail to take adequate steps to protect workers, but many physicians served as handmaidens to industry in covering up workplace disease and death. Dangerous substances made their way into the community, causing environmental health effects and considerable public fear. Like the workplace, the community suffered from lack of government and professional attention; organized lay groups pressured for official remediation. These developments, like the women's health movement, were examples of the impact of social movements on the health care system and on public attitudes toward health.

Medical sociology continues to offer alternatives to the medical model, a perspective which treats health and illness in a simplistic, linear fashion by focusing solely on biophysiological phenomena. Increasing numbers of modern medical sociologists see much of illness itself as a social construction, that is, a phenomenon caused by human and institutional beliefs and actions, rather than solely by a value-neutral physiological process. This has led scholars to examine the historical developments in disease rates. We have learned that morbidity and mortality for the acute diseases have been more affected by public health measures (e.g., sewers, clean water) and overall economic development (e.g., nutrition) than by medical treatments.

An alternative approach to the medical model emphasizes the effect of social structural factors—especially sex, class, and race—on epidemiology. In related fashion, a growing number of researchers examine the effects of social stresses, often mediated by race, class, and sex, as well as by social networks and social support. Another approach centers on how social structural factors affect illness behavior and the personal experience of illness, irrespective of health status.

Some scholars examine structural issues in the production of medical knowledge. The medical profession, as well as the public that seeks healing, has exaggerated the boundaries of medicine. Thus, sociological critics of medicalization, such as Irving Zola (1975) and Peter Conrad (1975), point to the unrealistic faith in medical explanations for many social phenomena (e.g., substance abuse, homosexuality). This critique of medicalization has played a major role in the field, depicting medicine as a field with elastic and expanding borders and outlining some of the downside of including social problems in medical jurisdictions.

A related strand of work is tied to an appreciation for the personal experience of illness in which people are viewed as feeling and acting on symptoms in many nonmedical ways. For instance, what may seem an illogical form of noncompliance with doctor's orders may be a well-thought-out plan to avoid medical and social side effects that might impair personal or work life. This perspective may be especially useful for chronic diseases, which have become our predominant health problems, and for which medical knowledge often lacks successful treatments. Sociologists have been especially interested in these chronic conditions, examining the various self-care options.

Scholars of the personal experience of illness continue to develop new approaches. Conversational analysis and discourse analysis examine micro-levels of clinical interaction to show inequalities of profession, gender, race, and class and to examine cognitive components of people's understanding of health and illness. Narrative analysis uses interviews with people about their experience of illness—qualitative autobiographical material—to get at the ways they make meaning of symptoms and at the social ramifications of illness and its social causes.

In providing alternatives to the biomedical model, medical sociologists do not doubt the significance of many advances in medical diagnosis and treatment. At the same time, they are cognizant of widespread unnecessary surgery and the many overuses and abuses of medical technology. Thus, medical sociologists study the discovery, diffusion, and social functions of drugs, technologies, and procedures. These processes of scientific discovery and practice are understood to be largely driven by the desire for professional self-advancement, for corporate profit, and social engineering rather than as the next advance in the linear development of a pure science.

Whereas the biomedical model separates mind and body, medical sociology attempts to integrate them. This holistic approach shows up in the burgeoning area of stress, coping, and social supports. Social and physical stresses can significantly affect health and mental health status, and these effects are themselves modified by the types of social supports people have. Recent research indicates that even major biomedical phenomena, such as cancer survival, can be affected by emotional responses and social networks.

In light of the increasing crises in health and the health care system, medical sociology has a large agenda. There is significant current research on the changing status of doctors and other members of the health work force. Tied to this is the trend toward health maintenance organizations (HMOs) and other forms of managed care, in which traditional professional and institutional roles have been altered. Scholars focus their attention on uncontrollable health costs and insurance premiums and examine the many ways in which the AIDS epidemic has affected the health care system and the society at large. Because medical sociology is so thoroughly steeped in a social context approach, it can contribute valuable knowledge about "risk" behaviors and preventive strategies, since these phenomena go far beyond the simple biomedical parameters of the disease.

Future Directions

Medical sociology as a subdiscipline has exhibited astonishing growth in the numbers of scholars engaged in it, in the topics studied, and in the range and sophistication of its theory. The field has always had strong connections to related health fields, such as epidemiology, medical anthropology, health services research, and medical history. While maintaining these connections, medical sociology is fostering new ones, with fields such as bioethics, gerontology, environmental sociology, and the sociology of science. Where it intersects with bioethics, it raises questions of professional and institutional controls over health and life, patient autonomy, governmental regulation, and philosophical views on the proper extent of medical intervention. With gerontology, it studies the many health problems of an aging population, especially with regard to chronic disease. With environmental sociology, it extends our attention to the social causes of disease. And with the sociology of science, it is concerned with the social construction of knowledge and the social functions of science and technology.

There is still a significant amount of what Robert Straus (1957) more than three decades ago termed "sociology in medicine," with sociologists working not only *in* medical institutions, but *for* them, in the sense that these sociologists eschew their broader academic and theoretical backgrounds for a somewhat circumscribed research role in service to the institution. The "sociology of medicine" approach examines medicine in its social context, usually looking from a more critical vantage point outside the institutions of medicine (though not all sociology *of* medicine is critical: Parsons and his contemporary supporters are uncritical observers).

Today's medical sociology cannot be categorized simply as sociology *of* or *in* medicine, since the field today covers so much more than *medicine.* Medical sociology increasingly eschews medical definitions of problems, looking instead at medicine as being like any other social institution, albeit an important one. Ranging beyond doctors, hospitals, nurses, and other elements of the health care system, the field's concern with health and illness covers an enormous range of topics. Just as sociology in general addresses personal, interpersonal, group, institutional, and political levels, so too does medical sociology examine the totality of issues concerning the health and illness of human beings.

Notes

1. In the interest of readability, I have minimized the number of citations to the literature. For those seeking a broader and more complete introduction to medical sociology texts (Wolinsky 1980; Cockerham 1989) and readers (Brown 1989; Conrad and Kern 1990; Freeman and Levine 1990) will be helpful.

2. *Symbolic interaction* is a term derived from the theoretical perspective that views beliefs, norms, and behaviors as coming from human interaction rather than from a positivistic set of facts and rules. In medical sociology this leads to an emphasis on interpersonal dynamics and the personal experience of health and illness.

References

Anderson, R. (1968). *A behavioral model of families' use of health services.* Chicago: Center for Health Administration Studies.

Becker, H. S., Greer, B., Hughes, E. C., & Strauss, A. (1961). *Boys in white: Student culture in medical school.* Chicago: University of Chicago Press.

Brown, P. (1989). *Perspectives in medical sociology.* Belmont, CA: Wadsworth.

Cockerham, W. C. (1989). *Medical sociology* (4th ed.). Englewood Cliffs, NJ: Prentice-Hall.

Conrad, P. (1975). The discovery of hyperkinesis: Notes on the medicalization of deviant behavior. *Social Problems, 23,* 12-21.

Conrad, P., & Kern, R. (1990). *The sociology of health and illness.* New York: St. Martin's.

Davis, F. (1963). *Passage through crisis.* Indianapolis: Bobbs-Merrill.

Ehrenreich, J., & Ehrenreich, B. (1971). *The American health empire: Power, profits, and politics.* New York: Vintage.

Fox, R. (1957). Training for uncertainty. In R. K. Merton, G. G. Reader, & P. Kendall (Eds.), *The student physician.* Cambridge: Harvard University Press.

Freeman, H. E., & Levine, S. (1990). *The handbook of medical sociology* (4th ed.). Englewood Cliffs, NJ: Prentice-Hall.

Freidson, E. (1970). *Profession of medicine.* New York: Dodd, Mead.

Goffman, E. (1961). *Asylums.* New York: Anchor.

Hollingshead, A., & Redlich, F. (1958). *Social class and mental illness.* New York: Wiley.

Kotelchuck, D. (1976). *Prognosis negative: crisis in the health care system.* New York: Vintage.

Mechanic, D. (1962). The concept of illness behavior. *Journal of Chronic Diseases, 15,* 189-194.

Merton, R. K., Reader, G. G., & Kendall, P. (1957). *The student physician.* Cambridge, MA: Harvard University Press.

Navarro, V. (1976). *Medicine under capitalism.* New York: Prodist.

Parsons, T. (1951). *The social system.* Glencoe, IL: Free Press.

Rosenstock, I. (1966). Why people use health services. *Milbank Memorial Fund Quarterly, 44,* 94-127.

Roth, J. (1963). *Timetables.* Indianapolis: Bobbs-Merrill.

Stanton, A., & Schwartz, M. S. (1954). *The mental hospital.* New York: Basic.

Straus, R. (1957). The nature and status of medical sociology. *American Sociological Review, 22,* 200-204.

Strauss, A., Schatzman, L., Bucher, R., Ehrlich, D., & Sab-shin, M. (1964). *Psychiatric ideologies and institutions.* New York: Free Press.

Suchman, E. A. (1965). Social patterns of illness and medical care. *Journal of Health and Human Behavior, 6,* 2-16.

Waitzkin, H. (1983). *The second sickness: Contradictions of capitalist health care.* New York: Free Press.

Wolinsky, F. D. (1980). *The sociology of health.* Boston: Little, Brown.

Zola, I. K. (1966). Culture and symptoms: An analysis of patients presenting complaints. *American Sociological Review, 31,* 615-630.

Zola, I. K. (1975). In the name of health and illness: on some socio-political consequences of medical influence. *Social Science and Medicine, 9,* 83-87.

3

Don Quixote, Machiavelli, and Robin Hood

Public Health Practice, Past and Present

Fitzhugh Mullan

Science and politics come face to face in the practice of public health. Public health practitioners, whether commissioners of public health departments or program staff, are assigned the task of putting the products of scientific discovery to work for the population as a whole. This they do not in a laboratory but in the public arena—a domain governed by political forces and politicians whose agendas are larger and more variable than those of the public health worker. Edwin Chadwick himself, the principal architect of British public health in the 19th century, discovered this when his energetic work as a commissioner of the General Board of Health led to its dissolution by Parliament in 1854, a mere 6 years after it was inaugurated.[1] Although Chadwick's American contemporary, Lemuel Shattuck, published his *Report of the Sanitary Commission of Massachusetts* in 1850, it was 19 years later (and after Shattuck's death) that his proposal for a health department in the state of Massachusetts was enacted.[2]

These 19th-century leaders, and many who worked with and after them, succeeded in coupling the growing understanding of science—particularly bacteriology, or "sanitary science"—to the engine of government to create the public health movement. Although born of government, this movement sought to disencumber itself from patronage and the venality of politicians and the political process. Early leaders of state and municipal boards of health included social reformers, politicians, and physicians, and progress in sanitation was often offset by corruption and scandal. These boards focused on issues such as sewage and waste removal, vaccination, and the testing of milk to ensure child health.[3]

In April 1872, Drs Stephen Smith and Elisha Harris of New York convened a small group of their colleagues to explore the formation of an organization in what is the first documented professional meeting of health officers. At a larger meeting on September 12 of that year, the American Public Health Association was founded, a seminal moment in the establishment of public health as a domain of professional practice. From that point on, the American Public Health Association was a strong supporter of the formation of boards of health and the professionalization of public health leadership.[4]

Most of the early boards of health functioned as advisory bodies, with little power to make changes in the face of competing interests. However, revolutionary discoveries made during the latter years of the 19th century, by Pasteur, Koch, and others, led to innovations in areas such as the production of diphtheria antitoxin and the control of tuberculosis, giving health officials increasing credibility and authority. By the early years of the 20th century formal health departments had emerged as the agencies of public health, most headed by physicians and staffed by sanitary engineers, bacteriologists, chemists, and trained inspectors. Their enterprises multiplied rapidly, encompassing contagious disease control, food inspection, plumbing, school health, child health, the licensing of physicians and midwives, and campaigns against specific conditions such as "social evil" (prostitution).[5]

Public health in this epoch gained an element of police power and enforcement that represented a degree of independence for public health officials that had not existed previously. It is difficult to measure this degree of independence compared with that of the current epoch, but many important early leaders—such as George Whipple of Massachusetts, Charles Chapin of Rhode Island, Victor Vaughn of Michigan, John Hurty of Indiana, and Oscar Dowling of Louisiana—held office for far longer than officials of today and provided significant public health leadership at the state and national levels.[6] Perhaps the most influential health official of this epoch was Hermann Biggs, who served as health commissioner of New York City and then New York State for almost 40 years. His tenure spanned the turn of the century, and he played a leadership role in tuberculosis control, use of diphtheria antitoxin, development of community health centers, and administrative reform.[7]

The Public Health Official in the 20th Century

The Progressive movement of the first years of the 20th century gave Biggs and his reformist colleagues an enormous boost. The movement focused attention on issues such as poverty, child labor, maternal and child health, and social insurance.[8] Political Progressivism melded scientific efficiency with moral compassion, creating an ideal environment for the growth of public health. Although a number of cities on the eastern seaboard had health boards beginning in the early 19th century, and Massachusetts established the first state health department in 1869, it was the final years of the 19th century and the first decades of the 20th that saw state and local health departments spread across the country and the role of the health official in public life become more important.

Two very important developments for the public health movement took place in the second decade of the 20th century. The first was the enactment of legislation in 1912 that changed the name of the Public Health and Marine Hospital Service to, simply, the Public Health Service. It also added to the mission of the newly named agency the investigation of "the diseases of man and propagation and spread thereof, including sanitation and sewage and the pollution either directly or indirectly of the navigable streams and lakes of the United States."[9] The mission of the Public Health Service, which had previously been limited to quarantine, medical research, and the care of merchant sailors, was dramatically expanded, creating a corps of federal public health officials who would serve as allies of state and local health officials working on local health, sanitation, and environmental problems. Indeed, in the years following the passage of this legislation Public Health Service personnel tackled multiple problems of rural sanitation and health, including hookworm, trachoma, and pellagra.[10]

The second portentous happening of this period for public health practice was the advent of county health departments—a development that would ultimately create the largest cadre of public health officials in the United States. The suburbanization of metropolitan areas provided the impetus for the formation of the first county health agencies, which occurred in 1908 in Jefferson County, Kentucky, where Louisville is located, and in 1911 in Guilford County, North Carolina, where Greensboro is located.[11] In 1911 a typhoid epidemic in Yakima, Washington, led the Public Health Service to dispatch Dr Leslie Lumsden, who, working with the state health department and local officials, performed a sanitary survey of the county. That survey led to the appointment of a fulltime Yakima County health officer and established a pattern of Public Health Service locality surveys that catalyzed the formation of many county health departments.[12]

Federal grants-in-aid to state and local public health departments began, cautiously, with the Sheppard-Towner Act of 1921, which provided support to child health programs through state health departments.[13] Congress killed the program in 1929 by denying it funding, but the Sheppard-Towner Act proved to be a precursor to Title V of the Social Security Act of 1935, which has fueled the national Maternal and Child Health program through state and local health departments since that time. Title VI of the Social Security Act provided state health departments for general public health purposes. This funding, coupled with Depression-driven programs such as the Works Progress Administration and the Public Works Administration, built a financial base under health departments that supported health surveys, new construction, and hiring of new personnel.[14] These developments armed public health officials with increased resources and larger constituencies, but they also made the work more complex and more political.

World War II and its aftermath saw major changes in both health science and the role of public health agencies. Prewar sanitary successes against infectious diseases, combined with the advent of antibiotics and the polio vaccine after the war, decreased the focus of health agencies and the public on contagious illnesses. Mental, occupational, and environmental health became the domain of health departments in a world dominated by the rapid growth of hospitals financed by the Hill-Burton program, private health insurance, and medical research funded through the National Institutes of Health. The administration of public health functions at the state and local level varied considerably from area to area, but as mental, occupational, and environmental health issues were joined in the mid-1960s by Medicaid (in some states), the situation called for public health officials with an increasing range of management and political skills.

From the 1960s on, federal agencies funded augmented levels of state and local health department activity—often with state matching-fund requirements—in areas such as maternal and child health, nutrition, immunization, control of sexually transmitted diseases, and health planning. Prevention and health education were increasingly important themes in public health work in areas such as tobacco use, seat-belt use, injury prevention, and gun control. Perhaps the most unexpected aspect of the life of the public health official in recent years has been the resurgence of infectious disease. HIV/AIDS is the most prominent of the new infections, but the emergence of Legionnaire disease, hantavirus infections, toxic shock syndrome, viral hemorrhagic fevers, and multidrug-resistant tuberculosis in today's mobile and heavily populated world has recommissioned the contemporary health officer as a soldier in the war against infectious disease.

Throughout the late 1930s and 1940s, the idea of national health insurance was hotly debated. Public health officials often found themselves in difficult positions, caught between their desire to serve the sick and the poor and the American Medical Association's aggressive opposition to any national health insurance program.[15] The legislative campaign eventually faltered, but the national debate continued, resulting ultimately in the passage of the Medicare and Medicaid programs in 1965. Although a number of the programs enacted in the 1960s to provide health services to disadvantaged populations (e.g., the Community and Migrant Health Center program and the National Health Service Corps) bypassed public health agencies, with federal grants given directly to communities,[16] a devolutionary emphasis in Washington and the growing prominence of state governments have put state and local health agencies back in the middle of the debate about health care for the increasingly large population of uninsured Americans.

The Multiple Roles of the Public Health Official

In 1945 the great public health scholar and philosopher C.E.A. Winslow assumed the editorship of the *American Journal of Public Health,* a position he would hold for a decade. He wrote: "*In the half of the century yet to come, the health officer must not be solely interested in syphilis, tuberculosis, or even heart disease and cancer. He must more and more concern himself with nutrition [and] housing. . . . He should lead in the elimination of substandard dwellings and participate actively in the planning for slum clearance, urban development and low-rent housing. He must concern himself with the living wage and the provision of a due measure of social security which is essential to both physiological and psychological health.*" In other words, public health which in its earliest days was an engineering science and has now become also a medical science must expand until it is, in addition, a social science.[17]

Winslow envisioned the health officer as someone who would take on not only the problems of ill health in the population but also the social circumstances that generate ill health. Undoubtedly, Winslow's vision will resonate with many individuals who took up the mantle of public health practice in the latter part of the 20th century. It is an ambitious and idealistic vision. Half a century later, how does life in public health practice compare with the challenge laid down by Winslow? What are the principles and challenges that face the public health official of today?

In the domain of public health at the outset of the 21st century, the stakes are very often high, and the life of a public health official is complex. He or she deals with some of society's toughest issues, including HIV/AIDS, environmental quality, abortion, addiction, and homelessness. Medicaid and Medicare, in particular, are big-ticket budget items, as are state-run institutions and government-sponsored community health and mental health centers. Even nonbudgetary health issues, such as tobacco policy and nursing home standards, involve large, politically organized industries. Needle exchange programs and physician-assisted suicide touch sensitive public nerves. Inevitably, public health practice becomes involved in the politics of the time and place, and public health practitioners are, perforce, political players.

These, of course, are issues that many others in our society engage as well. Public health officials, however, do not have the latitude of elected officials, who tackle these questions from their own political perspectives, mindful, presumably, of the preferences of their constituencies. Public health officials do not enjoy the certainty of business managers, whose approach to these issues is governed by market forces and technocratic imperatives. And public health officials, unlike clinicians, cannot base their decisions on biological science alone.

The public health official, in fact, must be politician, manager, and clinician in varying degrees at all times. Not only does this require a broad range of abilities and multiple databases, but the proportion of each of these skills that the public health leader exercises at any given time depends entirely on the circumstances. At the height of a legislative session, the public health official must be an adept politician, twisting arms and making pragmatic compromises with the best of them. Back at the office, he or she will be called on to make major management decisions about computer systems, labor relations, and risk management for departmental employees. Immunization strategies, HIV testing policy, and *Pfiesteria* outbreaks call on the public health official's clinical judgment and training. Although politics, management, and science make a heady brew and ensure that the job will never be dull, stepping regularly between these 3 walks of life can be awkward and hazardous—not to say fatiguing.

Don Quixote, Machiavelli, and Robin Hood

On a philosophical level, the challenge runs deeper. Many people enter the field of public health because it is a discipline that promises to give substance to their sense of altruism. As Winslow suggested, it is work that puts principle into action, that struggles toward the ideal even as it deals with some of society's most intransigent problems and most entrenched interests. For people coming of age in the post-Sputnik era, a career in public health blends science, the civil rights movement, and the Peace Corps experience. While solid waste and substandard nursing homes are more likely than windmills to be public health workers' targets, there needs to be a little Don Quixote in all public health practitioners—Don Quixote, the unabashed, unapologetic, unflappable idealist, locked in on his mission, undaunted by the doubters and the halfhearted.

But Don Quixote alone is not sufficient. The stakes are high, and the adversaries of public health have never heard of Don Quixote. Altruism does not motivate landlords to conduct lead paint abatement programs or restaurateurs to designate no-smoking areas in their establishments. Those who want to protect the quality of air and water invite altercations with some of society's largest and best-organized commercial interests. Battling—let alone besting—such interests requires cunning, daring, and doggedness in variable measures. Although issues such as these are sometimes joined in the courtroom, they are never matters for judicial review until laws have been passed proscribing certain behaviors as threats to the public health. Therefore, the first rounds of public health advocacy are always fought in the legislative chambers, meaning that the public health official must be adept at generating the alliances of political interests and support that will put public health statutes on the books. The proverbial horse trades and smoke-filled rooms must be part of the beat of the successful public health official.

In his 16th-century treatise *The Prince,* Machiavelli laid out for all time the rules of cunning and intrigue in the conduct of palace politics. Public health leaders who are ambitious for their programs would do well to read *The Prince* and carry a modicum of Machiavelli's pragmatic cynicism with them as they put their ideals to work for the public good. Public health work spans the geographic, social, and economic breadth of our society. Rich and poor, uptown and downtown, rural and urban, commercial and residential—all rely on the purity of the drinking water that is monitored by public health programs. Every citizen is affected by the quality of laboratories and nursing homes, as well as by the investigation of disease outbreaks. Historically, however, public health departments have maintained a special relationship with society's poor and less fortunate citizens, serving as an instrument to carry out programs of social equity that provide the poor with services that other citizens are able to purchase on the open market. Much of the work of public health departments today involves the provision of services to the vulnerable and the disadvantaged, for example, maternal and child health services, sexually transmitted disease programs, and the Special Supplemental Nutrition Program for Women, Infants, and Children (WIC).

The public health department is, therefore, an instrument of economic redistribution—a public agency that uses revenues generated by that part of the population that pays taxes to provide services to citizens who very often do not. The public health official is, perforce, an agent of and often a spokesperson for distributional justice. If public health programs are to be successful, they must draw funds from the public treasury and spend them on individuals who may be perceived by many as undeserving, troublesome, or even criminal. These programs will treat addicts, alcoholics, homeless persons, children born out of wedlock, and AIDS patients. These people are the clientele of the public health official, and to serve them well he or she must be prepared to assault the public purse on their behalf. Part of the public health official's professional identity must be that of Robin Hood, taking from the rich and giving to the poor, ambushing the public conscience and budget whenever possible to provide better and more humane services to the poor. Without such a sense of mission, a public health official runs the risk of becoming a warden and providing leadership impoverished of both finance and spirit.

The Public Health Official and the Executive

Keeping Don Quixote, Machiavelli, and Robin Hood in mind will help steer the public health official through the difficult and fascinating course that he or she must travel. A fourth person who must be kept in mind is the elected executive (president, governor, mayor, or county executive) for whom the health official works. The elected public official is as close as America comes to royalty. Public executives are potentates pro tem, and although not all of them act that way, most have the authority to command not only political loyalty but personal fealty. Elected executives (in contrast to elected legislators) have the apparatus of government as their responsibility and at their disposal, and the public health official is a beneficiary as well as a captive of that authority. A public health official who is of one mind with the executive will enjoy significant derivative power, but one whose person or program is out of favor with the executive will find that power greatly diminished, and most likely will be out of a job before long.

Being in league and in step with the executive is more than a matter of palace protocol. It is a requirement for professional effectiveness. It is also an arena in which the public health official enjoys a potential advantage over other public administrators, because a smart executive will recognize the technical nature of many of the issues in the health portfolio and will defer to the judgment of the public health official in a way that he or she might not with appointees who are less clearly professionally grounded.

The public health official will be called on to tangle with other members of the executive's cabinet on issues of economic or social contention in which the health perspective differs from that of other interests—when to shut down a convention because of Legionnaire disease, how to promote safe sex, when to declare a water source unsafe because of chemical or infectious contaminants. These circumstances raise issues for public health officials that do, indeed, invite the counsel of Machiavelli. The need to remain faithful to scientific and objective criteria for action must coexist with the necessary deference to elected political power. A public health official rarely succeeds in publicly stepping over his chief executive in pursuit of a public health issue, as Surgeon General C. Everett Koop did with President Reagan in the case of AIDS. The more common task of the public health official, and it is a crucial one, is to educate and persuade the executive at every opportunity. At stake are issues of style as well as substance, and the effective official will compromise far more often on issues of style than on those of substance.

Robin Hood at Risk

Although Don Quixote and Machiavelli are alive and well in the ranks of public health officials, there is reason to be concerned that Robin Hood is at risk. The role of health departments in the redistribution of wealth has always been open to some debate in the ranks of public health practitioners. There have always been public health leaders who have argued that the provision of medical care diverts public health from its real purpose and takes money from its coffers. Individuals holding this philosophy argued against public health involvement in early efforts to pass a national health insurance plan and prevented the formation of a medical care section in the American Public Health Association until 1949.[18] The same sentiments were extant in the ranks of the U.S. Public Health Service and were responsible for creating an environment in which Medicare and Medicaid, when enacted in 1965, were never candidates for inclusion in the Public Health Service. Those sentiments in the public health community, coupled with what is often an activist interest in medical care in the welfare community, are responsible for the fact that Medicaid was linked legislatively to public assistance from the outset and for the fact that the vast majority of Medicaid programs have always been run by state agencies other than the health department. Medicaid is the largest redistributional program in the health sphere, and, unhappily, in many instances the public health community has allowed the role of Robin Hood to be played by others.

The Institute of Medicine's landmark 1988 publication *The Future of Public Health* dealt judiciously with this issue.[19] That report declares that one of the 3 major functions of public health is "assurance," meaning that health departments should concern themselves with making sure that services get delivered to disadvantaged citizens. While this is a statesmanlike accommodation to the varied reality of attitudes about the delivery of medical services by health agencies, it does allow a fair amount of latitude to those who are disinclined to see health services delivery as an essential public health function.

Most recently there was President Clinton's failed health care reform initiative, which would have ensured that all Americans had a primary care provider available to deliver the full complement of preventive and curative services. Had such legislation been enacted, the need for health departments to play a role in health services delivery would have been greatly diminished. But this did not happen. Although Medicaid managed care requires the provision of full preventive and primary care services, it covers only a minority of poor and uninsured Americans—meaning that the role of public health agencies in the health care safety net will remain essential for the foreseeable future.

These historical trends, along with the impact of the welfare reform law, immigration policy, and the declining levels of free care provided by hospitals, mean that Robin Hood is embattled. Machiavelli and Don Quixote can provide Robin Hood with some assistance, but public health officials need to continue to speak out on behalf of their poor and disadvantaged clients, for whom the celebrated "marketplace" provides little and for whom publicly sponsored programs are increasingly the only option. It is easy to look beyond the health care needs of the moment to a time in the future when universal coverage will finally come to the United States—when health departments will be able to focus on assessment, policy development, and assurance. But that time is not now.

It is hard to be certain, of course, but it seems likely that our forebears in public health—the strategists Edwin Chadwick and Lemuel Shattuck, the quintessential practitioner Hermann Biggs, the scholar and historian C.E.A. Winslow, and the founder of the American Public Health Association, Stephen Smith—would share these apprehensions about the state of our system as we enter the 21st century, and that they would call on the Robin Hood in today's public health leaders to be active and vigilant.

Notes

1. George Rosen, *A History of Public Health* (New York, NY: MD Publications Inc, 1958), 197-228.

2. Lemuel Shattuck, *Report of the Sanitary Commission of Massachusetts* (1850; reprint, Cambridge, Mass: Harvard University Press, 1948).

3. The following review of the history of public health departments in the United States draws from Rosen, 294-496; John Duffy, *The Sanitarians: A History of Public Health* (Urbana and Chicago: University of Illinois Press, 1990), 126-316; and Paul Starr, *The Social Transformation of American Medicine* (New York, NY: Basic Books, 1982), 180-197.

4. Duffy, 130, 148.

5. Starr, 184-189; Duffy, 143, 205-206.

6. Duffy, 222.

7. Charles-Edward Avery Winslow, *The Life of Hermann Biggs* (Philadelphia, Pa: Lea & Febiger, 1929).

8. Commentaries by 3 important public health practitioners from the first quarter of the 20th century—B.S. Warren and Edgar Sydenstricker, "The Relation of Wages to the Public Health," and C.E.A. Winslow, "Public Health at the Crossroads"—have been reprinted in the *American Journal of Public Health* 89 (1999), 1641-1648.

9. Bess Furman, *A Profile of the United States Public Health Service, 1789-1948* (Washington, DC: U.S. Department of Health, Education, and Welfare, 1973), 286-287.

10. Fitzhugh Mullan, *Plagues and Politics: The Story of the United States Public Health Service* (New York, NY: Basic Books, 1989), 58-70.

11. Duffy, 232.

12. Ralph C. Williams, *The United States Public Health Service, 1798-1950* (Washington, DC: The Commissioned Officer Association of the United States Public Health Service, 1951), 141, 337-339.

13. Rosen, 363-364.

14. Duffy, 258-261.

15. Starr, 280-286; Duffy, 275-277.

16. Fitzhugh Mullan, "The National Health Service Corps and Health Personnel Innovations: Beyond Poorhouse Medicine," in *Reforming Medicine: Lessons*

of the Last Quarter Century, ed. Victor Sidel and Ruth Sidel (New York, NY: Pantheon, 1984), 176-200.

17. C.E.A. Winslow, quoted by Milton Terris in the introduction to the reprint edition of Winslow, *The Evolution and Significance of the Modern Public Health Campaign* (1923; reprint, New Haven, Conn: Yale University Press, 1984).

18. A. Viseltear, "Emergence of the Medical Care Section of the American Public Health Association, 1926-1948," *American Journal of Public Health* 63 (1972), 986-1007.

19. Institute of Medicine, *The Future of Public Health* (Washington, DC: National Academy Press, 1988).

4

Type A Botulism From Sautéed Onions

Clinical and Epidemiologic Observations

Kristine L. MacDonald, Robert F. Spengler,
Charles L. Hatheway, Nancy T. Hargrett, and Mitchell L. Cohen

Approximately 30 cases of food-borne botulism are reported in the United States each year. In most instances, illness is limited to one or two persons, and only two outbreaks involving 20 or more persons have been reported.[1,2] Investigation of such large outbreaks provides an opportunity to learn more about botulism, since persons with a range of clinical symptoms are identified, including those with mild illness. Canned products, primarily home canned, are the most frequent causes of botulism. In recent botulism outbreaks, however, foods not previously considered to be potential vehicles were mishandled in ways that provided adequate conditions for *Clostridium botulinum* growth and toxin production. This report describes the clinical and epidemiologic aspects of the third largest botulism outbreak in the United States in which another unusual vehicle—sautéed onions—was incriminated. The investigation emphasizes the importance of considering even theoretically unlikely food items as potential vehicles for botulinal toxin.

The Outbreak

During the evening of Saturday, Oct 15, 1983, three patients were hospitalized with signs and symptoms compatible with botulism. All three had eaten the same food items at a local restaurant the previous day: a patty-melt sandwich, French fries, lettuce, tomatoes, and a dill-pickle spear. Local health officials inspected the restaurant that evening. Because pickles were the only canned food item consumed by the three patients, the pickles were confiscated from the restaurant as the suspected vehicle. On

EDITORS' NOTE: From the *Journal of the American Medical Association, 253,* 1985, pp. 1275-1278.

Oct 16, six additional patients with similar symptoms were admitted to hospitals in the Peoria, Ill, area. The next day, the restaurant was closed pending further investigation.

Methods

Epidemiologic Investigation

For this investigation, a case of botulism was defined as an illness in any person who had eaten at the implicated restaurant on Friday, Saturday, or Sunday (Oct 14 through 16, 1983) and that included one of the following signs or symptom complexes: (1) onset of diplopia; (2) onset of any two of the following symptoms: dry mouth, blurred vision, dysphagia, or dysphonia; or (3) any one of these symptoms in combination with onset on physical examination of cranial nerve dysfunction, extremity weakness, or respiratory failure. All hospitals in Illinois were notified of the outbreak. The public was informed through the media and alerted to symptoms compatible with botulism. All emergency room records for the two major hospitals in Peoria were reviewed at the end of the outbreak period to identify any possible additional cases. Data on symptoms, therapy, and physical examination were obtained by reviewing the hospital records for all case-patients.

A standard questionnaire was administered to all persons considered case-patients. Information was obtained on food histories, time of eating, and seating location within the restaurant. Five case-control studies were conducted; all of the persons in the control groups had consumed food at the restaurant during the same three-day period as the case-patients. The first four studies compared food histories from case-patients with food histories from the following groups: restaurant employees working during the three-day period ($n = 24$), employees of shops in the mall where the restaurant is located ($n = 43$), persons who had used credit cards to pay for their meal on Oct 16, 1983 ($n = 14$), and companions who ate with the case-patients ($n = 38$). A strong association between eating a patty-melt sandwich and becoming ill was demonstrated in all studies; therefore, a fifth study was undertaken to determine which ingredient of the implicated sandwich was associated with illness. Controls were obtained through the media by asking all people who had eaten a patty-melt sandwich at the implicated restaurant during the time of potential exposure to call the local health department. These people were asked to describe the sandwich to verify that they had eaten a patty-melt. They were then questioned about food items they had eaten with their patty-melt sandwiches and any symptoms they might have experienced. Seventeen people who had eaten patty-melt sandwiches during the three-day period responded.

The implicated restaurant was inspected by state and local health officials and by investigators from the Food and Drug Administration (FDA). The owners, chefs, and other staff were questioned extensively about cooking practices, storage of food items, cleaning practices, and deliveries made to the restaurant. Food samples were collected for culturing and toxin testing.

Laboratory Investigation

Stool and/or serum specimens were collected from ill persons. Stool specimens were also collected from two control groups: restaurant employees and persons who had eaten the implicated sandwich but did not meet the case definition for botulism. Food specimens were also collected from the implicated restaurant. Stool and serum specimens were examined at the Centers for Disease Control (CDC), Atlanta, for botulinal toxin using the mouse bioassay, and stool specimens were examined for *C botulinum* organisms by inoculating chopped meat-glucose-starch medium, followed by anaerobic incubation, testing the cultures for mouse toxicity, and subsequent subculture onto egg-yolk agar.[3] Food specimens were examined at the CDC, the FDA, and the U.S. Department of Agriculture for toxin and *C botulinum.*

Results

Clinical and Epidemiologic Investigation

Twenty-eight people were found who met the case definition of botulism. Their mean age was 42 years (range, 20 to 73 years), and 20 were female. All patients were hospitalized, 12 required ventilatory support, and one died. The mean incubation period was 34 hours (range, 12 to 115 hours). The 12 patients with severe illness and who required ventilatory support had a shorter mean incubation period (21 hours) than did the other 16 patients (44 hours) ($P = .02$; Mann-Whitney U test). Of the 12 patients who required ventilatory support, five had a triad of neurologic signs on initial examination (in addition to other findings): extraocular muscle palsy, ptosis, and dilated or sluggishly reactive pupils. Of the remaining 16 patients with milder illness, this triad did not develop during the first week of hospitalization ($P = .008$; Fisher's exact test, two tailed). Of 27 patients with neurologic abnormalities on physical examination, 37% had sixth cranial nerve dysfunction. Twenty patients were each treated with two vials of trivalent ABE antitoxin. No acute hypersensitivity reactions occurred, but one patient had serum sickness several days after treatment.

All patients had eaten at the same restaurant over a three-day period. In 24 of 28 cases, the patients recalled having eaten a patty-melt sandwich. The remaining four had eaten a variety of other food items. The first four case-control studies showed a strong association between having eaten a patty-melt sandwich and development of botulism ($P < .0001$; Fisher's exact test, two tailed). In the fifth case-control study, we interviewed 41 customers (24 cases, 17 controls) who had eaten the patty-melt. Since we estimated that only 40 to 45 patty-melts were sold during the three-day period, we were able to interview most, if not all, of the persons who had eaten the sandwich. All 24 patients but only 10 of 17 controls ate the sautéed onions that were served on the sandwich ($P <. 001$; Fisher's exact test, two tailed). None of the 17 controls who ate patty-melts met our case definition for botulism, but three of them, all of whom had eaten sautéed onions, had new onset of dry mouth or muscle weakness within one week after eating the suspect meal.

A total of 1,863 people ate at the implicated restaurant over the three days of potential exposure, giving a total attack rate for restaurant patrons of 1.5%. Food tickets for the three-day period were not available; however, the estimated attack rate for developing botulism in restaurant patrons who ate the patty-melt, based on data obtained from controls, was 51% (24/47).

The patty-melt sandwich, as prepared by the implicated restaurant, was a hamburger patty served on toasted rye bread with two slices of melted American cheese and sautéed onions. Lettuce, tomato, and dill-pickle spear were served as a garnish, with a choice of French fries or potato salad. The onions were initially sliced and then cooked for 10 to 15 minutes with approximately 0.9 kg of margarine; garlic salt, paprika, and powdered chicken base were then added. The mixture was then poured into another pan so that the onions were covered by a thick layer of melted margarine and set on a grill for use during the day. The onions were not reheated before being served on the patty-melt sandwich. There was conflicting information as to whether the onion mixture was ever held overnight for serving the next day. While on the grill, the mixture had a pH of 5.6 and a temperature that stabilized at 41°C. A set of tongs was used to handle the sautéed onions and other food items.

Laboratory Investigation

Eighteen patients had type A *C botulinum* organisms or toxin detected: 14 had toxin detected in serum or stool and *C botulinum* isolated from stool; four others had *C botulinum* isolated but no toxin detected. Eleven of the 12 patients who required ventilatory support and only three of the remaining 16 less critically ill patients had toxin detected ($P = .001$; Fisher's exact test, two tailed).

None of the 23 stool specimens collected from restaurant employees (none of whom had eaten patty-melts) yielded type A toxin or *C botulinum.* Two of 14 stool specimens collected from controls who had eaten the implicated sandwich yielded type A *C botulinum,* but not its toxin. Both of these people had eaten sautéed onions with their sandwiches, but neither had any symptoms of botulism.

The original sautéed onions were not available for culture or testing for toxin; however, washings of a wrapper in which one of the ill persons had taken a patty-melt home yielded type A toxin and type A organisms. Type A *C botulinum* was cultured from five of 75 raw onions obtained from the restaurant. When other food specimens were tested, including multiple samples of spices, ketchup, mustard, ground beef, margarine, cheese, pickles, and bread, they did not yield preformed toxin or *C botulinum.*

COMMENT

All patients in this outbreak had eaten at the same restaurant over a three-day period, and the case-control studies strongly implicated sautéed onions served on a patty-melt sandwich as the vehicle for type A toxin. Four persons who met our case definition, however, did not recall having eaten the sautéed onions. The food histories for these four persons may have been incorrect, or cross-contamination of other foods may have occurred through the use of serving utensils. These four patients had mild symptoms and mild ptosis as the only abnormality noted on examination, which can be a subjective finding; none had laboratory confirmation of botulism. Such mild symptoms are consistent with the ingestion of a small dose of toxin, resulting from cross-contamination of food, or possibly with an incorrect diagnosis of botulism.

Observations of the clinical appearance of patients in this outbreak showed that a triad of oculomotor findings on initial examination predicted severity of illness for type A botulism. These three abnormalities are extraocular muscle palsy (all patients had medial rectus and lateral rectus weakness), pupillary dysfunction, and ptosis; they have previously been shown to be predictive for the development of respiratory failure in a large outbreak of type B botulism,[4] and our data show the same association for type A botulism. No other single finding or complex of findings on initial examination was predictive of prognosis in our study.

Severity of illness was inversely correlated with incubation period. The mean incubation period among patients requiring ventilatory support was approximately one-half that of the other patients. The incubation period has also been correlated with dose of toxin ingested,[5] but in this outbreak, the relationship between the severity of illness and the amount of onions ingested could not be evaluated, since the 24 case-patients ate similar amounts of onions. The variable incubation periods may reflect wide variations in the concentration of toxin within the onions or variability in host susceptibility. One patient, whose incubation period was 115 hours, had used a strong laxative shortly after consuming the patty-melt sandwich, which may have affected the amount of toxin absorbed.

The most remarkable feature of this outbreak was the unusual vehicle involved. The major requirements for germination of type A *C botulinum* spores and toxin production are an appropriate pH (> 4.6), a temperature of at least 10°C, sufficient availability of water (limited solute concentration), and an anaerobic environment.[6] These conditions could have been met in this situation, since the pH and temperature were appropriate, and the anaerobic environment could potentially have been created by the onions being immersed in margarine. *Clostridium botulinum* spores are quite heat resistant and can survive two hours in boiling water.[7] Since spores are common in soil,[8] we hypothesize that the raw onions were contaminated with spores from soil that were not destroyed by initial cooking; the spores subsequently germinated and formed toxin in the warm, anaerobic conditions provided by the margarine and the grill. The demonstration of *C botulinum* in the raw onions obtained from the restaurant and simulation experiments by the PDA (Donald A. Kautter, MS, oral communication, December 1983) support this hypothesis. Since type A botulism is more common in the western United States,[3] it is of interest that the onions supplied to the implicated restaurant had been grown in three western states.

Items other than canned foods have recently been implicated in several botulism outbreaks in the United States. In 1978, two outbreak investigations implicated potato salad, and in both outbreaks the potato salad was prepared (at least in part) from leftover baked potatoes (as seen by Seals et al.[9] and in unpublished data from the CDC). Laboratory experiments confirmed that toxin could be produced in potatoes inoculated with *C botulinum* spores, then baked and incubated.[10] Several cases of botulism have also resulted from baking commercial pot pies, holding them for prolonged periods at temperatures adequate for incubation of *C botulinum* spores, and then eating without reheating them.[11]

In this outbreak, pickles were initially suspected because they were the only canned food item common to the index cases. This investigation demonstrates the importance of considering theoretically unlikely food items as potential vehicles for botulinal toxin until epidemiologic and laboratory data have been collected and analyzed. The results also demonstrate the importance of appropriate holding conditions for foods potentially contaminated with C *botulinum* spores or organisms.

NOTES

1. Terranova W, Breman JG, Locey RP, et al.: Botulism type B: Epidemiologic aspects of an extensive outbreak. *Am J Epidemiol* 1978; 108:150-156.
2. Botulism in New Mexico. *MMWR* 1978; 27:138-145.
3. *Botulism in the United States, 1899-1977: Handbook for Epidemiologists, Clinicians, and Laboratory Workers.* Atlanta, Centers for Disease Control, 1979.
4. Terranova W, Palumbo JN, Breman JG: Ocular findings in botulism type B. *JAMA* 1979, 241:475-477.
5. Donadio JA, Gangarosa EJ, Faich GA: Diagnosis and treatment of botulism. *J Infect Dis* 1971; 124:108-112.
6. Schmidt CF: Spores of *C. botulinum:* Formation, resistance, germination, in Lewis KB, Cassel K (eds.): *Botulism: Proceedings of a Symposium,* publication 999-FP-l. Cincinnati. Public Health Service, 1964, pp. 69-88.
7. Dickson EC, Burke GS, Ward ES: A study of the resistance of the spores of *Bacillus botulinus* to various sterilizing agencies which are commonly employed in the canning of fruits and vegetables. *Arch Intern Med* 1919; 24:581-589.
8. Smith LDS: The occurrence of *Clostridium botulinum* and *Clostridium tctani* in the soil of the United States. *Health Lab Sci* 1978; 15:74-80.
9. Seals JE, Snyder JD, Edell TA, et al.: Restaurant-associated type A botulism: Transmission by potato salad. *Am J Epidemiol* 1981, 113:436-444.
10. Sugiyama H, Woodburn M, Yang KH, et al.: Production of botulinum toxin in inoculated pack studies of foil-wrapped baked potatoes. J *Food Protection* 1981; 44:800-898.
11. Botulism and commercial pot pie: California. *MMWR* 1983; 32:39-40, 45.

5

The Need for a New Medical Model

A Challenge for Biomedicine

George L. Engel

At a recent conference on psychiatric education, many psychiatrists seemed to be saying to medicine, "Please take us back and we will never again deviate from the 'medical model.'" For, as one critical psychiatrist put it, "Psychiatry has become a hodgepodge of unscientific opinions, assorted philosophies and 'schools of thought,' mixed metaphors, role diffusion, propaganda, and politicking for 'mental health' and other esoteric goals".[1] In contrast, the rest of medicine appears neat and tidy. It has a firm base in the biological sciences, enormous technologic resources at its command, and a record of astonishing achievement in elucidating mechanisms of disease and devising new treatments. It would seem that psychiatry would do well to emulate its sister medical disciplines by finally embracing once and for all the medical model of disease.

But I do not accept such a premise. Rather, I contend that all medicine is in crisis and, further, that medicine's crisis derives from the same basic fault as psychiatry's, namely, adherence to a model of disease no longer adequate for the scientific tasks and social responsibilities of either medicine or psychiatry. The importance of how physicians conceptualize disease derives from how such concepts determine what are considered the proper boundaries of professional responsibility and how they influence attitudes toward and behavior with patients. Psychiatry's crisis revolves around the

---

question of whether the categories of human distress with which it is concerned are properly considered "disease" as currently conceptualized and whether exercise of the traditional authority of the physician is appropriate for their helping functions. Medicine's crisis stems from the logical inference that since "disease" is defined in terms of somatic parameters, physicians need not be concerned with psychosocial issues which lie outside medicine's responsibility and authority. At a recent Rockefeller Foundation seminar on the concept of health, one authority urged that medicine "concentrate on the 'real' diseases and not get lost in the psychosociological underbrush. The physician should not be saddled with problems that have arisen from the abdication of the theologian and the philosopher." Another participant called for "a disentanglement of the organic elements of disease from the psychosocial elements of human malfunction," arguing that medicine should deal with the former only.[2]

The Two Positions

Psychiatrists have responded to their crisis by embracing two ostensibly opposite positions. One would simply exclude psychiatry from the field of medicine, while the other would adhere strictly to the "medical model" and limit psychiatry's field to behavioral disorders consequent to brain dysfunction. The first is exemplified in the writings of Szasz and others who advance the position that "mental illness is a myth" since it does not conform with the accepted concept of disease.[3] Supporters of this position advocate the removal of the functions now performed by psychiatry from the conceptual and professional jurisdiction of medicine and their reallocation to a new discipline based on behavioral science. Henceforth medicine would be responsible for the treatment and cure of disease, while the new discipline would be concerned with the reeducation of people with "problems of living." Implicit in this argument is the premise that while the medical model constitutes a sound framework within which to understand and treat disease, it is not relevant to the behavioral and psychological problems classically deemed the domain of psychiatry. Disorders directly ascribable to brain disorder would be taken care of by neurologists, while psychiatry as such would disappear as a medical discipline.

The contrasting posture of strict adherence to the medical model is caricatured in Ludwig's view of the psychiatrist as physician.[1] According to Ludwig, the medical model premises "that sufficient deviation from normal represents that *disease* is due to known or unknown natural causes, and that elimination of these causes will result in cure or improvement in individual patients" (Ludwig's italics). While acknowledging that most psychiatric diagnoses have a lower level of confirmation than most medical diagnoses, he adds that they are not "qualitatively different provided that mental disease is assumed to arise largely from 'natural' rather than metapsychological, interpersonal or societal causes." "Natural" is defined as "biological brain dysfunctions, either biochemical or neurophysiological in nature." On the other hand, "disorders such as problems of living, social adjustment reactions, character disorders, dependency syndromes, existential depressions, and various social deviancy conditions [would] be excluded from the concept of mental illness since these disorders arise in individuals with presumably intact neurophysiological functioning and are produced primarily by psychosocial variables." Such "nonpsychiatric disorders" are not properly the concern of the physician-psychiatrist and are more appropriately handled by nonmedical professionals.

In sum, psychiatry struggles to clarify its status within the mainstream of medicine, if indeed it belongs in medicine at all. The criterion by which this question is supposed to be resolved rests on the degree to which the field of activity of psychiatry is deemed congruent with the existing medical model of disease. But crucial to this problem is another, that of whether the contemporary model is, in fact, any longer adequate for medicine, much less for psychiatry. For if it is not, then perhaps the crisis of psychiatry is part and parcel of a larger crisis that has its roots in the model itself. Should that be the case, then it would be imprudent for psychiatry prematurely to abandon its models in favor of one that may also be flawed.

THE BIOMEDICAL MODEL

The dominant model of disease today is biomedical, with molecular biology its basic scientific discipline. It assumes disease to be fully accounted for by deviations from the norm of measurable biological (somatic) variables. It leaves no room within its framework for the social, psychological, and behavioral dimensions of illness. The biomedical model not only requires that disease be dealt with as an entity independent of social behavior, it also demands that behavioral aberrations be explained on the basis of disordered somatic (biochemical or neurophysiological) processes. Thus the biomedical model embraces both reductionism, the philosophic view that complex phenomena are ultimately derived from a single primary principle, and mind-body dualism, the doctrine that separates the mental from the somatic. Here the reductionistic primary principle is physicalistic; that is, it assumes that the language of chemistry and physics will ultimately suffice to explain biological phenomena. From the reductionist viewpoint, the only conceptual tools available to characterize and experimental tools to study biological systems are physical in nature.[4]

The biomedical model was devised by medical scientists for the study of disease. As such it was a scientific model; that is, it involved a shared set of assumptions and rules of conduct based on the scientific method, and constituted a blueprint for research. Not all models are scientific. Indeed, broadly defined, a model is nothing more than a belief system utilized to explain natural phenomena, to make sense out of what is puzzling or disturbing. The more socially disruptive or individually upsetting the phenomenon, the more pressing the need of humans to devise explanatory systems. Such efforts at explanation constitute devices for social adaptation. Disease par excellence exemplifies a category of natural phenomena urgently demanding explanation.[5] As Fabrega has pointed out, "disease" in its generic sense is a linguistic term used to refer to a certain class of phenomena that members of all social groups, at all times in the history of man, have been exposed to. "When people of various intellectual and cultural persuasions use terms analogous to 'disease,' they have in mind, among other things, that the phenomena in question involve a person-centered, harmful, and undesirable deviation or discontinuity . . . associated with impairment or discomfort".[5] Since the condition is not desired it gives rise to a need for corrective actions. The latter involve beliefs and explanations about disease as well as rules of conduct to rationalize treatment actions. These constitute socially adaptive devices to resolve, for the individual as well as for the society in which the sick person lives, the crises and uncertainties surrounding disease.[6]

Such culturally derived belief systems about disease also constitute models, but they are not scientific models. These may be referred to as popular or folk models. As efforts at social adaptation, they contrast with scientific models, which are primarily designed to promote scientific investigation. The historical fact we have to face is that in modern Western society biomedicine not only has provided a basis for the scientific study of disease, it has also become our own culturally specific perspective about disease, that is, our folk model. Indeed the biomedical model is now the dominant folk model of disease in the Western world.[5,6]

In our culture the attitudes and belief systems of physicians are molded by this model long before they embark on their professional education, which in turn reinforces it without necessarily clarifying how its use for social adaptation contrasts with its use for scientific research. The biomedical model has thus become a cultural imperative, its limitations easily overlooked. In brief, it has now acquired the status of *dogma*. In science, a model is revised or abandoned when it fails to account adequately for all the data. A dogma, on the other hand, requires that discrepant data be forced to fit the model or be excluded. Biomedical dogma requires that all disease, including "mental" disease, be conceptualized in terms of derangement of underlying physical mechanisms. This permits only two alternatives whereby behavior and disease can be reconciled: the *reductionist*, which says that all behavioral phenomena of disease must be conceptualized in terms of physicochemical principles; and the *exclusionist,* which says that whatever is not capable of being so explained must be excluded from the category of disease. The reductionists concede that some disturbances in behavior belong in the spectrum of disease. They categorize these as mental diseases and designate psychiatry as the relevant medical discipline. The exclusionists regard mental illness as a myth and would eliminate psychiatry from medicine. Among physicians and psychiatrists today the reductionists are the true believers, the exclusionists are the apostates, while both condemn as heretics those who dare to question the ultimate truth of the biomedical model and advocate a more useful model.

Historical Origins of the Reductionistic Biomedical Model

In considering the requirements for a more inclusive scientific medical model for the study of disease, an ethnomedical perspective is helpful.[6] In all societies, ancient and modern, preliterate and literate, the major criteria for identification of disease have always been behavioral, psychological, and social in nature. Classically, the onset of disease is marked by changes in physical appearance that frighten, puzzle, or awe, and by alterations in functioning, in feelings, in performance, in behavior, or in relationships that are experienced or perceived as threatening, harmful, unpleasant, deviant, undesirable, or unwanted. Reported verbally or demonstrated by the sufferer or by a witness, these constitute the primary data upon which are based first-order judgments as to whether or not a person is sick.[7] To such disturbing behavior and reports all societies typically respond by designating individuals and evolving social institutions whose primary function is to evaluate, interpret, and provide corrective measures.[5,6] Medicine as an institution and as a discipline, and physicians as professionals, evolved as one form of response to such social needs. In the course of history, medicine became scientific as physicians and other scientists developed a taxonomy and applied scientific methods to the understanding, treatment, and prevention of disturbances which the public first had designated as "disease" or "sickness."

Why did the reductionistic, dualistic biomedical model evolve in the West? Rasmussen identifies one source in the concession of established Christian orthodoxy to permit dissection of the human body some five centuries ago.[8] Such a concession was in keeping with the Christian view of the body as a weak and imperfect vessel for the transfer of the soul from this world to the next. Not surprisingly, the Church's permission to study the human body included a tacit interdiction against corresponding scientific investigation of man's mind and behavior. For in the eyes of the Church these had more to do with religion and the soul and hence properly remained its domain. This compact may be considered largely responsible for the anatomical and structural base upon which scientific Western medicine eventually was to be built. For at the same time, the basic principle of the science of the day, as enunciated by Galileo, Newton, and Descartes, was analytical, meaning that entities to be investigated be resolved into isolable causal chains or units, from which it was assumed that the whole could be understood, both materially and conceptually, by reconstituting the parts. With mind-body dualism firmly established under the imprimatur of the Church, classical science readily fostered the notion of the body as a machine, of disease as the consequence of breakdown of the machine, and of the doctor's task as repair of the machine. Thus the scientific approach to disease began by focusing in a fractional-analytic way on biological (somatic) processes and ignoring the behavioral and psychosocial. This was so even though in practice many physicians, at least until the beginning of the 20th century, regarded emotions as important for the development and course of disease. Actually, such arbitrary exclusion is an acceptable strategy in scientific research, especially when concepts and methods appropriate for the excluded areas are not yet available. But it becomes counterproductive when such strategy becomes policy and the area originally put aside for practical reasons is permanently excluded, if not forgotten altogether. The greater the success of the narrow approach the more likely is this to happen. The biomedical approach to disease has been successful beyond all expectations, but at a cost. For in serving as guideline and justification for medical care policy, biomedicine has also contributed to a host of problems, which I shall consider later.

Limitations of the Biomedical Model

We are now faced with the necessity and the challenge to broaden the approach to disease to include the psychosocial without sacrificing the enormous advantages of the biomedical approach. On the importance of the latter all agree, the reductionist, the exclusionist, and the heretic. In a recent critique of the exclusionist position, Kety put the contrast between the two in such a way as to help define the issues.[9] "According to the medical model, a human illness does not become a specific disease all at once and is not equivalent to it. The medical model of an illness is a process that moves from the recognition and palliation of symptoms to the characterization of a specific disease in which the etiology and pathogenesis are known and treatment is rational and specific." Thus taxonomy progresses from symptoms, to clusters of symptoms, to syndromes, and finally to diseases with specific pathogenesis and pathology. This sequence accurately describes the successful application of the scientific method to the elucidation and the classification into discrete entities of disease in its generic sense.[5,6]

The merit of such an approach needs no argument. What do require scrutiny are the distortions introduced by the reductionistic tendency to regard the specific disease as adequately, if not best, characterized in terms of the smallest isolable component having causal implications, for example, the biochemical; or even more critical, is the contention that the designation "disease" does not apply in the absence of perturbations at the biochemical level.

Kety approaches this problem by comparing diabetes mellitus and schizophrenia as paradigms of somatic and mental diseases, pointing out the appropriateness of the medical model for both. "Both are symptom clusters or syndromes, one described by somatic and biochemical abnormalities, the other by psychological. Each may have many etiologies and shows a range of intensity from severe and debilitating to latent or borderline. There is also evidence that genetic and environmental influences operate in the development of both." In this description, at least in reductionistic terms, the scientific characterization of diabetes is the more advanced in that it has progressed from the behavioral framework of symptoms to that of biochemical abnormalities. Ultimately, the reductionists assume schizophrenia will achieve a similar degree of resolution. In developing his position, Kety makes clear that he does not regard the genetic factors and biological processes in schizophrenia as are now known to exist (or may be discovered in the future) as the only important influences in its etiology. He insists that equally important is elucidation of "how experiential factors and their interactions with biological vulnerability make possible or prevent the development of schizophrenia." But whether such a caveat will suffice to counteract basic reductionism is far from certain.

The Requirements of a New Medical Model

To explore the requirements of a medical model that would account for the reality of diabetes and schizophrenia as human experiences as well as disease abstractions, let us expand Kety's analogy by making the assumption that a specific biochemical abnormality capable of being influenced pharmacologically exists in schizophrenia as well as in diabetes, certainly a plausible possibility. By obliging ourselves to think of patients with diabetes, a "somatic disease," and with schizophrenia, a "mental disease," in exactly the same terms, we will see more clearly how inclusion of somatic and psychosocial factors is indispensable for both; or more pointedly, how concentration on the biomedical and exclusion of the psychosocial distorts perspectives and even interferes with patient care.

1) In the biomedical model, demonstration of the specific biochemical deviation is generally regarded as a specific diagnostic criterion for the disease. Yet in terms of the human experience of illness, laboratory documentation may only indicate disease potential, not the actuality of the disease at

the time. The abnormality may be present, yet the patient not be ill. Thus the presence of the biochemical defect of diabetes or schizophrenia at best defines a necessary but not a sufficient condition for the occurrence of the human experience of the disease, the illness. More accurately, the biochemical defect constitutes but one factor among many, the complex interaction of which ultimately may culminate in active disease or manifest illness.[10] Nor can the biochemical defect be made to account for all of the illness, for full understanding requires additional concepts and frames of reference. Thus while the diagnosis of diabetes is first suggested by certain core clinical manifestations, for example, polyuria, polydipsia, polyphagia, and weight loss, and is then confirmed by laboratory documentation of relative insulin deficiency, how these are experienced and how they are reported by any one individual, and how they affect him, all require consideration of psychological, social, and cultural factors, not to mention other concurrent or complicating biological factors. Variability in the clinical expression of diabetes as well as of schizophrenia, and in the individual experience and expression of these illnesses, reflects as much these other elements as it does quantitative variations in the specific biochemical defect.

2) Establishing a relationship between particular biochemical processes and the clinical data of illness requires a scientifically rational approach to behavioral and psychosocial data, for these are the terms in which most clinical phenomena are reported by patients. Without such, the reliability of observations and the validity of correlations will be flawed. It serves little to be able to specify a biochemical defect in schizophrenia if one does not know how to relate this to particular psychological and behavioral expressions of the disorder. The biomedical model gives insufficient heed to this requirement. Instead it encourages bypassing the patient's verbal account by placing greater reliance on technical procedures and laboratory measurements. In actuality the task is appreciably more complex than the biomedical model encourages one to believe. An examination of the correlations between clinical and laboratory data requires not only reliable methods of clinical data collection, specifically high-level interviewing skills, but also basic understanding of the psychological, social, and cultural determinants of how patients communicate symptoms of disease. For example, many verbal expressions derive from bodily experiences early in life, resulting in a significant degree of ambiguity in the language patients use to report symptoms. Hence the same words may serve to express primary psychological as well as bodily disturbances, both of which may coexist and overlap in complex ways. Thus virtually each of the symptoms classically associated with diabetes may also be expressions of or reactions to psychological distress, just as ketoacidosis and hypoglycemia may induce psychiatric manifestations, including some considered characteristic of schizophrenia. The most essential skills of the physician involve the ability to elicit accurately and then analyze correctly the patient's verbal account of his illness experience. The biomedical model ignores both the rigor required to achieve reliability in the interview process and the necessity to analyze the meaning of the patient's report in psychological, social, and cultural as well as in anatomical, physiological, or biochemical terms.[7]

3) Diabetes and schizophrenia have in common the fact that conditions of life and living constitute significant variables influencing the time of reported onset of the manifest disease as well as of variations in its course. In both conditions this results from the fact that psychophysiologic responses to life change may interact with existing somatic factors to alter susceptibility and thereby influence the time of onset, the severity, and the course of a disease. Experimental studies in animals amply document the role of early, previous, and current life experience in altering susceptibility to a wide variety of diseases even in the presence of a genetic predisposition.[11] Cassel's demonstration of higher rates of ill health among populations exposed to incongruity between the demands of the social system in which they are living and working and the culture they bring with them provides another illustration among humans of the role of psychosocial variables in disease causation.[12]

4) Psychological and social factors are also crucial in determining whether and when patients with

the biochemical abnormality of diabetes or of schizophrenia come to view themselves or be viewed by others as sick. Still other factors of a similar nature influence whether or not and when any individual enters a health care system and becomes a patient. Thus the biochemical defect may determine certain characteristics of the disease, but not necessarily the point in time when the person falls ill or accepts the sick role or the status of a patient.

5) "Rational treatment" (Kety's term) directed only at the biochemical abnormality does not necessarily restore the patient to health even in the face of documented correction or major alleviation of the abnormality. This is no less true for diabetes than it will be for schizophrenia when a biochemical defect is established. Other factors may combine to sustain patienthood even in the face of biochemical recovery. Conspicuously responsible for such discrepancies between correction of biological abnormalities and treatment outcome are psychological and social variables.

6) Even with the application of rational therapies, the behavior of the physician and the relationship between patient and physician powerfully influence therapeutic outcome for better or for worse. These constitute psychological effects which may directly modify the illness experience or indirectly affect underlying biochemical processes, the latter by virtue of interactions between psychophysiological reactions and biochemical processes implicated in the disease.[11] Thus insulin requirements of a diabetic patient may fluctuate significantly depending on how the patient perceives his relationship with his doctor. Furthermore, the successful application of rational therapies is limited by the physician's ability to influence and modify the patient's behavior in directions concordant with health needs. Contrary to what the exclusionists would have us believe, the physician's role is, and always has been, very much that of educator and psychotherapist. To know how to induce peace of mind in the patient and enhance his faith in the healing powers of his physician requires psychological knowledge and skills, not merely charisma. These too are outside the biomedical framework.

The Advantages of a Biopsychosocial Model

This list surely is not complete, but it should suffice to document that diabetes mellitus and schizophrenia as paradigms of "somatic" and "mental" disorders are entirely analogous and, as Kety argues, are appropriately conceptualized within the framework of a medical model of disease. But the existing biomedical model does not suffice. To provide a basis for understanding the determinants of disease and arriving at rational treatments and patterns of health care, a medical model must also take into account the patient, the social context in which he lives, and the complementary system devised by society to deal with the disruptive effects of illness, that is, the physician role and the health care system. This requires a biopsychosocial model. Its scope is determined by the historic function of the physician to establish whether the person soliciting help is "sick" or "well"; and if sick, why sick and in which ways sick; and then to develop a rational program to treat the illness and restore and maintain health.

The boundaries between health and disease, between well and sick, are far from clear and never will be clear, for they are diffused by cultural, social, and psychological considerations. The traditional biomedical view, that biological indices are the ultimate criteria defining disease, leads to the present paradox that some people with positive laboratory findings are told that they are in need of treatment when in fact they are feeling quite well, while others feeling sick are assured that they are well, that is, they have no "disease."[5,6] A biopsychosocial model which includes the patient as well as the illness would encompass both circumstances. The doctor's task is to account for the dysphoria and the dysfunction which lead individuals to seek medical help, adopt the sick role, and accept the status of patienthood. He must weight the relative contributions of social and psychological as well as of biological factors implicated in the patient's dysphoria and dysfunction as well as in his decision to accept or not accept patienthood and with it the responsibility to cooperate in his own health care.

By evaluating all the factors contributing to both illness and patienthood, rather than giving primacy to biological factors alone, a biopsychosocial model would make it possible to explain why some individuals experience as "illness" conditions which others regard merely as "problems of living," be they emotional reactions to life circumstances or somatic symptoms. For from the individual's point of view his decision between whether he has a "problem of living" or is "sick" has basically to do with whether or not he accepts the sick role and seeks entry into the health care system, not with what, in fact, is responsible for his distress. Indeed, some people deny the unwelcome reality of illness by dismissing as "a problem of living" symptoms which may in actuality be indicative of a serious organic process. It is the doctor's, not the patient's, responsibility to establish the nature of the problem and to decide whether or not it is best handled in a medical framework. Clearly the dichotomy between "disease" and "problems of living" is by no means a sharp one, either for patient or for doctor.

When Is Grief a Disease?

To enhance our understanding of how it is that "problems of living" are experienced as illness by some and not by others, it might be helpful to consider grief as a paradigm of such a borderline condition. For while grief has never been considered in a medical framework, a significant number of grieving people do consult doctors because of disturbing symptoms, which they do not necessarily relate to grief. Fifteen years ago I addressed this question in a paper entitled "Is Grief a Disease? A Challenge for Medical Research."[13] Its aim too was to raise questions about the adequacy of the biomedical model. A better title might have been, "When Is Grief a Disease?" just as one might ask when schizophrenia or when diabetes is a disease. For while there are some obvious analogies between grief and disease, there are also some important differences. But these very contradictions help to clarify the psychosocial dimensions of the biopsychosocial model.

Grief clearly exemplifies a situation in which psychological factors are primary; no preexisting chemical or physiological defects or agents need be invoked. Yet as with classic diseases, ordinary grief constitutes a discrete syndrome with a relatively predictable symptomatology which includes, incidentally, both bodily and psychological disturbances. It displays the autonomy typical of disease; that is, it runs its course despite the sufferer's efforts or wish to bring it to a close. A consistent etiologic factor can be identified, namely, a significant loss. On the other hand, neither the sufferer nor society has ever dealt with ordinary grief as an illness even though such expressions as "sick with grief" would indicate some connection in people's minds. And while every culture makes provisions for the mourner, these have generally been regarded more as the responsibility of religion than of medicine.

On the face of it, the arguments against including grief in a medical model would seem to be the more persuasive. In the 1961 paper I countered these by comparing grief to a wound. Both are natural responses to environmental trauma, one psychological, the other physical. But even at the time I felt a vague uneasiness that this analogy did not quite make the case. Now 15 years later a better grasp of the cultural origins of disease concepts and medical care systems clarifies the apparent inconsistency. The critical factor underlying man's need to develop folk models of disease, and to develop social adaptations to deal with the individual and group disruptions brought about by disease, has always been the victim's ignorance of what is responsible for his dysphoric or disturbing experience.[5,6] Neither grief nor a wound fits fully into that category. In both, the reasons for the pain, suffering, and disability are only too clear. Wounds or fractures incurred in battle or by accident by and large were self-treated or ministered to with folk remedies or by individuals who had acquired certain technical skills in such matters. Surgery developed out of the need for treatment of wounds and injuries and has different historical roots than medicine, which was always closer in origin to magic and religion. Only later in Western history did surgery and medicine merge as healing arts. But even from earliest times there were people who behaved as though grief-stricken, yet seemed not to have suffered any loss; and others who developed what for all the world looked like wounds or fractures, yet had not been subjected to any known trauma. And there were people who suffered losses whose grief deviated in one way or another from what the culture had come to accept as the normal course; and others whose wounds failed to heal or festered or who became ill even though the wound had apparently healed. Then, as now, two elements were crucial in defining the role of patient and physician and hence in determining what should be regarded as disease. For the patient it has been his not knowing why he felt or functioned badly or what to do about it, coupled with the belief or knowledge that the healer or physician did know and could provide relief. For the physician in turn it has been his commitment to his professional role as healer. From these have evolved sets of expectations which are reinforced by the culture, though these are not necessarily the same for patient as for physician.

A biopsychosocial model would take all of these factors into account. It would acknowledge the fundamental fact that the patient comes to the physician because either he does not know what is wrong or, if he does, he feels incapable of helping himself. The psychobiological unity of man requires that the physician accept the responsibility to evaluate whatever problems the patient presents and recommend a course of action, including referral to other helping professions. Hence the physician's basic professional knowledge and skills must span the social, psychological, and biological, for his decisions and actions on the patient's behalf involve all three. Is the patient suffering normal grief or melancholia? Are the fatigue and weakness of the woman who recently lost her husband conversion symptoms, psychophysiological reactions, manifestations of a somatic disorder, or a combination of these? The patient soliciting the aid of a physician must have confidence that the M.D. degree has indeed rendered that physician competent to make such differentiations.

A Challenge for Both Medicine and Psychiatry

The development of a biopsychosocial medical model is posed as a challenge for both medicine and psychiatry. For despite the enormous gains which have accrued from biomedical research, there is a growing uneasiness among the public as well as among physicians, and especially among the younger generation, that health needs are not being met and that biomedical research is not having a sufficient impact in human terms. This is usually ascribed to the all too obvious inadequacies of existing health care delivery systems. But this certainly is not a complete explanation, for many who do have adequate access to health care also complain that physicians are lacking in interest and understanding, are preoccupied with procedures, and are insensitive to the personal problems of patients and their families. Medical institutions are seen as cold and impersonal; the more prestigious they are as centers for biomedical research, the more common such complaints.[14] Medicine's unrest derives from a growing awareness among many physicians of the contradiction between the excellence of their biomedical background on the one hand and the weakness of their qualifications in certain attributes essential for good patient care on the other.[7] Many recognize that these cannot be improved by working within the biomedical model alone.

The present upsurge of interest in primary care and family medicine clearly reflects disenchantment among some physicians with an approach to disease that neglects the patient. They are now more ready for a medical model which would take psychosocial issues into account. Even from within academic circles are coming some sharp challenges to biomedical dogmatism.[8,15] Thus Holman ascribes directly to biomedical reductionism and to the professional dominance of its adherents over the health care system such undesirable practices as unnecessary hospitalization, overuse of drugs, excessive surgery, and inappropriate utilization of diagnostic tests. He writes, "While reductionism is a powerful tool for understanding, it also creates profound misunderstanding when unwisely applied. Reductionism is particularly harmful when it neglects the impact of nonbiological circumstances upon biologic processes." And, "Some medical outcomes are inadequate not because appropriate technical interventions are lacking but because our conceptual thinking is inadequate."[15] How ironic it would be were psychiatry to insist on subscribing to a medical model which some leaders in medicine already are beginning to question.

Psychiatrists, unconsciously committed to the biomedical model and split into the warring camps of reductionists and exclusionists, are today so preoccupied with their own professional identity and status in relation to medicine that many are failing to appreciate that psychiatry now is the only clinical discipline within medicine concerned primarily with the study of man and the human condition. While the behavioral sciences have made some limited incursions into medical school teaching programs, it is mainly upon psychiatrists, and to a lesser extent clinical psychologists, that the responsibility falls to develop approaches to the understanding of health and disease and patient care not readily accomplished within the more narrow framework and with the specialized techniques of traditional biomedicine. Indeed, the fact is that the major formulations of more integrated and holistic concepts of health and disease proposed in the past 30 years have come not from within the biomedical establishment, but from physicians who have drawn upon concepts and methods which originated within psychiatry, notably the psychodynamic approach of Sigmund Freud and psychoanalysis and the reaction-to-life-stress approach of Adolf Meyer and psychobiology.[16] Actually, one of the more lasting contributions of both Freud and Meyer has been to provide frames of reference whereby psychological processes could be included in a concept of disease. Psychosomatic medicine—the term itself a vestige of dualism—became the medium whereby the gap between the two parallel but independent ideologies of medicine, the biological and the psychosocial, was to be bridged. Its progress has been slow and halting, not only because of the extreme complexities intrinsic to the field itself, but also because of unremitting pressures, from within as well as from without, to conform to scientific methodologies basically mechanistic and reductionistic in conception and inappropriate for many of the problems under study. Nonetheless, by now a sizable body of knowledge based on clinical and experimental studies of man and animals has accumulated. Most, however, remains unknown to the general medical public and to the biomedical community and is largely ignored in the education of physicians. The recent solemn pronouncement by an eminent biomedical leader[2] that "the emotional content of organic medicine [has been] exaggerated" and "psychosomatic medicine is on the way out" can only be ascribed to the blinding effects of dogmatism.

The fact is that medical schools have constituted unreceptive if not hostile environments for those interested in psychosomatic research and teaching, and medical journals have all too often followed a double standard in accepting papers dealing with psychosomatic relationships.[17] Further, much of the work documenting experimentally in animals the significance of life circumstances or change in altering susceptibility to disease has been done by experimental psychologists and appears in psychology journals rarely read by physicians or basic biomedical scientists.[11]

General Systems Theory Perspective

The struggle to reconcile the psychosocial and the biological in medicine has had its parallel in biology, also dominated by the reductionistic approach of molecular biology. Among biologists too have emerged advocates of the need to develop holistic as well as reductionistic explanations of life processes, to answer the "why?" and the "what for?" as well as the "how?"[18,19] Von Bertalanffy, arguing the need for a more fundamental reorientation in scientific perspectives in order to open the way to holistic approaches more amenable to scientific inquiry and conceptualization, developed general systems theory.[20] This approach, by treating sets of related events collectively as systems manifesting functions and properties on the specific level of the whole, has made possible recognition of isomorphies across different levels of organization, as molecules, cells, organs, the organism, the person, the family, the society, or the biosphere. From such isomorphies can be developed fundamental laws and principles that operate commonly at all levels of organization, as compared to those which are unique for each. Since systems theory holds that all levels of organization are linked to each other in a hierarchical relationship so that change in one affects change in the others, its adoption as a scientific approach should do much to mitigate the holist-reductionist dichotomy and improve communication across scientific disciplines. For medicine, systems theory provides a conceptual approach suitable not only for the proposed biopsychosocial concept of disease but also for studying disease and medical care as interrelated processes.[10,21] If and when a general-systems approach becomes part of the basic scientific and philosophic education of future physicians and medical scientists, a greater readiness to encompass a biopsychosocial perspective of disease may be anticipated.

Biomedicine as Science and as Dogma

In the meantime, what is being and can be done to neutralize the dogmatism of biomedicine and all the undesirable social and scientific consequences that flow therefrom? How can a proper balance be established between the fractional analytic and the natural history approaches, both so integral for the work of the physician and the medical scientist?[22] How can the clinician be helped to understand the extent to which his scientific approach to patients represents a distinctly "human science," one in which "reliance is on the integrative powers of the observer of a complex nonreplicable event and on the experiments that are provided by history and by animals living in particular ecological settings," as Margaret Mead puts it?[23] The history of the rise and fall of scientific dogmas throughout history may give some clues. Certainly mere emergence of new findings and theories rarely suffices to overthrow well-entrenched dogmas. The power of vested interests, social, political, and economic, are formidable deterrents to any effective assault on biomedical dogmatism. The delivery of health care is a major industry, considering that more than 8 percent of our national economic product is devoted to health.[2] The enormous existing and planned investment in diagnostic and therapeutic technology alone strongly favors approaches to clinical study and care of patients that emphasize the impersonal and the mechanical.[24] For example, from 1967 to 1972 there was an increase of 33 percent in the number of laboratory tests conducted per hospital admission.[25] Planning for systems of medical care and their financing is excessively influenced by the availability and promise of technology, the application and effectiveness of which are often used as the criteria by which decisions are made as to what constitutes illness and who qualifies for medical care. The frustration of those who find what they believe to be their legitimate health needs inadequately met by too technologically oriented physicians is generally misinterpreted by the biomedical establishment as indicating "unrealistic expectations" on the part of the public rather than being recognized as reflecting a genuine discrepancy between illness as actually experienced by the patient and as it is conceptualized in the biomedical mode.[26] The professionalization of biomedicine constitutes still another formidable barrier.[8,15] Professionalization has engendered a caste system among health care personnel and a peck order concerning what constitute appropriate areas for medical concern and care, with the most esoteric disorders at the top of the list. Professional dominance "has perpetuated prevailing practices, deflected criticisms, and insulated the profession from alternate views and social relations that would illuminate and improve health care" (p. 21).[15] Holman argues, not unconvincingly, that "the Medical establishment is not primarily engaged in the disinterested pursuit of knowledge and the translation of that knowledge into medical practice; rather in significant part it is engaged in special interest advocacy, pursuing and preserving social power" (p. 11).[15]

Under such conditions it is difficult to see how reforms can be brought about. Certainly contributing another critical essay is hardly likely to bring about any major changes in attitude. The problem is hardly new, for the first efforts to introduce a more holistic approach into the undergraduate medical curriculum actually date back to Adolph Meyer's program at Johns Hopkins, which was initiated before 1920.[27] At Rochester, a program directed to medical students and to physicians during and after their residency training, and designed to inculcate psychosocial knowledge and skills appropriate for their future work as clinicians or teachers, has been in existence for 30 years.[28] While difficult to measure outcome objectively, its impact, as indicated by a questionnaire on how students and graduates view the issues involved in illness and patient care, appears to have been appreciable.[29] In other schools, especially in the immediate post–World

War II period, similar efforts were launched, and while some flourished briefly, most soon faded away under the competition of more glamorous and acceptable biomedical careers. Today, within many medical schools there is again a revival of interest among some faculty, but they are few in number and lack the influence, prestige, power, and access to funding from peer review groups that goes with conformity to the prevailing biomedical structure.

Yet today, interest among students and young physicians is high, and where learning opportunities exist they quickly overwhelm the available meager resources. It would appear that given the opportunity, the younger generation is very ready to accept the importance of learning more about the psychosocial dimensions of illness and health care and the need for such education to be soundly based on scientific principles. Once exposed to such an approach, most recognize how ephemeral and insubstantial are appeals to humanism and compassion when not based on rational principles. They reject as simplistic the notion that in past generations doctors understood their patients better, a myth that has persisted for centuries.[30] Clearly, the gap to be closed is between teachers ready to teach and students eager to learn. But nothing will change unless or until those who control resources have the wisdom to venture off the beaten path of exclusive reliance on biomedicine as the only approach to health care. The proposed biopsychosocial model provides a blueprint for research, a framework for teaching, and a design for action in the real world of health care. Whether it is useful or not remains to be seen. But the answer will not be forthcoming if conditions are not provided to do so. In a free society, outcome will depend upon those who have the courage to try new paths and the wisdom to provide the necessary support.

Summary

The dominant model of disease today is biomedical, and it leaves no room within its framework for the social, psychological, and behavioral dimensions of illness. A biopsychosocial model is proposed that provides a blueprint for research, a framework for teaching, and a design for action in the real world of health care.[31]

References and Notes

1. A. M. Ludwig (1975).

2. *AF Illustrated, 3,* 5 (1976).

3. T. S. Szasz, *The Myth of Mental Illness* (Harper & Row, New York, 1961); E. F. Torrey, *The Death of Psychiatry* (Chilton, Radnor, Pa., 1974).

4. R. Rosen, in *The Relevance of General Systems Theory,* E. Laszlo, Ed. (Braziller, New York, 1972), p. 45.

5. H. Fabrega, *Arch. Gen. Psychiatry 32,* 1501 (1972).

6. ______, *Science, 189,* 969 (1975).

7. G. L. Engel, *Ann. Intern. Med. 78,* 587 (1973).

8. H. Rasmussen, *Pharos 38,* 53 (1975).

9. S. Kety, *Am. J. Psychiatry 131,* 957 (1974).

10. G. L. Engel, *Perspect. Biol. Med. 3,* 459 (1960).

11. R. Ader, in *Ethology and Development,* S. A. Barnett, Ed. (Heinemann, London, 1973), p. 37; G. L. Engel, *Gastroenterology 67,* 1085 (1974).

12. J. Cassel, *Am. J. Public Health 54,* 1482 (1964).

13. G. L. Engel, *Psychosom. Med. 23,* 18 (1961).

14. R. S. Duff and A. B. Hollingshead, *Sickness and Society* (Harper & Row, New York, 1968).

15. H. R. Holman, *Hosp. Pratt. 11,* 11 (1976).

16. K. Menninger, *Ann. Intern. Med. 29,* 318 (1948); J. Romano, *J. Am. Med. Assoc. 143,* 409 (1950); G. L. Engel, *Midcentury Psychiatry,* R. Grinker, Ed. (Thomas, Springfield, Ill., 1953), p. 33; H. Wolff, Ed., *An Outline of Man's Knowledge* (Doubleday, New York, 1960), p. 41; G. L. Engel, *Psychological Development in Health and Disease* (Saunders, Philadelphia, 1962).

17. G. L. Engel and L. Salzman, *N. Engl. J. Med. 288,* 44 (1973).

18. R. Dubos, *Mirage of Health* (Harper & Row, New York, 1959); *Reason Awake* (Columbia Univ. Press, New York, 1970); E. Mayr, in *Behavior and Evolution,* A. Roe and G. G. Simpson, Eds. (Yale Univ. Press, New Haven, Conn., 1958), p. 341; *Science 134,* 1501 (1961); *Am. Sci. 62,* 650 (1974); J. T. Bonner, *On Development. The Biology of Form* (Harvard Univ. Press, Cambridge, Mass., 1974); G. G. Simpson, *Science 139,* 1 (1963).

19. R. Dubos, *Man Adapting* (Yale Univ. Press, New Haven, Conn., 1965).

20. L. von Bertalanffy, *Problems of Life* (Wiley, New York, 1952); *General Systems Theory* (Braziller, New York, 1968). See also E. Laszlo, *The Relevance of General Systems Theory* (Braziller, New York, 1972); *The Systems View of the World* (Braziller, New York, 1972); Dubos.[19]

21. K. Menninger, *The Vital Balance* (Viking, New York, 1963); A. Sheldon, in *Systems and Medical Care,* A. Sheldon, F. Baker, C. P. McLaughlin, Eds. (MIT Press, Cambridge, Mass., 1970), p. 84; H. Brody, *Perspect. Biol. Med. 16,* 71 (1973).

22. G. L. Engel, in *Physiology, Emotion, and Psychosomatic Illness,* R. Porter and J. Knight, Eds. (Elsevier-Excerpta Medica, Amsterdam, 1972), p. 384.

23. M. Mead, *Science 191,* 903 (1976).

24. G. L. Engel, *J. Am. Med. Assoc. 236,* 861 (1976).

25. J, M. McGinnis, *J. Med. Educ. 51,* 602 (1976).

26. H. Fabrega and P. R. Manning, *Psychosom. Med. 35,* 223 (1973).

27. A. Meyer, *J. Am. Med. Assoc. 69,* 861 (1917).

28. A. H. Schmale, W. A. Greene, F. Reichsman, M. Kehoe, and G. L. Engel, *Adv. Psychosom. Med. 4,* 4 (1964); G. L. Engel, *J. Psychosom. Res. 11,* 77 (1967); L. Young, *Ann. Intern. Med. 83,* 728 (1975).

29. G. L. Engel, *J. Nerv. Ment. Dis. 154,* 159 (1972); *Univ. Rochester Med. Rev.* (winter 1971-1972), p. 10.

30. ______, *Pharos 39,* 127 (1976).

31. This article was adapted from material presented as the Loren Stephens Memorial Lecture, University of Southern California Medical Center, 1976; the Griffith McKerracher Memorial Lecture at the University of Saskatchewan, 1976; the Annual Hutchings Society Lecture, State University of New York-Upstate Medical Center, Syracuse, 1976. Also presented during 1975 to 1976 at the University of Maryland School of Medicine, University of California-San Diego School of Medicine, University of California-Los Angeles School of Medicine, Massachusetts Mental Health Center, and the 21st annual meeting of Midwest Professors of Psychiatry, Philadelphia. The author is a career research awardee in the U.S. Public Health Service.

6

The Discovery of Hyperkinesis

Notes on the Medicalization of Deviant Behavior

Peter Conrad

Introduction

The increasing medicalization of deviant behavior and the medical institution's role as an agent of social control has gained considerable notice (Friedson, 1970; Pitts, 1968; Kitterie, 1971; Zola, 1972). By medicalization we mean defining behavior as a medical problem or illness and mandating or licensing the medical profession to provide some type of treatment for it. Examples include alcoholism, drug addiction, and treating violence as a genetic or brain disorder. This redefinition is not a new function of the medical institution: psychiatry and public health have always been concerned with social behavior and have traditionally functioned as agents of social control (Foucault, 1965; Szasz, 1970; Rosen, 1972). Increasingly sophisticated medical technology has extended the potential of this type of social control, especially in terms of psychotechnology (Chorover, 1973). This approach includes a variety of medical and quasi-medical treatments or procedures: psychosurgery, psychotropic medications, genetic engineering, antibuse, and methadone.

This paper describes how certain forms of behavior in children have become defined as a medical problem and how medicine has become a major agent for their social control since the discovery of hyperkinesis. By discovery we mean both origin of the diagnosis and treatment for this disorder, and discovery of children who exhibit this behavior. The first section analyzes the discovery of hyperkinesis and why it suddenly became popular in the 1960's. The second section will discuss the medicalization of deviant behavior and its ramifications.

The Medical Diagnosis of Hyperkinesis

Hyperkinesis is a relatively recent phenonenon as a medical diagnostic category. Or in the past two decades has it been available as a recognized diagnostic category and only in the last decade has it received widespread notice and medical popularity. However, the roots of the diagnosis and treatment of this clinical entity are found earlier.

Hyperkinesis is also known as Minimal Brain Dysfunction, Hyperactive Syndrome, Hyperkinetic Disorder of Childhood, and by several other diagnostic categories. Although the symptoms and the presumed etiology vary, in general the behaviors are quite similar and greatly overlap.[1] Typical symptom patterns for diagnosing the disorder include: extreme excess of motor activity (hyperactivity); very short attention span (the child flits from activity to activity); restlessness; fidgetiness; often wildly oscillating mood swings (he's fine one day, a terror the next); clumsiness; aggressive-like behavior; impulsivity; in school he cannot sit still, cannot comply with rules, has low frustration level; frequently there may be sleeping problems and acquisition of speech may be delayed (Stewart et al., 1966; Stewart, 1970; Wender, 1971). Most of the symptoms for the disorder are deviant behaviors.[2] It is six times as prevalent among boys as among girls. We use the term hyperkinesis to represent all the diagnostic categories of this disorder.

The Discovery of Hyperkinesis

It is useful to divide the analysis into what might be considered clinical factors directly related to the diagnosis and treatment of hyperkinesis and social factors that set the context for the emergence of the new diagnostic category.

Clinical Factors

Bradley (1937) observed that amphetamine drugs had a spectacular effect in altering the behavior of school children who exhibited behavior disorders or learning disabilities. Fifteen of the thirty children he treated actually became more subdued in their behavior. Bradley termed the effect of this medication paradoxical, since he expected that amphetamines would stimulate children as they stimulated adults. After the medication was discontinued the children's behavior returned to premedication level.

A scattering of reports in the medical literature on the utility of stimulant medications for "childhood behavior disorders" appeared in the next two decades. The next significant contribution was the work of Strauss and his associates (Strauss & Lehtinen, 1947) who found certain behavior (including hyperkinesis behaviors) in postencephaletic children suffering from what they called minimal brain injury (damage). This was the first time these behaviors were attributed to the new organic distinction of minimal brain damage.

This disorder still remained unnamed or else it was called a variety of names (usually just "childhood behavior disorder"). It did not appear as a specific diagnostic category until Laufer, Denhoff, and Solomons (1957) described it as the "hyperkinetic impulse disorder" in 1957. Upon finding "the salient characteristics of the behavior pattern . . . are strikingly similar to those with clear cut organic causation" these researchers described a disorder with no clear-cut history or evidence for organicity (Laufer et al., 1957).

In 1966 a task force sponsored by the U.S. Public Health Service and the National Association for Crippled Children and Adults attempted to clarify the ambiguity and confusion in terminology and symptomology in diagnosing children's behavior and learning disorders. From over three dozen diagnoses, they agreed on the term "minimal brain dysfunction" as an overriding diagnosis that would include hyperkinesis and other disorders (Clements, 1966). Since this time M.B.D. has been the primary formal diagnosis or label.

In the middle 1950's a new drug, Ritalin, was synthesized, that has many qualities of amphetamines without some of their more undesirable side effects. In 1961 this drug was approved by the FDA for use with children. Since this time there has been much research published on the use of Ritalin in the treatment of childhood behavior disorders. This medication became the "treatment of choice" for treating children with hyperkinesis.

Since the early sixties, more research appeared on the etiology, diagnosis and treatment of hyperkinesis (cf. DeLong, 1972; Grinspoon & Singer, 1973; Cole, 1975)—as much as three-quarters concerned with drug treatment of the disorder. There had been increasing publicity of the disorder in the mass media as well. The Reader's Guide to Periodical Literature had no articles on hyperkinesis before 1967, one each in 1968 and 1969, and a total of forty for 1970 through 1974 (a mean of eight per year).

Now hyperkinesis has become the most common child psychiatric problem (Gross & Wilson, 1974, p. 142); special pediatric clinics have been established to treat hyperkinetic children, and substantial federal funds have been invested in etiological and treatment research. Outside the medical profession, teachers have developed a working clinical knowledge of hyperkinesis' symptoms and treatment (cf. Robin & Bosco, 1973); articles appear regularly in mass circulation magazines and newspapers so that parents often come to clinics with knowledge of this diagnosis. Hyperkinesis is no longer the relatively esoteric diagnostic category it may have been twenty years ago; it is now a well-known clinical disorder.

Social Factors

The social factors affecting the discovery of hyperkinesis can be divided into two areas: (1) The Pharmaceutical Revolution; (2) Government Action.

1. *The Pharmaceutical Revolution.* Since the 1930's the pharmaceutical industry has been synthesizing and manufacturing a large number of psychoactive drugs, contributing to a virtual revolution in drug making and drug taking in America (Silverman & Lee, 1974).

Psychoactive drugs are agents that affect the central nervous system. Benzedrine, Ritalin, and Dexedrine are all synthesized psychoactive stimulants which were indicated for narcolepsy, appetite control (as "diet pills"), mild depression, fatigue, and more recently hyperkinetic children.

Until the early sixties there was little or no promotion and advertisement of any of these medications for use with childhood disorders.[3] Then two major pharmaceutical firms (Smith, Kline and French, manufacturer of Dexedrine, and CIBA, manufacturer of Ritalin) began to advertise in medical journals and through direct mailing and efforts of the "detail men." Most of this advertising of the pharmaceutical treatment of hyperkinesis was directed to the medical sphere; but some of the promotion was targeted for the educational sector also (Hentoff, 1972). This promotion was probably significant in disseminating information concerning the diagnosis and treatment of this newly discovered disorder.[4] Since 1955 the use of psychoactive medications (especially phenothiazines) for the treatment of persons who are mentally ill, along with the concurrent dramatic decline in in-patient populations, has made psychopharmacology an integral part of treatment for mental disorders. It has also undoubtedly increased the confidence in the medical profession for the pharmaceutical approach to mental and behavioral problems.

2. *Government Action.* Since the publication of the USPHS report on MBD there have been at least two significant governmental reports on treating school children with stimulant medications for behavior disorders. Both of these came as a response to the national publicity created by the *Washington Post* report (1970) that five to ten percent of the 62,000 grammar school children in Omaha, Nebraska were being treated with "behavior modification drugs to improve deportment and increase learning potential" (quoted in Grinspoon & Singer, 1973). Although the figures were later found to be a little exaggerated, it nevertheless spurred a Congressional investigation (U.S. Government Printing Office, 1970) and a conference sponsored by the Office of Child Development (1971) on the use of stimulant drugs in the treatment of behaviorally disturbed school children.

The Congressional Subcommittee on Privacy chaired by Congressman Cornelius E. Gallagher held hearings on the issue of prescribing drugs for hyperactive school children. In general, the committee showed great concern over the facility in which the medication was prescribed; more specifically that some children at least were receiving drugs from general practitioners whose primary diagnosis was based on teachers' and parents' reports that the child was doing poorly in school. There was also a concern with the absence of follow-up studies on the long-term effects of treatment.

The HEW committee was a rather hastily convened group of professionals (a majority were M.D.'s) many of whom already had commitments to drug treatment for children's behavior problems. They recommended that only M.D.'s make the diagnosis and prescribe treatment, that the pharmaceutical companies promote the treatment of the disorder only through medical channels, that parents should not be coerced to accept any particular treatment, and that long-term follow-up research should be done. This report served as blue ribbon approval for treating hyperkinesis with psychoactive medications.

Discussion

We will focus discussion on three issues: How children's deviant behavior became conceptualized as a medical problem; why this occurred when it did; and what are some of the implications of the medicalization of deviant behavior.

How does deviant behavior become conceptualized as a medical problem? We assume that before the discovery of hyperkinesis this type of deviance was seen as disruptive, disobedient, rebellious, antisocial, or deviant behavior. Perhaps the label "emotionally disturbed" was sometimes used, when it was in vogue in the early sixties, and the child was usually managed in the context of the family or the school or in extreme cases, the child guidance clinic. How then did this constellation of deviant behaviors become a medical disorder?

The treatment was available long before the disorder treated was clearly conceptualized. It was twenty years after Bradley's discovery of the "paradoxical effect" of stimulants on certain deviant children that Laufer named the disorder and described its characteristic symptoms. Only in the late fifties were both the diagnostic label and the pharmaceutical treatment available. The pharmaceutical revolution in mental health and the increased interest in child psychiatry provided a favorable background for the dissemination of knowledge about this new disorder. The latter probably made the medical profession more likely to consider behavior problems in children as within their clinical jurisdiction.

There were agents outside the medical profession itself that were significant in "promoting" hyperkinesis as a disorder within the medical framework. These agents might be conceptualized in Decker's terms as "moral entrepreneurs," those who crusade for creation and enforcement of the rules (Decker, 1963).[5] In this case the moral entrepreneurs were the pharmaceutical companies and the Association for Children with Learning Disabilities.

The pharmaceutical companies spent considerable time and money promoting stimulant medications for this new disorder. From the middle 1960's on, medical journals and the free "throwaway" magazines contained elaborate advertising for Ritalin and Dexedrine. These ads explained the utility of treating hyperkinesis and urged the physician to diagnose and treat hyperkinetic children. The ads run from one to six pages. For example, a two-page ad in 1971 stated:

> MBD . . .MEDICAL MYTH OR DIAGNOSABLE DISEASE ENTITY
>
> What medical practitioner has not, at one time or another, been called upon to examine an impulsive, excitable hyperkinetic child? A child with difficulty in concentrating. Easily frustrated. Unusually aggressive. A classroom rebel. In the absence of any organic pathology, the conduct of such children was, until a few short years ago, usually dismissed as . . . spunkiness, or evidence of youthful vitality. But it is now evident that in many of these children the hyperkinetic syndrome exists as a distinct medical entity. This syndrome is readily diagnosed through patient histories, neurologic signs, and psychometric testing—has been classified by an expert panel convened by the United States Department of Health, Education and Welfare as Minimal Brain Dysfunction, MBD.

The pharmaceutical firms also supplied sophisticated packets of "diagnostic and treatment" information on hyperkinesis to physicians, paid for professional conferences on the subject, and supported research in the identification and treatment of the disorder. Clearly these corporations had a vested interest in the labeling and treatment of hyperkinesis; CIBA had $13 million profit from Ritalin alone in 1971, which was 15 percent of the total gross profits (Charles, 1971; Hentoff, 1972).

The other moral entrepreneur, less powerful than the pharmaceutical companies, but nevertheless influential, is the Association for Children with Learning Disabilities. Although its focus is not specifically on hyperkinetic children, it does include it in its conception of Learning Disabilities along with aphasia, reading problems like dyslexia, and perceptual motor problems. Founded in the early 1950's by parents and professionals, it has functioned much as the National Association for Mental Health does for mental illness: promoting conferences, sponsoring legislation, providing social support. One of the main functions has been to disseminate information concerning this relatively new area in education, Learning Disabilities. While the organization does have a more educational than medical perspective, most of the literature indicates that for hyperkinesis members have adopted the medical model and the medical approach to the problem. They have sensitized teachers and schools to the conception of hyperkinesis as a medical problem.

The medical model of hyperactive behavior has become very well accepted in our society. Physicians find treatment relatively simple and the results sometimes spectacular. Hyperkinesis minimizes parents' guilt by emphasizing "It's not their fault, it's an organic problem" and allows for non-punitive management or control of deviance. Medication often makes a child less disruptive in the classroom and sometimes aids a child in learning. Children often like their "magic pills" which make their behavior more socially acceptable and they probably benefit from a reduced stigma also. There are, however, some other, perhaps more subtle ramifications of the medicalization of deviant behavior.

The Medicalization of Deviant Behavior

Pitts has commented that "Medicalization is one of the most effective means of social control and that it is destined to become the main mode of formal social control" (1971, p. 391). Kitterie (1971) has termed it "the coming of the therapeutic state."

Medicalization of mental illness dates at least from the seventeenth century (Foucault, 1965; Szasz, 1970). Even slaves who ran away were once considered to be suffering from the disease drapetomania (Chorover, 1973). In recent years alcoholism, violence, and drug addiction as well as hyperactive behavior in children have all become defined as medical problems, both in etiology or explanation of the behavior and the means of social control or treatment.

There are many reasons why this medicalization has occurred. Much scientific research, especially in pharmacology and genetics, has become technologically more sophisticated, and found more subtle correlates with human behavior. Sometimes these findings (as in the case of XYY chromosomes and violence) become etiological explanations for deviance. Pharmacological technology that makes new discoveries affecting behavior (e.g., antibuse, methadone, and stimulants) are used as treatment for deviance. In part this application is encouraged by the prestige of the medical profession and its attachment to science. As Friedson notes, the medical profession has first claim to jurisdiction over anything that deals with the functioning of the body and especially anything that can be labeled illness (1970, p. 251). Advances in genetics, pharmacology, and "psychosurgery" also may advance medicine's jurisdiction over deviant behavior.

Second, the application of pharmacological technology is related to the humanitarian trend in the conception and control of deviant behavior. Alcoholism is no longer sin or even moral weakness, it is now a disease. Alcoholics are no longer arrested in many places for "public drunkenness," they are now somehow "treated," even if it is only to be dried out. Hyperactive children are now considered to have an illness rather than to be disruptive, disobedient, overactive problem children. They are not as likely to be the "bad boy" of the classroom; they are children with a medical disorder. Clearly there are some real humanitarian benefits to be gained by such a medical conceptualization of deviant behavior. There is less condemnation of the deviants (they have an illness, it is not their fault) and perhaps less social stigma. In some cases, even the medical treatment itself is more humanitarian social control than the criminal justice system.

There is, however, another side to the medicalization of deviant behavior. The four aspects of this side of the issue include (1) the problem of expert control; (2) medical social control; (3) the individualization of social problems; and (4) the "depoliticization" of deviant behavior.

1. *The Problem of Expert Control.* The medical profession is a profession of experts; they have a monopoly on anything that can be conceptualized as illness. Because of the way the medical profession is organized and the mandate it has from society, decisions related to medical diagnoses and treatment are virtually controlled by medical professionals.

Some conditions that enter the medical domain are not ipso facto medical problems, especially deviant behavior, whether alcoholism, hyperactivity, or drug addiction, By defining a problem as medical it is removed from the public realm where there can be discussion by ordinary people and put on a plane where only medical people can discuss it. As Reynolds states,

> The increasing acceptance, especially among the more educated segments of our populace, of technical solutions—solutions administered by disinterested politically and morally neutral experts—results in the withdrawal of more and more areas of human experience from the realm of public discussion. For when drunkenness, juvenile delinquency, sub par performance and extreme political beliefs are seen as symptoms of an underlying illness or biological defect the merits and drawbacks of such behavior or beliefs need not be evaluated. (1973, pp. 220-221)

The public may have their own conceptions of deviant behavior but that of the experts is usually dominant.

2. *Medical Social Control.* Defining deviant behavior as a medical problem allows certain things to be done that could not otherwise be considered; for example, the body may be cut open or psychoactive medications may be given. This treatment can be a form of social control.

In regard to drug treatment Lennard points out: "Psychoactive drugs, especially those legally prescribed, tend to restrain individuals from behavior and experience that are not complementary to the requirements of the dominant value system" (1971, p. 57). These forms of medical social control presume a prior definition of deviance as a medical problem. Psychosurgery on an individual prone to violent outbursts requires a diagnosis that there was something wrong with his brain or nervous system. Similarly, prescribing drugs to restless, overactive, and disruptive school children requires a diagnosis of hyperkinesis. These forms of social control, what Chorover (1973) has called "psychotechnology," are very powerful and often very efficient means of controlling deviance. These relatively new and increasingly popular forms of social control could not be utilized without the medicalization of deviant behavior. As is suggested from the discovery of hospice, if a mechanism of medical social control seems useful, then the deviant behavior it modifies will develop a medical label or diagnosis. No overt malevolence on the part of the medical profession is implied: rather it is part of a complex process, of which the medical profession is only a part. The larger process might be called the individualization of social problems.

3. *The Individualization of Social Problems.* The medicalization of deviant behavior is part of a larger phenomenon that is prevalent in our society, the individualization of social problems. We tend to look for causes and solutions to complex social problems in the individual rather than in the social system. This view resembles Ryan's (1971) notion of "blaming the victim," seeing the causes of the problem in individuals rather than in the society where they live. We then seek to change the "victim" rather than the society. The medical perspective of diagnosing an illness in an individual lends itself to the individualization of social problems. Rather than seeing certain deviant behaviors as symptomatic of problems in the social system, the medical perspective focuses on the individual diagnosing and treating the illness, generally ignoring the social situation.

Hyperkinesis serves as a good example. Both the school and the parents are concerned with the child's behavior; the child is very difficult at home and disruptive in school. No punishments or rewards seem consistently to work in modifying the behavior; and both parents and school are at their wit's end. A medical evaluation is suggested. The diagnosis of hyperkinetic behavior leads to prescribing stimulant medications. The child's behavior seems to become more socially acceptable, reducing problems in school and at home.

But there is an alternate perspective. By focusing on the symptoms and defining them as hyperkinesis we ignore the possibility that behavior is not an illness but an adaptation to a social situation. It diverts our attention from the family or school and from seriously entertaining the idea that the "problem" could be in the structure of the social system. And by giving medications we are essentially supporting the existing systems and do not allow this behavior to be a factor of change in the system.

4. *The Depoliticization of Deviant Behavior.* Depoliticization of deviant behavior is a result of both the process of medicalization and individualization of social problems. To our Western world, probably one of the clearest examples of such a depoliticization of deviant behavior occurred when political dissenters in the Soviet Union were declared mentally ill and confined in mental hospitals (cf. Conrad, 1972). This strategy served to neutralize the meaning of political protest and dissent, rendering it the ravings of mad persons.

The medicalization of deviant behavior depoliticizes deviance in the same manner. By defining the overactive, restless and disruptive child as hyperkinetic we ignore the meaning of behavior in the context of the social system. If we focused our analysis on the school system we might see the child's behavior as symptomatic of some "disorder" in the school or classroom situation, rather than symptomatic of an individual neurological disorder.

Conclusion

I have discussed the social ramifications of the medicalization of deviant behavior, using hyperkinesis as the example. A number of consequences of this medicalization have been outlined, including the depoliticization of deviant behavior, decision-making power of experts, and the role of medicine as an agent of social control. In the last analysis medical social control may be the central issue, as in this role medicine becomes a de facto agent of the status quo. The medical profession may not have entirely sought this role, but its members have been, in general, disturbingly unconcerned and unquestioning in their acceptance of it. With the increasing medical knowledge and technology it is likely that more deviant behavior will be medicalized and medicine's social control function will expand.

Notes

1. The USPHS report (Clements, 1966) included 38 terms that were used to describe or distinguish the conditions that it labeled Minimal Brain Dysfunction. Although the literature attempts to differentiate MBD, hyperkinesis, hyperactive syndrome, and several other diagnostic labels, it is our belief that in practice they are almost interchangeable.

2. For a fuller discussion of the construction of the diagnosis of hyperkinesis, see Conrad (1976), especially Chapter 6.

3. The American Medical Association's change in policy in accepting more pharmaceutical advertising in the late fifties may have been important. Probably the PDA approval of the use of Ritalin for children in 1961 was more significant. Until 1970, Ritalin was advertised for treatment of "functional behavior problems in children." Since then, because of an PDA order, it has only been promoted for treatment of MBD.

4. The drug industry spends fully 25 percent of its budget on promotion and advertising. See Coleman, Katz, & Menzel (1966) for the role of the detail men and how physicians rely upon them for information.

5. Friedson also notes the medical professional role as moral entrepreneur in this process also: "The profession does treat the illnesses laymen take to it, but it also seeks to discover illness of which the laymen may not even be aware. One of the greatest ambitions of the physician is to discover and describe a 'new' disease or syndrome. . . ." (1970, p. 252).

References

Becker, H. S. (1963). *The outsiders.* New York: Free Press.

Bradley, C. (1937, March). The behavior of children receiving Benzedrine. *American Journal of Psychiatry, 94,* 577-585.

Charles, A. (1971, October). The case of Ritalin. *New Republic, 23,* 17-19.

Chorover, S. L. (1973, October). Big brother and psychotechnology. *Psychology Today,* pp. 43-54.

Clements, S. D. (1966). *Task force I: Minimal brain dysfunction in children* (National Institute of Neurological Diseases and Blindness, Monograph No. 3). Washington, DC: U.S. Department of Health, Education, and Welfare.

Cole, S. (1975, January). Hyperactive children: The use of stimulant drugs evaluated. *American Journal of Orthopsychiatry, 45,* 28-37.

Coleman, J., Katz, E., & Menzel, H. (1966). *Medical innovation.* Indianapolis: Bobbs-Merrill.

Conrad, P. (1972). *Ideological deviance: An analysis of the Soviet use of mental hospitals for political dissenters.* Unpublished manuscript.

Conrad, P. (1976). *Identifying hyperactive children in the medicalization of deviant behavior.* Lexington, MA: D. C. Heath & Co.

DeLong, A. R. (1972, February). What have we learned from psychoactive drugs research with hyperactives? *American Journal of Diseases in Children, 123,* 177-180.

Foucault, M. (1965). *Madness and civilization.* New York: Pantheon.

Friedson, E. (1970). *Profession of medicine.* New York: Harper & Row.

Grinspoon, L., & Singer, S. (1973, November). Amphetamines in the treatment of hyperactive children. *Harvard Educational Review, 43,* 515-555.

Gross, M. B., & Wilson, W. E. (1974). *Minimal brain dysfunction.* New York: Brunner/Mazel.

Hentoff, N. (1972, May). Drug pushing in the schools: The professionals. *Village Voice, 22,* 21-23.

Kitterie, N. (1971). *The right to be different.* Baltimore, MD: Johns Hopkins University Press.

Laufer, M. W., Denhoff, E., & Solomons, G. (1957, January). Hyperkinetic impulse disorder in children's behavior problems. *Psychosomatic Medicine, 19,* 38-49.

Lennard, H. L., & Associates. (1971). *Mystification and drug misuse.* New York: Harper & Row.

Office of Child Development. (1971, January 11-12). *Report of the conference on the use of stimulant drugs in treatment of behaviorally disturbed children.* Washington, DC: Department of Health, Education, and Welfare, January 11-12.

Pitts, J. (1968). Social control: The concept. In D. Sills (Ed.), *International encyclopedia of the social sciences* (Vol. 14). New York: Macmillan.

Reynolds, J. M. (1973). The medical institution. In L. T. Reynolds & J. M. Henslin (Eds.), *American society: A critical analysis* (pp. 198-324). New York: David McKay.

Robin, S. S., & Bosco, J. J. (1973, December). Ritalin for school children: The teachers' perspective. *Journal of School Health, 47,* 624-628.

Rosen, G. (1972). The evolution of social medicine. In H. E. Freeman, S. Levine, & L. Reeder (Eds.), *Handbook of medical sociology* (pp. 30-60). Englewood Cliffs, NJ: Prentice-Hall.

Ryan, W. (1971). *Blaming the victim.* New York: Vintage.

Silverman, M., & Lee, P. R. (1974). *Pills, profits and politics.* Berkeley: University of California Press.

Sroufe, L. A., & Stewart, M. (1973, August). Treating problem children with stimulant drugs. *New England Journal of Medicine, 289,* 407-421.

Stewart, M. A. (1970, April). Hyperactive children. *Scientific American, 222,* 794-798.

Stewart, M. A., Ferris, A., Pitts, N. P., & Craig, A. G. (1966, October). The hyperactive child syndrome. *American Journal of Orthopsychiatry, 36,* 861-867.

Strauss, A. A., & Lehtinen, L. E. (1947). *Psychopathology and education of the brain-injured child* (Vol. 1). New York: Grune & Stratton.

Szasz, T. (1970). *The manufacture of madness.* New York: Harper & Row.

U.S. Government Printing Office. (1970, September 29). *Federal involvement in the use of behavior modification drugs on grammar school children of the right to privacy inquiry: Hearing before a subcommittee of the committee on government operations.* Washington, DC, 91st Congress, 2nd session.

Wender, P. (1971). *Minimal brain dysfunction in children.* New York: John Wiley.

Zola, I. (1972, November). Medicine as an institution of social control. *Sociological Review, 20,* 487-504.

7

Behavior as the Central Outcome in Health Care

Robert M. Kaplan

Health psychology and behavioral medicine are among the most rapidly developing areas of psychological research and practice. Although no one model has dominated the field, the biomedical disease model has guided most thinking. According to this model, syndromes expressed as signs and symptoms are associated with lesions or some underlying pathology. This pathology is the focus of research and the target of treatment. Interventions are made to eradicate the lesion or prevent its pathogenesis. The lesion, however, is the central focus of examination.

Reviews of the emerging field of behavioral medicine and health psychology often emphasize the role of behavior in the onset, maintenance, and treatment of disease (Miller, 1983). Many of these reviews characterize the role of stress on bodily processes. Krantz, Grunberg, and Baum (1985) emphasized the links between behavior and health through basic physiological mechanisms. Their review concluded with an emphasis on new technologies for assessing physiologic, rather than behavioral, health outcomes. For example, they pointed to the availability of portable blood-withdrawal pumps, blood pressure monitors, and biochemical assessment tools. Rodin and Salovey (1989) underscored the importance of disease end points. They encouraged health psychologists to focus on placement in specific disease categories such as cancer or coronary heart disease. These reviews characterize the field as emphasizing the impact of behavior on identified lesions or specific disease states.

Progressive versions of the medical model acknowledge that the cause of illness might be environmental or the lesion psychosocial. Even the

EDITORS' NOTE: From *American Psychologist, 46,* pp. 1211-1220.

biopsychosocial model (Engel, 1976), however, concentrates on sickness and its causes. Attention is directed toward the psychological or environmental etiology and the physiological lesion (White, 1988). These models have directed measurement toward assessment of disease categories, characteristics of lesions, and disease risk factors.

In their efforts to be in the mainstream, many behavioral research investigators also focus their studies on the health outcomes measured by physicians and other health care providers. Typically, these are measures of blood chemistry, physical characteristics, and blood or tissue sensitivity to medication. In this article I argue that the only important indicators of health and wellness are behavioral. Thus, outcome measures in health and medicine should be anchored in their relations with behavior. In this context the definition of behavior is general, as offered by Atkinson, Atkinson, Smith, and Hilgard (1987) in their widely used introductory psychology textbook. They define behavior as "those activities of an organism that can be observed by another organism or by an experimenter's instruments" (p. 657). Included in behavior are verbal reports about subjective conscious experiences. In this article, I refer to biological measures as measures of physiological state. Biological measures and disease classifications are important precisely because they are predictors or mediators of behavioral outcomes.

In the following sections, I argue that there has been too much concentration on purely biological measures and that the importance of behavioral health outcomes has been undervalued.

Behavioral Health Outcomes

The conceptualization and measurement of health status has interested scholars for many decades. After the Eisenhower administration, a report of the President's Commission on National Goals (1960) identified health status measurement as an important objective. In his influential book, *The Affluent Society,* John Kenneth Galbraith (1958) described the need to measure the effect of the health care system on quality of life. In recent years there have been many attempts to define and measure health status.

The movement toward behavioral measures is an old one. When Sullivan (1966) reviewed the literature on health measurement nearly a quarter of a century ago, he emphasized the importance of behavioral outcomes. Bolstered by the accomplishments of behavioral scientists, Sullivan developed a convincing argument that behavioral indicators such as absenteeism, bed-disability days, and institutional confinement were the most important consequences of disease and disability. Ability to perform activities at different ages could be compared with societal standards for these behaviors. Restrictions in usual activity were seen as prima facie evidence of deviation from well-being. Health conditions affect behavior, and in this article behavioral health outcomes are conceptualized as observable behavioral consequences of a health state. Arthritis, for example, may be associated with difficulty in walking, observable limping, or problems in using the hands. Even a minor illness, such as the common cold, might result in disruptions in daily activities, alterations in activity patterns, and decreased work capacity.

Diseases and disabilities are important for two reasons. First, illness may cause a truncation of the life expectancy. In other words, those in specific disease categories may die prematurely. Death is a behavioral outcome. It can be defined as the point at which there is no observable behavior. Second, diseases and disabilities may cause behavioral dysfunctions as well as other symptoms. Biomedical studies typically refer to health outcomes in terms of mortality (death) and morbidity (dysfunction) and sometimes to symptoms.

Mortality remains the major outcome measure in most epidemiologic studies and clinical trials. In order to make informed decisions about the nation's health, Congress receives various reports of statistical indicators from the National Center for Health Statistics. These include the crude mortality rate, the infant mortality rate, and years of potential life lost. Although important, each of these measures ignores dysfunction while people are alive. The National Center for Health Statistics provides information on a variety of states of morbidity. For example, it considers disability, defined as a temporary or long-term reduction in a person's activity.

Over the last 15 years, medical and health services researchers have developed new ways to assess health status quantitatively. These measures are often called *quality of life* measures. Because they are used exclusively to evaluate health status, the more descriptive *health-related quality of life* is preferred (Kaplan & Bush, 1982). Some approaches to the measurement of health-related quality of life combine measures of morbidity and mortality to express health outcomes in units analogous to years of life. The years-of-life figure, however, is adjusted for diminished quality of life associated with diseases or disabilities (Kaplan & Anderson, 1988).

Modern measures of health outcome consider future as well as current health status. Cancer, for example, may have very little impact on current functioning but may have a substantial impact on behavioral outcomes in the future. Today, a person with a malignant tumor in a leg may be functioning very much like a person with a leg muscle injury. However, the cancer patient is more likely to remain dysfunctional in the future. Comprehensive expressions of health status need to incorporate estimates of future behavioral dysfunction as well as to measure current status (Kaplan & Anderson, 1988).

The spectrum of medical care ranges from public health, preventive medicine, and environmental control through diagnosis to therapeutic intervention, convalescence, and rehabilitation. Many programs affect the probability of occurrence of future dysfunction rather than alter present functional status. In many aspects of preventive care, for example, the benefit of the treatment cannot be seen until many years after the intervention. A supportive family that instills proper health habits in its children, for example, may also promote better health in the future, even though the benefit may not be realized for years. The concept of health must consider not only the ability to function now but also the probability of future changes in function or probabilities of death. A person who is functional and asymptomatic today may harbor a disease with a poor prognosis. Thus, many individuals are at high risk of dying from heart disease even though they are perfectly functional today. Should we call them healthy? The term *severity of illness* should take into consideration both dysfunction and prognosis. Comprehensive models that combine morbidity, mortality, and prognosis have been described in the literature (Kaplan & Anderson, 1988). A behavioral conceptualization of health status can represent this prognosis by modeling disruptions in behavior that might occur in the future.

Many medical treatments may cause near-term dysfunction to prevent future dysfunction. For example, coronary artery bypass surgery causes severe dysfunction for a short period of time, yet the surgery is presumed to enhance function or decrease mortality at a later time. Patients may be incapacitated following myocardial infarction and restricted to coronary care units. Yet the treatment is designed to help them achieve better future outcomes. Pap smears and hysterectomies are performed in order to decrease the probability of future deaths due to cancer. Much of health care involves looking into the future to enhance behavioral outcomes over the life span. Therefore, it is essential to divide health into current and future components.

In appraising the importance of behavioral outcomes, we must ask why there is concern about diseases, injuries, and disabilities. The behavioral perspective suggests that the only reasons are the following: (a) Life expectancy may be shortened, (b) quality of life may be compromised either now or at some time prior to death, or (c) some combination of a and b. A disease that has no impact on either life expectancy or life quality would be unimportant. In fact, disease states gain their importance precisely to the degree to which they correlate with decreased longevity or impaired health-related quality of life.

The importance of behavioral outcomes has not been disregarded by the traditional medical community. In fact, recognition of the centrality of behavioral outcomes has been emphasized in several articles and editorials recently featured in *The New England Journal of Medicine* (Ellwood, 1988; Greenfield, 1989; Shortell & McNerney, 1990). Despite the growing recognition of the importance of behavioral outcomes by the medical community (Advances in Health Status Assessment, 1987; Bergner, 1989; Institutes of Medicine, 1989; Quality of Life Assessment, 1988a, 1988b; Shumaker,

Furberg, Czajkowski, & Schron, in press; Walker & Rosser, 1988), behavioral scientists manifest a paradoxical reluctance to follow this trend. Instead, the trend has been to focus on measures of biological process.

Trend Toward Biological Variables as Opposed to Behavioral Indexes

We are witnessing a trend toward the biologicalization of both behavioral and biomedical sciences. Reviews of the health psychology literature criticize studies that do not focus on some aspect of blood chemistry or those that do not use disease categories (Baum, Grunberg, & Singer, 1982). Measures of biological process are seen to be more pure, more reliable, and more valid than are behavioral indicators. Thus, an increasing number of studies assess health status through measures of blood cholesterol, blood pressure, or characteristics of the immune response, including natural killer-cell and t-cell activity. W. T. Kelvin created the doctrine that measurement is the prerequisite to science. For most of this century, scientists and clinicians followed the doctrine and attempted to use measures, even when the validity of the measures was unknown. Feinstein (1967) suggested that modern trends represent the "curse of Kelvin." The fact that there is a measure for some variable does not always mean that the measure is useful. Clinicians have been more attracted to blood pressure and cardiac output than to headache and anxiety. Clearly, the former are easier to quantify, but are they more meaningful?

It is important to emphasize that not all biological variables are measures of health status or health outcome. They are, however, predictive of some health outcomes. Elevated blood pressure, for example, is important because it predicts premature mortality or behavioral dysfunction resulting from coronary heart disease and from stroke. If blood pressure were unrelated to these behavioral outcomes, it would be a matter of little concern. There are many aspects of blood chemistry that bear no relation to clinical outcomes. Even common clinical tests, such as urine analysis, serum phosphorus, and alkaline phosphatase, have only weak and inconsistent relations to outcomes in all but the most extreme cases. Amberg, Schneiderman, Berry, and Zettner (1982), for example, demonstrated empirically that the alkaline phosphatase screening test provides essentially no information relevant to health outcome. Elevated blood cholesterol may be predictive of future bad outcomes, including early mortality from heart disease. However, other lipids in blood such as very low-density lipoproteins or chylomicrons may bear little relation to health outcomes in all but the most extreme cases. Modest elevation in these fractions of blood lipids may be of little concern.

Recently there has been a significant growth of interest in the relation between stress and measurable aspects of immune function. Temoshok, Soloman, and Jenkins (1989) cautioned scientists against overinterpreting these immunologic measures. Normal oscillations in most immune parameters are still poorly understood. Immunologists are uncertain about whether absolute numbers or percentages of cell subtypes are most meaningful. Most important, the immune system is a genuine system in which various components adjust to changes in one another, and some important aspects of the system may remain to be identified. Our understanding of the relation between immune parameters and health is still very sketchy.

Biological measures are also assumed to be more reliable than behavioral tests. Often however, the reliability of these measures is not assessed. When data are available, the results can be discouraging. Many investigators, fascinated by blood pressure as an outcome measure, have criticized behavioral measures for being nonphysiologic and unreliable. Yet the reliability of blood pressure is equally open to question because conventional sphygmomanometric measurements have poor test-retest coefficients. This leads to misclassification, incorrect diagnosis, and potentially damaging labeling (Hla, Vokaty, & Feussner, 1986; Patterson, 1934). There are many sources of error in blood pressure measurement. These include misreading biases, time sampling problems (blood pressure changes minute to minute), and situational factors. For example, it has been demonstrated that some patients have specific arousal of blood pressure in the presence of physicians. The condition has now been given the diagnostic label *white coat hypertension* (Pickering et al., 1988). Low reliability is not limited to blood pressure. It also characterizes measures of blood cholesterol, glucose, and a large number of other biochemical assays.

One of the important appeals of biological measures is that they focus on objectively defined events. Behavioral outcomes are often not measured objectively. Observer bias common to behavioral measures may be less common with biological measures. However, at a conceptual level, behavioral outcomes can represent defined events such as exercise or role performance. Subjective events, such as pain or discomfort, are characterized in pain behaviors and through verbal behaviors. It is tempting to assume that biological measures are more valid and reliable because they have less observer bias. However, they may include several other sources of measurement error, and they do not necessarily have evidence for validity.

To summarize, in order to avoid known problems with behavioral measures, researchers and clinicians have been attracted to outcomes that can be measured with biochemical assays, mechanical devices, or auto-analyzer machines. Although these measures are not subject to the same errors as behavioral tests, they have their own sources of error and often have low reliability and questionable validity. Establishing the validity of biological measures requires a model that relates them to health status.

Are Medical Measures More Valid or Meaningful?

It is often assumed that the relation between the biologic variables and health outcomes is nearly perfect. However, there is a remarkable variability in behavioral health outcomes within fixed levels of many biological variables. There are numerous examples, of which only three will be considered: biologic measures of arthritis, blood pressure, and blood cholesterol. The arthritis example emphasizes current behavioral health outcomes, whereas the latter two focus on future behavioral outcomes and mortality.

Arthritis. Clinical outcomes in studies of rheumatology have been difficult to evaluate (Deyo, 1988). Clinical measures often include joint tenderness, grip strength, and joint circumference. Some studies have shown that the reliability of these measures is often poor (Buchanan, 1982). Fries (1983) questioned the validity and reliability of a variety of traditional outcome measures, ranging from laboratory measures of erythrocyte sedimentation rate (ESR), latex fixation titer, and hemoglobin. It has been shown that rheumatoid arthritis patients may develop serological abnormalities that are poorly correlated with joint inflammation (McCarty, 1986). In addition, Fries suggested that traditional clinical measures such as grip strength, walking time, and patient global assessment are merely surrogates for the true outcomes in arthritis, which he argued are disability, physical discomfort, and financial loss. An elevated ESR means little to a patient who feels fine and can conduct his or her life without pain. The ESR characterizes current inflammation but does not give information about future dysfunction. Conversely, a patient with disabling arthritis pain is not well when the ESR is normal. Clinical tests are useful only when they identify treatment to remedy current dysfunction or predict future problems. Fries asserted that pain and functional outcomes are meaningful to the patients and that clinical measures are of less importance. As a result, a growing number of rheumatologists are focusing attention on behavioral or functional health outcomes (Anderson, Firschein, & Meenan, 1989).

Blood Pressure. Elevated blood pressure is a serious problem in the United States and in most other developed countries. Following the Hypertension Detection and Follow-up Program (HDFP), elevated blood pressure came to be defined as systolic pressure exceeding 140 mmHg or diastolic pressure (DBP) exceeding 90 mmHg. Using these guidelines, it has been estimated that as many as 58 million adults (about 30% of the adult population) have hypertension (Joint National Committee on Detection, Evaluation, and Treatment of High Blood Pressure, 1985). Investigators are concerned about elevated blood pressure because of its relation to future behavioral health outcomes. Several major epidemiologic studies have documented the relation between elevated blood pressure and both morbidity and mortality (National Heart, Lung and Blood Institute, 1984). In addition, evidence from the HDFP (1979) has demonstrated that reductions in blood pressure result in reductions in deaths due to heart disease. People are often not concerned about high blood pressure because it may produce no symptoms or current behavioral dysfunction. High blood pressure does have a bad prognosis, with affected individuals being at risk for behavioral dysfunction or death later in life. However, the relation between blood pressure and both mortality and morbidity are far from uniform. Severe elevated blood pressure is a severe risk for mortality, whereas blood pressure in the mild hypertension range (DBP = 90-104 mmHg) is a less significant risk (Rocella, Bowler, & Horan, 1987). Indeed, most of those with mild hypertension, even those untreated, have normal life expectancies with no complications.

Although high blood pressure is associated with risks, the treatment of high blood pressure may cause some problems. Significant numbers of patients experience dizziness, tiredness, and impotence when treated with medications (Breckenridge, 1988). Thus, the treatment of high blood pressure can cause undesirable health outcomes. Treatment, like hypertension, is a factor that may influence behavioral health outcomes, sometimes in the negative direction. Studies that measure only blood pressure and neglect these behavioral side effects will overestimate the net benefit. Conversely, too much focus on side effects might lead to an incorrect judgment that the treatment should be avoided. There may be considerable advantage in translating the side effects and benefits into common behavioral units and weighing them against one another in the treatment decision process (Kaplan & Atkins, 1989). The role of the clinician is to balance carefully the benefits and consequences of treatment (Aderman & Madhavan, 1981).

In summary, blood pressure is an important risk factor for heart disease and stroke. Systematic efforts to reduce blood pressure are advisable and effective. Yet, blood pressure is not a health outcome. It gains its importance through validity studies that demonstrate the association between blood pressure and behavioral outcomes including mortality, dysfunction, and symptomatic disturbances. Blood pressure is important because it provides probabilistic information about behavioral outcomes.

Cholesterol. The United States is currently experiencing a massive societal response to the presence of cholesterol in the diet. Numerous commercial products are promoted because they have no cholesterol. The term *hypercholesterolemia* suggests an increased concentration of cholesterol in blood. Total cholesterol values above 200 mg/dl are now considered to be diagnostic (Expert Panel on Detection, Evaluation, and Treatment of High Blood Cholesterol in Adults, 1988). Several epidemiologic studies have identified elevated blood cholesterol as a risk factor for cardiovascular disease mortality (Kannel, Castelli, Gordon, & McNamara, 1971). Yet the connection between dietary cholesterol and serum cholesterol has been less clearly established. Studies in metabolic wards and selected experimental studies do demonstrate that dietary manipulation can reduce serum cholesterol in the short run, although longer term changes have not been clearly documented. Furthermore, although there have been ecological correlations between estimated total fat consumption and total heart disease mortality across cultures, correlations within countries have not been systematically observed (Kaplan, 1985). A variety of explanations can be suggested for these "nonfindings." For example, measurement error in both dietary cholesterol and serum cholesterol may account for the null results (Jacobs, Anderson, & Blackburn, 1979). But the availability of an explanation for a nonfinding is not a demonstration that a significant association exists (Kaplan, 1988). Thus, the relation between dietary cholesterol and serum cholesterol is somewhat ambiguous.

Stallones (1983) criticized the diet-heart-disease connection, suggesting that there is no zero-order relation between diet and mortality. The problems with the cholesterol interventions have been reviewed in several earlier articles (Fries, Green, & Levine, 1989; Kaplan, 1984, 1985). These positions are regarded as controversial, but they are related to the current issue.

The reason that cholesterol is important is that elevated cholesterol is a risk factor for behavioral health outcomes. If it were not, why would one care? The important point is that the outcome itself must be considered. The role of the investigator is to determine the relation between modifiable habits (dietary patterns) and outcomes as mediated through the channel of serum cholesterol. Serum cholesterol can serve as a target for modification, but one must be assured that modifying serum cholesterol improves outcome and does not adversely affect health status.

Deaths in General Versus Deaths From Specific Causes

Some investigators, recognizing the problems with measures of disease process, turn their attention toward the ultimate medical outcome—death. As noted earlier in this review, vital status is considered to be a behavioral outcome. However, the behavioral approach differs from the traditional medical model in its emphasis on life-death status without reference to medical cause of death. The emphasis is on observable outcome rather than on disease category.

Many medical studies confuse outcome with placement in disease categories. Results from several recent clinical trials illustrate this point. In one widely cited study (Steering Committee of the Physicians' Health Study Research Group (1988, 1989), physician subjects were assigned to take aspirin (325 mg/day) or placebo in order to prevent myocardial infarctions. The ultimate aim, of course, was to reduce the number of deaths associated with heart disease. Indeed, there was a significant reduction in deaths from myocardial infarctions over an eight-year follow-up period. This result was highly publicized and even earned aspirin the description of a "miracle drug" on the cover of *Newsweek* magazine (Clark, Gosnell, Hager, Carroll, & Gordon, 1988). Yet closer inspection of the data reveals that there was no advantage of aspirin for the crucial behavioral outcome—life or death. Myocardial infarctions were compensated for by increases in death from other cardiovascular causes. There was a trend toward more hemorrhagic strokes among those taking aspirin, and there was the suggestion that aspirin may cause these strokes because it reduces blood clotting. Overall, aspirin did not reduce the number of deaths but changed the distribution among categories (Kaplan, 1989b).

A similar result [is seen] for the Coronary Primary Prevention Trial (Lipid Research Clinics Coronary Prevention Trial Results, 1984). In this study, a group of about 1,900 men at risk for coronary heart disease was given cholestyramine, a resin that binds bial acids and lowers serum cholesterol, whereas another group of about 1,900 men was given a placebo. Among the 3,800 male participants, 38 (2%) in the control group and 30 (1.6%) in the experimental group died of heart disease. The study is widely cited as the crucial evidence for cholesterol reduction. In addition, data from the study have been used to argue that a 1% reduction in cholesterol results in a 2% reduction in mortality. This has come to be known in health promotion campaigns as the *1% to 2% rule.* The exact calculation of this 1% to 2% rule, so often cited in public statements, is difficult to follow. Forming a ratio of these small percentages of deaths and subtracting from 1.0 gives the estimate of about a 21% reduction in mortality (1.0 - [.0157/.022]). This combined with an observed 12% reduction in cholesterol yields the 1% to 2% rule.

This important study represents the scientific basis for the current campaign toward cholesterol reduction. A stacking histogram does suggest a significant reduction in heart disease deaths among those randomly assigned to cholestyramine. Yet the entire height of the bars in the stacking histogram shows that there was no advantage of treatment for total mortality. According to the behavioral conceptualization, the treatment had no benefit. Reductions in death from heart disease were compensated for by increases in death from other causes.

Similar results [are noted] from the Helsinki Heart Study, which evaluated a similar drug called gemfibrozil (Frick et al., 1987). In the Helsinki study, 2,051 men were randomly assigned to take gemfibrozil twice daily, whereas another 2,030 men were given a placebo. After six years, 19 of the men in the placebo group had died of ischemic heart disease, whereas only 14 of those in the drug-treated group had died. This significant difference led the authors to conclude that gemfibrozil caused a 26% reduction in ischemic heart disease deaths. The

26% is calculated as follows: In the drug group, 0.68% (14/2,051) died, whereas in the placebo group 0.93% (19/2,030) died of ischemic heart disease. The actual difference is about one fourth of one percent. However, the ratio (.0068/.0093) subtracted from 1.0 yields about a 26% reduction. Furthermore, the total number of deaths in the gemfibrozil group was actually higher than those in the placebo group (45 vs. 42).

Some argue that cholesterol-lowering drugs should still be regarded as efficacious because there is no biological model that would explain why decreased cholesterol should lead to increased deaths in nondisease categories. However, the finding that cholesterol lowering does not reduce total mortality has now been reported in several different studies (Fries et al., 1989). The burden of proving benefit rests with the treatment advocates. Those who adopt the traditional disease-specific view might be satisfied with reductions in cardiovascular deaths. However, the more comprehensive behavioral model requires a reduction in total mortality. Adoption of this model might stimulate new research designed to explain the increased deaths in nondisease categories.

In all three of these important clinical trials, there was a highly publicized benefit of treatment, However, the benefit only occurs for a specific disease category. There was no benefit of treatment with regard to the important life-death outcome. Investigators and the lay press often focus on improvements in a specific cause of death. Yet families of the deceased may be more concerned that the subject is dead than they are about the specific cause of demise. Focus on specific categories can obscure the most important behavioral outcomes. Research directed toward specific disease categories or aspects of a biological process may not capture global concerns about health. That task requires a comprehensive behavioral model.

Can a Behavioral Conceptualization Influence Research and Practice?

Focus on biological rather than behavioral outcomes has led many investigators down the wrong path. For example, elevated levels of protein in urine suggest that the kidneys are misfiltering and removing some proteins that the body needs. Many years ago, when physicians measured high levels of protein in urine, they advised their patients to eat less protein. That advice led to poorer health outcomes because the body was already protein deprived. Ultimately, identifying the manipulations that led to better behavioral health outcomes led to more effective treatments. Another example involves the diagnosis and treatment of back pain. Legal definitions of disability sometimes require a physical diagnosis, and the medical evaluation often identifies a structural problem. This leads to the incorrect conclusion that the prognosis is poor. Thus, the medical model reinforces dysfunction, even though rehabilitation is common. A comprehensive view of health can reveal when new treatment approaches are needed, whereas focus on specific processes might misdirect treatment.

The traditional approach leads to a focus on risk factors rather than on health outcomes. Yet, modification of risk factors may not necessarily improve health. For example, many epidemiologic studies have failed to find a relation between coffee consumption and death due to heart disease. Several very thorough evaluations have shown that those who drink coffee have the same life expectancies as those who abstain (Wilson, Garrison, Kannel, McGee, & Costelli, 1989). On the other hand, some investigators have reported that coffee increases low density lipoprotein cholesterol or blood pressure (Thelle, Heyden, & Fodor, 1987). Because cholesterol and blood pressure are risk factors for heart disease, people are advised to give up the coffee they enjoy. The logic behind this advice might be challenged, however, as coffee does not increase the risk of heart disease or other behavioral health outcomes.

Treatment of factors suspected of causing undesirable behavioral outcomes is usually advisable. Yet change in these risk factors does not assure that the behavioral goal will be achieved. One recent example is the treatment of cardiac arrhythmias. Research had demonstrated that adults who had suffered a heart attack were at risk for sudden death if they experienced asymptomatic cardiac arrhythmias (Bigger, Fleiss, Kleiger, Miller, & Rolnitzky, 1984). Drugs were available to suppress these cardiac arrhythmias, and these products were used often. In what many thought was a demonstration of the obvious, the National Institutes of Health initiated a major clinical study involving 1,455 post–myocardial infarction patients in a variety of major medical centers (Cardiac Arrhythmia Suppression Trial [CAST] Investigators, 1989). The patients were randomly assigned to take anti-arrhythmic medication or placebos. All of the participants had been screened and demonstrated to experience suppression of their arrhythmia in response to the medication. Over an average of 10 months of follow-up, however, those assigned to the active drug had a significantly higher rate of death from arrhythmia than those assigned to the placebo. In addition, those in the active medication group had a higher overall death rate. If the investigators had only measured the response of the heart rhythm to anti-arrhythmic drugs, they would have concluded that the drug produced a benefit. Following the patients through the behavioral outcome (mortality) inspired them to stop the trial early and declare the medications unsafe.

The important point is that physiologic and biochemical measures do not necessarily have meaning. They gain their meaning through systematic correlations with health outcome. Attention directed at behavioral health outcomes can clarify the importance of biological processes.

Pathways to Health Outcomes

In this article I have argued that the only important outcomes in health and illness are behavioral. Clearly, these outcomes are deserving of one's attention. People expend tremendous resources in order to achieve better health status. In fact, in the United States, more is spent on health care than on food (Kaplan, 1989a). How might one realize the best return on one's investments in terms of health outcomes?

There are at least two ways to achieve better health outcomes. The first is through the modification of mediators of the behavioral outcomes. This is accomplished by identifying tissue pathology and seeking its remedy. Thus, those with diabetes experience poor health outcomes because of a problem in insulin production or insulin action. By supplying more insulin or by tuning up insulin receptors, better health outcomes may be achieved. Those with tumors may experience better health outcomes with the tumors excised. There is nothing wrong with the medical model. In fact, direct treatment of pathology (lesions) remains one of the best methods for improving health outcomes. The traditional practice of medicine and surgery should be viewed as a set of methods designed to improve behavioral outcomes.

Another pathway for improving health outcomes involves modification of behavior, independent of the disease pathway. For example, patients with chronic obstructive pulmonary disease may face a situation in which there are no known medical or surgical remedies. However, behavior modification programs may enhance functioning independent of improvement in disease state (Atkins, Kaplan, Reinsch, Lotback, & Timms, 1984; Kaplan & Atkins, 1988). Pain treatment may also benefit from this conceptualization. Substantial evidence now suggests that pain and suffering are distinct. Pain behavior can continue after the injury that initiated the pain has healed. Several studies have shown that behavior modification can alter behavioral health outcomes for those with back pain, even though it does not affect back physiology in measurable ways (Fordyce, 1988). Health outcomes are behavioral, and one way to improve them is to modify behavior.

The behavioral conceptualization does not disregard the traditional medical model. Indeed, medicines and surgeries are excellent methods for improving behavioral health outcomes. However, the behavioral model is broader. Medicines, surgeries, and behavioral interventions are complementary methods for enhancing behavioral health outcomes. Often one alternative is superior in terms of efficacy or efficiency. For example, hernias can be surgically repaired and it would be inappropriate to use behavioral treatment to modify outcomes related to these problems. On the other hand, several disabilities do not respond to medicines or surgeries. For these, behavioral interventions may be the best alternative for producing a health benefit. Using behavioral outcomes as the target of care allows different alternatives to compete. Ultimately, treatments should be favored if they produce the most benefit at the lowest cost.

Summary

Physicians have long recognized that disease categories provide minimal information about the impact of illness upon patient experiences (Ellwood, 1988). A diagnosis is important because it may identify a course of treatment. Yet within specific diagnoses, patients differ considerably in how they are affected. Multiple sclerosis, for example, may have essentially no impact on behavioral dysfunction or it could have devastating implications. The impact of the disease on the daily life of the patient may be more important than naming the condition. A recent editorial in the *Journal of the American Medical Association* concluded that physicians need to learn to "treat the patient, not the disease" (Riesenberg & Glass, 1989, p. 943).

There are only two health outcomes that are of importance. First, there is life expectancy. Second, there is function or quality of life during the years that people are alive. Biological and physical events are mediators of these behavioral outcomes. Individuals are concerned about cancer, high blood pressure, high cholesterol, or other problems because they may shorten the life expectancy or make life less desirable prior to death. There is a growing consensus that these behavioral outcomes are central in studies of health care and medicine. Yet refinement of these measures requires active participation of behavioral scientists. Although behavioral outcomes are gaining a stronger foothold in medical research, psychologists and behavioral scientists have shown minimal interest. A behavioral conceptualization of health outcomes may suggest important new directions for research and practice.

References

Aderman, M. H., & Madhavan, S. (1981). Management of the hypertensive patient: A continuing dilemma. *Hypertension, 3,* 192-197.

Advances in Health Status Assessment. (1987). Conference proceedings. *Journal of Chronic Disease, 40*(Suppl. 1).

Amberg, J., Schneiderman, L. J., Berry, C. C., & Zettner, A. (1982). The "abnormal" outpatient chemistry panel serum alkaline phosphatase: Analysis of physician response, outcome, cost and health effectiveness. *Journal of Chronic Disease, 35,* 81-88.

Anderson, J. J., Firschein, H. E., & Meenan, R. E. (1989). Sensitivity of a health status measure to short-term clinical changes in arthritis. *Arthritis and Rheumatism, 32,* 844-850.

Atkins, C. J., Kaplan, R. M., Reinsch, S., Lotback, K., & Timms, R. M. (1984). Behavioral exercise programs in the management of patients with chronic obstructive pulmonary disease. *Journal of Consulting and Clinical Psychology, 52,* 591-603.

Atkinson, R. L., Atkinson, R. C., Smith, E. E., & Hilgard, E. R. (1987). *Introduction to psychology* (9th ed.). San Diego, CA: Harcourt Brace Jovanovich.

Baum, A., Grunberg, N. E., & Singer, J. E. (1982). The use of psychological and neuroendocrinological measurements in the study of stress. *Health Psychology, 1,* 217-236.

Bergner, M. (1989). Health status as a measure of health promotion and disease prevention: Unresolved issues and the agenda for the 1990's. *Proceedings of the 1989 Public Health Conference on Records and Statistics.* Rockville, MD: National Center for Health Statistics.

Bigger, J. T., Fleiss, J. L., Kleiger, R., Miller, J. P., & Rolnitzky, L. M. (1984). Multicenter post-infarction research group: The relationships among ventricular arrhythmias, left ventricular dysfunction and mortality in the two years after myocardial infarction. *Circulation, 69,* 250-258.

Breckenridge, A. (1988). Current controversies in the treatment of hypertension. *American Medicine, 84*(Suppl. 1B), 36-46.

Buchanan, W. W. (1982). Assessment of joint tenderness, grip strength, digital joint circumference and morning stiffness in rheumatoid arthritis. *Journal of Rheumatology, 9,* 763-766.

Cardiac Arrhythmia Suppression Trial (CAST) Investigators. (1989). Preliminary report: The effect of encanide and flecainide on mortality in a randomized trial of arrhythmia suppression after myocardial infarction. *The New England Journal of Medicine, 321,* 406-412.

Clark, M., Gosnell, M., Hager, M., Carroll, G., & Gordon, J. (1988, February 8). What you should know about heart attacks. *Newsweek,* pp. 50-54.

Deyo, R. A. (1988). Measuring the quality of life of patients with rheumatoid arthritis. In S. R. Walker &

R. M. Rosser (Eds.), *Quality of life: Assessment and application* (pp. 205-222). London: MTP Press.

Ellwood, P. M. (1988). Outcomes management: A technology of patient experience. *The New England Journal of Medicine,* 318, 1549-1556.

Engel, G. L. (1976). The need for a new medical model: A challenge for biomedicine. *Science, 196,* 129-136.

Expert Panel on Detection, Evaluation, and Treatment of High Blood Cholesterol in Adults. (1988). Report on the national cholesterol education program. *Archives of Internal Medicine, 148,* 36-69.

Feinstein, A. R. (1967). *Clinical judgment.* Huntington, NY: Kreiger.

Fordyce, W. E. (1988). Pain and suffering: A reappraisal. *American Psychologist, 43,* 276-283.

Frick, M. K., Elo, O., Haapa, K., Heinonen, O. P., Heinsalmi, P., Helo, P., Huttunen, J. K., Kaitaniemi, R., Koskinen, P., & Manninen, V. (1987). Helsinki Heart Study: Primary prevention trial with gemfibrozil in middle-aged men with dyslipidemia. *The New England Journal of Medicine, 317,* 1237-1245.

Fries, J. E (1983). Toward an understanding of patient outcome measurement. *Arthritis & Rheumatism, 26,* 697-704.

Fries, J. E., Green, L. W., & Levine, S. (1989). Health promotion and the compression of morbidity. *Lancet, 1,* 481-483.

Galbraith, J. K. (1958). *The affluent society.* Boston: Houghton Mifflin.

Greenfield, S. (1989). The state of outcome research: Are we on target? *The New England Journal of Medicine, 320,* 17, 1142-1143.

Hla, K. M., Vokaty, K. A., & Feussner, J. (1986). Observer error in systolic blood pressure measurement in the elderly: A case for automatic requarters. *Archives of Internal Medicine, 146,* 2373-2376.

Hypertension Detection and Follow-up Program Cooperative Group (HDFP). (1979). Five-year findings of the hypertension, detection, and follow-up program: 1. Reduction in mortality of persons with high blood pressure, including mild hypertension. *Journal of the American Medical Association, 242,* 2562-2576.

Institutes of Medicine. (1989). Advances in health status assessment: Conference proceedings. *Medical Care, 27*(Suppl.), S1-S293.

Jacobs, D. R., Anderson, J. T., & Blackburn, H. (1979). Diet and serum cholesterol: Do zero correlations negate the relationship? *American Journal of Epidemiology, 110,* 77-87.

Joint National Committee on Detection, Evaluation, and Treatment of High Blood Pressure. (1985). Hypertension prevalence and the status of awareness, treatment, and control in the United States. *Hypertension, 7,* 457-468.

Kannel, W. B., Castelli, W. P., Gordon, T., & McNamara, P. M. (1971). Serum cholesterol, lipoproteins and the risk of coronary heart disease. *Annals of Internal Medicine, 74,* 1.

Kaplan, R. M. (1984). The connection between clinical health promotion and health status: A critical review. *American Psychologist, 39,* 755-765.

Kaplan, R. M. (1985). Behavioral epidemiology, health promotion, and health services. *Medical Care, 23,* 564-583.

Kaplan, R. M. (1988). The value dimension in studies of health promotion. In S. Spacapan & S. Oskamp (Eds.), *The social psychology of health* (pp. 207-236). Beverly Hills, CA: Sage.

Kaplan, R. M. (1989a). Health outcome models for policy analysis. *Health Psychology, 8,* 723-735.

Kaplan, R. M. (1989b). Physicians' health study: Aspirin and primary prevention of heart disease. *The New England Journal of Medicine, 321,* 1826-1827.

Kaplan, R. M., & Anderson, J. P. (1988). The general health policy model: Update and application. *Health Services Research, 23,* 203-235.

Kaplan, R. M., & Atkins, C. J. (1988). Behavioral interventions for patients with COPD. In J. McSweeney & I. Grant (Eds.), *Chronic obstructive pulmonary disease: A behavioral perspective* (pp. 701-740). New York: Marcel Dekker.

Kaplan, R. M., & Atkins, C. J. (1989). The well-year of life as a basis for patient-decision making. *Patient and Education Counseling, 13,* 281-295.

Kaplan, R. M., & Bush, J. W. (1982). Health-related quality of life measurement for evaluation research and policy analysis. *Health Psychology, 1,* 621-680.

Krantz, D. S., Grunberg, N. E., & Baum, A. (1985). Health psychology. *Annual Review of Psychology, 36,* 349-383.

Lipid Research Clinics Coronary Prevention Trial Results. (1984). 1. Reduction in incidence in coronary heart disease. *Journal of the American Medical Association, 251,* 351-364.

McCarty, D. J. (1986). Clinical assessment of arthritis. In D. J. McCarty (Ed.), *Arthritis and allied conditions* (9th ed., pp. 131-147). Philadelphia: Lea & Febiger.

Miller, N. E. (1983). Behavioral medicine: Symbiosis between laboratory and clinic. *Annual Review of Psychology, 34,* 1-31.

National Heart, Lung and Blood Institute. (1984). *Tenth report of the director: Vol. 1. Progress and promise*

(NIH Publication No. 84-2356). Bethesda, MD: National Institutes of Health.

Patterson, H. R. (1984). Sources of error in recording blood pressure of patients with hypertension in general practice. *British Medical Journal, 289,* 1661-1664.

Pickering, T. G., James, G. D., Boddie, C., Harshfield, G. A., Blank, S., & Laragh, J. H. (1988). How common is white coat hypertension? *Journal of the American Medical Association, 259,* 225-228.

President's Commission on National Goals. (1960). Report. (Available from Robert Kaplan, Division of Health Care Sciences, M-022, School of Medicine, University of California, San Diego, La Jolla, CA 92093-0622)

Quality of life assessment. (1988a, Fall). *Quality of Life in Cardiovascular Care, 4*(3).

Quality of life assessment. (1988b, Winter). *Quality of Life in Cardiovascular Care, 4*(4).

Riesenberg, D., & Glass, R. M. (1989). The medical outcomes study. *Journal of the American Medical Association, 262,* 943.

Rocella, E. J., Bowler, A. E., & Horan, N. (1987). Epidemiologic considerations in defining hypertension. *Medical Clinics of North America, 71,* 785-801.

Rodin, J., & Salovey, P. (1989). Health psychology. *Annual Review of Psychology, 40,* 533-579.

Shortell, S. M., & McNerney, W. J. (1990). Criteria and guidelines for reforming the U.S. Health Care System. *The New England Journal of Medicine, 322,* 463-467.

Shumaker, S., Furberg, C., Czajkowski, S., & Schron, E. (in press). *Quality of life in cardiovascular disease.* New York: Wiley.

Stallones, R. A. (1983). Ischemic heart disease and lipids in blood and diet. *Annual Review of Nutrition, 3,* 155-185.

Steering Committee of the Physicians' Health Study Research Group. (1988). Preliminary report: Findings from the aspirin component of the ongoing Physicians' Health Study. *The New England Journal of Medicine, 318,* 262-264.

Steering Committee of the Physicians' Health Study Research Group. (1989). Final report on the aspirin component of the ongoing Physicians' Health Study. *The New England Journal of Medicine, 321,* 129-135.

Sullivan, D. E. (1966). *Conceptual problems in developing an index of health* (Monograph Series II, No. 17). Washington, DC: Office of Health Statistics, National Center for Health Statistics.

Temoshok, L., Soloman, G. E., & Jenkins, S. (1989, August). *Methodological issues in research on psychoneuroimmunology.* Paper presented at the 97th Annual Convention of the American Psychological Association, New Orleans, LA.

Thelle, D. S., Heyden, S., & Fodor, J. G. (1987). Coffee and cholesterol in epidemiological and experimental studies. *Atherosclerosis, 67,* 97-103.

Walker, S., & Rosser, R. (Eds.). (1988). *Quality of life: Assessment and applications.* London: MTP Press.

White, N. E. (1988). Medical and graduate education in behavioral medicine and the evolution of health care. *Annals of Behavioral Medicine, 10,* 23-29.

Wilson, P. W., Garrison, R. J., Kannel, W. B., McGee, D. L., & Castelli, W. P. (1989). Is coffee consumption a contributor to cardiovascular disease? Insights from the Framingham study. *Archives of Internal Medicine, 149,* 1169-1172.

PART II

Health Attitude Change

Essay: Social Theory, Conforming, and the Change of Health Attitudes and Behaviors

William D. Marelich and Jeff S. Erger

> Well you know, smoking takes ten years off your life. It's the ten WORST years, isn't it, folks? It's the ones at the end. It's the wheelchair, adult diaper, kidney dialysis . . . years. You can have those years!
>
> Comedian Denis Leary

Conforming to Social Environments

Behavior change is a difficult and complicated process, and altering *health* behaviors is no different. Adopting and maintaining health promotion behaviors such as exercise or altering health-compromising behaviors such as smoking are notorious as things people know they should do, but cannot seem to keep doing. Take a moment to think about the times in the last year you decided to change some type of behavior pattern. Maybe you made a New Year's resolution that required doing something different or stopping some behavior or activity (Can you even remember what your last New Year's resolution was?) Maybe you promised yourself to eat healthier, or try exercising a little bit more, or even adopt yoga into your everyday routine, as one of your text authors says he is going to do each and every January.

Was making the change easy? We bet that the first few days, you were probably "gung ho" to change, yet by the end of the first couple of weeks, you may have found adhering to the change a challenge. Did your "zeal" for making the change diminish over time? Did you find that the change persisted after the first few weeks—or the first month? Did you find yourself reverting back to your old patterns? Did your promise of adopting yoga turn into television watching?

Don't think we are preaching at you, telling you that you are weak for your failures, that you are deficient for not being healthy, or that you simply are uninformed of the relevant theory, and that once you are better informed, your life will be much healthier. We are just as subject to the social and psychological factors that make behavior change difficult. As noted above, one of us has a standing New Year's resolution: to start and finish a 30-day yoga exercise plan. He has a book that lays out all the daily programs and discusses the benefits of doing the exercise. Over the past decade, he has averaged sticking to the plan a whopping 3 days in a row before something "comes up" that puts Day 4 off until tomorrow. Then, after a few hit-or-miss days, the program ends. One year, he did all 30 days, and it felt great! Then he stopped. This is despite the exercise program doing wonders for how he feels and the fact that he recommends the program to many people when the topic comes up.

Changing health behaviors can be a long and even arduous process because existing behavior patterns are heavily influenced by the social and physical environment in which we find ourselves. In other words, sometimes we perform particular behaviors because the social system pressures us to conform. This may sound rather draconian ("Where is free will?" you ask), yet a host of social psychological observations and studies suggest that individuals conform to the perceived normative behavior patterns and/or to behavior-setting programs. A classic example of such conformity you may recall from an introductory psychology or sociology course is *The Stanford Prison Study.* (If you are not familiar with the study, there is a great Web site that overviews the study and its implications at: http://www.prisonexp.org.)

You still say, "Ha! I make my own choices!" Well, let's take a common health behavior example from college life and see. Say you are out with a number of your friends, and a couple of them are having cigarettes. Everyone is having a good time, and even though you are a nonsmoker, one of your friends suggests you give it a try. You struggle a bit with the decision, and finally you give in, telling yourself, "Just this once." If this has happened to you, then indeed you have fallen prey to your social environment. You may dislike smoking and know that smoking is bad for your health, yet you were coaxed into giving it a try. "But wait," you exclaim, "I had consumed some alcohol, so my judgment was affected!" Well, this, too, helped you to conform. Alcohol was part of the social environment. And you just attributed the reason why you smoked to the influence of alcohol, which was part of the social environment you were in. You are still conforming, albeit in an impaired state.

If you still don't buy this social pressure and conforming argument, think for a moment about the number of friends and acquaintances you know who are "social smokers": In other words, how many people do you know who smoke only when at parties? We bet you know a few, and probably the strongest reason they smoke in this social setting is simply to conform and fit in.

In another example, say you are trying to eat healthier and decide to make an effort to avoid fast foods and junk foods. Yet your school schedule, work, and social obligations make it very tough to adopt this "healthy" food regimen. You try to seek out healthy foods at school, but the choices are rather mundane. This assumes you have healthy choices at all—we suspect that for some of you, this would be quite challenging since colleges are notorious for having limited selections of healthy foods. Furthermore, if you commute to your university, you are no doubt tempted by available fast-food options near you or even on campus. Indeed, at one of our universities, at least eight fast-food opportunities are within walking distance, and two are actually on campus.

At work, you are surrounded by quick-snack machines and the inevitable "food runs" that take place at many offices, which probably don't include healthy alternatives. And at play, how often do you find yourself requesting a "thin-crust cheese pizza" when all your friends are enjoying a pizza with everything? Do you really want to be the "odd person out?" Getting the pizza with "everything" is the easiest and probably most appeasing to you and your peers. And then there are the late night "study" pizzas. Count the number of pizza deliveries to a college dorm on some Sunday night, or simply count the number of pizza boxes in the trash the next day, and then consider the calories involved. If everyone in your study group wants pizza, are you going to say no and eat carrot sticks?

You see, avoiding unhealthy behaviors or adopting healthy behaviors can be a challenge, especially when the social environment works against you.

Health Behaviors and Health Habits

Beyond the noticeable pressures to conform, some of our health behaviors (both good and bad) can become "habits." This simply means that many of the ways in which you behave operate automatically, without you really thinking about what you are doing. Health habits start off as health behaviors influenced and supported by the social environment. Given time and repetition, these behaviors become part of our everyday behaviors; social environment pressures no longer need to be present for the health habit to occur.

For example, health-promoting behaviors that have become automatic for many in our society include brushing your teeth at night before going to bed or putting your seat belt on before you drive in an automobile. These behaviors for many individuals have become habituated, done automatically without purposeful forethought. Another health behavior, albeit health compromising, would be the normative behavior many of us engage in that entails drinking multiple cups of coffee in the morning, then rushing out the door without eating breakfast. You wake up, wander bleary-eyed into the kitchen to make coffee, fill your mug with the dark brew, and head off to class or work. Or maybe you are like a friend of one of your authors, who has to walk his dog Jake and subsequently goes to the local coffee house to get his "fix." Later in the morning, after your coffee "buzz" has turned into nervous hunger, you seek food. This almost daily pattern of behaviors is probably performed by some of you without much thought. The only time you may realize this pattern is when something interferes with the pattern, such as running out of coffee, which disrupts the morning routine.

Health habits can be harder to change than typical health behaviors because they are ingrained in our behavior patterns. Since habits are automatic, we are generally unaware that we are doing them. To test this, we challenge you to change your current tooth-brushing schedule. Try brushing your teeth at 7 p.m. instead of before going to bed, or at 10 a.m. instead of right after you wake up. We think that within a 7-day period, you'll "slip" and brush your teeth at your normal time at least once without thinking. This is evidence for the strength of health habits even in the face of willful attempts at changing them.

Overview of Change Strategies

There is an old joke told about psychologists: "How many psychologists does it take to change a light bulb?" The answer, "Well first, the light bulb has to WANT to change." We think that change is partially a function of individuals *wanting* to change and the social influences, perceptions, and rewards that influence change. As hard as it is to change health behaviors, change can indeed be implemented and sustained.

The current section of readings addresses health behavior change in terms of theoretical applications. Although some may respond to applying theory as a waste of time—"Who needs theory? Just tell the person to change!"—in fact, applying formal theory leads to more successful and pronounced change. In social psychology, theories help us to understand the underlying issues that drive the health-compromising behaviors or the barriers to healthy behavior adoption, predict when the behavior will occur, and enable us to eventually effect change. The goals with theory, then, are to understand, predict, effect, and control behavior.

Theories provide a cause-and-effect explanation of phenomena. Without underlying theory, we are left with a series of change components that do not provide cause-and-effect evidence. This has been termed the "black-box" problem. Even though change components are applied and behavior change does indeed occur, we are unable to say "X causes Y" because we lack an underlying theoretical explanation for *why X caused the change Y.*

For example, if we wanted to change one of your current health behaviors such as eating junk food, we could provide you with information and educate you about the positive or negative aspects of the health behavior. We could inform you that eating junk food is unhealthy because increased empty-calorie intake leads to fat production and varies insulin rates, creating body instability. Furthermore, we could tell you that healthy individuals eat junk food at much lower rates than do those who are obese. Yet to simply say that this information alone will change your health behaviors would not be correct: Something else will also be at work. In fact, most health behavior studies show that increasing knowledge by itself does not effect change. Indeed, if we were to claim that knowledge alone effected change, then we have fallen prey to the black-box effect.

To fully understand, predict, and control behaviors, we need to explain what is operating inside the black box. In the example above, instead of surmising that information alone will cause change, we can fully explain the black-box components through the use of an attitude/behavior change theory such as the *theory of reasoned action.* The information or knowledge about junk food influences two of the model's components: *attitudes* (i.e., your like/dislike of the object or behavior) and *subjective norms* (i.e., your perceptions of what others think about the object or behavior that pressures you to conform). Attitudes and subjective norms directly influence another component, your *intent* to change the behavior. Finally, behavioral intent influences adoption of the new behavior.

Applying this theory and assuming that being healthy is a goal of yours, we can now suggest that your attitude toward junk food will be influenced by the negative information presented to you and your subjective norms will be influenced by the information that healthy people eat less junk food. These two components will influence your intent to eat junk food, which will subsequently lead you to eat less junk food. This now is clearly a causal model of health behavior change, and the behavior change components can be supported as a "whole" by underlying theory. If we find that the model works for changing behaviors about fast food, it should generalize to other health-related behaviors such as exercise and smoking. This is the power of using theory as a basis for action, and you don't have to reinvent the wheel to get rolling.

Health behavior change strategies may take place at various levels: the individual level, the group and social normative level, and the legislative/societal level. The Marelich and Rotheram-Borus article summarizes many of these approaches and may be viewed as a general overview of many strategies used for behavior change. Its inclusion here is to offer a succinct overview of these strategies and their applications. Individual behavior change is partitioned into a series of components, including *behavioral intent, environmental constraints, outcome expectations, social norms, emotion/attitude,* and *self-efficacy.* Each of these is then related back to its original theory. Behavior change as a product of social norms is presented next and reviews a series of strategies, ranging from innovation diffusion via media to sexual ecology. Legislative/societal change, also known as *macrochange,* is also addressed, looking at legislative changes that have influenced health-related outcomes, such as driving-while-intoxicated laws. (Part V of this text more broadly addresses legislative/policy influences.)

Furthermore, Marelich and Rotheram-Borus suggest that the future of many of these behavior change strategies lies in their "manualized" application in various health settings, including children's mental health service delivery, mental retardation services, and psychiatric rehabilitation. Service to such populations has required streamlining due to cost constraints, and hence, many organizations have adopted a model of service delivery that utilizes medical/clinical professionals in management roles who oversee paraprofessionals to implement the specific health service. If you are a graduate medical, nursing, or public health student, you may currently be in the "management" role noted above or in the future may be part of such an organization that uses this model. If you are an undergraduate student reading these pages, you may actually be one of the "paraprofessionals" mentioned in the article who follow a prescribed manual of services under the guidance of a health manager. In fact, just recently, one of your authors discovered that two of his undergraduates were implementing manualized protocols in their current internships on two populations, autistic children and abused adolescents.

Individual and Group Change Models

The next section focuses on some of the more commonly used and accepted individual and group change models. Most of these center on changing attitudes in various ways. Attitudes are considered to be the affective or emotional considerations a person has about something. For example, you may have a positive attitude or affect toward smoking ("I like to smoke"), and this attitude can be a strong predictor of whether you will smoke in the future. Hence, getting you to change your attitude toward smoking is an important step in changing your smoking behavior. Attitude change is influenced by many components, including perceived social norms and peer group influences.

The articles represented in this section were chosen because we feel they nicely illustrate the behavior change principles employed, adhere to the ideals of the intended models, and are generally easy to read. The articles provide a good amount of detail on the model components and how the components influence behavioral intent and, ultimately, health behaviors.

The section begins with an article by Larson, Bergan, Heidrich, Alvin, and Schneeweiss, which presents an application of the *health belief model,* a formidable model with strong results over the past 30 years. Here, they apply the model by using postcard reminders to address the component "cues to action." Wulfert and Wan summarize the concept of *self-efficacy* in their article on condom use, which links self-efficacy and other cognitive-behavioral intervention components to increasing condom use. The article also comments on Bandura's *social learning theory,* which underscores the importance of individuals modeling their behaviors on the behaviors of others.

Hausenblas, Carron, and Mack explore two very similar models, the *theory of reasoned action* and the *theory of planned behavior,* in application to exercise behavior. Note that for these theories, *behavioral intent* is an important component and can be seen as a keystone in how these models function. This article, unlike the others presented in this section, uses a statistical technique called "meta-analysis," which essentially aggregates research findings from different articles. The technique allows one to ask, "Summarizing across many studies, does the model change behavior, and if so, how much change or effect is noted?"

These first three articles summarize what is sometimes referred to as *individual* attitude and behavior change models. The next article focuses on *group* or *social normative* change. Kelly, Lawrence, Diaz, et al. apply a *diffusion of innovations* framework to change social norms regarding HIV risk behaviors. The diffusion framework may be used to initiate change by devising new behavior strategies that can be easily adopted by members of a social group and subsequently diffused through the rest of the group members through simple communication channels. Here, safe-sex behaviors are the new set of behaviors to be adopted, and diffusion is facilitated through *opinion leaders* who are respected social group members.

After reading these articles, one exercise you can undertake is to ponder what they have in common and where they differ. You will probably notice quite a bit of overlap across models, or in some instances, the labels may differ, but the underlying concepts may be similar. Such overlaps in components are normal in social psychology. New behavior change models are generated from older models. For example, the *theory of planned behavior* was an extension of the *theory of reasoned action.* In other instances, new models arrive from nonsocial psychological areas and hence have components similar to existing models, but with different names. The *health belief model* comes from the medical sciences yet has components very similar to the two models listed above. In all, getting a sense of "What came first" or "What area of science the model comes from" will help explain overlap, and the articles' reference sections will be the most helpful in this endeavor. Also, noting model differences may be enlightening: Do all models end with behavior change? Is behavior intent disregarded in any of the models?

Designing Health Behavior Interventions

At this point, you may be saying to yourself, "Okay, so I want to change a health behavior, and I need to make it theory driven. I have selected a theory, so now I'm ready to implement an intervention and make people healthier!" Indeed, if research were only this simple. Certainly, the first few steps in planning an intervention are to figure out exactly what behavior you want to change and to pick a framework or theory to apply. However, once these steps have been addressed, one has to design *how* the intervention will be implemented, and this takes a certain amount of care and planning. Research methods are the building blocks toward interpreting and evaluating behaviors.

One element of planning and implementing research that we wanted to underscore in this text regards how health messages are constructed or "framed." As you might have noticed from the earlier articles, *knowledge* is a key component in many of the health behavior change models. Hence, how that knowledge or information is conveyed is an important issue. You might not think that the simple wording of a message can have a big effect on behavior, but take a moment to see whether you can recall any "health messages" that led you to engage in a new healthy behavior or to reduce an unhealthy behavior. Maybe a billboard that you saw or a posted flyer at your university that led to you altering your behavior?

Here's a real applied example of this process. Recently, one of your textbook authors was involved in designing a health message to inform students where they can purchase condoms on campus. Now, simply putting up a notice might have sufficed. Yet here was an opportunity to try and change students' attitudes and behaviors toward condom use, with the goal being that if students were sexually active, they should feel compelled to use condoms. A message was constructed to convey the importance of condom use, followed by locations where condoms could be obtained on campus. The constructed message read, "Using condoms can better protect you from HIV and STDs, and can be obtained from our health center on campus." Notice how the information on condoms is worded? Do you think this would have motivated you to have a condom available the next time you are intimate with a new partner?

To help you understand the import of message framing, we present in this section an article by Rothman, Martino, Bedell, Detweiler, and Salovey, which focuses on how to "frame" health behavior messages to elicit behavior change. Their approach is based on Kahneman and Tversky's *prospect theory,* which attempts to understand individuals' decision making as it relates to their perceptions of risk (i.e., either risk-averse or risk-seeking). The Rothman et al. findings suggest that if the purpose of the health message is for prevention (e.g., to prevent sunburn), then the message should be associated with risk aversion and therefore should be "gain framed." Gain-framed messages are worded in such a way as to ensure better health or add additional protection: "If you use sunscreen with a higher SPF, you will be better protected against sunburn and skin cancer." Notice that the message is selling the "sure thing" of better protection.

If, however, the health message is intended to motivate individuals to get tested or screened for a disease (e.g., breast cancer), then the message should be associated with risk taking and should be "loss framed." Loss-framed messages are worded in such a way as to highlight the *costs* or risks associated with not getting tested; "If you don't do a self-breast exam, there is a chance of developing breast cancer and other problems." Here, the message underscores the risk of not taking the chance and undertaking the detection behavior. Even the simple choice of phrasing a message in terms of gains or losses, or benefits or risks, can be crucial in the effectiveness of that message in changing people's behavior. When the goal is to save lives and make those lives healthier and free from pain and sickness, the responsibility of the researcher trying to make those changes happen is not to be taken lightly.

After reading Rothman et al., return for a moment to the example health message that one of your textbook authors thought was a great opportunity to entice students to use condoms if they are sexually active. Given that the goal was to get students to use condoms, do you think the provided message was *gain framed* or *loss framed?* Why? What does the wording of the message tell you? Given the goal, was the correct framing applied? We hope you give this some thought before moving to our next section on the health care setting.

A. Overview of Change Strategies

8

FROM INDIVIDUAL TO SOCIAL CHANGE

Current and Future Directions of Health Interventions

WILLIAM D. MARELICH AND MARY JANE ROTHERAM-BORUS

As the new millennium approaches, intervention strategies that focus on improving health have been aggressively pursued by medical and social/behavioral practitioners. The emergence and application of the biopsychosocial model has led to the realization that health-related behaviors are interdependent with psychological and social factors (e.g., diabetes and schizophrenia are driven by both medical and psychological factors; see Engel, 1977). Hence, solutions for changing health behaviors encompass social-environmental factors as well as psychological issues.

Shaping or changing health behaviors can be a monumental task. Whether the behavior is simple (e.g., brushing one's teeth every day) or complex (e.g., adhering to a 6-month tuberculosis drug regimen), individuals must make an effort to maintain healthy behaviors and avoid unhealthy behaviors. Often, barriers in complying with the new behavior or lack of confidence with adherence leads to failure (Janz & Becker, 1984). In particular, the early stages of behavior change are the most crucial because habituation of the replacement behaviors has not occurred; hence, constant reinforcement is

EDITORS' NOTE: Previously published in Gullota, R. L. et al., *Child and Family Health Care: Issues for the Year 2000 and Beyond,* pp. 169-196.

required for the new behaviors to persist. However, behavior change can and does take place given time, the individual's willingness to comply, and the acceptability of the new behavior within cultural norms (Rogers, 1962).

Health behavior interventions focus on both individual behavior change (e.g., changing an individual's attitudes, behavioral intentions, and actions) and social change (e.g., changing population attitudes and behaviors). Together, these interventions address different parts of the epidemiologic spectrum of disease and infection gradient, yet are interdependent. Individual-level intervention strategies (e.g., case-level interventions or small group interventions) have been very successful in changing behaviors (for broad reviews, see McGuire, 1985, and Oskamp, 1991; for applications to health issues, see Taylor, 1995). Since health intervention research may be viewed as applied or action oriented, these intervention strategies typically are applied to individuals manifesting a disease (i.e., at risk for spreading the disease) or those at risk for infection.

However, this emphasis on high-profile cases is analogous to treating the "tip of the iceberg" of a disease (Lilienfeld & Lilienfeld, 1980), whereby cases that manifest the disease receive individual treatment, but those with unapparent infections (i.e., infected cases that show no symptoms) remain untreated. The AIDS epidemic in the United States is a good example of the "iceberg" phenomenon and individual behavior change interventions. HIV/AIDS health interventions focus on those individuals practicing high-risk behaviors such as unprotected intercourse with multiple partners or unsterile needle sharing, and include changing the attitudes, intentions, and actions of those at high risk for HIV However, regardless of these interventions, incidence rates continued to increase through the 1980s and have remained at high levels through the 1990s. Although the people at highest risk are being addressed, many infected individuals continue to bridge into the uninfected population and perpetuate the epidemic.

Other health change interventions focus on broader social change strategies, where normative social behaviors and attitudes of the population are altered through mass appeals, social activism, and public policy (Stokols, 1992; Susser, 1995). These interventions are intended to influence the entire population, including those at high risk for disease spread or infection and those at low risk. One key to societal adoption of healthy behaviors (e.g., daily exercise or quitting smoking) may lie in discovering the "tipping point" for mass acceptance of the behavior. Gladwell (1996) has illustrated this principle with the metaphor, "Tomato ketchup in a bottle—none will come and then the lot'll" (p. 36). In other words, social change may appear slow or even stagnant at first, yet over time momentum builds and change "spills" into the normative behaviors of the population. Recent examples of population-wide changes in health-related behaviors include declines in smoking and increases in the use of vehicle restraints.

Together, individual and social change strategies are important tools for influencing health-enhancing behaviors and deterring unhealthy or risky health behaviors. The current chapter provides an overview of successful health behavior interventions addressing individual and societal change. The first part presents theory-driven intervention strategies applied at the level of the individual. The second part reviews health interventions from a social influence perspective, focusing on changes in behavioral norms of communities and the larger U.S. population. These interventions can have wide-ranging social impact, yet have received little attention. The final section of the chapter elaborates on the future of health interventions, including how the individual and social influence approaches need to be expanded to address providers, managed care settings, and legislative changes.

Behavioral Interventions at the Individual Level

Over the past 30 years, health researchers have undertaken the task of making sense of an individual's health behaviors and his or her interconnectivity to surrounding systems. Using a biopsychosocial model, the physical, mental, and social factors that affect health have been investigated. Health behavior change research and interventions have focused on a wide range of issues, including heart disease (Farquhar et al., 1990; Miller, Smith, Turner,

Guijarro, & Hallet, 1996), HIV/AIDS sexual behaviors (Kalichman, Carey, & Johnson, 1996), smoking (Bruvold, 1993), weight loss (Black, Gleser, & Kooyers, 1990) and eating disorders (Mann, Nolen-Hoeksema, Huang, & Burgard, 1997), cancer (Meyer & Mark, 1995), obesity (Kirsch, Montgomery, & Sapirstein, 1995), exercise behavior (Hausenblas, Carron, & Mack, 1997), and health/work issues (Donaldson, Cooler, & Weiss, 1998).

This section will focus on individual-based models of behavior and behavior change that have been shown to be effective. To date, there have been a number of excellent reviews that have addressed many of these models and their application to health issues (e.g., Glanz, Lewis, & Rimer, 1990; Rodin & Salovey, 1989; Taylor, 1995). Hence, this section provides a brief sample of various theories and models. In addition, models based on social/behavioral theory are given preference for coverage because they illustrate or explain the "black box" (i.e., causal mechanisms) of behavioral intervention strategies (Lipsey, 1993; Scott & Sechrest, 1989), thereby providing powerful, replicable explanations for health behaviors and health behavior change (Van Ryn & Heaney, 1992). For example, in their review of HIV/AIDS behavior change studies, Fisher and Fisher (1992) found that a majority of studies utilized informal conceptual approaches to behavioral intervention as opposed to formal theory-driven approaches. They concluded that "AIDS-risk-reduction interventions that are conceptually based and group specific and that focus on providing AIDS-risk-reduction information, motivation, and behavioral skills are the most impactful and sound bases for intervention" (p. 463). Similar findings have been shown for theory-driven drug adherence interventions (Haynes, McKibbon, & Kanani, 1996) and theory-driven behavioral outcomes and HIV-risk reduction (Kalichman et al., 1996).

Some of the most successful theories of individual health behavior change include the health belief model (Janz & Becker, 1984), the theory of reasoned action (Fishbein & Ajzen, 1975; Fishbein et al., 1993), and the theory of planned behavior (Ajzen & Madden, 1986). In general, these models may be considered attitudinal models of behavior change (Taylor, 1995). If an individual's attitude (emotive or affective response) toward the faulty behavior can be changed, then the individual should strive to change the behavior and replace it with a healthy response. Other theories of behavior change include social cognitive theory (Bandura, 1986) and the transtheoretical model of stages and processes of change (Prochaska, DiClemente, & Norcross, 1992). These theories tend to be broader in scope than the attitudinal models, often encompassing attitudinal and cognitive-behavioral components and decision-making processes.

All the models noted above have received considerable empirical support. As such, the task of overviewing each of these models may seem inhibitive. However, there is considerable overlap across these competing models, especially when examining factors that may impede health behavior change, future goals, and health outcome expectations (Bandura, 1997). The most successful components from these and other models (see Fishbein et al., 1991; see also Bandura, 1997) include the following:

- intentions
- environmental constraints (i.e., barriers)
- outcome expectations
- social norms
- emotion
- self-efficacy

Intentions. An intention is the cognitive antecedent to a behavior, and may be seen as the mediating factor between attitudes (i.e., affective association toward an object or a person) and behavioral actions (which historically have shown only weak causal links; see Wicker, 1969). Behavioral change comes from altering the individual's intention of performing the behavior. Intentions are altered by influencing attitudes and beliefs. The models most associated with behavioral intentions are the theories of reasoned action (Fishbein & Ajzen, 1975), planned behavior (Ajzen & Madden, 1986), and stages/processes of change (Prochaska et al., 1992).

Environmental Constraints (Barriers). Environmental constraints are those mental or physical barriers that hinder performance or adoption of healthy behaviors. Behavioral change comes from removal of the barriers or by showing the individual how to work around the offered constraints. Barriers are a major factor in the health belief model (Janz & Becker, 1984) and social cognitive theory (Bandura, 1997), and have been shown to play an important role in health interventions (Janz & Becker, 1984).

Outcome Expectations. Outcome expectations are the beliefs "that a particular course of action will produce certain outcomes" (Bandura, 1977, p. 193). In other words, if the benefits to behavior change outweigh the costs, then the probability of behavior change is increased. Therefore, behavior change comes from bolstering perception of benefits and downplaying costs. Most models of behavior change focus on at least one facet of outcomes, either physical/health improvements, improvements in social relations, or self-evaluation (Bandura, 1997).

Social Norms. Social norms are the individual's perceptions of the normative behavioral pressures surrounding the individual (e.g., from peers or family members). Behavior change is instigated either by changing the individual's perception of normative influences, or by restructuring the individual's social environment (e.g., changing peer groups). All the models noted above contain a social-norm component.

Emotion. The emotional reaction (positive or negative) of the individual when confronted with making a behavior change can also determine whether the change is successful or unsuccessful. Behavior intervention is thus undertaken by promoting positive emotional reactions (e.g., coping strategies; see Lazarus & Folkman, 1984). Since attitudes are, by nature, affective (Oskamp, 1991), all the attitudinal models of behavior change contain this component. In addition, social cognitive theory and the stages/processes of change model also incorporate emotion.

Self-Efficacy. Self-efficacy is a cognitive component and may be defined as the individual's self-perception of his or her capability to perform the required behavior change. Therefore, self-efficacy is antecedent to behavioral intention and action. However, self-efficacy has also been shown directly to influence behavior above and beyond behavioral intentions (Ajzen & Madden, 1986). Behavioral change comes from training individuals that they are capable of making the requested behavior change. Models of behavioral change associated with self-efficacy include social cognitive theory, the theory of planned behavior, and the stages/processes of change model.

Although we have presented components from various models, it is important to note that the use of these components without their respective theories, known as eclecticism, may suffer from inherent philosophical problems (Slife & Williams, 1995). For example, by measuring the effects of barriers, applied researchers are forced to accept the underlying assumptions associated with the health belief model even though none of the other components of the model may be addressed. Theories such as the health belief model are intended to explain health behavior and behavior change by themselves, and are often derived from different theoretical frameworks and assumptions. Indeed, "every part [of a theory component] brings with it the whole of the host of hidden ideas that any theory always has" (Slife & Williams, 1995, p. 48).

It has been argued that transtheoretical models bridge theoretical accounts of behavior and the goal of helping individuals alter or solve their behavioral problems (Slife & Williams, 1995). For example, Prochaska and DiClemente (1992) have provided excellent evidence for the utility of their transtheoretical model of stages/processes of change in "describing, predicting, and explaining changes in a broad range of behavior problems" (p. 204). However, as noted earlier, behavior change interventions that are theory based produce more reliable and valid results than those that are not (e.g., Fisher & Fisher, 1992; Haynes et al., 1996). Indeed, as Bandura (1997) has concisely stressed, "scientific progress is better achieved by encompassing more fully the determinants within an integrated theory than by creating conglomerate models with constructs picked from divergent theories with the attendant problems of redundancy, fractionation, and theoretical disconnectedness" (p. 286).

Interventions at the Group Level: Effecting Social Change

> There must be no letup to social action against . . . known health hazards.
>
> (Susser, 1995, p. 158)

Although interventions aimed at affecting the individual's attitudes and behaviors have produced the bulk of empirical findings, those aimed at influencing social change have an important place in changing health behaviors and in maintaining behavior change across time. Broad social change in regard to health behaviors and promotion have been noted for smoking, diet, and exercise in recent years, with changes in social normative behaviors suggested for these changes (McGinnis, Richmond, Brandt, Windom, & Mason, 1992; Stokols, 1992; Taylor, 1995).

How are social norms changed? One suggestion is that normative behaviors are changed in small, incremental steps, also known as "small wins" (Weick, 1984). Applied to health behavior change and interventions, the small wins approach functions to ease individuals into changing their health behaviors through small, controllable actions. This approach is analogous to the "foot-in-the-door" phenomenon (Freedman & Fraser, 1966). The foot-in-the-door approach suggests that if an individual commits to a lesser request, then he or she is likely to perform a more costly act in order to remain in consonance with his or her earlier action (Oskamp, 1991). For example, Freedman and Fraser (1966) found that individuals who acquiesced to having a small, driver safety sign placed in their window were more likely to allow a large "drive carefully" sign placed on their lawns compared to a control group that were asked only to display the large sign.

Weick (1984) has cited a number of non-health-related examples to support the small wins approach to societal change. For example, the Task Force on Gay Liberation succeeded in having the Library of Congress reclassify works on the gay liberation movement from "abnormal sexual relations" to "sexual life," thus winning a small battle that raised public consciousness about the acceptability of being gay. In another example, Weick (1984) suggests that although feminists have suffered setbacks in big win situations (e.g., equal rights legislation), they have been successful with small wins in degendering the English language. These small wins, in turn, will affect public consciousness and, subsequently, future legislation.

In regard to health promotion and societal change, Stokols (1992) notes that "incremental health promotion . . . can exert a positive, albeit gradual, influence on the quality and healthfulness" (p. 6) of individuals. For example, Corea (1992) illustrated how social activism and empirical research culminated in changing the AIDS diagnostic definition to include clinical symptoms specifically related to women. McGinnis et al. (1992) cited gradual changes in social norms as the reason why smoking has declined since 1980 and for increases in seat belt use (e.g., from 1975 to 1995, seat belt use has seen an almost tenfold increase; National Highway Traffic Safety Administration, 1996). In another study, Berger and Marelich (1997) also suggested incremental changes in societal norms as the salient factor behind steep declines in alcohol-impaired driving attitudes, beliefs, and behaviors, comparing two cross-sectional samples of California drivers from 1983 to 1994.

What types of intervention strategies best effect social change? From social learning theory, we know that individuals acquire new behaviors and change old ones through direct experience and positive feedback offered by others, through self-reinforcement, or through indirect or vicarious experiences of others being reinforced (or not punished) for particular behaviors (Bandura, 1986). Further, individuals exist as part of larger social webs of interdependencies. These "loose couplings" (Weick, 1979) allow for some individual differences, yet underscore the importance of social networks that surround and influence behavior. Hence, intervention strategies that focus on altering individuals' perceptions of social-normative behaviors may have the greatest effect.

Social change may best be shaped by exposing individuals to health prevention or health change messages over time using communication channels such as the mass media (e.g., television and radio). Media communication influences how individuals perceive the world, and can be viewed as a "belief" cultivation process (Roberts & Maccoby, 1985). Further, the media can forge cohesiveness of individuals by generating shared experiences and social comparison (Meyrowitz, 1985).

Once a core group of individuals has been exposed, the new information filters or diffuses its way into society and social acceptance (Rogers, 1962). For example, say a town is exposed to a series of health-promotion messages over a one-month period. The messages will filter their way around the community due to simple communication processes. Those who comprehended the message will pass the information along to those who did not attend to the message and to those who attended but did not comprehend. Finally, message adherence will slowly occur as more and more individuals begin to conform.

Community-based health interventions using mass media often show positive results. For example, in a well-documented study by Farquhar et al. (1990), reductions in cardiovascular disease were noted in a communitywide intervention. The intervention focused on educational strategies, including mass media campaigns that included television, radio, newspaper, and other print media, and interpersonal training programs. Two California cities served as treatments and two as controls. Results also indicated modest significant decreases in cholesterol level and blood pressure. It was also noted that the media intervention accelerated smoking declines in the treatment cities. Other community health interventions using mass media have also shown positive results (see Lando et al., 1995; Multiple Risk Factor Intervention Trial Research Group, 1982; Owen, Bauman, Booth, Oldenburg, & Magnus, 1995).

However, community-based interventions can also fail to have an impact (Susser, 1995). For example, COMMIT (Community Intervention Trial for Smoking Cessation; COMMIT Research Group, 1995a, 1995b) focused on smoking cessation in 11 matched community pairs, with cessation of smoking for heavy smokers as one of the target outcomes. The intervention consisted of educational messages presented through different mediums (e.g., mass media, community events, work sites, and health care providers). Results indicated that quit rates for heavy smokers (the main target group) were not affected by the intervention.

The successes and failures of these and other mass media interventions may be attributed to a number of factors. One reason for null results is because the society may not be prepared to take such large steps, with individuals taking big countermeasures against change (Weick, 1984). Indeed, an individual's behavior is bound by attitudes and behaviors of his or her social group (Mead, 1934), and instability or dissonance is experienced when there is a "lack of correspondence" between the normative expectations of society and the individual's behavior (Schneiderman, 1988, p. 71). Hence, behaviors that are embedded and accepted in society, albeit unhealthy or risky, are by nature hard to alter due to the initial dissonance individuals experience in making the changes.

For example, Rotello (1997, p. 56) has suggested that the AIDS epidemic in U.S. gay males could be attenuated if gay men adopted a more monogamous lifestyle, thereby limiting "bridging" or sexual mixing of high HIV-risk core group members with those outside the core. He notes further, however, that modern gay culture tolerates multiple sexual partners as part of its ideology. Moving the culture toward a monogamous lifestyle would encounter resistance from many group members because of violation of cultural norms.

Another reason for the null results is the complex nature of information communication. According to McGuire (1985), there are five key factors that affect attention and communication of information: source, message, channel, receiver, and target. Source focuses on who the source of the message is. Message indicates the type of message, for example, fear-related or informational. Channel refers to the route by which the message is delivered, such as radio, television, and so on. Receiver indicates who is going to receive the information, for example, children or adults. Finally, target indicates the target behavior that takes place. These five factors must be met for messages to be attended to. Further, individuals need to process the received information, understand it, and retain the information in order for the message to have an effect.

Social marketers of health promotion messages note similar concerns with communication. In their overview of the social marketing of AIDS education, Rabin and Porter (1996) suggested a number of factors that must be present for social marketing to work. First, the consumer should want what is being marketed. If the goal is increasing condom use, social marketers must provide a message that indicates the benefits of condom use and creates a need for the condoms. Second, consideration should be given to consumer acceptance of the particular product. This may include increasing the comfortableness of condom wear or providing alternative products (e.g., the female condom).

Third, price or investment should be considered. This includes not only actual cost of the product, but also access issues and emotional barriers. Fourth, message delivery must be considered. In other words, effort should be placed on the particular communication channels that are used for the health messages. Fifth, the target audience should be considered. If the purpose of the intervention is to influence condom use in gay men, then communication channels and products should be marketed with this in mind. Sixth, the socially marketed message needs to be constantly promoted and redesigned. Single or short-term interventions, although cost-effective, generally produce weaker effects than longer interventions. In addition, constant exposure (i.e., mere exposure) to the same message can lead to message disregard (Zajonc, 1968). Therefore, new messages must continue to be generated that pique the consumer's interest.

By integrating the small wins approach, communication factors, and social marketing, we may attribute the success of large-scale interventions to successful diffusion of new information, ideas, or innovations into society. Rogers (1962) has summarized a strong body of empirical research in this area, labeling this approach the diffusion of innovations framework. An innovation is simply an idea "perceived" as new to those exposed to the idea, while diffusion is the spread of the innovation (i.e., new idea) across individuals. For diffusion to take place, the innovation must be adopted by individuals. This adoption process occurs in steps, which include awareness of the innovation, interest, evaluation of the innovation before adoption, a trial-run period (i.e., "dry run"), and finally adoption of the innovation by the individual. Hence, the diffusion process consists of interdependent components, including the innovation or idea, communication of the innovation from person to person, a social system that encourages communication across individuals, and time for the idea to filter through the society or community (Smith, 1976).

In a demonstration of the diffusion of innovations framework, Kelly et al. (1992) used a multiple-baseline health-related intervention to change social norms and HIV-risk behaviors. In their study, community opinion leaders (called "trendsetters") in three cities were trained to disseminate risk-reduction information in informal social settings (e.g., nightclubs or bars). Findings showed that HIV-risk behaviors declined over a 2-month period. In addition, changes in perceived social norms were noted, with greater peer acceptance of safer sex and precautionary measures noted over a 2-month period in all three cities. Other direct applications of diffusion of HIV-prevention messages have also shown positive results (see Kelly et al., 1997; also see Rotheram-Borus et al., 1998).

The Future of Health Behavior Interventions

The vast majority of interventions for the health behaviors described in the first part of this chapter were typically targeted at individuals at high risk and typically used a group delivery format. In general, these interventions have focused on Phase 3 research (i.e., demonstrating that a program can be efficacious with the target population). However, Phase 4 research trials (i.e., those that evaluate whether the implementation of an intervention program in real-world settings is effective) have been few and have often had equivocal results. As noted in the second part of the chapter, programs such as The Stanford Heart Trial (Maccoby, Farquhar, & Fortmann, 1985), the Community Intervention Trial for Smoking Cessation (COMMIT; Commit Research Group, 1995a, 1995b), and the Medical Outcome Study (MOS; Wells, Hayes, et al., 1989; Wells, Stewart, et al., 1989) are examples of large scale intervention projects that emphasized individuals' behaviors over time when multifaceted, multilevel interventions are mounted.

A primary issue in each of these trials has been the fidelity of the intervention that is being implemented when the intervention is diffused to community settings.

These individual- and group-level interventions have offered many theories and behavioral tools to affect health outcomes. However, what will the future of health interventions bring? What should be the focus of future interventions, and what kinds of changes need to be made? This final section will address important, yet underemphasized facets related to health behavior interventions: intervention providers, managed care, and legislative changes.

Intervention Providers and the Managed Care System

Intervention providers (i.e., those actually implementing the intervention) are often ignored by social scientists in the planning of successful intervention programs. Many good intervention programs have failed to be replicated and disseminated by failing to address providers' needs (Weisz & Weiss, 1993). Children's mental health service delivery is one example. A number of effective programs have been shown to improve children's behavioral outcomes (Hibbs & Jensen, 1996b). These include adolescent suicide attempters (Rotheram-Borus, Piacentini, Cantwell, Belin, & Song, in press; Rotheram-Borus, Piacentini, Van Rossem, et al., in press), children with attention deficit disorder (Anastopoulos, Barkley, & Sheldon, 1996; Barkley, Guevremont, Anastopoulos, & Fletcher, 1992), children with depressive disorders (Brent, Holder, Kolko, Birmaher, et al., 1997; Silverman & Kurtines, 1996), conduct disordered children (Patterson, Dishion, & Chamberlain, 1993), anxious children (Barrett, Dadds, & Rapee, 1996; Kendall, 1994; Kendall & Southam-Gerow, 1996), and those with obsessive compulsive disorder (March, Mulle, & Herbel, 1994). Each of the successful programs is cognitive-behavioral in orientation, lasts between 12 and 20 sessions, includes the involvement of adults in the children's environments, and has clearly targeted outcomes. However, practice in community-based clinics does not follow these general guidelines that have demonstrated positive outcomes (Weisz & Weiss, 1993).

One challenge for implementation of effective programs comes from the provider community, whose training, experience, and expertise is inconsistent with the emerging consensus in the research literature on how to deliver effective programs. For example, many providers of care (e.g., those psychodynamically oriented) are not trained in brief treatment techniques and do not set goals that can be defined as achieved or not achieved (Weisz & Weiss, 1993). Although each of the successful programs noted above were guided by a manual, very few providers are actually trained to implement interventions by following such a guide. Providers are typically socialized to believe that the quality and conditions of the interpersonal relationship established between the client and themselves is the key element influencing behavior change (Strupp, 1977). This expectation is not supported by the empirical literature, and perpetuates a failure to implement effective programs (Beckman & Fischer, 1997).

A second challenge for implementation of effective programs comes from managed care. In contrast to the small wins approach that has characterized the implementation of interventions for individuals, there are major changes currently occurring in the organization and financing of physical and mental health care in the United States (Remarks on the Advisory Commission, 1997). These changes in the organization of the health care system result in substantial revisions in the process of delivering care. The primary concerns driving these changes are improved cost-efficiency with a desire simultaneously to improve quality of care.

There has been far less attention to methods of guiding the behavior of the health care providers in the specific process of delivering their interventions. The failure to have a strong empirical basis for the providers' behavior creates the opportunity for health care companies and management concerns to alter the process of care without anticipating or being constrained by information that would force the organization and delivery of care to be addressed in a very different fashion. Therefore, it is important to determine standards of care in key disease areas. Then managed care organizations must provide that standard of care.

One area in which potential standards could be developed is the area of children's mental health services. Recently, effective programs were reviewed and identified by Hibbs and Jensen (1996b). Each of the effective programs was 12 to 20 sessions in length (Hibbs & Jensen, 1996a). In no case was a program identified that could be successfully implemented in under 10 sessions (Giles & Marafiote, 1998). However, Miller (1996) reports that managed care administrators are pressuring providers to complete treatment in 3 to 4 sessions.

One example where standards of care need further development is in the treatment of depression in children, which is typically addressed in primary health care within managed care settings (Starfield, 1992). Similar to adults (Wells, Sturm, Sherbourne, & Meredith, 1996), the existing research documenting positive outcomes for children with depressive disorders has been conducted primarily in mental health clinics (Weisz & Weiss, 1993). There are at least three different manual-based interventions for the treatment of depressed adolescents (Brent, Holder, Kolko, Birmaher, et al., 1997; Moreau & Mufson, 1997; Rotheram-Borus, Piacentini, Miller, Graae, & Castro-Blanco, 1994), but none of these programs could be effectively implemented within a primary health care setting. Most youth have mental health symptoms that remit relatively quickly (Rotheram-Borus, Piacentini, Cantwell, et al., in press); therefore, treatment of the depression is not likely to differ significantly from a brief intervention delivered in primary health care settings. However, the interrelatedness of symptoms among adolescents is rarely examined, particularly when evaluating depressed youth in medical settings. Adolescent problem behaviors cluster (Ensminger, 1987). Therefore, youth who are depressed are also likely to be attempting suicide, using drugs, having problems in school, and are at higher risk for teenage pregnancy and sexually transmitted diseases.

These problems will not be noticed within a medical setting that focuses solely on remitting symptoms of depression. The long-term negative outcomes for depressed youth are a key issue that needs some way of being assessed and monitored within managed care settings. The status of treatment research in the area of adolescent depression is similar to the status of research in most areas for preventive interventions with children. There are very few domains where the standards for quality care have been identified and evaluations have been conducted and replicated for positive outcomes of preventive interventions (Institute of Medicine, 1992).

When no standards of care exist that are well documented, managed care organizations have a huge opportunity to restructure the service delivery system in a manner consistent with high-quality care. The existing literature on preventive and clinical interventions for children point us to delivering preventive services in short-term interventions (12-20 sessions) by highly trained paraprofessionals using a structured and specific manual to guide the delivery of the intervention. In contrast, care is being delivered by Ph.D. and M.D. practitioners over a much briefer period (3-6 sessions) in an open-ended format that lacks clear guidelines (Weisz & Weiss, 1993).

Neither the current practice of preventive interventions in field settings nor the practices of mental health and psychosocial aspects of care being delivered (or being proposed to be delivered) in managed care settings follows these practice guidelines. Managed care settings are generally providing preventive care for both physical and mental health problems in primary health care settings by nurses and family practitioners. When mental health care is authorized, there are seldom manual-based interventions that are being systematically implemented. Instead, the dose of the interventions is being decreased with little attention to the content or the quality of the care. The level of professional, typically a licensed person with a professional degree, and the associated costs of care are reduced by providing large numbers of patients at reduced reimbursement rates to providers. Thus, costs are being constrained, but the primary area of cost containment is duration, or number of sessions of care. The quality of services is rarely addressed, especially at the level of provider specialization and training.

An alternative strategy for the field of psychosocial- or mental health–focused preventive interventions is to consider a major revision in the certification and licensing of providers. Two fields offer excellent prototypes for these types of changes over the past 20 years: mental retardation (Szymanski, 1987) and psychiatric rehabilitation (Fairweather & Fergus, 1993; Risley & Reid, 1996). In regard to mental retardation, retarded children as recently as the 1950s were sent to mental hospitals that were staffed by nurses and doctors where they would remain in inpatient settings throughout their lifetime. Today, there are interdisciplinary teams of talented paraprofessionals who provide the great majority of care. Training is provided to these paraprofessionals through specialized training programs. Hospitalizations are time limited and behavior focused; for example, to receive toilet training or eating skills, or learn eye contact and smiling behaviors. Once skills are acquired, daily life is managed in community settings (Jacobson, Burchard, & Carling, 1992). Many who previously would have been maintained for life in a hospital setting now hold jobs and assist in providing for themselves with support from the community support companion (Wolfe, Kregel, & Wehman, 1996). The training of almost all professionals in this field is behaviorally based. This is a very different, nonmedical approach to the organization of care for a subgroup covered by the public safety net.

Similar shifts have occurred in the field of psychiatric rehabilitation (Liberman & Yager, 1994). Persons with behaviorally based psychotic disorders who typically would have been maintained in hospital settings often can exist in assisted living programs (Drake et al., 1998; Rosenheck & Neale, 1998; Salyers, Masterton, Fekete, Picone, & Bond, 1998). Disordered individuals can share jobs and compensate for each other when symptoms impair daily functioning in a way that demands withdrawal from the job for a period of time.

These two fields present potential models for the field of prevention. It is possible that higher quality of care can be provided by persons with lower levels of degrees, but delivered by persons with higher levels of specialized training within a specific area. The costs of care would drop not because professional skills were being discounted, as is currently happening in Independent Physicians Associations (IPAs) and Preferred Provider Organizations (PPOs), but because the level of training has been reduced. The quality of care would more closely resemble the standards that are implemented and demonstrated to be appropriate within the research literature. Over time, it would be expected that general competence of the field consistently to manage persons with mental health problems in a more effective fashion would increase.

The fields of mental retardation and psychiatric rehabilitation provide alternative models for organizing care that do not typify the current organization of care in preventive, psychosocial, or mental health care (Pulcini & Howard, 1997). These fields also present us with a model of the problems that society must avoid if imitating the organization of care. Both the mentally retarded and the psychiatrically disturbed need a continuum of levels of support services for different points in their illness that has the potential for being comprehensive. While these needs are clearly recognized for severely impaired populations, the funding levels are so low in appropriations for persons with these problems that it is impossible to provide the continuum of care (Austad, Hunter, & Morgan, 1998). If preventive services were to adapt models similar to these subspecialties, the policies would have to include sufficient funds to implement the programs in the manner that is designed (Minihan, Dean, & Lyons, 1993).

For example, in California, services for the mentally retarded are typically subcontracted to behavioral health care organizations that receive a capitated payment for each of the disabled served by the program. The greatest amount of the care is provided by community support companions who attempt to teach clients skills in coping with stressful hassles that accompany everyday life: scheduling doctor appointments, changing the water in a fish bowl, fixing a meal, going to a movie. These companions accompany the clients to doctors' appointments, taking public transportation on a bus, and resolve interpersonal conflicts and clarify understanding between the provider and clients. The funds allocated for these programs are so low, however, that only those willing to accept the lowest paid jobs accept the position, although considerably greater skills are needed. The low rates of compensation, high levels of overtime work required, high turnover rates of employees, and low status of the field lead to poor services often being delivered to the persons in community settings. It is not clear whether the care received is of lower quality overall to persons in community settings versus in inpatient settings. However, the failure to operationalize and fund the services at a viable level is leading to much poorer care than would be anticipated given the research literature that has demonstrated interventions to be efficacious when funded at appropriate levels. Thus, if these models are to be emulated, the problems that have plagued these systems of care (Gardner, 1992; Johnston & Shook, 1993) need to be anticipated and addressed in the planning stage.

Legislation and Health Behavior Change

There are many possibilities in the ongoing reorganization of delivery and financing of care for providers dramatically to shift their roles, responsibilities, and the content of the care provided. For such a revolution to occur within preventive services, major shifts will need to occur. Legislation is one area that may result in significant benefits to reorganization of the systems for the delivery of care and result in major societal changes regarding healthy behaviors and disease prevention. Indeed, legislative changes and related sanctions have been shown to have strong effects on health issues, including alcohol consumption, smoking, vehicle accidents, and child safety issues (Stokols, 1992; Susser, 1995). In addition, broader legislation has had an indirect impact on health through public safety concerns such as air quality, toxic waste cleanup, and clean water.

Legislation change, however, may have only short-term effects. For example, Ross (1994) found that increased sanctions had at most a limited effect on deterrence of alcohol-impaired driving. In addition, Rogers and Schoenig (1994) found that legislative changes alone could not account for reductions in drinking and driving witnessed in the early 1980s in California. Indeed, factors such as personal morality (i.e., a sense of an internalized obligation of what is right and wrong) and socialization of preventative habits may be the strongest operatives on behavior even in the absence of punishment threat (Andenaes, 1977; Gibbs, 1975).

Further, legislative changes and levied sanctions can be implemented only when issues of public safety or concern are raised. For example, public safety issues surrounding alcohol-impaired driving (for both the driver and passenger) have been a priority of state legislators due to high death and injury rates (17,274 alcohol-related fatalities in 1995; National Highway Traffic Safety Administration, 1996). This is evidenced by a constant retooling of state legislation toward stricter sanctions (e.g., from 1981 to 1985, over 450 new alcohol-impaired driving laws were passed by state legislation; National Commission Against Drunk Driving, 1985).

For legislation to be accepted, arguments must be made for the public safety. Although progress has been made for sanction intervention for issues such as smoking in public places and bicycle helmet use for children (Stokols, 1992), other areas will probably never be addressed. For example, how would the public react to forced physical exercise programs? Even when these programs are offered in the workplace, few employees participate in such programs (Donaldson et al., 1998). Could sanctions be levied against those who consume high levels of dietary fat? Even when an individual's disease leads to a public health threat (e.g., an active tuberculosis patient refuses to adhere to his or her drug regimen and continues to expose others to infection, or an HIV-positive individual continues to have unprotected sexual relations), prosecution is difficult and rare.

Susser (1995) has suggested an approach that integrates social action and legislative changes. Health prevention and protection must start at the nongovernmental level. As the social movement gains strength, legislation can be introduced. For example, Rogers and Schoenig (1994) concluded that reductions in alcohol-impaired driving witnessed in the 1980s could be attributed to the initiation and popularity of MADD (Mothers Against Drunk Driving), a volunteer organization intent on reducing alcohol-impaired driving. Further, MADD increased public awareness of drinking and driving, no doubt leading to changes in legislation over the past 20 years.

In addition, community interventions should be continued, with constant refinements made to interventions that have shown null or marginal results

(Susser, 1995). Even null results may, over time, filter through the population, given that diffusion of an idea or message often takes years (Rogers, 1962). This constant "poking" at the society resembles the aforementioned small wins approach, with small unassuming wins eventually leading to larger societal changes.

Summary

This chapter has been an attempt to understand the current state of health intervention strategies and to suggest future paths. The exploration of past and current interventions has revealed that health behavior change may be successfully effected through individual and societal change strategies. As for the future of health-related interventions, we have suggested an emphasis on the intervention provider and changes in the current managed care system, and we have underscored the importance of legislative changes that can have strong effects on health behavior. Although often overlooked, these areas can play a pivotal role in the success of an intervention and may be expected to offer the best hope for efficient and effective health interventions in the future.

As has been noted, there are many theories that address health behavior change. Whether through attitudinal pressures on the individual or diffusion of societal norms, people will and do change their behavior. With this in mind, it appears the tools are available to help "tip" our society toward healthy behaviors, and to reach those with unapparent infections to keep them from "bridging" (see Rotello, 1997) into uninfected populations. Further, these tools may be used to perpetuate the societal acceptance of healthy behaviors (e.g., exercise, limiting dietary fat consumption) and to avoid risky health behaviors (e.g., needle sharing). The emphasis now lies on (a) how to integrate successfully the existing health-related research and knowledge developed, (b) the providers who will use these theoretical and behavioral tools in applied settings, (c) the managed care system in which the providers operate, and (d) future legislation that can impact individuals directly, their providers, and the existing care system.

Although there are no simple solutions to changing health behaviors, the past 50 years have offered much in the areas of social theory and program evaluation. The emergence of the biopsychosocial model and the fields of health psychology and program evaluation (Shadish, Cook, & Leviton, 1991) together have provided successful paradigms for investigating and evaluating health-related behaviors and their psychosocial components. The next millennium no doubt will have much to offer—and much to consider.

References

Ajzen, I., & Madden, T. J. (1986). Prediction of goal-directed behavior: Attitudes, intentions, and perceived behavioral control. *Journal of Experimental Social Psychology, 22,* 453-474.

Anastopoulos, A. D., Barkley, R. A., & Sheldon, T. L. (1996). Attention deficit disorder. In E. D. Hibbs & E. S. Jensen (Eds.), *Psychosocial treatments for child and adolescent disorders: Empirically based strategies for clinical practice* (pp. 267-284). New York: American Psychological Association.

Andenaes, J. (1977). The moral or educative influence of criminal law. In J. L. Tapp & F. J. Levine (Eds.), *Law, justice, and the individual in society: Psychological and legal issues* (pp. 50-59). New York: Holt, Rinehart & Winston.

Austad, C. S., Hunter, R. D. A., & Morgan, T. C. (1998). Managed health care, ethics, and psychotherapy. *Clinical Psychology, 5,* 67-76.

Bandura, A. (1977). Self-efficacy: Toward a unifying theory of behavioral change. P*sychological Review, 84*(2), 191-215.

Bandura, A. (1986). *Social foundations of thought and action: A social cognitive theory.* Englewood Cliffs, NJ: Prentice Hall.

Bandura, A. (1997). *Self-efficacy: The exercise of control.* New York: Freeman.

Barkley, R. A., Guevremont, D. C., Anastopoulos, A. D., & Fletcher, K. E. (1992). A comparison of three family therapy programs for treating family conflicts in adolescents with attention-deficit hyperactivity disorder. *Journal of Consulting & Clinical Psychology, 60,* 450-462.

Barrett, P. M., Dadds, M. R., & Rapee, R. M. (1996). Family treatment of childhood anxiety: A controlled trial. *Journal of Consulting and Clinical Psychology, 64,* 333-342.

Beckman, E. A., & Fischer, T. J. (1997). Negotiating managed care contracts. *Comprehensive Therapy, 23,* 554-559.

Berger, D. E., & Marelich, W. D. (1997). Legal and social control of alcohol-impaired driving in California: 1983-1994. *Journal of Studies on Alcohol, 58*(5), 518-523.

Black, D. R., Gleser, L. J., & Kooyers, K. (1990). A meta-analysis of couples weight-loss programs. *Health Psychology, 9,* 330-347.

Brent, D. A., Holder, D., Kolko, D., Birmaher, B., et al. (1997). A clinical psychotherapy trial for adolescent depression comparing cognitive, family, and supportive therapy. *Archives of General Psychiatry, 54*(9), 877-885.

Bruvold, W. H. (1993). A meta-analysis of adolescent smoking prevention programs. *American Journal of Public Health, 83,* 872-880.

COMMIT Research Group. (1995a). Community intervention trial for smoking cessation (COMMIT): I. Cohort results from a four-year community intervention. *American Journal of Public Health, 85,* 183-192.

COMMIT Research Group. (1995b). Community intervention trial for smoking cessation (COMMIT): II. Changes in adult cigarette smoking prevalence. *American Journal of Public Health, 85,* 193-200.

Corea, G. (1992). *The invisible epidemic: The story of women and AIDS.* New York: HarperCollins.

Donaldson, S. I., Cooler, L. E., & Weiss, R. (1998). Promoting health and well-being through work: Science and practice. In X. B. Arriaga & S. Oskamp (Eds.), *Addressing community problems: Research and intervention* (pp. 160-194). Thousand Oaks, CA: Sage.

Drake, R. E, McHugo, G. J., Clark, R. E., Teague, G. B., Xie, H., Miles, K., & Ackerman, T. H. (1998). Assertive community treatment for patients with co-occurring severe mental illness and substance use disorder: A clinical trial. *American Journal of Orthopsychiatry, 68,* 201-215.

Ensminger, M. E. (1987). Adolescent sexual behavior as it relates to other transition behaviors in youth. In S. L. Hofferth & C. D. Hayes (Eds.), *Risking the future: Adolescent sexuality, pregnancy, and child-bearing* (pp. 36-55). Washington DC: National Academy of Sciences.

Engel, G. L. (1977). The need for a new medical model: A challenge for biomedicine. *Science, 196,* 129-136.

Fairweather, G. W., & Fergus, E. O. (1993). *Empowering the mentally ill.* Austin, TX: Fairweather Publishing.

Farquhar, J. W., Fortmann, S. P., Flora, J. A., Taylor, B., Haskell, W. L., Williams, P. T., Maccoby, N., & Wood, P. D. (1990). Effects of communitywide education on cardiovascular disease risk factors: The Stanford Five-City Project. *Journal of the American Medical Association, 264*(3), 359-365.

Fishbein, M., & Ajzen, I. (1975). *Relief, attitude, intention, and behavior: An introduction to theory and research.* Reading, MA: Addison-Wesley.

Fishbein, M., Bandura, A., Triandis, H. C., Kanfer, F. H., Becker, M. H., Middlestadt, S. E., & Eicher, A. (1992). *Factors influencing behavior and behavior change: Final report—Theorist's Workshop.* Rockville, MD: NIMH.

Fishbein, M., Chan, D. K.-S., O'Reilly, K., Schnell, D., Wood, R., Beeker, C., & Cohn, D. (1993). Factors influencing gay men's attitudes, subjective norms, and intentions with respect to performing sexual behaviors. *Journal of Applied Social Psychology, 23*(6), 417-438.

Fisher, J. D., & Fisher, W. A. (1992). Changing AIDS-risk behavior. *Psychological Bulletin, 111*(3), 455-474.

Freedman, J. L., & Fraser, S. C. (1966). Compliance without pressure: The foot-in-the-door technique. *Journal of Personality and Social Psychology, 4,* 195-202.

Gardner, J. F. (1992). Quality, organization design, and standards. *Mental Retardation, 30*(3), 173-177.

Gibbs, J. P. (1975). *Crime, punishment, and deterrence.* New York: Elsevier.

Giles, T. R., & Marafiote, R. A. (1998). Managed care and the practitioner: A call for unity. *Clinical Psychology, 5*(1), 41-50.

Gladwell, M. (1996, June 3). The tipping point: Why is the city suddenly so much safer—Could it be that crime really is an epidemic? *The New Yorker,* pp. 32-38.

Glanz, K., Lewis, F. M., & Rimer, B. K. (Eds.). (1990). *Health behavior and health education: Theory, research, and practice* (2nd ed.). San Francisco: Jossey-Bass.

Haynes, R. B., McKibbon, K. A., & Kanani, R. (1996). Systematic review of randomised trials of interventions to assist patients to follow prescriptions for medications. *Lancet, 348,* 383-387.

Hausenblas, H. A., Carron, A. V., & Mack, D. E. (1997). Application of the theories of reasoned action and planned behavior to exercise behavior: A meta-analysis. *Journal of Sport and Exercise Psychology, 19,* 36-51.

Hibbs, E. D., & Jensen, E. S. (1996a). Analyzing the research: What this book is about. In E. D. Hibbs & E. S. Jensen (Eds.), *Psychosocial treatments for child and adolescent disorders: Empirically based strategies for clinical practice* (pp. 3-8). New York: American Psychological Association.

Hibbs, E. D., & Jensen, E. S. (Eds.). (1996b). *Psychosocial treatments for child and adolescent disorders: Empirically based strategies for clinical practice.* New York: American Psychological Association.

Institute of Medicine. (1992). *Toward a national health care survey: A data system for the 21st century.* Washington, DC: National Academy Press.

Jacobson, J. W., Burchard, S. N., & Carling, P. J. (Eds.). (1992). *Community living for people with developmental and psychiatric disabilities.* Baltimore, MD: Johns Hopkins University Press.

Janz, N. K., & Becker, M. H. (1984). Health belief model: A decade later. *Health Education Quarterly, 11*(1), 1-47.

Johnston, J. M., & Shook, G. L. (1993). Model for the statewide delivery of programming services. *Mental Retardation, 31*(3), 127-139.

Kalichman, S. C., Carey, M. P., & Johnson, B. T. (1996). Prevention of sexually transmitted HIV infection: A meta-analytic review of the behavioral outcome literature. *Annals of Behavioral Medicine, 18*(1), 6-15.

Kelly, J. A., Murphy, D. A., Sikkema, K. J., McAuliffe, T. L., Roffman, R. A., Solomon, L. J., Winett, R. A., & Kalichman, R. A. (1997). Outcomes of a randomized controlled community-level HIV prevention intervention: Effects on behavior among at-risk gay men in small U.S. cities. *Lancet, 350,* 1500-1504.

Kelly, J. A., St. Lawrence, J. S., Stevenson, L. Y., Hauth, A. C., Kalichman, S. C., Diaz, Y. E., Brasfield, T. L., Koob, J. J., & Morgan, M. G. (1992). Community AIDS/HIV risk reduction: The effects of endorsements by popular people in three cities. *American Journal of Public Health, 82*(11), 1483-1489.

Kendall, P. C. (1994). Treating anxiety disorders in children: Results of a randomized clinical trial. *Journal of Consulting and Clinical Psychology, 62,* 100-110.

Kendall, P. C., & Southam-Gerow, M. A. (1996). Long-term follow-up of a cognitive-behavioral therapy for anxiety-disordered youth. *Journal of Consulting and Clinical Psychology, 64,* 724-730.

Kirsch, L., Montgomery, G., & Sapirstein, G. (1995). Hypnosis as an adjunct to cognitive-behavioral psychotherapy: A meta-analysis. *Journal of Consulting and Clinical Psychology, 63*(2), 214-220.

Lando, H. A., Pechacek, T. R., Pirie, P. L., Murray, D. M., Mittlemark, M. B., Lichtenstein, E., Nothwehr, F., & Gray, C. (1995). Changes in adult cigarette smoking in the Minnesota Heart Health Program. *American Journal of Public Health, 85*(2), 201-208.

Lazarus, R. S., & Folkman, S. (1984). *Stress, appraisal, and coping.* New York: Springer.

Liberman, R. P., & Yager, J. (Eds.). (1994). *Stress in psychiatric disorders.* New York: Springer.

Lilienfeld, A. M., & Lilienfeld, D. E. (1980). *Foundations of epidemiology* (2nd ed.). New York: Oxford University Press.

Lipsey, M. W. (1993). Theory as method: Small theories of treatments. *New Directions for Program Evaluation, 57,* 5-38.

Maccoby, N., Farquhar, J. W., & Fortmann, S. P. (1985). The community studies of the Stanford Heart Disease Prevention Program. In R. M. Kaplan & M. H. Criqui (Eds.), *Behavioral epidemiology and disease prevention* (NATO ASI Series A: Life Sciences, Vol. 84, pp. 385-400). New York: Plenum.

Mann, T., Nolen-Hoeksema, S., Huang, K., & Burgard, D. (1997). Are two interventions worse than none? Joint preliminary and secondary prevention of eating disorders in college females. *Health Psychology, 16*(3), 215-225.

March, J. S., Mulle, K., & Herbel, B. (1994). Behavioral psychotherapy for children and adolescents with obsessive-compulsive disorder: An open trial of new protocol-driven treatment package. *Journal of the American Academy of Child and Adolescent Psychiatry, 33,* 333-341.

McGinnis, J. M., Richmond, J. B., Brandt, E. N. Jr., Windom, R. E., & Mason, J. O. (1992). Health progress in the United States: Results of the 1990 objectives for the nation. *Journal of the American Medical Association, 268*(18), 2545-2552.

McGuire, W. J. (1985). Attitudes and attitude change. In G. Lindzey & E. Aronson (Eds.), *The handbook of social psychology* (3rd ed., Vol. 2, pp. 233-346). New York: Random House.

Mead, G. H. (1934). *Mind, self, and society.* Chicago: University of Chicago Press.

Meyer, T. J., & Mark, M. M. (1995). Effects of psychosocial interventions with adult cancer patients: A meta-analysis of randomized experiments. *Health Psychology, 14*(2), 101-108.

Meyrowitz, J. (1985). *No sense of place: The impact of electronic media on social behavior.* New York: Oxford University Press.

Miller, I. J. (1996). Managed care is harmful to outpatient mental health services: A call for accountability. *Professional Psychology: Research and Practice, 27,* 349-363.

Miller, T. Q., Smith, T. W, Turner, C. W., Guijarro, M. L., & Hallet, A. J. (1996). A meta-analytic review of research on hostility and physical health. *Psychological Bulletin, 119*(2), 322-348.

Minihan, E. M., Dean, D. H., & Lyons, C. M. (1993). Managing the care of patients with mental retardation: A survey of physicians. *Mental Retardation, 31,* 239-246.

Moreau, D., & Mufson, L. (1997). Interpersonal psychotherapy for depressed adolescents. *Child and Adolescent Psychiatric Clinics of North America, 6,* 97-110.

Multiple Risk Factor Intervention Trial Research Group. (1982). Multiple Risk Factor Intervention Trial: Risk factor changes and mortality results. *Journal of the American Medical Association, 248,* 1465-1477.

National Commission Against Drunk Driving. (1985). *A progress report on the implementation of recommendations by the Presidential Commission on Drunk Driving* (DOT HS-806-885). Washington, DC: National Highway Traffic Safety Administration.

National Highway Traffic Safety Administration. (1996). *Traffic safety facts 1995: A compilation of motor vehicle crash data from the fatal accident reporting system and the general estimates system* (DOT HS-808-471). Washington, DC: Government Printing Office.

Oskamp, S. (1991). *Attitudes and opinions* (2nd ed.). Englewood Cliffs, NJ: Prentice Hall.

Owen, N., Bauman, A., Booth, M., Oldenburg, B., & Magnus, P. (1995). Serial mass-media campaigns to promote physical activity: Reinforcing or redundant? *American Journal of Public Health, 85*(2), 244-248.

Patterson, G., Dishion, T., & Chamberlain, P. (1993). Outcomes and methodological issues relating to treatment of antisocial children. In T. Giles (Ed.), *Handbook of effective psychotherapy* (pp. 43-88). New York: Plenum.

Prochaska, J. O., & DiClemente, C. C. (1992). States of change in the modification of problem behaviors. *Progress in Behavior Modification, 28,* 183-218.

Prochaska, J. O., DiClemente, C. C., & Norcross, J. C. (1992). In search of how people change: Applications to addictive behaviors. *American Psychologist, 47*(9), 1102-1114.

Pulcini, J., & Howard, A. M. (1997). Framework for analyzing health care models serving adults with mental retardation and other developmental disabilities. *Mental Retardation, 35,* 209-217.

Rabin, S. A., & Porter, R. W. (1996). Application of social marketing principles to AIDS education. In M. Gluck, E. Rosenthal, H. Gelband, R. Colindres, L. Esslinger, C. J. Behney, & S. R. Tunis (Eds.), *The effectiveness of AIDS prevention efforts* (pp. 277-308). Washington, DC: Office of Technology Assessment, American Psychological Association Office of AIDS.

Remarks on the Advisory Commission on Consumer Protection and Quality in the Health Care Industry. (1997, March 31). *Weekly compilation of presidential documents: 1997 Presidential Documents Online via GPO access.* [Available: http://frwebgate3.access.gpo.gov/cgi-bin/waisgate.cgi?WAISdocID = 4462922964+0+0+0&WAISaction = retrieve]. Washington, DC: Government Printing Office.

Risley, T. R., & Reid, D. R. (1996). Management and organizational issues in the delivery of psychological services for people with mental retardation. In J. W., Jacobson & J. A. Mulick (Eds.), *Manual of diagnosis and professional practice in mental retardation* (pp. 383-391). Washington, DC: American Psychological Association.

Roberts, D. F., & Maccoby, N. (1985). Effects of mass communication. In G. Lindzey & E. Aronson (Eds.), *The handbook of social psychology: Vol. 2. Special fields and applications* (pp. 539-598). Reading, MA: Addison-Wesley.

Rodin, J., & Salovey, P. (1989). Health psychology. *Annual Review of Psychology, 40,* 533-579.

Rogers, E. M. (1962). *Diffusion of innovations.* New York: Free Press.

Rogers, P. N., & Schoenig, S. E. (1994). A time series evaluation of California's 1982 driving-under-the-influence legislative reforms. *Accident Analysis and Prevention, 26,* 63-78.

Rosenheck, R., & Neale, M. (1998). Intersite variation in the impact of intensive psychiatric community care on hospital use. *American Journal of Orthopsychiatry, 68,* 191-200.

Ross, H. L. (1994). *Confronting drunk driving.* New Haven, CT: Yale University Press.

Rotello, G. (1997). *Sexual ecology: AIDS and the destiny of gay men.* New York: E. P. Dutton.

Rotheram-Borus, M. J., Piacentini, J., Cantwell, C., Belin, T. R., & Song, J. (in press). The long-term impact of an emergency room intervention for adolescent suicide attempters. *Journal of the American Academy of Child and Adolescent Psychiatry.*

Rotheram-Borus, M. J., Piacentini, J., Miller, S., Graae, F., & Castro-Blanco, D. (1994). Brief cognitive-behavioral treatment for adolescent suicide attempters and their families. *Journal of the American Academy of Child & Adolescent Psychiatry, 33*(4), 508-517.

Rotheram-Borus, M. J., Piacentini, J., Van Rossem, R., Graae, F., Cantwell, C., Castro-Blanco, D., & Feldman, J. (in press). Treatment adherence among Latina female adolescent suicide attempters. *Suicide and Life-Threatening Behavior.*

Rotheram-Borus, M. J., Towns, B., Lightfoot, M., Cline, T. R., Webber, D., & Murphy, D. A. (1998). *Diffusing HIV prevention messages through religious groups.* Manuscript submitted for publication.

Salyers, M. E., Masterton, T. W., Fekete, D. M., Picone, J. J., & Bond, G. R. (1998). Transferring clients from intensive case management: Impact on client functioning. *American Journal of Orthopsychiatry, 68,* 233-245.

Schneiderman, L. (1988). *The psychology of social change.* New York: Human Sciences Press.

Scott, A. G., & Sechrest, L. (1989). Strength of theory and theory of strength. *Evaluation and Program Planning, 12,* 329-336.

Shadish, W. R., Cook, T. D., & Leviton, L. C. (1991). *Foundations of program evaluation: Theories of practice.* Newbury Park, CA: Sage.

Silverman, W. K., & Kurtines, W. (1996). Transfer of control: A psychosocial intervention model for internalizing disorders in youth. In E. D. Hibbs & R. S. Jensen (Eds.), *Psychosocial treatments for child and adolescent disorders: Empirically based strategies for clinical practice* (pp. 267-284). New York: American Psychological Association.

Slife, B. D., & Williams, R. N. (1995). *What's behind the research? Discovering hidden assumptions in the behavioral sciences.* Thousand Oaks, CA: Sage.

Smith, A. D. (1976). *Social change: Social theory and historical processes.* New York: Longman.

Starfield, B. (1992). *Primary care: Concept, evaluation, and policy.* New York: Oxford University Press.

Stokols, D. (1992). Establishing and maintaining healthy environments: Toward a social ecology of health promotion. *American Psychologist, 47*(1), 6-22.

Strupp, H. (1977). A reformulation of the dynamics of the therapist's contribution. In A. Gurmant & A. Rugin (Eds.), *Effective psychotherapy: A handbook of research.* Elmsdale, NY: Pergamon.

Susser, M. (1995). The tribulations of trials—Intervention in communities [Editorial]. *American Journal of Public Health, 85*(2), 156-158.

Szymanski, L. S. (1987). *Prevention of psychosocial dysfunction in persons with mental retardation.* Sterling D. Garrard Memorial Symposium: Community Health Care Services for Adults With Mental Retardation (1986, Auburn, MA). *Mental Retardation, 25,* 215-218.

Taylor, S. E. (1995). *Health psychology* (3rd ed.). New York: McGraw-Hill.

Van Ryn, M., & Heaney, C. A. (1992). What's the use of theory? *Health Education Quarterly, 19*(3), 315-330.

Weick, K. (1979). *The social psychology of organizing* (2nd ed.). New York: McGraw-Hill.

Weick, K. (1984). Redefining the scale of social problems. *American Psychologist, 39*(1), 40-49.

Weisz, J. R., & Weiss, B. (1993). *Effects of psychotherapy with children and adolescents.* Newbury Park, CA: Sage.

Wells, K., Hays, R. D., Burnam, M. A., Rogers, W., Greenfield, S., & Ware, J. E. Jr. (1989). Detection of depressive disorder for patients receiving prepaid or fee-for-service care: Results from the Medical Outcomes Study. *Journal of the American Medical Association, 262,* 3298-3302.

Wells, K., Stewart, A. L., Hays, R. D., Burnam, M. A., Rogers, W., Daniels, M., Berry, S., Greenfield, S., & Ware, J. E. Jr. (1989). The functioning and well-being of depressed patients: Results from the Medical Outcomes Study. *Journal of the American Medical Association, 262,* 914-949.

Wells, K. B., Sturm, R., Sherbourne, C. D., & Meredith L. S. (1996). *Caring for depression.* Cambridge, MA: Harvard University Press.

Wicker, A. W. (1969). Attitudes versus actions: The relationship of verbal and overt behavioral responses to attitude objects. *Journal of Social Issues, 25*(4), 41-78.

Wolfe, P., Kregel, J., & Wehman, P. (1996). Service delivery. In P. J. McLaughlin & P. Wehman (Eds.), *Mental retardation and developmental disabilities* (2nd ed., pp. 3-27). Austin, TX: Pro-Ed.

Zajonc, R. B. (1968). Attitudinal effects of mere exposure. *Journal of Personality and Social Psychology, 9*(2), 1-27.

9

Do Postcard Reminders Improve Influenza Vaccination Compliance?

A Prospective Trial of Different Postcard "Cues"

Eric B. Larson, James Bergman, Fred Heidrich,
Barbara L. Alvin, and Ronald Schneeweiss

Annual influenza immunizations have been recommended since 1964 for persons over the age of 65 and for persons with cardiac, pulmonary, renal and metabolic diseases. Immunization is intended to prevent the excess mortality associated with influenza epidemics in this high-risk group.[1] However, overall vaccination rates among high-risk patients have been as low as 10 to 15 percent according to the Centers for Disease Control (CDC).[2] These low rates have prompted us to study influenza vaccination to learn more about the general subject of health behavior and to find effective means to promote healthy behavior.[3] Although research efforts over the years have used different constructs to explain the effects of personal, psychosocial and environmental elements on health and illness behavior,[4-8] we chose to study the Health Belief Model (HBM) as formulated by Hochbaum, Beeker, Rosenstock and others.[8]

The HBM is a blend of social and psychologic theories, particularly value expectancy theory. The model predicts that an individual's perception of (1) susceptibility to a disease, (2) severity of the disease, and (3) benefits and costs of the action to prevent the disease will determine the likelihood of the individual undertaking that action. The HBM suggests two common determinants of impulses to

EDITORS' NOTE: *Medical Care, 20,* 1982, pp. 639-648. Reprinted with permission from Lippincott Williams & Wilkins.

action: (1) the value placed by an individual on a particular outcome or goal and (2) the individual's estimate of the likelihood that a particular action will produce the desired outcome.[9]

The model has been tested in a variety of settings involving symptomatic and asymptomatic health behaviors.[10-14] Our initial study of influenza vaccination behavior during the 1975 vaccination period validated a variation of the HBM (Fig. 9.1), and showed positive correlations with compliance and the elements of the model.[3] The study also demonstrated that a reminder postcard or "cue" was an effective means of promoting vaccination. Our study, like many others, was retrospective, but even in this retrospective study, the model explained a relatively small amount of variance.

Two more recent studies reported higher rates of correlation of the HBM with compliance in the Swine Flue immunization program. Using logit analysis of data collection retrospectively, Rundall and Wheeler[15] reported that the HBM accounted for 34 percent of the variance in the use of vaccine by senior citizens. Cummings et al.,[16] in a prospective study of Swine Flu vaccination, explained more than 40 percent of the variance with predictor variables, which included the HBM, measures of behavioral intention, social influence, physician's advice, socio-economic status and past experience with flu shots. Path analysis revealed that most of the influence of HBM variables on behavior was mediated through behavioral intention and that physician recommendations showed a substantial direct effect on vaccination behavior. Sackett[17] has reported that, in contrast to retrospective studies, prospective studies of the HBM have shown inconsistent results. He believes these results to suggest that patients' health beliefs may result from, rather than cause, compliance. In the Canadian study of compliance with antihypertensive theory, beliefs changed to coincide with compliance: after six months of therapy but not before, compliant patients perceived hypertension to be a more serious disease that benefited from drug therapy.[18] The findings of Sackett[17,18] and Cummings et al.,[16] therefore, suggest that behavioral intent and subsequent behavior could be influenced by efforts directed at changing relevant health beliefs and support the rationale for our prospective trial of three postcard cues, each containing a different message (Fig. 9.1).

Postcard cues have been shown to lower broken appointment rates[19-21] and have been retrospectively correlated with vaccination compliance.[3] We reasoned that a postcard containing information emphasizing those health beliefs that correlated with vaccinations might be used to change behavioral intentions, thereby promoting vaccination compliance. We also wondered whether a postcard with a personal message from a patient's primary care physician might improve compliance because of the previously demonstrated effect of physician recommendations on health and vaccination behavior. Accordingly, we designed and executed a randomized prospective trial of the effect of cue postcards on vaccination behavior that compares vaccination rates of patients receiving a "neutral" postcard, an "HBM" postcard, a "personal" postcard, and no postcard. The purpose of the trial was to compare the effect of the HBM postcard with the effect of no postcard or a neutral postcard and to make similar comparisons for the personal postcard. The study also allows us to observe trends in influenza vaccination among outpatients following the national "Swine Flu" vaccination debacle of 1976, which we anticipated would lower overall vaccination rate.

Methods

The study was conducted at the University of Washington Family Medical Center (FMC). The study population consisted of those patients identified as being at high risk for serious complications from influenza infection': patients over 65 years of age and/or patients with chronic heart disease, bronchopulmonary disease, renal disease and diabetes mellitus, based on ICDA-8 diagnosis codes stored in the FMC's computer.

Three hundred ninety-five patients were identified and selected for study. These patients were randomly assigned to one of four groups: a control group receiving no postcard, a group receiving a neutral postcard, a group receiving an HEM postcard and a group receiving a personal postcard. When the 1978-1979 influenza vaccine became

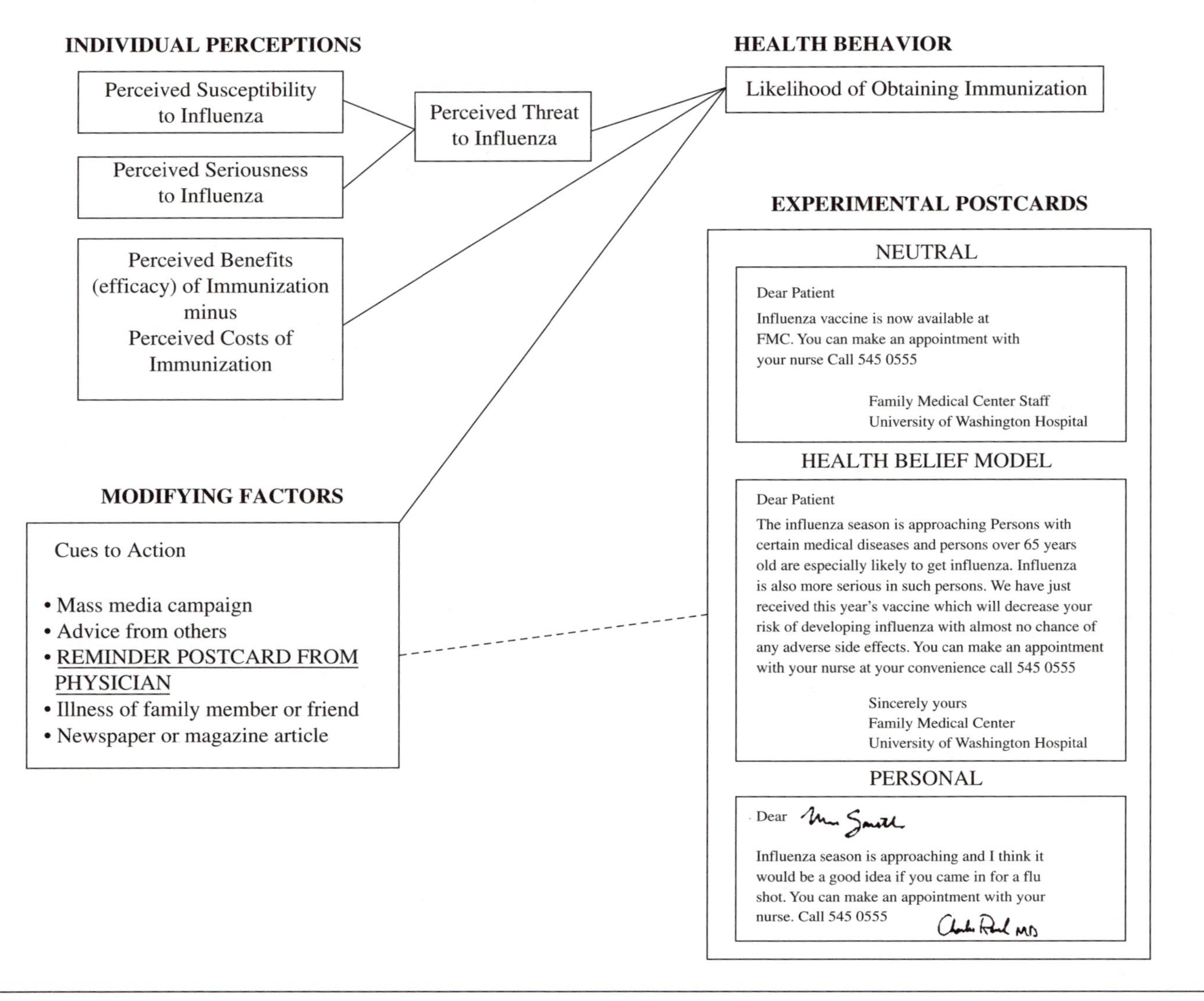

Figure 9.1 "Health Belief Model" and experimental postcards.

available, the postcards shown in Fig. 9.1 were mailed to patients. The HBM postcard obviously emphasizes the severity of influenza, the susceptibility of older persons to influenza and the benefits of vaccination. We did not intend to imply that older patients are more likely than younger patients to get influenza.

Initial demographic data were recorded when patients were assigned to experimental groups. Thereafter, data gathering occurred either when study patients came to the FMC for vaccination or in mid-December when they were called and interviewed by phone. At that time, patients in the control group were called to determine if they had been vaccinated. They were also reminded of the availability of vaccine. Telephone interviewing was necessary because only 36.0 percent of patients were vaccinated in the FMC.

Of 395 patients originally selected for study, 88 were unavailable for analysis because they had moved, died, were hospitalized, had withdrawn from the practice or had no phone. Of the remaining 301 patients, data were gathered on 283.

Results

Only 36.6 percent of patients were vaccinated at the FMC. and only 20.1 percent of those vaccinated were at routine appointment. Other vaccination sites included the place of residence, Public Safety Building, and other sites including physicians' offices, fire stations, school and work places.

The vaccination rates for each of the four experimental groups are displayed in Figure 9.2. Patients receiving the HBM postcard had a higher vaccination rate (51.4 percent) than control patients (20.2 percent) and than patients receiving a neutral postcard (25.0 percent). Patients receiving a personal postcard also had a higher vaccination rate (41.0 percent) than control patients.

Because the groups differed with respect to past vaccination experience, vaccination rates were computed separately for patients with different vaccination histories. The Health Belief Model group consistently had the highest vaccination rate, no matter how the groups were divided. However, smaller and unequal cell sizes resulted in differences

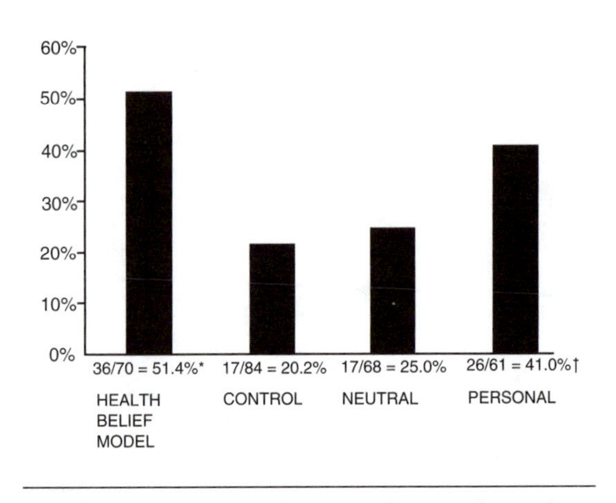

Figure 9.2 Vaccination Rates for Experimental Groups

that were statistically significant ($0.05 < p < 0.1$) for some comparisons.

Linear logistic regression was then used to test the statistical significance of the variation of vaccination probability with the following variables of interest: age, sex, experimental group, vaccination status last year (VLY), disease classification, history of adverse reactions to influenza vaccine, history of influenza in the past and utilization status. Age, vaccination status last year and experimental group were the only variables that were found to have a significant effect on the likelihood of being vaccinated.

After adjusting for age and VLY, the hypothesis that there is no difference in the vaccination rate among the four groups reviving either no postcard or one of the three types of postcards was tested. The HBM appears to be effective compared with no postcard or the neutral postcard.

Discussion

Physicians and dentists commonly use postcards to remind patients of appointments. Studies have consistently demonstrated that postcards do lower broken appointment rates.[19-21]

The elements of HBM have been shown to correlate with a variety of preventive health behaviors, including influenza immunization. Our study tests the hypothesis that the combination of a cue postcard and a message emphasizing the elements of the HBM are more effective than no postcard or than a postcard containing what we have called a neutral massage, simply announcing the availability of vaccine. The HBM postcard was more effective than either no postcard or the neutral postcard, and remained so after adjusting for age and prior vaccination history. Furthermore, subgroup analysis showed that this effect persisted without exception in the various subgroups analyzed. The consistency of the increased vaccination rates in the group receiving the HBM postcard suggests that the HBM postcard is more effective than a neutral or no postcard.

Studies of vaccination and other preventive health behaviors have also shown that physician advice correlates with compliance.[16] Nonetheless, a personal postcard, designed to provide a message from the patient's personal physician, although effective overall, was not more effective after adjusting for age and prior vaccination experience. This observation does not argue that physician advice is not effective, but that the personal postcard substitute for direct physician advice used in this study was not demonstrably more effective than no postcard or the neutral postcard. Given the methodologic problems we encountered, we hope this type of cue will be restudied.

We know of no other study that has tested various postcard reminders in this fashion. The finding that the HBM postcard was more effective is of some theoretical interest to scholars interested in the general development of the model. The general observation that retrospective studies find higher correlations between the HBM than prospective studies[17,24,25] and the results of Cummings et al.[16] showing that the HBM variables influence behavior through behavioral intention suggested that health beliefs change and may be changeable. The postcard emphasizing those elements of the HBM that were correlated with vaccination in our earlier studies might have changed persons' "subjective probabilities"[9] or expectations that a particular action will produce a desired outcome, perhaps by interacting with or reinforcing certain preexistent health beliefs. The change was presumably great enough to promote the desired behavior.

The results support the notion that the HBM is effective as a source of material for health-related advertising campaigns. In addition, for the practitioner, the observed effectiveness of the HBM postcard suggests that the HBM may be a useful approach in counseling designed to change unhealthy behaviors. Inui et al.[26] included the HBM in physician tutorials designed to improve physicians' effectiveness as managers and educators of patients with essential hypertension. Patients of tutored physicians were more compliant with drug regimens and had better control of blood pressures than patients of untutored physicians.

Our study suggests that an HBM postcard is one effective way for practitioners to promote vaccines for high-risk patients in their practice. Reminder postcards can be designed to explain that patients are at high risk (i.e., *susceptible* to a potentially severe disease) for the disease for which an effective low-risk vaccine is available. A health-belief-based reminder postcard promoting influenza vaccination among high-risk patients would probably be effective in promoting other vaccines like pneumococcal vaccine.

References

1. Influenza vaccine: preliminary statement. *Morbidity Mortality Weekly Rep* 1978; 27:205.

2. Influenza vaccine: recommendation of the Public Health Services Advisory Committee on Immunization Practices. *Morbidity Mortality Weekly Rep* 1975; 24:197.

3. Larson EB, Olsen E, Cole W. The relationship of health beliefs and a postcard reminder to influenza vaccination. *J Fam Med* 1979; 8:1207.

4. Kasl SV, Cobb S. Health behavior, illness behavior, and sick role behavior. *Arch Environ Health* 1966; 12:246.

5. Andersen R. *A Behavioral Model of Families' Use of Health Services.* Center for Health Administration Studies, University of Chicago, Research Series 25, 1968.

6. Anderson JG, Bartkus DE. Choice of medical care: a behavioral model of health and illness behavior. *J Health Soc Behav* 1973; 14:348.

7. Fabrega H. Toward a model of illness behavior. *Med Care* 1973; 11:470.

8. Becker M, ed. The health belief model and personal health behavior. *Health Educ Monogr* 1974; 2:236.

9. Maiman LA, Becker MH. The health belief model: origins and correlates in psychological theory. *Health Educ Monogr* 1974; 2:336

10. Kegeles SS. Some motives for seeking preventive dental care. *J Am Dent Assoc* 1963; 67:90.

11. Heinzelmann F. Factors in prophylaxis behavior in treating rheumatic fever: an exploratory study. *J Health Human Behav* 1960; 1:183.

12. Hochbaum GM. *Public Participation in Medical Screen Programs: A Socio-Psychological Study.* Washington, D.C., United States Government Printing Office, 1958. Public Health Service, Public Health Service Publication No. 572.

13. Kirscht JP, Becker MH, Eveland JP. Psychological and social factors as predictors of medical behavior. *Med Care* 1976; 5:422.

14. Becker MH, Drachman RH, Kirscht JP. Predicting mothers' compliance with pediatric medical regimens. *J Perdiatr* 1972; 81:843.

15. Rundall TG, Wheeler JRC. Factors associated with utilization of the swine flu vaccination program among seniors in Tompkins County. *Med Care* 1979; 17:191.

16. Cummings KM, Jette AM, Brock BM, Haefher DP. Psychosocial determinants of immunization behavior in a swine influenza campaign. *Med Care* 1979; 17:639.

17. Sackett DL. Patients and therapies: getting the two together. *N Engl J Med* 1978; 298:278.

18. Taylor DW. A test of the health belief model in hypertension. In: Haynes RD, Sackett DL, Taylor DW, eds. *Compliance in health care.* Baltimore: Johns Hopkins University Press, 1979; 105-109.

19. Schroeder SA. Lowering broken appointment rates at a medical clinic. *Med Care* 1973; 11:75.

20. Shepard DS, Mosely TAB. Mailed versus telephoned appointment reminder to reduce broken appointments in a hospital outpatient department. *Med Care* 1976; 14:268.

21. Nazarian LF, Mechaber J, Chamey E. Effect of a mailed appointment reminder on appointment keeping. *Pediatrics* 1974; 53:349.

22. Armitage P. *Statistical methods in medical research.* New York: Wiley, 1971.

23. Cox DR. *Analysis of binary data.* London: Wiley, 1970; 14-29.

24. Becker MH, Maiman LA, Kirscht JP, et al. Patient perceptions and compliance: recent studies, the health belief model. In: Haynes RB, Sackett DI Taylor DW, eds. *Compliance in health care.* Baltimore: Johns Hopkins University Press, 1979; 78.

25. Haynes RB. A critical review of the "determinants" of patient compliance with therapeutic regimens. In: Sackett DL, Haynes RB, eds. *Compliance with therapeutic regimens.* Baltimore: Johns Hopkins University Press, 1978; 35.

26. Inui TS, Yourtee EL, Williamson JW. Improved outcomes in hypertension after physician tutorials: a controlled trial. *Ann Intern Med,* 1976; 84:646.

10

CONDOM USE

A Self-Efficacy Model

EDELGARD WULFERT AND CHOI K. WAN

Since the epidemic spread of the human immunodeficiency virus (HIV) was first recognized, massive educational campaigns have informed the public how the virus is transmitted and how sexual transmission can be prevented. An emerging body of literature documents that the response to these educational efforts has been varied: Apparently, gay men have substantially modified their sexual behavior, although high-risk activities continue to present a major source for new infections (see Stall, Coates, & Hoff, 1988, for a review); risk reduction efforts among intravenous (IV) drug users have been much less successful (Des Jarlais & Friedman, 1988); and many non-monogamous heterosexual men and women do not even consider themselves at risk for HIV infection and are not changing their behavior (Leigh, 1990; Siegel & Gibson, 1988).

These findings underscore the need for a better understanding of why so many people persist in sexual high-risk practices. Unfortunately, to date many behavioral acquired immunodeficiency syndrome (AIDS) studies have focused on demographic and psychosocial characteristics of risk group members rather than on identifying the psychological processes involved in sexual risk taking. A few studies that sought to elucidate these psychological processes were conducted within the general framework of the health belief model (Rosenstock, 1974) and arrived at conflicting results (see Montgomery et al., 1989, for a review). This has led some researchers to conclude that the HIV epidemic may not fit well within the conceptual framework of the health belief model (Brown, DiClemente, & Reynolds, 1991).

Recently, Bandura (1990) has proposed a self-efficacy (SE) model of safer sex behavior that examines HIV prevention from the perspective of social-cognitive theory (Bandura, 1977, 1986). In the past, this theory has led to thoughtful analyses

EDITORS' NOTE: From *Health Psychology, 12,* pp. 346-353.

of a wide range of health behaviors and has generated powerful interventions for behaviors that are notoriously difficult to change, such as alcohol abuse or smoking (e.g., Marlatt & Gordon, 1985; Monti, Abrams, Kadden, & Cooney, 1989; Perry, Klepp, & Shultz, 1988). Yet, surprisingly, social-cognitive theory to date has not been systematically applied to an empirical analysis of HIV prevention (a few studies have incorporated SE beliefs into the health belief model, e.g., Aspinwall, Kemeny, Taylor, Schneider, & Dudley, 1991; see also Stall et al., 1988, for a discussion of two unpublished studies).

When sexual risk reduction is analyzed from a social-cognitive perspective, knowledge and skills to exercise self-protective behaviors are necessary but not sufficient (Bandura, 1990). People may know how the virus is transmitted and have the skills to negotiate condom use but still engage in unprotected sexual intercourse. According to Bandura, this happens because behavior is not directly a result of knowledge or skills. Rather, it is mediated by a process of cognitive appraisal by which people integrate knowledge, outcome expectancies, emotional states, social influences, and past experiences to form a judgment of their ability to master a difficult situation. This judgment of SE mediates behavior and determines whether people initiate an action, how much effort they expend, and how long they persist in the face of difficulty. Hence, people will practice safer sex only to the degree that they believe they can protect themselves when needed.

The present study applied Bandura's SE theory to condom use. It was guided by the conceptual model presented in Figure 10.1, which accords SE the role of a final common pathway, integrating the effects of several cognitive variables that have been thought to play a role in safer sex behavior. Before we explain these variables in more detail, a word of caution is necessary. The reader must keep in mind that one cannot determine the direction of causality between two variables by using recursive causal modeling techniques (Asher, 1983). In the model in Figure 10.1, we imposed directionality between the constructs consistent with social-cognitive theory. Whereas social-cognitive theory views SE beliefs as causal, in our study we neither imposed a temporal sequence between any of the variables included in the model nor did we experimentally manipulate the predictor variables. Consequently, the linkages between the constructs are correlational, and our study cannot make causal claims. However, the model itself serves as a useful heuristic device, which allows one to determine how well social-cognitive theory is able to explain the data. With this in mind, let us now turn to the constructs included in the model.

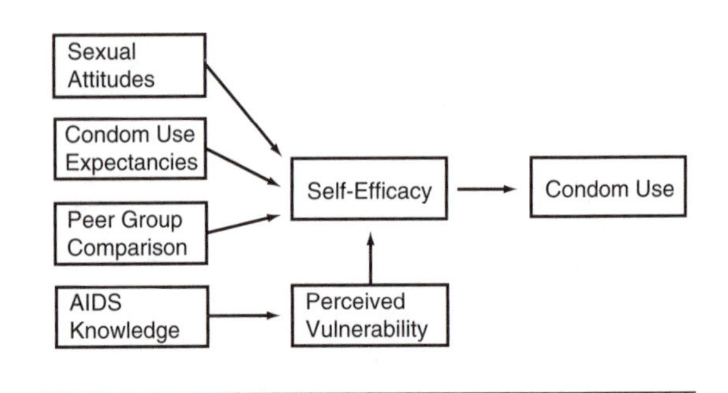

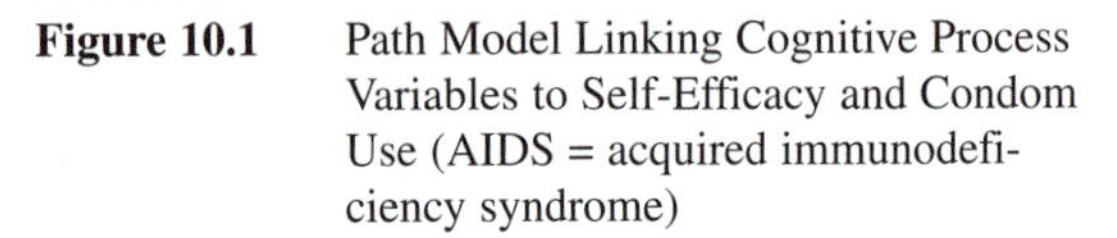

Figure 10.1 Path Model Linking Cognitive Process Variables to Self-Efficacy and Condom Use (AIDS = acquired immunodeficiency syndrome)

The first variable in the model is sexual attitudes. To date, no reports have appeared that examine the relationship of sexual attitudes to SE, but the relationship of sexual attitudes to behavior has been extensively researched, often with conflicting results. Some studies found negative sexual attitudes to be associated with embarrassment when purchasing contraceptives (Fisher, Fisher, & Byrne, 1971), difficulty communicating with a partner about condoms (Fisher, Miller, Byrne, & White, 1980), and failure to use contraceptives (Byrne, 1983; Fisher, 1984). However, other research found no relationship (e.g., Baffi, Schroeder, Redican, & McCluskey, 1989), and one study even reported a link between positive sexual attitudes and not using condoms (Carpenter, Stulbaum, Jones, & Barlow, 1988). These inconsistencies could be reconciled if the attitude-behavior relationship were viewed as mediated by SE beliefs: Some people, for example, may have positive attitudes toward sex but low SE, because they know they forget about protection once they become highly aroused; others, in contrast, may have negative attitudes but feel very sure about using condoms because they fear catching a disease. We therefore hypothesized that sexual attitudes would be related to SE but would not directly predict condom use.

A variable of important implications in an SE model is outcome expectancies. The role of outcome expectancies is somewhat ambiguous in light of the lingering controversy that outcome expectancies cannot be properly discriminated from SE beliefs (e.g., Eastman & Marzillier, 1984; Lee, 1989). Attempts to provide a clear distinction between outcome expectancies and SE beliefs on a conceptual level have been unsatisfactory, but on a practical level the constructs can be discriminated if they are carefully defined and operationalized (Haaga & Stewart, 1992). In the present study, we defined SE as the degree of confidence people reported in their ability to use condoms during a 6-month period and outcome expectancies as the consequences people expected to result from using condoms. Outcome expectancies were not conceptualized as direct predictors of condom use as one can hold positive and negative expectancies at the same time (e.g., believing that condoms protect users from disease but also believing that condoms interfere with pleasure); instead, we assumed outcome expectancies to have motivational status (Annis & Davis, 1988) through their effects on SE beliefs. We hypothesized that positive expectancies would motivate individuals to practice safer sex by enhancing their sense of SE and that negative expectancies would be related to risk behavior by decreasing SE.

As social-cognitive theory places great emphasis on the social origin of most complex human actions, influences from a person's peer group were considered another important source of variability. According to Bandura (1990), people form beliefs about their own capabilities, in part, by comparing themselves with others whom they regard as similar and by observing how effective these individuals behave in a given situation. Therefore, in the present study, we assumed that our subjects were influenced by their perceptions of their peers' safer sex practices. Specifically, we hypothesized that those who compared their own condom use favorably to their peers' condom use would report an increased sense of SE and therefore use condoms more consistently.

Finally, we predicted that knowledge about AIDS would play no significant role in an SE model because social-cognitive theory does not view education as a sufficient cause of self-motivated behavior change. This view has received empirical support from studies that have generally found little or no relationship between people's knowledge about AIDS and risk reduction (e.g., Baldwin & Baldwin, 1988; Becker & Joseph, 1988; DiClemente, Forest, & Mickler, 1989). Recently, it was suggested that knowledge may act as a cue and heighten perceived vulnerability to HIV infection (Maticka-Tyndale, 1990). However, the role of perceived vulnerability is itself unclear because it sometimes has (e.g., Baldwin & Baldwin, 1988; DiClemente et al., 1989) and sometimes it has not (e.g., Montgomery et al., 1989) predicted risk reduction. As with the framework of social-cognitive theory, these cognitive factors can affect behavior only indirectly through their influence on SE. Consequently, we examined the relationship between knowledge, perceived vulnerability, and SE.

In summary, the purpose of the present study was to investigate psychological factors associated with sexual risk behavior. The study was conceptually guided by Bandura's social-cognitive theory and examined whether an SE model (see Figure 10.1) is capable of predicting condom use from outcome expectancies, social influences, attitudes, risk perception, and AIDS-related knowledge.

Method

Subjects

Three hundred and fifty undergraduate students from advanced psychology classes completed an anonymous survey for extra course credit. In the analyses reported here, only students who described themselves as single, heterosexual, and currently sexually active were included. These criteria eliminated 16 homosexual or bisexual, 16 married, and

83 sexually inactive respondents (56 virgins and 27 individuals who had not had sexual intercourse during the past 6 months). In addition, 23 respondents were eliminated for missing data on one or more variables, leaving a final sample of 212 respondents (103 men and 109 women). The ethnic composition of the sample was 83% Caucasian, 8% African-American, 3% Hispanic, and 6% other or unidentified. The students' stated religious affiliation was 28% Catholic, 37% Jewish, 24% Protestant, and 11% other or unidentified. The mean age of the respondents was 21.4 years (men = 21.8 years; women = 21.1 years).

Instrument Development

A self-report questionnaire was developed to gather information about sexual practices, condom use SE, condom use, peer group comparison, expectancies about condoms, sexual attitudes, knowledge about AIDS, perceived risk for HIV infection, and social desirability.

The behavioral and expectancy items were developed through pilot work with 54 men and 42 women, who anonymously completed an open-ended questionnaire about their sexual behavior, beliefs about condoms, and reasons for using or not using condoms. Additional items were adapted from published studies. Available questionnaires on sexual attitudes (Fisher, Byrne, & White, 1983), AIDS knowledge (Sherr, 1987), and social desirability (Tellegen, 1982) were included. The complete instrument was pretested by six research assistants for clarity and readability and then administered twice to 78 men and 75 women with a test-retest interval of 3 weeks. All variables demonstrated adequate test-retest reliability (condom use SE = .78; condom use = .91; peer group comparison = .71; three expectancy factors = .78, .72, and .76; sexual attitudes = .87; perceived HIV risk = .74; and social desirability = .72), except for the AIDS knowledge test (.63). This rather low coefficient may have been due to true differences as the subjects could have informed themselves between test and retest about items they were unsure of. Part of the unreliability may also have reflected the effects of restricted range, because 85% of the sample correctly responded to at least 8 of the 10 items.

Measures

Besides standard demographic data and information about sexual behaviors not included in the model (e.g., number of past sex partners and reasons for condom use), data were gathered on social desirability and on the following seven major constructs:

Condom Use. Self-reported condom use was the main criterion variable in our model. We defined condom use as the proportion of times an individual engaged in protected sexual intercourse relative to the total number of times intercourse occurred. As our study was cross-sectional rather than longitudinal, we were unable to assess condom use prospectively and therefore employed condom use during the past 6 months as an estimate of future use. Subjects were asked to respond on a 7-point scale ranging from never (1) to always (7) to the following question: Over the past 6 months, of all the times you had vaginal intercourse, how often did you use condoms?

Inferring future condom use from use over the past 6 months seems reasonable in light of Epstein's (1979) demonstration that a variety of behaviors can be predicted with correlations in the vicinity of .80 or .90, as long as the behaviors in question are aggregated over a sufficient number of occurrences. The 6-month estimation interval used in the present study appeared more than adequate for two reasons: First, unpublished longitudinal research has shown that stable estimates for condom use by heterosexual men and women can be obtained over a 3-month period (Jaccard & Wan, 1992). Second, published research (Lex, Palmieri, Mello, & Mendelson, 1988) showed that women's patterns of sexual activity over a prospective 3-month interval were highly consistent.

SE. This construct was assessed with a measure imported from research in addictive behaviors, which found that a global SE rating of one's ability to abstain over 1 year was a highly accurate predictor of long-term abstinence (e.g., Erickson, Tiffany, Martin, & Baker, 1983). Using a similarly global measure, we asked subjects to respond on a 7-point scale ranging from not at all confident (1) to extremely confident (7) to the following question: How confident are you that you will be able to use condoms for vaginal intercourse over the next 6 months?

Outcome Expectancies. Twenty expected consequences of condom use were each scored on a 7-point scale ranging from completely disagree (1) to completely agree (7). From these statements, three factors were extracted with principal component analysis; varimax and oblique rotations yielded comparable results. The negative expectancies factor (e.g., "Condoms interfere with romance" and "Condoms reduce sensation") explained 21.3% of the variance; the disease prevention factor (e.g., "Condoms reduce the risk of AIDS" and "Condoms prevent sexually transmitted diseases") accounted for 18.0% of the variance; and the pregnancy prevention factor (e.g., "Condoms prevent unwanted pregnancies" and "My partner insists on condoms") for 9.6% of the variance in the data. The three factors had acceptable levels of internal consistency with alphas of .90, .93, and .69, respectively. Scores for each factor were obtained by summing across individual items and calculating the mean.

Sexual Attitudes. The Sexual Opinion Questionnaire (Fisher, Byrne, & White, 1983), which purports to measure a bipolar personality dimension termed erotophobia-erotophilia, was included to assess general sexual attitudes. It consists of 21 statements (e.g., "Seeing a pornographic movie would be sexually arousing to me" and "Masturbation can be an exciting experience"), which are answered on a 7-point scale ranging from completely agree (1) to completely disagree (7). Scores are derived according to a formula and have a possible range from 0 to 126. The scale has established psychometric properties and norms, and research concerning this instrument has been summarized by Fisher, Byrne, White, and Kelley (1988).

Peer Group Comparison. Bandura's theory strongly emphasizes the effects of social influences on SE beliefs that result when individuals compare themselves with those whom they perceive as similar. To examine peer group influences on condom use, subjects were asked the following question: When you compare yourself with your close friends, do you believe you use condoms equally, more, or less often? Subjects responded on a 3-point scale: less often (1), same (2), and more often (3).

AIDS Knowledge. From an AIDS knowledge test developed by Sherr (1987) 10 true-false statements were selected (e.g., "By donating blood, the donor can acquire the AIDS virus" and "The AIDS virus can be passed during sexual intercourse from an infected woman to a man"). Scores were expressed as the number of items answered correctly, with a possible range from 0 to 10.

Perceived Vulnerability. Subjects expressed their perceived risk of contracting the AIDS virus on a 7-point scale ranging from extremely unlikely (1) to extremely likely (7) in answer to the following question: Considering all the different factors that may contribute to AIDS, what would you say are your chances of getting AIDS?

Social Desirability. The Desirable Response Inconsistency Scale (DRIN; Tellegen, 1982), a 22-item true-false questionnaire (e.g., "I am a warm person rather than cool and detached"), served as an indicator of response bias due to social desirability.

RESULTS

The men and women in the study reported a mean number of 1.8 sex partners during the past 6 months and a mean number of 5.4 sex partners during the past 3 years. Only 29% of the subjects reported consistently having used condoms during the past 6 months. As the main reason for using condoms, 73% stated pregnancy prevention and only 17% mentioned fear of AIDS. That AIDS was not a big concern was also reflected in the answers of 80% of the students who perceived themselves not at all or only slightly at risk for HIV infection.

On the basis of theoretical considerations, the structural model presented in Figure 10.1 was formally tested. As social-cognitive theory assigns a pivotal role to SE, any contributions of the cognitive variables to condom use were expected to occur through their influence on SE. To control for a possible bias due to social desirability, the DRIN scale scores were used as a covariate in the analysis, but social desirability is not formally represented in the figure.

The fit of our model was evaluated with LISREL VII by using the sample covariance matrix as input and a maximum likelihood solution. The model was statistically overidentified. As we worked with single indicators, all the measures were subject to measurement error, which can introduce bias in the estimates of the structural coefficients. The effects of such error were explicitly modeled by using a strategy suggested by Hayduk (1987). This involved constraining the theta delta and theta epsilon matrices to predetermined values corresponding to a priori determined levels of error variance. By using this strategy, the test-retest reliability coefficients obtained from our pilot study were used to determine the error variances.

Although the model fit was very good (GFI = .95), an inspection of the modification indices for gamma showed one very strong indicator with a value of 24.63, suggesting that the overall fit could be improved by adding a path from peer group comparison to condom use. We therefore revised the conceptual model and formulated the new model. This model, with a direct path leading from peer group comparison not only to SE but also to condom use, was reevaluated with LISREL VII. The new analysis resulted in an overall improved model fit.

The variables in the model accounted for 46% of the variance in condom use and for 53% of the variance in SE. Seven of the path coefficients were statistically significant. Consistent with social-cognitive theory, condom use was predicted by SE beliefs (note that in the present context predict is to be taken in a strict statistical, not causal, sense); but, in addition, it was also significantly predicted by peer group comparison, a finding not entirely consistent with social-cognitive theory (according to social-cognitive theory, social models influence behavior indirectly by affecting SE beliefs). The central mediating variable, SE, was predicted by self-comparisons with one's peer group and by outcome expectancies: Favorable comparisons and positive expectancies about condom use (i.e., disease and pregnancy prevention) were directly related to SE, whereas negative expectancies (e.g., reduction of pleasure) were inversely associated with SE. Consistent with our predictions, AIDS knowledge was unrelated to condom use. Similar to previous research (Maticka-Tyndale, 1990), we found a positive correlation between AIDS knowledge scores and perceived vulnerability to HIV infection, but perceived vulnerability was not a significant predictor of either SE or condom use. General sexual attitudes (as determined by the erotophobia-erotophilia personality dimension) did not account for any significant portion of the variance in the model.

Discussion

The results of the present study indicate that the SE paradigm is a useful conceptual framework for understanding important psychological factors involved in sexual risk behavior. The following conclusions can be drawn from the findings.

First, the men and women in our study were well-informed about the facts and myths of HIV transmission; but whereas greater knowledge was related to an increased awareness of susceptibility to HIV infection, we observed no appreciable effect of knowledge on safer sex behavior. Like other researchers (Leigh, 1990; Siegel & Gibson, 1988), we found that most of the heterosexual men and women in our study did not feel at risk for contracting the AIDS virus. At the same time, 70% of them used condoms inconsistently or not at all, and the average subject reported having had sexual intercourse with 5.4 partners during the 3 years preceding this study. These findings indicate that the majority of these well-educated men and women underestimate the risk involved in their sexual behavior and engage in actions that can potentially lead to HIV infection.

Second, whether sexually active men and women practiced safer sex was associated with certain beliefs and expectations about using condoms. Consistent with social-cognitive theory, we found that outcome expectancies were related to condom use indirectly through SE. More specifically, beliefs that using condoms has negative consequences, such as diminished sexual pleasure, were correlated with decreased SE and less consistent condom use, whereas beliefs that condoms effectively prevent pregnancy and disease were associated with greater SE and more consistent condom use. Furthermore, the majority of the men and women in our study reported using condoms mainly for contraception rather than disease prevention, a finding consistent with other studies (e.g., Baffi et al., 1989; Maticka-Tyndale, 1990). This highlights the need for a fundamental attitude change toward condom use among nonmonogamous or serially monogamous heterosexual men and women.

Third, condom use was related to social modeling influences. Subjects who compared themselves favorably with their peers and believed they were using condoms at least as frequently as their peers reported greater SE and more consistent condom use. This suggests, not surprisingly, that the social network of young adults plays an important role in their sexual behavior. Comparison with one's peers was the only variable in our model that was directly associated with condom use, above and beyond its relationship to SE. This indicates that some individuals believe they use condoms more frequently than their peers and in fact use them rather consistently, despite low SE, and vice versa. We speculate that these cases reflect the fact that condom use is not exclusively determined by a person's cognitive structure but also by his or her sex partner. For example, some individuals may report low SE because they find it difficult to stop themselves once they become sexually aroused; nevertheless, they may believe they use condoms more often than their peers because they are in a relationship with a partner who refuses intercourse without protection.

Fourth, general sexual attitudes were neither related to SE nor to condom use. Viewed in light of the long-standing debate about the relationship between attitudes and behavior, this finding is not too surprising. Various researchers have argued that general attitude measures are not useful for predicting specific actions and should be replaced by behavior-specific attitude measures (e.g., Ajzen & Fishbein, 1977). This raises the question of whether a condom-specific attitude measure, such as Brown's (1984) Attitude Toward the Condom scale, would add to the predictive power of an SE model. It would seem worthwhile to examine this question in future research.

In summary, the findings supported an SE model of safer sex behavior. Within the context of this model, SE functioned as a central mediator through which other cognitive factors, including expectancies and self-comparison with one's peers, exerted their influence on condom use. These findings suggest some general guidelines for the design of educational programs to promote condom use among sexually active young adults. Such programs should target SE beliefs and attempt to enhance them, for example, by increasing positive and decreasing negative expectancies associated with condom use. Furthermore, group-based interventions with peer models who demonstrate effective behavior might be especially useful as they would provide a social context within which more adaptive peer norms could develop.

Despite the fit between our conceptual model and the data, some caveats are necessary as the study suffered from several limitations. One weakness was that the core construct of our conceptual model, SE, was measured in a nontraditional way as one global belief. Because SE was originally formulated in the context of phobic disorders (e.g., Bandura & Adams, 1977), it has traditionally been expressed as confidence ratings across a series of hierarchically arranged behavioral attainments (e.g., looking at a snake, approaching it, touching it, and holding it). A recently published 28-item questionnaire, the Condom Use SE Scale for college populations (Brafford & Beck, 1991), would have fulfilled the traditional requirement as it presents a more fine-grained analysis of condom use SE (e.g., purchasing a condom, having one available, negotiating its use with a partner, and using one). Unfortunately, this instrument was not available at the time the present study was conducted. Although it is an empirical question of whether a composite measure of SE can account for more variance in condom use, a more fine-grained SE analysis would have been preferable from a practical vantage point because it permits identifying possible sources of resistance toward condom use. For example, some individuals may feel unable to plan ahead and have condoms available when needed, even though they could negotiate condom use with a partner; others may have no problems planning ahead but feel embarrassed about discussing condom use with a partner. Identifying such differences in SE would be important if one were to design interventions that promote safer sex behavior.

Another limitation of the study relates to the generality of its findings. The variables correlated with safer sex behavior in college-age heterosexual men and women may not be relevant for other groups at risk for HIV infection, including gay men, IV drug users, and minorities from economically disadvantaged backgrounds. For example, concerns about birth control, which significantly enhanced the SE beliefs of the heterosexual men and women in the present study, are of no concern to gay or lesbian individuals. Similarly, fitting in with one's peer group may be especially important for college students for whom peer acceptance and group belonging are vital aspects of everyday living; but it may be of much lesser importance to independently living adults. This is not to say that for individuals with different backgrounds SE does not occupy the role of a central mediator in behavior, but cognitive variables other than those identified in the present study could be associated with SE beliefs. Future research should therefore clarify the generality of an SE model of sexual risk-taking behavior.

A final word of caution is necessary because of the correlational nature of our study. Even though social-cognitive theory makes causal assertions, we would like to reiterate that our design does not justify the conclusion that we demonstrated a causal effect of SE on condom use. Demonstrating causality would have required the experimental manipulation of SE beliefs and a test of their effects on condom use in a prospective rather than cross-sectional design.

A second issue related to the correlational nature of our design requires clarification: In principle, it would be possible to reverse the arrows in our conceptual model. To illustrate, one might argue that individuals who use condoms more frequently also report a higher sense of SE and hold more positive expectancies about condoms. This assertion would not only be logically but also theoretically justifiable, given that social-cognitive theory is based on a model of reciprocal determinism. It holds that behavioral, cognitive, and environmental factors, as well as other personal factors, interact as triadic determinants of each other (Bandura, 1977, 1986). In a real-world situation, experience with condoms most likely affects an individual's SE beliefs and outcome expectancies, and these cognitions, in turn, will influence whether the individual uses condoms. Unfortunately, the continuous flow between behavior, cognition, and environment is difficult to capture as, for practical limitations, one cannot study every possible interaction in a triadic causal model. However, reciprocal causal factors do not operate all at once, and one can gain an understanding of behavior by studying individual segments in a chain of events (Bandura, 1986). The present study examined how cognitions relate to condom use, and we were able to demonstrate a fit between our conceptual model and the data. But good fit does not mean that we "confirmed" our model; it simply means that, given our data, we did not reject the model (Loehlin, 1987). Therefore, our results do not preclude that other models would have fit the data equally well or even better.

References

Ajzen, I., & Fishbein, M. (1977). Attitudinal and normative variables as predictors of specific behaviors. *Journal of Personality and Social Psychology, 27,* 41-57.

Annis, H. M., & Davis, D. S. (1988). Assessment of expectancies. In D. M. Donovan & G. A. Marlatt (Eds.), *Assessment of addictive behaviors* (pp. 84–111). New York: Guilford.

Asher, H. B. (1983). *Causal modeling* (2nd ed.). Newbury Park, CA: Sage.

Aspinwall, L. G., Kemeny, M. E., Taylor, S. E., Schneider, S. T., & Dudley, J. P. (1991). Psychosocial predictors of gay men's AIDS risk-reduction behavior. *Health Psychology, 10,* 432-444.

Baffi, C. R., Schroeder, K. K., Redican, K. J., & McCluskey, L. (1989). Factors influencing selected heterosexual male college students' condom use. *Journal of American College Health, 38*(3), 137-141.

Baldwin, J., & Baldwin, J. (1988). Factors affecting AIDS-related sexual risk-taking behavior among college students. *The Journal of Sex Research, 25,* 181-196.

Bandura, A. (1977). *Social learning theory.* Englewood Cliffs, NJ: Prentice Hall.

Bandura, A. (1986). *Social foundations of thought and action: A social cognitive theory.* Englewood Cliffs, NJ: Prentice Hall.

Bandura, A. (1990). Perceived self-efficacy in the exercise of control over AIDS infection. *Evaluation and Program Planning, 13,* 9-17.

Bandura, A., & Adams, N. E. (1977). Analysis of self-efficacy theory of behavioral change. *Cognitive Therapy and Research, 1*(4), 287-310.

Becker, M., & Joseph, J. (1988). AIDS and behavioral change to reduce risk: A review. *American Journal of Public Health, 78,* 394-410.

Brafford, L. J., & Beck, K. H. (1991). Development and validation of a condom self-efficacy scale for college students. *Journal of American College Health, 39*(5), 219-225.

Brown, I. S. (1984). Development of a scale to measure attitude toward the condom as a method of birth control. *Journal of Sex Research, 20*(3), 255-263.

Brown, L. K., DiClemente, R. J., & Reynolds, L. A. (1991). HIV prevention for adolescents: Utility of the health belief model. *AIDS Education and Prevention, 3*(1), 50-59.

Byrne, D. (1983). Sex without contraception. In D. Byrne & W. A. Fisher (Eds.), Adolescents, sex, and contraception (pp. 3—31). Hillsdale, NJ: Erlbaum.

Carpenter, K., Stulbaum, S., Jones, J. C., & Barlow, D. H. (1988, November). *Relationship between AIDS information, sexual attitudes, and risky sexual behavior in heterosexual college students.* Poster presented at the 22nd annual meeting of the Association for the Advancement of Behavior Therapy, New York.

Des Jarlais, D. C., & Friedman, S. R. (1988). The psychology of preventing AIDS among intravenous drug users: A social learning conceptualization. *American Psychologist, 43,* 865-870.

DiClemente, C. D., Forest, K., & Mickler, S. (1989). Differential effects of AIDS knowledge and perceived susceptibility on the reduction of high-risk sexual behaviors among college adolescents. In *Fifth International AIDS Conference: Abstracts* (p. 742). International AIDS Association.

Eastman, C., & Marzillier, J. S. (1984). Theoretical and methodological difficulties in Bandura's self-efficacy theory. *Cognitive Therapy and Research, 8,* 213-229.

Epstein, S. (1979). The stability of behavior: On predicting most of the people much of the time. *Journal of Personality and Social Psychology, 37,* 1097-1126.

Erickson, L. M., Tiffany, S. T., Martin, E. M., & Baker, T. B. (1983). Aversive smoking therapies: A conditioning analysis of therapeutic effectiveness. *Behaviour Research and Therapy, 21,* 595-611.

Fisher, W. A. (1984). Predicting contraceptive behavior among university men: The role of emotions and behavioral intentions. *Journal of Applied Social Psychology, 14,* 104-123.

Fisher, W. A., Byrne, D., & White, L. A. (1983). Emotional barriers to contraception. In D. Byrne & W. A. Fisher (Eds.), *Adolescents, sex, and contraception* (pp. 207—239). Hillsdale, NJ: Erlbaum.

Fisher, W. A., Byrne, D., White, L. A., & Kelley, K. (1988). Erotophobia—erotophilia as a dimension of personality. *The Journal of Sex Research, 25,* 123-151.

Fisher, W. A., Fisher, J. D., & Byrne, D. (1971). Consumer reactions to contraceptive purchasing. *Personality and Social Psychology Bulletin, 3,* 293-296.

Fisher, W. A., Miller, C. T., Byrne, D., & White, L. A. (1980). Talking dirty: Responses to communicating a sexual message as a function of situational and personality factors. *Basic and Applied Social Psychology, 1,* 115-126.

Haaga, D. A. F., & Stewart, B. L. (1992). How do you know an act when you see one? A response to Devins (1992). *Journal of Consulting and Clinical Psychology, 60,* 32-33.

Hayduk, L. A. (1987). *Structural equation modeling with LISREL: Essentials and advances.* Baltimore: Johns Hopkins University Press.

Jaccard, J. J., & Wan, C. K. (1992). *Self-report of behaviors related to AIDS.* Unpublished manuscript, University at Albany, State University of New York, Department of Psychology.

Lee, C. (1989). Theoretical weaknesses lead to practical problems: The example of self-efficacy theory. *Journal of Behavior Therapy and Experimental Psychiatry, 20,* 115-123.

Leigh, B. C. (1990). The relationship of substance use during sex to high-risk sexual behavior. *The Journal of Sex Research, 27,* 199-213.

Lex, P. W., Palmieri, S. L., Mello, N. K., & Mendelson, J. H. (1988). Alcohol use, marihuana smoking, and sexual activity in women. *Alcohol, 5,* 21-25.

Loehlin, J. C. (1987). Latent variable models: An introduction to factor, path, and structural analysis. Hillsdale, NJ: Erlbaum.

Marlatt, G. A., & Gordon, J. R. (Eds.). (1985). *Relapse prevention: Maintenance strategies in the treatment of addictive behaviors.* New York: Guilford.

Maticka-Tyndale, E. (1990). Sexual scripts and AIDS prevention: Variations in adherence to safer-sex guidelines by heterosexual adolescents. *The Journal of Sex Research, 28,* 45-66.

Montgomery, S. B., Joseph, J. G., Becker, M. H., Ostrow, D. G., Kessler, R. C., & Kirscht, J. P. (1989). The health belief model in understanding compliance with preventive recommendations for AIDS: How useful? *AIDS Education and Prevention, 1*(4), 303-323.

Monti, P. M., Abrams, D. B., Kadden, R. M., & Cooney, N. L. (1989). *Treating alcohol dependence.* New York: Guilford.

Perry, C. L., Klepp, K. I., & Shultz, J. M. (1988). Primary prevention of cardiovascular disease: Community-wide strategies for use. *Journal of Consulting and Clinical Psychology, 56,* 358-364.

Rosenstock, I. M. (1974). The health belief model and preventive health behavior. *Health Education Monographs, 2,* 354-386.

Sherr, L. (1987). An evaluation of the UK government health education campaign on AIDS. *Psychology and Health, 1,* 61-72.

Siegel, K., & Gibson, W. C. (1988). Barriers to the modification of sexual behavior among heterosexuals at risk for acquired immunodeficiency syndrome. *New York State Journal of Medicine, 88,* 66-70.

Stall, R. D., Coates, T. J., & Hoff, C. (1988). Behavioral risk reduction for HIV infection among gay and bisexual men: A review of results from the United States. *American Psychologist, 43,* 878-885.

Tellegen, A. (1982). *Brief manual for the Differential Personality Questionnaire.* Unpublished manuscript.

11

Application of the Theories of Reasoned Action and Planned Behavior to Exercise Behavior

A Meta-Analysis

Heather A. Hausenblas, Albert V. Carron, and Diane E. Mack

Considerable evidence exists to support the suggestion that exercise and physical activity participation contribute positively to both physical and psychological health (cf. Wankel, 1993). These benefits, however, are realized by only a small percentage of the population; those individuals who exercise regularly (Berger & McInman, 1993). Despite the numerous benefits of exercise, only 37% of the American adult population follow a regular exercise program (Harris & Associates, cited in Berger & McInman, 1993). Also, a major problem with exercise programs—whether designed for the general public, the elderly, psychiatric patients, the obese, or coronary rehabilitation patients—is participant nonadherence (Andrew et al., 1981; Dishman & Gettman, 1980; Massie & Shephard, 1971; Oldridge, 1979). That is, approximately 50% of those who begin a physical activity program withdraw within the first 6 months (Dishman, 1988).

Over the past decade, researchers have attempted to gain a better understanding of the antecedents of individual adherence in physical activity (Godin, 1993). Some of the theoretical models that have attracted the interest of researchers are the health belief model (e.g., Heinzelmann & Bagley, 1970), self-efficacy theory (e.g., Poag-DuCharme & Brawley, 1993), protection

EDITORS' NOTE: Reprinted, by permission, from H.A. Hausenblas, A.V. Carron, and D.E. Mack, 1997, "Application of the Theories of Reasoned Action and Planned Behavior to Exercise Behavior: A Meta-Analysis," *Journal of Sport & Exercise Psychology, 19*(1): pp. 36-51.

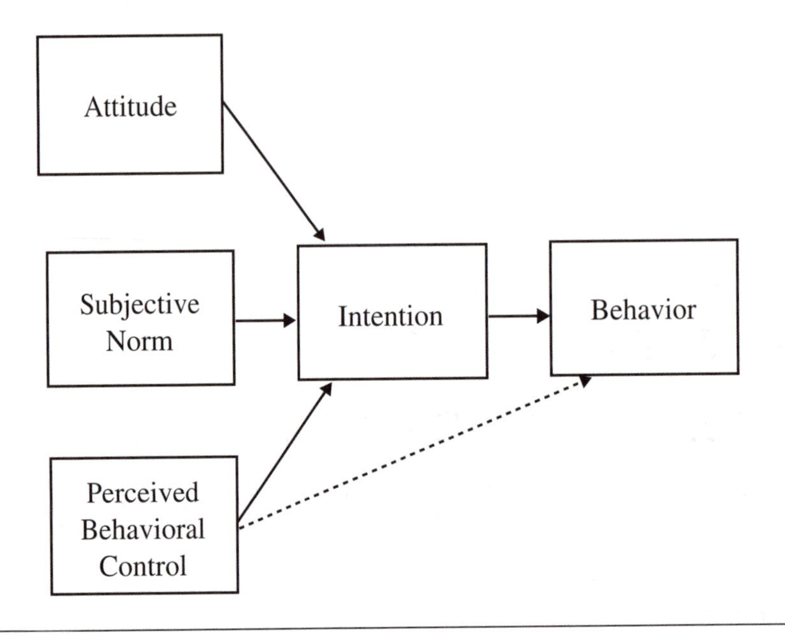

Figure 11.1 Schematic Representation of the Theory of Planned Behavior

motivation theory (e.g., Wurtele & Maddux, 1987), physical activity model (cf. Dishman, 1993), and self-regulatory theory (cf. Dishman, 1993). According to Maddux (1993), however, it is the theory of reasoned action (TRA) (Ajzen & Fishbein, 1980; Fishbein & Ajzen, 1975) and the theory of planned behavior (TPB) (Ajzen, 1985, 1988, 1991) that have guided the majority of the research on health and exercise behavior. Figure 11.1 provides an overview of TRA and TPB in a schematic format.

TRA, which developed as a framework to explain volitional behavior, is based on the assumption that people behave in a sensible and rational manner by taking into account available information and considering the potential implications of their behavior. The basis of TRA is an expectancy by value summation of beliefs about performing a particular behavior. The cornerstone of the theory is intention—a motivational construct that represents how hard people are willing to try and how much effort they are planning to exert in order to perform a behavior. Intention is hypothesized to be the direct determinant of behavior and is, in turn, determined by the attitude toward performing the behavior and perceived social pressures to perform the behavior (subjective norm). These latter determinants of intention (attitude and subjective norm) are founded on behavioral beliefs and normative beliefs, respectively, that form the expectancy-value base.

Attitude toward performing a behavior is a function of a cognitive belief structure that embraces two subcomponents: the individual's beliefs about the consequences of carrying out the behavior and the positive or negative evaluation of those consequences. Thus, for example, an individual's beliefs about exercise behavior could be represented by both positive (i.e., improve personal health) and negative expectations (i.e., feel considerable discomfort from physical exertion). In addition to these evaluative components (i.e., good, bad), behavioral beliefs also contain a strength component (i.e., how much improvement in personal health, discomfort, or both is expected). Thus, an individual's attitude toward exercise behavior would be determined by multiplying the evaluation of each expected outcome by the strength of the belief that performing the behavior would lead to the outcome.

Subjective norm is considered a joint product of an individual's normative beliefs, which are perceptions about the expectations of important others (e.g., family, friends) and motivation to comply with those expectations. Thus, as was the case with attitudes, subjective norms are composed of a strength component and a motivation to comply component.

Ajzen (1985) has contended that intention cannot be the only predictor of behavior in situations where the actor's control over the behavior is incomplete. To take into account limitations (real or perceived) in performing a given behavior, Ajzen (1985, 1988, 1991) added a third element to the original Fishbein and Ajzen model: the concept of perceived behavioral control. The revised model is referred to as the theory of planned behavior (TPB). Perceived behavioral control is conceptualized as the perceived ease or difficulty of performing a behavior (Ajzen, 1988). Perceived behavioral control is considered to have both a direct effect on behavior and an indirect effect through behavioral intentions. Antecedents to perceived behavioral control are the weighted sum of control beliefs (which are facilitating or obstructing factors) and the perceived power of a particular control factor to facilitate or inhibit performance of the behavior (Ajzen & Driver, 1991).

Two recent narrative reviews have summarized the results of studies examining TRA and TPB for exercise behavior (Blue, 1995; Godin, 1993). In regard to antecedents of behavioral intention in the TRA, both Blue (1995) and Godin (1993) concluded that attitude was the most important variable and that intention to exercise was not strongly influenced by social pressure.

In regards to TPB, Godin (1993) reviewed eight published studies and reported that an additional 4-20% of the variance (with an average of 8%) in exercise intention can be explained by perceived behavioral control. Further, Blue (1995) found that perceived behavioral control added to the prediction of intention beyond attitude and subjective norm. She thus concluded that TPB may be superior to the TRA in that "TPB (a) has more predictive qualities for exercise intention and (b) does not make the assumption that control for exercise behavior rests solely in the individual" (Blue, 1995, p. 115).

Godin's (1993) and Blue's (1995) attempts to quantify the research on the TRA and TPB constitute what has been referred to as a vote counting procedure (Light & Smith, 1971). In vote counting, reviewers sort the results of each study into positive, negative, and nonsignificant categories and make conclusions based on the resulting tallies.

As Hedges and Olkin (1980) pointed out, vote counting is attractive because it is easy to use, requires a minimal amount of statistical data for integration, and permits the merging of analysis from different studies. They also noted, however, that the power of the procedure is low and actually decreases as the number of studies reviewed increases. As an alternate procedure, numerous authors have recommended meta-analysis as a more appropriate approach for research synthesis (Hedges & Olkin, 1980; Wolfe, 1986). As Glass, McGraw, and Smith (1981) stated, a "meta analysis is nothing more than the attitude of data analysis applied to quantitative summaries of individual studies" (p. 217). Thus, as Glass et al. noted, meta-analysis provides for the integration of numerous and diverse studies using the full power of statistical methods.

Thus, the primary purpose of the present study was to apply the statistical procedures of meta-analysis to summarize research that has used TRA, TPB, or both to examine exercise intentions and behaviors. Specifically, the magnitude of the relationships among the various constructs of TRA and TPB was quantified. The construct of perceived behavioral control was added to the TRA in an attempt to improve the predictive validity of the model (Ajzen, 1985). Thus, a secondary purpose, somewhat related to the primary purpose, was to compare the relative utility of TRA and TPB by quantifying the relationships between perceived behavioral control and both intention and exercise behavior.

Fishbein and Ajzen (1975; Ajzen & Fishbein, 1980; Ajzen & Madden, 1986) have argued that the predictive power of an intention should vary inversely with the time between the measurement of that intention and the observation of the behavior. Their underlying logic is that the longer the interval, the more likely an intention will change as new information becomes available. Thus, another secondary purpose of the present study was to examine the issue of proximity of measurement and predictive utility in the intention-behavior relationship.

A controversial issue exists regarding the distinction (or, more accurately, the failure to distinguish) between intention and expectation (cf. Courneya & McAuley, 1993a, 1993b, 1994; Sheppard, Hartwick, & Warshaw, 1988; Warshaw & Davis, 1985). Warshaw and Davis (1985) noted that most research on intention has failed to define the construct, and when it has been defined, it is often framed (and subsequently measured) as an expectation. In an attempt to clarify the distinction, Warshaw and Davis (1985) defined behavioral intention as "the degree to which a person has formulated conscious plans to perform or not perform the behavior" (p. 214). On the other hand, behavioral expectation was defined as "the individual's estimation of the likelihood that he or she will actually perform some specified behavior" (Warshaw & Davis, 1985, p. 125). It was also pointed out that the formation of an expectation may involve a variety of factors not presented in an intention, including anticipated changes in intention, noncognitive habits, ability limitations, and environmental facilitators or constraints. Based on these arguments, it has been suggested that expectation might be a better predictor for behaviors that are not completely volitional (Sheppard et al., 1988). Consequently, a third secondary purpose of the present study was to contrast the results from research that has measured an intention-behavior relationship versus research where an expectation-behavior relationship was assessed.

Although Farley et al. (1981) and Sheppard et al. (1988) have conducted meta-analyses on research focusing on TRA, the present study extended their work in two principle ways. First, the focus in the present investigation was on exercise intentions and behaviors. Farley et al. and Sheppard et al. were concerned with assessing the utility of TRA for explaining and predicting volitional behaviors in general. It is not possible from their results to determine the utility of the TRA constructs for the explanation and prediction of exercise intentions and behaviors. Second, given the relatively recent introduction of the TPB, neither Farley et al. nor Sheppard et al. were able to assess the degree to which perceived behavior control—the principal construct which differentiates TRA and TPB—provides for an increased understanding in behavior.

Method

Selection and Inclusion of Studies

The data were obtained from studies identified from three principle sources: computer searches, manual searches, and journal searches. The computer searches included *PsychLIT* (1975 to the present), *MEDLINE* (1975 to the present), *SPORTdiscus* (1975 to the present), and *Dissertation Abstract Ondisc* (DAO) (1975 to the present). The year 1975 was chosen as a starting point to coincide with the date when the TRA was introduced by Fishbein and Ajzen (1975). Also, manual searches were conducted using the reference lists from recent comprehensive empirical and narrative reviews (e.g., Blue, 1995; Godin, 1993). And finally, 12 journals considered likely to have pertinent research were searched: *Canadian Journal of Applied Sport Psychology, Health Psychology, International Journal of Sport Psychology, Journal of Applied Sport Psychology, Journal of Behavioral Medicine, Journal of Sport & Exercise Psychology, Journal of Sport Behavior, Journal of Sport Medicine and Physical Fitness, Journal of Sport Sciences, Perceptual and Motor Skills, Research Quarterly for Exercise and Sport,* and *The Sport Psychologist.*

The two principal criteria for initial selection were that the study (a) focused on exercise (i.e., participants were not identified as athletes, activity was not identified as sport, participants were not on teams or in organized leagues) and (b) incorporated at least two of the constructs contained in TRA or TPB. Those criteria notwithstanding, studies were discarded from further consideration if they failed to provide usable statistics to compute an effect size (ES).

An examination of the studies revealed that some contained repeated measures of some constructs. Thus, for example, a study examining the relationship of intention to exercise might have obtained assessments of exercise behavior at 3 months, 6 months, and one year. In this case, three ESs would have been available for the intention-behavior relationship. Wolfe (1986) has suggested that to ensure that one study does not have an inordinate impact on the overall ES, a composite value is more appropriate. Thus, in the above example, an average ES would have been calculated to represent the magnitude of the intention-behavior relationship over the three time periods.

Although it makes sense to combine different time point assessments for statistical purposes, theoretically, it negated the purpose of prospective exercise studies designed to observe changes over time relationship. Therefore, repeated measures of TRA/TPB were also kept separate to assess them. A total of 31 studies were used which yielded 162 ESs, based on $N = 10{,}621$ participants.

Intention Versus Expectation

As indicated above, a comparison was made between studies that have operationally defined the construct of intention as either an intention or an expectation. Studies examining intention were those that measured the extent to which a person "intends," "plans," "is determined," or "has decided" to perform the behavior. Studies examining expectation were those that measured the "probability" or "likelihood" of performing the behavior (cf. Blue, 1995; Courneya & McAuley, 1994).

Coding the Data

The characteristics of the study, the program of exercise, the participants, and the measures were coded for each research article. Information included in the study category included: sample size, response rate, client selection (random, volunteer, target), location (university, home, corporation, fitness club), psychometrics (internal consistency, test-retest reliability), and theory tested (TRA or TPB). The program category included the duration of the treatment (in weeks) and its frequency (times per week). The participant category involved coding for gender (male, female, both), age (adolescent, university, adult, senior), mean age, occupation, socioeconomic status, ethnicity, special population (pregnant women, disabled), and training status (trained, untrained). The measure category included the specific relationship—for example, intention and exercise behavior, perceived behavioral control and exercise behavior, and so on.

Results

Description of the Data

Study Characteristics. Insofar as the studies are concerned, 41.9% examined TPB and 58.1% examined the TRA. A major strength of the TRA and TPB is that an elicitation study forms the basis for instrument development. In accordance with the Ajzen and Fishbein (1980) protocol, elicitation studies were reported for constructing an instrument only 51.5% of the time.

The psychometric properties of the scales used were reported in 83.9% of the studies. That is, 58.1% reported internal consistency values, 12.9% reported test-retest reliabilities, and 12.9% reported both. The majority of the studies were conducted in a university setting (50%), followed by corporations (6.5%), fitness clubs (6.5%), the community (16.1%), and home (16.1%).

Sample Characteristics. The majority of the participants were volunteers (64.5%), followed by target groups (22.6%), and random assignment (9.7%). Only 9.7% of the studies reported on ethnicity, 19.4% reported on participant occupation, 19.4% on social economic status, and 48.4% reported the response rate of the participants.

In regards to gender, the majority of the studies (83.3%) utilized mixed samples of males and females. Special populations examined were pregnant women (3.2%), cardiac patients (12.9%), and disabled (3.2%). Due to the low number of ESs, no comparisons were possible on the basis of these participant characteristics.

General Analyses

The Theory of Reasoned Action. The direct determinant of exercise behavior according to the TRA is intention. A large ES of 1.09 was found between intention and behavior. This finding is in line with Davis, Jackson, Kronenfeld, and Blair (1984), who concluded that behavioral intention is "one of the most important and one of the most consistently relevant predictors of continued participation in health improvement programs" (p. 362).

According to TRA, the direct determinants of an intention to adopt an exercise behavior are the constructs of attitude and subjective norm. Attitude was over two times more useful as a predictor of intention to exercise, ES = 1.22, *SD* = .05, than was subjective norm, ES = 0.56, *SD* = .07; $t(44) = 33.87$, $p < .001$.

As a general interest, the direct relationships between attitude and exercise behavior and between subjective norm and exercise behavior were examined (cf. Rentier & Speckart, 1981). A large relationship was present between attitude and exercise behavior (ES = 0.84), whereas the subjective norm-behavior relationship was zero-order (ES = 0.18). The difference was statistically significant, $t(28) = 22.28$, $p < .001$. These results support a conclusion that while subjective norm is a useful construct for predicting intention to exercise, it is not a useful direct predictor of exercise.

A note of caution concerning the interpretation of the results is warranted. The constructs within TRA and TPB are interrelated (and ordered in a specific manner in the respective models). The ESs reported here undoubtedly overestimate the magnitude of the overall relationships within these models. It would have been beneficial to examine the predictive utility of both TRA and TPB using hierarchical regression or path analysis. However only 14 ESs were available to examine the complete TRA model, and 8 ESs were available to examine the complete TPB model. Consequently, due to insufficient power, neither a hierarchical regression nor a path analysis were computed (cf. Green, 1991).

The Utility of Perceived Behavioral Control. As indicated earlier, perceived behavioral control was added to TRA by Ajzen (1985)—thereby producing TPB—in an attempt to improve the predictive validity of the model. There is strong support for this addition insofar as exercise behavior is concerned. Perceived behavioral control had a large relationship with both exercise behavior (ES = 1.01) and intention to exercise (ES = 0.97). The results of the present study clearly support a conclusion that TPB is superior to TRA for predicting and explaining exercise intentions and behaviors.

Proximal and Distal Measures. As indicated above, Fishbein and Ajzen (1975) proposed that the predictive power of an intention will vary inversely with the time between the measurement of that intention and the observation of the behavior. Thus, the issue of proximity of measurement and prediction in the intention-behavior relationship was examined in those studies (n - 4) where multiple measures of subsequent behavior were available. No differences were observed between the magnitude of the ES for the intention-proximal behavior relationship (ES = 1.10, *SD* = .06) and the intention-distal behavior relationship (ES = 1.10, *SD* = .08). These results should be treated with some caution, however, given the small number of studies that have addressed the issue.

Intention Versus Expectation. As was pointed out above. Sheppard et al. (1988) have suggested that expectation might be a better predictor than intention for behaviors where there are constraints on involvement (i.e., barriers to exercise). The published reports available for the meta-analysis did not provide for an opportunity to distinguish between studies focusing on volitional versus non-volitional exercise behavior. It was possible, however, to contrast those studies that measured an intention-behavior relationship (74.2%) with those studies that measured an expectation-behavior relationship (22.6%). The results indicated a significantly larger relationship, $r(30) = 8.24$, $p < .001$, was present for the expectation-exercise behavior relationship, ES = 1.26, *SD* = .06, $n = 8$, than for the intention-exercise behavior relationship, ES = 1.04, *SD* = .08, $n = 24$. Thus, a researcher interested in examining general predictions emanating from TRA or TPB should use the construct of intention. On the other hand, if the primary interest is in predicting exercise behavior, the construct of expectation appears to be more useful.

Discussion

The TRA and TPB provide a theoretical structure for examining exercise behavior in a number of settings and populations. The purpose of the present investigation was to use meta-analysis to statistically examine the utility of TRA and TPB for explaining and predicting of exercise behavior. The results provide strong general support for the validity of TRA and TPB. A number of specific results bear reemphasizing. First, the results showed that intention has a large effect (ES = 1.09) on exercise behavior. There is little doubt that after individuals have formed the intention, exercise behavior results.

Second, the results also showed that attitude has a large effect on intention to exercise (ES = 1.22), whereas subjective norm has only a moderate effect on intention to exercise (ES = 0.56). These results are not inconsistent with TRA and TPB. That is, both TRA and TPB contain the proposition that some intentions are more likely to be under attitudinal control and, therefore, be better predicted by attitude, whereas intentions to perform other behaviors are more likely to be under normative control and be better predicted by subjective norms (Ajzen & Fishbein, 1980). The present results illustrate that, insofar as exercise behavior is concerned, the construct of intention is more strongly related to the construct of attitude. What is not clear at this point, however, is the underlying reasons. A number of authors have questioned how subjective norm has been operationally defined (cf. Grube, Morgan, & McGree, 1986; Miniard & Cohen, 1981). Thus, insofar as the explanation of exercise behavior is concerned, subjective norm either may be a less useful construct than attitude (as well as perceived behavioral control and intention) or it may be that there have been limitations in its operationalization.

As a secondary purpose, the utility of TRA and TPB were compared by quantifying the relationships between perceived behavioral control and both intention and exercise behavior. The results showed that perceived behavioral control is an important construct for understanding exercise involvement; it has a large effect on both intention to exercise (ES = 0.97) and exercise behavior itself (ES = 1.01). Ajzen (1985) has argued that TRA, which relies on intention as the sole predictor of behavior, is insufficient whenever control over the behavioral goal is incomplete (i.e., even though people may have a strong intent to perform the behavior, other factors may interfere with their ability to do so). Therefore, it was proposed that an individual's perceived control over the behavior must be assessed to ensure accurate prediction of intentions and behaviors (Ajzen, 1985). The present investigation provides support for the greater predictive utility of TPB over TRA.

The role of perceived behavioral control is important for the explanation and prediction of exercise involvement for a number of reasons. First, the strong relationship between perceived behavioral control and intention contributes to the suggestion that the more the attainment of a behavioral goal is considered to be under personal volitional control, the stronger will be the relationship with an intention to perform the behavior. Considered together, perceived behavioral control and intention add to the explanation and understanding of exercise behavior.

Second, the strong relationship between perceived behavioral control and exercise behavior is consistent with Ajzen's (1985) proposition that perceived behavioral control can influence behavior independent of the mediating effect of intention (which is contrary to the propositions of TRA). Therefore, at this very preliminary stage, TPB demonstrates promise for the explanation and prediction of exercise behavior above and beyond that afforded by TRA (Willis & Campbell, 1992, pp. 79-91). TPB accommodates one of the more difficult problems associated with exercise adherence—the fact that there are general barriers to regular exercise participation.

Third, the strong relationships between exercise behavior and both perceived behavioral control and attitude contribute to the suggestion that individuals have the greatest commitment to exercise when they hold favorable beliefs about exercise and believe that they can successfully perform the behavior. The direct influence of attitude on exercise behavior has been commented upon previously by Bentler and Speckart (1981), who found that attitudes were more important than intentions for the prediction of exercise behavior. This reinforces the suggestion that variables other than intentions have an effect on future behavior (Godin, 1993).

As another secondary purpose, the question of the proximity of the measurement of intention to behavior and the resulting effectiveness of prediction was examined. Contrary to the intuitively logical postulation of Fishbein and Ajzen (1975), the present results supported a conclusion that the predictive power of an intention does not vary inversely with the time between the measurement of that intention and the observation of the behavior. This conclusion must be treated with caution, however, due to the small number of ESs available to test the postulation. A third and final secondary purpose involving a comparison of the expectation-behavior relationship and the intention-behavior relationship found larger ES for the former. Expectation is the probability of the behavior being performed, whereas intention involves making a behavioral commitment to perform (or not perform) the behavior. The formation of an expectation may involve a variety of factors (e.g., anticipated changes in intention, noncognitive habits, ability limitations, and environmental facilitators or constraints) that could influence behavior beyond that of intention (Courneya & McAuley, 1993b).

Areas of future research became evident through the meta-analysis. Researchers should continue to examine the TPB in exercise behavior with a view to determining potential moderator variables (e.g., age, gender, and training status) that are related to physical activity levels. The sample of research available for the present meta-analysis was not sufficient to validly examine the role of these potential moderators. Also, future studies, in accordance with the Ajzen and Fishbein (1980) protocol, should report elicitation studies and psychometric properties of the scales used. Finally, future studies should examine the predictive power of an intention to exercise behavior over time. Are intentions to exercise stable over time, or unstable over time due to changes in attitude, subjective norm, or perceived behavioral control?

The results of the current meta-analysis have implications not only for TRA and TPB, but for various social cognitive models (i.e., self-efficacy theory, protection motivation theory, and health belief model) used to examine exercise behavior (Brawley, 1993; Maddux, 1993; Maddux, Brawley, & Boykin, 1995; Maddux & DuCharme, in press; Weinstein, 1993). These models "share a number of specific components or ingredients that should compel researchers to view these models not as competitors to be pitted against one another, but rather as complementary and amenable to integration" (Maddux et al., 1995, p. 186). For example, the importance of perceived behavioral control (PBC) as a predictor of behavior is supported by research on self-efficacy—a construct similar, but not identical to PBC (Maddux & DuCharme, in press).

Maddux (1993; Maddux & DuCharme, in press; Maddux et al., 1995) have suggested that an improved approach in the theoretical examination of exercise behavior is to incorporate the major features of the models mentioned above into a single model and then attempt to determine the relative importance of the various constructs. TPB is proposed as the vehicle for integration because it contains most of the major components of the other models. If this integration is undertaken, the results of the current study will have implications for the proposed integrated model. Finally, the results of the present study should have implications for health professionals. The constructs embedded in the TPB—attitude, subjective norm, perceived behavioral control, and intention—have considerable utility in predicting and explaining exercise behavior. A knowledge of TPB could help exercise practitioners understand the key elements associated with initiating and maintaining exercise behavior. It could also help them evaluate changes in exercise behaviors that occur as a result of planned interventions. As Kurt Lewin (1951) has proposed, "there is nothing so practical as a good theory" (p. 169). The results from the present study provide strong evidence that the theory of reasoned action is a good theory; its extension, the theory of planned behavior, is an even better theory.

References

Ajzen, I. (1985). From intention to actions: A theory of planned behavior. In J. Kuhl & J. Beckman (Eds.), *Action control: From cognition to behavior* (pp. 11-39). Heidelberg: Springer.

Ajzen, I. (1988). *Attitudes, personality, and behavior.* Chicago, IL: Nasey.

Ajzen, I. (1991). The theory of planned behavior. *Organizational Behavior and Human Decision Processes, 50,* 179-211.

Ajzen, I., & Driver, B. L. (1991). Prediction of leisure participation from behavior, normative, and control beliefs: An application of the theory of planned behavior. *Leisure Sciences, 13,* 185-204.

Ajzen, I., & Fishbein, M. (1980). *Understanding attitudes and predicting social behavior.* Englewood Cliffs, NJ: Prentice-Hall.

Ajzen, I., & Madden, T. J. (1986). Prediction of goal directed behavior: Attitudes, intentions, and perceived behavioral control. *Journal of Experimental Social Psychology, 22,* 453-474.

Andrew, G. M., Oldridge, N. B., Parker, J. O., Cunningham, D. A., Rechnitzer, P. A., Jones, N. L., Buck, C., Kavanagh, T., Shephard, R. J., Sutton, J. R., & McDonald, W. (1981). Reasons for dropout from exercise programs in post coronary patients. *Medicine and Science in Sports and Exercise, 13,* 164-168.

Bentler, P. A., & Speckart, G. (1981). Attitudes "cause" behavior: A structural equation analysis. *Journal of Personality and Social Psychology, 40,* 226-238.

Berger, E. G., & McInman, A. (1993). Exercise and the quality of life. In R. N. Singer, M. Murphy, & L. K. Tennant (Eds.), *Handbook of research on sport psychology* (pp. 729-760). New York: Macmillan.

Blue, C. L. (1995). The predictive capacity of the theory of reasoned action and the theory of planned behavior in exercise research: An integrated literature review. *Research in Nursing and Health, 18,* 105-121.

Brawley, L. R. (1993). The practicality of using social psychological theories for exercise and health research and intervention. *Journal of Applied Sport Psychology, 5,* 99-115.

Cohen, J. (1969). *Statistical power analysis for the behavioral sciences.* New York: Academic.

Cohen, J. (1992). A power primer. *Psychological Bulletin, 112,* 115-119.

Courneya, K. S., & McAuley, E. (1993a). Can short-range intentions predict physical activity participation? *Perceptual and Motor Skills, 77,* 115-122.

Courneya, K. S., & McAuley, E. (1993b). Predicting physical activity from intention: Conceptual and methodological issues. *Journal of Sport & Exercise Psychology, 15,* 50-62.

Courneya, K. S., & McAuley, E. (1994). Factors affecting the intention-physical activity relationship: Intention versus expectation and scale correspondence. *Research Quarterly for Exercise and Sport, 65,* 280-285.

Davis, K. E., Jackson, K. L., Kronenfeld, J. J., & Blair, S. N. (1984). Intent to participation in worksite health promotion activities: A model of risk factors and psychosocial variables. *Health Education Quarterly, 11,* 361-377.

Dishman, R. K. (1988). Epilogue and future directions. In R. K. Dishman (Ed.), *Exercise adherence: Its impact on public health* (pp. 417-426). Champaign, IL: Human Kinetics.

Dishman, R. K. (1993). Exercise adherence. In R. N. Singer, M. Murphy, & L. K. Tennant (Eds.), *Handbook of research on sport psychology* (pp. 779-798). New York: Macmillan.

Dishman, R. K., & Gettman, L. R. (1980). Psychobiological influences on exercise adherence. *Journal of Sport Psychology, 2,* 295-310.

Farley, J. U., Lehmann, D. R., & Ryan, M. J. (1981). Generalizing from imperfect replication. *Journal of Business, 54,* 597-610.

Fishbein, M., & Ajzen, I. (1975). *Belief, attitude, intention and behavior.* Don Mills, NY: Addison Wesley.

Glass, G. V., McGraw, B., & Smith, M. L. (1981). *Meta-analysis in social research.* Newbury Park, CA: Sage.

Godin, G. (1993). The theories of reasoned action and planned behavior: Overview of findings, emerging research problems and usefulness for exercise promotion. *Journal of Applied Sport Psychology, 5,* 141-157.

Green, S. B. (1991). How many subjects does it take to do a regression analysis? *Multivariate Behavioral Research, 20,* 449-510.

Grube, J. W., Morgan, M., & McGree, S. T. (1986). Attitudes and normative beliefs as predictors of smoking intentions and behaviors: A test of three models. *British Journal of Social Psychology, 25,* 81-93.

Hedges, L. V. (1981). Distribution theory for Glass's estimates of effect size and related estimates. *Journal of Educational Statistics, 6,* 107-128.

Hedges, L. V. (1982). Fitting categorical models to effect sizes from a series of experiments. *Journal of Educational Statistics, 7,* 114-137.

Hedges, L. V., & Olkin, I. (1980). Vote counting methods in research synthesis. *Psychological Bulletin, 88,* 359-369.

Hedges, L. V., & Olkin, I. (1985). *Statistical methods for meta-analysis.* New York: Academic.

Heinzelmann, P., & Bagley, R. W. (1970). Response to physical activity programs and their effects on health behaviors. *Public Health Reports, 85,* 905-911.

Hunter, I. E., & Schmidt, F. L. (1990). *Methods of meta-analysis: Correcting error and bias in research findings.* Newbury Park, CA: Sage.

Lewin, K. (1951). *Field theory in social science.* New York: Harper.

Light, R. J., & Smith, P. V. (1971). Accumulating evidence: Procedures for resolving contractions among different research studies. *Harvard Educational Review, 41,* 429-471.

Maddux, J. E. (1993). Social cognitive models of health and exercise behavior: An introduction. *Journal of Applied Sport Psychology, 5,* 116-140.

Maddux, J. E., Brawley, L., & Boykin, A. (1995). Self-efficacy and healthy behavior: Prevention, promotion, and detection. In J. E. Maddux (Ed.), *Self-efficacy, adaptation, and adjustment: Theory, research, and application* (pp. 173-202), New York: Plenum.

Maddux, J. E., & DuCharme, K. A. (in press). Behavioral intentions in theories of health behavior. In D. Gochman (Ed.), *Handbook of health behavior research.* New York: Plenum.

Massie, J. F., & Shephard, R. (1971). Physiological and psychological effects of training: A comparison of individual and gymnasium programs, with a characterization of the exercise "drop out." *Medicine and Science in Spans and Exercise, 3,* 110-117.

Miniard, P. W., & Cohen, J. B. (1981). An examination of the Fishbein-Ajzen behavioral-intention model's concepts and measures. *Journal of Experimental Social Psychology, 17,* 309-339.

Oldridge, N. B. (1979). Compliance of post myocardial infarction patients to exercise programs. *Medicine and Science in Sports and Exercise, 11,* 373-375.

Poag-DuCharme, K. A., & Brawley, L. R. (1993). Self-efficacy theory: Use in the prediction of exercise behavior in the community setting. *Journal of Applied Sport Psychology, 5,* 178-194.

Rosenthal, R. (1979). The "file drawer" problem and tolerance for null results. *Psychological Bulletin, 86,* 638-641.

Rosenthal, R. (1995). Writing meta-analytic reviews. *Psychological Bulletin, 118,* 183-192.

Sheppard, B. H., Hartwick, J., & Warshaw, P. R. (1988). The theory of reasoned action: A meta-analysis of past research with recommendations and future research. *Journal of Consumer Research, 15,* 325-343.

Thomas, J. R., & French, K. E. (1986). The use of meta-analysis in exercise and sport: A tutorial. *Research Quarterly for Exercise and Sport, 57,* 196-204.

Wankel, L. M. (1993). The importance of enjoyment to adherence and psychological benefits from physical activity: Special issues. Exercise and psychological well-being. *International Journal of Sport Psychology, 24,* 151-169.

Warshaw, P. R., & Davis, F. D. (1985). Disentangling behavioral intention and behavioral expectation. *Journal of Experimental Social Psychology, 21,* 213-228.

Weinstein, N. D. (1993). Testing four competing theories of health-protective behavior. *Health Psychology, 12,* 324-333.

Willis, J. D., & Campbell, L. F. (1992). *Exercise psychology.* Champaign, IL: Human Kinetics.

Wolfe, P. M. (1986). *Meta-analysis: Quantitative methods for research synthesis.* London: Sage.

Wurtele, S. K., & Maddux, J. E. (1987). Relative contributions of protection motivation theory components in predicting exercise intentions and behavior. *Health Psychology, 6,* 453-466.

12

HIV Risk Behavior Reduction Following Intervention With Key Opinion Leaders of Population

An Experimental Analysis

Jeffrey A. Kelly, Janet S. St. Lawrence, Yolanda E. Diaz, L. Yvonne Stevenson, Allan C. Hauth, Ted L. Brasfield, Seth C. Kalichman, Joseph E. Smith, and Michael E. Andrew

Introduction

Experience in many health promotion areas supports the importance of social influence as a determinant of population risk behavior patterns.[1-3] Gay men who successfully implement risk reduction report greater peer support for behavior change than their unsuccessful counterparts,[4-6] while beliefs that one's friends have already made precautionary changes and that these changes will be well accepted predict compliance with acquired immunodeficiency syndrome (AIDS) risk reduction recommendations,[5-6] condom use or other safer-sex modifications.[7-8]

Persons frequently seek the advice of friends concerning steps needed to reduce risk for AIDS.[9] Diffusion of innovation theory posits that trends and innovations are often initiated by a relatively small segment of opinion leaders in the population.[10]

Once visibly modeled and accepted by natural opinion leaders, innovations then diffuse throughout a population, influencing others. The purpose of this investigation was to experimentally test an AIDS prevention intervention based on diffusion of innovation/social influence principles. Because HIV (human immunodeficiency virus) risk behavior levels remain high among gay men in small cities[5,6,11] and because geographically isolated communities constitute compact environments where it is feasible to experimentally evaluate community-level intervention of this kind, the project targeted homosexual men in small cities.

Methods

Setting and Baseline Survey

The study was conducted late in 1989 in Biloxi and Hattiesburg, Mississippi, and Monroe, Louisiana, selected because they are relatively small (populations of 50,000 to 75,000 residents), separated by at least 60 miles from one another or from any other city of larger size, and because each city had one or two large gay bars. Due to the geographical isolation of the cities and the paucity of other meeting places, these clubs tend to attract large, stable crowds of homosexual men and serve as the primary social setting in each city's gay community. An earlier survey of men patronizing clubs in these cities revealed alarmingly high rates of high-risk sexual behavior.[6] AIDS incidence data for the cities are not compiled, but data from local health department HIV testing sites indicate relatively low seroprevalence rates (approximately 2 percent) among all men who seek testing in the cities. This suggests that HIV infection prevalence is still moderate but will increase unless behavior changes among gay men are quickly implemented.

To obtain baseline data on population AIDS risk characteristics, men entering each city's clubs were initially surveyed over three consecutive nights. The survey measure was completed anonymously and individually at small tables located near the club entrances; men who completed the questionnaire on one night did not complete it again during the same three-night sampling period. In addition to demographic information, the measure assessed:

- knowledge about AIDS risk behaviors and risk reduction steps using a 23-item true/false test;[12]
- perceived social norms concerning the acceptability of adopting safer sex precautions measured by endorsement on 5-point Likert scales of five, statements (example: "My gay male friends insist on using condoms when they have intercourse") and yielding scores of 5 to 25;[5-6] and
- personal sexual behavior occurring over the past two months, including number of occurrences and different partners for unprotected insertive and receptive anal intercourse, anal intercourse with condoms, and other low-risk practices (frottage, mutual masturbation, and similar activities). This measure was pilot tested extensively and has been successfully used in prior surveys of gay men's risk behavior.[5,6,11]

The same survey procedure was repeated in a second three-day sampling period four months later at each club in each city to establish baseline stability in population risk characteristics. A preliminary review of survey data revealed that AIDS risk knowledge scores were consistently high among men in each city ($M = 21$ of 23 items answered correctly) so basic knowledge items were deleted from subsequent surveys. Counts were made of the total number of men who entered clubs to determine the proportion of the entire population successfully surveyed.

Study Design and Intervention Procedures

Following baseline population assessments in all cities, one community (Biloxi) was randomly selected to receive the intervention while the other two communities served as comparison cities. The comparison cities received no specific intervention, although AIDS prevention posters and brochures were generally available in gay clubs in the cities. No significant differences in population risk behavior were found between the two comparison cities.

In the intervention city, a three-stage process identified, trained, and then contracted with popular opinion leaders among gay men to endorse behavior change to their peers.

Identification of Opinion Leaders. To identify key popular people, four club bartenders familiar with population members were trained to observe social interaction patterns within the city's gay clubs. Each made unobtrusive behavioral observations in the clubs for one week, recording first names and a physical identifier for 30 persons observed to socialize and be greeted positively most often by men in the clubs. Recording sheets were cross-matched for repeated mention; 36 of a total of 82 names received multiple nominations and were considered key popular people. Twenty-two were located, entered in the program, and asked to invite one friend also considered to be highly popular with gay men and not already a participant. The total training group consisted of 39 men and four women with a mean age of 30 years and a mean education level of 13.8 years; 91 percent of the group was White and 9 percent African-American or Hispanic.

Training the Opinion Leaders. The training consisted of four weekly, 90-minute group sessions led by a male and a female leader. In session one, the leaders reviewed basic epidemiology of HIV infection, high-risk behavior, and precautionary changes needed to reduce risk and misconceptions concerning risk. They discussed the steps that can be used to successfully implement risk reduction, including: keeping condoms readily available if sexually active; avoiding excessive intoxicant use before sex; discussing precautions in advance with sexual partners; resisting coercions to engage in high-risk practices; and self-reinforcing for behavior change efforts.

Session two described characteristics of effective health promotion messages: sensitizing others to the potential threat of AIDS; stressing that HIV infection can be prevented by behavior change; identifying specific behavior changes needed to reduce risk; suggesting strategies for implementing these changes; using self as an example in order to avoid a "preachy" tone (i.e., beginning statements with "I am learning to . . ." rather than "You should . . ."); and personally endorsing the positive value and desirable benefits of behavior change.

In the third session, leaders modeled conversational examples which incorporated the characteristics discussed in session two. Following discussion of the enactments, participants role-played how they would initiate conversations, incorporating these message characteristics. Group leaders and assistants observed this social skill rehearsal, providing feedback and suggestions. After becoming proficient in the role-plays, each participant identified four gay male friends with whom he or she could initiate an endorsement conversation in the next week. Monitoring forms were provided for recording descriptions of these conversations.

Session four reviewed outcomes of the real-life conversations; most participants reported positive reactions from others. The leaders and participants then problem-solved persons, settings, strategies, and times which would afford opportunities to initiate additional conversational contacts with other peers. All members agreed to initiate and monitor at least 10 more peer conversations over the next two weeks. The session concluded with further discussion emphasizing the participants' important role in stressing the benefits of behavior changes to prevent HIV infection among gay men in their own community. Of the 43 opinion leaders who began the intervention, 35 attended all the sessions.

Later review of participants' self-monitoring forms indicated that 371 peer conversations were monitored over the two-week period. This probably underestimates the number of conversations which actually took place because peer conversations were likely to have continued beyond the monitoring phase. In addition, before and after the training program, each opinion leader was asked to role-play standard, simulated peer educational conversations. Ratings of the tape recorded role-plays were made by trained judges, naive to whether practice conversations were pre- or postintervention. These rates revealed that, after training, the opinion leaders more frequently exhibited skills taught in the program (data available on request to author). These checks confirm social skill acquisition and conversational assignment compliance by the opinion leaders.

To stimulate opportunities for initiating peer conversations, posters with a traffic light logo (red, yellow, and green circles) but no printed explanation were placed throughout the clubs shortly before the end of the intervention. Each training participant was given a small lapel button with the same logo and asked to wear it. Participants reported that this cueing device led many people to inquire about the meaning of the symbol. These questions, in turn, stimulated opportunities to explain precautionary changes from the traffic light scheme (high-risk, moderate-risk, low-risk) and endorse these changes in the conversational style that was practiced in training. The lapel buttons also served as visual cues which reinforced the endorsement of behavior change by well-known and popular individuals.

Several months after the intervention's completion, participants were recontacted by telephone, encouraged to continue their peer education conversations, and commended for their continued efforts.

Determining Change in Population Risk Characteristics. Surveys of all male club patrons in all cities were repeated in the same manner as at baseline three months and again six months after the end of the training period. Responses of training participants were excluded. Intervention city men reported they were approached to initiate a mean of 7.1 conversations, demonstrating that the conversations encouraged in the training program occurred frequently.

Results

A total of 659 surveys were completed at the two baseline survey periods (intervention city *N* = 328, comparison cities *N* = 331), and 608 men completed surveys at the two postintervention periods (intervention city *N* = 278, comparison cities *N* = 330). This was an average of 81 percent (range = 68 to 88 percent) of all men patronizing each city's clubs during the survey periods. Between 24 and 47 percent of the men who completed measures on one occasion were the same men who completed them earlier; over 70 percent of respondents lived in the city where the survey was conducted. The mean age of all men surveyed was 29.1 years; the mean education level 14.9 years; 86 percent of men were White and 14 percent African-American or Hispanic. There were no significant differences between intervention and comparison city populations, nor were there systematic changes over time within a city's surveyed population, for these characteristics.

For purposes of brevity, results of the two baseline surveys and the three- and six-month postintervention surveys are averaged as a single figure. Populations in the intervention and comparison cities were initially comparable in risk characteristics. At the postintervention surveys, the proportion of men who engaged in unprotected anal intercourse decreased by about 30 percent from their initial levels. Much less change was evident in the population of men in the comparison cities. Similarly, there was an increase in proportion of all anal intercourse occasions when condoms were used only in the intervention city. Finally, the intervention produced a decrease in the proportion of intervention city men who reported having multiple sexual partners in the preceding two months, an effect not found in the comparison cities.

Percentage distribution for number of sexual partners in the intervention and comparison populations before and after intervention [show] some shifts reflecting an increased proportion of intervention city men who had either one or no sexual partner from pre- to postintervention and slight general decreases in the proportion of men who had two or more partners. Survey responses of the male opinion leaders, examined separately, showed that in the two months before training, 39 percent of opinion leaders engaged in unprotected anal intercourse; in the postintervention survey, 24 percent engaged in this practice.

Distinctive changes in social norm measure scores were not associated with the intervention; only a general and modest pre- to posttest increase in scores was found (from *M* = 15.6 to 17.0). However, intervention city men who refrained from unprotected anal intercourse reported in posttest surveys receiving health message conversations from peers more (*M* = 6.3 conversations) than men who still engaged in unprotected receptive anal intercourse (*M* = 3.5) or in any unprotected anal intercourse (*M* = 4.8).

Discussion

To the best of our knowledge, this constitutes the first report of an experimentally controlled study evaluating a community-level field test of an intervention for HIV risk reduction. This study found that engaging key opinion leaders popular with gay men in small cities to serve as behavior change endorsers to their peers produced reductions in the proportion of men in the population who engaged in high-risk activities and produced concomitant, population-wide increases in precaution-taking. The magnitude of these shifts compares favorably to those commonly found following mass, community-based population intervention for other health behavior problems such as cigarette smoking and cardiovascular risk reduction. This suggests a cost-effective HIV prevention model that may be of benefit in interventions with gay men, intravenous drug users, adolescents, and other groups.

Several findings in this study were of particular interest. First, AIDS risk behavior knowledge scores were high among men in each city even before intervention, suggesting that lack of knowledge about AIDS was not a critical dimension in the populations studied and that intervention methods which induce behavior change implementation and social acceptability of changes are needed. Second, while we anticipated that the intervention would alter perceptions of social norms, the norm measure did not reflect changes parallel to the population behavior shifts. Generalized changes in sexual behavior may precede peer norm changes rather than cause the initial adoption of risk reduction. In that case, elements of the intervention responsible for population behavior change may have included frequent safety prompts delivered by credible peers, conversational dissemination of suggestions for implementing precautionary changes, legitimization of making risk reduction changes by opinion leaders, or other factors.

While the study's results are highly promising, a number of cautions must be raised. We studied only men who patronized clubs and relied on self-reports of behavior. However, the geographical isolation of the study cities, the stability of club populations over time, and the function of clubs as the major social setting for gay men in these communities supports the relevance of data collection at these sites. While self-report behavior measures are essential in large-scale HIV risk behavior research, other data corroborating population behavior change—such as changes in community STD (sexually transmitted disease) incidence, condom purchasing patterns, or HIV testing requests and infection incidence—are needed to substantiate future conclusions about intervention impact. Finally, only a small number of cities were involved in this demonstration. Wider-scale clinical field trials of such experimental models in multiple cities and with larger populations are needed to establish their generalizability.

References

1. Report of the Surgeon General: Reducing the health consequences of smoking: Twenty-five years of progress. Rockville, MD: U.S. Dept. of Health and Human Services, 1989.

2. Fredericksen LW, Solomon LC, Brehony KA: Marketing Health Behavior. New York: Plenum Publishing, 1984.

3. Rogers EM: Communication Strategies for Family Planning. New York: Free Press, 1973.

4. McKusick L, Coates TJ, Wiley J, Morin S, Stall R: Prevention of HIV infection among gay and bisexual men. Paper presented at the International Conference on AIDS, Washington, DC, 1987.

5. Kelly JA, St. Lawrence JS, Brasfield TL, Lemke A, Amidei T, Roffman RE, Hood HV, Smith JE, Kilgore H, McNeill C: Psychological factors which predict AIDS high-risk versus AIDS precautionary behavior. J Consult Clin Psychol 1990; 58:117-120.

6. Kelly JA, St Lawrence JS, Brasfield TL, Stevenson LY, Diaz Y, Hauth AC: AIDS risk behavior patterns among men in small cities. Am J Public Health 1990; 80:416-418.

7. Joseph JG, Montgomery SB, Emmons C, Kessier RC, Ostrow D, Wortman CB, O'Brien K, Eller M, Eshleman S: Magnitude and determinants of behavioral risk reduction: Longitudinal analysis of a cohort at risk for AIDS. Psychol Health 1987; 1:73-96.

8. McKusick L, Wiley JA, Coates TJ, Stall R, Saika G, Morin S, Charles K, Horstman W, Conant MA: Reported changes in the sexual behavior of men at risk for AIDS,

San Francisco, 1982-1984. Public Health Rep 1985; 100:622-629.

9. Ross MW, Carson JA: Effectiveness of distribution of information on AIDS: A national study of six media in Australia. NY State J Med 1988; 88: 239-241.

10. Rogers EM: Diffusion of Innovations. New York: Free Press, 1983.

11. St. Lawrence JS, Hood HV, Brasfield TL, Kelly JA: Differences in gay men's AIDS risk knowledge and behavior patterns in high and low AIDS prevalence cities. Public Health Rep 1989; 104:391-395.

12. Kelly JA, St. Lawrence JS, Hood HV, Brasfield TL: An objective test of AIDS risk behavior knowledge: Scale development, validation, and norms. J Behav Ther Exp Psychiatry 1989; 20:227-234.

13

The Systematic Influence of Gain- and Loss-Framed Messages on Interest in and Use of Different Types of Health Behavior

Alexander J. Rothman, Steven C. Martino, Brian T. Bedell, Jerusha B. Detweiler, and Peter Salovey

There is little question that persuading people to make healthier behavioral choices would provide substantial reductions in illness morbidity and premature mortality (Department of Health and Human Services, 1991). Yet the development of effective persuasive appeals has proved to be rather difficult. Even when a persuasive intervention has been shown to be effective in a particular health domain, more often than not it has been developed in the absence of a theoretical framework that could guide the application of the intervention more generally (Salovey, Rothman, & Rodin, 1998). Are there specific strategies that can be adopted to maximize the effectiveness of messages designed to promote healthy behavior?

Over the past 10 years, researchers have focused on the relative effectiveness of messages that emphasize the benefits of performing a behavior

EDITORS' NOTE: Reprinted from *Personality and Social Psychology Bulletin, 25,* pp. 1355-1369, copyright © 1999. Reprinted by permission of Sage Publications, Inc.

(gain-framed messages) and messages that emphasize the costs of not performing a behavior (loss-framed messages) (e.g., Meyerowitz & Chaiken, 1987; Rothman, Salovey, Antone, Keough, & Martin, 1993; see Rothman & Salovey, 1997, for a review). Although aspects of this approach can be traced back to earlier research on fear appeals (Leventhal, 1970), this particular line of research has been grounded in the basic tenets of Kahneman and Tversky's (1979; Tversky & Kahneman, 1981) prospect theory. The framing postulate of prospect theory states that people's decisions are sensitive to how information is presented. Specifically, people are risk-seeking in their preferences when considering loss-framed information but are risk-averse in their preferences when considering gain-framed information.

Consistent with the underlying tenets of prospect theory, Rothman and Salovey (1997) provided a taxonomy of situations that afford predictions as to when gain- or loss-framed health appeals are maximally persuasive. They proposed that when people are considering a behavior that they perceive involves some risk or uncertainty (e.g., it may detect a health problem), loss-framed appeals are more persuasive, but when people are considering a behavior that they perceive involves a relatively certain outcome (e.g., it prevents the onset of a health problem), gain-framed appeals are more persuasive. Current support for this framework is based on comparisons of the relative effectiveness of gain- and loss-framed appeals that have been drawn across studies conducted in different health domains. In this article, we describe two experiments that provide the first systematic tests of these predictions within the same health domain.

Integrating Message Framing and Health Promotion

Meyerowitz and Chaiken (1987) were the first investigators to examine the relative influence of gain- and loss-framed information on health behavior. They modified a pamphlet that promoted breast self-examination (BSE) so that it provided a series of either loss- or gain-framed statements about breast cancer and BSE. Consistent with their predictions, women who had received the loss-framed pamphlet were more likely to have performed the behavior over a 4-month follow-up period as compared to women who had read the gain-framed pamphlet. Several subsequent studies have similarly observed that providing people with loss-framed information is an effective way to promote the performance of or preferences for mammography (Banks et al., 1995), HIV-testing (Kalichman & Coley, 1995), amniocentesis (Marteau, 1989), skin cancer examinations (Block & Keller, 1995; Rothman, Pronin, & Salovey, 1996), and blood-cholesterol screening (Maheswaran & Meyers-Levy, 1990).[1] However, investigators also have found that providing people with gain-framed information is a more effective way to promote healthy behavioral practices, such as requests for a free sample of sunscreen (Detweiler, Bedell, Salovey, Pronin, & Rothman, 1999; Rothman et al., 1993), the use of infant car seats (Christophersen & Gyulay, 1981), and intentions to use condoms (Linville, Fischer, & Fischhoff, 1993).

How might these diverging findings be reconciled? Rothman and Salovey (1997) have proposed that the relative effectiveness of a gain- or loss-framed appeal is contingent on the type of behavior that is promoted. Loss-framed messages should be an effective means to promote behavior but only if engaging in that behavior is perceived to be risky or uncertain. Recall that Meyerowitz and Chaiken (1987) predicted an advantage for loss-framed messages because women reported that engaging in BSE was a risky behavior. In fact, a subsequent study (Meyerowitz, Wilson, & Chaiken, 1991) revealed that a loss-framed message about breast cancer promoted BSE only among those women who previously reported that they perceived BSE to be a risky behavior. If people perceived all health behaviors as risky, one would expect a consistent advantage for loss-framed appeals. However, not all health behaviors are perceived as risky or uncertain.

An important distinction between health behaviors can be made based on the function that they serve. Detection behaviors such as BSE or mammography serve to detect the presence of a health problem, and because they can inform people that they may be sick, initiating the behavior may be considered a risky decision. Although detection behaviors such as mammography provide critical long-term benefits, characterizing them as risky accurately captures people's subjective assessment of these behaviors (e.g., Hill, Gardner, & Rassaby, 1985; Mayer & Solomon, 1992; Meyerowitz & Chaiken, 1987). In contrast, prevention behaviors such as the regular use of sunscreen or condoms forestall the onset of an illness and maintain a person's current health status. In fact, these behaviors are risky only to the extent that one chooses not to take action. This distinction is important because it provides a useful heuristic to predict which behaviors people tend to perceive as risky and which behaviors people tend to perceive as relatively certain or safe (for a discussion of these issues, see Rothman & Salovey, 1997). Moreover, it suggests that loss-framed appeals would be more effective in promoting detection behaviors but gain-framed appeals would be more effective in promoting prevention behaviors.

To date, conclusions concerning the relative effectiveness of gain- and loss-framed appeals have had to rely on comparisons drawn across studies and across health domains. That these effects have been obtained across a variety of health threats is encouraging with respect to the generalizability of this approach to health promotion. However, the numerous differences between the health domains and health behaviors studied make it difficult to assert unequivocally that the relative influence of gain- and loss-framed appeals is contingent on the function of the behavior. Even within a single health domain, prevention and detection behaviors (e.g., condoms and HIV testing) can differ on dimensions such as cost, familiarity, difficulty, frequency, and the need for trained personnel to perform the behavior. These substantial differences leave open the possibility of alternative explanations for the observed pattern of findings. Studies are needed that experimentally manipulate both the framing of a health message and the function of a specific health behavior.

The following two experiments provide the empirical evidence needed to support the theoretical framework proposed by Rothman and Salovey (1997). Experiment 1 tested the proposed framework in the context of a hypothetical disease. The use of a hypothetical disease afforded the opportunity to construct a single health behavior that could be presented as either a prevention or a detection behavior. Of course, there are limitations to any study that relies on a hypothetical, and consequently unfamiliar, health problem. Experiment 2 complemented and extended the findings obtained in Experiment 1 by testing the proposed framework in the context of real health problems, tooth decay and gum disease, and using real health behaviors that differed only in terms of their described function (prevention vs. detection).

Experiment 1: The Letrolisus Virus

To test the prediction that gain-framed messages should be used to promote prevention behaviors and loss-framed messages should be used to promote detection behaviors, a scenario describing a hypothetical disease, the letrolisus virus, was developed. Participants were led to believe that the letrolisus virus was a real, highly contagious illness and were provided with either gain- or loss-framed information about an action to be taken that, depending on condition, was presented as a detection behavior (i.e., it determined whether you were infected with the virus) or a prevention behavior (i.e., it prevented you from becoming infected with the virus).

Because participants were reading about an illness that they had never heard of, we were concerned about variability in how thoroughly people processed the framed information. Any failure to sufficiently attend to the framed information constrains the formation of the different construals afforded by the two framed messages. Prior experimental work has shown that in the absence of situational pressures to attend to a persuasive message, the degree to which participants are dispositionally inclined to think deeply (i.e., score highly on a measure of need for cognition [NEC]) determines whether framing effects are obtained (Wegener, Petty, & Klein, 1994). Given that the health issue in this study had no prior relevance to participants, it was quite possible that any differential effects of gain- and loss-framed information on participants' behavioral intentions would be limited to those participants who were predisposed to process the messages deeply.

Likewise, although all participants were told that the illness was real and highly contagious, there was likely to be considerable variability in the degree to which participants felt at risk for both being and becoming infected with the virus. Any variability in perceived risk is important because interest in both a behavior that detects a viral infection and a behavior that prevents a viral infection should depend on feeling personally at risk for infection (Weinstein, Rothman, & Nicolich, 1998). People who believe that there is no chance that they are or will become infected should have little interest in a detection or a prevention behavior, regardless of how information about the behavior was framed. Ideally, to control for differences in perceived risk of infection, perceptions of risk for the virus should be assessed prior to the presentation of the framed information. However, this was not possible given that prior to the experimental manipulation, none of the participants had ever heard of the disease. Perceptions of risk for the new virus were thus measured after participants had read information about the virus and the recommended behavior.

Experiment 1 provided an opportunity to test the relative influence of gain- and loss-framed health information on intentions to perform a prevention and a detection behavior in a hypothetical health domain. We predicted that participants would express a greater willingness to perform the detection behavior after having read a loss-framed message but a greater willingness to perform the prevention behavior after having read a gain-framed message. Moreover, the predicted effect of message frame on behavioral intentions should be more pronounced for those participants who were likely to focus and elaborate on the message.

Method

Participants

The participants consisted of 176 undergraduates who volunteered to participate in this study (72 men, 95 women, and 9 who failed to report their gender). Participants were assigned randomly to one of four conditions in a 2 (behavior: prevention, detection) x 2 (message frame: gain, loss) between-participants design.

Materials

Health Information About the Letrolisus Virus. Participants were provided with the following brief summary of the letrolisus virus:

> The letrolisus virus is a highly contagious illness that is transmitted in much the same way as the common flu virus, but it has far more damaging consequences. The initial symptoms include mild to severe congestion in the nose, throat, and lungs along with difficulty breathing. Over time, however, the condition gradually gets worse, resulting in chronic lung problems and in some cases death.

Information About a Precautionary Behavior. Participants were provided with information about a way either to prevent or to detect the letrolisus virus. Half of the participants read the following about a behavior that was said to be a detection behavior:

> Doctors recommend that everyone make an appointment to be tested. When you arrive at your appointment you will receive a small injection of inactive viral material. Three days later, you must return to your doctor for a brief follow-up. If your skin has had a positive reaction to the injection, you will receive an oral medication that will eliminate the virus.

The remaining participants read the following about a behavior that was said to be a prevention behavior:

> Doctors recommend that everyone receive a complete inoculation. To do so, you will need to make an appointment to receive a single injection of the letrolisus virus. Three days later, you must return to your doctor for a brief follow-up and to receive a second, oral dose of the vaccine.

These behavioral descriptions were constructed so that the two behaviors were essentially equivalent yet retained the detection-prevention distinction. The one objective difference between the two behaviors was that in the detection procedure, taking the oral medication at the second visit is contingent on a positive skin reaction to the initial injection. This difference reflects a defining characteristic of a detection procedure (i.e., one is undergoing a diagnostic procedure that may indicate a need for treatment). Furthermore, the diagnostic criterion (i.e., a skin reaction) and the treatment (i.e., a single dose of an oral medication) were kept relatively innocuous to keep the two behaviors as similar as possible.

Message-Framing Manipulation. The description of each precautionary behavior contained three persuasive elements that were either gain- or loss-framed: a title, an introductory statement, and a concluding statement. In the gain-frame condition, these statements emphasized the benefits associated with performing the recommended health behavior (e.g., "Detection makes effective treatment possible. . . . If you detect the *letrolisus* virus early, you can get treatment to eliminate the infection without delay" and "Prevention ensures you of your health. . . . Getting an inoculation against the *letrolisus* virus is the best way to reduce your risk of infection and increase your body's resistance to the illness"). The loss-framed message emphasized the costs associated with not performing the recommended health behavior (e.g., "Failing to detect the virus may undermine effective treatment. If you detect the letrolisus virus too late, you greatly reduce the potential for effective treatment" and "Failing to prevent the virus may undermine your health. . . . Unless you get an inoculation against the letrolisus virus, your risk of infection will be very high and your body will have little resistance to the illness").

Dependent Variables

Behavioral Intentions. Three items assessed participants' intentions to perform the recommended behavior: (a) How likely would you be to get [the inoculation/ a test for the viral infection] sometime soon? (b) If you were faced with the decision of whether to get [the inoculation/tested for the viral infection] today, how likely is it that you would do so? and (c) How tempted would you be to put off getting [the inoculation/a test for the viral infection]? Each item was assessed on a 7-point scale ranging from 1 (*not at all*) to 7 (*extremely*). The items were combined into a single index with the third item reverse-scored ($\alpha = .83$).

Perceived Risk. One item assessed participants' perceived risk for developing the illness. Ratings were made on a 7-point scale ranging from 1 (*not at all*) to 7 (*extremely*).

NFC. At the end of the experiment, participants completed the 18-item NFC scale that assessed the degree to which individuals enjoy thinking about and elaborating on persuasive messages (Cacioppo, Petty, & Kao, 1984). Participants rated their agreement with each item on a 7-point scale ranging from 1 (*strongly disagree*) to 7 (*strongly agree*) ($\alpha = .87$). To avoid categorizing participants as low in NFC because of missing values, each participant's average score was multiplied by the total number of questions (18). Based on a median split, participants were categorized as either high ($N = 82$) or low ($N = 92$) in NFC.

Procedure

Participants were told that they would be reading a health alert concerning a real illness, although the details of this illness had been modified somewhat for this experiment. They were instructed to take the illness very seriously and to imagine vividly being at risk for contracting the disease. All participants read a brief description of the letrolisus virus. Next, participants read about either a prevention behavior (i.e., an inoculation) or a detection behavior (i.e., a diagnostic test). In each condition, half of the participants received gain-framed information about the behavior and half received loss-framed information about the behavior. After reading the health information, each participant completed a packet of measures.

Results

Perceived Risk for Contracting the Virus

Because perceived risk had to be assessed after participants had learned about the virus, a series of analyses was conducted to evaluate its status as a covariate in our subsequent analysis of the influence of message framing on participants' behavioral intentions. Consistent with the premise that participants' interest in a behavior would be contingent on their feeling at risk for contracting the virus, there was a significant positive correlation between perceived risk and behavioral intentions, $r(174) = .55$, $p < .001$. Perceptions of personal risk were analyzed in a 2 (NFC) x 2 (message frame) x 2 (behavior) ANOVA that revealed no significant main effect for or interactions involving message frame, *F*s < 1. The only significant effect obtained was a main effect of behavior such that participants who read about the prevention behavior reported a higher level of risk ($M = 4.51$, $SD = 1.50$) than did those who read about the detection behavior ($M = 3.86$, $SD = 1.42$), $F(1, 172) = 9.19$, $p < .01$.

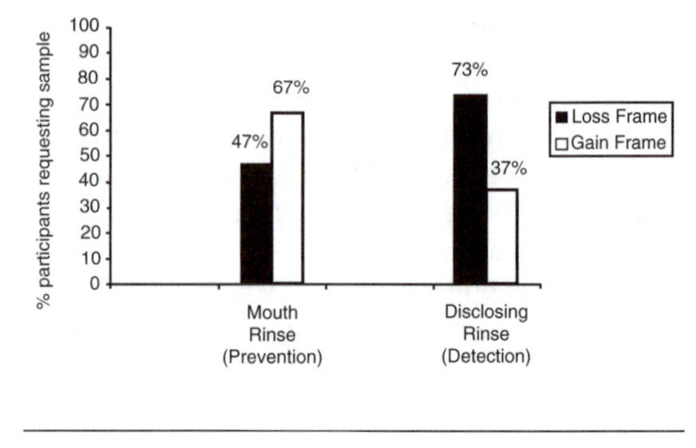

Figure 13.1 Intention to Perform the Recommended Behavior as a Function of Message Frame and Behavior for Participants High in Need for Cognition, Experiment 1

Intentions to Perform the Recommended Behavior

We predicted that participants would express stronger intentions to perform the detection behavior after having read loss-framed information about the health issue, whereas participants would express stronger intentions to perform the prevention behavior after having read gain-framed information about the issue. Moreover, this pattern of results was expected to be limited to those participants who would have thought systematically about the issue. Behavioral intentions were analyzed in a 2 (NFC) x 2 (message frame) x 2 (behavior) ANCOVA with perceived risk for contracting the virus included as a covariate. Consistent with predictions, the NFC x Frame x Behavior interaction was significant, $F(1, 165) = 4.37$, $p < .05$. Further analyses were conducted separately for people high and people low in NFC.

For those participants who were high in NFC, the predicted interaction between message frame and behavior was obtained, $F(1, 77) = 3.69$, $p < .06$. Participants expressed stronger intentions to perform the detection behavior after having read the loss-framed information than after having read the gain-framed message, $t(39) = 2.20$, $p < .05$. As expected, the pattern of means reversed when the behavior was said to be a prevention behavior, although this difference was not statistically reliable.

The behavioral intentions reported by participants who tended not to think about or elaborate on persuasive messages (i.e., low in NFC) were unaffected by either the frame or the behavior manipulation. (See Figure 13.1.)

Discussion

In this experiment, participants learned about a new health threat, the letrolisus virus, and were then provided with information about a precautionary behavior that was said to be either a prevention behavior (i.e., an inoculation) or a detection behavior (i.e., a diagnostic test). The information that participants received included three statements that systematically emphasized either the benefits of performing the behavior (gain-framed information) or the costs of not performing the behavior (loss-framed information). The results obtained in Experiment 1 were consistent with our predictions. Participants who were high in NFC (i.e., who enjoy thinking about and elaborating on persuasive messages) reported reliably greater intentions to perform a detection behavior after having read loss-framed information and somewhat greater intentions to perform a prevention behavior after having read gain-framed information.

Although the findings obtained across a series of previous studies have been consistent with the framework offered by Rothman and Salovey (1997), this experiment provided the first experimental demonstration of the contingent relation between message frame and type of behavior. The use of a hypothetical illness afforded the opportunity to present participants with prevention or detection behaviors that were nearly identical save for their different functions. However, the hypothetical nature of the illness and associated behaviors does place some limitations on the conclusions that can be drawn from this experiment, especially its generalizability. Because participants were unfamiliar with the health issue and, therefore, were not likely to find the issue particularly involving, the predicted findings were obtained only for those participants who—based on the individual difference measure of NFC—could be expected to think about and elaborate on the health information that was provided. Although the observation that participants low in NFC were unaffected by the experimental manipulations is consistent with the broader literature on the relation between NFC and persuasion (Cacioppo, Petty, Feinstein, Jarvis, & Blair, 1996), we sought to examine a real issue that would be involving for all people.

Experiment 2: Dental Health and Gum Disease

Are there any real health behaviors that can be understood to differ only in terms of the function they serve? In the area of dental hygiene, the answer is yes. People regularly use mouth rinses to prevent the buildup of dental plaque and the development of gum disease (Adams & Addy, 1994). However, other mouth rinses—called disclosing rinses—are used to detect the presence of dental plaque and the onset of gum disease.[2] In either case, the behavior can be easily incorporated into someone's regular dental hygiene habits. All one has to do is place a small amount of the rinse in one's mouth, swish it around, and then spit it out. In the case of prevention, the mouth rinse inhibits plaque from developing on a person's teeth. In the case of detection, the disclosing rinse identifies those areas of one's teeth where plaque has accumulated and indicates the areas at risk that need to be targeted for a thorough brushing.

In Experiment 2, participants were provided with either a gain- or a loss-framed pamphlet about plaque and gum disease that recommended an oral hygiene behavior that was said to either prevent plaque (a mouth rinse) or detect plaque (a disclosing rinse). By focusing on a familiar health problem and real health behaviors, this experiment addressed concerns that the findings obtained in Experiment 1 could not be generalized beyond a hypothetical disease. Because most, if not all, people are concerned about the accumulation of plaque and the development of cavities and gum disease, we expected that our participants would be motivated to attend to and process the framed material. Attention to the framed information also should be heightened by the fact that it was presented in a professionally designed pamphlet that was purportedly developed by the University of Minnesota Dental Health Communications Project. Finally, the use of real behaviors allowed us to offer participants the opportunity to mail in a postage-paid postcard to request a free sample of the recommended product. The rate at which people requested free samples provides a strong test of participants' interest in the product.

Not only did Experiment 2 test the framework outlined by Rothman and Salovey (1997) in the context of a real health issue but it also extended previous research in this area in several ways. Prior studies have provided people with gain- and loss-framed information, but there has been little attempt to include any assessment of the framing manipulation (but see Block & Keller, 1995). In this study, framing manipulation checks were included to ensure that the two framing conditions were correctly perceived as having emphasized gains or losses.

Immediately after reading the pamphlet, participants provided a complete list of the thoughts and feelings that they had had while reading the pamphlet. Investigators have routinely used thought listings to assess the extent to which participants have processed a persuasive communication (Eagly & Chaiken, 1993). This task provided an opportunity to examine whether exposure to gain- and loss-framed information elicits a similar degree of message elaboration. Some investigators have suggested that people may be less likely to process gain-framed information systematically (Maheswaran & Meyers-Levy, 1990; Smith & Petty, 1996). The thought-listing task also enabled us to test whether participants' cognitive responses to the information mediated the effect that the gain- and loss-framed messages had on interest in the recommended health behavior. Although investigators have successfully identified when gain- and loss-framed messages should be effective, they have had difficulty identifying the constructs that mediate their impact on behavior.

Method

Overview

The present experiment tested the relative effectiveness of gain- and loss-framed messages to promote the performance of detection and prevention behaviors in a 2 (message frame: gain, loss) x 2 (behavior: prevention, detection) between-participants design. Participants read a gain- or loss-framed pamphlet that described an oral hygiene behavior that either prevents or detects dental health problems. Subsequently, participants indicated their own attitudes and intentions concerning the behavior and were provided an opportunity to request a free sample of the recommended product.

Participants

Participants included 120 undergraduates (89 women, 31 men) from the University of Minnesota who responded to an advertisement for a study on communication and health behavior. Participants received $5 as compensation for completing the experiment.

Dental Hygiene Pamphlets

The dental health information was presented in a four-page pamphlet that was designed to appear professional and was attributed to the University of Minnesota Dental Health Communications Project. Four different versions of the pamphlet were developed. Two pamphlets promoted the use of a prevention behavior (mouth rinse), and two pamphlets promoted the use of a detection behavior (disclosing rinse). The two behaviors were operationalized such that they required the same actions (i.e., swishing liquid in one's mouth and spitting it out).

Of the participants who read about a standard mouth rinse, half read gain-framed information about the behavior (e.g., "People who use a mouth rinse daily are taking advantage of a safe and effective way to reduce plaque accumulation") and half read loss-framed information (e.g., "People who do not use a mouth rinse daily are failing to take advantage of a safe and effective way to reduce plaque accumulation"). Likewise, of the people who read about disclosing rinse, half read gain-framed information (e.g., "Using a disclosing rinse before brushing enhances your ability to detect areas of plaque accumulation") and half read loss-framed information (e.g., "Failing to use a disclosing rinse before brushing limits your ability to detect areas of plaque accumulation").

Care was taken to ensure that the gain- and loss-framed versions of the pamphlets provided the same information. Aside from specific details about the particular behavior promoted, all pamphlets presented the same general information about dental health. The pamphlet was divided into five sections: (a) how plaque is formed and how a cavity develops, (b) the development of gum disease, (c) proper oral hygiene behavior, (d) how mouth rinse (disclosing rinse) works, and (e) a recommendation to use mouth rinse (disclosing rinse).

Measures

Premanipulation Measures. There were three groups of premanipulation measures.[3]

1. *Demographics.* A series of items assessed general demographic information, including participants' age, gender, ethnic background, and educational background.

2. *Dental history.* A series of items assessed participants' dental hygiene practices and dental health background. These items included questions about how often participants brushed their teeth, flossed, and visited a dentist for routine examinations. Participants also reported their history of dental procedures as well as the number of cavities they recalled having had filled. Finally, participants were asked if they had ever suffered from any form of gum disease.

3. *Perception of risk and severity of gum disease.* Participants rated how likely they were to develop some form of gum disease if they continued their current dental hygiene practices. This rating was made on a 9-point scale ranging from 1 (*extremely unlikely*) to 9 (*extremely likely*). Participants also reported how worried they were about developing gum disease and how serious a problem developing gum disease would be. Each rating was made on a 9-point scale ranging from 1 (*not at all*) to 9 (*extremely*).

Postmanipulation Measures. There were six groups of postmanipulation measures.

1. *Thought-listing task.* Participants were asked to list the thoughts that they had while reading the pamphlet. Participants were instructed to list only one thought per box and that they need not use all of the boxes provided. Two judges, who were blind to framing condition, independently coded the thoughts listed on two different dimensions. First, judges coded the thoughts as either favorable (i.e., a statement expressing a positive reaction to the information contained in the pamphlet), unfavorable (i.e., a statement expressing a negative reaction to the information contained in the pamphlet), neutral (i.e., a statement about the information in the pamphlet expressing a reaction that was neither clearly positive nor clearly negative), or unrelated (i.e., a statement not associated with the information presented in the pamphlet). Interrater agreement on this dimension was high (r = .85), and disagreements were resolved through discussion.

The judges also coded each statement as to whether it indicated feelings of concern about the participant's own dental health (e.g., "My gums have been feeling sore lately") or feelings of reassurance about one's health (e.g., "I'm glad I take good care of my teeth"). Thoughts about dental health that expressed neither concern nor reassurance were classified as neutral, and thoughts not about dental health were classified as unrelated. Interrater agreement on this second dimension was acceptable (r = .79), and disagreements were resolved through discussion.

2. *Affective reactions to the pamphlet.* On a series of seven positive (assured, calm, cheerful, happy, hopeful, relaxed, relieved) and seven negative (anxious, afraid, discouraged, disturbed, sad, troubled, worried) adjective scales, participants indicated how they felt while reading the pamphlet. Ratings were made on a 7-point scale ranging from 1 (*not at all*) to 7 (*extremely*). Ratings of the negative items were reverse scored and an affective reaction index was constructed (α = .86).

3. *Perceptions of risk and severity of gum disease.* The three items included in the premanipulation measures were repeated in the postmanipulation questionnaire.

4. *Attitude toward the behavior.* Four questions assessed participants' attitude toward performing the behavior about which they had read. Participants rated the effectiveness of the behavior, how important it is to perform the behavior, how beneficial it is to perform the behavior, and how favorable they felt toward engaging in the behavior. Ratings were made on a 9-point scale ranging from 1 (*not at all*) to 9 (*extremely*). These questions were combined into a single index (α = .83).

5. *Behavioral intentions.* Three questions assessed participants' intentions regarding the behavior about which they had read. Using a 9-point scale ranging from 1 (*I have no intention of doing this*) to 9 (*I am certain that I will do this*), participants indicated how likely it was that they would buy the product within the next week and how likely it was that they would use the product in the next week. Using an open-ended response format, participants indicated how much they would pay for a 12-ounce bottle of the product.

6. *Evaluations of the pamphlet.* A series of five questions assessed participants' evaluation of the pamphlet. Participants indicated how interesting, involving, and informative they found the pamphlet. In each case, ratings were made on a 9-point scale ranging from 1 (*not at all*) to 9 (*extremely*). These three ratings were collapsed into a single index representing participants' evaluation of the quality of the pamphlet (α = .82).

Two questions provided a check on the framing manipulation. Participants judged the tone of the information included in the pamphlet on a 9-point scale ranging from -4 (*mostly negative*) to +4 (*mostly positive*), with the midpoint labeled *neutral.* Participants also indicated whether the pamphlet emphasized the benefits associated with doing the behavior or the costs associated with not doing the behavior. This rating was made on a 9-point scale ranging from -4 (*costs*) to +4 (*benefits*), with the midpoint labeled *equally emphasized.*

7. *Behavioral measure: Request for "free sample of product."* At the end of the experiment, participants were given a postage-paid postcard that they could mail in to receive a free sample of the promoted product (mouth rinse or disclosing rinse).

Procedure

Participants were scheduled individually or in groups of two to five individuals. The experimenter explained that the purpose of the experiment was to evaluate the effectiveness of pamphlets promoting proper dental hygiene. After signing a consent form, participants completed a packet of measures and were randomly given one of four pamphlets to read. Participants were instructed to take as much time as they wanted reading the pamphlet. When a participant was finished reading, the pamphlet was collected and the postmanipulation measures were distributed. At the close of the experiment, participants were given a postcard to mail in for a free sample of the product about which they had read.

Results

An initial set of analyses was conducted to determine whether any of the demographic or dental history variables moderated the effect of message frame and behavior on the postmanipulation measures. Because no moderating effects were obtained, all analyses are presented collapsed over these factors.

Evaluation of the Pamphlet and Manipulation Checks

Participants' evaluations of the pamphlet were examined to confirm that the pamphlets differed only in terms of how the health information was framed. Analyses revealed that participants' ratings of the quality of the pamphlet were unaffected by the framing manipulation, $F(1, 116) = 1.50, p > .20$, by the type of behavior promoted in the pamphlet ($F < 1$), or by the interaction between these two factors ($F < 1$).

To assess whether the framing manipulation was perceived as intended, participants rated whether the pamphlet placed more emphasis on the benefits associated with doing the behavior or the costs associated with not doing the behavior. Participants in the loss-framed condition judged the pamphlet as emphasizing costs more than benefits, whereas participants in the gain-framed condition judged the pamphlet as emphasizing benefits over costs, $F(1, 116) = 27.14, p < .001$. An examination of participants' ratings of the tone of the pamphlet revealed a similar pattern of results. Participants who read loss-framed information judged the tone of the pamphlet to be significantly more negative than did those who read gain-framed information, $F(1, 116) = 6.19, p < .05$. Finally, participants' affective reaction to the pamphlet was consistent with their perception of its tone. Participants reported having a more positive affective reaction to the gain-frame pamphlet than to the loss-framed pamphlet, $F(1, 116) = 8.39, p < .01$. No other effects on these measures approached significance, all Fs < 1.88.

Perceptions of Risk and Severity

Several items assessed participants' perceptions of the likelihood that they would develop some form of gum disease and the perceived severity of its development. Analyses of each of these measures controlled for participants' responses prior to reading the pamphlet. Participants first estimated the likelihood that they would develop some form of gum disease if they continued their current dental hygiene practices. An analysis of covariance controlling for participants' initial perceptions revealed a main effect of message frame, $F(1, 114) = 13.90, p < .001$. Participants who read loss-framed pamphlets felt more at risk for developing some form of gum disease provided they continued their current hygiene practices than did those who read gain-framed pamphlets. Participants in the loss-framed condition similarly reported that they were more worried about developing gum disease, $F(1, 114) = 7.41$, $p < .01$, and that the development of gum disease was a more serious problem, $F(1, 114) = 3.28$, $p < .08$. There were no other significant effects on any of these measures, $Fs < 1$.

Thought Reactions to the Pamphlet

The total number of issue-relevant thoughts listed by participants was examined to determine whether there were differences across conditions in amount of cognitive responding to the pamphlet. Participants listed the same number of thoughts in response to the pamphlet regardless of which behavior was promoted or how the information was framed (all $Fs < 1$).

We also examined the types of thoughts that participants had while reading the pamphlet. The overall valence of the thoughts that participants listed was determined by subtracting the number of unfavorable thoughts from the number of favorable thoughts. Participants who read the loss-framed pamphlet listed somewhat more favorable responses to the message than did participants who read the gain-framed pamphlet, $F(1, 116) = 3.46$, $p = .06$. The effect of behavior and the interaction between message frame and behavior were both not significant, $Fs < 1$. Further analyses were conducted separately on the number of favorable and unfavorable reactions that participants had listed. Although participants in the loss-framed condition listed more favorable reactions to the pamphlet than did those in the gain-framed conditions, $F(1, 116) = 3.42$, $p = .06$, there was no difference across conditions in the number of unfavorable reactions listed by participants, $F(1, 116) = 1.56$, $p > .20$.

To determine the valence of the thoughts that participants had about their own dental health, the number of negative thoughts about dental health that had been listed was subtracted from the number of positive thoughts listed. An analysis of this index revealed that participants who read loss-framed pamphlets listed more negative thoughts about their current dental health than did those who read gain-framed pamphlets, $F(1, 116) = 8.78$, $p < .005$. The effect of behavior and the interaction between message frame and behavior were both not significant, $Fs(1, 116) = 1.34$ and 0.73, $ps > .25$. Separate analyses of positive and negative statements about dental health also were conducted. Participants in the loss-framed conditions listed more thoughts expressing concern about their teeth and gums than did those in the gain-framed conditions, $F(1, 116) = 7.47$, $p < .01$. Although there was a tendency for people in the loss-framed condition to express fewer favorable thoughts about their dental health, this comparison was only marginally significant, $F(1, 116) = 2.88$, $p < .10$.

Attitude Toward the Behavior

Participants evaluated the behavior about which they had read on a series of four dimensions, and these ratings were combined into a single index. Participants' attitudes toward the behavior were found to be affected by both the type of behavior recommended, $F(1, 116) = 9.21$, $p < .01$, and how the information about the behavior was framed, $F(1, 116) = 13.46$, $p < .0001$. Participants reported holding more favorable attitudes toward the prevention behavior (mouth rinse) ($M = 7.13$, $SD = 1.58$) than toward the detection behavior (disclosing rinse) ($M = 6.11$, $SD = 1.55$). Participants who had read a loss-framed pamphlet held more favorable attitudes toward performing the behavior ($M = 7.04$, $SD = 1.48$) than did those who had read a gain-framed pamphlet ($M = 6.20$, $SD = 1.69$), regardless of which behavior was promoted in the pamphlet. The interaction between message frame and behavior was not significant, $F < 1$.

Behavioral Intentions

Several indicators assessed participants' intentions regarding the dental hygiene product about which they had read. We predicted that participants who read a gain-framed pamphlet that promoted mouth rinse would report stronger intentions to purchase and make use of the product than would participants who read a loss-framed version of the pamphlet. In contrast, for participants who read about disclosing rinse, we predicted that those who had read the loss-framed pamphlet would report stronger intentions regarding the product than would those who had read the gain-framed pamphlet.

Participants first reported their intentions to buy the product with in the next week. Consistent with predictions, the interaction between message frame and behavior was significant, $F(1, 116) = 7.22$, $p <. 01$. When participants read a pamphlet promoting the use of mouth rinse, those individuals who read gain-framed information reported stronger intentions to purchase the product ($M = 6.67$, $SD = 3.01$) than did those who read loss-framed information ($M = 5.33$, $SD = 2.81$). Conversely, when participants read about disclosing rinse, those individuals who read loss-framed information reported stronger intentions to purchase the product ($M = 4.43$, $SD = 2.58$) than did those who read gain-framed information ($M = 3.10$, $SD = 2.44$). There was also a main effect of behavior such that participants who read about mouth rinse reported stronger intentions to purchase the product ($M = 6.00$, $SD = 2.96$) than did those who read about disclosing rinse ($M = 3.77$, $SD = 2.58$), $F(1, 116) = 20.24$, $p <. 001$.

Participants' intentions to use the product about which they had read within the next week revealed a similar, albeit marginally, significant interaction between message frame and behavior, $F(1, 116) = 3.50$, $p = .06$. The pattern of the interaction was as predicted. In the prevention behavior condition, participants who read gain-framed information reported greater intentions to use mouth rinse within the next week ($M = 6.63$, $SD = 2.79$) than did those who read loss-framed information ($M = 5.83$, $SD = 2.70$), whereas in the detection behavior condition, participants who read loss-framed information reported greater intentions to use disclosing rinse within the next week ($M = 3.87$, $SD = 2.73$) than did those who read gain-framed information ($M = 2.87$, $SD = 2.30$). Overall, participants reported greater intentions to use mouth rinse within the next week ($M = 6.23$, $SD = 2.75$) than disclosing rinse ($M = 3.37$, $SD = 2.55$), $F(1, 116) = 35.48$, $p <. 001$.

Finally, participants reported how much they would be willing to pay for a 12-ounce bottle of the product. The ANOVA yielded the predicted interaction between message frame and behavior, $F(1, 116) = 4.24$, $p < .05$. Participants who read gain-framed pamphlets promoting the use of mouth rinse indicated that they were willing to pay more for the product ($M =$ \$3.23, $SD = 1.72$) than did participants who read loss-framed pamphlets ($M =$ \$2.89, $SD = 1.10$). Conversely, participants who read loss-framed pamphlets about disclosing rinse were willing to pay more for the product ($M =$ \$3.56, $SD = 1.96$) than did participants who read gain-framed pamphlets ($M =$ \$2.67, $SD = 1.59$). No other effects were significant.

Requests for Product Samples

All participants received a postcard that they could mail in to request a free sample of the recommended product. We predicted that participants would be more likely to request a sample of mouth rinse if they had read a gain-framed pamphlet than if they had read a loss-framed pamphlet but that participants would be more likely to request a sample of disclosing rinse if they had read a loss-framed pamphlet than if they had read a gain-framed pamphlet. Because the behavioral data were categorical, log-linear analysis was used. As predicted, the saturated model that contained the three-way interaction between message frame, behavior, and request provided the best fit of the data; moreover, removing the three-way interaction from the model significantly reduced the fit of the model.[4] Of those participants who read pamphlets promoting the use of mouth rinse, a greater percentage of participants in the gain-framed condition returned postcards requesting free samples (67%) than did those in the loss-framed condition (47%). Conversely, of those participants who read pamphlets promoting the use of disclosing rinse, a significantly greater percentage of participants in the loss-framed condition requested a sample of the product (73%) than did those in the gain-framed condition (37%, see Figure 13.2).

Mediational Analyses

Although there is substantial empirical evidence that the manner in which health information is framed influences behavioral decisions, little is known about the factors that mediate framing effects. Rothman and Salovey (1997) suggested several potential mediators that were assessed in this experiment: participants' affective reactions to

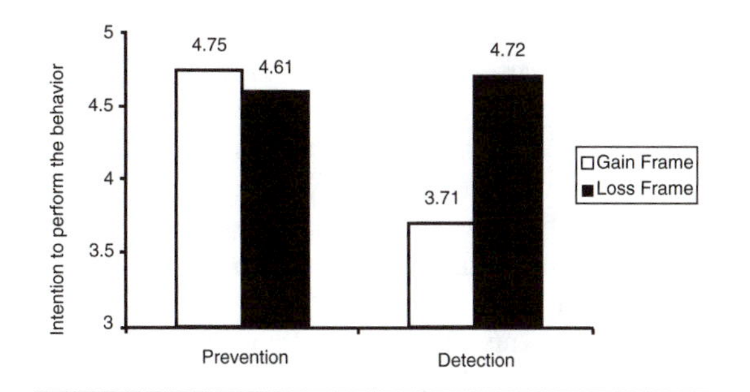

Figure 13.2 The Influence of Message Frame and Behavior on Requests for a Free Sample of the Recommended Dental Product, Experiment 2

the framed material, their cognitive responses to the material, their attitudes toward the recommended behavior, and their perceptions of risk and concern about the health threat. Mediational analyses were conducted to examine the effect of message frame on participants' behavioral intentions and their requests for a free sample of the recommended product. Because of the interaction between message frame and behavior, analyses were conducted separately for each behavior.

Detection Behavior (Disclosing Rinse). To test for mediation, the message-framing manipulation must have influenced the outcome variable, and the potential mediator must be both affected by the framing manipulation and related to the outcome variable (Baron & Kenny, 1986). Our analyses first focused on participants' behavioral intentions. To simplify the analysis, the three measures of behavioral intention were standardized and combined into a single index ($\alpha = .78$). Regression analysis revealed that participants' behavioral intentions were stronger after having read a loss-framed pamphlet than after having read a gain-framed pamphlet, B = .27, t(58) = 2.16, p < .05. Furthermore, participants' attitude toward the product and the overall valence of their thoughts about the material were each significantly affected by the framing manipulation (Bs = .36 and .26, *ps* < .05, respectively) and significantly related to the behavioral intention index (Bs = .65 and .47, *ps* < .0001, respectively).

To test for mediation, participants' behavioral intentions were first regressed onto the potential mediator and then message frame (coded -1 [gain-frame], 1 [loss-frame]) was entered into the regression model. When participants' attitudes toward the recommended product were included in the regression, there was a significant reduction in the effect that message frame had on behavioral intentions, B = .04, $t(57) = .41$, $p = .68$; $z = 4.25$, $p < .0001$.[5] Similar, albeit somewhat weaker, findings were obtained when the valence of participants' thoughts about the framed material was included as a mediator, B = .17, $t(57) = 1.46$, $p = .15$; $z = 1.63$, p < .05.

Mediational analyses also were conducted to test the relation between message frame and participants' request for a free sample of the recommended product (coded 0 [no], 1 [yes]). However, analyses revealed no significant relation between any of the potential mediators and requests for a free sample. Even the relation between behavioral intention and sample requests was only marginally significant, B = .18, $t(58) = 1.43$, $p < .16$. This pattern of findings precluded any further tests of a mediational model with respect to the sample requests.

Prevention Behavior (Mouth Rinse). Separate mediational analyses were conducted for participants' behavioral intentions and their requests for a free sample. Unexpectedly, none of the potential mediators satisfied the criteria necessary for testing a mediational model for the relation between message frame and behavioral intentions concerning mouth rinse. However, participants' behavioral intentions did satisfy the criteria necessary to test its role as a mediator for the influence of message frame on requests for a free sample of mouth rinse. When card requests were regressed on behavioral intention and message frame, there was a marginally significant reduction in the effect of message frame on card requests, B = -.13, $t(57) = 1.08$, $p = .28$; $z = 1.26$, p < .10, whereas the relation between behavioral intention and card request remained significant, B = .34, $t(57) = 2.74$, $p < .01$.

Discussion

The results obtained in Experiment 2 not only replicated those of Experiment 1 but also revealed the predicted relation between message frame and behavior in the context of a real health concern. When the use of mouth rinse was promoted, it was more effective to have participants read a gain-framed than a loss-framed pamphlet about gum disease. However, the loss-framed pamphlet was more effective when the use of disclosing rinse was promoted. This pattern of results provides strong empirical evidence in support of our conceptual framework.

Prior tests of the influence of framed information on attitudes and behavior have generally failed to confirm that the framed appeals were perceived to differ in their relative emphasis on benefits and costs (Rothman, Martino, & Jeffery, 1997). In the current experiment, participants' perception of the framed material was assessed. Although participants perceived all four versions of the pamphlet to be of equal quality, they correctly identified the tone and emphasis that the pamphlets were designed to convey.

The gain- and loss-framed pamphlets also elicited different cognitive responses from participants. Although people reported a similar number of thoughts, the loss-framed pamphlets elicited more favorable thoughts from participants, perhaps indicating that people are more familiar, and thus more comfortable with, health materials that focus on potential losses. However, regarding specific thoughts about their own dental health, the loss-framed pamphlets elicited more negative thoughts about participants' teeth and gums, whereas the gain-framed pamphlets elicited more reassuring thoughts about one's teeth and gums.

Participants' thoughts about the persuasive message and their attitudes toward the recommended behavior were more favorable when they had read the loss-framed as compared to the gain-framed pamphlet. The discrepancy between these results and the differential effect of frame on subsequent behavior is striking but is consistent with prior research (e.g., Banks et al., 1995; Rothman et al., 1993; but see Meyerowitz & Chaiken, 1987). This pattern of findings constrained attempts to identify the processes that underlie the persuasive influence of message framing on behavior. Analyses indicated that the influence of loss-framed messages on behavioral intentions was mediated by participants' attitude toward the behavior and the valence of their thoughts about the pamphlet. However, participants' behavioral intentions did not mediate the effect of message frame on requests for a free sample of disclosing rinse. Conversely, although none of the variables measured in this study mediated the effect of gain-framed information on intentions regarding mouth rinse, there was some evidence that participants' reported behavioral intentions mediated the influence of message frame on requests for a free sample of mouth rinse. Given the strong and consistent pattern of behavioral findings, the consistently weak evidence for mediation is a clear indication that a more systematic account of how framed information influences behavior is needed.

General Discussion

A number of investigators have asserted that framing messages systematically in terms of either benefits or costs can provide an effective way to promote health behaviors (e.g., Banks et al., 1995; Kalichman & Coley, 1995; Meyerowitz & Chaiken, 1987; Rothman et al., 1993). Perhaps because of its similarity to a traditional fear appeal, it was initially assumed that loss-framed appeals would consistently be more effective than gain-framed appeals. However, based on a review of the empirical literature, Rothman and Salovey (1997) argued that the relative influence of gain- and loss-framed messages is contingent on how people perceive the behavior promoted. Specifically, do they perceive performing the behavior to be risky or uncertain? Because people tend to perceive choosing to perform a detection behavior to be risky but choosing to perform a prevention behavior to be safe, the observed advantage for loss- and gain-framed messages should depend on the type of behavior promoted. The two experiments reported in this article provided the first direct test of this conceptual model by using an experimental paradigm in which the frame of the message and the type of behavior were manipulated. Each experiment provided empirical evidence consistent with predictions: gain-framed appeals proved to be more effective in promoting a prevention behavior, whereas loss-framed appeals proved to be more effective in prompting a detection behavior.

The Distinction Between Prevention and Detection Behaviors

Although the relation between message frame and behavior type has proved quite robust, the predictions laid out by Rothman and Salovey (1997) do not rest on features that are intrinsic to prevention and detection behaviors. The finding that loss-framed appeals are a more effective way to promote detection behaviors relies on the fact that society consistently teaches people to perceive behaviors such as BSE and mammography as illness detecting.[6] However, it is possible for these behaviors to be reframed as health-affirming behaviors (i.e., a woman could get a mammogram to affirm that her breasts are healthy). In fact, people who regularly follow a set of preventive behaviors (e.g., brush and floss their teeth) should have little reason to be concerned about a screening exam. To the extent that people perceive performing a detection behavior to be a safe, health-affirming practice, a gain-framed rather than a loss-framed appeal should be more persuasive. Consistent with this outlook, two studies that assessed how people perceived a detection behavior found that the predicted advantage for a loss-framed appeal was limited to those people who believed that engaging in the behavior would be risky (Meyerowitz et al., 1991; Rothman et al., 1996).

A further distinction also could be made among detection behaviors. Research has consistently focused on behaviors that screen for health problems (e.g., HIV, cancer). With advances in fields such as genetic testing, tests may be developed that identify factors that are health promoting. Given the tendency to construe detection behaviors in terms of what they are designed to detect, people may not perceive behaviors that screen for healthy attributes as risky (i.e., one no longer runs the risk of finding something wrong). Under these conditions, a gain-framed appeal should be more effective.

What about the prediction that gain-framed messages should be used to promote prevention behaviors? To the extent that adopting a prevention behavior is not perceived as a safe or certain option, gain-framed appeals should become less effective. Consistent with this proposition, Block and Keller (1995, Experiment 1) found that a loss-framed appeal heightened participants' attitude toward and interest in a prevention behavior when the behavior was said to be only 20% effective. The perceived effectiveness of a prevention or a detection behavior may contribute to whether choosing to perform the behavior is considered a risky or safe proposition.

How Do Gain- and Loss-Framed Messages Influence Behavior?

There is little question that providing people with either gain- or loss-framed health information influences the decisions they make and the behaviors they choose to perform. Moreover, framed information has been shown to influence behaviors taken both soon after the information has been presented and up to 12 months after participants have viewed a framed presentation (e.g., Banks et al., 1995). In contrast to the behavioral findings, investigators have had difficulty identifying the psychological processes that mediate the influence of framed information on behavior. Although some evidence of mediational processes was obtained in Experiment 2, the findings were inconsistent across the two behavior conditions. Why would participants' intentions and behavior be more closely linked for a prevention behavior compared to a detection behavior? Perhaps the feelings of concern and anxiety that people associate with adopting a detection behavior undermines their determination to act on their intentions. Although investigators have long been interested in the premise that too much fear will undermine behavior (e.g., Janis, 1967), this perspective has received minimal empirical support (Sutton, 1982). In fact, in the current study, participants in the detection behavior condition who received loss-framed information reported the highest proportion of card requests. Of course, we have no information as to the proportion of participants across the experimental conditions who actually used the product that they were mailed.

Some researchers have suggested that a message-processing approach may help elucidate the influence that message framing has on behavior (e.g., Maheswaran & Meyers-Levy, 1990; Smith & Petty, 1996). Specifically, any observed advantage for either gain- or loss-framed messages may rest on the fact that people have processed one version of the message more extensively than the other. Smith and Petty (1996, Experiment 2) found that information that is framed in an unexpected manner (e.g., people expect a loss-framed but are given a gain-framed message) is processed more extensively than information framed in an expected manner, and consequently had a stronger influence on people's attitudes and intentions. However, this effect was limited to those people who were otherwise not motivated to process the message (i.e., people low in NFC). People who were dispositionally motivated to process the message were unaffected by the expectancy manipulation. It is not clear how a differential processing perspective could account for the fact that framing effects on behavior have been obtained with people who were highly involved in a health issue and therefore likely to have systematically processed the information they received regardless of how it was framed (e.g., Banks et al., 1995; Detweiler et al., 1999; Rothman et al., 1993). Moreover, in Experiment 2, participants appeared to process the gain- and loss-framed pamphlets in a similar manner, although in the predicted behavior condition, each frame was shown to be more effective than the other. However, comparisons of the total amount of cognitive responding provide only a general assessment of cognitive elaboration (Smith & Petty, 1996). Measures of participants' responses to strong and weak framed arguments provide a more sophisticated assessment of message processing, and including these measures in subsequent research should help to clarify these issues.

Conclusion

Rothman and Salovey (1997) proposed a conceptual framework designed to assist investigators in developing interventions to promote healthy behavior. Although a number of field experiments had revealed findings consistent with this framework, the studies reported in this article provide the first direct confirmation of the predicted relation between message frame and behavior. Despite the fact that we have developed an increasingly sophisticated understanding of when gain- and loss-framed messages are likely to be effective, the processes through which framed messages influence decision making and behavior are still not well understood. Identifying these processes will improve both the theoretical bases of message framing effects and the ability to provide people with health information that is maximally persuasive.

Notes

1. Loss-framed information about a blood-cholesterol test was effective only when college undergraduates were informed that coronary heart disease was a problem for people younger than 25 years old. Students who believed that coronary heart disease was not a relevant health threat were more persuaded by gain-framed information (Maheswaran & Meyers-Levy, 1990; see Rothman & Salovey, 1997, for a broader analysis of this finding).

2. Generally, people chew on disclosing tablets to detect plaque accumulation. However, it is possible to dissolve these tablets in water to produce a rinse that serves the same function. We included the latter form of the behavior in our pamphlets so that it would be consistent with the mouth rinse behavior.

3. Several personality constructs as well as beliefs about dental issues (e.g., self-esteem, dispositional optimism, perceived prevalence of gum disease) were included in the premanipulation packet; however, they were unrelated to the findings reported in this article. Additional information about these measures can be obtained from the first author.

4. The results of the log-linear analysis were consistent with those obtained with ANOVA. An analysis of the percentage of postcards returned revealed the predicted Message Frame x Behavior Interaction, $F(1, 116) = 10.36$, $p < .005$.

5. The z score provides a direct test of the strength of the proposed mediator and is derived based on Baron and Kenny's (1986) modification of a test developed by Sobel (1982).

6. The general tendency to construe detection behaviors in terms of their ability to detect the presence rather than the absence of a problem is consistent with research that has shown that people have an easier time processing and reasoning about the presence rather than the absence of features (McGuire & McGuire, 1991).

References

Adams, D., & Addy, M. (1994). Mouthrinses. *Advanced Dental Research, 5,* 291-301.

Banks, S. M., Salovey, P., Greener, S., Rothman, A. J., Moyer, A., Beauvais, J., & Eppel, E. (1995). The effects of message framing on mammography utilization. *Health Psychology, 14,* 178-184.

Baron, R. M., & Kenny, D. A. (1986). The moderator-mediator variable distinction in social psychological research: Conceptual, strategic, and statistical considerations. *Journal of Personality and Social Psychology, 51,* 1173-1182.

Block, L. G., & Keller, P. A. (1995). When to accentuate the negative: The effects of perceived efficacy and message framing on intentions to perform a health-related behavior. *Journal of Research, 32,* 192-203.

Cacioppo, J. T., Petty, R. E., Feinstein, J. A., Jarvis, W., & Blair, G. (1996). Dispositional differences in cognitive motivation: The life and times of individuals varying in need for cognition. Psychological Bulletin, 119, 197-253.

Cacioppo, J. T., Petty, R. E., & Kao, C. F. (1984). The efficient assessment of need for cognition. *Journal of Personality Assessment, 48,* 306-307.

Christophersen, E. R., & Gyulay, J. E. (1981). Parental compliance with car seat usage: A positive approach with long-term follow-up. *Journal of Pediatric Psychology, 6,* 301-312.

Department of Health and Human Services. (1991). *Healthy people 2000: National health promotion and disease prevention objectives.* Washington, DC: Government Printing Office.

Detweiler, J. B., Bedell, B. T., Salovey, P., Pronin, E., & Rothman, A. J. (1999). Message framing and sunscreen use: Gain-framed messages motivate beach-goers. *Health Psychology, 18,* 189-196.

Eagly, A. H., & Chaiken, S. (1993). *The psychology of attitudes.* Fort Worth, TX: Harcourt Brace Jovanovich.

Hill, D., Gardner, G., & Rassaby, J. (1985). Factors predisposing women to take precautions against breast and cervix cancer. *Journal of Applied Social Psychology, 15,* 59-79.

Janis, I. L. (1967). Effects of fear arousal on attitude change: Recent developments in theory and experimental research. In L. Berkowitz (Ed.), *Advances in experimental social psychology* (Vol. 3, pp. 166-224). San Diego, CA: Academic Press.

Kahneman, D., & Tversky, A. (1979). Prospect theory: An analysis of decisions under risk. *Econometrica, 47,* 263-291.

Kalichman, S. C., & Coley, B. (1995). Context framing to enhance HIV-antibody-testing messages targeted to African American women. *Health Psychology, 14,* 247-254.

Leventhal, H. (1970). Findings and theory in the study of fear communications. In L. Berkowitz (Ed.), *Advances in experimental social psychology* (Vol. 5, pp. 119-186). San Diego, CA: Academic Press.

Linville, P. W., Fischer, G. W., & Fischhoff, B. (1993). AIDS risk perceptions and decision biases. In J. B. Pryor & G. D. Reeder (Eds.), *The social psychology of HIV infection* (pp. 5-38). Hillsdale, NJ: Lawrence Erlbaum.

Maheswaran, D., & Meyers-Levy, J. (1990). The influence of message framing and issue involvement. *Journal of Marketing Research, 27,* 361-367.

Marteau, T. M. (1989). Framing of information: Its influence upon decisions of doctors and patients. *British Journal of Social Psychology, 28,* 89-94.

Mayer, J. A., & Solomon, L. (1992). Breast self-examination skill and frequency: A review. *Annals of Behavioral Medicine, 14,* 189-196.

McGuire, W. J., & McGuire, C. V. (1991). The content, structure, and operation of thought systems. In R. S. Wyer Jr., & T. K. Srull (Eds.), *Advances in social cognition* (Vol. 4, pp. 1-78). Hillsdale, NJ: Lawrence Erlbaum.

Meyerowitz, B. E., & Chaiken, S. (1987). The effect of message framing on breast self-examination attitudes, intentions, and behavior. *Journal of Personality and Social Psychology, 52,* 500-510.

Meyerowitz, B. E., Wilson, D. K, & Chaiken, S. (1991, June). *Loss-framed messages increase breast self-examination for women who perceive risk.* Paper presented at the annual convention of the American Psychological Society, Washington, D.C.

Rothman, A. J., Martino, S. C., & Jeffery, R. W. (1997). *Predicting preferences in the domains of gains and losses: The importance of knowing when a gain is a gain and a loss is a loss.* Unpublished manuscript, University of Minnesota, Minneapolis.

Rothman, A. J., Pronin, E., & Salovey, P. (1996, October). *The influence of prior concern on the persuasiveness of loss-framed messages about skin cancer.* Paper presented at the annual meeting of the Society of Experimental Social Psychology, Sturbridge, MA.

Rothman, A. J., & Salovey, P. (1997). Shaping perceptions to motivate healthy behavior: The role of message framing. *Psychological Bulletin, 121,* 3-19.

Rothman, A. J., Salovey, P., Antone, C., Keough, K., & Martin, C. D. (1993). The influence of message framing on intentions to perform health behaviors. *Journal of Experimental Social Psychology, 29,* 408-433.

Salovey, P., Rothman, A. J., & Rodin, J. (1998). Health behavior. In D. Gilbert, S. Fiske, & G. Lindzey

(Eds.), *Handbook of social psychology, 4th edition* (Vol. 2, pp. 633-683). New York: McGraw-Hill.

Smith, S. M., & Petty, R. E. (1996). Message framing and persuasion: A message processing analysis. *Personality and Social Psychology Bulletin, 22,* 257-268.

Sobel, M. E. (1982). Asymptotic confidence intervals for indirect effects in structural models. In S. Leinhardt (Ed.), *Sociological methodology 1982* (pp. 290-312). San Francisco: Jossey-Bass.

Sutton, S. R. (1982). Fear-arousing communications: A critical examination of theory and research. In J. R. Eiser (Ed.), *Social psychology and behavioral medicine* (pp. 303-337). New York: John Wiley.

Tversky, A., & Kahneman, D. (1981). The framing of decisions and the rationality of choice. *Science, 221,* 453-458.

Wegener, D. T., Petty, R. E., & Klein, D. J. (1994). Effects of mood on high elaboration attitude change: The mediating role of likelihood judgments. *European Journal of Social Psychology, 24,* 25-43.

Weinstein, N. D., Rothman, A. J., & Nicolich, M. (1998). Use of correlational data to examine the effects of risk perceptions on precautionary behavior. *Psychology & Health, 13,* 479-501.

PART III

THE HEALTH CARE SETTING

Essay: Health Care Settings and Their Social Dynamics

Jeff S. Erger and William D. Marelich

Doctors prescribe medicine of which they know little, to cure diseases of which they know less, in human beings of which they know nothing.

Voltaire

Going to the doctor is rarely a pleasant thing. It involves at best, inconvenience, and at worst, great pain and suffering. Of course, the same can be said of going to the post office, or the bank to clear up a problem with an account, or just about any interaction we might have within any social institution. One reason for this is that the setting of social institutions is constructed by and for the purpose and advantage of those who inhabit it on a daily basis, not those who visit it on occasion. However, when it comes to the medical setting, there is a critical difference from most institutions: When we step into a doctor's office or hospital, we do not have the option of walking out if we don't like what we hear. In fact, we are more likely to stay when we hear bad news. With that in mind, consider a visit to the doctor's office but look at it from the perspective of a social psychologist.

First, your visit begins long before you go to the office. A phone call to the doctor will meet with a list of questions about you and the scheduling of an appointment. The questions will revolve not only around the nature of the visit (routine checkup, back pain, chronic illness, etc.) but also the status of your health insurance. If this is your first visit to the office, they will know quite a bit about you from the answers to those questions before you arrive. You will know next to nothing about them. You might want to know about the doctor, and you might have sought information from friends or coworkers on what doctor to choose. However, have you ever asked a physician whether he or she graduated at the top or bottom of his or her class? What training does that person complete to keep up to speed on the latest developments in medicine? If you are going to put your life in their hands, don't you want to know the answers to these questions? Why don't you ask?

Upon arrival at the office, you will check in with the receptionist, who often wears a medical "uniform." You will be asked many questions and perhaps fill out some forms. Then, you will wait. And wait. And wait some more. Think about what is being communicated to you during this time. First, you must check in with someone who is most likely behind a window. Behind that receptionist are row upon row of files, each one containing the details of a human life. These files are "secure" behind that window, and that is symbolic of the fact that your privacy will be treated with seriousness even as you are baring yourself in a very nonprivate way. Second, you are the one waiting, and waiting in many cases long beyond your scheduled appointment time. Your time is not the important resource in this context; you are not in control. Third, while you wait, you can look around the office and most likely see posters, flyers, and bulletin board postings, all with health-related themes. This environment, the uniforms worn, and the language used all make the waiting time serve to orient you toward the task at hand.

After waiting, you will be called and pass through a door. Here, there will be a maze of corridors and rooms with many people walking around, each in different-colored "uniforms." There will be very expensive machines making whirring and pinging noises. You will follow where you are led, and then you will be shown into a room and told what to do. Usually, this is to wait some more. After a time, someone will enter and do some preliminary tasks, such as taking blood pressure and weighing you. You will be asked questions, which you will answer. This will soon end with a direction for you to disrobe and wait for the doctor.

After all this waiting, you are now almost naked and sitting on a piece of tissue paper on an exam table. Consider that you have done exactly what you were told to do since making the phone call to schedule your appointment. And you ended up in your underwear. You have not questioned a single directive. You might feel highly anxious to be unclothed in front of strangers, or you might feel slightly odd, or you might not think twice about it. The question is, would you automatically do as you were told by strangers and strip down in any other situation? The end result—you in your underwear—is a very concrete demonstration of the power of the medical setting to control our behavior.

Now, let's set aside consideration of the patient's perspective for a moment and consider chess players. Have you ever seen a chess grand master play in a demonstration where they oppose 20 people at the same time? They must have incredible minds to hold so much information at once! Twenty separate games, 20 separate board positions. The grand masters will walk around the circle from table to table, and when they come to a board, they will make a move within 5 seconds or so. They must have been planning what to do well in advance, thinking ahead. This perception is understandable but completely wrong. Chess grand masters who engage in this kind of exhibition do not hold 20 games in their minds; they don't even hold a single game in their minds. Instead, they look at the board and evaluate it *as it stands,* then choose their move based on that evaluation.

Now, let's consider the physician who is going to examine you. What has she been doing since you arrived at the office? She has been busy. She has been seeing patients, writing prescriptions, analyzing test results, talking on the phone, and generally going about the business of being a doctor. Has she thought about you? Has she looked at your records the night before and contemplated how she should deal with your case? Probably not. In fact, while you have been focused on this examination for days or even weeks, the physician will start to think about the exam when she stands outside the door of the exam room in which you sit on that exam table. While walking through the maze of the offices, did you happen to notice that exam room doors have slots on them where medical files can be placed? The doctor will stand at your door, pull your file, read it, then enter and call you by name. She will evaluate your case *as it stands.*

The doctor will ask you many questions, physically examine you, and tell you what she thinks should be done in your case. At this point, you will be asked if you have any questions. If you are like most people, you will not ask any. Some will ask for clarification of a statement the doctor has made. Almost no one will ask more than two questions during this time. After a total of 10 to 15 minutes or so, the doctor will tell you to get dressed, and you will be out of the doctor's mind. Another staff person will enter, and you will go with them and do what you are told. This might be to take some tests, or it might be to leave the office. You will do as you are told. Such is the power of the situation and our typical reaction to it.

There are three main forces working on those in the health care setting, and we can look at each in turn. We can focus on the patient, the provider, or the setting itself. Each of these approaches has advantages and drawbacks when taken to extremes.

Looking at things from the patient's point of view is something we can all relate to; after all, we have all been patients at one time or another. If our goal is to understand health, then seeing how sick people go through a health care system and come out the other side healthy seems straightforward. However, focusing primarily on the patient has a significant drawback. It treats the health care system as a static environment that the patient encounters and reacts to. From this perspective, the health care system is simply "there," and patients react to whatever they encounter while wandering through, seeking the goal of health. The health care system throws stimuli at the patient, and the patient responds. The question to be investigated is why patients respond as they do. If this were a book strictly addressing health psychology, we would fill this section with readings looking at exactly this reaction of patients to the setting.

We can focus on the health care provider, and this makes a great deal of sense as well. After all, the doctors make the decisions, the staff provides the care, and to the extent that they do a good job, people will get healthy. So the questions we might ask, among others, might include the following: What makes for the good provision of care? What makes for good decision making? How do doctors get patients to comply with their decisions? Here, the patient is not important; it is the characteristics and actions of the health care provider that are critical to the health outcome. If this book were designed for a nursing program or medical school, we might have many articles focused on providers and their actions. However, patients do act, sometimes in small ways and sometimes in a very extreme manner, and medical workers must respond to patients' actions. If we focus only on providers, we will miss the often critical actions and influences of patients on what happens in the medical setting.

If we see the setting as dominant, then both patient and provider are being swept along by it. Both are subject to larger social forces that act upon them, tossing them first one way, then the other. Health outcomes are determined by factors such as race, gender, class, institutional culture, the insurance industry, the economics of health care, and other large-scale social structures and systems. Were this a book used only in medical sociology courses, we would include a great deal of research from this perspective. Yet there are problems with this perspective. Consider two middle-class Hispanic males with HMO insurance who both see female physicians at the same medical practice. One receives very good care, actively participates in care decisions, and is extremely happy with the doctor. The other receives adequate care, rarely speaks during exams, and does not like his doctor. In this case, race, gender, insurance status, the nature of the institution, and culture cannot account for the differences in care, participation, or satisfaction with physician.

As we keep saying, we are social psychologists, and so we reject both the purely small- and the purely large-scale focus. We see value in looking at only the large or small, and in some cases, a great deal of value. However, we never forget that the large is made up of the small, and the small is affected by the large. Indeed, when thinking about the health care setting, we focus on the *interactions* that happen in a specific *context.* The patients and providers and their individual perspectives certainly matter, but they matter in that they affect the interaction of and the meeting between the two; these interactions produce health care decisions and outcomes. When the physician is talking, the patient is responding, and the doctor is altering his or her behavior based on the patient's actions. Communication is never a one-way street.

These interactions do not take place in a vacuum, but rather in a specific culture and organizational setting. This context shapes the interaction in sometime subtle and sometimes obvious ways—like getting you to sit in your underwear on a table! Health care settings are primarily about health care and the delivery of that care, but a major concept that threads its way through the interactions that happen in these settings is *control.* Where control is an issue, so is *power.*

The Patient-Provider Interaction

The readings in this section focus on this power and how it is enacted through interaction and are included because they nicely illustrate the various angles by which an interaction can be negotiated and affected. You may have noticed there are only three readings in this section. We felt that the readings cover the patient-provider interaction sequence well and reference many other excellent articles on this sequence that you may find useful.

The first offering looks at a situation of routine health care, that of a gynecological examination. Some of you might find the Emerson reading to be a little strange. Men probably have never contemplated gynecological examinations in much detail, and many women will no doubt think it odd that all the physicians seem to be male. Keep in mind that this article was written in 1970, but that does not make the observations out-of-date.

The major point of this article is that the definition of what is going on in the medical examination is being contested in an interactive way, that patients and medical staff are often at odds as to what should happen and is happening, and that the medical team works together to maintain control over the definition of the situation.

The extreme case of male gynecologists examining women in 1970 brings this process to the forefront and makes it easier to analyze, but the critical thing to keep in mind is that the definition of the situation is *always* contested. Physicians often must perform actions that could be seen by patients as demeaning, invasive, or sexual in nature. Physicians must constantly work at keeping the actions defined as "medical," "necessary," and "not that bad." Have you ever heard your doctor say to you, "This may cause you some discomfort?" Why that choice of words rather than "This is really going to hurt!" Emerson shows how choice of words and actions help to keep the definition of the situation as the doctor wants it to be during the interactions. Word choice, setting, and, perhaps most important, teamwork are all critical tools the medical staff use to maintain control over the situation. Thus, power is exerted throughout the course of the interaction.

While Emerson looks at the *process* of interaction and how the medical definition is maintained, the next reading looks at both the process and how this process can influence the *outcomes* of medical interactions, and the implication for quality of care. Erger, Grusky, Mann, and Marelich look at the interactions between HIV-positive patients and health care providers when the initial treatment decision for HIV is being made. Given its qualitative nature, this article provides an interesting view into the patient-provider interaction sequence and how these interactions can ultimately affect treatment.

During the time frame of this study, the Department of Health and Human Services had guidelines for the prescribing of antiretroviral drugs, and these guidelines included the discussion of benefits and risks of starting and delaying medication. However, Erger et al. show that discussion of options in this context is rare to nonexistent. Instead, they find that health care providers use verbal techniques to produce the outcome they see as best, while keeping patient resistance and questioning to a minimum. This echoes the findings of Emerson, showing that language is a tool of power to keep the interaction on the ground where the health care provider wishes it to be.

Another point to consider in this article is that the interactions are strongly shaped by the *contexts* in which they occur. The organizational structure affected the content and outcomes of the interactions in several ways. The status differences between the primary health care providers (physician assistants and nurse practitioners) and the supervising physicians were a source of stress and pressure looming over the meetings with patients. This power dynamic has important implications for all medical care as health systems seek to reduce costs by having lower-cost workers take up increasing activity and responsibility for care provision. Another contextual influence is that the nonmedical organizational elements in the clinics, specifically the office of research, influenced the content and process of interactions and likely the medical decisions being made.

Setting Defining the Illness

The final reading in this section concentrates on the setting and nature of the institution and how that setting affects the definitions, interactions, and outcomes of the medical process. Many of you no doubt are familiar with Rosenhan's classic work from both psychology and sociology but probably have not read the original article (which we provide here, albeit in abbreviated form). Rosenhan discusses what happens when average people who are "normal" are placed in a psychiatric hospital.

After gaining admittance, these "pseudopatients" acted in as normal and cooperative a manner as they could. Despite this, their every behavior was interpreted in light of their assumed psychiatric condition to the point where routine everyday behavior is seen as symptomatic of their "condition." Writing becomes "[compulsive] writing behavior." Waiting for lunch by the cafeteria becomes an indication of "the oral-acquisitive nature of the syndrome." Because of this, it took the pseudopatient from 7 to 52 days to be released, and not one of them was released as "sane," but rather as being in "remission." The medical label is a sticky one that once applied, is impossible to remove.

Rosenhan shows that the process of interaction in a psychiatric hospital is very much shaped by the situation rather than other factors of the interaction, such as the people, status differences, or the behaviors that occur. However, the situation does not shape the definitions applied by everyone in the situation. Patients quickly labeled the pseudopatients as "normal." Why is it that the mentally ill saw the "reality" of the situation, while trained professionals could not?

Final Note

Please keep two things in mind as you read this set of articles on "The Health Care Setting." First, you are a consumer of health care. You have and will deal with the health care system both for yourself and for your family. Knowing about the dynamics of the health care setting will help you to negotiate the system in a smooth way, avoiding pitfalls while gaining your goals. We know of a case where a man stayed awake for almost a week. No one knows why this person failed to sleep during this time, but the effects of sleep deprivation, most importantly hallucinations, manifested. After being admitted to the hospital, diagnosed as schizophrenic, and given antipsychotic medication and sedatives, he slept for 24 hours. Upon waking up, the doctors on the case said that the antipsychotic medication would be required for the rest of his life. Clearly, since they gave him the medication and his hallucinations stopped, the diagnosis was correct and the medication worked! If it were not for a relative showing up and literally demanding that the psychiatrists consider sleep deprivation as the cause of the hallucinations and other behavior and sleeping as the cure, this person would have still been on that unneeded medication today, many years later.

The second thing to keep in mind is that you might very well end up working in the medical profession, either as a care provider or as an administrator of some kind. If this is the case, you will be in a position to make improvements in the system to which you belong. In this way, you can improve the care that many people receive every day, not only while you are working in that organization but even after you have gone on to other things. Try to keep these twin goals in mind as you read about the problems in health care settings. Don't stop at focusing on the problems, but as you turn the page, keep asking yourself, "How can this be fixed?"

A. The Patient-Provider Interaction

14

BEHAVIOR IN PRIVATE PLACES

Sustaining Definitions of Reality in Gynecological Examinations

JOAN P. EMERSON

INTRODUCTION

In *The Social Construction of Reality,* Berger and Luckmann discuss how people construct social order and yet construe the reality of everyday life to exist independently of themselves.[1] Berger and Luckmann's work succeeds in synthesizing some existing answers with new insights. Many sociologists have pointed to the importance of social consensus in what people believe; if everyone else seems to believe in something, a person tends to accept the common belief without question. Other sociologists have discussed the concept of legitimacy, an acknowledgment that what exists has the right to exist, and delineated various lines of argument which can be taken to justify a state of affairs. Berger and Luckmann emphasize three additional processes that provide persons with evidence that things have an objective existence apart from themselves. Perhaps most important is the experience that reality seems to be out there before we arrive on the scene. This notion is fostered by the nature of language, which contains an all-inclusive scheme of categories, is shared by a community, and must be learned laboriously by each new member. Further, definitions of reality are continuously validated by apparently trivial features of the social scene, such as details of the setting, persons' appearance and demeanor, and "inconsequential" talk. Finally, each part of a systematic world view serves as evidence for all the other parts, so that reality is solidified by a process of intervalidation of supposedly independent events.

EDITORS' NOTE: Emerson, J.P. (1970). Behavior in private places: Sustaining definitions of reality in gynecological examinations. In P. Dreitsel (Ed.), *Recent Sociology* (pp. 74–97). New York: Macmillan.

Because Berger and Luckmann's contribution is theoretical, their units of analysis are abstract processes. But they take those processes to be grounded in social encounters. Thus, Berger and Luckmann's theory provides a framework for making sense of social interaction. In this paper, observations of a concrete situation will be interpreted to show how reality is embodied in routines and reaffirmed in social interaction.

Situations differ in how much effort it takes to sustain the current definition of the situation. Some situations are relatively stable; others are precarious.[2] Stability depends on the likelihood of three types of disconforming events. Intrusions on the scene may threaten definitions of reality, as when people smell smoke in a theater or when a third person joins a couple and calls one member by a name the second member does not recognize. Participants may deliberately decline to validate the current reality, like Quakers who refused to take off their hats to the king. Sometimes participants are unable to produce the gestures which would validate the current reality. Perhaps a person is ignorant of the relevant vocabulary of gestures. Or a person, understanding how he should behave, may have limited social skills so that he cannot carry off the performance he would like to. For those who insist on "sincerity," a performance becomes especially taxing if they lack conviction about the trueness of the reality they are attempting to project.

A reality can hardly seem self-evident if a person is simultaneously aware of a counter-reality. Berger and Luckmann write as though definitions of reality were internally congruent. However, the ordinary reality may contain not only a dominant definition, but in addition counterthemes opposing or qualifying the dominant definition. Thus, several contradictory definitions must be sustained at the same time. Because each element tends to challenge the other elements, such composite definitions of reality are inherently precarious even if the probability of disconfirming events is low.

A situation where the definition of reality is relatively precarious has advantages for the analysis proposed here, for processes of sustaining reality should be more obvious where that reality is problematic. The situation chosen, the gynecological examination,[3] is precarious for both reasons discussed above. First, it is an excellent example of multiple contradictory definitions of reality, as described in the next section. Second, while intrusive and deliberate threats are not important, there is a substantial threat from participants' incapacity to perform.

Dramaturgical abilities are taxed in gynecological examinations because the less convincing reality internalized by secondary socialization is unusually discrepant with rival perspectives taken for granted in primary socialization.[4] Gynecological examinations share similar problems of reality-maintenance with any medical procedure, but the issues are more prominent because the site of the medical task is a woman's genitals. Because touching usually connotes personal intimacy, persons may have to work at accepting the physician's privileged access to the patient's genitals.[5] Participants are not entirely convinced that modesty is out of place. Since a woman's genitals are commonly accessible only in a sexual context, sexual connotations come readily to mind. Although most people realize that sexual responses are inappropriate, they may be unable to dismiss the sexual reaction privately and it may interfere with the conviction with which they undertake their impersonal performance. The structure of a gynecological examination highlights the very features which the participants are supposed to disattend. So the more attentive the participants are to the social situation, the more the unmentionable is forced on their attention.

The next section will characterize the complex composition of the definition of reality routinely sustained in gynecological examinations. Then some of the routine arrangements and interactional maneuvers which embody and express this definition will be described. A later section will discuss threats to the definition which arise in the course of the encounter. Measures that serve to neutralize the threats and reaffirm the definition will be analyzed. The concluding section will turn to the theoretical issues of precariousness, multiple contradictory definitions of reality, and implicit communication.

The Medical Definition and Its Counterthemes

Sometimes people are in each other's presence in what they take to be a "gynecological examination."

What happens in a gynecological examination is part of the common stock of knowledge. Most people know that a gynecological examination is when a doctor examines a woman's genitals in a medical setting. Women who have undergone this experience know that the examination takes place in a special examining room where the patient lies with her buttocks down to the edge of the table and her feet in stirrups, that usually a nurse is present as a chaperone, that the actual examining lasts only a few minutes, and so forth. Besides knowing what equipment to provide for the doctor, the nurse has in mind a typology of responses patients have to this situation, and a typology of doctors' styles of performance. The doctor has technical knowledge about the examining procedures, what observations may be taken to indicate, ways of getting patients to relax, and so on.

Immersed in the medical world where the scene constitutes a routine, the staff assume the responsibility for a credible performance. The staff take part in gynecological examinations many times a day, while the patient is a fleeting visitor. More deeply convinced of the reality themselves, the staff are willing to convince skeptical patients. The physician guides the patient through the precarious scene in a contained manner: taking the initiative, controlling the encounter, keeping the patient in line, defining the situation by his reaction, and giving cues that "this is done" and "other people go through this all the time."

Not only must people continue to believe that "this is a gynecological examination," but also that "this is a gynecological examination going right." The major definition to be sustained for this purpose is "this is a medical situation" (not a party, sexual assault, psychological experiment, or anything else). If it is a medical situation, then it follows that "no one is embarrassed"[6] and "no one is thinking in sexual terms."[7] Anyone who indicates the contrary must be swayed by some nonmedical definition.

The medical definition calls for a matter-of-fact stance. One of the most striking observations about a gynecological examination is the marked implication underlying the staff's demeanor toward the patient: "Of course, you take this as matter-of-factly as we do." The staff implicitly contend: "In the medical world the pelvic area is like any other part of the body; its private and sexual connotations are left behind when you enter the hospital." The staff want it understood that their gazes take in only medically pertinent facts, so they are not concerned with an aesthetic inspection of a patient's body. Their nonchalant pose attempts to put a gynecological examination in the same light as an internal examination of the ear.

Another implication of the medical definition is that the patient is a technical object to the staff. It is as if the staff work on an assembly line for repairing bodies; similar body parts continually roll by and the staff have a particular job to do on them. The staff are concerned with the typical features of the body part and its pathology rather than with the unique features used to define a person's identity. The staff disattend the connection between a part of the body and some intangible self that is supposed to inhabit the body.

The scene is credible precisely because the staff act as if they have every right to do what they are doing. Any hint of doubt from the staff would compromise the medical definition. Since the patient's nonchalance merely serves to validate the staff's right, it may be dispensed with without the same threat. Furthermore, the staff claim to be merely agents of the medical system, which is intent on providing good health care to patients. This medical system imposes procedures and standards which the staff are merely following in this particular instance. That is, what the staff do derives from external coercion—"We have to do it this way"—rather than from personal choices which they would be free to revise in order to accommodate the patient.

The medical definition grants the staff the right to carry out their task. If not for the medical definition, the staff's routine activities could be defined as unconscionable assaults on the dignity of individuals. The topics of talk, particularly inquiries about bodily functioning, sexual experience, and death of relatives, might be taken as offenses against propriety. As for exposure and manipulation of the patient's body, it would be a shocking and degrading invasion of privacy were the patient not defined as a technical object. The infliction of pain would be mere cruelty. The medical definition justifies the request that a presumably competent adult give up most of his autonomy to persons often subordinate in age, sex, and social class. The patient needs the medical definition to minimize the threat to his dignity; the staff need it in order to inveigle the patient into cooperating.

Yet definitions that appear to contradict the medical definition are routinely expressed in the course of gynecological examinations. Some gestures acknowledge the pelvic area as special; other gestures acknowledge the patient as a person. These counterdefinitions are as essential to the encounter as the medical definition. We have already discussed how an actor's lack of conviction may interfere with his performance. Implicit acknowledgments of the special meaning of the pelvic area help those players hampered by lack of conviction to perform adequately. If a player's sense of "how things really are" is implicitly acknowledged, he often finds it easier to adhere outwardly to a contrary definition.

A physician may gain a patient's cooperation by acknowledging her as a person. The physician wants the patient to acknowledge the medical definition, cooperate with the procedures of the examination, and acknowledge his professional competence. The physician is in a position to bargain with the patient in order to obtain this cooperation. He can offer her attention and acknowledgment as a person. At times he does so.

Although defining a person as a technical object is necessary in order for medical activities to proceed, it constitutes an indignity in itself. This indignity can be canceled or at least qualified by simultaneously acknowledging the patient as a person.

The medical world contains special activities and special perspectives. Yet the inhabitants of the medical world travel back and forth to the general community where modesty, death, and other medically relevant matters are regarded quite differently. It is not so easy to dismiss general community meanings for the time one finds oneself in a medical setting. The counterthemes that the pelvic area is special and that patients are persons provide an opportunity to show deference to general community meanings at the same time that one is disregarding them.

Sustaining the reality of a gynecological examination does not mean sustaining the medical definition, then. What is to be sustained is a shifting balance between medical definition and counterthemes.[8] Too much emphasis on the medical definition alone would undermine the reality, as would a flamboyant manifestation of the counterthemes apart from the medical definition. The next three sections will suggest how this balance is achieved.

Sustaining the Reality

The appropriate balance between medical definition and counterthemes has to be created anew at every moment. However, some routinized procedures and demeanor are available to participants in gynecological examinations. Persons recognize that if certain limits are exceeded, the situation would be irremediably shattered. Some arrangements have been found useful because they simultaneously express medical definition and countertheme. Routine ways of meeting the task requirements and also dealing with "normal trouble" are available. This section will describe how themes and counterthemes are embodied in routinized procedures and demeanor.

The pervasiveness of the medical definition is expressed by indicators that the scene is enacted under medical auspices.[9] The action is located in "medical space" (hospital or doctor's office). Features of the setting such as divisions of space, decor, and equipment are constant reminders that it is indeed "medical space." Even background details such as the loudspeaker calling, "Dr. Morris. Dr. Armand Morris" serve as evidence for medical reality (suppose the loudspeaker were to announce instead, "Five minutes until post time"). The staff wear medical uniforms, don medical gloves, use medical instruments. The exclusion of lay persons, particularly visitors of the patient who may be accustomed to the patient's nudity at home, helps to preclude confusion between the contact of medicine and the contact of intimacy.[10]

Some routine practices simultaneously acknowledge the medical definition and qualify it by making special provision for the pelvic area. For instance, rituals of respect express dignity for the patient. The patient's body is draped so as to expose only that part which is to receive the technical attention of the doctor. The presence of a nurse acting as "chaperone" cancels any residual suggestiveness of male and female alone in a room.[11]

Medical talk stands for and continually expresses allegiance to the medical definition. Yet certain features of medical talk acknowledge a nonmedical delicacy. Despite the fact that persons present on a gynecological ward must attend to many topics connected with the pelvic area and various bodily functions, these topics are generally discussed. Strict conventions dictate unmentionables are to be acknowledged under what circumstances. However, persons are exceptionally free to refer to the genitals and related matters on the obstetrics gynecology service. If technical matters in regard to the pelvic area come up, they are to be discussed nonchalantly.

The special language found in staff-patient contacts contributes to depersonalization and desexualization of the encounter. Scientific-sounding medical terms facilitate such communication. Substituting dictionary terms for everyday words adds formality. The definite article replaces the pronoun adjective in reference to body parts, so that for example, the doctor refers to "the vagina" and never "your vagina." Instructions to the patient in the course of the examination are couched in language which bypasses sexual imagery; the vulgar connotation of "spread your legs" is generally metamorphosed into the innocuous "let your knees fall apart."

While among themselves, the staff generally use explicit technical terms, explicit terminology is often avoided in staff-patient contacts.[12] The reference to the pelvic area may be merely understood, as when a patient says: "I feel so uncomfortable there right now" or "They didn't go near to this area, so why did they have to shave it?" In speaking with patients, the staff frequently uses euphemisms. A doctor asks: "When did you first notice difficulty down below?" and a nurse inquires: "Did you wash between your legs?" Persons characteristically refer to pelvic examinations euphemistically in staff-patient encounters. "The doctors want to take a peek at you," a nurse tells a patient. Or "Dr. Ryan wants to see you in the examining room."

In one pelvic examination, there was a striking contrast between the language of staff and patient. The patient was graphic; she used action words connoting physical contact to refer to the examination procedure: feeling, poking, touching, and punching. Yet she never located this action in regard to her body, always omitting to state where the physical contact occurred. The staff used impersonal medical language and euphemisms: "I'm going to examine you"; "I'm just cleaning out some blood clots"; "He's just trying to fix you up a bit."

Sometimes the staff introduce explicit terminology to clarify a patient's remark. A patient tells the doctor, "It's bleeding now" and the doctor answers, "You? From the vagina?" Such a response indicates the appropriate vocabulary, the degree of freedom permitted in technically oriented conversation, and the proper detachment. Yet the common avoidance of explicit terminology in staff-patient contacts suggests that despite all the precautions to assure that the medical definition prevails, many patients remain somewhat embarrassed by the whole subject. To avoid provoking this embarrassment, euphemisms and understood references are used when possible.

Highly specific requirements for everybody's behavior during a gynecological examination curtail the leeway for the introduction of discordant notes. Routine technical procedures organize the event from beginning to end, indicating what action each person should take at each moment. Verbal exchanges are also constrained by the technical task, in that the doctor uses routine phrases of direction and reassurance to the patient. There is little margin for ad-libbing during a gynecological examination.

The specifications for demeanor are elaborate. Foremost is that both staff and patient should be nonchalant about what is happening. According to the staff, the exemplary patient should be "in play": showing she is attentive to the situation by her bodily tautness, facial expression, direction of glance, tone of voice, tempo of speech and bodily movements, timing and appropriateness of responses. The patient's voice should be controlled, mildly pleasant, self-confident, and impersonal. Her facial expression should be attentive and neutral, leaning toward the mildly pleasant and friendly side, as if she were talking to the doctor in his office, fully dressed and seated in a chair. The patient is to have an attentive glance upward, at the ceiling or at other persons in the room, eyes open, not dreamy or "away," but ready at a second's notice to revert to the doctor's face for a specific verbal exchange. Except for such a verbal exchange, however, the patient is supposed to avoid looking into the doctor's eyes during the actual examination because direct eye contact between the two at this time is provocative. Her role calls for passivity and self-effacement. The patient should show willingness to relinquish control to the doctor. She should refrain from speaking at length and from making inquiries which would require the doctor to reply at length. So as not to point up her undignified position, she should not project her personality profusely. The self must be eclipsed in order to sustain the definition that the doctor is working on a technical object and not a person.

The physician's demeanor is highly stylized. He intersperses his examination with remarks to the patient in a soothing tone of voice: "Now relax as much as you can"; "I'll be as gentle as I can"; "Is that tender right there?" Most of the phrases with which he encourages the patient to relax are routine even though his delivery may suggest a unique relationship. He demonstrates that he is the detached professional, and the patient demonstrates that it never enters her mind that he could be anything except detached. Since intimacy can be introduced into instrumental physical contact by a "loving" demeanor (lingering, caressing motions and contact beyond what the task requires), a doctor must take special pains to insure that his demeanor remains a brisk, no-nonsense show of efficiency.[13]

Once I witnessed a gynecological examination of a forty-year-old woman who played the charming and scatterbrained Southern belle. The attending physician stood near the patient's head and carried on a flippant conversation with her while a resident and medical student actually performed the examination. The patient completely ignored the examination, except for brief answers to the examining doctor's inquiries. Under these somewhat trying circumstances she attempted to carry off a gay, attractive pose and the attending physician cooperated with her by making a series of bantering remarks.

Most physicians are not so lucky as to have a colleague conversing in cocktail-hour style with the patient while they are probing her vagina. Ordinarily, the physician must play both parts at once, treating the patient as an object with his hands while simultaneously acknowledging her as a person with his voice. In this incident, where two physicians simultaneously deal with the patient in two distinct ways, the dual approach to the patient usually maintained by the examining physician becomes more obvious.[14]

The doctor needs to communicate with the patient as a person for technical reasons. Should he want to know when the patient feels pain in the course of examination or information about other medical matters, he must address her as a person. Also the doctor may want to instruct the patient on how to facilitate the examination. The most reiterated instruction refers to relaxation. Most patients are not sufficiently relaxed when the doctor is ready to begin. He then reverts to a primitive level of communication and treats the patient almost like a young child. He speaks in a soft, soothing voice, probably calling the patient by her first name, and it is not so much the words as his manner which is significant. This caressing voice is routinely used by hospital staff members to patients in critical situations, as when the patient is overtly frightened or disoriented. By using it here, the doctor heightens his interpersonal relation with the patient, trying to reassure her as a person in order to get her to relax.

Moreover, even during a gynecological examination, failing to acknowledge another as a person is an insult. It is insulting to be entirely instrumental about instrumental contacts. Some acknowledgment of the intimate connotations of touching must occur. Therefore, a measure of "loving" demeanor is subtly injected. A doctor cannot employ the full gamut of loving insinuations that a lover might infuse into instrumental touching. So he indirectly implies a hint of intimacy which is intended to counter the insult and make the procedure acceptable to the woman. The doctor conveys this loving demeanor not by lingering or superfluous contact, but by radiating concern in his general manner, offering extra assistance, and occasionally by sacrificing the task requirements to "gentleness."

In short, the doctor must convey an optimal combination of impersonality and hints of intimacy that simultaneously avoid the insult of sexual familiarity and the insult of unacknowledged identity. The doctor must manage this even though the behavior emanating from each definition is contradictory. If the doctor can achieve this feat, it will contribute to keeping the patient in line. In the next section, we will see how the patient may threaten this precarious balance.

Precariousness in Gynecological Examinations

Threats to the reality of a gynecological examination may occur if the balance of opposing definitions is not maintained as described above. Reality in gynecological examinations is challenged mainly by patients. Occasionally, a medical student, who might be considerably more of a novice than an experienced patient, seemed uncomfortable in the scene.[15] Experienced staff members were rarely observed to undermine the reality.

Certain threatening events which could occur in any staff-patient encounter bring an added dimension of precariousness to a gynecological examination because the medical aegis screens so much more audacity at that time. In general, staff expect patients to remain poised and in play like a friendly office receptionist; any show of emotion except in a controlled fashion is objectionable. Patients should not focus on identities of themselves or the staff outside those relevant to the medical exchange. Intractable patients may complain about the pain, discomfort, and indignities of submitting to medical treatment and care. Patients may go so far as to show they are reluctant to comply with the staff. Even if they are complying, they may indirectly challenge the expert status of the staff, as by "asking too many questions."

Failure to maintain a poised performance is a possible threat in any social situation. Subtle failures of tone are common, as when a performer seems to lack assurance. Performers may fumble for their lines: hesitate, begin a line again, or correct themselves. A show of embarrassment, such as blushing, has special relevance in gynecological examinations. On rare occasions when a person shows signs of sexual response, he or she really has something to blush about. A more subtle threat is an indication that the actor is putting an effort into the task of maintaining nonchalant demeanor; if it requires such an effort, perhaps it is not a "natural" response.

Such effort may be indicated, for example, in regard to the direction of glance. Most situations have a common visual focus of attention, but in a gynecological examination the logical focus, the patient's internal organs, is not accessible; and none of the alternatives, such as staring at the patient's face, locking glances with others, or looking out the window are feasible. The unavailability of an acceptable place to rest the eyes is more evident when the presence of several medical students creates a "crowd" atmosphere in the small cubicle. The lack of a visual focus of attention and the necessity to shift the eyes from object to object requires the participants to remain vaguely aware of their directions of glance. Normally, the resting place of the eyes is a background matter automatically managed without conscious attention. Attentiveness to this background detail is a constant reminder of how awkward the situation is.

Certain lapses in patients' demeanor are so common as hardly to be threatening. When patients express pain it can be overlooked if the patient is giving other signs of trying to behave well, because it can be taken that the patient is temporarily overwhelmed by a physiological state. The demonstrated presence of pain recalls the illness framework and counters sexual connotations. Crying can be accredited to pain and dismissed in a similar way. Withdrawing attention from the scene, so that one is not ready with an immediate comeback when called upon, is also relatively innocuous because it is close to the required passive but in-play demeanor.

Some threats derive from the patient's ignorance of how to strike an acceptable balance between medical and nonmedical definitions, despite her willingness to do so. In two areas in particular, patients stumble over the subtleties of what is expected: physical decorum (proprieties of sights, sounds, and smells of the body) and modesty. While the staff is largely concerned with behavioral decorum and not about lapses in physical decorum, patients are more concerned about the latter, whether due to their medical condition or the procedure. Patients sometimes even let behavioral decorum lapse in order to express their concern about unappealing conditions of their bodies, particularly discharges and odors. This concern is a vestige of a nonmedical definition of the situation, for an attractive body is relevant only in a personal situation and not in a medical one.

Some patients fail to know when to display their private parts unashamedly to others and when to conceal them like anyone else. A patient may make an "inappropriate" show of modesty, thus not granting the staff the right to view what medical personnel have the right to view and others do not. But if patients act as though they literally accept the medical definition, this also constitutes a threat. If a patient insists on acting as if the exposure of her breasts, buttocks, and pelvic area are no different from exposure of her arm or leg, she is "immodest." The medical definition is supposed to be in force only as necessary to facilitate specific medical tasks. If a patient becomes nonchalant enough to allow herself to remain uncovered for much longer than is technically necessary, she becomes a threat. This also holds for verbal remarks about personal matters. Patients who misinterpret the license by exceeding its limits unwittingly challenge the definition of reality.[16]

Neutralizing Threatening Events

Most gynecological examinations proceed smoothly and the definition of reality is sustained without conscious attention.[17] Sometimes subtle threats to the definition arise, and occasionally staff and patient struggle covertly over the definition throughout the encounters.[18] The staff take more preventive measures where they anticipate the most trouble: young, unmarried girls; persons known to be temporarily upset; and persons with reputations as uncooperative. In such cases, the doctor may explain the technical details of the procedure more carefully and offer direct reassurance. Perhaps he will take extra time to establish personal rapport, as by medically related inquiries ("How are you feeling?" "Do you have as much pain today?"), personal inquiries ("Where do you live?"), addressing the patient by her first name, expressing direct sympathy, praising the patient for her behavior in this difficult situation, speaking in a caressing voice, and affectionate gestures. Doctors also attempt to reinforce rapport as a response to threatening events.

The foremost technique in neutralizing threatening events is to sustain a nonchalant demeanor even if the patient is blushing with embarrassment, blanching from fear, or moaning in pain. The patient's inappropriate gestures may be ignored as the staff convey, "We're waiting until you are ready to play along." Working to bring the scene off, the staff may claim that this is routine, or happens to patients in general; invoke the "for your own good" clause; counterclaim that something is less important than the patient indicates; assert that the unpleasant medical procedure is almost over; and contend that the staff do not like to cause pain or trouble to patients (as by saying, "I'm sorry" when they appear to be causing pain). The staff may verbally contradict a patient, give an evasive answer to a question, or try to distract the patient. By giving a technical explanation or rephrasing in the appropriate hospital language something the patient has referred to in a nonmedical way, the staff member reinstates the medical definition.

Redefinition is another tactic available to the staff. Signs of embarrassment and sexual arousal in patients may be redefined as "fear of pain." Sometimes sexual arousal will be labeled "ticklishness." After one examination, the doctor thanked the patient, presumably for her cooperation, thus typifying the patient's behavior as cooperative and so omitting a series of uncooperative acts which he had previously acknowledged.

Humor may be used to discount the line the patient is taking. At the same time, humor provides a safety valve for all parties whereby the sexual connotations and general concern about gynecological examinations may be expressed by indirection. Without taking the responsibility that a serious form of the message would entail, the participants may communicate with each other about the events at hand. They may discount the derogatory implications of what would be an invasion of privacy in another setting by dismissing the procedure with a laugh. If a person can joke on a topic, he demonstrates to others that he possesses a laudatory degree of detachment.

For example, in one encounter, a patient vehemently protests, "Oh, Dr. Raleigh, what are you doing?" Dr. Raleigh, exaggerating his southern accent, answers, "Nothin'." His levity conveys: "However much you may dislike this, we have to go on with it for your own good. Since you know that perfectly well, your protest could not be calling for a serious answer." Dr. Raleigh also plays the seducer claiming innocence, thus obliquely referring to the sexual connotations of where his hand is at the moment. In another incident, Doctor Ryan is attempting to remove some gauze which has been placed in the vagina to stop the bleeding. He flippantly announces that the remaining piece of gauze has disappeared inside the patient. After a thorough search, Doctor Ryan holds up a piece of gauze on the instrument triumphantly: "Well, here it is. Do you want to take it home and put it in your scrapbook?" By this remark, Doctor Ryan ridicules the degree of involvement in one's own medical condition which would induce a patient to save this kind of memento. Later in the same examination, Dr. Ryan announces he will do a rectal examination and the (elderly) patient protests, "Oh, honey, don't bother." Dr. Ryan assures her jokingly, "It's no bother, really." The indirect message of all three jokes is that one should take gynecological procedures casually. Yet simultaneously an undercurrent of each joke acknowledges a perspective contrary to the medical definition.

While in most encounters, the nurse remains quietly in the background, she comes forward to deal actively with the patient if the definition of reality is threatened. In fact, one of the main functions of her presence is to provide a team member for the doctor in those occasional instances where the patient threatens to get out of line. Team members can create a more convincing reality than one person alone. Doctor and nurse may collude against an uncooperative patient, as by giving each other significant looks. If things reach the point of staff collusion, however, it may mean that only by excluding the patient can the definition of reality be reaffirmed. A more drastic form of solidifying the definition by excluding recalcitrant participants is to cast the patient into the role of an "emotionally disturbed person." Whatever an "emotionally disturbed person" may think or do does not count against the reality the rest of us acknowledge.

Perhaps the major safeguard of reality is that challenge is channeled outside the examination. Comments about the unpleasantness of the procedure and unaesthetic features of the patient's body occur mainly between women, two patients, or a nurse and a patient. Such comments are most frequent while the patient gets ready for the examination and waits for the doctor or after the doctor leaves. The patient may establish a momentary "fellow-woman aura" as she quietly voices her distaste for the procedure to the nurse. "What we women have to go through" the patient may say. Or, "I wish all gynecologists were women." Why? "They understand because they've been through it themselves." The patient's confiding manner implies: "I have no right to say this, or even feel it, and yet I do." This phenomenon suggests that patients actually have strong negative reactions to gynecological examinations which belie their acquiescence in the actual situation. Yet patients' doubts are expressed in an innocuous way which does not undermine the definition of reality when it is most needed.

To construct the scene convincingly, participants constantly monitor their own behavior and that of others. The tremendous work of producing the scene is contained in subtle maneuvers in regard to details which may appear inconsequential to the layman. Since awareness may interfere with a convincing performance, the participants may have an investment in being as unselfconscious as possible. But the sociologist is free to recognize the significance of "inconsequential details" in constructing reality.

Conclusion

In a gynecological examination, the reality sustained is not the medical definition alone, but a dissonance of themes and counterthemes. What is done to acknowledge one theme undermines the others. No theme can be taken for granted because its opposite is always in mind. That is why the reality of a gynecological examination can never be routinized, but always remains precarious.

The gynecological examination should not be dismissed as an anomaly. The phenomenon is revealed more clearly in this case because it is an extreme example. But the gynecological examination merely exaggerates the internally contradictory nature of definitions of reality found in most situations. Many situations where the dominant definition is occupational or technical have a secondary theme of sociality which must be implicitly acknowledged (as in buttering up the secretary, small talk with sales clerks, or the undertaker's show of concern for the bereaved family). In "business entertaining" and conventions of professional associations, a composite definition of work and pleasure is sustained. Under many circumstances, a composite definition of action as both deviant and unproblematic prevails. For example, while Donald Ball stresses the claim of respectability in his description of an abortion clinic, his material illustrates the interplay of the dominant theme of respectability and a countertheme wherein the illicitness of the situation is acknowledged.[19] Internally inconsistent definitions also are sustained in many settings on who persons are and what their relation is to each other.

Sustaining a sense of the solidness of a reality composed of multiple contradictory definitions takes unremitting effort. The required balance among the various definitions fluctuates from moment to moment. The appropriate balance depends on what the participants are trying to do at that moment. As soon as one matter is dealt with, something else comes into focus, calling for a different balance. Sometimes even before one issue is completed, another may impose itself as taking priority. Further, each balance contains the seeds of its own demise, in that a temporary emphasis on one theme may disturb the long-run balance unless subsequent emphasis on the countertheme negates it. Because the most effective balance depends on many unpredictable factors, it is difficult to routinize the balance into formulas that prescribe a specific balance for given conditions. Routinization is also impractical because the particular forms by which the themes are expressed are opportunistic. That is, persons seize opportunities for expression according to what would be a suitable move at each unique moment of an encounter. Therefore, a person constantly must attend to how to express the balance of themes via the currently available means.

Multiple contradictory realities are expressed on various levels of explicitness and implicitness. Sustaining a sense of solidness of reality depends on the right balance of explicit and implicit expressions of each theme through a series of points in time. The most effective gestures express a multitude of themes on different levels. The advantages of multiple themes in the same gesture are simultaneous qualification of one theme by another, hedging (the gesture lacks one definite meaning), and economy of gestures.

Rational choices of explicit and implicit levels would take the following into account. The explicit level carries the most weight, unless countered by deliberate effort. Things made explicit are hard to dismiss or discount compared to what is left implicit. In fact, if the solidification of explication is judged to be nonreversible, use of the explicit level may not be worth the risk. On the other hand, when participants sense that the implicit level is greatly in use, their whole edifice of belief may become shaken. "I sense that a lot is going on underneath" makes a person wonder about the reality he is accepting. There must be a lot he does not know, some of which might be evidence which would undermine what he currently accepts.

The invalidation of one theme by the concurrent expression of its countertheme must be avoided by various maneuvers. The guiding principle is that participants must prevent a definition that a contradiction exists between theme and countertheme from emerging. Certain measures routinely contribute to this purpose. Persons must try to hedge on both theme and countertheme by expressing them tentatively rather than definitely and simultaneously alluding to and discounting each theme. Theme and countertheme should not be presented simultaneously or contiguously on the explicit level unless it is possible to discount their contradictory features. Finally, each actor must work to keep the implicit level out of awareness for the other participants.

The technique of constructing reality depends on good judgment about when to make things explicit and when to leave them implicit, how to use the implicit level to reinforce and qualify the explicit level, distributing themes among explicit and implicit levels at any one moment, and seizing opportunities to embody messages. To pursue further these tentative suggestions on how important explicit and implicit levels are for sustaining reality, implicit levels of communication must be explored more systematically.

Notes

1. P. Berger & T. Luckmann (1966), *The social construction of reality,* Garden City, NY: Doubleday.

2. The precarious nature of social interaction is discussed throughout the work of Erving Goffman.

3. The data in this article are based on observations of approximately 75 gynecological examinations conducted by male physicians on an obstetrics-gynecology ward and some observations from a medical ward for comparison. For a full account of this study, see J. P. Emerson (1963), "Social functions of humor in a hospital setting," unpublished doctoral dissertation, University of California at Berkeley. For a sociological discussion of a similar setting, see W. P. Rosengren & S. DeVault (1963), "The sociology of time and space in an obstetrical hospital," in E. Freidson (Ed.), *The hospital in modern society* (pp. 266–292), New York: Free Press of Glencoe.

4. "It takes severe biographical shocks to disintegrate the massive reality internalized in early childhood; much less to destroy the realities internalized later. Beyond this, it is relatively easy to set aside the reality of the secondary internalizations." Berger & Luckmann (1966), p. 142.

5. As stated by Lief and Fox: "The amounts and occasions of bodily contact are carefully regulated in all societies, and very much so in ours. Thus, the kind of access to the body of the patient that a physician in our society has is a uniquely privileged one. Even in the course of a so-called routine physical examination, the physician is permitted to handle the patient's body in ways otherwise permitted only to special intimates, and in the case of procedures such as rectal and vaginal examinations in ways normally not even permitted to a sexual partner." H. I. Lief & R. C. Fox (1963), "Training for 'detached concern' in medical students," in H. I. Lief et al. (Eds.), *The psychological basis of medical practice,* New York: Harper & Row, p. 32. As Edward Hall remarks, North Americans have an inarticulated convention that discourages touching except in moments of intimacy. E. T. Hall (1959), *The silent language,* Garden City, NY: Doubleday, p. 149.

6. For comments on embarrassment in the doctor-patient relation, see M. Balint (1957), *The doctor, his patient, and the illness,* New York: International Universities Press, p. 57.

7. Physicians are aware of the possibility that their routine technical behavior may be interpreted as sexual by the patient. The following quotation states a view held by some physicians: "It is not unusual for a suspicious hysterical woman with fantasies of being seduced to misinterpret an ordinary movement in the physical examination as an amorous advance." E. Weiss & O. S. English (1949), *Psychosomatic medicine,* Philadelphia: W. B. Saunders; quoted in M. Hollender (1958), *The psychology of medical practice,* Philadelphia: W. B. Saunders, p. 22. An extreme case suggests that pelvic examinations are not without their hazards for physicians, particularly during training: "A third-year student who had prided himself on his excellent adjustment to the stresses of medical school developed acute anxiety when about to perform, for the first time, a pelvic examination on a gynecological patient. Prominent in his fantasies were memories of a punishing father who would unquestionably forbid any such explicitly sexual behavior." S. Bojar (1961), "Psychiatric problems of medical students," in G. B. Glaine, Jr., et al. (Eds.), *Emotional problems of the student.* Garden City, NY: Doubleday, p. 248.

8. Many other claims and assumptions are being negotiated or sustained in addition to this basic definition of the situation. Efforts in regard to some of these other claims and assumptions have important consequences for the fate of the basic definition. That is, in the actual situation, any one gesture usually has relevance for a number of realities, so that the fates of the various realities are intertwined with each other. For example, each participant is putting forth a version of himself which he wants validated. A doctor's jockeying about claims about competence may reinforce the medical definition and so may a patient's interest in appearing poised. But a patient's ambition to "understand what is really happening" may lead to undermining of the medical definition. Understanding that sustaining the basic definition of the situation is intertwined with numerous other projects, however, we will proceed to focus on that reality alone.

9. Compare Donald Ball's account of how the medical definition is conveyed in an abortion clinic, where it serves to counter the definition of the situation as deviant. D. W. Ball (1967, Winter), "An abortion clinic ethnography" *Social Problems, 14,* 293–301.

10. Glaser and Strauss discuss the hospital prohibition against examinations and exposure of the body in the presence of intimates of the patient. B. Glaser & A. Strauss (1965), *Awareness of dying,* Chicago: Aldine, p. 162.

11. Sudnow reports that at the county hospital he studied, male physicians routinely did pelvic examinations without nurses being present, except in the emergency ward. D. Sudnow (1967), *Passing on: The social organization of dying,* Englewood Cliffs, NJ: Prentice Hall, p. 78.

12. The following quotation suggests that euphemisms and understood references may be used because the staff often has the choice of using "lewd words" or not being understood. "Our popular vocabulary for describing sexual behavior has been compounded of about equal

parts of euphemism and obscenity, and popular attitude and sentiment have followed the same duality. Among both his male and female subjects, the interviewers found many who knew only the lewd words for features of their own anatomy and Physiology." N. N. Foote (1955), "Sex as play," in J. Himelhock & S. F. Fava, *Sexual behavior in American society,* New York: Norton, p. 239.

13. The doctor's demeanor typically varies with his experience. In his early contacts with patients, the young medical student may use an extreme degree of impersonality generated by his own discomfort in his role. By the time he has become accustomed to doctor-patient encounters, the fourth-year student and intern may use a newcomer's gentleness, treating the scene almost as an intimate situation by relying on elements of the "loving" demeanor previously learned in nonprofessional situations. By the time he is a resident and focusing primarily on the technical details of the medical task, the physician may be substituting a competent impersonality, although he never reverts to the extreme impersonality of the very beginning. The senior doctor, having mastered not only the technical details but an attitude of detached concern as well, reintroduces a mild gentleness, without the involved intimacy of the intern.

14. The management of closeness and detachment in professional-client relations is discussed in C. Kadushin (1962, March), "Social distance between client and professional," *American Journal of Sociology, 67,* 517–531. Wilensky and Lebeaux discuss how intimacy with strangers in the social worker-client relation is handled by accenting the technical aspects of the situation, limiting the relationship to the task at hand, and observing the norms of emotional neutrality, impartiality, and altruistic service. H. L. Wilensky & C. N. Lebeaux (1958), *Industrial society and social welfare,* New York: Russell Sage Foundation, pp. 299–303.

15. For a discussion of the socialization of medical students toward a generally detached attitude, see Lief & Fox (1963), pp. 12–35. See also M. J. Daniels (1960, November), "Affect and its control in the medical intern," *American Journal of Sociology, 66,* 259–267.

16. The following incident illustrates how a patient may exceed the limits. Mrs. Lane, a young married woman, was considered by the physicians a "seductive patient," although her technique was subtle and her behavior never improper. After examining Mrs. Lane, an intern privately called my attention to a point in the examination when he was pressing on the patient's ovaries and she remarked to the nurse: "I have this pain in intercourse until my insides are about to come out." The intern told me that Mrs. Lane said that to the nurse, but she wanted him to hear. He didn't want to know that, he said; it wasn't necessary for her to say that. The intern evidently felt that Mrs. Lane's remark had exceeded the bounds of decorum. A specific medical necessity makes the imparting of private information acceptable, the doctor's reaction suggests, and not merely the definition of the situation as medical.

17. There is reason to think that those patients who would have most difficulty in maintaining their poise generally avoid the situation altogether. Evidence that some uncool women avoid pelvic examinations is found in respondents' remarks quoted by Rainwater: "I have thought of going to a clinic for a diaphragm, but I'm real backward about doing that. I don't even go to the doctor to be examined when I'm pregnant. I never go until about a month before I have the baby." "To tell you frankly, I'd like a diaphragm but I'm just too embarrassed to go get one." L. Rainwater (1960), *And the poor get children,* Chicago: Quadrangle, pp. 10, 31.

18. An example of such a struggle is analyzed in J. P. Emerson (1970), "Nothing unusual is happening," in T. Shibutani (Ed.), *Human nature and collective behavior.* Papers in honor of Herbert Blumer, Englewood Cliffs, NJ: Prentice Hall.

19. Donald Ball (1967).

15

HIV Health Care Provider-Patient Interaction

Observations on the Process of Providing Antiretroviral Treatment

Jeff Erger, Oscar Grusky, Traci Mann, and William Marelich

Power and status have strong effects on communication, and this is especially true in the health care arena. Interactions between patients and health care providers are not straightforward, but fraught with barriers and tensions on both sides. Pressures on the busy provider to get to the next patient and pressures on the patient to cope with serious medical conditions compound basic difficulties in communication created by status and power differences. The goal of this pilot study is to describe the interaction of HIV+ patients and health care providers at the meeting when treatment options are first discussed. This meeting is critical to the development of the patient-provider relationship, as it is the first time there can be any action discussed or plans made. In general, this meeting and the decisions made during the meeting set the stage for years of complex and changing medical treatments. Specifically, we hypothesize that this meeting influences who receives and who does not receive antiretroviral treatment. There are many factors that influence the interaction between patients and health care providers and the decisions made during these meetings. These factors include but are not limited to communication, power, status, and perceptions of the likeliness that the patient will comply with treatment.

Meetings between patients and health care providers are situations where the task is primarily one of communication. The patient tries to explain

EDITORS' NOTE: Previously published in *AIDS Patient Care and STDs, 14,* pp. 259-268. Copyright ©2000. Reprinted with permission.

his problems and the health care provider tries to explain what can be done about those problems. Given that these interactions are where much of the work of health care gets done, where diagnoses are made and treatments prescribed, it is not surprising that a great deal of research has been done in this area (DiMatteo, Hayes, & Prince, 1986; DiMatteo et al., 1993; Hall, Roter, & Rand, 1981; Roter, 1984; Roter & Hall, 1992). However, not much attention has been paid to interactions in the *HIV/AIDS* setting specifically.

While observational studies of patient-provider interactions in HIV/AIDS are relatively few, the factors that have been shown to affect the quality and quantity of communication in the health care setting in general should give insight into the HIV/AIDS setting. Severity and acuteness of illness alter the pattern of interaction, with chronic illness being treated with a more balanced interaction pattern and acute illness resulting in a more physician-dominated interaction (Szasz & Hollender, 1956). Many studies have found a failure to explain a patient's condition and treatment in terms the patient can easily understand (Allman, Yoels, & Clair, 1993; Clair, 1993; Coe, 1978; Davis, 1972; Fisher & Todd, 1990). Physicians report two primary reasons for not communicating fully with their patients; the inability to understand and the potentially negative effect of threatening information (Davis, 1972; Howard & Strauss, 1975). Doctors tend towards evasiveness or technical language when communicating threatening information.

Some health care providers are effective communicators. In general, conversations involve both active speaking and active listening, with the speaker and listener roles constantly being exchanged (Zimmerman & West, 1975). Nods, verbal encouragement to "go on," questions, and a lack of interruptions are consistent with being a good listener. Nonverbal skills increase patient compliance and patient satisfaction with care (DiMatteo et al., 1986) Information is best used in the medical treatment setting when it reduces uncertainty, provides a basis for action, and/or strengthens the patient-provider relationship (Cassell, 1985).

Status factors have been shown to contribute to *mis*-communication in the health care setting. Cultural factors often influence communication, with members of some ethnic groups understating symptoms, while others tend to overstate symptoms; some groups give concise descriptions of maladies, while others give very detailed descriptions (Zola, 1966). Poorly educated patients are more likely to have their questions ignored (Atkinson, 1995). The class of the provider is also important, with providers from an upper-middle class background tending to communicate more information than providers from lower or working class backgrounds (Waitzkin, 1991).

Perhaps the main factors that shape interaction in the health care setting are power and status (Atkinson, 1995). The health care provider seeks to take control over the patient's problem, and what should be done about it. The focus during meetings is typically limited to medical issues. Social and personal factors are usually marginal to the task at hand (Waitzkin, Britt, & Williams, 1994).

An issue strongly related to power and particularly important in the treatment of HIV/AIDS is the issue of adherence, especially with complex highly active antiretroviral therapies (HAART). As providers are aware of this, they tend to use adherence as a major factor in organizing their decision making (Marelich et al., 2000). Providers look at the question of adherence as one of "Will the patient comply with what I tell them to do?" placing the burden of adherence strictly on the patient. However the patient-provider *relationship* can affect adherence, and this relationship is forged from the first meeting (Conference Report, 1997). Adherence is increased if there is clear communication between the patient and provider, if the connection is empathic, if rapport is established, and if there is systematic follow-up by the provider (Becker & Maiman, 1975; DiMatteo et al., 1993; O'Brien, Petrie, & Raeburn, 1992).

Because the communication between patient and provider is particularly important during the meeting at which treatment decisions are made, in the current study, we attempt to assess what factors influence the treatment decision process in the HIV/AIDS care setting. In addition, we attempt to describe in detail the features that typify these interactions. Our goal is to describe *what* happens in these meetings, and try to understand *why* it happens as it does.

Methods

Participants

Participants were 10 HIV patients (9 male) ranging in age from 28 to 50 (mean 34.5). All patients were on public assistance, and 4 patients were African-American, 5 were Caucasian, and 1 was Latino. To be eligible for the study, patients had to have never before received combination antiretroviral therapy for HIV, be age 18 or older, be new patients at the clinics under study, be asymptomatic, and speak enough English so that their interactions with the provider would be in English. The purpose of the interactions was to make a decision about the appropriate treatment protocol for each patient (Mann et al., in press).

The patients were seen by one of four female health care providers. Two of the providers were nurse practitioners, and two were physicians' assistants. The providers worked at one of two managed care clinics whose clients were limited to HIV patients.

Clinic A served an urban, ethnically diverse population (60% of clients receive Ryan White benefits; 35% Caucasian, 16% African-American, 48% Latino, 1% Asian/Pacific Islander). Both physicians' assistants worked at Clinic A. There are a total of 5 full-time primary care providers at Clinic A, and the two providers included in this study see approximately 50% of Clinic A's patients between them. Clinic A serves approximately 540 patients per month and receives 40 new patients per month.

Clinic B served a more affluent population (50% of clients receive Ryan White benefits; 50% Caucasian, 23% African-American, 20% Latino, and 7% Asian/Pacific Islander). There are a total of three full-time primary care providers at Clinic B, and the two providers included in this study (both nurse practitioners) see approximately 60% of Clinic B's patients between them. Clinic B serves approximately 800 patients per month and receives 30 new patients per month.

Procedures

Eligible patients were invited to participate by clinic staff, and if patients were interested, two researchers described the study to them and obtained their consent. All 10 patients contacted agreed to participate. Five cases were observed where HAART was prescribed and five where it was not. Providers gave consent to participate before the researchers approached patients. After consenting to participate, providers were given a copy of the Department of Health and Human Services (DHHS) Guidelines for the Use of Antiretroviral Agents.

Two observers (the same researchers that obtained patient consent) accompanied each patient to an examination room where the interaction took place. Both observers were seated on chairs in the corners of the rooms during the interactions, and did not speak unless asked a direct question by the patient or provider. The interaction was a conversation and hence did not involve a medical examination or medical tests. The observers coded the interactions using the Discussion Topic Checklist (Mann et al., in press). In addition to coding interaction *behaviors,* such as interruptions, smiles, backchanneling, etc., the checklist was designed to enable the observers to keep track of all relevant *topics* that were discussed during the interaction. The checklist listed the five benefit items and the six risk items that the DHHS guidelines indicate should be mentioned when HAART is discussed, as well as items about treatment protocols (e.g., treatment options, drug adherence). If the items were discussed during the interaction, the observers checked them off on the list. The Discussion Topic Checklist was pretested and refined using mock provider-patient interactions. The observers were willing to leave the room if either the patient or the provider asked them to do so, and were asked to leave one time so that a provider could examine a patient.

After the observation stage, the observers and patient left the room. Each observer separately audiotaped a narrative of the interaction based on notes, ratings, and recollections from the interaction. The observers then met to review the Discussion Topic Checklist and to come to a consensus on the Discussion Topic items. Original responses were retained so that reliability analyses could be conducted. Observers' initial assessment of the Discussion Topic Checklist items were in agreement 89% of the time.

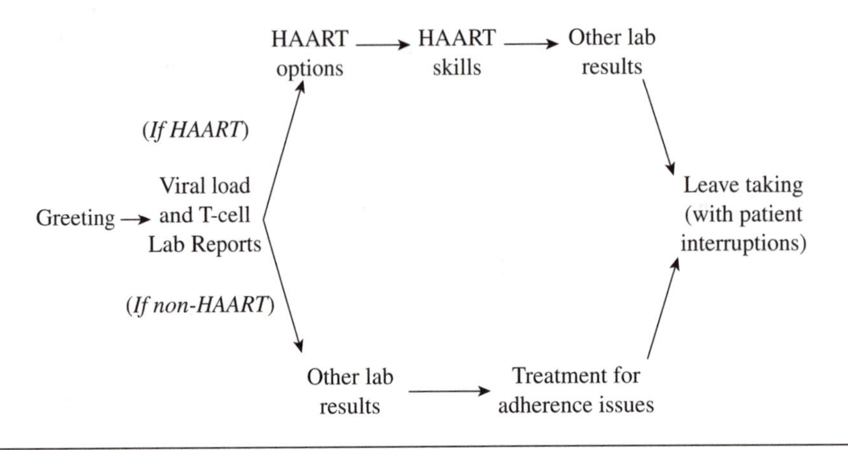

Figure 15.1 Typical Interaction Sequences for Highly Active Antiretroviral Therapy (HAART) and Non-HAART Treatment Discussions

RESULTS

The findings of this preliminary investigation show certain patterns in the *interaction sequence* that vary according to the treatment decision. We also found differences in *interactional style* between providers at the two clinics. Additionally, we found that the introduction of a *single treatment option* is common to these interactions regardless of the treatment decision. Providers focused on the *will and skills* that patients need in order to adhere to complex treatment regimens. Finally, we found strong pressures in the *organizational structure* on the primary health care providers to channel patients into clinical trials.

The Interaction Sequence

One of the primary goals of this research project is to describe the interaction between patients and health care providers when they meet to make the initial treatment decisions. The interactions follow one of two general patterns, differing according to the treatment decision (see Figure 15.1).

Overall, the sessions lasted from 8 to 40 minutes, with a mean duration of 26.4 minutes. In cases where HAART was deferred, the mean time of interaction was 25.0 minutes, and in cases where HAART was prescribed, the mean interaction time was 27.8 minutes.[1]

Interactions began in the same way, with a very brief greeting sequence. This greeting ranged from momentary eye contact, to a simple exchange of "hello" and a nod, to more involved exchanges of small talk. Greeting sequences took at most 60 seconds before the next stage occurred.

After the greeting, the first issue for discussion was the result of the patient's t-cell count and viral load lab tests. Providers typically look at the patient's chart and say "Your t-cells were X and your viral load was Y." This uniformity of pattern should not be surprising as the stated purpose of the meeting is to discuss these test results and to come to a decision about treatment. It is at this point that the patient is first called upon to provide input into the process. That these interactions follow the same pattern up to this point indicates a reliance on the patient medical history in the provider's organization of the situation, to the point that the provider has made a treatment decision before entering the exam room and beginning the interaction. Interviews of health care providers show a strong reliance on medical charts in these situations (Marelich et al., 2000).

After stating the test results, the provider might ask, "Do you know what those mean?" or the patient might say, "That is good, right?" or "That is pretty high." Typically those who are newly infected have little knowledge of what the test results mean in terms of the immune system or their prognosis, while those who have been infected for some time have better understanding. This is a key opportunity for the provider to assess the current level of knowledge of the patient, as well as the patient's ability to comprehend medical issues in general. The meaning of the test results for the patient's health is then discussed, with providers explaining in greater or lesser detail according to the level of knowledge displayed by the patient.

It is at this point in the interaction that the sequence of events diverges for those who are prescribed HAART and those who are not. Turning first to those that are prescribed HAART (the upper path in Figure 15.1), discussion proceeds to which options are available for combination therapy. This stage in the interaction begins with either a question such as "How do you feel about medication?" or a statement ". . . but I think we should put you on medications." The varieties of combination therapy that are available are then discussed, and the interaction segues to the next stage, that of the skills needed to successfully comply with HAART regimens.

During the discussion of various HAART regimens, questions about work schedules, presence of refrigerators, diet schedules, roommates' attitudes about HIV medication, and other issues relevant to adherence are investigated. Generally the focus is on pill-taking behavior and what might interfere with pill taking. Once a decision is arrived upon, pill acquisition (clinic procedures, pill cases, pharmacy choice, etc.) is discussed.

The last stage in interaction for these cases is discussion of other lab results and any other medical problems the patient may be experiencing. It is not unusual for the provider to signal that the session is drawing to a close, have the patient bring up some health concern, and have a discussion of that issue for 5 minutes or so. When the provider ends the session, it is typically with a summation of what needs to be done by the patient ("Go see the case worker to fill out these forms") and a reminder of the next scheduled meeting ("I will see you in 3 months").

The interactions where there are no HAART prescribed (lower path in Figure 15.1) differ a bit in sequence and content. After the discussion of t-cell and viral load lab results, it is far more likely that the rest of the lab results are then discussed. Following this is a discussion of problems the patient has that would interfere with a HAART regimen. These issues include substance abuse and mental disorders, and the majority of the patient-provider interaction is dedicated to emphasizing the importance of treating these disorders so that HAART therapy will be effective. In addition, this is where the groundwork is often laid for future HAART discussions. This includes such things as the distribution and emphasis on literature (e.g., pamphlets) and praise for the efficacy of HAART regimens in helping patients.

Overall, the interaction sequence in both the HAART and non-HAART interactions shows the emphasis on HAART as the end point in the treatment process. Providers believe that all patients will eventually be on HAART, if not now, then some time in the future. This perceived end point or goal shapes the observed interaction, and likely shapes the future interactions as well to a great degree.

Interactional Styles

There were several differences in interaction patterns between the two clinics. Clinic A employed physician's assistants, while Clinic B used nurse practitioners. However, the differences observed between the two settings cannot with certainty be attributed to the status of the provider, the clientele, or the procedures of the clinics.

The physicians' assistants consistently spent more time with patients, used more "personal" interaction styles, smiled more, and directed their gazes at the patient more than the nurse practitioners. The nurse practitioners used more "professional" and impersonal interaction styles. The physicians' assistants also questioned patients more on aspects of the patient's lives, such as living arrangements, presence of roommates in the household, and transportation problems. In contrast, the nurse practitioners employed more of a medical model of the patient (Siegler & Osmond, 1974), focusing on the direct issues of viral load and t-cell counts, as well as pill-taking behavior, to the near exclusion of other issues.

The organizational structure and clinic setting also affected the interactions. The clinic where the physicians' assistants practiced was noisier and busier (as seen by more patients in the waiting room and longer delays for patients waiting to see the providers). It serves a population more at risk and more diverse than the clinic where the nurse practitioners practice.

The combination of lower status of both physicians' assistants and the population they serve contributes to the observed differences. A diverse and marginalized client base presents more problems to effective treatment by making communication more difficult. These clients are more likely to have characteristics indicating lower likelihood of adherence to medications. Providers must be aware of the individual characteristics of each patient, and look for and be ready to probe for indications of troublesome conditions in each patient. In contrast, the relatively higher status of the nurse practitioners and the uniformity and higher status of the population they serve lead to a more routinized pattern of interaction.

While the description of the interaction in these meetings is important, several major themes influencing the decision-making process emerged from our observations. We believe these factors to be of primary importance in determining what treatment decision is made during these sessions. The presentation of a *single treatment option* to the patient and the provider's search for patient *will and skills* needed for successful therapy were both important in these sessions. Additionally, some evidence of *organizational structure* channeling patients into clinical trials was seen.

Single Treatment Option

The introduction of potential treatments was performed by the provider. In those cases when HAART was prescribed, the provider presented one type of treatment as possible. For example, "We are going to start you on a cocktail" or, " . . . but I think we should start you on medications." Similarly, in cases where HAART was not prescribed, one treatment type was mentioned by providers. For example, in a case where the patient was a methamphetamine user, the provider said she was going to refer him to a psychiatrist for his depression, and to support groups to help with his drug problem. After stating this was what she was going to do, she asked "Well, what do you think of this plan?" In cases where t-cell counts were high and viral loads were low, providers typically would state, "We will just keep an eye on things, 'cause your numbers look good."

In each case, one type of treatment was presented to the patient for the patient's approval or disapproval. The provider did not present a range of options and the risks and benefits associated with each option. By presenting limited options, the provider better controls the situation and presents himself/herself as knowledgeable. This control is an act that maintains the power of the provider by minimizing any opportunity for the patient to contest the recommendation of the provider. Providers often employ interactional strategies that seek to minimize "trouble" (Emerson, 1970).

Will and Skills

While the patterns of interaction follow the general pattern according to HAART/non-HAART treatment decision and the presentation of a single option, the specific details of the interactions vary a great deal. When patients are clearly not candidates for medication (e.g., t-cell 860, viral load 513) the interaction is straightforward. However, for the majority of cases, one general theme did emerge from the observation of patient-provider meetings; providers are looking to see if patients have the *will* to begin therapy, and if they have the *skills* to adhere to a complex regimen of medications.

The assessment of will happens quickly, and early in the interaction. Sometimes it is a direct question from the provider, such as "How do you feel about medications?" and other times it comes from patients' statements, "I am ready to do whatever it takes." If patients express doubts, fears, or concerns about medications, the provider attempts to address these concerns. For example, some patients have heard bad things about AZT, and providers typically address these concerns by putting the "trouble" with AZT in historical context, often pointing out that AZT once was used alone, but now is used in combination with other medications with much better results. The provider is looking for a statement of willingness to act and will attempt to overcome any objections to action.

The assessment of skills is more complex. The skills needed for patients are an understanding of medication schedule, the understanding of requirements for each specific medication, and the ability to arrange their daily schedules so that pills can be taken at the time and under the conditions required. The primary source of information used by the provider in skill assessment is the medical history of the patient. Substance abuse and mental disorders are seen as interfering in the employment of skills needed to adhere to HAART regimens. Providers use this language when emphasizing the necessity of programs such as AA or referrals to psychiatric care to the patient. "We need to get this under control so that the medications will work." In general, the treatment decision was made by the provider before she met with the patient. This is clear from the single case where the provider did *not* have access to the patient chart before the meeting. This interaction lacked focus until the chart arrived, at which point after a glance at the chart, the provider clearly made a decision (defer treatment and refer to psychiatric care).

Additional information about skills is gained through the interaction. By pointing at pictures of pills, preparing a schedule of medications with the patient, giving the patient pamphlets and other materials about HAART therapy, providers can determine the level at which patients understand what they need to do. Misunderstandings can be corrected, and the importance of adherence can be mentioned repeatedly.

Often information is available in the interaction that indicates a *lack* of skill, but because of the placement of this information in the meeting sequence, this information is not seen as particularly problematic by the provider. Patient confusion was clear several times regarding the complex regimens of HAART that were being prescribed. After several attempted explanations, the provider might state that "all of this will be in the pamphlets I will give you." As the decision on treatment is agreed to by both patient and provider early in the meeting, providers fit new information into terms of the already-made decision and do not use emergent information to alter the decision.

The reliance on pamphlets to communicate the details of HAART can be especially problematic when the patient is poorly educated; the patient that is confused in the verbal description may be the patient that is *least* likely to benefit by written materials. Additionally, by glossing over the confusion of the patient, providers risk being seen as aloof, uncaring about the patient's confusion, and may miss a chance to strengthen the patient-provider relationship. A simple statement such as "I know this is very confusing to take in all at once, so look over the pamphlets I will give you over the next few days. If you have any questions, call" can go a long way in helping the patient feel better about the confusion produced by so much new information.

Organizational Structure

There was an indication of a strong push from the providers' superiors to enroll patients in clinical trials. On three separate occasions, there was mention of clinical trials. In the first, a provider said "We're going to start you on a cocktail because your viral load is so high, we are not going to screen you for research." This suggested that the clinic is organized to screen everyone for clinical trials. On another occasion, a physician joined a patient-provider session, and after the nurse practitioner informed him what they had discussed thus far, his first question was "Did you discuss clinical trials?" Finally, the clinic's research coordinator was observed stopping a nurse practitioner in the hallway to ask if a certain patient met the criteria for a clinical trial.

The transformation of the nurse practitioners and physician's assistants from expert to subordinate when interacting with their superiors in the organization was striking. They went from being active, talking, exhibiting highly confident body language, and controlling the situation, to passive, subservient observers. Their bodies drew in to take up less space, they directed their gaze at the superiors, and nodded in support of statements made by those superiors.

Nurse practitioners and physician's assistants are not passive and unaware actors in terms of power. On the contrary, they are very aware of their dual position in the organization. One physician's assistant commented on her not wearing a white lab coat, saying "I try to establish a relationship, and I don't want that coat getting in the way." The same provider later said, "I had to make sure to be professional with him, because he is a straight white male, and I don't want him to think of me as a woman, but as someone who knows what he needs to do." Other comments showed an awareness of the higher status of physicians, such as stating that when a physician said something to a patient, it really hit home.

From the perspective of the organization, the inclusion of patients in clinical trials is a good thing for many reasons: The patient receives close monitoring, the clinic saves resources that can be used for other patients, and clinical trials can lead to new medications that can help many people.

Conclusion and Discussion

As this is an exploratory study, any conclusions drawn are preliminary and should be taken with caution. Given the small number of providers, patients, and clinics included, it would be inappropriate to generalize these findings to the larger HIV/AIDS care system. We would expect managed care clinics such as those studied here to differ from fee-for-service providers. Additionally, as these interactions were at the first meeting between the provider and patient, this study looks at one small slice of a broad and ongoing process. Previous experience with health care systems by the patient, patient knowledge of and attitudes about health care issues, and future interactions between patient and provider all have important ramifications on the outcome of treatment; these and other potentially important factors are not considered in this study. However, given the limitations of the data, some interesting conclusions can be drawn.

First, the sequence of events in the interactions shows the health care providers to be primarily focused on medical aspects of the patient and that the health care provider is focused on an end goal of successfully getting the patient on a HAART regimen. From the provider's perspective, those patients not immediately prescribed HAART will eventually be on HAART, and this assumption of medication strongly shapes the interaction.

Second, providers use a two-stage model to determine a patient's suitability for HAART. Initial focus is on t-cell and viral load as medical indicators of disease progression. After these test results indicate HAART is medically desirable, providers then try to assess the patient's will to begin therapy as well as if they have the skills needed to adhere to complex HAART regimens. When patients are seen as not ready for HAART, the provider attempts to prepare the patient to eventually begin HAART. When patients are not willing to begin treatment, due to fear of specific medications or medications in general, the provider attempts to convince the patient that medications are a good idea. When patients are perceived as being at risk of not adhering to treatment regimens, the provider attempts to overcome any lack of skill or condition that causes that risk.

Third, there are strong organizational pressures to include patients in clinical trials. This pressure reveals the complexity of the treatment decision in that it is not simply a case of the individual choosing the best option, or of a patient and provider negotiating a treatment option, but rather one where many factors influence the treatment decision at many levels. The position of the nurse practitioners and physician's assistants in these organizations is a difficult one, in that they do much of the work with patients but are under the supervision of physicians. Thus, they must present themselves to patients as knowledgeable experts, while presenting themselves to their supervising physicians as deferential and obedient. That they sometimes must interact with both patients and physicians at the same time complicates their role and leads to a great deal of role strain.

The results of this study indicate some directions for future research, both in patient-provider interaction and at the level of the organization. This study focused on medical aspects of the patient (as that is what the providers focused on), but other patient characteristics (e.g., gender, race) may affect the interaction and the treatment decision. More important, interactional styles of the patient may be critical to the outcome of the treatment decision. In this study, we looked at the initial meeting between patient and provider, but the ongoing interactions between patient and provider are more important than the first meeting. As patients gain knowledge about their condition, they are more likely to challenge the advice of the provider. How is this conflict handled? How does conflict between the patient and provider affect the treatment decisions made and the relationship between the patient and provider?

At the organizational level, there are many factors of potential interest. How does the training health care practitioners receive affect treatment decisions and interactional style? What organizational procedures and policies direct the treatment decisions, and how are these policies created, maintained, and changed?

The findings of this study suggest that power and status are key features in the early stages of the development of the treatment relationship between health care provider and patient. Power and status relations between patient and provider, as well as the power and status processes between the provider and the health care organization, shape the interaction between patient and provider when treatment options are discussed. These interactions show a tendency toward a presentation of options to the patient that are less than complete. To the extent that it is desirable that patients make decisions about their health care under conditions of full information, health care providers and health care organizations need to make special efforts to communicate treatment options, and the risks and benefits of those options, in terms that patients can understand.

Note

1. In only one case was the duration under 20 minutes, a case where treatment was deferred. Eliminating this outlier gives a mean interaction time for deferred treatment cases of 29.3 minutes.

References

Allman, R., Yoels, W., & Clair, J. (1993). Reconciling the agendas of physicians and patients. In J. Clair & R. Allman (Eds.), *Sociomedical perspectives on patient care.* Lexington KY: University of Kentucky Press.

Atkinson, P. (1995). *Medical talk and medical work.* London: Sage.

Becker, M., & Maiman, L. (1975). Sociobehavioral determinants of compliance with health and medical care recommendations. *Medical Care, 23,* 10-24.

Cassell, E. (1985). *Talking with patients* (Vol. 2). Cambridge, MA: MIT Press.

Clair, J. (1993). The application of social science to medical practice. In J. Clair & R. Allman (Eds.), *Sociomedical perspectives on patient care.* Lexington, KY: University of Kentucky Press.

Coe, R. (1978). *Sociology of medicine* (2nd ed.). New York: McGraw-Hill.

Conference Report. (1997). *Adherence to new HIV therapies: A research conference.* Washington, D.C.

Davis, F. (1972). *Illness, interaction and the self.* Belmont, CA: Wadsworth.

DiMatteo, M., Hayes, R., & Prince, L. (1986). Relationship of physicians' nonverbal communication skill to patient satisfaction, appointment noncompliance, and physician workload. *Health Psychology, 5,* 581-593.

DiMatteo, M., Sherbourne, C., Hays, R., Ordway, L., Kravitz, R., & McGlynn, E. (1993). Physicians' characteristics influence patients' adherence to medical treatment: Results from the medical outcomes study. *Health Psychology, 12,* 93-102.

Emerson, J. (1970). Behavior in private places: Sustaining definitions of reality in gynecological examinations. In P. Drietsel (Ed.), *Recent sociology.* New York: Macmillian.

Fisher, S., & Todd, A. (1990). *The social organization of doctor-patient communication* (2nd ed.). Norwood, NJ: Ablex.

Hall, J., Roter, D., & Rand, C. (1981). Communication of affect between physician and patient. *Journal of Health and Social Behavior, 22,* 18-30.

Howard, J., & Strauss, A. (Eds.). (1975). *Humanizing health care.* New York: Wiley-Interscience.

Mann, T., Grusky, O., Marelich, W., & Erger, J. (in press). The implementation of the DHHS guidelines for the use of antiretroviral agents in HIV-infected adults: A pilot study. *AIDS Care.*

Marelich, W. D., Grusky, O., Mann, T., Erger, J., & Roberts, K. J. (2000). Medical markers, adherence myths, and organizational structure: A two-stage model of HIV healthcare provider decision making. In J. J. Kronenfeld (Ed.), *Research in the Sociology of Health Care: Health care providers, institutions, and patients—Changing patterns of care provision and care delivery* (Vol. 17, pp. 99-117). Stamford, CT: JAI Press.

O'Brien, M., Petrie, K., & Raeburn, J. 1992. Adherence to medication regimens: Updating a complex medical issue. *Medical Care Review, 49*(4), 435-454.

Roter, D. (1984). Patient question asking in physician-patient interaction. *Health Psychology, 3,* 395-409.

Roter, D., & Hall, J. (1992). *Doctors talking with patients/patients talking with doctors: Improving communication in medical visits.* Westport, CT: Auburn House.

Siegler, M., & Osmond, H. (1974). *Models of madness, models of medicine.* New York: Macmillan.

Szasz, T., & Hollender, M. (1956). A contribution to the philosophy of medicine: The basic models of the doctor-patient relationship. *Journal of the American Medical Association, 97,* 585-588.

Waitzkin, H. (1991). *The politics of medical encounters.* New Haven, CT: Yale University Press.

Waitzkin, H., Britt, T., & Williams, C. (1994). Narratives of aging and social problems in medical encounters with older persons. *Journal of Health and Social Behavior, 35,* 322-348.

Zimmerman, D., & West, C. (1975). Sex roles, interruptions and silences in conversation. In B. Thorne & N. Henley (Eds.), *Language and sex: Differences and dominance* (pp. 105-129). Rowley, MA: Newbury House.

Zola, I. (1966). Culture and symptoms—an analysis of patients' presenting complaints. *American Sociological Review, 31,* 615-630.

16

ON BEING SANE IN INSANE PLACES

D. L. ROSENHAN

If sanity and insanity exist, how shall we know them?

The question is neither capricious nor itself insane. However much we may be personally convinced that we can tell the normal from the abnormal, the evidence is simply not compelling. It is commonplace, for example, to read about murder trials wherein eminent psychiatrists for the defense are contradicted by equally eminent psychiatrists for the prosecution on the matter of the defendant's sanity. More generally, there are a great deal of conflicting data on the reliability, utility, and meaning of such terms as "sanity," "insanity," "mental illness," and "schizophrenia."[1] Finally, as early as 1934, Benedict suggested that normality and abnormality are not universal.[2] What is viewed as normal in one culture may be seen as quite aberrant in another. Thus, notions of normality and abnormality may not be quite as accurate as people believe they are.

To raise questions regarding normality and abnormality is in no way to question the fact that some behaviors are deviant or odd. Murder is deviant. So, too, are hallucinations. Nor does raising such questions deny the existence of the personal anguish that is often associated with "mental illness." Anxiety and depression exist. Psychological suffering exists. But normality and abnormality, sanity and insanity, and the diagnoses that flow from them may be less substantive than many believe them to be.

At its heart, the question of whether the sane can be distinguished from the insane (and whether degrees of insanity can be distinguished from each other) is a simple matter: Do the salient characteristics that lead to diagnoses reside in the patients themselves or in the environments and contexts in which observers find them? From Bleuler, through Kretchmer, through the formulators of the recently revised *Diagnostic and Statistical Manual of the*

American Psychiatric Association, the belief has been strong that patients present symptoms, that those symptoms can be categorized, and, implicitly, that the sane are distinguishable from the insane. More recently, however, this belief has been questioned. Based in part on theoretical and anthropological considerations, but also on philosophical, legal, and therapeutic ones, the view has grown that psychological categorization of mental illness is useless at best and downright harmful, misleading, and pejorative at worst. Psychiatric diagnoses, in this view, are in the minds of the observers and are not valid summaries of characteristics displayed by the observed.[3-5]

Gains can be made in deciding which of these is more nearly accurate by getting normal people (that is, people who do not have, and have never suffered, symptoms of serious psychiatric disorders) admitted to psychiatric hospitals and then determining whether they were discovered to be sane and, if so, how. If the sanity of such pseudopatients were always detected, there would be prima facie evidence that a sane individual can be distinguished from the insane context in which he is found. Normality (and presumably abnormality) is distinct enough that it can be recognized wherever it occurs, for it is carried within the person. If, on the other hand, the sanity of the pseudopatients were never discovered, serious difficulties would arise for those who support traditional modes of psychiatric diagnosis. Given that the hospital staff was not incompetent, that the pseudopatient had been behaving as sanely as he had been outside of the hospital, and that it had never been previously suggested that he belonged in a psychiatric hospital, such an unlikely outcome would support the view that psychiatric diagnosis betrays little about the patient but much about the environment in which an observer finds him.

This article describes such an experiment. Eight sane people gained secret admission to 12 different hospitals.[6] Their diagnostic experiences constitute the data of the first part of this article; the remainder is devoted to a description of their experiences in psychiatric institutions. Too few psychiatrists and psychologists, even those who have worked in such hospitals, know what the experience is like. They rarely talk about it with former patients, perhaps because they distrust information coming from the previously insane. Those who have worked in psychiatric hospitals are likely to have adapted so thoroughly to the settings that they are insensitive to the impact of that experience. And while there have been occasional reports of researchers who submitted themselves to psychiatric hospitalization,[7] these researchers have commonly remained in the hospitals for short periods of time, often with the knowledge of the hospital staff. It is difficult to know the extent to which they were treated like patients or like research colleagues. Nevertheless, their reports about the inside of the psychiatric hospital have been valuable. This article extends those efforts.

Pseudopatients and Their Settings

The eight pseudopatients were a varied group. One was a psychology graduate student in his 20's. The remaining seven were older and "established." Among them were three psychologists, a pediatrician, a psychiatrist, a painter, and a housewife. Three pseudopatients were women, five were men. All of them employed pseudonyms, lest their alleged diagnoses embarrass them later. Those who were in mental health professions alleged another occupation in order to avoid the special attentions that might be accorded by staff, as a matter of courtesy or caution, to ailing colleagues.[8] With the exception of myself (I was the first pseudopatient, and my presence was known to the hospital administrator and chief psychologist and, so far as I can tell, to them alone), the presence of pseudopatients and the nature of the research program was not known to the hospital staffs.[9]

The settings were similarly varied. In order to generalize the findings, admission into a variety of hospitals was sought. The 12 hospitals in the sample were located in five different states on the East and West coasts. Some were old and shabby, some were quite new. Some were research-oriented, others not. Some had good staff-patient ratios, others were quite understaffed. Only one was a strictly private hospital. All of the others were supported by state or federal funds or, in one instance, by university funds.

After calling the hospital for an appointment, the pseudopatient arrived at the admissions office complaining that he had been hearing voices. Asked what the voices said, he replied that they were often unclear, but as far as he could tell they said "empty," "hollow," and "thud." The voices were unfamiliar and were of the same sex as the pseudopatient. The choice of these symptoms was occasioned by their apparent similarity to existential symptoms. Such symptoms are alleged to arise from painful concerns about the perceived meaninglessness of one's life. It is as if the hallucinating person were saying, "My life is empty and hollow." The choice of these symptoms was also determined by the absence of a single report of existential psychoses in the literature.

Beyond alleging the symptoms and falsifying name, vocation, and employment, no further alterations of person, history, or circumstances were made. The significant events of the pseudopatient's life history were presented as they had actually occurred. Relationships with parents and siblings, with spouse and children, with people at work and in school, consistent with the aforementioned exceptions, were described as they were or had been. Frustrations and upsets were described along with joys and satisfactions. These facts are important to remember. If anything, they strongly biased the subsequent results in favor of detecting sanity, since none of their histories or current behaviors were seriously pathological in any way.

Immediately upon admission to the psychiatric ward, the pseudopatient ceased simulating any symptoms of abnormality. In some cases, there was a brief period of mild nervousness and anxiety, since none of the pseudopatients really believed that they would be admitted so easily. Indeed, their shared fear was that they would be immediately exposed as frauds and greatly embarrassed. Moreover, many of them had never visited a psychiatric ward; even those who had, nevertheless had some genuine fears about what might happen to them. Their nervousness, then, was quite appropriate to the novelty of the hospital setting, and it abated rapidly.

Apart from that short-lived nervousness, the pseudopatient behaved on the ward as he "normally" behaved. The pseudopatient spoke to patients and staff as he might ordinarily. Because there is uncommonly little to do on a psychiatric ward, he attempted to engage others in conversation. When asked by staff how he was feeling, he indicated that he was fine, that he no longer experienced symptoms. He responded to instructions from attendants, to calls for medication (which was not swallowed), and to dining-hall instructions. Beyond such activities as were available to him on the admissions ward, he spent his time writing down his observations about the ward, its patients, and the staff. Initially these notes were written "secretly," but as it soon became clear that no one much cared, they were subsequently written on standard tablets of paper in such public places as the dayroom. No secret was made of these activities.

The pseudopatient, very much as a true psychiatric patient, entered a hospital with no foreknowledge of when he would be discharged. Each was told that he would have to get out by his own devices, essentially by convincing the staff that he was sane. The psychological stresses associated with hospitalization were considerable, and all but one of the pseudopatients desired to be discharged almost immediately after being admitted. They were, therefore, motivated not only to behave sanely, but to be paragons of cooperation. That their behavior was in no way disruptive is confirmed by nursing reports, which have been obtained on most of the patients. These reports uniformly indicate that the patients were "friendly," "cooperative," and "exhibited no abnormal indications."

The Normal Are Not Detectably Sane

Despite their public "show" of sanity, the pseudopatients were never detected. Admitted, except in one case, with a diagnosis of schizophrenia,[10] each was discharged with a diagnosis of schizophrenia "in remission." The label "in remission" should in no way be dismissed as a formality, for at no time during any hospitalization had any question been raised about any pseudopatient's simulation. Nor are there any indications in the hospital records that the pseudopatient's status was suspect. Rather, the evidence is strong that, once labeled schizophrenic, the pseudopatient was stuck with that label. If the pseudopatient was to be discharged, he must naturally be "in remission"; but he was not sane, nor, in the institution's view, had he ever been sane.

The uniform failure to recognize sanity cannot be attributed to the quality of the hospitals, for, although there were considered variations among them, several are considered excellent. Nor can it be alleged that there was simply not enough time to observe the pseudopatients. Length of hospitalization ranged from 7 to 52 days, with an average of 19 days. The pseudopatients were not, in fact, carefully observed, but this failure clearly speaks more to traditions within psychiatric hospitals than to lack of opportunity.

Finally, it cannot be said that the failure to recognize the pseudopatients' sanity was due to the fact that they were not behaving sanely. While there was clearly some tension present in all of them, their daily visitors could detect no serious behavioral consequences—nor, indeed, could other patients. It was quite common for the patients to "detect" the pseudopatients' sanity. During the first three hospitalizations, when accurate counts were kept, 35 of a total of 118 patients on the admissions ward voiced their suspicions, some vigorously. "You're not crazy. You're a journalist, or a professor [referring to the continual note-taking]. You're checking up on the hospital." While most of the patients were reassured by the pseudopatient's insistence that he had been sick before he came in but was fine now, some continued to believe that the pseudopatient was sane throughout his hospitalization.[11] The fact that the patients often recognized normality when staff did not raises important questions.

Failure to detect sanity during the course of hospitalization may be due to the fact that physicians operate with a strong bias toward what statisticians call the type 2 error.[5] This is to say that physicians are more inclined to call a healthy person sick (a false positive, type 2) than a sick person healthy (a false negative, type 1). The reasons for this are not hard to find: It is clearly more dangerous to misdiagnose illness than health. Better to err on the side of caution, to suspect illness even among the healthy.

But what holds for medicine does not hold equally well for psychiatry. Medical illnesses, while unfortunate, are not commonly pejorative. Psychiatric diagnoses, on the contrary, carry with them personal, legal, and social stigmas.[12] It was therefore important to see whether the tendency toward diagnosing the sane insane could be reversed. The following experiment was arranged at a research and teaching hospital whose staff had heard these findings but doubted that such an error could occur in their hospital. The staff was informed that at some time during the following 3 months, one or more pseudopatients would attempt to be admitted into the psychiatric hospital. Each staff member was asked to rate each patient who presented himself at admissions or on the ward according to the likelihood that the patient was a pseudopatient. A 10-point scale was used, with a 1 and 2 reflecting high confidence that the patient was a pseudopatient.

Judgments were obtained on 193 patients who were admitted for psychiatric treatment. All staff who had had sustained contact with or primary responsibility for the patient—attendants, nurses, psychiatrists, physicians, and psychologists—were asked to make judgments. Forty-one patients were alleged, with high confidence, to be pseudopatients by at least one member of the staff. Twenty-three were considered suspect by at least one psychiatrist. Nineteen were suspected by one psychiatrist and one other staff member. Actually, no genuine pseudopatient (at least from my group) presented himself during this period.

The experiment is instructive. It indicates that the tendency to designate sane people as insane can be reversed when the stakes (in this case, prestige and diagnostic acumen) are high. But what can be said of the 19 people who were suspected of being "sane" by one psychiatrist and another staff member? Were these people truly "sane," or was it rather the case that in the course of avoiding the type 2 error the staff tended to make more errors of the first sort—calling the crazy "sane"? There is no way of knowing. But one thing is certain: Any diagnostic process that lends itself so readily to massive errors of this sort cannot be a very reliable one.

The Stickiness of Psychodiagnostic Labels

Beyond the tendency to call the healthy sick—a tendency that accounts better for diagnostic behavior on admission than it does for such behavior after a lengthy period of exposure—the data speak to the massive role of labeling in psychiatric assessment. Having once been labeled schizophrenic, there is nothing the pseudopatient can do to overcome the tag. The tag profoundly colors others' perceptions of him and his behavior.

From one viewpoint, these data are hardly surprising, for it has long been known that elements are given meaning by the context in which they occur. Gestalt psychology made this point vigorously, and Asch[13] demonstrated that there are "central" personality traits (such as "warm" versus "cold") which are so powerful that they markedly color the meaning of other information in forming an impression of a given personality.[14] "Insane," "schizophrenic," "manic-depressive," and "crazy" are probably among the most powerful of such central traits. Once a person is designated abnormal, all of his other behaviors and characteristics are colored by that label. Indeed, that label is so powerful that many of the pseudopatients' normal behaviors were overlooked entirely or profoundly misinterpreted. Some examples may clarify this issue.

Earlier I indicated that there were no changes in the pseudopatient's personal history and current status beyond those of name, employment, and, where necessary, vocation. Otherwise, a veridical description of personal history and circumstances was offered. Those circumstances were not psychotic. How were they made consonant with the diagnosis of psychosis? Or were those diagnoses modified in such a way as to bring them into accord with the circumstances of the pseudopatient's life, as described by him?

As far as I can determine, diagnoses were in no way affected by the relative health of the circumstances of a pseudopatient's life. Rather, the reverse occurred: The perception of his circumstances was shaped entirely by the diagnosis. A clear example of such translation is found in the case of a pseudopatient who had had a close relationship with his mother but was rather remote from his father during his early childhood. During adolescence and beyond, however, his father became a close friend, while his relationship with his mother cooled. His present relationship with his wife was characteristically close and warm. Apart from occasional angry exchanges, friction was minimal. The children had rarely been spanked. Surely there is nothing especially pathological about such a history. Indeed, many readers may see a similar pattern in their own experiences, with no markedly deleterious consequences. Observe, however, how such a history was translated in the psychopathological context, this from the case summary prepared after the patient was discharged.

> "This white 39 year-old male . . . manifests a long history of considerable ambivalence in close relationships, which begins in early childhood. A warm relationship with his mother cools during his adolescence. A distant relationship to his father is described as becoming very intense. Affective stability is absent. His attempts to control emotionality with his wife and children are punctuated by angry outbursts and, in the case of the children, spankings. And while he says that he has several good friends, one senses considerable ambivalence embedded in those relationships also. . . ."

The facts of the case were unintentionally distorted by the staff to achieve consistency with a popular theory of the dynamics of a schizophrenic reaction.[15] Nothing of an ambivalent nature had been described in relations with parents, spouse, or friends. To the extent that ambivalence could be inferred, it was probably not greater than is found in all human relationships. It is true the pseudopatient's relationships with his parents changed over time, but in the ordinary context, that would hardly be remarkable—indeed, it might very well be expected. Clearly, the meaning ascribed to his verbalizations (that is, ambivalence, affective instability) was determined by the diagnosis: schizophrenia. An entirely different meaning would have been ascribed if it were known that the man was "normal."

All pseudopatients took extensive notes publicly. Under ordinary circumstances, such behavior would have raised questions in the minds of observers, as, in fact, it did among patients. Indeed, it seemed so certain that the notes would elicit suspicion that elaborate precautions were taken to remove them from the ward each day. But the precautions proved needless. The closest any staff member came to questioning these notes occurred when one pseudopatient asked his physician what kind of medication he was receiving and began to write down the response. "You needn't write it," he was told gently. "If you have trouble remembering, just ask me again."

If no questions were asked of the pseudopatients, how was their writing interpreted? Nursing records for three patients indicate that the writing was seen as an aspect of their pathological behavior. "Patient engages in writing behavior" was the daily nursing comment on one of the pseudopatients who was never questioned about his writing. Given that the patient is in the hospital, he must be psychologically disturbed. And given that he is disturbed, continuous writing must be a behavioral manifestation of that disturbance, perhaps a subset of the compulsive behaviors that are sometimes correlated with schizophrenia.

One tacit characteristic of psychiatric diagnosis is that it locates the sources of aberration within the individual and only rarely within the complex of stimuli that surrounds him. Consequently, behaviors that are stimulated by the environment are commonly misattributed to the patient's disorder. For example, one kindly nurse found a pseudopatient pacing the long hospital corridors. "Nervous, Mr. X?" she asked.

"No, bored," he said.

The notes kept by pseudopatients are full of patient behaviors that were misinterpreted by well-intentioned staff. Often enough, a patient would go "berserk" because he had, wittingly or unwittingly, been mistreated by, say, an attendant. A nurse coming upon the scene would rarely inquire even cursorily into the environmental stimuli of the patient's behavior. Rather, she assumed that his upset derived from his pathology, not from his present interactions with other staff members. Occasionally, the staff might assume that the patient's family (especially when they had recently visited) or other patients had stimulated the outburst. But never were the staff found to assume that one of themselves or the structure of the hospital had anything to do with a patient's behavior. One psychiatrist pointed to a group of patients who were sitting outside the cafeteria entrance half an hour before lunchtime. To a group of young residents, he indicated that such behavior was characteristic of the oral-acquisitive nature of the syndrome. It seemed not to occur to him that there were very few things to anticipate in a psychiatric hospital besides eating.

A psychiatric label has a life and an influence of its own. Once the impression has been formed that the patient is schizophrenic, the expectation is that he will continue to be schizophrenic. When a sufficient amount of time has passed, during which the patient has done nothing bizarre, he is considered to be in remission and available for discharge. But the label endures beyond discharge, with the unconfirmed expectation that he will behave as a schizophrenic again. Such labels, conferred by mental health professionals, are as influential on the patient as they are on his relatives and friends, and it should not surprise anyone that the diagnosis acts on all of them as a self-fulfilling prophecy. Eventually, the patient himself accepts the diagnosis, with all of its surplus meanings and expectations, and behaves accordingly.[5]

The inferences to be made from these matters are quite simple. Much as Zigler and Phillips have demonstrated that there is enormous overlap in the symptoms presented by patients who have been variously diagnosed,[16] so there is enormous overlap in the behaviors of the sane and the insane. The sane are not "sane" all of the time. We lose our tempers "for no good reason." We are occasionally depressed or anxious, again for no good reason. And we may find it difficult to get along with one or another person again for no reason that we can specify. Similarly, the insane are not always insane. Indeed, it was the impression of the pseudopatients while living with them that they were sane for long periods of time—that the bizarre behaviors upon which their diagnoses were allegedly predicated constituted only a small fraction of their total behavior. If it makes no sense to label ourselves permanently depressed on the basis of an occasional depression, then it takes better evidence than is presently available to label all patients insane or schizophrenic on the basis of bizarre behaviors or cognitions. It seems more useful, as Mischel[17] has pointed out, to limit our discussions to behaviors, the stimuli that provoke them, and their correlates.

It is not known why powerful impressions of personality traits, such as "crazy" or "insane" arise. Conceivably, when the origins of and stimuli that give rise to a behavior are remote or unknown, or when the behavior strikes us as immutable, trait labels regarding the behavior arise. When, on the other hand, the origins and stimuli are known and available, discourse is limited to the behavior itself. Thus, I may hallucinate because I am sleeping, or I may hallucinate because I have ingested a peculiar drug. These are termed sleep-induced hallucinations, or dreams, and drug-induced hallucinations, respectively. But when the stimuli to my hallucinations are unknown, that is called craziness, or schizophrenia—as if that inference were somehow as illuminating as the others.

The Consequences of Labeling and Depersonalization

Whenever the ratio of what is known to what needs to be known approaches zero, we tend to invent "knowledge" and assume that we understand more than we actually do. We seem unable to acknowledge that we simply don't know. The needs for diagnosis and remediation of behavioral and emotional problems are enormous. But rather than acknowledge that we are just embarking on understanding, we continue to label patients "schizophrenic," "manic-depressive," and "insane," as if in those words we had captured the essence of understanding. The facts of the matter are that we have known for a long time that diagnoses are often not useful or reliable, but we have nevertheless continued to use them. We now know that we cannot distinguish insanity from sanity. It is depressing to consider how that information will be used.

Not merely depressing, but frightening. How many people, one wonders, are sane but not recognized as such in our psychiatric institutions? How many have been needlessly stripped of their privileges of citizenship, from the right to vote and drive to that of handling their own accounts? How many have feigned insanity in order to avoid the criminal consequences of their behavior, and, conversely, how many would rather stand trial than live interminably in a psychiatric hospital—but are wrongly thought to be mentally ill? How many have been stigmatized by well-intentioned, but nevertheless erroneous, diagnoses? On the last point, recall again that a "type 2 error" in psychiatric diagnosis does not have the same consequences it does in medical diagnosis. A diagnosis of cancer that has been found to be in error is cause for celebration. But psychiatric diagnoses are rarely found to be in error. The label sticks, a mark of inadequacy forever.

References and Notes

1. P. Ash, J. Abnorm. *Soc. Psychol.* 44, 272 (1949); A. T. Beck, *Amer. J. Psychiat.* 119, 210 (1962); A. T. Boisen, *Psychiatry* 2, 233 (1938); N. Kreitman, *J. Ment. Sci.* 107, 876 (1961); N. Kreitman, P. Sainsbury, J. Morrisey, J. Towers, J. Scrivener, *ibid.,* p, 887; H. O. Schmitt and C. P. Fonda, J. *Abnorm. Soc. Psychol.* 52, 262 (1956); W. Seeman, *J. Nerv. Ment. Dis.* 118, 541 (1953). For an analysis of these artifacts and summaries of the disputes, see J. Zubin, *Annu. Rev. Psychol.* 18, 373 (1967); L. Phillips and J. G. Draguns, *ibid.* 22, 447 (1971).

2. R. Benedict (1934), *J. Gen Psychol.* 10, 59 (1934).

3. See in this regard H. Becker, *Outsiders: Studies in the Sociology of Deviance* (Free Press, New York, 1963); B. M. Braginsky, D. D. Braginsky, K. Ring, *Methods of Madness: The Mental Hospital as a Last Resort* (Holt, Rinehard & Winston. New York, 1969); G. M. Crocetti and P. V. Lemkau, *Amer. Sociol. Rev.* 30, 577 (1965); E. Goffman, *Behavior in Public Places,* (Free Press, New York, 1964); R. D. Laing, *The Divided Self: A Study of Sanity and Madness* (Quadrangle, Chicago, 1960); D. L. Phillips, *Amer. Sociol. Rev.* 28, 963 (1963); T. R. Sarbin, *Psychol. Today* 6, 18 (1972); E. Schur, *Amer. J. Sociol.* 75, 309 (1969); T. Szasz, *Law, Liberty and Psychiatry* (Macmillan, New York, 1963); *The Myth of Mental Illness: Foundations of a Theory of Mental Illness* (Hoeber-Harper, New York, 1963). For a critique of some of these views, see W. R. Gove, *Amer. Sociol. Rev.* 35, 873 (1970).

4. E. Goffman, *Asylums* (Doubleday, Garden City, N.Y., 1961).

5. T. J. Scheff, *Being Mentally Ill: A Sociological Theory* (Aldine, Chicago, 1966).

6. Data from a ninth pseudopatient are not incorporated in this report because, although his sanity went undetected, he falsified aspects of his personal history, including his marital status and parental relationships. His experimental behaviors therefore were not identical to those of the other pseudopatients.

7. A. Barry, *Bellevue Is a State of Mind* (Harcourt Brace Jovanovich, New York, 1971); I. Belknap, *Human Problems of a State Mental Hospital* (McGraw-Hill,

New York, 1956); W. Caudill, F. C., Redlich, H. R. Gilmore, E. B. Brody, *Amer. J. Orthopsychiat.* 22, 314 (1952); A. R. Goldman, R. H. Bohr, T. A. Steinberg, *Prof. Psychol.* 1, 427 (1970); unauthored, *Roche Report* 1 (No. 13), 8 (1971).

8. Beyond the personal difficulties that the pseudopatient is likely to experience in the hospital, there are legal and social ones that, combined, require considerable attention before entry. For example, once admitted to a psychiatric institution, it is difficult, if not impossible, to be discharged on short notice, state law to the contrary notwithstanding. I was not sensitive to these at the outset of the project, nor to the personal and situational emergencies that can arise, but later a writ of habeas corpus was prepared for each of the entering pseudopatients and an attorney was kept "on call" during every hospitalization. I am grateful to John Kaplan and Robert Bartels for legal advice and assistance in these matters.

9. However distasteful such concealment is, it was a necessary first step to examining these questions. Without concealment, there would have been no way to know how valid these experiences were; nor was there any way of knowing whether whatever detections occurred were a tribute to the diagnostic acumen of the staff or to the hospital's rumor network. Obviously, since my concerns are general ones that cut across individual hospitals and staffs, I have respected their anonymity and have eliminated clues that might lead to their identification.

10. Interestingly, of the 12 admissions, 11 were diagnosed as schizophrenic and one, with the identical symptomatology, as manic-depressive psychosis. This diagnosis has a more favorable prognosis, and it was given by the only private hospital in our sample. On the relations between social class and psychiatric diagnosis, see A. deB. Hollingshead and F.C. Redlich, *Social Class and Mental Illness: A Community Study* (Wiley, New York, 1958).

11. It is possible, of course, that patients have quite broad latitudes in diagnosis and therefore are inclined to call many people sane, even those whose behavior is patently aberrant. However, although we have no hard data on this matter, it was our distinct impression that this was not the case. In many instances, patients not only singled us out for attention, but came to imitate our behaviors and styles.

12. J. Cumming and E. Cumming, *Community Ment. Health* 1, 135 (1965); A. Farina and K. Ring, *J. Abnorm. Psychol.* 70, 47 (1965); H. E. Freeman and O. G. Simmons, *The Mental Patient Comes Home* (Wiley, New York, 1963); W. J. Johannsen, *Ment. Hygiene* 53, 218 (1969); A. S. Linsky, *Soc. Psychiat.* 5, 166 (1970).

13. S. E. Asch, *J. Abnormal Soc. Psychol.* 41, 258 (1946); *Social Psychology* (Prentice-Hall, New York, 1952).

14. See also I. N. Mensh and J. Wishner, J. Personality 16, 188 (1947); J. Wishner, *Psychol. Rev.* 67, 96 (1960); J. S. Bruner and R. Tagiuri, in *Handbook of Social Psychology,* C. Lindzey, Ed. (Addison-Wesley, Cambridge, Mass., 1954), Vol. 2, pp. 634-654; J. S. Bruner, D. Shapiro, R. Tagiuri, in *Person Perception and Interpersonal Behavior,* R. Tagiuri and L. Petrullo, Eds. (Stanford Univ. Press, Stanford, Calif., 1958), pp. 277-288.

15. For an example of a similar self-fulfilling prophecy, in this instance dealing with the "central" trait of intelligence, see R. Rosenthal and L. Jacobson, *Pygmalion in the Classroom* (Holt, Rinehart & Winston, New York, 1968).

16. E. Zigler and L. Phillips, *J. Abnorm. Soc. Psychol.* 63, 69 (1961). See also R. K. Freudenberg and J. P. Robertson, A.M.A. *Arch. Neurol. Psychiatr.* 76, 14 (1956).

17. W. Mischel, *Personality and Assessment* (Wiley, New York, 1968).

PART IV

Stress, Coping, and Social Relationships

Essay: The Process of Stress, Coping, and Empowerment

William D. Marelich and Jeff S. Erger

> Good friends are good for your health.
>
> Irwin Sarason

Taking an exam is stressful, isn't it? Even if you are totally prepared and know the material cold, you will still feel a bit worried about it. Now, think about final exams. Finals week means days of exams, all dealing with different courses. There is a buildup the week before, cramming, late-night study sessions. Students wander from exam to exam, bleary-eyed, shoulders hunched with the weight of the world, peppered with uncertainty. And when these exams are all over, what happens? You get sick.

Many experience the "after-exams" cold or flu. Do the exams cause illness? Well, not directly. Studying for exams in conjunction with everything else you have to do generates stress. In addition, there is an inherent uncertainty associated with studying for exams that can elevate stress. "Is the material I'm studying the correct material? Am I studying enough? Are my notes complete? Am I getting everything? If I don't do well on the exam, how will this affect my grade?" As you experience stress, you are in fact experiencing a negative emotional state. Furthermore, as this negative state increases, your body physiologically becomes affected, with increasing amounts of stress weakening your immune system. And given that microbes take a number of days to work their nasty magic, you get sick a few days after your stress levels were at their highest.

Now, what happens when finals come around and you break up with the person you were dating? It probably makes things worse. What if your parent goes into the hospital? What if your rent is coming due and you don't have the money? These are situations that students face with regularity. Some students crack under the strain, failing courses, and perhaps even dropping out of school. Other students manage somehow to work through all of the stress, coping successfully with the situation and its effects on them, and pass all of their classes. What causes the difference between coping well, barely coping, and not managing to deal with a situation at all?

Of course, there are stressors in the environment other than exams. In fact, stress can be caused by any number of events. Stress can be due to salient *life events,* such as changing jobs, the end of a romantic relationship, or death of a family member, and can have unsettling effects on individuals and their surrounding social systems. *Daily hassles* may also lead to stress. Hassles are the small stressors that over time build up and lead individuals to experience higher levels of stress. Examples of hassles include traffic jams, conflicts with your roommates or neighbors, and even daily chores. These are situations that we know are stressful, but often we forget that even positive life events can be sources of stress. Getting married is a very positive event, yet the process of committing to a relationship, telling family and friends, and planning a wedding creates a huge amount of stress in people's lives for months and even years. Researchers have attempted to identify those life events and daily hassles that can contribute most to stress, and such measurement scales are available in the research literature.

Findings with such "stress lists," however, have been modest at best. The problem with these lists lies in how individuals appraise potentially stressful events; for some individuals, an event may be appraised as stressful, yet for others, that same event may be benign. For example, believe it or not, some students really enjoy studying and taking exams because they can demonstrate how much they know about a topic. Although individuals ending romantic relationships generally experience great amounts of stress, especially those going through divorces, some are actually relieved when the relationship ends and experience less stress. In another example, one of your textbook authors recently embraced the idea that what makes living in southern California so unique is the experience of traffic. By reframing the traffic situation, he no longer stresses about being in traffic.

What makes an event such as a traffic jam or the end of a relationship a stressor for some individuals but not others? Borrowing from Lazarus and Folkman's work in this section, when a potentially stressful event occurs within the individual's social/physical environment, a *primary appraisal* of the event is undertaken to discern whether the event is positive or negative for the individual, and if negative, how harmful or threatening the event appears to be. If the event is deemed nonthreatening, little or no stress is experienced. If an event is deemed threatening, a *secondary appraisal* is undertaken to ascertain the individual's available resources and ability to handle or cope with the stressor. If the individual perceives that he or she can adequately address or control the event, then little stress is experienced. However, if the individual perceives that he or she does not have adequate resources to handle the event, then the event will lead to greater levels of stress.

Imagine sitting in your apartment, and all of a sudden you notice a noxious smell. At this point, primary appraisal is undertaken (e.g., "Can this smell harm me? Is exposure to this noxious odor good for my health?"). After a few moments, you discern that possibly the smell is harmful (e.g., "It smells like ammonia"). Secondary appraisal is next undertaken to assess your coping abilities and resources to deal with the threat (e.g., "Can I identify where the smell is coming from so I can stop it? Can I deal with this? I don't know what to do. . . . I'm helpless!"). Once you have evaluated whether you have the ability and resources to address the threat, then action can be taken to minimize the threat. In this example, you have evaluated the noxious smell as possibly being ammonia and have determined you don't know what to do. Stress, therefore, will be elevated since you feel you have little control over exposure to the smell.

As stress levels increase, various strategies are undertaken to reduce the stress, and these stress reduction efforts are referred to as *coping*. Think again about all your studying prior to final exams week. During that time, did you take off a couple of hours to go to the gym, play a sport, "veg-out" in front of the television, or go shopping? Did you take an entire evening off and hang out with friends and have a few beers? Maybe you even read a pleasure book or just decided to take a nap? If you did any of these in the midst of your growing stress, then, indeed, you adopted a form of coping. Some of you may be wondering how "vegging-out" in front of the television or hanging out with your friends are forms of coping. Coping takes many forms; in the face of stress, television watching is a form of escape, as is taking a nap, while hanging out with friends may be considered a form of seeking social support.

Coping consists of resources and strategies. *Coping resources* are the factors that individuals rely on in times of stress. These resources can vary across individuals and include personality factors (e.g., self-esteem, hardiness), personal characteristics (e.g., race/ethnicity), social support (e.g., social networks), and broader social factors (e.g., socioeconomic status). As secondary appraisals are undertaken, resource availability moderates the experience of stress. For example, those from low socioeconomic areas who need to see a health care provider for the flu may struggle with trying to locate low-cost health care near their neighborhoods, and furthermore, may need to take a few days off work without pay since many jobs for this population do not provide health care benefits. Hence, getting ill can generate a great deal of stress associated with treatment access, paying for treatment, and time off work without pay. However, those from high socioeconomic-status neighborhoods who get the flu have the freedom to visit physicians of their choice and take time off work with pay, without detrimental effects. Thus, getting ill for this group of individuals generates much less stress.

Coping strategies are the cognitive-behavioral reactions individuals adopt to cope with increasing levels of stress. Two strategies have been identified. *Problem-focused coping* entails trying to solve the problems or issues that are stressful—in other words, trying to reduce stress through viewing the stressor as a problem that can be fixed. *Emotion-focused coping* entails regulation of one's emotional reaction to the stressor. Depending on the stressor, individuals have been shown to either use both strategies or to favor one strategy over the other. For example, there is some evidence to suggest that emotion-focused coping is preferred when stressors are health related. However, as we will see later in this section on empowerment, once individuals understand that they can influence their health care, problem-focused strategies are also enacted.

Depending on the coping strategy adopted, health and illness may be either improved or made worse. This statement may seem somewhat odd because it suggests that some coping strategies used to reduce stress may actually be harmful and subsequently increase stress. If a friend of yours was just diagnosed with HIV, how do you think they might react over the next month? Maybe your friend would seek council with you and other peers to help alleviate stress. Or perhaps he or she will become increasingly religious and seek solace in greater forces. Both of these strategies may be viewed as positive and may lead to increased well-being and better health outcomes. However, it is possible your friend may adopt the dictum that "it's better to burn out than fade away" and engage in destructive behaviors such as alcohol and drug use as a form of escape. Stress might be alleviated temporarily while the individual is intoxicated, but once that person is sober, the stress returns along with possible physical deterioration associated with alcohol and drug use.

In the example above, one of the options your friend may adopt is to seek social support, which illustrates the coping resource of *social relationships.* Talking with friends is indeed a common coping strategy. We also rely on friends and family for many things, such as caring for pets while we are away from home, providing transportation to and from appointments, and even connecting us to others who might help us in some way (e.g., "I know a doctor who works at the hospital, and you should talk to her"), and all of these can be very beneficial to our health. Social relationships act to moderate potential stressors and function as an available resource that may be used if stress becomes elevated. Social psychologists argue that we need social relationships; they are required to help us define reality and to define ourselves. In fact, through social interactions with others, the rules, norms, and societal structures are defined and communicated, and our roles within society are negotiated. Without social relationships, reality becomes disfigured, and what we believe to be true cannot be confirmed.

What constitutes a social relationship? Almost any type of association in which there is *behavioral interdependence* and *emotional attachment* with another person may be considered a social relationship. For example, as one of your textbook authors writes this section, he is sitting in a small coffeehouse embedded within a larger red brick building. It's midmorning, the sun is shining and warm, and people are walking their dogs by a nearby park. Folks are wandering in the front door to have their orders served by a 70s retro-guy behind the counter who, in between orders, talks to a 90s grunge-guy coworker. A patron's cell phone rings, and she answers it saying, "Hello, honey. . . ." and exits to have more privacy. Within this setting, social relationships are evident. Coworkers are interacting, someone is speaking to a loved one over the phone, and the dogwalkers are engaged with their domestic quadrupeds. Even patrons who are sitting alone carry with them the current memories of their own existing social relationships. Indeed, as your author sits here alone writing these words, the knowledge that his family, friends, and dog "Lucy" are available for support is comforting.

As noted earlier, social relationships act to moderate stress, and this may be explained by the available resources that social relationships offer. A prime example of such effects is the *marriage benefit* often noted by sociologists in regard to health outcomes and mortality. Those who are married tend to live longer compared with those who are not married, have better well-being, and in general are healthier. However, there can be a downside to marriage and social relationships. Having an "unhappy" marriage can actually increase stress levels and subsequently negatively effect health and well-being. Obligatory responsibilities associated with social relationships (i.e., things you have to do for your partner or family), especially when these interfere with individual plans and goals, can also increase stress.

The social relationships and interactions presented so far have focused on those in which you have some type of emotional ties and interdependence. There are, however, tertiary interactions that can also affect the type of health care you receive, especially the interactions with those embedded within the health care setting. As was noted earlier in Part III, when visiting a health care provider, typically, you do what you are told. Part of this is due to "the authority stature" of someone in a white coat. Another contributor is that when you seek health care, there is a good chance that you are rather ill or have a painful injury, and hence you want to be taken care of as quickly as possible. Asking questions about your ailment or your treatment options only slows down the process of getting treatment, you think. Also, you may not know much about your ailment, so although you might want to ask questions, you don't know which questions to ask.

Such passive behavior is unfortunate, because patients who tend to ask questions and take an active role in their treatments may actually receive superior health care compared with those who acquiesce or act helpless. Such active behaviors are sometimes referred to as *empowered behaviors* and encompass actions such as question asking, knowledge seeking, "doctor shopping," and a general motivation toward one's personal health. Patients adopting such behaviors are provided a sense of personal responsibility for the care they receive, and this can be very satisfying and reinforcing.

Think about it this way. Have you ever felt a sense of accomplishment after completing a complex task? Maybe you gave an outstanding presentation in a class or had to give a solo music performance? You succeeded because you worked hard on the task, and no doubt you had to figure out how to navigate the task complexities. In the end, you made the decisions, and the end result was a satisfying experience.

Being proactive in your health care can provide the same positive experience. If you are proactive in the health care you receive, then you and your health care provider are working in tandem to make you healthy. And you may be surprised to discover that your health care provider would actually welcome your participation and motivation. If he or she sees that you are highly motivated to get better, you may be prescribed a more aggressive treatment because the provider believes you can meet the challenge. However, if you are passive, then you are simply being "worked on" and are a bystander to your care. Certainly, you will be given adequate treatment, but the provider may prescribe a treatment that is less aggressive and easier to adhere to.

Stressful Life Events and the Structure of Coping

The first article in this section looks at stress and life events. The Rabkin and Struening article starts with a review of the effects of life events on stress and illness, with a particular focus on the *Social Readjustment Rating Scale* (SSRS). The SSRS has been a popular measure of life events since the late 1960s and comprises 43 stressful life events in a checklist format. Each life event is assigned a score (e.g., death of a spouse = 100; pregnancy = 40), with higher summed scores indicative of greater stress and probability of illness. Rabkin and Struening note that although life events do affect stress levels and subsequently affect health, the size of the effect or impact of life events on illness is small, accounting for maybe "9% of the variance in illness." In other words, at best, about 9% of the reason individuals become ill may be accounted for by the stressful events in their lives. However, this amount is still notable. They rightly state that research needs to focus on "the circumstances under which such effects occur and do not occur." The focus of the article then moves into factors that can mediate the experience of stress given particular life events, including stressor characteristics, personal factors, and external factors such as social environments.

The next article investigates the process of coping. Folkman and Lazarus (leaders in the field) suggest that psychological stress be viewed through a transactional lens, through which the individual and environment are seen as affecting each other in a reciprocal fashion. Two processes mediate this person-environment interaction: appraisal and coping. As noted earlier, primary and secondary appraisals are made to ascertain threat and available resources. Coping is the second process, consisting of both behavioral and cognitive efforts to (a) manage or alter "the person-environment relationship that is the sources of stress," referred to as problem-focused coping, or (b) regulate stressful emotions, referred to as emotion-focused coping. These ideas are subsequently evaluated using a sample of community-residing men and women.

Before you move on to the next section, we suggest taking a moment to become introspective about your own personal reactions to past stressful events. Whether the stress came from a neighbor who plays his music too loud, the death of a family pet, or the end of a romantic relationship, what did you do to cope with the event? Did you use both problem-focused and emotion-focused coping strategies? What coping responses did you actually perform? We know that such a task might seem odd, but taking a couple of minutes to apply these ideas to your personal experiences should act to strengthen your understanding of these concepts and maybe alleviate exam stress in the future.

On Social Relationships and Health

Recall that social relationships are viewed by many researchers as a coping resource that functions to moderate the experience of stress. The House, Landis, and Umberson article is a classic work from 1988 that shows that disease morbidity and mortality are higher for those with low quantities and qualities of social relationships. The authors make several suggestions for understanding and improving the dynamics of social relationships within the *stress-social relationship-illness* model, including the adoption of frameworks, such as those by Lazarus and Folkman, which view social relationships as part of an appraisal-coping process.

Personal Responsibility and the Empowered Patient

The first article in this section is a study by Langer and Rodin looking at the effects of enhanced personal responsibility on health and well-being. Social psychology has shown that offering personal control and choice to individuals generally leads to anxiety reduction and increased confidence. The study focuses on residents of a nursing home, where typically many rules and restrictions limit their choices and freedoms. This study is an excellent example of experimental research in an applied setting, which is why we included it here. Interestingly, one of your textbook authors was sitting at a graduation ceremony just recently, and the keynote speaker (a graduate from the university in the early 1980s) mentioned this study as one that he remembered because of its controversial flavor. We hope it has the same lasting effect on you.

Since this was an experiment, residents were divided into two groups: those who were provided additional freedoms (the enhanced personal responsibility group) and those in a comparison group who simply followed the existing rules and norms. The enhanced personal responsibility group was told that they had the power to alter a number of factors in this behavior setting, ranging from how their social time would be spent to how they wanted their rooms arranged. Furthermore, these residents were reminded that if they had any complaints about their current living situation, they should make their complaints known so that things could be changed to their liking.

Overall, the enhanced personal responsibility group fared much better than the comparison group. Those who were given responsibility showed various health-related improvements, including being more active and reporting greater levels of happiness. The comparison group, on the other hand, reported higher levels of debilitation. These findings underscore the importance of individuals being involved in their living situations, which can have positive mental and physical health outcomes.

The last reading in this section is by Marelich, Roberts, Murphy, and Callari, who investigate the ways in which those with HIV/AIDS involve themselves in their medication decisions. This qualitative paper illustrates many of the empowered behaviors noted earlier and also some initial barriers to empowered behavior. Patients reported working actively with their health care providers toward treatment decisions, being active knowledge gatherers, and even reporting total influence over their treatment decisions in some instances. However, when initially diagnosed with HIV/AIDS, some patients reported acting passively with their providers due to the uncertainty surrounding their new diagnosis and illness status. This suggests that empowerment is a developing process in which the longer individuals interact with their providers and live with their illness, the more proactive they become regarding their treatment and care.

A. Stressful Life Events and the Structure of Coping

17

LIFE EVENTS, STRESS, AND ILLNESS

J.G. RABKIN AND E.L. STRUENING

Studies relating social factors and life events to illness appear with remarkable regularity in the major psychological, psychiatric, psychosomatic, and sociological journals, and to a lesser extent in those of clinical medicine and epidemiology. While some of these publications derive from the cumulative efforts of investigators who have worked in this field for many years, concern has been expressed that many recent studies repeat both the findings and the flaws of earlier ones, delaying a hierarchical growth and development of knowledge in the field.

Accordingly, there is a need for critical evaluation of this literature, taking in issues of method as well as content. In this article our goals are (i) to review selectively the research literature on the relations of life events, stress, and the onset of illness; (ii) to delineate trends in its development; (iii) to evaluate the conceptual and methodological approaches employed; (iv) to identify major variables mediating the impact of stressful events on individuals and groups; and (v) to recommend more comprehensive approaches to substantive issues.

Despite historical recognition of the predisposing role of social factors in the onset of illness, it is only during the last 40 years that scientists have attempted to study these phenomena systematically. In 1936 Hans Selye articulated his concept of stress as the "general adaptation syndrome," a set of nonspecific physiological reactions to various noxious environmental agents.[1] This formulation was largely responsible for popularizing the concept of stress in the scientific vocabulary of medicine, and it initiated an era of research and theoretical development conducted with accelerating enthusiasm on an international scale in numerous branches of the medical and later the social sciences. Also in the 1930's Franz Alexander and his psychoanalytic colleagues in Chicago became interested in relating personality characteristics to selected organic syndromes within the framework of psychosomatic theory. Development of the stress and psychosomatic models of illness has proceeded apace, with a gradual convergence of interest and assumptions so that today stress research and psychosomatic research are to some extent overlapping.

The notion of socially induced stress as a precipitating factor in chronic diseases is gaining acceptance among a wide spectrum of scientists. It is becoming recognized that stress can be one of the components of any disease, not just of those designated as "psychosomatic." As Dodge and Martin[2] have expressed it, "the diseases of our times, namely the chronic diseases, are etiologically linked with excessive stress and in turn this stress is a product of specific socially structured situations inherent in the organization of modern technological societies." Even susceptibility to microbial infectious diseases is thought to be a function of environmental conditions culminating in physiological stress on the individual, rather than simply of exposure to an external source of infection.[3]

In the formulation of a revised etiological model, illness onset is generally associated with a number of potential factors, including the presence of stressful environmental conditions, perception by the individual that such conditions are stressful, the relative ability to cope with or adapt to these conditions, genetic predisposition to a disease, and the presence of a disease agent. In this context the stress concept does not only explain why some people are more prone to illness than others. Stress, like anxiety, is a broad and general concept describing the organism's reactions to environmental demands. Its utility derives from its role in identifying productive lines of research on the etiology of disease, encompassing external events that influence individuals and populations and also their appraisals and interpretations of such events. Accordingly, we will turn to a consideration of the body of research that has focused on the correspondence between life changes, stress, and illness onset.

In the following review we limit our attention to life changes of a primarily personal nature. Changes caused by widespread social processes also heighten the individual's vulnerability to stress and stress-related diseases, but we shall consider only life events which are experienced primarily on an individual level, such as changes in family status or occupation.

Definitions

We consider the following sequence of conditions: social stressors, mediating factors, stress, onset of illness. In the present context the term "social stressors" refers to personal life changes, such as bereavement, marriage, or loss of job, which alter the individual's social setting. A more specific definition is proposed by Holmes and Rahe,[4] who define as social stressors any set of circumstances the advent of which signifies or requires change in the individual's ongoing life pattern. According to this conception, exposure to social stressors does not cause disease but may alter the individual's susceptibility at a particular period of time and thereby serve as a precipitating factor.

"Mediating factors" are those characteristics of the stressful event, of the individual, and of his social support system that influence his perception of or sensitivity to stressors. Some are long-term predisposing factors which heighten the individual's risk of becoming ill, such as high serum cholesterol in relation to myocardial infarction. Others may render the individual less vulnerable to stress, such as prior experience with the stressor. In general, consideration of mediating variables contributes to an understanding of differential sensitivities to social stressors.

"Stress" is the organism's response to stressful conditions or stressors, consisting of a pattern of physiological and psychological reactions, both immediate and delayed. "Onset of illness" is defined by the appearance of clinical symptoms of disease.

"Predisposing factors" are longstanding behavior patterns, childhood experiences, and durable personal and social characteristics that may alter the susceptibility of the individual to illness. "Precipitating factors," in contrast, influence the timing of illness onset; the term refers for the most part to more or less transient changes in current conditions or characteristics, and it is such changes that constitute our present subject of inquiry. "Chronic disease" refers here very generally to syndromes which are of long duration and are noninfectious. It is the chronic diseases rather than the acute, infectious ones that are usually thought to be particularly influenced by the experience of stress.

Life Events Research

The role of stressful life events in the etiology of various diseases has been a field of research for the last 25 years. Derived from William B. Cannon's early observations of bodily changes related to emotions and Adolph Meyer's interest in the life chart as a tool in medical diagnosis, the field was first given formal recognition at the 1949 Conference on Life Stress and Bodily Disease sponsored by the Association for Research in Nervous and Mental Diseases. Since then several groups of investigators have adopted this general framework in independent long-term projects.

In general, the purpose of life events research is to demonstrate a temporal association between the onset of illness and a recent increase in the number of events that require socially adaptive responses on the part of the individual. The impact of such events is presumed to be additive; more events are expected to have greater effect. The underlying assumption is that such events serve as precipitating factors, influencing the timing but not the type of illness episodes. Onset of psychiatric as well as physical disorders and accidents have been studied in both retrospective and prospective designs within the life events framework. Most investigators working in this field have adopted in original or modified form a 43-item checklist developed by Holmes, Rahe, and their colleagues. The checklist items are intended to represent fairly common situations arising from family, personal, occupational, and financial events that require or signify change in ongoing adjustment. Scores on the first version, known as the Schedule of Recent Experience (SRE), consisted of the number of items checked. Subsequently, weights were assigned to each item based on ratings by a standardization sample of judges who were asked to rate the life events "as to their relative degree of necessary readjustment . . . the intensity and length of time necessary to accommodate to a life event."[5] On this scale, known as the Social Readjustment Rating Scale (SRRS), death of spouse, for example, is weighted at 100 (the highest point on the scale), marriage at 50, change in recreation at 19, vacation at 12. This and comparable checklists, usually covering the previous 6 to 24 months, are typically used as the measure of stressful life events. Modified forms have been developed for specific populations such as children, college students, and athletes.

The most elaborate and extensive program of life events research has been conducted by Rahe, Holmes, Gunderson, and their colleagues. Their work, originally based largely on American naval shipboard personnel, has been extended on an international basis to other naval samples and to diverse civilian groups, and has evoked considerable comment in the literature, both positive and negative. This brief description of their overall approach and representative findings is intended to illustrate the kinds of research and major issues and problems in the field.

In their early retrospective studies, Rahe and his colleagues[6] asked over 2,000 navy personnel to report their life changes and histories of illness during the previous 10 years. Number of illness episodes was related to scores on the SRRS; these scores are referred to as life change units or LCU's. In general, according to these investigators, those who recorded fewer than 150 LCU's for a given year reported good health for the following year; of those with annual LCU's between 150 and 300, about half reported illness in the next year; and when annual LCU scores exceeded 300, as they did for a small proportion of the respondents, illness followed in 70 percent of the cases, and furthermore tended to entail multiple episodes.

In prospective studies of 2,500 American naval personnel aged 17 to 30, life events that occurred in the 6 months prior to shipboard tours of duty were compared with shipboard medical records of the 6-month cruise. Respondents were grouped into quartiles based on their precruise LCU scores, and mean rates of illness were computed for each group. Those in the first quartile had a mean of 1.4 recorded illnesses, those in the fourth quartile 2.1 recorded illnesses, a statistically significant difference. Similar results were obtained with a sample consisting of 821 Norwegian sailors[7] and in a study of the entire crew of 1,005 men on a warship on combat duty off Vietnam.[8]

Numerous other studies by various investigators have similarly shown associations between number and intensity of life events and the probability of specific illnesses in the near future [see Notes (5) or

(6) for extensive lists of references]. In many of these studies data about life events and illness episodes were gathered from large, heterogeneous samples by means of questionnaires in conjunction with medical records. In addition to military personnel, employees of large corporations and clinic or hospital patients have been popular subjects in retrospective studies because of the availability of long-term records.

In both retrospective and prospective investigations, modest but statistically significant relationships have been found between mounting life change and the occurrence or onset of sudden cardiac death, myocardial infarctions, accidents, athletic injuries, tuberculosis, leukemia, multiple sclerosis, diabetes, and the entire gamut of minor medical complaints.[6,9] High scores on checklists of life events have also been repeatedly associated with psychiatric symptoms and disorders, and such scores have been found to differ between psychiatric and other samples.[10,11]

It has been further noted that life events may be related to the course of illness and recovery, whatever the etiology of the primary disease.[12] In addition, periodic analyses of life events may serve to monitor and help predict the course of illness, as illustrated in a post-hospital follow-up of mental patients by Michaux et al.[13]

Statistical Issues

Is it, then, reliably established that stressful life events commonly precede the onset of a wide variety of physical and psychiatric disorders in populations? As presented in the literature, the results are impressive. Their sheer number, the variety of populations studied, and the range of disorders implicated together suggest that this is a useful and meaningful procedure for predicting illness and, more generally, for learning more about vulnerability to illness. However, closer scrutiny of methodological and theoretical aspects of the research, as well as the actual data that have been reported, uncovers a host of serious issues. These are attracting increasing attention both from critics of the life events approach and from investigators who use the method.

The most immediate issue, and one which has received only cursory attention from investigators in this field, concerns the size and practical significance of the correlation between number and nature of life events and subsequent illness episodes. The vast majority of life events studies have, until very recently, relied on statistical methods of the most rudimentary nature to analyze this relationship. Between-group differences are often reported only in percentages, or else exclusively in terms of statistical significance (*P* levels). Given the very large sample sizes characteristic of life events research, even very small correlations of no practical utility may pass tests of statistical significance.

Reports of obtained correlation coefficients are often conspicuously missing. When present, they are typically below .30, suggesting that life events may account at best for 9 percent of the variance in illness. In Rahe's naval data, coefficients of correlation between life events and illness were consistently around .12,[7] and other investigators have reported equally low, albeit statistically significant, correlations.[11,14,15] Similarly, when statistically significant differences in illness rates are reported for groups classified in terms of prior life event scores, or groups of differing health status are compared with respect to number of prior life events, attention is often focused exclusively on group means. Variability of scores within groups tends to be overlooked, even when it is extreme, as observed by Wershow and Reinhart.[16] In practical terms, then, life events scores have not been shown to be predictors of the probability of future illnesses.

Psychometric Issues

It seems likely that stronger relationships between life events and illness episodes might be obtained if the psychometric properties of the measuring instrument were improved and the outcome criteria refined. Although few studies of the reliability and validity of life events checklists have been published, available evidence suggests weaknesses in both these respects. Rahe[7] reports correlations ranging from .26 to .90 in test-retest reliability of the SRRS. He attributes such wide variation to variations in intervals between questionnaire administration, differences in sample characteristics, and complexity of wording used in the questions. As Sarason et al.[17] have concluded, by any reasonable standard the reliability of the SRE is low.

Rahe et al.[7] report that wives' independent scores of their husbands' recent life changes show correlations with the husbands' self-reports ranging from .50 to .75. Other questions about validity concern respondents' errors of omission or commission and definition of the criteria of illness with which checklist scores are correlated. Brown[18] has referred to the problem of "retrospective contamination" where respondents may exaggerate past events from a need to justify subsequent illnesses. He cites a study of mongolism, published in 1958 before chromosomal abnormalities were associated with the syndrome, which "demonstrated" the etiologic importance of stressors of the mother during pregnancy. On the other hand, Rahe[7] reported that in studies of patients with coronary heart disease where recent life changes were gathered both by questionnaire and interview, the patients rarely if ever listed life changes in the questionnaires that were not substantiated in the interviews.

Another form of contamination that may be a more significant source of error is that a given life event and an illness perceived or reported shortly thereafter may be products of the same phenomenon, so that one cannot be said to distinctly precede or precipitate the other. This problem may arise when the cause and the effect of a life event are both at least a partial result of the actor's behavior, as, for example, in the case of a college student who drops out of school and then manifests psychiatric symptoms. Divorce can be regarded as a life change contributing to depression, but depression in some cases may be a contributory factor in divorce. Although the problem of clearly differentiating between life change and observed outcome has not been ignored in the literature, satisfactory solutions have not yet been achieved. According to Hudgens,[19] 29 of 43 events on the SRRS checklist are often the symptoms or consequences of illness, and as such are possible sources of contamination.

Several investigators have wondered whether life event checklist scores are actually associated with care-seeking behavior rather than with the onset of illness. Since care-seeking—that is, the fact of a medical record—is frequently used as the operational definition of illness onset in college populations, naval shipboard studies, and elsewhere, the issue is not easily resolved. Cadoret[20] and Hudgens,[19] in their studies of life events and psychiatric depression, both suggest that mounting life changes precipitate psychiatric hospitalization, not the appearance of symptoms. Hudgens noted that while causal relations have been found between stressful life events and worsening of psychiatric conditions already existing, and between life events and subsequent admission to treatment facilities, he has not found it convincingly demonstrated that ordinary life events cause illness. Instead, it may be that life changes lead people to seek medical treatment, that they are equivalent, perhaps, in their etiological role to the availability of medical facilities or funds with which to pay for treatment. Mechanic,[21] studying the use of outpatient medical services, has also suggested that stress helps to trigger use of a medical facility, if not the development of symptoms. This distinction between illness onset and treatment-seeking behavior may apply to disorders of gradual onset and to those which often go untreated, such as colds and headaches. The issue is, however, irrelevant to the association of life changes with accidents, suicide, mortality rates, and episodes of acute, severe illness such as myocardial infarctions. It is perhaps in the realm of psychiatric disorder that the most care is warranted in handling this issue.

Content Validity

Investigators using the life events approach have differences of opinion about the nature of the events to be included in checklists. Though the various instruments in use have overlapping items, they vary in length, content, relative number of positive and negative items, and number of items over which respondents have no control (such as "death of a friend," in contrast to "marriage"). Most checklists selectively emphasize events of young adulthood, undesirable events, and subjectively evaluated events; this may make it difficult to interpret findings when various groups are being compared. Holmes and Masuda,[13] Dekker and Webb,[22] and Uhlenhuth et al.[23] found, for example, that young adults aged 20 to 30 reported twice as many life changes as those over 60, and throughout the age range a significant inverse relationship prevails. It is unclear, however, whether this finding is due to the character of the scale or to greater degrees of stress in early adulthood. The former possibility is supported by data from the Midtown Manhattan Community Survey of 1660 adults which showed that stresses accumulated with advancing age.[24]

The "common" events represented on life events checklists may be largely irrelevant to certain groups, or else those groups experience far fewer changes than are usually reported. For example, findings of very few life changes were reported by Wershow and Reinhart[16] in their study of 88 chronically ill, marginally employed men who were consecutively admitted for medical reasons to a southern Veterans Administration hospital. In this study, the mean LCU score for the year preceding hospitalization was very low, and 19 percent of the sample reported absolutely no life events at all, apart from Christmas. Before concluding that this population indeed experienced few ordinary life changes, it is necessary to verify the appropriateness and relevance of the checklist items for these particular respondents. This question can be extended to consider the appropriateness of various life event items for members of different socioeconomic and ethnic groups.

In attempting to evaluate the adequacy of item selection, Dohrenwend[25] asked samples of community residents, community leaders, psychiatric patients, and convicts to respond to an open-ended question regarding "the last major event in your life that . . . changed your usual activities" and then to the standard checklists of life events for the preceding year. He found that surprisingly few of the events reported in the checklist were previously described by respondents as events they considered major. Further, his different samples cited different kinds of events. He concluded that there really are several domains of life events, and those to be sampled must depend on the goals of a given study.

Considering the same issue, Kellam[26] regards the present checklists as too simple and conceptually deficient. He suggests the stratification of life events with items representing the following categories: age group, stage of life, locus of control (fate or personal responsibility), positive versus negative events, and level of social organization involved (such as family, neighborhood, community).

Considerable attention has been devoted to the question of whether an event must be unfavorable to evoke stress. In their original work, Holmes and Rahe scaled life events in terms of "the intensity and length of time necessary to accommodate to a life event, regardless of its desirability"; B. S. Dohrenwend[27] also endorses this position, which is supported by extensive clinical work on normal life events such as engagement and marriage.[28] Gersten et al.,[15] however, disagree; they regard undesirability rather than simply total amount of change as the better definition of stressor. On the basis of community survey data about nearly 700 children, they have concluded that the number of undesirable life events or a balanced scale (sum of undesirable events minus sum of desirable events) is a better predictor of behavioral impairment than is the total number of changes.

Another unresolved issue concerns the scoring of life event checklists. Some investigators assume that there is only one population of events and so measure stress additively by counting number of events that have occurred in a specified time interval. Others believe that subcategories and weights are preferable. The most common method, noted earlier, is to apply weights derived from judge samples that showed strong convergence of opinions regarding appropriate weighting for particular items. More recently some investigators have asked subjects to rate events in terms of the subjective distress these caused and to indicate the number of times each occurred within the period under study. These subjective ratings were then used as weights in arriving at a total score. Rubin et al.[8] found that weights derived by stepwise multiple regression analysis of questionnaires provided by naval personnel enhanced the correlations between total scores of the life events measure and counts of subsequent illness episodes of their naval respondents. Finally, the factorial structures of the most commonly used checklists have not been adequately explored; it would be useful to determine empirically how many dimensions are included in their scope and whether separate factor scores may be more useful than the single total score currently employed.

Confounding Variables

Another issue in life events research that warrants further attention is the possibility of interaction between life changes and other factors, such as availability of social support systems to serve as protective buffers for the affected individual. As defined by Caplan,[29] social support systems consist of enduring interpersonal ties to a group of people who can be relied upon to provide emotional sustenance, assistance, and resources in times of need, who provide feedback, and who share standards and values. Ideally, one belongs to several supportive groups situated at home, at work, in church, and in a series of recreational or avocational sites. Cassel[30] has observed that deficiencies in support systems will not in themselves contribute to susceptibility to illness in the absence of social stressors. The converse is also probable: Social stressors in the presence of strong social support systems will have only minor effects on health. An excellent illustration of the value of measuring the interaction of these sets of variables is provided by Nuckolls et al.,[31] who studied life changes and social supports for women during pregnancy, in relation to complications of later pregnancy and delivery. Neither the life change score alone nor the social support score alone was related to complications. When the two scores were considered jointly, however, significant findings emerged: 90 percent of the women with high life change scores but low social support scores had one or more complications, whereas only 33 percent of women with equally high life change scores but with high social support scores had any complications. The social support scores were irrelevant in the absence of high life change scores. These results clearly document the need for more analytical approaches.

Questions have been raised about the composition of samples in many life events studies. Wershow and Reinhart[16] refer to the common failure to "disaggregate groups," as in the study where patients attending a dermatology clinic and those with coronary heart disease are together classified as suffering from chronic disorders, or where protocols of respondents with vastly different backgrounds and life styles are combined for analysis. In the earlier naval studies of Holmes and Rahe, for example, the only distinction made between respondents was based on the ship to which they were assigned. Draftees, career military men, officers and enlisted men, newcomers and old-timers, and those with hazardous and not hazardous jobs were all grouped together. (In recent publications some of these distinctions have been taken into consideration.)

Another design issue concerns the advisability of controlling the variables of socioeconomic status and ethnicity in sample selection and data analysis. Preliminary work by Holmes and Rahe[4] suggests that respondents grouped by social class or color rank life events similarly in terms of their perceived impact or magnitude. More direct evidence has been compiled by Dohrenwend and Dohrenwend,[32] who addressed the issue of a possible relationship between class, ethnicity, and differential experience of life events. After reviewing a wide variety of published studies on class and ethnic differences, they concluded that both class and ethnicity influence exposure to stressful events. They found that lower-class members experience more severe though not more frequent stressful events than do middle-class members. Within social class, stressful situations are both more frequent and more severe for blacks than for whites. Thus far such relationships have been only tentatively explored.

It must be noted that the extensive critical appraisals of life events studies are possible primarily because of the relatively large and coherent body of research that has been published. The fact that different groups of investigators have produced coordinated and cumulative research programs over many years provides critics with an adequate picture of how far work has progressed, what are current deficiencies and weaknesses, and what remains to be done. The field of life events research, like that of psychotherapy research, seems to evoke almost as much critical commentary as empirical data. In life events research, however, communication channels are evidently effective. The quality of recent work surpasses that of earlier studies, and many suggestions have been incorporated into research programs. Increasing numbers of studies are prospective in design, and the researchers concern themselves with sample selection, seek appropriate and relevant items in their checklists, try to refine their outcome criteria, and use multivariate statistical methods in data analyses. With these improvements in design and methods, investigators may be able to demonstrate more accurately the nature of the relationship between life events and subsequent illness episodes than has been done to date.

We would conclude that the life events approach to the measurement of stress and subsequent illness offers a method that is attractive in its simplicity, directness, ease of data collection, and common sense appeal or "face validity." Much work remains to be done in a psychometric sense as well as conceptually, to improve the reliability and validity of the measuring instruments, to develop stratified domains of life events, and to select for investigation only those events that are relevant to the topic and population being studied. It might be profitable to study conditions under which the probability of illness is enhanced by the occurrence of prior life changes in contrast to those where such changes have little impact. Comparison of groups who handle life changes effectively with those who appear to break down with little apparent provocation may also further our understanding of the possible role of life changes in precipitating illness. Another helpful approach might be the extension of the dependent variables examined after the occurrence of life changes.

In short, instead of trying repeatedly to answer the question whether life events play a precipitating role in illness, the next step in the progressive development of this field entails examination of the circumstances under which such effects occur and do not occur.

Mediating Factors

Some people develop chronic diseases and psychiatric disorders after exposure to stressful conditions, and others do not. Indeed, most people do not become disabled even when terrible things happen to them, as Hudgens[19] has observed. Exposure to stressors alone is almost never a sufficient explanation for the onset of illness in ordinary human experience, and other factors that influence their impact require consideration. These may be grouped in three broad categories: characteristics of the stressful situation, individual biological and psychological attributes, and characteristics of the social support systems available to the individual that serve as buffers.

Before turning to a review of these mediating factors, it is important to emphasize both their cumulative impact and the reciprocal relationship between them. That is, the more rigorous and severe the external situation, the less significant are social and individual characteristics in determining the likelihood and nature of response. When conditions are sufficiently harsh, as in some wartime situations, prolonged sensory deprivation, or concentration camps, breakdown is virtually universal and individual variations are reflected only in the length of time before the reaction occurs and perhaps in subsequent recovery time. When the stressful situation is less severe, social supports and individual characteristics contribute to an understanding of why some people become ill and others do not. Finally, although it seems probable that extreme environmental conditions can induce disability even in those who do not have social or personal deficits, vulnerability alone, in the absence of stressful conditions, does not precipitate chronic disease or psychiatric disorder.

Stressor Characteristics

Formal characteristics of stressful events that have been found to influence illness onset include their magnitude (departure from baseline conditions), intensity (rate of change), duration, unpredictability, and novelty. The most widely studied of these is magnitude, which has been investigated among survivors of extreme experiences such as internment in concentration camps or as prisoners of war. A linear correspondence has been observed repeatedly between magnitude of the stressor and extent of both psychiatric and physical disability.[33,34] It is now widely agreed that stressors of sufficient intensity and duration will induce an acute stress reaction in all so exposed, regardless of predisposition. There has been less consensus concerning long-term or permanent disabilities, but recent longitudinal data from concentration camp survivors have shown that profound and protracted stressful conditions may have irreversible effects on all.[35]

Speed of change, prolonged exposure, lack of preparedness, and lack of prior experience have each been found to heighten the impact of stressful events.[36,37] Cumulatively these findings suggest that the formal properties of stressors constitute a significant source of variation affecting their influence on individuals.

Individual Characteristics as Mediating Factors

A critical factor in evaluating the impact of stressful events is the individual's perception of them. Such perception depends on personal characteristics determining the appraisal of the significance of potentially harmful, challenging, or threatening events. It is this cognitive process which differentiates a stressor from a stimulus and which determines the nature of the stress reaction and subsequent coping activities.[38]

The perception of stressful events is mediated by two broad categories of variables, one consisting of personal or "internal" factors and the other of interpersonal or external ones, following the Dohrenwends'[32] conceptualization. Personal factors include, for example, biological and psychological threshold sensitivities, intelligence, verbal skills, morale, personality type, psychological defenses, past experience, and a sense of mastery over one's fate.[7,32,34] Demographic characteristics such as age, education, income, and occupation may also contribute to the individual's evaluation of stressful conditions and his response to them.[23]

The effects of most personal variables in mediating stressful conditions are fairly obvious: Persons with more skills, assets, and resources and with more versatile defenses and broader experience tend to fare better. In general, the more competence individuals have demonstrated in the past, the more likely it is that they will cope adaptively with a current stressor. The more experience they have had previously with a particular stressor, the more probable that their present responses will be effective.[37]

The correspondence of personality type to stress reactions and to vulnerability to disease is less clear-cut. As noted in the introductory section, the subject has been of major interest among those concerned with the psychosomatic approach. Over the years, investigators have proposed several models to account for the impact of intrapsychic factors on bodily function, such as Adler's concept of organ inferiority,[39] Alexander's idea that specific emotional conflicts are determinants of disordered function in a particular organ,[40] and Dunbar's that personality constellations are associated with specific psychosomatic disorders.[41] With the passage of time and accumulation of experience, these approaches to the understanding of personality and illness have become less popular. Investigators who have continued to work within this tradition have turned their attention to the delineation of broad life styles and behavior patterns rather than specific intrapsychic constellations and conflicts. A major focus within this framework has been on personal correlates of premature coronary heart disease, myocardial infarction, and sudden death. Studies of the behavior of individuals prone to coronary disease have identified distinctive behavioral and characterological styles which may serve as predisposing factors.[42] The extensive research on clustering of life events in association with myocardial infarction and sudden cardiac death does not contradict these findings, since such life events apparently serve as triggering or precipitating elements influencing the timing rather than the risk of illness onset.

External Mediating Variables

Another broad set of contingencies, or mediating variables, in the stress equation which may be considered social or transactional in nature consists of the buffers and supports accessible to the individual in his social environment. The social positions individuals or groups occupy in a community can materially influence their experience of stress and presumably, therefore, their vulnerability to a broad range of chronic diseases. While the effects of exposure to stressful events may be reduced for those who are effectively embedded in social networks or support systems,[29,43] they are commonly exacerbated by deficiencies or impairments of such systems. Three such categories—social isolation, social marginality (minority membership), and status inconsistency—may be considered in this context.

Urban sociologists recognized years ago that deteriorating areas of the central city had disproportionately high rates of disorders, both medical and psychiatric.[44] More recently, social isolation has been delineated as a major factor in increased risk of disease. There is now considerable evidence to suggest that those who live alone and are not involved with people or organizations have for this very reason a heightened vulnerability to a variety of chronic diseases.[45-47] A generalized "failure to thrive" among institutionalized children is often associated with a lack of meaningful relationships to other people.[48] Also in this context, it has been observed that bereavements are a potential source of ill health, apparently in relation to the social isolation created by the loss of a spouse.[49]

While social isolation is perhaps the most extreme example of impairment of one's position in the community, marginal social status due to membership in a low-status group or simply in one that constitutes a numerical minority in the area has also been associated with increased health risks.[47] Sheer numerical size of a given group, sometimes referred to as ethnic density, has been found to be inversely related to psychiatric hospitalization rates: As a given ethnic group constitutes a smaller proportion of the total population in a particular area, diagnosed rates of mental illness increase in comparison both to the rates for other ethnic groups in that area and to the rates of the same ethnic group in neighborhoods where its members constitute a significant proportion or majority. This observation has been made with respect to Chinese in Canada,[50] French and English minorities in neighboring Quebec towns,[51] Italians in different Boston areas,[52] and black and white residents of various census tracts in Baltimore.[53] Presumably the smaller the community of ethnically similar members, the less the social support available to any one member. Equivalent findings have been noted for socially marginal groups with respect to such diseases as tuberculosis.[45]

The third social variable, status inconsistency, refers to the situation where an individual occupies two or more distinct social statuses or roles that involve incompatible social expectations. For example, mother-married-adult are three compatible statuses, in contrast to mother-unmarried-adolescent. Other forms of inconsistency may entail lack of fit between education and occupation, or between age or sex and employment. Studies exploring the stressful effects of status incongruence have been conducted both with individuals in survey format and with populations for which aggregate data are derived from public records.[2]

Studies of individuals have dealt with observed discrepancies between education and income level, or education and occupational rank, which were presumed to generate role conflict. While a few investigators have failed to find an association between status incongruence and measures of health,[54] several have found it, using different kinds of samples and measures of health.[55]

Hinkle and his colleagues at the Human Ecology Study Program at Cornell[56] analyzed the medical histories of 2,600 semiskilled workers who worked for the New York City telephone company continuously for 20 years. Admittedly, this is an atypical group in terms of geographical and employment stability and consequent lack of exposure to social change. The investigators found an enormous range in the number of illness episodes recorded, from fewer than 5 days a year of absence due to illness to an average of 50 days a year for 20 years. The very healthy workers were found to be people whose social backgrounds, aspirations, and interests coincided with their present circumstances, whose family, educational, and occupational statuses were consistent. This was not the case for the frequently ill workers, whose educational or family status was often inappropriately high for the kind of work they were doing. Hinkle did not invoke the concept of status inconsistency in his conceptual analysis, but his findings lend themselves to an understanding in this context.

The literature concerning variables that mediate the impact of stressful events on individuals derives from so many sources that a general critical appraisal would be unsuitable. Some of it represents conventional, well-executed laboratory studies with clearly defined independent and dependent variables. Other studies, such as those of concentration camp survivors, are necessarily retrospective in design, based on samples of convenience and ad hoc measures of change. However, most of the findings so briefly summarized here have been reported by several investigators working independently, with different populations. The results are therefore cumulatively persuasive, and open a variety of areas for future exploration.

Summary

Although conceptual and theoretical orientations should play an important preparatory role in the design and execution of empirical studies, this does not often appear to be the case in the literature reviewed on the relation of life events, stress, and illness. It is clearly recognized that illness onset is the outcome of multiple characteristics of the individual interacting with a number of interdependent factors in the individual's social context in the presence of a disease agent. The conceptual model is comprehensive, multicausal, and interactive; empirical designs should consider this complexity. In spite of the repeatedly observed trivial relationships between measures of change in life events and illness onset (or care-seeking behavior), many investigators continue to focus on linear relationships between independent and dependent variables without consideration or control of intervening and mediating variables, some of which easily lend themselves to standard measurement procedures. To advance the accurate prediction and understanding of illness onset, the design and execution of empirical studies must take into account, as Mechanic and others have stressed, the complexity of the phenomena being studied.

Crucial in the measurement process are the psychometric properties of the measures used and the methods of collecting data that are employed. Investigators in the area of life events research are vulnerable in their operational definitions of both independent and dependent variables.

More emphasis should be placed on a thorough conceptualization and sampling of the universe of life events, followed by multidimensional scaling of item samples in a variety of respondent samples drawn from theoretically meaningful populations to identify common dimensions of life events. The internal consistency and test-retest reliability of summary scales derived from those analyses should be studied across samples to determine the true variance and stability of these measures over a variety of populations.

The use of unidimensional scales with questionable content validity continues to be a problem in the operational definition of such complex domains as reported symptoms of illness or mental illness. The continued use of one measure to represent an obviously complex domain of symptoms will frequently lead to limited and erroneous conclusions. An extensive literature also indicates that symptoms of mental and physical illness are not unidimensional.

In retrospective studies important sources of error in the measurement of life events include selective memory, denial of certain events, and overreporting to justify a current illness. In prospective studies, the subjective evaluation of the significance of a life event to the respondent has been neglected.

The data analytic procedures used in life events research do not adequately inform the reader of the nature of obtained results. Certain procedures crucial to the understanding of results seldom have been undertaken. For example, not one instance of an estimate of the internal consistency reliability of a life events scale was discovered in this review, though such values are important in the evaluation of measures and in the interpretation of the magnitude of relationships. Further, the application of similar data analytic procedures to the data of a number of studies would enhance the comparability and communication of results and the possibility of making generalizations. It is concluded that improvement in data analytic procedures remains a major challenge for life events investigators.

Refinements of method and content in this field are to be encouraged, in the expectation that they will contribute to a better understanding of the disease process and also to the development of techniques of primary prevention of illness and rehabilitation of the chronically ill.

References

1. H, Selye, *The Stress of Life* (McGraw-Hill, New York, 1956).
2. D. Dodge and W. Martin, *Social Stress and Chronic Illness* (Univ. of Notre Dame Press, Notre Dame, Ind., 1970).
3. R. Diibos, *Man Adapting* (Yale Univ. Press, New Haven, Conn., 1965).
4. T. Holmes and R. Rahe, *J. Psychosom. Res.* 11, 213 (1967).
5. T. Holmes and M. Masuda, in *Stressful Life Events,* B. S. Dohrenwend and B. P. Dohrenwend, Eds. (Wiley, New York, 1974), p. 49.
6. R. Rahe, *Ann. Clin. Res.* 4, 250 (1972).
7. ____, in *Stressful Life Events,* B. S. Dohrenwend and B. P. Dohrenwend, Eds. (Wiley, New York, 1974), p. 73.
8. R. Rubin, E. Gunderson, R. Arthur, *J. Psychosom. Res.* 15, 89 (1971).
9. S. Bramwell, M. Masuda, N. Wagner, T. Holmes, *J. Hum. Stress* 1, 6 (1975); A. Antonovsky and R. Kats, *J. Health Soc. Behav.* 8, 15 (1967); R. Rahe and E. Lind, J. *Psychosom. Res.* 15, 19 (1971); R. Rahe, *ibid.* 8, 35 (1964); M. Selzer and A. Vinokur, *Am. J. Psychiatry* 131, 903 (1974); T. Theorell and R. Rahe, *J. Psychosom. Res.* 15, 25 (1971).
10. D. Dekker and J. Webb, *J. Psychosom. Res,* 18, 125 (1974); E. Jaco, in *Social Stress,* S. Levine and N. Scotch, Eds. (Aldine, Chicago, 1970), p. 210; J. Myers, J. Lindenthal, M. Pepper, D. Ostrander, *J. Health Soc. Behav.* 13, 398 (1972); E. Paykel, in *Stressful Life Events,* B. S. Dohrenwend and B. P. Dohrenwend, Eds. (Wiley, New York, 1974), p. 135; ____, B. Prusoff, J. Myers, *Arch. Gen. Psychiatry* 32, 327 (1975); E. Uhlenhuth and E. Paykel, *ibid.* 28, 473 (1973).
11. R. Markush and R. Favero, in *Stressful Life Events,* B. S. Dohrenwend and B. P. Dohrenwend, Eds. (Wiley, New York, 1974), p. 171.
12. A. Kagan and L. Levi, *Soc. Sci. Med.* 8, 225 (1974).
13. W. Michaux, K. Gansereit, O. McCabe, A. Kurland, *Comm. Ment. Health J.* 3, 358 (1967).
14. L. Bieliavskas and J. Webb, *J. Psychosom. Res.* 18, 115 (1974).
15. J. Gersten, T. Langner, J. Eisenberg, L. Orzek, in *Stressful Life Events,* B. S. Dohrenwend and B. P. Dohrenwend, Eds. (Wiley, New York, 1974), p. 159.
16. H. Wershow and G. Reinhart, *J. Psychosom. Res,* 18, 393 (1974).
17. I. Sarason, C. de Monchaux, T. Hunt, in *Emotions: Their Parameters and Measurement,* L. Levi, Ed. (Raven, New York, 1975), p. 499.
18. G. Brown, in *Stressful Life Events,* B. S. Dohrenwend and B. P. Dohrenwend, Eds. (Wiley, New York, 1974), p. 217.
19. R. Hudgens, in *ibid.,* p. 119.
20. R. J. Cadoret, G. Winokur, J. Dorzab, M. Baker, *Arch. Gen. Psychiatry* 26, 133 (1972).
21. D. Mechanic, in *Stressful Life Events,* B, S. Dohrenwend and B. P. Dohrenwend, Eds. (Wiley, New York, 1974).
22. D. Dekker and J. Webb, J. *Psychosom. Res.* 18, 125 (1974).
23. E. Uhlenhuth, R. Lipman, M. Baiter, M. Stern, *Arch. Gen. Psychiatry* 31, 759 (1974).
24. T. Langner and S. Michael, *Life Stress and Mental Health* (Collier-Macmillan, London, 1963).
25. B. P. Dohrenwend, in *Stressful Life Events,* B. S. Dohrenwend and B. P. Dohrenwend, Eds. (Wiley, New York, 1974), p. 275.
26. S. Kellam, in *ibid.,* p. 207.
27. B. S. Dohrenwend, *J. Health Soc, Behav,* 14, 167 (1973).
28. R. Rapoport, *Fam. Process* 2, 68 (1963).
29. J. Caplan, *Support Systems and Community Mental Health* (Behavioral Publications, New York, 1974).
30. J. Cassel, in *Handbook of Evaluation Research,* E. Struening and M. Guttentag, Eds. (Sage, Beverly Hills, Calif., 1975), p. 537.
31. C. Nuckolls, J. Cassel, B. Kaplan, *Am. J. Epidemiol.* 95, 431 (1972).
32. B. P. Dohrewend and B. S. Dohrenwend, *Social Status and Psychological Disorder* (Wiley Interscience, New York, 1969).
33. R. Arthur, in *Life Stress and Illness,* E. Gunderson and R. Rahe, Eds., (Thomas, Springfield, Ill., 1974), p. 195; L. Eitinger, in *Society, Stress and Disease,* L. Levi, Ed. (Oxford Univ. Press, London, 1971), vol. 1; F. Hocking, *Am. J.Psychother.* 24, 4 (1970).
34. S. Wolf and H. Goodell, Eds., *Harold G. Woljfs Stress and Disease* (Thomas, Springfield, Ill., ed. 2, 1968).
35. M. Horowitz, *Stress Response Syndromes* (Aronson, New York, 1976).
36. J. Cassel, in *Social Stress,* S. Levine and N. Scotch, Eds. (Aldine, Chicago, 1970), p. 189; J. Coleman, *Am. J. Occup. Ther.* 27, 169 (1973); R. Lauer, *Soc. Forces* 52, 510 (1974).
37. N. Miller, in *Psychopathology of Human Adaptation,* G. Serban and A. Kling, Eds. (Plenum, New York, in press).
38. J. Groen, in *Society, Stress and Disease,* L. Levi, Ed. (Oxford Univ. Press, London, 1971), vol. 1, p. 91;

M. Jacobs, A. Spilken, M. Norman, *Psychosom. Med.* 31, 31 (1969).

39. H. Ansbacher and R. Ansbacher, Eds., *The Individual Psychology of Alfred Adler* (Basic Books, New York, 1956).

40. F. Alexander, T. French, G. Pollack, *Psychosomatic Specificity* (Univ. of Chicago Press, Chicago, 1968), vol. 1.

41. F. Dunbar, *Psychosomatic Diagnosis* (Hoeber, New York, 1943).

42. M. Friedman and R. Rosenman, *Type A Behavior and Your Heart* (Knopf, New York, 1974); R. Rosenman et a*l., J. Am. Med. Assoc,* 233, 872 (1975); S. Wolf, in *Society, Stress and Disease,* L. Levi, Ed. (Oxford Univ. Press, London, 1971), vol. 1.

43. J. Cassel, *Mt. Sinai J, Med.* 40, 539 (1973).

44. R. Faris and H. Dunham, *Mental Disorders in Urban Areas* (Univ. of Chicago Press, Chicago, 1939).

45. T. H, Holmes, in *Personality, Stress and Tuberculosis,* P. J. Sparer, Ed. (International Universities Press, New York, 1956), p. 65.

46. L. Levy and L. Rowitz, *The Ecology of Mental Disorder* (Behavioral Publications, New York, 1973); J. Cassel and A. Leighton, in *Mental Health Considerations in Public Health,* S. E. Goldston, Ed. (Government Printing Office, Washington, D.C., 1969), p. 67.

47. A. Linsky, *Soc. Psychiatry* 5, 166 (1970).

48. R. Spitz, *Psychoanal. Study Child* 2, 113 (1946); A. Schmale, S. Meyerowitz, D. Tinling, *in Modern Trends in Psychosomatic Medicine,* O. W. Hill, Ed. (Appleton-Century-Crofts, New York, 1970), p. 1.

49. P. Clayton, *Arch. Gen. Psychiatry* 30, 747 (1974); *Am. J, Psychiatry* 132, 133 (1975); S. Kiritz and R. Moos, *Psychosom. Med.* 36, 96 (1974); C. Parkes, in *Modern Trends in Psychosomatic Medicine,* O. W. Hill, Ed. (Appleton-Century-Crofts, New York, 1970), vol. 2, p. fl; C. Parks, B. Benjamin, R. Fitzgerald, *Br. Med. J.* 1, 740 (1969).

50. H. B. M. Murphy, *Milbank Mem. Fund Q.* 39, 385(1961).

51. I. Rootman and D. Sydiaha, *Psychiatr. Q.* 43, 131 (1969).

52. N. Mintz and D. Schwartz, *Int. J. Soc. Psychiatry* 10, 101 (1964).

53. G. Klee, E. Spiro, A. Bahn, K. Gorwitz, in *Psychiatric Epidemiology and Mental Health Planning,* R. Monroe, G. Klee, and E. Brody, Eds. (American Psychiatric Association, Washington, D.C., 1967), p. 107.

54. R. Meile and P. Haese, *J. Health Soc. Behav.* 10, 237 (1969).

55. J. Abramson, *Milbank Mem. fund Q.* 44, 23 (1966); E. F. Jackson, *Am. Sociol. Rev. 27,* 469 (1962); S. King and S. Cobb, *J. Chronic Dis.* 7, 466 (1958); S. Cobb and S. Kasl, *Am. J. Public Health 56,* 1657 (1966); S. King and S. Cobb, *J. Chronic Dis,* 7, 466 (1958).

56. L. E. Hinkle and H. G. Wolff, in *Explorations in Social Psychiatry,* A. Leighton, J. Clausen, R. Wilson, Eds. (Basic Books, New York, 1957), p. 105; L. Hinkle, in *Stressful Life Events,* B. S. Dohrewend and B. P. Dohrenwend, Eds. (Wiley, New York, 1974), p. 9.

18

An Analysis of Coping in a Middle-Aged Community Sample

Susan Folkman and Richard S. Lazarus

There is a growing conviction that the ways people cope with stress affect their psychological, physical, and social well-being (for reviews see Antonovsky, 1979; Coelho et al., 1974; Cohen and Lazarus, 1979; Janis and Mann, 1977; Moos, 1977). Despite the ground swell of interest in coping, little is known about how it plays this mediating role. A major reason is that most coping research has been concerned with unusual populations (for example, those exhibiting some form of pathology or, less frequently, exceptionally good adjustment) or with unusual or special events (such as tornadoes, parachute jumps, doctoral examinations, and spinal injuries). With the exception of a study by Pearlin and Schooler (1978), attention has not been given to the ways most people—those who do not exhibit either pathology or superperson characteristics—cope with the ordinary stressful events of their day-to-day lives. Measures devised to assess coping have been inadequate or inappropriate for this latter task. Without suitable assessment strategies, little progress can be made in understanding how coping mediates the relationship between the stresses of everyday living and psychological, physical, and social well-being.

Our purpose here is twofold: to report a study of the ways 100 community-residing men and women aged 45-64 coped with the stressful events of daily living during the course of a year, and thereby to present an approach to the assessment of coping that we think holds promise for coping research.

In this study we sought to answer two basic questions about the coping process. First, to what extent are people consistent in coping with the diverse stressful events of ordinary living? If coping is determined primarily by person variables, intraindividual coping patterns should be highly consistent across stressful encounters. On the other

EDITORS' NOTE: Previously published in the *Journal of Health and Social Behavior,* 1980, pp. 219-239. Reprinted with permission.

hand, if situation variables are the major determinants, coping patterns will be situation-specific, and there will be low consistency. Second, what are the actual factors that influence the coping process? Five were considered: certain situational factors, including what the event was about, who was involved, and how the event was appraised, and two demographic variables, age and gender.

This report does not examine the relationships between coping processes and adaptational outcomes, such as morale, social functioning, and somatic illness. Before this can be done, it is necessary to have a workable approach to the measurement of coping, and to have at least a preliminary understanding of the consistency of the coping process across stressors and of some of the determinants of coping. This report should, therefore, be regarded as a necessary first step in programmatic research on coping and adaptational outcome.

Approaches to the Measurement of Coping

Current approaches to measurement are based on three broad perspectives, namely, coping conceptualized in terms of ego processes (e.g., Haan, 1977; Vaillant, 1977), coping conceptualized as traits (e.g., Lazarus et al., 1974), and coping conceptualized in terms of the special demands of specific kinds of situations, such as illness (e.g., Moos, 1977), natural disasters (e.g., Lucas, 1969), and bereavement (e.g., Parkes, 1972). A brief discussion of each of these perspectives will make clear why the measures of coping that have evolved are unsatisfactory.

Conceptualizing coping in terms *of defensive* or *ego processes* poses several difficulties for our understanding of the relationship between the coping process and the adaptational outcome.

Usually defenses are hierarchically organized on an evaluative dimension. Vaillant (1977), for example, orders defense processes from primitive to mature according to their "relative theoretical maturity and pathological import" (p. 80). Menninger (1963) speaks of five orders of regulatory devices representing levels of disorganization, and Haan (1977) ranks ego processes as indicating ego-failure, defense, or coping according to their adherence to an objective reality. The placement of an ego process on an evaluative dimension is often made on the basis of information about how well the person functions. This leads to the first major difficulty, namely, a confounding between the process and the adaptational outcome.

Two examples are the studies of Wolff et al. (1964) concerning "well-defended" parents of children with terminal illness, and the more recent work of Vaillant (1977). In the study by Wolff et al., the parents' degree of defense ("well-defendedness") was used to predict their stress hormone level. However, the measure of well-defendedness was based partially on evidence of lack of distress. It is no great surprise, therefore, that the outcome measure of stress level, corticosteroid secretion, was also correlated with well-defendedness.

Vaillant's procedure for assigning defense level scores to behaviors in his longitudinal study of the adaptive processes of male graduates of an Eastern university also illustrates this problem of the confounding of process and outcome. Behaviors at times of crisis and conflict in each man's life were described, and these behaviors were assigned a defense rating according to their relative maturity. Raters were given a life-style summary to assist them in rating the behavior—in other words, a defense was rated in the context of the man's overall functioning. Level of defense (i.e., maturity of defense) was subsequently used to distinguish outcome groups. However, when there is interdependence between the process and the adaptational outcome, as in the case of Vaillant's study, the process cannot be used to explain the outcome.

Another difficulty is that adequate interrater reliability in assigning labels to ego processes is difficult to attain. This problem is noted by Vaillant (1971) and by Morrissey (1977) in his review of studies employing Haan's tripartite arrangement of ego processes. Raters' disagreements stem in large part from the amount of inference that is often required to label an ego process. For example, Vaillant (1977) defines reaction formation as behavior in a fashion diametrically opposed to an unaccepted instinctual impulse. This mechanism includes overtly caring for someone else when one wishes to be cared for oneself, "hating" someone or something one really likes, or "loving" a hated rival or unpleasant duty (p. 385).

Altruism, on the other hand, is defined as vicarious but constructive and instinctually gratifying service to others. It includes benign and constructive reaction formation, philanthropy, and well-repaid service to others. Altruism differs from . . . reaction formation in that it leaves the person using the defense partly gratified (p. 386).

Gratification seems to be the key to knowing when a behavior represents one or the other of the defenses, but how would an observer know whether the person was really gratified (altruism) or merely pretending gratification (reaction formation)? To reduce the amount of inference required to answer this question, Vaillant looks for information about the consequences of the event in subsequent life history. This, of course, leads to the problem mentioned earlier, namely, confounding of outcome with process.

Finally, by treating coping as a defense system whose purpose is to reduce tension and restore equilibrium, attention is focused on tension reduction rather than problem-solving. Although maintaining emotional equilibrium is an important function of coping (Cohen and Lazarus, 1979; White, 1974), so is problem-solving (see Janis and Mann, 1977; Mechanic, 1962; Murphy, 1974). A comprehensive definition of coping needs to include both emotion-regulating *and* problem-solving functions.

A second way to conceptualize coping is as a personality *trait*. This overlaps the first type of conceptualization whenever the traits are derived from defense theory, as, for example, in the case of repression-isolation (cf. Gardner et al., 1959; Levine and Spivack, 1964; Luborsky et al., 1965; Schafer, 1954), repression-sensitization (cf. Byrne, 1964; Welsh, 1956), and coping-avoidance (Goldstein, 1959, 1973). Byrne's (1964) repression-sensitization scale, Goldstein's (1959) sentence-completion test, and a defense mechanisms inventory by Gleser and Ihilevich (1969) are examples of defense-oriented measures also based on a trait approach. (For a comprehensive review of trait measures of coping, see Moos, 1974.) Traits differ from defensive processes, however, in that they refer not to a defensive response per se, but to the dispositional or personality attributes that lead to the response (cf. Lazarus, 1974).

Overall, trait measures are poor predictors of coping processes (Cohen and Lazarus, 1973; Lazarus et al., 1974). Trait measures are based on the assumption that people are behaviorally (also attitudinally and cognitively) consistent across situations. However, substantial consistency has seldom been found in personality research. There are arguments that most people are consistent under certain situational conditions, but even the use of person-by-situation interactions does not greatly improve the extent to which traits predict behavior (cf. Bowers, 1973; Ekehammar, 1974; Magnusson and Endler, 1977; Pervin and Lewis, 1978). The consistency of the coping process has never been addressed systematically in research, but has been, in the main, assumed.

Further, the unidimensional quality of most trait measures does not adequately reflect the multidimensional quality of actual coping processes. Naturalistic observation (e.g., Mechanic, 1962; Murphy, 1974; Visotsky et al., 1961) indicates that coping is a complex amalgam of thoughts and behaviors (cf. Lazarus, in press). Moos and Tsu (1977), for example, point out that in coping with physical illness a patient must deal with many sources of stress, including pain and incapacitation, hospital environments, and the demands imposed by the professional staff and special treatment procedures. At the same time, the patient must also preserve emotional balance, a satisfactory self-image, and good relationships with family and friends. These multiple tasks require an array of coping strategies, the complexity of which simply cannot be captured in a unidimensional measure.

Coping is also a *shifting* process (cf. Lazarus, in press) in which a person must, at certain times, rely more heavily on one form of coping, say, defensive strategies, and at other times on problem-solving strategies, as the status of the situation changes. It is difficult to see how the unfolding nature of most stressful encounters, and the concomitant changes in coping, could be adequately described by a presumably *static* measure of a general trait or personality disposition.

Situation-oriented researchers approach the study of coping from a third perspective. They usually describe the ways people cope with specific situations, for example, with cancer (e.g., Weisman and

Worden, 1976-77), polio (Visotsky et al., 1961), burns (e.g., Andreasen and Norris, 1972), spinal cord injury (e.g., Bulman and Wortman, 1977), parachute jumping (Epstein, 1962), and changes in institutional residence (Aldrich and Mendkoff, 1963). In these studies, coping strategies are often grouped into functional categories, for example, strategies for maintaining or restoring interpersonal relationships, seeking information, feeling better, maintaining self-esteem, and making good decisions. Although the coping strategies often include defenses, they are not organized around defense theory. Instead, defenses are described in terms of the particular function they serve in a specific situation. The "comforting cognitions" described by Mechanic (1962) in his study of doctoral students preparing for their qualifying examinations represent a good example. They include self-statements such as:

I'm as bright and knowledgeable as other students who have passed these examinations; I've handled test situations in the past—there's no good reason why not now; I am doing all I can to prepare—the rest is not up to me; I wouldn't have gotten this far unless I knew something; I'm well liked in this department; I've already demonstrated my competence on past work, they will pass me; You can't really fail these examinations unless you really mess up (p. 121).

These statements are specific to the exam situation and are grouped by function, in this case, the reduction of anxiety. The situation-oriented approach has certain virtues. By not limiting the definition of coping to defensive or trait-relevant processes, a more inclusive and comprehensive description of coping is possible. This is particularly evident in Mechanic's (1962) study, in which descriptions are given about how students managed the source of stress, i.e., the examination, by allocating time, choosing test areas, and developing test-taking skills, and also regulated feeling states through the use of comforting cognitions, favorable social comparisons, humor, being a member of a supportive group, and the search for support from other students, friends, the spouse, faculty, the investigator, "and sometimes anyone present" (p. 140).

There are problems with this approach, however. Because these studies are usually designed to identify coping strategies that mediate adaptational outcomes in *unusual* situations, and not to analyze coping cross-situationally, findings tend not to be generalizable to other contexts. In other words, situation-oriented research on coping tends also to be situation-specific.

In this connection, a recent study by Pearlin and Schooler (1978) differs in important ways from other situation-oriented research. Rather than focusing on unusual events, these researchers were concerned with the ordinary stresses people encounter. Further, rather than studying a single event, they asked their subjects about the ways they coped with stresses associated with four social roles: marriage partner, household economic manager, parent, and worker. Pearlin and Schooler found that people used a broad range of strategies in coping with the demands associated with these roles. They identified 17 coping factors, each made up of at least three specific strategies. Certain coping responses, such as engaging in selective perception and making positive comparisons, were found in all four role areas, suggesting that they have fairly universal application, whereas others appeared only in one area. Such differences are important because they imply that there may be both consistency *and* variability when coping is viewed across situations (see also Moos, 1974; Sidle et al., 1969).

There are two limitations to the Pearlin and Schooler (1978) study. First, most of the analyses were based on questions that asked how the respondents *usually* coped with *general* sources of stress, and not how they actually coped in specific situations. Questions about sources of stress and coping are illustrative. One question asked:

> How strongly do you agree or disagree that: 1. I cannot completely be myself around my spouse? 2. My marriage doesn't give me enough opportunity to become the sort of person I'd like to be? 3. My spouse appreciates me just as I am? (p. 19)

And another asked:

> How often do you: 1. Tell yourself that marital difficulties are not important? 2. Try to overlook your spouse's faults and pay attention only to good points? 3. Try to ignore difficulties by looking only at good things? (p. 20)

When a situational source of stress is defined in terms of a general quality, such as social atmosphere, we learn about an enduring aspect of a cluster of specific situations that in this case includes opportunity for self-expression and spousal appreciation or the lack thereof. These are general, abstract qualities of situations and do not inform us of the specific demands with which the person is coping. Similarly, when a person is asked about how he or she *usually* copes, information is being solicited about a personality disposition. At this level of abstraction, measurement poses the same problems encountered in the trait approach to measurement discussed above. Overall, there is usually a poor relationship between what people say they usually do and what they actually do in specific instances. The best way to learn about the demands of situations (such as a personal criticism or a manifestation of interpersonal coolness or hostility) and how people cope with them (e.g., by counterhostility, avoidance, or withdrawal of interest) is to describe how people *actually* cope in *specific* stressful encounters.

The second limitation of Pearlin and Schooler's study is its concern with persistent life-strains, that is, enduring and hence unresolved problems "that have the potential for arousing threat . . ." (p. 3). Subjects were not asked about stresses they had resolved or were successful in overcoming. As a result, a large domain of coping responses, those effective in changing the situation out of which the strainful experience arose, was ignored. This orientation toward enduring problems might help explain why responses to modify the situation represented only 3 of the 17 coping responses elicited, a finding that seemed to surprise the authors.

The conceptualization of coping used in the present study falls within the cognitive-phenomenological theory of psychological stress developed by Lazarus and his colleagues (e.g., Lazarus, 1966; Lazarus, in press; Coyne and Lazarus, in press; Folkman et al., 1979; Lazarus et al., 1980; Lazarus and Launier, 1978). The overall theoretical framework is transactional in that the person and the environment are seen in an ongoing relationship of reciprocal action, each affecting and in turn being affected by the other. Lazarus has defined two processes that mediate this relationship: appraisal and coping.

Appraisal is the cognitive process through which an event is evaluated with respect to what is at stake (primary appraisal) and what coping resources and options are available (secondary appraisal). There are three major types of stressful appraisals: harm-loss, which refers to damage that has already occurred; threat, which refers to harm or loss that has not yet occurred but is anticipated; and challenge, which refers to an anticipated opportunity for mastery or gain. The degree to which a person experiences psychological stress, that is, feels harmed, threatened, or challenged, is determined by the relationship between the person and the environment in that specific encounter as it is defined both by the evaluation of what is at stake *and* the evaluation of coping resources and options.

Coping is defined as the cognitive and behavioral efforts made to master, tolerate, or reduce external and internal demands and conflicts among them. Such coping efforts serve two main functions: the management or alteration of the person-environment relationship that is the source of stress (problem-focused coping) and the regulation of stressful emotions (emotion-focused coping). These functions of coping are also recognized by George (1974), Kahn et al. (1964), Murphy and Moriarty (1976), Murphy (1974), White (1974), Mechanic (1962), and Pearlin and Schooler (1978).

Coping efforts are made in response to stress appraisals. However, appraisal and coping continuously influence each other throughout an encounter. For example, an appraisal of harm/loss, threat, or challenge stimulates coping efforts that change the person-environment relationship by altering the relationship itself (problem-focused coping) and/or by regulating emotional distress (emotion-focused coping). The changed relationship leads to new appraisals or reappraisals, which in turn engender further coping efforts, and so on. The identification of appraisal as a determinant of coping, or coping as a determinant of appraisal, is thus provisional depending upon where one interrupts the ongoing, dynamic relationship between the two.

The term *coping processes* refers to what the person actually thinks and does in a particular encounter and to changes in these efforts as the encounter unfolds during a single episode or across episodes that are in some sense part of a common stressful encounter, as in bereavement. This study focuses on just one aspect of these processes, namely, what the person thinks and does to cope with the demands of a specific stressful encounter. Shortly we shall explain how we combine a person's complex coping efforts to provide a summary description of coping processes in that particular encounter. What we do not have is a description of how the coping efforts are ordered in time or how they change in relation to shifts in the person-environment relationship. We are currently analyzing open-ended interview material with a view to studying these complex time-related changes in coping processes. The analysis we report here should be regarded as an effort to set the stage for this more ambitious undertaking.

Method

Sample

The sample consisted of 100 respondents (52 women, 48 men), aged 45-64, who participated in a 12-month study of stress, coping, and emotions. The participants were white and primarily Protestant (93; 6 Catholic and 1 Jewish), had at least a ninth-grade level of education (mean = 13.7 years) and at least "adequate" income ($7,000 or above in 1974; mean = $11,313), and were not severely disabled. Age was further stratified into four 5-year periods: 45-49 (N = 27), 50-54 (N = 25), 55-59 (N = 24), and 60-64 (N = 24). These persons were selected from a population previously surveyed by the Alameda County Human Population Laboratory (HPL).[1] In 1965, the HPL completed a survey of physical, mental, and social health in Alameda County (Hochstim, 1970). The sampling frame consisted of all (over 7,000) adults aged 20 or over living in a probability sample area of 4,735 housing units. This population was resurveyed by HPL in 1974, and it was from the 1974 panel sample (N = 4,864) that our participants were drawn. A total of 216 people were initially contacted by phone, 109 of whom agreed to be in the study. Over the course of the study, nine of these dropped out. A comparison of the 109 in the original sample with those who refused to participate on income, religion, physical status, and education revealed that those refusing were less educated ($\chi^2 = 11.21$, df = 3, $p < .02$), with more falling within the education level of 8-12 years. Of the nine who dropped out, four were women, and they came from the youngest three age groups (three from each).

The Response Measure: The Ways of Coping[2]

The "Ways of Coping" is a checklist of 68 items describing a broad range of behavioral and cognitive coping strategies that an individual might use in a specific stressful episode. The strategies were derived from the framework suggested by Lazarus and his colleagues (Lazarus, 1966; Lazarus and Launier, 1978) and from suggestions offered in the coping literature (Mechanic, 1962; Sidle et al., 1969; Weisman and Worden, 1976-77). They include items from the domains of defensive coping (e.g., avoidance, intellectualization, isolation, suppression), information-seeking, problem-solving, palliation, inhibition of action, direct action, and magical thinking. The checklist is binary, yes or no, and is always answered with a specific stressful event in mind.

The items on the Ways of Coping checklist were classified into two categories: problem-focused and emotion-focused. The problem-focused category includes items that describe cognitive problem-solving efforts and behavioral strategies for altering or managing the source of the problem. Examples are:

- Got the person responsible to change his or her mind.
- Made a plan of action and followed it.
- Stood your ground and fought for what you wanted.

The emotion-focused category includes items that describe cognitive and behavioral efforts directed at reducing or managing emotional distress. Examples are:

- Looked for the "silver lining," so to speak; tried to look on the bright side of things.
- Accepted sympathy and understanding from someone.
- Tried to forget the whole thing.

Reporting of Stressful Events

Participants were interviewed seven times at 4-week intervals about stressful events that had occurred during the previous month and were perhaps still going on. Details were sought about what had led up to the event, who was involved, what it was about, what happened, what was at stake, and the ways the participant coped. At the conclusion of the account, the participant indicated on the Ways of Coping checklist those strategies that had been or were being used in the event. In the first interview, participants were asked to describe three events. In subsequent sessions, they were asked to describe one event.

In addition, participants filled out a Coping Questionnaire during the third week following each interview. The Coping Questionnaire asked the person to think of the most stressful event experienced during the month, to give a written description of it, and then to indicate on the Ways of Coping checklist those strategies that were used in the episode. Initially participants were asked to fill out two questionnaires each month. However, after 2 months the number was reduced to one.

Most participants did not report the maximum number of stressful incidents our interview and questionnaire procedures permitted. Sometimes a participant would discuss the same incident in an interview that he or she had reported on a questionnaire, and at other times a participant would report that nothing stressful had happened in the previous month. As a consequence, the number of episodes reported by the participants varied from 4 to 18. In all, 1,524 episodes were collected, an average of 15.2 for each person, although not all were used in the analysis for reasons given in the next section.

Classification of Coping Episodes

Each coping episode was classified as to what it was about, who was involved, and how it was appraised. Four broad categories were used to describe what each coping episode was primarily about: health, work, family matters, and other. These categories describe the *"context"* of an event. Four categories were also established to describe who was involved: self only, person(s) at work, family member(s), and others. These categories describe the *"person involved."*

The classification of episodes as to their context and the person involved was made by a team of three coders—one of the writers (SF), a graduate student, and an undergraduate student. In the early stages of coding, agreement among the coders ranged from .85 to .96. Any episode that was not coded the same way by all three coders was discussed, and a code was agreed upon. A reliability check was made after approximately 600 episodes had been coded, and the range of agreement was .87 to .97. A third reliability check was made after 1,200 had been coded; the range of agreement was .90 to .97.

Episodes were classified as to *"appraisal"* by the participants, who indicated on the final page of the Ways of Coping checklist which of four statements described the situation for which they had just completed the checklist: In general, is this situation one

1. that you could change or do something about?
2. that must be accepted or gotten used to?
3. that you needed to know more about before you could act?
4. in which you had to hold yourself back from doing what you wanted to do?

In many instances the participants checked more than one statement, in which case they were asked to underline the one that best described the situation. Only those episodes that could be coded for all three factors—context, the person involved, and appraisal—were included in the analysis. In all, 192, or 13%, were eliminated because they could not be coded for all three factors; 1,332 remained, an average of 13.3 for each person.

Results and Discussion

The Dual Functions of Coping

One of the major theoretical tenets underlying this investigation is that the coping process involves both problem-focused and emotion-focused functions. Therefore, the finding that both problem- *and* emotion-focused coping were used in virtually every stressful encounter is important. Of the 1,332 coping episodes analyzed, there were less than 2% in which only one type of coping was used. This points up dramatically the earlier theme that conceptualizing coping solely in terms of defensive processes or problem-solving processes is inadequate. Defensive processes refer primarily to the emotion-focused function of coping, but in the stressful encounters reported here, problem-focused coping was also used in nearly every instance. Similarly, researchers who emphasize the problem-solving aspect of coping are dealing with a limited aspect of the coping process as it presents itself in ordinary living. For example, in Janis and Mann's (1977) decision-making model, although emotion is seen as a source of interference with good decision-making, little attention is given to the strategies people use to regulate it. Snyder et al. (1962) and George (1974) have called attention to the need to look at coping devices that decision-makers can use to minimize the psychological tensions accompanying decision-making under emergency conditions or under conditions of uncertainty or ambiguity. This is not to say that there is no place for research on defensive processes or decision-making. However, when *coping* is the subject of investigation, it is best seen as a complex process involving both the problem-solving and emotion-regulating functions, as Lazarus (in press; Note 1) has argued.

Consistency of Coping Patterns

A second major theoretical tenet is that coping is best understood as being determined by the relationship *between* the person and the environment, rather than by independent person or situation factors. The findings of this study offer strong support for this position and demonstrate its usefulness in understanding the coping process. The degree of consistency of coping patterns is a key feature of this issue, since the higher such consistency, the greater the role independent person factors must have as determinants.

A *coping pattern* was defined here as the combined proportion of problem- and emotion-focused coping used in a specific episode. Scores on the P-scale (24 items) ranged from 0 to 23, with a mean of 8.6, a median of 8.4, and a standard deviation of 4.4. Scores on the E-scale (40 items) ranged from 0 to 37, with a mean of 13.4, a median of 13.2, and a standard deviation of 6.1. Since the two distributions were normal, each with an N of 1,332 episodes, they were divided into approximately equal thirds. The operational definition of pattern thus involved classifying each P-score and E-score as high, medium, or low and combining the rankings to form nine possible patterns ranging from high on both scales to low on both scales.

Consistency scores were calculated through a combinatorial analysis in which the number of pattern repetitions was calculated *intraindividually* as a proportion of maximum possible repetitions. Perfect consistency (a score of 1) was defined as the repetition of one pattern across all episodes. Perfect variability (a score of 0) was defined as the absence of any repetitions. This method of analysis took into account the varying numbers of episodes that individuals reported by using that figure as the denominator in the ratio. For example, for an individual reporting 16 episodes, the increased likelihood of pattern repetitions owing to the large number of episodes is controlled for by the increased number of possible repetitions the large number of episodes would contain.

A small number of participants were highly consistent in their use of coping patterns. A closer look at the episodes reported by the 5% of the sample with the highest consistency scores (ranging from .714 to 1.00) revealed that for each person there was great variety among episodes with respect to what they were about, who was involved, and how they were appraised. This suggests that high consistency is a function of a personality factor or trait rather than the result of the person experiencing the same situation over and over again. However, the consistency scores of most of the sample suggest that, on the whole, coping patterns are not greatly determined by person factors, nor are they determined entirely by situation factors.

These generalizations with respect to coping consistency must be tentative, for we have examined only one of several possible coping patterns. "Pattern" here refers to the *relative proportions* of problem- and emotion-focused coping used in a particular episode. As such, it ignores the specific problem- and emotion-focused strategies brought to bear in a given encounter. For example, within the emotion-focused category are numerous, more specific coping strategies, such as trying to see humor in the situation, avoidance, detachment, assignment of blame (to self or others), fatalism, projection, and fantasy. Specific strategies within the problem-focused category include seeking information, trying to get help, inhibiting action, and taking direct action. Further analysis of these or other specific strategies would provide the possibility for testing consistency or variability in patterns other than those employed here.

Similarly, the problem-focused and emotion-focused functions of coping were selected for study because of their theoretical importance as reflected in relatively independent major research literatures, e.g., industrial-social psychology (Kahn et al., 1964), sociology (Mechanic, 1962), and developmental psychology (Murphy, 1974). However, they are only two of several functions that could have been considered. Other possibilities include whether coping is directed at oneself or another, whether it is active or passive (cf. Rothbaum et al., 1979), and whether it produces a solution (an "exit," to use the term of Miller et al., 1960) or merely a deferral of solution. Examination of these functions might increase the likelihood of observing coping styles, which can be thought of as clusters of patterns or profiles.

It may be that to identify coping styles that transcend situational contexts, we must look at another level of abstraction for ways people think about themselves or relate to others of a particular sort, for example, the powerful or powerless, friendly or hostile, controlling or permissive. Intuitively, we sense the existence of such styles. For example, most of us know people who seem to be assaultive yet simultaneously vulnerable, a pattern of coping that allows them to be demanding and at the same time wards off counterdemands by implying that such counterdemands would "do them in." We are persuaded that such complex and subtle coping styles do exist, but it may not be possible to identify them through the Ways of Coping checklist.

In the present data set, such styles are not readily apparent. When pattern is defined simply in terms of proportions of problem- and emotion-focused coping, variability rather than consistency predominates, and as the findings will show, problem- and emotion-focused coping are differentially influenced by situational factors—i.e., who was involved in the coping episode, what its context was, and how the episode was appraised—and by the age and gender of the participant.

The Influence of Situational Factors on Coping

Three sets of analyses were performed on problem- and emotion-focused coping scores. The first set examined the effects of who was involved in the episode (person involved), the second examined the effects of what it was about (context), and the third examined the effects of how it was appraised (appraisal). The category "other" within the factors of context and person involved was not included in this analysis, since the meaning of any differences for this category would not have been clear. Within every set of analyses, each category was entered into multiple comparisons—e.g., episodes that had to do with health were compared with episodes that were work-related and with episodes that were family-related. Because of the multiple testing, the significance level for rejecting the null hypothesis of no difference between the means was set conservatively at .02 to reduce the increased chance of a Type I error.

The Person Involved. Of the three situational factors considered, the person involved in the coping episode was the factor having the least influence on coping. Epiodes involving people at work generated increased problem-focused coping compared with episodes involving the self only or family members. There was no effect on emotion-focused coping.

The Context. The context of the episode, that is, whether it was work-related, family-related, or health-related, differentially influenced problem- and emotion-focused coping. Work was associated with higher levels of problem-focused coping, and health was associated with increased emotion-focused coping.

The increase in problem-focused coping associated with the work context is particularly interesting when the findings about work in Pearlin and Schooler's (1978) study are considered. Pearlin and Schooler were puzzled by the infrequent use of strategies directed at changing the situation, and by the resistance of problems at work to amelioration through coping efforts. They suggested that this might be due to the impersonal and chronic nature of problems in the work arena. As noted earlier, another reason might be that a domain of interpersonal work-related problems in which there existed the potential for problem-solving, or at least problem-managing, was not tapped in their research.

Of the 310 work episodes in the study reported here, 184 (59%) involved a specific other person. In addition, 32% of the problems at work were appraised as permitting something to be done to change them. Pearlin and Schooler may be correct in saying that impersonal, chronic problems at work, such as noise and depersonalization, may be resistant to amelioration, and may therefore generate emotion- rather than problem-focused forms of coping. But work-related problems can also be interpersonal, and can be appraised as holding the potential for amelioration through problem-focused coping.

The increase in emotion-focused coping associated with health problems is consonant with findings from situation-oriented studies of coping with physical illness and disabilities (for reviews see Cohen and Lazarus, 1973; Lipowski, 1970; Moos, 1977). These studies have shown that much coping is directed toward managing feelings of anxiety, fear, and dread, and toward restoration of self-esteem and interpersonal relationships. To a large extent, these coping efforts fall under the rubric of emotion-focused coping. However, even though emotion-focused coping was particularly frequent in health-related stressful episodes, we must not lose sight of the fact that problem-focused coping was also used in these episodes. Studies of illness and disability should investigate both forms of coping.

The family context, that is, stressful encounters involving family concerns, did not have a clear impact on either problem- or emotion-focused coping. This may be due to the heterogeneity of episodes grouped within this category. Family-related episodes ranged from minor concerns about holiday meals and family celebrations to major concerns about financial security and the welfare of aging parents. These diverse experiences should each be considered separately; however, there were not enough instances in each category to permit their separation for purposes of analysis. In any future investigation with larger samples, such a breakdown should be made.

Appraisal. Lazarus and his colleagues (Folkman et al., 1979; Lazarus, 1966, in press; Lazarus et al., 1970, 1974; Lazarus and Launier, 1978) ascribe great importance to appraisal and consider it the critical determinant of the coping process. According to appraisal theory, in a threatening or harmful situation that is appraised as holding few possibilities for beneficial change, the person will employ emotion-focused modes of coping. On the other hand, when a situation is appraised as having the potential for amelioration by action, the person will use problem-focused coping to alter the troubled relationship that produced the emotional distress.

Precisely as this analysis predicts, situations in which something constructive could be done and in which more information was needed generated higher levels of problem-focused coping than situations that had to be accepted. Situations that had to be accepted, on the other hand, and in which the person had to hold back from acting, generated higher levels of emotion-focused coping than those in which something constructive could be done. These findings offer clear support for the theory of cognitive appraisal as a determinant of coping.

Not only are our field study findings on appraisal and coping nicely in accord with a cognitive-phenomenological model of stress process, but they are also consistent with the findings of a number of laboratory studies. For example, given the chance, most subjects will attempt to control an aversive stimulus as long as it does not cause conflict in some other area (e.g., Averill et al., 1977; Averill and Rosenn, 1972); on the other hand, under conditions of no control, palliative (emotion-focused) forms of coping increase and appear successful in lowering distress and somatic disturbance (Folkins, 1970; Monat et al., 1972).

How an event was appraised and its context turned out to be the most potent situational factors in accounting for coping variability. However, the way an event is appraised might be related to its context, resulting in a confounding. Health-related episodes, for example, might most often be appraised as having to be accepted, and work-related episodes might most often be appraised as permitting one to do something constructive. Indeed, examination of the relationship between context and appraisal indicated a significant (χ^2 = 34.3, df = 9, p = .03) but weak (Cramer's V = .09) relationship.[3] Because the large sample size (number of episodes = 1,332) influences the significance of the chi-square statistic (Marascuilo, 1971), attention was given to the estimated strength of the relationship as opposed to the level of significance. The strength of the relationship as estimated by Cramer's V statistic (.09) was so weak that it is reasonable to consider the two factors virtually unrelated. Thus the context of an event and how it is appraised seem relatively independent in affecting the coping process.

The Influence of Age on Coping

The participants in this study were between the ages of 45 and 64. Two one-way analyses of variance, using a mean P- and E-score for each person as dependent variables, were performed to examine the relationship between age and coping. When we used four 5-year age groups, no effect was found in either problem- or emotion-focused coping. Since it was possible that 5-year periods of age stratification are too small to reflect age effects, analyses were also performed with two 10-year groups. There was still no relationship between age and coping.

Such negative results about age must be taken as suggestive at best because of the highly restricted age range of the sample. Had our sample included a wider age distribution, extended both at the older and younger age levels, there might well have been age effects. For example, even though a chi-square analysis indicated there was very little relationship between what an episode was about (χ^2 = 19.7, df = 9, p = .02, Cramer's V = .07) or how it was appraised (χ^2 = 17.4, df = 9, p = .04, Cramer's V = .07) and age,[4] there was a trend in which older participants reported more health-related episodes and fewer family and work episodes than younger ones. This suggests that as sources of stress begin to change with advancing age, differences in coping might emerge as a function of changes in sources of stress. That is, emotion-focused coping might increase and problem-focused coping decrease because of more concern about health and less concern about work.

Suggesting that changes in coping may be associated with age-related changes in sources of stress is different from suggesting that coping changes as a direct function of age, that is, as a function of personality development (cf. Clark and Anderson, 1967; Gutmann, 1974; Jung, 1933). Comparisons with more elderly samples are needed to determine if there are indeed changes in coping associated with aging, and if so, whether these changes are better understood as a function of changes in sources of stress or of changes in personality.

The Influence of Gender on Coping

Conventional wisdom has it that men are taught to emphasize instrumental, analytic, problem-solving skills, and that women are socialized to be more emotionally sensitive, expressive, and dependent than men (cf. Bakan, 1966; Bem, 1974; Parsons and Bales, 1955). In the language of coping, men can be expected to use more problem-focused coping and women more emotion-focused coping.

In this study, women reported more stressful episodes having to do with health (61% of such episodes were reported by women, 39% by men) and more family episodes (68% by women, 32% by men) than men. Men, on the other hand, reported more work episodes than women (69.5% by men, 30.5% by women). A chi-square analysis[5] indicated that these differences were significant (χ^2 = 101.76, df = 3, p = .000) and reflected a moderate relationship (Cramer's V = .28).

In contrast, men and women differed very little in the way they appraised events. For example, 374 episodes were appraised as permitting something to be done to alter the situation. Of these, 176, or 47%, were reported by men. Similarly, 681 situations were appraised as having to be accepted, of which 301, or 44%, were reported by men. A chi-square analysis confirmed the weak relationship (χ^2 = 8.79, df = 3, p = .03, Cramer's V = .08) between gender and appraisal. Nevertheless, because of the gender differences in the factor of context, gender differences in coping were examined within each of the situational factors to prevent confounding gender differences in sources of stress with differences in coping.

T-tests were used to compare males and females with respect to problem- and emotion-focused coping within each of the situational factors. The results offer relatively little confirmation for the gender differences that conventional wisdom leads us to expect. Men did use more problem-focused coping than women, but only differences in the use of emotion-focused coping at work and in situations. Contrary to our stereotypic beliefs, men and women coped quite similarly. Moreover, gender differences in problem-focused coping in the work context probably reflect gender differences in jobs rather than a general disposition on the part of males to use more problem-focused coping than females. Women more often than men hold lower-level jobs where there are fewer opportunities to engage in problem-solving processes (cf. Colligan and Murphy, 1979; Kreps, 1976). To properly examine gender differences in coping at work would require having a sample of males and females drawn from similar jobs and settings. Whether differences in coping are a function of gender per se (through socialization) or the pressures of the work setting could then be determined more rigorously.

The most puzzling gender difference was the finding that men used more problem-focused coping than women in situations that had to be accepted. Perhaps men persevere in problem-focused coping longer than women before deciding that nothing can be done; and even when nothing can be done, men may be disposed to think about the problem more than women. The data analyzed here offer no clues about these alternative possibilities.

The important point is that to address the issue of gender differences in coping, differences in sources of stress must be distinguished from those in coping. If one looked only at coping, it would appear there was a difference due to gender in emotion-focused coping. Actually, these differences are attributable to sources of stress rather than gender per se. For example, women reported more health-related episodes than men, and health, as was noted, was associated with elevated emotion-focused coping. *Within* health-related episodes, however, there were *no* gender differences in emotion-focused coping. In other words, women and men do not differ in their use of emotion-focused coping within similar contexts of living, but they do differ in the contexts in which their stressful encounters occur.

Final Comments on the Measurement of Coping

As we have noted, the measurement approach used in this study needs to be extended in several ways. Very simple patterns of coping and only two of many coping functions were analyzed. Different, possibly more complex patternings must be examined, and other functions should be considered, perhaps in combination with the two we have defined. In addition, efforts have to be made to capture the ways that coping efforts change throughout an encounter. Until the dynamic quality of coping is described, our assessment procedures will remain incomplete.

Despite its present limitations, however, the approach to measurement adopted here, the Ways of Coping checklist, offers certain advantages presently unavailable to those who wish to study coping. First, it is designed to assess coping in a specific encounter and can be used for both intraindividual and comparative analyses. Second, it allows the person to characterize his or her coping thoughts and actions complexly, since for any given encounter the person can indicate as many such thoughts and actions as are relevant. Third, as a checklist, the measure is easy to use and requires little training.

Assessing coping confronts us with the difficulties of getting information from people about how they cope. It is probably not fruitful to ask them to tell us this directly, for we cannot expect people to know what we mean by coping, or to tell us, for example, whether they used intellectualization, avoidance, denial, or direct action. The approach used here is a bit more indirect, but not greatly so. We asked participants what they thought and did in recent encounters, and then applied the concepts of coping to these statements.

The findings of this study depend, therefore, on self-reports. By using recent encounters we minimized the problem of memory and retrospective falsification in these reports. Also, by repeatedly sampling the person's domain of coping strategies (an average of 13 times), we theoretically increased the reliability of our findings (cf. Epstein, 1977, 1979). However, the assessment of coping will always have to face the issue of self-report versus observational and inferential techniques (cf. Lazarus, in press). The larger study from which the present findings come also contains information from interviews in which there was the opportunity to make such inferences. At some point it should therefore be possible to compare the self-report material with clinical observation. Whatever its shortcomings, and there are many, the measurement approach described in this research is offered as an alternative for studying the coping process. We believe the adoption of this approach, and the theoretical framework within which it was developed, could greatly facilitate obtaining answers to many of the perplexing questions about stress, coping, and adaptational outcome that have hitherto been difficult to address.

NOTES

1. We appreciate the generosity of the Alameda County Human Population Laboratory staff, who made their archives available to us and helped facilitate this research.

2. The assessment tools used in this research were developed during 1976-77 as a group effort in which Patricia Benner, Judith Cohen, Susan Folkman, Alien Kanner, Richard S. Lazarus, Catherine Schaefer, Judith Wrubel, and others participated. However, the major responsibility for collecting and formulating the items on the Ways of Coping checklist was borne by Catherine Schaefer.

3. These tests of independence were performed on coping episodes, and not on persons. As a result, there is some degree of dependence in the data. That is, there are 100 independent sets of data, each set representing a person, but within a set are dependent data due to person, which violates the assumption of independence required for the chi-square test. However, because (1) the analyses were performed to gather information and not to test hypotheses, (2) there were a large number of independent sets of data, and (3) there was variability within each set, the best alternative was to use the chi-square procedure in order not to lose a major portion of the data. Moreover, in the cases of age and gender, these analyses were used to separate sources of variability, and the inflation of relationships that might have been caused by the dependency in the data only led to more cautious statistical procedures, as can be seen in the case of gender.

4. See Note 3.

5. See Note 3.

REFERENCES

Aldrich, C. K., and E. Mendkoff 1963 "Relocation of the aged and disabled: A mortality study." *Journal of the American Geriatrics Society 11:*401-8.

Andreasen, N. J. C., and A. S. Norris 1972 "Long-term adjustment and adaptation mechanisms in severely burned adults." *Journal of Nervous and Mental Disease 154:*352-62.

Antonovsky, Aaron 1979 *Health, Stress, and Coping.* San Francisco: Jossey-Bass.

Averill, J. R., O'Brien, L. and G. W. DeWitt 1977 "The influence of response effectiveness on the preference for warning and on psychophysiological stress reactions." *Journal of Personality 45:*395-418.

Averill, J. R., and M. Rosenn 1972 "Vigilant and nonvigilant coping strategies and psychophysiological stress reactions during the anticipation of electric shock." *Journal of Personality and Social Psychology 23:*128-41.

Bakan, David 1966 *The Duality of Human Existence.* Chicago: Rand McNally.

Bern, S. L. 1974 "The measurement of psychological androgyny." *Journal of Consulting and Clinical Psychology* 42:155-62.

Bowers, K. S. 1973 "Situationism in psychology: An analysis and a critique." *Psychological Review 80:*307-36.

Bulman, R. J., and C. B. Wortman 1977 "Attributions of blame and coping in the 'Real World': Severe accident victims react to their lot." *Journal of Personality and Social Psychology 35:*351-63.

Byrne, D. 1964 "Repression-sensitization as a dimension of personality." Pp. 170-220 in Brendan A. Maher (ed.), *Progress in Experimental Personality Research,* vol. 1. New York: Academic Press.

Clark, Margaret, and B. G. Anderson 1967 *Culture and Aging: An Anthropological Study of Older Americans.* Springfield, Ill.: Charles C Thomas.

Coelho, George V., David A. Hamburg, and John E. Adams (eds.) 1974 *Coping and Adaptation.* New York: Basic Books.

Cohen, F., and R. S. Lazarus 1973 "Active coping processes, coping dispositions, and recovery from surgery." *Psychosomatic Medicine 35:*375-89.

Colligan, M. J., and L. R. Murphy 1979 "Mass psychogenic illness in organizations: An overview." *Journal of Occupational Psychology 52:*77-90.

Coyne, J., and R. S. Lazarus 1979 In "Cognition, stress, and coping: A press transactional perspective." In I. L. Kutash and L. B. Schlesinger (eds.), *Pressure Point: Perspectives on Stress and Anxiety.* San Francisco: Jossey-Bass.

Cronbach, L. J. 1951 "Coefficient alpha and the internal structure of tests." *Psychometrika 16:*287-334.

Ekehammar, B. 1974 "Interactionism in personality from a historical perspective." *Psychological Bulletin 81:*1026-48.

Epstein, S. 1962 "The measurement of drive and conflict in humans: Theory and experiment." Pp. 127-209 in Marshall R. Jones (ed.), *Nebraska Symposium on Motivation.* Lincoln: University of Nebraska Press.

______ 1977 "Traits are alive and well." Pp. 83-98 in David Magnusson and Norman W. Endler (eds.), *Personality at the Crossroads.* Hillsdale, N.J.: Erlbaum.

______ 1979 "The stability of behavior: I. On predicting most of the people much of the time." *Journal of Personality and Social Psychology 37:*1097-1126.

Folkins, C. 1970 "Temporal factors and the cognitive mediators of stress reactions." *Journal of Personality and Social Psychology 14:*173-84.

Folkman, S., C. Schaefer, and R. S. Lazarus 1979 "Cognitive processes as mediators of stress and coping." Pp. 265-98 in Vernon Hamilton and David M. Warburton (eds.), *Human Stress and Cognition.* Chichester, England: Wiley.

Gardner, R. W., P. S. Holzman, G. S. Klein, H. B. Linton, and D. P. Spence 1959 "Cognitive control, a study of individual consistencies in cognitive behavior." *Psychological Issues 1*(4).

George, A. L. 1974 "Adaptation to stress in political decision making: The individual, small group, and organizational contexts." Pp. 176-245 in George V. Coelho, David A. Hamburg, and John E. Adams (eds.), *Coping and Adaptation.* New York: Basic Books.

Gleser, G. C., and D. Ihilevich 1969. "An objective instrument for measuring defense mechanisms." *Journal of Consulting and Clinical Psychology 33:*51-60.

Goldstein, M. J. 1959 "The relationship between coping and avoiding behavior and response to fear-arousing propaganda." *Journal of Abnormal and Social Psychology 58:*247-52.

______ 1973 "Individual differences in response to stress." *American Journal of Community Psychology 1:*113-37.

Gutmann, D. L. 1974 "The country of old men: Cross-cultural studies in the psychology of later life." Pp. 95-127 in R. A. LeVine (ed.), *Culture and Personality.* Chicago: Aldine.

Haan, Norma. 1977. *Coping and Defending.* New York: Academic Press.

Hochstim, J. R. 1970 "Health and ways of living." Pp. 149-76 in I. J. Kessler and M. L. Levin (eds.), *The Community as an Epidemiological Laboratory.* Baltimore: Johns Hopkins Press.

Janis, Irving, and Leon Mann 1977 *Decision Making.* New York: Free Press.

Jung, Carl G. 1933 *Modern Man in Search of a Soul.* New York: Harcourt Brace and World.

Kahn, Robert L., Donald M. Wolfe, Robert P. Quinn, and J. Diedrick Snoek 1964 *Organizational Stress: Studies in Role Conflict and Ambiguity.* New York: Wiley.

Kreps, Juanita 1976. Women and the American Economy. Englewood Cliffs, N.J.: Prentice-Hall.

Lazarus, Richard S. 1966 Psychological Stress and the Coping Process. New York: McGraw-Hill. In "The stress and coping paradigm." In Carl Press Eisdorfer, Donna Cohen, Arthur Kleinman, and Peter Maxim (eds.), *Theoretical Bases for Psychopathology.* New York: Spectrum.

Lazarus, R. S., J. R. Averill, and E. M. Opton, Jr. 1970 "Toward a cognitive theory of emotion." Pp. 207-32 in Magda B. Arnold (ed.), *Feelings and Emotions.* New York: Academic Press.

______ 1974 "The psychology of coping: Issues of research and assessment." Pp. 249-315 in George V. Coelho, David A. Hamburg, and John E. Adams (eds.), *Coping and Adaptation.* New York: Basic Books.

Lazarus, R. S., A. Kanner, and S. Folkman 1980 "Emotions: A cognitive-phenomenological analysis." Pp. 189-217 in Robert Plutchik and Henry Kellerman (eds.), *Theories of Emotion.* New York: Academic Press.

Lazarus, R. S., and R. Launier 1978 "Stress-related transactions between person and environment." Pp. 287-327 in Lawrence A. Pervin and Michael Lewis (eds.), *Perspectives in Interactional Psychology.* New York: Plenum.

Leigh, C. A. 1979 "*The problem-focused and emotion-focused scales of the Ways of Coping questionnaire: A construct-validity study.*" Unpublished master's thesis, University of California, Berkeley.

Levine, M., and G. Spivack 1964 *The Rorschach Index of Repressive Style.* Springfield, Ill.: Charles C Thomas.

Lipowski, Z. J. 1970 "Physical illness, the individual and the coping processes." *Psychiatry in Medicine 1:*91-102.

Luborsky, L., B. Blinder, and J. Schimek 1965 "Looking, recalling and GSR as a function of defense." *Journal of Abnormal Psychology 70:*270-80.

Lucas, Rex A. 1969 *Men in Crisis.* New York: Basic Books.

Magnusson, David, and Norman S. Endler (eds.) 1977 *Personality at the Crossroads.* Hillsdale, N.J.: Erlbaum.

Marascuilo, Leonard A. 1971 *Statistical Methods for Behavioral Science Research.* New York: McGraw-Hill.

Mechanic, David. 1962 *Students Under Stress.* New York: The Free Press of Glencoe.

Menninger, Karl. 11963 *The Vital Balance: The Life Process in Mental Health and Illness.* New York: Viking.

Miller, George A., Eugene H. Galanter, and Karl Pribram 1960 *Plans and the Structure of Behavior.* New York: Holt.

Monat, A., J. R. Averill, and R. S. Lazarus 1972 "Anticipatory stress and coping reactions under various conditions of uncertainty." *Journal of Personality and Social Psychology 24:*237-53.

Moos, Rudolf 1974 "Psychological techniques in the assessment of adaptive behavior." Pp. 334-99 in George V. Coelho, David A. Hamburg, and John E. Adams (eds.), *Coping and Adaptation.* New York: Basic Books.

______ 1977 *Coping with Physical Illness.* New York: Plenum.

Moos, R., and V. D. Tsu 1977 "The crisis of physical illness: An overview." Pp. 1-22 in Rudolf Moos (ed.), *Coping with Physical Illness.* New York: Plenum.

Morrissey, R. F. 1977 "The Haan model of ego functioning: An assessment of empirical research." Pp. 250-79 in Norma Haan, *Coping and Defending.* New York: Academic Press.

Murphy, L. B. 1974 "Coping, vulnerability, and resilience in childhood." Pp. 69-100 in George V. Coelho, David A. Hamburg, and John E. Adams (eds.), *Coping and Adaptation.* New York: Basic Books.

Murphy, Lois B., and Alice E. Moriarty 1976 *Vulnerability, Coping, and Growth.* New Haven, Conn.: Yale University Press.

Parkes, Colin Murray 1972 *Bereavement: Studies of Grief in Adult Life.* New York: International Universities Press.

Parsons, Talcott, and Robert F. Bales 1955 *Family, Socialization, and Interaction Processes.* Glencoe, Ill.: Free Press.

Pearlin, L., and C. Schooler 1978 "The structure of coping." *Journal of Health and Social Behavior 19:*2-21.

Pervin, Lawrence A., and Michael Lewis (eds.) 1978 *Perspectives in Interactional Psychology.* New York: Plenum.

Rothbaum, F., J. Wolfer, and M. Visintainer 1979 "Coping behavior and locus of control in children." *Journal of Personality 47:*118-35.

Schafer, Roy 1954 *Psychoanalytic Interpretations in Rorschach Testing.* New York: Grune & Stratton.

Sidle, A., R. Moos, J. Adams, and P. Cady 1969 "Development of a coping scale: A preliminary study." *Archives of General Psychiatry 20:*226-32.

Snyder, R. C., H. W. Bruck, and B. Sapin 1962 *Foreign Policy Decision-Making.* New York: Free Press.

Stone, George C., Frances Cohen, and Nancy E. Adler (eds.) 1979 "Coping with the stresses of illness." Pp. 217-54 in *Health Psychology.* San Francisco: Jossey-Bass.

Vaillant, George 1971 "Theoretical hierarchy of adaptive ego mechanisms." *Archives of General Psychiatry 24:*107-18.

______ 1977 *Adaptation to Life.* Boston: Little, Brown.

Visotsky, H. M., D. A. Hamburg, M. E. Goss, and B. A. Lebovits 1961 "Coping behavior under extreme stress." *Archives of General Psychiatry 5:*423-48.

Weisman, A., and J. W. Worden 1976 The existential plight in cancer: 77 Significance of the first 100 days." *International Journal of Psychiatry in Medicine* 7(1):1-15.

Welsh, G. S. 1956 "Factor dimensions A and R." In George S. Welsh and W. Grant Dahlstrom (eds.), *Basic Reading on the MMPI in Psychology and Medicine.* Minneapolis: University of Minnesota Press.

White, R. 1974 "Strategies of adaptation: An attempt at systematic description." Pp. 47-68 in George V. Coelho, David A. Hamburg, and John E. Adams (eds.), *Coping and Adaptation.* New York: Basic Books.

Wolff, C. T., S. B. Friedman, M. A. Hofer, and J. W. Mason 1964 "Relationship between psychological defenses and mean urinary 17-hydroxy-corticosteroid excretion rates: I. A predictive study of parents of fatally ill children." *Psychosomatic Medicine 26:*576-91.

B. On Social Relationships and Health

19

SOCIAL RELATIONSHIPS AND HEALTH

JAMES S. HOUSE, KARL R. LANDIS, AND DEBRA UMBERSON

. . . my father told me of a careful observer, who certainly had heart-disease and died from it, and who positively stated that his pulse was habitually irregular to an extreme degree; yet to his great disappointment it invariably became regular as soon as my father entered the room.

— Charles Darwin[1]

Scientists have long noted an association between social relationships and health. More socially isolated or less socially integrated individuals are less healthy, psychologically and physically, and more likely to die. The first major work of empirical sociology found that less socially integrated people were more likely to commit suicide than the most integrated.[2] In subsequent epidemiologic research age-adjusted mortality rates from all causes of death are consistently higher among the unmarried than the married.[3-5] Unmarried and more socially isolated people have also manifested higher rates of tuberculosis,[6] accidents,[7] and psychiatric disorders such as schizophrenia.[8,9] And as the above quote from Darwin suggests, clinicians have also observed potentially health-enhancing qualities of social relationships and contacts.

The causal interpretation and explanation of these associations has, however, been less clear. Does a lack of social relationships cause people to become ill or die? Or are unhealthy people less likely to establish and maintain social relationships? Or is there some other factor, such as a

EDITORS' NOTE: Reprinted with permission from *Science, 241,* pp. 540-545.

misanthropic personality, which predisposes people both to have a lower quantity or quality of social relationships and to become ill or die?

Such questions have been largely unanswerable before the last decade for two reasons. First, there was little theoretical basis for causal explanation. Durkheim[2] proposed a theory of how social relationships affected suicide, but this theory did not generalize to morbidity and mortality from other causes. Second, evidence of the association between social relationships and health, especially in general human populations, was almost entirely retrospective or cross-sectional before the late 1970s. Retrospective studies from death certificates or hospital records ascertained the nature of a person's social relationships after they had become ill or died, and cross-sectional surveys of general populations determined whether people who reported ill health also reported a lower quality or quantity of relationships. Such studies used statistical control of potential confounding variables to rule out third factors that might produce the association between social relationships and health, but could do this only partially. They could not determine whether poor social relationships preceded or followed ill health.

In this article, we review recent developments that have altered this state of affairs dramatically: (i) emergence of theoretical models for a causal effect of social relationships on health in humans and animals; (ii) cumulation of empirical evidence that social relationships are a consequential predictor of mortality in human populations; and (iii) increasing evidence for the causal impact of social relationships on psychological and physiological functioning in quasi-experimental and experimental studies of humans and animals. These developments suggest that social relationships, or the relative lack thereof, constitute a major risk factor for health—rivaling the effects of well-established health risk factors such as cigarette smoking, blood pressure, blood lipids, obesity, and physical activity. Indeed, the theory and evidence on social relationships and health increasingly approximate that available at the time of the U.S. Surgeon General's 1964 report on smoking and health,[10] with similar implications for future research and public policy.

The Emergence of "Social Support" Theory and Research

The study of social relationships and health was revitalized in the middle 1970s by the emergence of a seemingly new field of scientific research on "social support." This concept was first used in the mental health literature,[11,12] and was linked to physical health in separate seminal articles by physician-epidemiologists Cassel[13] and Cobb.[14] These articles grew out of a rapidly developing literature on stress and psychosocial factors in the etiology of health and illness.[15] Chronic diseases have increasingly replaced acute infectious diseases as the major causes of disability and death, at least in industrialized countries. Consequently, theories of disease etiology have shifted from ones in which a single factor (usually a microbe) caused a single disease, to ones in which multiple behavioral and environmental as well as biologic and genetic factors combine, often over extended periods, to produce any single disease, with a given factor often playing an etiologic role in multiple diseases.

Cassel[13] and Cobb[14] reviewed more than 30 human and animal studies that found social relationships protective of health. Recognizing that any one study was open to alternative interpretations, they argued that the variety of study designs (ranging from retrospective to experimental), of life stages studied (from birth to death), and of health outcomes involved (including low birth weight, complications of pregnancy, self-reported symptoms, blood pressure, arthritis, tuberculosis, depression, alcoholism, and mortality) suggested a robust, putatively causal, association. Cassel and Cobb indicated that social relationships might promote health in several ways, but emphasized the role of social relationships in moderating or buffering potentially deleterious health effects of psychosocial stress or other health hazards. This idea of "social support," or something that maintains or sustains the organism by promoting adaptive behavior or neuroendocrine responses in the face of stress or other health hazards, provided a general, albeit simple, theory of how and why social relationships should causally affect health.[16]

Publications on "social support" increased almost geometrically from 1976 to 1981. By the late 1970s, however, serious questions emerged about the empirical evidence cited by Cassel and Cobb and the evidence generated in subsequent research. Concerns were expressed about causal priorities between social support and health (since the great majority of studies remained cross-sectional or retrospective and based on self-reported data), about whether social relationships and supports buffered the impact of stress on health or had more direct effects, and about how consequential the effects of social relationships on health really were.[17-19] These concerns have been addressed by a continuing cumulation of two types of empirical data: (i) a new series of prospective mortality studies in human populations and (ii) a broadening base of laboratory and field experimental studies of animals and humans.

Prospective Mortality Studies of Human Populations

Just as concerns began to surface about the nature and strength of the impact of social relationships on health, data from long-term, prospective studies of community populations provided compelling evidence that lack of social relationships constitutes a major risk factor for mortality. Berkman and Syme[20] analyzed a probability sample of 4,775 adults in Alameda County, California, who were between 30 and 69 in 1965 when they completed a survey that assessed the presence or extent of four types of social ties—marriage, contacts with extended family and friends, church membership, and other formal and informal group affiliations. Each type of social relationship predicted mortality through the succeeding 9 years. A combined "social network" index remained a significant predictor of mortality (with a relative risk ratio for mortality of about 2.0, indicating that persons low on the index were twice as likely to die as persons high on the index) in multivariate analyses that controlled for self-reports in 1965 of physical health, socioeconomic status, smoking, alcohol consumption, physical activity, obesity, race, life satisfaction, and use of preventive health services. Such adjustment or control for baseline health and other risk factors provides a conservative estimate of the predictive power of social relationships, since some of their impact may be mediated through effects on these risk factors.

The major limitation of the Berkman and Syme study was the lack of other than self-reported data on health at baseline. Thus, House et al.[21] sought to replicate and extend the Alameda County results in a study of 2,754 adults between 35 and 69 at their initial interview and physical examinations in 1967 through 1969 by the Tecumseh (Michigan) Community Health Study. Composite indices of social relationships and activities (as well as a number of the individual components) were inversely associated with mortality during the succeeding 10- to 12-year follow-up period, with relative risks of 2.0 to 3.0 for men and 1.5 to 2.0 for women, after adjustment for the effects of age and a wide range of biomedically assessed (blood pressure, cholesterol, respiratory function, and electrocardiograms) as well as self-reported risk factors of mortality. Analyzing data on 2,059 adults in the Evans County (Georgia) Cardiovascular Epidemiologic Study, Schoenbach et al.[22] also found that a social network index similar to that of Berkman and Syme[20] predicted mortality for an 11- to 13-year follow-up period, after adjustment for age and baseline measures of biomedical as well as self-reported risk factors of mortality. The Evans County associations were somewhat weaker than those in Tecumseh and Alameda County, and as in Tecumseh were stronger for males than females.

Studies in Sweden and Finland have described similar results. Tibblin, Welin, and associates[23,24] studied two cohorts of men born in 1913 and 1923, respectively, and living in 1973 in Gothenberg, Sweden's second largest city. After adjustments for age, baseline levels of systolic blood pressure, serum cholesterol, smoking habits, and perceived health status, mortality in both cohorts through 1982 was inversely related to the number of persons in the household and the men's level of social and outside home activities in 1973. Orth-Gomer et al.[25] analyzed the mortality experience through 1981 of a random sample of 17,433 Swedish adults aged 29 to 74 at the time of their 1976 or 1977 baseline interviews. Frequency of contact with family, friends, neighbors, and coworkers in 1976-77 was predictive of mortality through 1981, after

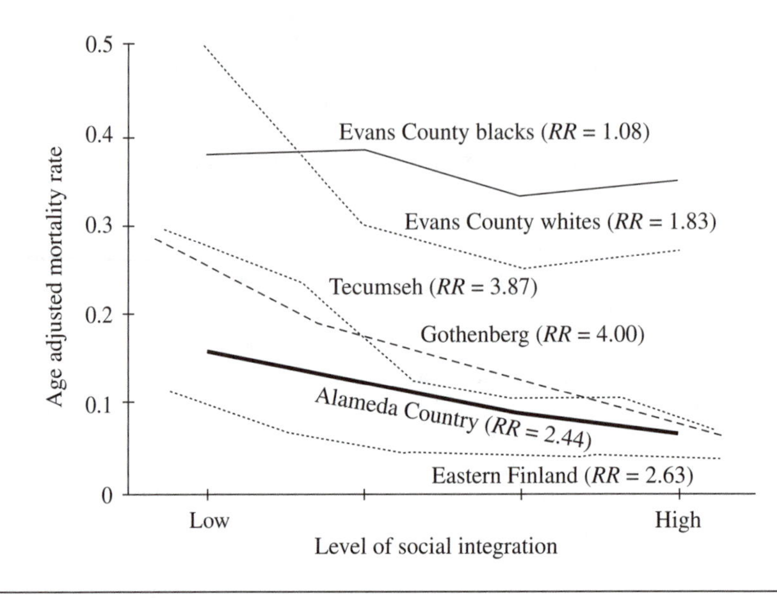

Figure 19.1 Level of Social Integration and Age-Adjusted Mortality for Males in Five Prospective Studies. RR, the Relative Risk Ratio of Mortality at the Lowest Versus Highest Level of Social Integration.

adjustment for age, sex, education, employment status, immigrant status, physical exercise, and self-reports of chronic conditions. The effects were stronger among males than among females, and were somewhat nonlinear, with the greatest increase in mortality risk occurring in the most socially isolated third of the sample. In a prospective study of 13,301 adults in predominantly rural eastern Finland, Kaplan et al.[26] found a measure of "social connections" similar to those used in Alameda County, Tecumseh, and Evans County to be a significant predictor of male mortality from all causes during 5 years, again after adjustments for other biomedical and self-reported risk factors. Female mortality showed similar, but weaker and statistically nonsignificant, effects.

These studies manifest a consistent pattern of results, as shown in Figs. 19.1 and 19.2, which show age-adjusted mortality rates plotted for the five prospective studies from which we could extract parallel data. The report of the sixth study[25] is consistent with these trends. The relative risks (RR) in Figs. 19.1 and 19.2 are higher than those reported above because they are only adjusted for age. The levels of mortality in Figs. 19.1 and 19.2 vary greatly across studies depending on the follow-up period and composition of the population by age, race, and ethnicity, and geographic locale, but the patterns of prospective association between social integration (that is, the number and frequency of social relationships and contacts) and mortality are remarkably similar, with some variations by race, sex, and geographic locale.

Only the Evans County study reported data for blacks. The predictive association of social integration with mortality among Evans County black males is weaker than among white males in Evans County or elsewhere (Fig. 19.1), and the relative risk ratio for black females in Evans County, although greater than for Evans County white females, is smaller than the risk ratios for white females in all other studies (Fig. 19.2). More research on blacks and other minority populations is necessary to determine whether these differences are more generally characteristic of blacks compared to whites.

Modest differences emerge by sex and rural as opposed to urban locale. Results for men and

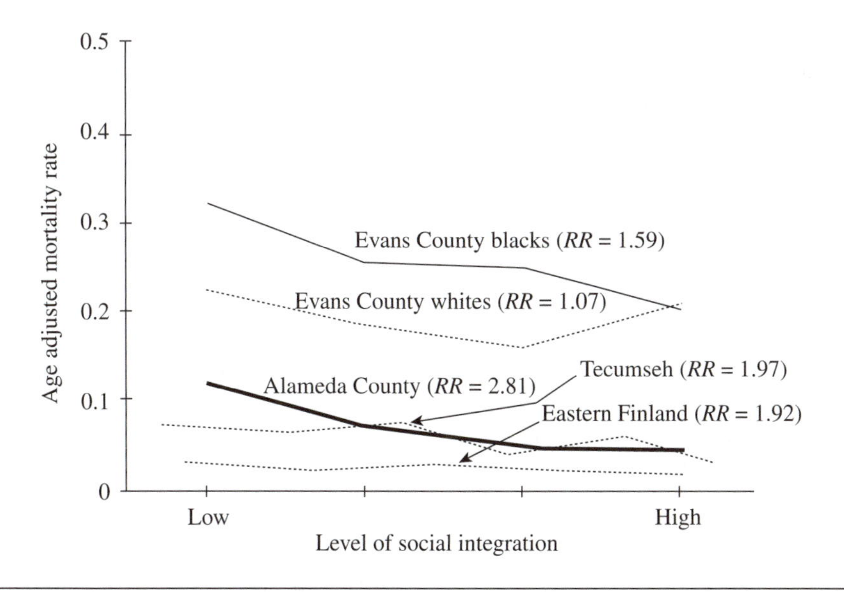

Figure 19.2 Level of Social Integration and Age-Adjusted Mortality for Females in Five Prospective Studies. RR, the Relative Risk Ratio of Mortality at the Lowest Versus Highest Level of Social Integration.

women are strong, linear, and similar in the urban populations of Alameda County (that is, Oakland and environs) and Gothenberg, Sweden (only men were studied in Gothenberg). In the predominantly small-town and rural populations of Tecumseh, Evans County, and eastern Finland, however, two notable deviations from the urban results appear: (i) female risk ratios are consistently weaker than those for men in the same rural populations (Figs. 19.1 and 19.2), and (ii) the results for men in more rural populations, although rivaling those in urban populations in terms of risk ratios, assume a distinctly nonlinear, or threshold, form. That is, in Tecumseh, Evans County, and eastern Finland, mortality is clearly elevated among the most socially isolated, but declines only modestly, if at all, between moderate and high levels of social integration.

Explanation of these sex and urban-rural variations awaits research on broader regional or national populations in which the same measures are applied to males and females across the full rural-urban continuum. The current results may have both substantive and methodological explanations. Most of the studies reviewed here, as well as others,[27-29] suggest that being married is more beneficial to health, and becoming widowed more detrimental, for men than for women. Women, however, seem to benefit as much or more than men from relationships with friends and relatives, which tend to run along same-sex lines.[20,30] On balance, men may benefit more from social relationships than women, especially in cross-gender relationships. Small communities may also provide a broader context of social integration and support that benefits most people, except for a relatively small group of socially isolated males.

These results may, however, have methodological rather than substantive explanations. Measures of social relationships or integration used in the existing prospective studies may be less valid or have less variance in rural and small town environments, and for women, thus muting their relationship with mortality. For example, the data for women in Fig. 19.2 are similar to the data on men if we assume that women have higher quality relationships and hence that their true level of social integration is moderate even at low levels of quantity. The social context of small communities may similarly provide a moderate level of social integration for everyone except quite isolated males. Thus measures of frequency of social contact may be poorer indices of social integration for women and more rural populations than for men and urban dwellers.

Variations in the results in Figs. 19.1 and 19.2 should not, however, detract from the remarkable consistency of the overall finding that social relationships do predict mortality for men and women in a wide range of populations, even after adjustment for biomedical risk factors for mortality. Additional prospective studies have shown that social relationships are similarly predictive of all-cause and cardiovascular mortality in studies of people who are elderly[31-33] or have serious illnesses.[34,35]

Experimental and Quasi-Experimental Research

The prospective mortality data are made more compelling by their congruence with growing evidence from experimental and clinical research on animals and humans that variations in exposure to social contacts produce psychological or physiological effects that could, if prolonged, produce serious morbidity and even mortality. Cassel[13] reviewed evidence that the presence of a familiar member of the same species could buffer the impact of experimentally induced stress on ulcers, hypertension, and neurosis in rats, mice, and goats, respectively; and the presence of familiar others has also been shown to reduce anxiety and physiological arousal (specifically secretion of free fatty acids) in humans in potentially stressful laboratory situations.[36,37] Clinical and laboratory data indicate that the presence of or physical contact with another person can modulate human cardiovascular activity and reactivity in general, and in stressful contexts such as intensive care units (pp. 122-141).[38] Research also points to the operation of such processes across species. Affectionate petting by humans, or even their mere presence, can reduce the cardiovascular sequelae of stressful situations among dogs, cats, horses, and rabbits (pp. 163-180).[38] Nerem et al.[39] found that human handling also reduced the arteriosclerotic impact of a high fat diet in rabbits. Recent interest in the potential health benefits of pets for humans, especially the isolated aged, is based on similar notions, although the evidence for such efforts is only suggestive.[40]

Bovard[41] has proposed a psychophysiologic theory to explain how social relationships and contacts can promote health and protect against disease. He reviews a wide range of human and animal studies suggesting that social relationships and contacts, mediated through the amygdala, activate the anterior hypothalamic zone (stimulating release of human growth hormone) and inhibit the posterior hypothalamic zone (and hence secretion of adrenocorticotropic hormone, cortisol, catecholamines, and associated sympathetic autonomic activity). These mechanisms are consistent with the impact of social relationships on mortality from a wide range of causes and with studies of the adverse effects of lack of adequate social relationships on the development of human and animal infants.[42] This theory is also consistent with sociobiological processes which, due to the survival benefit of social relationships and collective activity, would promote genetic selection of organisms who find social contact and relatedness rewarding and the lack of such contact and relatedness aversive.[43]

The epidemiologic evidence linking social relationships and supports to morbidity in humans is limited and not fully consistent. For example, although laboratory studies show short-term effects of social relationships on cardiovascular functioning that would, over time, produce cardiovascular disease, and prospective studies show impacts of social relationships on mortality from cardiovascular disease, the link between social relationships and the incidence of cardiovascular morbidity has yet to be firmly demonstrated.[19,44] Overall, however, the theory and evidence for the impact of social relationships on health are building steadily.[45,46]

Social Relationships as a Risk Factor for Health: Research and Policy Issues

The theory and data reviewed above meet reasonable criteria for considering social relationships a cause or risk factor of mortality, and probably morbidity, from a wide range of diseases[10,46] (pp. 289-321).[47] These criteria include strength and consistency of statistical associations across a wide range of studies, temporal ordering or prediction from cause to effect, a gradient of response (which may in this case be nonlinear), experimental data on animals and humans consistent with nonexperimental human data, and a plausible theory[41] of biopsychosocial mechanisms explaining the observed associations.

The evidence on social relationships is probably stronger, especially in terms of prospective studies, than the evidence which led to the certification of the Type A behavior pattern as a risk factor for coronary heart disease.[48] The evidence regarding social relationships and health increasingly approximates the evidence in the 1964 Surgeon General's report[10] that established cigarette smoking as a cause or risk factor for mortality and morbidity from a range of diseases. The age-adjusted relative risk ratios shown in Figs. 19.1 and 19.2 are stronger than the relative risks for all cause mortality reported for cigarette smoking.[10] There is, however, less specificity in the associations of social relationships with mortality than has been observed for smoking, which is strongly linked to cancers of the lung and respiratory tract (with age-adjusted risk ratios between 3.0 and 11.0). Better theory and data are needed on the links between social relationships and major specific causes of morbidity and mortality.

Although a lack of social relationships has been established as a risk factor for mortality, and probably morbidity, three areas need further investigation: (i) mechanisms and processes linking social relationships to health, (ii) determinants of levels of "exposure" to social relationships, and (iii) the means to lower the prevalence of relative social isolation in the population or to lessen its deleterious effects on health.

Mechanisms and Processes Linking Social Relationships to Health

Although grounded in the literature on social relationships and health, investigators on social support in the last decade leaped almost immediately to the interpretation that what was consequential for health about social relationships was their supportive quality, especially their capacity to buffer or moderate the deleterious effects of stress or other health hazards.[13,14] Many recent studies have reported either a general positive association between social support and health or a buffering effect in the presence of stress,[49] but these studies are problematic because the designs are largely cross-sectional or retrospective and the data usually self-reported. The most compelling evidence of the causal significance of social relationships on health has come from the experimental studies of animals and humans and the prospective mortality studies reviewed above—studies in which the measures of social relationships are merely the presence or absence of familiar other organisms, or relative frequency of contact with them, and which often do not distinguish between buffering and main effects. Thus, social relationships appear to have generally beneficial effects on health, not solely or even primarily attributable to their buffering effects, and there may be aspects of social relationships other than their supportive quality that account for these effects.

We now need a broader theory of the biopsychosocial mechanisms and processes linking social relationships to health than can be provided by extant concepts or theories of social support. That broader theory must do several things. First, it must clearly distinguish between (i) the existence or quantity of social relationships, (ii) their formal structure (such as their density or reciprocity), and (iii) the actual content of these relationships such as social support. Only by testing the effects on health of these different aspects of social relationships in the same study can we understand what it is about social relationships that is consequential for health.

Second, we need better understanding of the social, psychological, and biological processes that link the existence, quantity, structure, or content of social relationships to health. Social support—whether in the form of practical help, emotional sustenance, or provision of information—is only one of the social processes involved here. Not only may social relationships affect health because they are or are not supportive, they may also regulate or control human thought, feeling, and behavior in ways that promote health, as in Durkheim's[2] theory relating social integration to suicide. Current views based on this perspective suggest that social relationships affect health either by fostering a sense of meaning or coherence that promotes health[50] or by facilitating health-promoting behaviors such as proper sleep, diet, or exercise, appropriate use of alcohol, cigarettes, and drugs, adherence to medical regimens, or seeking appropriate medical care.[51] The negative or connective aspects of social relationships need also to be considered, since they may be detrimental to the maintenance of health and of social relationships.[52]

We must further understand the psychological and biological processes or mechanisms linking social relationships to health, either as extensions of the social processes just discussed [for example, processes of cognitive appraisal and coping[53]] or as independent mechanisms. In the latter regard, psychological and sociobiological theories suggest that the mere presence of, or sense of relatedness with, another organism may have relatively direct motivational, emotional, or neuroendocrinal effects that promote health either directly or in the face of stress or other health hazards but that operate independently of cognitive appraisal or behavioral coping and adaptation[42,43,54] (pp. 87-180).[38]

Determinants of Social Relationships: Scientific and Policy Issues

Although social relationships have been extensively studied during the past decade as independent, intervening, and moderating variables affecting stress or health or the relations between them, almost no attention has been paid to social relationships as dependent variables. The determinants of social relationships, as well as their consequences, are crucial to the theoretical and causal status of social relationships in relation to health. If exogenous biological, psychological, or social variables determine both health and the nature of social relationships, then the observed association of social relationships to health may be totally or partially spurious. More practically, Cassel,[13] Cobb,[14] and others became interested in social support as a means of improving health. This, in turn, requires understanding of the broader social, as well as psychological or biological, structures, and processes that determine the quantity and quality of social relationships and support in society.

It is clear that biology and personality must and do affect both people's health and the quantity and quality of their social relationships. Research has established that such factors do not, however, explain away the experimental, cross-sectional, and prospective evidence linking social relationships to health.[55] In none of the prospective studies have controls for biological or health variables been able to explain away the predictive association between social relationships and mortality. Efforts to explain away the association of social relationships and supports with health by controls for personality variables have similarly failed.[56,57] Social relationships have a predictive, arguably causal, association with health in their own right.

The extent and quality of social relationships experienced by individuals is also a function of broader social forces. Whether people are employed, married, attend church, belong to organizations, or have frequent contact with friends and relatives, and the nature and quality of those relationships, are all determined in part by their positions in a larger social structure that is stratified by age, race, sex, and socioeconomic status and is organized in terms of residential communities, work organizations, and larger political and economic structures. Older people, blacks, and the poor are generally less socially integrated,[58] and differences in social relationships by sex and place of residence have been discussed in relation to Figs. 19. and 19.2. Changing patterns of fertility, mortality, and migration in society affect opportunities for work, marriage, living, and working in different settings, and having relationships with friends and relatives, and can even affect the nature and quality of these relations.[59] These demographic patterns are themselves subject to influence by both planned and unplanned economic and political change, which can also affect individuals' social relationships more directly—witness the massive increase in divorce during the last few decades in response to the women's movement, growth in women's labor force participation, and changing divorce law.[60,61]

In contrast with the 1950s, adults in the United States in the 1970s were less likely to be married, more likely to be living alone, less likely to belong to voluntary organizations, and less likely to visit informally with others.[62] Changes in marital and childbearing patterns and in the age structure of our society will produce in the 21st century a steady increase of the number of older people who lack spouses or children—the people to whom older people most often turn for relatedness and support.[59] Thus, just as we discover the importance of social relationships for health, and see an increasing need for them, their prevalence and availability may be declining. Changes in other risk factors (for example, the decline of smoking) and improvements in medical technology are still producing overall improvements on health and longevity, but the improvements might be even greater if the quantity and quality of social relationships were also improving.[63]

Notes and References

1. C. Darwin, *Expression of the Emotions in Man and Animals* (Univ. of Chicago Press, Chicago, 1965 [1872]).

2. E. Durkheim, *Suicide* (Free Press, New York, 1951 [1897]).

3. A. S. Kraus and A. N. Lilienfeld, *J Chronic Dis.* 10, 207 (1959).

4. H. Carter and P. C. Click, *Marriage and Divorce: A Social and Economic Study* (Harvard Univ. Press, Cambridge, MA, 1970).

5. E. M. Kitigawa and P. M. Hauser, *Differential Mortality in the United States: A Study in Socio-Economic Epidemiology* (Harvard Univ. Press, Cambridge, MA, 1973).

6. T. H. Holmes, in *Personality, Stress and Tuberculosis,* P. J. Sparer, Ed. (International Univ. Press, New York, 1956).

7. W. A. Tillman and G. E. Hobbs, *Am. Psychiatr.* 106, 321 (1949).

8. R. E. L. Paris, *Am. Social.* 39, 155 (1934).

9. M. L. Kohn and J. A. Clausen, *Am. Social Rev.* 20, 268 (1955).

10. U.S. Surgeon General's Advisory Committee on Smoking and Health, *Smoking and Health* (U.S. Public Health Service, Washington, DC, 1964).

11. G. Caplan, *Support Systems and Community Mental Health* (Behavioral Publications, New York, 1974).

12. President's Commission on Mental Health, *Report to the President* (Government Printing Office, Washington, DC, 1978), vols. 1 to 5.

13. J. Cassel, *Am. Epidemiol.* 104, 107 (1976).

14. S. Cobb, *Psychosomatic Med.* 38, 300 (1976).

15. J. Cassel, in *Social Stress, S.* Levine and N. A. Scotch, Eds. (Aldine, Chicago, 1970), pp. 189-209.

16. J. S. House, *Work Stress and Social Support* (Addison-Wesley, Reading, MA, 1981).

17. K. Heller, in *Maximizing Treatment Gains: Transfer Enhancement in Psychotherapy,* A. P. Goldstein and F. H. Kanter, Eds. (Academic Press, New York, 1979), pp. 353-382.

18. P. A. Thoits, *J. Health Soc. Behav.* 23, 145 (1982).

19. D. Reed et al., *Am. Epidemiol.* 117, 384 (1983).

20. L. F. Berkman and S. L. Syme, *ibid.* 109, 186 (1979).

21. J. S. House, C. Robbins, H. M. Metzner, *ibid.* 116, 123 (1982).

22. V. J. Schoenbach et al, *ibid.* 123, 577 (1986).

23. G. Tibblin et al., in *Social Support: Health and Disease,* S. O. Isacsson and L. Janzon, Eds. (Almqvist & Wiksell, Stockholm, 1986), pp. 11-19.

24. L. Welin et al., *Lancet* i, 915 (1985).

25. K. Orth-Gomer and J. Johnson, *J. Chron. Dis.* 40, 949 (1987).

26. G. A. Kaplan et al., *Am. J. Epidemiol.,* in press.

27. M. Stroebe and W. Stroebe, *Psychol. Bull.* 93, 279 (1983).

28. W. R. Gove, *Soc. Forces* 51, 34 (1972).

29. K. J. Helsing and M. Szklo, *Am. Epidemiol.* 114, 41 (1981).

30. L. Wheeler, H. Reis, J. Nezlek, *J. Pers. Soc. Psychol.* 45, 943 (1983).

31. D. Blazer, *Am. Epidemiol.* 115, 684 (1982).

32. D. M. Zuckerman, S. V. Kasl, A. M. Ostfeld, *ibid.* 119, 410 (1984).

33. T. E. Seeman et al., *ibid.* 126, 714 (1987).

34. W. E. Ruberman et al., *N. Engl. J. Med.* 311, 552 (1984).

35. K. Orth-Gomer in *Social Support: Health and Disease,* S. O. Isacsson and L. Janzon, Eds. (Almqvist & Wiksell, Stockholm, 1986), pp. 21-31.

36. L. S. Wrightsman, Jr., *J. Abnorm. Soc. Psychol.* 61, 216 (1960).

37. K. W. Back and M. D. Bogdonoff, *Behav. Sci.* 12, 384 (1967).

38. J. J. Lynch, *The Broken Heart* (Basic Books, New York, 1979).

39. R. M. Nerem, M. J. Levesque, J. F. Cornhill, *Science* 208, 1475 (1980).

40. J. Goldmeier, *Gerontologist* 26, 203 (1986).

41. E. W. Bovard, in *Perspectives on Behavioral Medicine,* R. B. Williams (Academic Press, New York, 1985), vol. 2.

42. J. Bowlby, in *Loneliness: The Experience of Emotional and Social Isolation,* R. S. Weiss, Ed. (MIT Press, Cambridge, MA, 1973).

43. S. P. Mendoza, in *Social Cohesion: Essays Toward a Sociophysiological Perspective,* P. R. Barchas and S. P. Mendoza, Eds. (Greenwood Press, Westport, CT, 1984).

44. S. Cohen, *Health Psychol. 7,* 269 (1988).

45. L. F. Berkman, in *Social Support and Health,* S. Cohen and S. L. Syme, Eds. (Academic Press, New York, 1985), pp. 241-262.

46. W. E. Broadhead et al., *Am. Epidemiol.* 117, 521 (1983).

47. A. M. Lilienfeld and D. E. Lilienfeld, *Foundations of Epidemiology* (Oxford Univ. Press, New York, 1980).

48. National Heart, Lung and Blood Institute, *Circulation* 63, 1199 (1982).

49. S. Cohen and S. L. Syme, *Social Support and Health* (Academic Press, New York, 1985).

50. A. Antonovsky, *Health, Stress and Coping* (Jossey-Bass, San Francisco, 1979).

51. D. Umberson, *J. Health Soc. Behav.* 28, 306 (1987).

52. K. Rook, J. Pars. *Soc. Psychol.* 46, 1097 (1984).

53. R. S. Lazarus and S. Folkman, *Stress, Appraisal, and Coping* (Springer, New York, 1984).

54. R. B. Zajonc, *Science* 149, 269 (1965).

55. J. S. House, D. Umberson, K. Landis, *Annu. Rev. Sochi.,* in press.

56. S. Cohen, D. R. Sherrod, M. S. Clark, J. *Pers. Soc. Psychol.* 50, 963 (1986).

57. R. Schultz and S. Decker, *ibid.* 48, 1162 (1985).

58. J. S. House, *Socio. Forum* 2, 135 (1987).

59. S. C. Watkins, J. A. Menken, J. Bongaarts, *Am. Sociol. Rev.* 52, 346 (1987).

60. A. Cherlin, *Marriage, Divorce, Remarriage* (Harvard Univ. Press, Cambridge, MA, 1981).

61. L. J. Weitzman, *The Divorce Revolution* (Free Press, New York, 1985).

62. J. Veroff, E. Douvan, R. A. Kulka, *The Inner American: A Self-Portrait from 1957 to 1976* (Basic Books, New York, 1981).

63. Supported by a John Simon Guggenheim Memorial Foundation Fellowship and NIA grant 1-PO1-AG05561 (to J.S.H.), NIMH training grant 5-T32-MH16806-06 traineeship (to K.R.L.), NIMH training grant 5-T32-MH16806-05 and NIA 1-F32-AG05440-01 postdoctoral fellowships (to D.U.). We are indebted to D. Buss, P. Converse, G. Duncan, R. Kahn, R. Kessler, H. Schuman, L. Syme, and R. Zajonc for comments on previous drafts, to many other colleagues who have contributed to this field, and to M. Klatt for preparing the manuscript.

C. Personal Responsibility and the Empowered Patient

20

THE EFFECTS OF CHOICE AND ENHANCED PERSONAL RESPONSIBILITY FOR THE AGED

A Field Experiment in an Institutional Setting

ELLEN J. LANGER AND JUDITH RODIN

The transition from adulthood to old age is often perceived as a process of loss, physiologically and psychologically (Birren, 1958; Gould, 1972). However, it is as yet unclear just how much of this change is biologically determined and how much is a function of the environment. The ability to sustain a sense of personal control in old age may be greatly influenced by societal factors, and this in turn may affect one's physical well-being.

Typically the life situation does change in old age. There is some loss of roles, norms, and reference groups, events that negatively influence one's perceived competence and feeling of responsibility (Bengston, 1973). Perception of these changes in addition to actual physical decrements may enhance a sense of aging and lower self-esteem (Lehr & Puschner, 1963). In response to internal developmental changes, the aging individual may come to see himself in a position of lessened mastery relative to the rest of the world, as a passive object manipulated by the environment (Neugarten & Gutman, 1958). Questioning whether these factors can be counteracted, some studies have suggested that more successful aging—measured by decreased mortality, morbidity, and psychological

EDITORS' NOTE: From *Journal of Personality and Social Psychology, 34*, pp. 191-198.

disability—occurs when an individual feels a sense of usefulness and purpose (Bengston, 1973; Butler, 1967; Leaf, 1973; Lieberman, 1965).

The notion of competence is indeed central to much of human behavior. Adler (1930) has described the need to control one's personal environment as "an intrinsic necessity of life itself" (p. 398). deCharms (1968) has stated that "man's primary motivation propensity is to be effective in producing changes in his environment. Man strives to be a causal agent, to be the primary locus of, causation for, or the origin of, his behavior; he strives for personal causation" (p. 269).

Several laboratory studies have demonstrated that reduced control over aversive outcomes increases physiological distress and anxiety (Geer, Davison, & Gatchel, 1970; Pervin, 1963) and even a nonveridical perception of control over an impending event reduces the aversiveness of that event (Bowers, 1968; Glass & Singer, 1972; Kanfer & Seidner, 1973). Langer, Janis, and Wolfer (1975) found that by inducing the perception of control over stress in hospital patients by means of a communication that emphasized potential cognitive control, subjects requested fewer pain relievers and sedatives and were seen by nurses as evidencing less anxiety.

Choice is also a crucial variable in enhancing an induced sense of control. Stotland and Blumenthal (1964) studied the effects of choice on anxiety reduction. They told subjects that they were going to take a number of important ability tests. Half of the subjects were allowed to choose the order in which they wanted to take the tests, and half were told that the order was fixed. All subjects were informed that the order of the tests would have no bearing on their scores. They found that subjects not given the choice were more anxious, as measured by palmar sweating. In another study of the effects of choice, Corah and Boffa (1970) told their subjects that there were two conditions in the experiment, each of which would be signaled by a different light. In one condition they were given the choice of whether or not to press a button to escape from an aversive noise, and in the other one they were not given the option of escaping. They found that the choice instructions decreased the aversiveness of the threatening stimulus, apparently by increasing perceived control. Although using a very different paradigm, Langer (1975) also demonstrated the importance of choice. In that study it was found that the exercise of choice in a chance situation, where choice was objectively inconsequential, nevertheless had psychological consequences manifested in increased confidence and risk taking.

Lefcourt (1973) best summed up the essence of this research in a brief review article dealing with the perception of control in man and animals when he concluded that "the sense of control, the illusion that one can exercise personal choice, has a definite and a positive role in sustaining life" (p. 424). It is not surprising, then, that these important psychological factors should be linked to health and survival. In a series of retrospective studies, Schmale and his associates (Adamson & Schmale, 1965; Schmale 1953; Schmale & Iker, 1966) found that ulcerative colitis, leukemia, cervical cancer, and heart disease were linked with a feeling of helplessness and loss of hope experienced by the patient prior to the onset of the disease. Seligman and his coworkers have systematically investigated the learning of helplessness and related it to the clinical syndrome of depression (see Seligman, 1975). Even death is apparently related to control-relevant variables. McMahon and Rhudick (1964) found a relationship between depression or hopelessness and death. The most graphic description of this association comes from Bettelheim (1943), who in his analysis of the "Muselmanner," the walking corpses in the concentration camps, described them as:

> Prisoners who came to believe the repeated statements of the guards—that there was no hope for them, that they would never leave the camp except as a corpse—who came to feel that their environment was one over which they could exercise no influence whatsoever. . . . Once his own life and the environment were viewed as totally beyond his ability to influence them, the only logical conclusion was to pay no attention to them whatsoever. Only then, all conscious awareness of stimuli coming from the outside was blocked out, and with it all response to anything but inner stimuli.

Death swiftly followed and, according to Bettelheim,

> [survival] depended on one's ability to arrange to preserve some areas of independent action, to keep control of some important aspects of one's life despite an environment that seemed overwhelming and total.

Bettelheim's description reminds us of Richter's (1957) rats, who also "gave up hope" of controlling their environment and subsequently died.

The implications of these studies for research in the area of aging are clear. Objective helplessness as well as feelings of helplessness and hopelessness—both enhanced by the environment and by intrinsic changes that occur with increasing old age—may contribute to psychological withdrawal, physical disease, and death. In contrast, objective control and feelings of mastery may very well contribute to physical health and personal efficacy.

In a study conceived to explore the effects of dissonance, Ferrare (1962; cited in Seligman, 1975; Zimbardo & Ruch, 1975) presented data concerning the effects of the ability of geriatric patients to control their place of residence. Of 17 subjects who answered that they did not have any other alternative but to move to a specific old age home, 8 died after 4 weeks of residence and 16 after 10 weeks of residence. By comparison, among the residents who died during the initial period, only one person had answered that she had the freedom to choose other alternatives. All of these deaths were classified as unexpected because "not even insignificant disturbances had actually given warning of the impending disaster."

As Zimbardo (Zimbardo & Ruch, 1975) suggested, the implications of Ferrare's data are striking and merit further study of old age home settings. There is already evidence that perceived personal control in one's residential environment is important for younger and noninstitutional populations. Rodin (in press), using children as subjects, demonstrated that diminished feelings of control produced by chronic crowding at home led to fewer attempts to control self-reinforcement in the laboratory and to greater likelihood of giving up in the face of failure.

The present study attempted to assess directly the effects of enhanced personal responsibility and choice in a group of nursing home patients. In addition to examining previous results from the control-helplessness literature in a field setting, the present study extended the domain of this conception by considering new response variables. Specifically, if increased control has generalized beneficial effects, then physical and mental alertness, activity, general level of satisfaction, and sociability should all be affected. Also, the manipulation of the independent variables, assigning greater responsibility and decision freedom for relevant behavior, allowed subjects real choices that were not directed toward a single behavior or stimulus condition. This manipulation tested the ability of the subjects to generalize from specific choices enumerated for them to other aspects of their lives, and thus tested the generalizability of feelings of control over certain elements of the situation to more broadly based behavior and attitudes.

Method

Subjects

The study was conducted in a nursing home, which was rated by the state of Connecticut as being among the finest care units and offering quality medical, recreational, and residential facilities. The home was large and modern in design, appearing cheerful and comfortable as well as clean and efficient. Of the four floors in the home, two were selected for study because of similarity in the residents' physical and psychological health and prior socioeconomic status, as determined from evaluations made by the home's director, head nurses, and social worker. Residents were assigned to a particular floor and room simply on the basis of availability, and on the average, residents on the two floors had been at the home about the same length of time. Rather than randomly assigning subjects to experimental treatment, a different floor was randomly selected for each treatment. Since there was not a great deal of communication between floors, this procedure was followed in order to decrease the likelihood that the treatment effects would be contaminated. There were 8 males and 39 females in the responsibility-induced condition (all fourth-floor residents) and 9 males and 35 females in the comparison group (all second-floor residents). Residents who were either completely bedridden or judged by the nursing home staff to be completely noncommunicative (11 on the experimental floor and 9 on the comparison floor) were omitted from the sample. Also omitted was one woman on each floor, one 40 years old and the other 26 years old, due to their age. Thus, 91 ambulatory adults, ranging in age from 65 to 90, served as subjects.

Procedure

To introduce the experimental treatment, the nursing home administrator, an outgoing and friendly 33-year-old male who interacts with the residents daily, called a meeting in the lounge of each floor. He delivered one of the following two communications at that time:

> *[Responsibility-induced group]* I brought you together today to give you some information about Arden House. I was surprised to learn that many of you don't know about the things that are available to you and more important, that many of you don't realize the influence you have over your own lives here. Take a minute to think of the decisions you can and should be making. For example, you have the responsibility of caring for yourselves, of deciding whether or not you want to make this a home you can be proud of and happy in. You should be deciding how you want your rooms to be arranged—whether you want it to be as it is or whether you want the staff to help you rearrange the furniture. You should be deciding how you want to spend your time, for example, whether you want to be visiting your friends who live on this floor or on other floors, whether you want to visit in your room or your friends' room, in the lounge, the dining room, etc., or whether you want to be watching television, listening to the radio, writing, reading, or planning social events. In other words, it's your life and you can make of it whatever you want.
>
> This brings me to another point. If you are unsatisfied with anything here, you have the influence to change it. It's your responsibility to make your complaints known, to tell us what you would like to change, to tell us what you would like. These are just a few of the things you could and should be deciding and thinking about now and from time to time everyday. You made these decisions before you came here and you can and should be making them now.
>
> We're thinking of instituting some way for airing complaints, suggestions, etc. Let [nurse's name] know if you think this is a good idea and how you think we should go about doing it. In any case let her know what your complaints or suggestions are.
>
> Also, I wanted to take this opportunity to give you each a present from the Arden House. [A box of small plants was passed around, and patients were given two decisions to make: first, whether or not they wanted a plant at all, and second, to choose which one they wanted. All residents did select a plant.] The plants are yours to keep and take care of as you'd like.
>
> One last thing, I wanted to tell you that we're showing a movie two nights next week, Thursday and Friday. You should decide which night you'd like to go, if you choose to see it at all.

> [*Comparison group*] I brought you together today to give you some information about the Arden House. I was surprised to learn that many of you don't know about the things that are available to you; that many of you don't realize all you're allowed to do here. Take a minute to think of all the options that we've provided for you in order for your life to be fuller and more interesting. For example, you're permitted to visit people on the other floors and to use the lounge on this floor for visiting as well as the dining room or your own rooms. We want your rooms to be as nice as they can be, and we've tried to make them that way for you. We want you to be happy here. We feel that it's our responsibility to make this a home you can be proud of and happy in, and we want to do all we can to help you.
>
> This brings me to another point. If you have any complaints or suggestions about anything, let [nurse's name] know what they are. Let us know how we can best help you. You should feel that you have free access to anyone on the staff, and we will do the best we can to provide individualized attention and time for you.
>
> Also, I wanted to take this opportunity to give you each a present from the Arden House. [The nurse walked around with a box of plants and each patient was handed one.] The plants are yours to keep. The nurses will water and care for them for you.
>
> One last thing, I wanted to tell you that we're showing a movie next week on Thursday and Friday. We'll let you know later which day you're scheduled to see it.

The major difference between the two communications was that on one floor, the emphasis was on the residents' responsibility for themselves, whereas on the other floor, the communication stressed the staff's responsibility for them. In addition, several other differences bolstered this treatment: Residents in the responsibility-induced group were asked to give their opinion of the means by which complaints were handled rather than just being told that any complaints would be handled by staff members; they were given the opportunity to select their own plant and to care for it themselves, rather than being given a plant to be taken care of by someone else; and they were given their choice of a movie night, rather than being assigned a particular night, as was typically the case in the old age home. However, there was no difference in the amount of attention paid to the two groups.

Three days after these communications had been delivered, the director visited all of the residents in their rooms or in the corridor and reiterated part of the previous message. To those in the responsibility-induced group he said, "Remember what I said last Thursday. We want you to be happy. Treat this like your own home and make all the decisions you used to make. How's your plant coming along?" To the residents of the comparison floor, he said the same thing omitting the statement about decision making.

Dependent Variables

Questionnaires. Two types of questionnaires were designed to assess the effects of induced responsibility. Each was administered 1 week prior to and 3 weeks after the communication. The first was administered directly to the residents by a female research assistant who was unaware of the experimental hypotheses or of the specific experimental treatment. The questions dealt with how much control they felt over general events in their lives and how happy and active they felt. Questions were responded to along 8-point scales ranging from 0 (none) to 8 (total). After completing each interview, the research assistant rated the resident on an 8-point scale for alertness.

The second questionnaire was responded to by the nurses, who staffed the experimental and comparison floors and who were unaware of the experimental treatments. Nurses on two different shifts completed the questionnaires in order to obtain two ratings for each subject. There were nine 10-point scales that asked for ratings of how happy, alert, dependent, sociable, and active the residents were as well as questions about their eating and sleeping habits. There were also questions evaluating the proportion of weekly time the patient spent engaged in a variety of activities. These included reading, watching television, visiting other patients, visiting outside guests, watching the staff, talking to the staff, sitting alone doing nothing, and others.

Behavioral Measures. Since perceived personal control is enhanced by a sense of choice over relevant behaviors, the option to choose which night the experimental group wished to see the movie was expected to have measurable effects on active participation. Attendance records were kept by the occupational therapist, who was unaware that an experiment was being conducted.

Another measure of involvement was obtained by holding a competition in which all participants had to guess the number of jelly beans in a large jar. Each patient wishing to enter the contest simply wrote his or her name and estimate on a piece of paper and deposited it in a box that was next to the jar.[1]

Finally, an unobtrusive measure of activity was taken. The tenth night after the experiment, the right wheels of the wheelchairs belonging to a randomly selected subsample of each patient group were covered with 2 inches (.05 m) of white adhesive tape. The following night, the tape was removed from the chairs and placed on index cards for later evaluation of amount of activity, as indicated by the amount of discoloration.

Results

Questionnaires. Before examining whether or not the experimental treatment was effective, the pretest ratings made by the subjects, the nurses, and the interviewer were compared for both groups. None of the differences approached significance, which indicates comparability between groups prior to the start of the investigation.

In response to direct questions about how happy they currently were, residents in the responsibility-induced group reported significantly greater increases in happiness after the experimental treatment than did the comparison group, $t(43) = 1.96$, $p < .05$.[2] Although the comparison group heard a communication that had specifically stressed the home's commitment to making them happy, only 23% of them reported feeling happier by the time of the second interview, whereas 48% of the experimental group did so.

The responsibility-induced group reported themselves to be significantly more active on the second interview than the comparison group, $t(43) = 2.67$, $p < .01$. The interviewer's ratings of alertness also showed significantly greater increase for the experimental group, $t(43) = 2.40$, $p < .025$. However, the questions that were relevant to perceived control showed no significant changes for the experimental group. Since over 20% of the patients indicated that they were unable to understand what we meant by control, these questions were obviously not adequate to discriminate between groups.

The second questionnaire measured nurses' ratings of each patient. The correlation between the two nurses' ratings of the same patient was .68 and .61 (p's $< .005$) on the comparison and responsibility-induced floors, respectively.[3] For each patient, a score was calculated by averaging the two nurses' ratings for each question, summing across questions, and subtracting the total pretreatment score from the total posttreatment score.[4] This yielded a positive average total change score of 3.97 for the responsibility-induced group as compared with an average negative total change of -2.37 for the comparison group. The difference between these means is highly significant, $t(50) = 5.18$, $p < .005$. If one looks at the percentage of people who were judged improved rather than at the amount of judged improvement, the same pattern emerges: 93% of the experimental group (all but one subject) were considered improved, whereas only 21% (six subjects) of the comparison group showed this positive change ($\chi^2 = 19.23$, $p < .005$).

The nurses' evaluation of the proportion of time subjects spent engaged in various interactive and noninteractive activities was analyzed by comparing the average change scores (post-precommunication) for all of the nurses for both groups of subjects on each activity. Several significant differences were found. The experimental group showed increases in the proportion of time spent visiting with other patients (for the experimental group, $M = 12.86$ vs. -6.61 for the comparison group), $t(50) = 3.83$, $p < .005$; visiting people from outside of the nursing home (for the experimental group, $M = 4.28$ vs. -7.61 for the comparison group), $t(50) = 2.30$, $p < .05$; and talking to the staff (for the experimental group, $M = 8.21$ vs. 1.61 for the comparison group), $t(50) = 2.98$, $p < .05$.[5] In addition, they spent less time passively watching the staff (for the experimental group, $M = -4.28$ vs. 9.68 for the comparison group), $t(50) = 2.60$, $p < .05$. Thus, it appears that the treatment increased active, interpersonal activity but not passive activity such as watching television or reading.

Behavioral Measures. As in the case of the questionnaires, the behavioral measures showed a pattern of differences between groups that was generally consistent with the predicted effects of increased responsibility. The movie attendance was significantly higher in the responsibility-induced group than in the control group after the experimental treatment ($z = 1.71$, $p < .05$, one-tailed), although a similar attendance check taken one month before the communications revealed no group differences.[6]

In the jelly-bean-guessing contest, 10 subjects (21%) in the responsibility-induced group and only 1 subject (2%) from the comparison group participated ($\chi^2 = 7.72$, $p < .01$). Finally, very little dirt was found on the tape taken from any of the patients' wheelchairs, and there was no significant difference between the two groups.

Discussion

It appears that inducing a greater sense of personal responsibility in people who may have virtually relinquished decision making, either by choice or necessity, produces improvement. In the present investigation, patients in the comparison group were given a communication stressing the staff's desire to make them happy and were otherwise treated in the sympathetic manner characteristic of this high-quality nursing home. Despite the care provided for these people, 71% were rated as having become more debilitated over a period of time as short as 3 weeks. In contrast with this group, 93% of the people who were encouraged to make decisions for themselves, given decisions to make, and given responsibility for something outside of themselves, actually showed overall improvement. Based on their own judgments and by the judgments of the nurses, with whom they interacted on a daily basis, they became more active and felt happier. Perhaps more important was the judged improvement in their mental alertness and increased behavioral involvement in many different kinds of activities.

The behavioral measures showed greater active participation and involvement for the experimental group. Whether this directly resulted from an increase in perceived choice and decision-making responsibility or from the increase in general activity and happiness occurring after the treatment cannot be assessed from the present results. It should also be clearly noted that although there were significant differences in active involvement, the overall level of participation in the activities that comprised the behavioral measures was low. Perhaps a much more powerful treatment would be one that is individually administered and repeated on several occasions. That so weak a manipulation had any effect suggests how important increased control is for these people, for whom decision making is virtually nonexistent.

The practical implications of this experimental demonstration are straightforward. Mechanisms can and should be established for changing situational factors that reduce real or perceived responsibility in the elderly. Furthermore, this study adds to the body of literature (Bengston, 1973; Butler, 1967; Leaf, 1973; Lieberman, 1965) suggesting that senility and diminished alertness are not an almost inevitable result of aging. In fact, it suggests that some of the negative consequences of aging may be retarded, reversed, or possibly prevented by returning to the aged the right to make decisions and a feeling of competence.

Notes

1. We also intended to measure the number of complaints that patients voiced. Since one often does not complain after becoming psychologically helpless, complaints in this context were expected to be a positive indication of perceived personal control. This measure was discarded, however, since the nurses failed to keep a systematic written record.

2. All of the statistics for the self-report data and the interviewers' ratings are based on 43 subjects (25 in the responsibility-induced group and 20 in the comparison group), since these were the only subjects available at the time of the interview.

3. There was also significant agreement between the interviewer's and nurses' ratings of alertness ($r = .65$).

4. Since one nurse on the day shift and one nurse on the night shift gave the ratings, responses to the questions regarding sleeping and eating habits were not included in the total score. Also, in order to reduce rater bias, patients for whom there were ratings by a nurse on only one shift were excluded from this calculation. This left 24 residents from the experimental group and 28 from the comparison group.

5. This statistic is based only on the responses of nurse on duty in the evening.

6. Frequencies were transformed into arcsines and analyzed using the method that is essentially the same as that described by Langer and Abelson (1972).

References

Adamson, J., & Schmale, A. Object loss, giving up, and the onset of psychiatric disease. *Psychosomatic Medicine*, 1965, 27, 557-576.

Adler, A. Individual psychology. In C. Murchinson (Ed.), *Psychologies of 1930*. Worcester, Mass.: Clark University Press, 1930.

Bengston, V. L. Self determination: A social and psychological perspective on helping the aged. *Geriatrics*, 1973.

Bettelheim, B. Individual and mass behavior in extreme situations. *Journal of Abnormal and Social Psychology*, 1943, 38, 417-452.

Birren, J. Aging and psychological adjustment. *Review of Educational Research,* 1958, 8, 475-490.

Bowers, K. Pain, anxiety, and perceived control. *Journal of Consulting and Clinical Psychology*, 1968, 32, 596-602.

Butler, R. Aspects of survival and adaptation in human aging. *American Journal of Psychiatry*, 1967, 123, 1233-1243.

Corah, N., & Boffa, J. Perceived control, self-observation, and response to aversive stimulation. *Journal of Personality and Social Psychology*, 1970, 16, 1-4.

deCharms, R. *Personal causation*. New York: Academic Press, 1968.

Geer, J., Davison, G., & Gatchel, R. Reduction of stress in humans through nonveridical perceived control of aversive stimulation. *Journal of Personality and Social Psychology,* 1970, 16, 731-738.

Glass, D., & Singer, J. *Urban stress.* New York: Academic Press, 1972.

Gould, R. The phases of adult life: A study in developmental psychology. *American Journal of Psychiatry,* 1972, 129, 521-531.

Kanfer, R., & Seidner, M. Self-control: Factors enhancing tolerance of noxious stimulation. *Journal of Personality and Social Psychology*, 1973, 25, 381-389.

Langer, E. J. The illusion of control. *Journal of Personality and Social Psychology*, 1975, 2, 311-328.

Langer, E. J., & Abelson, R. P. The semantics of asking a favor: How to succeed in getting help without really dying. *Journal of Personality and Social Psychology*, 1972, 24, 26-32.

Langer, E. J., Janis, I. L., & Wolfer, J. A. Reduction of psychological stress in surgical patients. *Journal of Experimental Social Psychology*, 1975, 11, 155-165.

Leaf, A. Threescore and forty. *Hospital Practice,* 1973, 34, 70-71.

Lefcourt, H. The function of the illusion of control and freedom. *American Psychologist*, 1973, 28, 417-425.

Lehr, K., & Puschner, I. *Studies in the awareness of aging.* Paper presented at the 6th International Congress on Gerontology, Copenhagen, 1963.

Lieberman, M. Psychological correlates of impending death: Some preliminary observations. *Journal of Gerontology*, 1965, 20, 181-190.

McMahon, A., & Rhudick, P. Reminiscing, adaptational significance in the aged. *Archives of General Psychiatry*, 1964, 10, 292-298.

Neugarten, B., & Gutman, D. Age-sex roles and personality in middle age: A thematic apperception study. *Psychological Monographs*, 1958 72(17, Whole No. 470).

Pervin, L. The need to predict and control under conditions of threat. *Journal of Personality*, 1963, 31, 570-585.

Richter, C. On the phenomenon of sudden death in animals and man. *Psychosomatic Medicine*, 1957, 19, 191-198.

Rodin, J. Crowding, perceived choice, and response to controllable and uncontrollable outcomes. *Journal of Experimental Social Psychology*, in press.

Schmale, A. Relationships of separation and depression to disease. I.: A report on a hospitalized medical population. *Psychosomatic Medicine*, 1953, 20, 259-277.

Schmale, A., & Iker, H. The psychological setting of uterine cervical cancer. *Annals of the New York Academy of Sciences*, 1966, 125, 807-813.

Seligman, M. E. P. *Helplessness*. San Francisco: Freeman, 1975.

Stotland, E., & Blumenthal, A. The reduction of anxiety as a result of the expectation of making a choice. *Canadian Review of Psychology*, 1964, 18, 139-45.

Zimbardo, P. G., & Ruch, F. L. *Psychology and life* (9th ed.). Glenview, Ill.: Scott, Foresman, 1975.

21

HIV/AIDS Patient Involvement in Antiretroviral Treatment Decisions

W.D. Marelich, K.J. Roberts, D.A. Murphy, and T. Callari

Introduction

Medical decisions, especially those involving antiretroviral treatment regimens, may be thought of as the end result of a series of interactions between patients and their health care providers. Health care providers have become increasingly trained to include patient concerns and opinions when making medical decisions (Coulehan & Block, 1997), while patients have been actively encouraged through media campaigns not only to seek treatment for various illnesses but also to request specific drug treatments (Gerth & Stolberg, 2000; Heussner & Salmon, 1988). Although some research has addressed patient involvement in treatment decisions across various disease types (Degner & Sloan, 1992; Nease & Brooks, 1995; Strull et al., 1984), to date no studies have exclusively examined HIV-positive patients' decision-making preferences.

Understanding how involved patients are (or want to be) in their medication-treatment decisions and how free they are to discuss treatment options with their providers is especially important for those infected with HIV. Antiretroviral medications and their strict regimens can have both personal- and health-related consequences (i.e., medication side effects and lifestyle inconveniences) that should be communicated by patients (Murphy et al., 2000). These issues, if unreported by patients, may act as barriers to antiretroviral medication adherence. Nonadherence, in turn, can lead to virus mutations that are resistant to current drug treatments (Carpenter et al., 1997). Further, unclear or "murky" patient-provider communications may result in less-than-optimal treatment for those with HIV/AIDS (Marelich et al., 2000).

How involved do patients want to be in their treatment decisions? Passive models of patient involvement suggest that when sick, individuals will seek exemption from normal social role responsibilities and want others to take care of them (Parsons, 1964). Although many of the tenets of Parson's "sick role" model have been formally criticized (Cockerham, 1982; West, 1984), some patients, including long-term or terminal care patients, prefer that their providers make all their treatment decisions (Degner & Sloan, 1992; Strull et al., 1984). This preference may be associated with illness severity: The more severely ill individuals are, the less involved they tend to want to be in their treatment decisions (Nease & Brooks, 1995). In addition, other research suggests that passivity may be an initial state for patients, followed by more active involvement (Strull et al., 1984). For example, in summarizing open-ended items from their study, Strull and colleagues noted, "that although [patients] rely on their clinicians to make initial decisions about treatment, they wish to play an active role later, after they have had experience with the medications" (p. 2993).

Recent observations have noted a growing trend toward patient empowerment in medical care and treatment decisions in the USA (Roberts, 1999). Patients are becoming better informed and more aware of treatment options, in some cases "taking charge" of their medical care (Reiser, 1993; Roberts, 1999). Information regarding medical care and treatments has become more accessible through media-related outlets such as the World Wide Web (Akatsu & Kuffner, 1998), thus allowing patients to readily access medical information. This trend toward empowerment has been generally positive for patients, with increased patient participation in health care decisions yielding positive health-related outcomes (Kaplan et al., 1989; Starfield et al., 1981).

Although two related studies have recently addressed HIV/AIDS health care providers' decision making and antiretroviral therapies (Erger et al., 2000; Marelich et al., 2000), no studies have specifically addressed HIV/AIDS patient involvement in these decisions. The purpose of this study was to investigate HIV/AIDS patients' involvement with their providers concerning antiretroviral treatment therapies, including how much input patients have regarding their drug-treatment decisions. Focus groups were conducted with HIV-infected patients currently receiving antiretroviral medications. Patients were asked a series of questions regarding contribution to their antiretroviral regimen selections with their health care providers. A qualitative analysis of transcripts was used to derive emergent themes (Strauss & Corbin, 1990).

Method

Participants

Focus group participants were recruited through an advertisement in an HIV/AIDS publication and directly from an HIV/AIDS clinic. Criteria for participation included being 18 years of age or older, having an HIV diagnosis, and currently being prescribed antiretroviral therapy. Overall, 54 individuals were invited to participate in the focus group interviews. Of these, nine refused to participate (due to time constraints), and six did not show for their scheduled group, resulting in a final sample size of 39.

Race/ethnicity composition of focus group participants included 44% African-American, 39% White, 6% Latino and 6% other or mixed race. Age of participants ranged from 33 to 54 years (M = 40.9, SD = 5.5), with males comprising 69% of the sample. Length of time receiving antiretroviral therapy ranged from two months to 12 years (M = 4.3, SD = 3.3). The most frequently used antiretroviral medications included D4T (56% of the sample), 3TC (49%), Nelfinavir (33%), and Ritonavir (33%). The most common three-drug combination therapies included Nelfinavir, DDI, D4T (n = 4), D4T, 3TC, Nelfinavir (n = 4), and Ritonavir, D4T, Saquinavir (n = 4).

Procedures

With approval of the Institutional Review Board at the University, individuals interested in participating in the study were given an enrollment interview where the study was explained further and informed consent conducted. As soon as a sufficient number of participants were identified, a focus group was scheduled (a total of four focus groups were conducted). All focus groups were audiotaped and transcribed, with participants receiving $30 for participation and refreshments at the group session. Two facilitators led the group interviews (a male and a female) and followed a structured script with response probes.

Participants were asked a series of closed- and open-ended questions regarding their current antiretroviral regimen, difficulties in taking their medication, and barriers to adherence (see Murphy et al., 2000, for analysis of these issues). In addition to these items, participants were asked a series of open-ended items addressing their involvement in deciding their current antiretroviral regimen. These items were structured around the following questions: (a) How did participants prefer to make their health care decisions? (b) did participants take an active role in decision making or prefer having medical professionals make their decisions for them? and (c) did participants' health care providers involve them in the decision about their current therapy?

Analysis

Qualitative analyses were conducted using Ethnograph, a software program for computer-based text search and retrieval. A line-by-line review of the transcripts was performed deriving first-level codes (descriptors of important components of the interviews). These were then printed and reviewed, and subcodes were established to divide the first-level codes into small categories. The subsequent results of the qualitative analyses reflect emergent categories.

Results

Focus group participants were asked, "When you were prescribed your current HIV therapy, how much did your doctor or health care provider involve you in that decision? That is, did you feel like you were part of the decision-making process?" Four primary themes emerged from the data: (1) *joint decision making* (i.e., patients and providers working together); (2) *patients taking control* and making up their own minds; (3) *initial passivity, then involvement* (i.e., patients' initial lack of involvement in treatment decisions followed by increased involvement); and (4) *patients as knowledge gatherers.* The first two themes focus on patients' involvement with their health care providers regarding antiretroviral treatment decisions. The third theme addresses temporal changes in patients' levels of involvement over the course of their disease treatment. The final theme focuses on where HIV/AIDS patients obtain their treatment-related information.

Joint Decision Making: "We work as a team"

Most focus group participants reported at least some level of participation with their health care providers in antiretroviral treatment decisions, with only one participant (who was newly diagnosed at the time of the study) noting little involvement (i.e., letting her provider make all the decisions). Sometimes, the patient and the provider both contributed to the final treatment decision. As one participant noted, "There's a marriage there, ya know? We're constantly learning from each other. I learn something, I tell him. He learns something, he tells me."

Some participants described their relationship with their providers as teamwork, where they and their providers worked together to discuss and resolve issues. For example, one participant noted, "Every doctor that I have, we work as a team. If we can't work as a team we don't work." Another person commented, "Well, it's a team . . . it's teamwork and my doctor's always there for me in answering the questions. . . . I have no problem discussing issues with my doctor or treatment with my doctor." Finally, one participant mentioned the importance of communication, focusing on the "relationship" formed between the patient and the provider, "The two of us are very in sync. We've created quite a relationship between the two of us. . . . I've been on [protease inhibitors] for five years . . . and whatever idiosyncrasies you can think of I came down with . . . and [we] fine tuned . . . where I'm at today."

Other examples of joint involvement included patients working with their providers to make a drug regimen change, or keeping the current regimen they were on. For example, one participant noted, "I told [my health care provider] I want to get off these . . . drugs. I specified which ones I want to get off of. And over time, we have gotten off of those drugs . . . so it works both ways . . . it's not just the doctor [who is in charge]." Another patient, who had acceptable t-cell and viral load levels, reported the following interaction, "They wanted to add another regimen, and I told them that I appreciate what they're trying to do, and I understand, but let's wait. Let's wait until the first of the year and see . . . take another test and see where we're at. So I always interact with their decision. I don't let the doctor make full decisions for me."

Patients Taking Control

Being Assertive: "I push for something, I get it." In some instances, study participants reported playing a very assertive role in requesting the treatment options they want. For example, a number of study participants reported being aggressive and "pushing" for particular antiretroviral medication regimens. One participant noted, "I essentially probably take the more aggressive role, and I think the doctors [at the clinic] attest to that. I get quite feisty in terms of dictating what I want." Another patient echoed, "I push for something, I get it, and I try it out and if it works for me, it works for me. If it doesn't work, I let the doctor know to do something different." Still, another patient stated, "I basically pushed my doctor to switch from Crixivan to Viracept, because it was easy [as a regimen]." These comments are indicative of patients jostling with their providers for control of treatments rendered.

Listening, Then Deciding: "I choose it myself." Instead of pushing for regimen changes, a few patients noted listening to their providers' recommendations, then making up their own minds. As one participant put it, "I usually just listen to what the doctors will say, but then make up my own mind. . . . I was given choices of what [regimen type] would work best for me. And I chose the schedule I'm on right now. I chose it myself." Another patient added, "I listen to the doctor . . . [but] I feel that I pretty much get to make the decisions as to what I want or don't want to take." This approach, albeit less aggressive than pushing for treatments, retains decision power for the patients, yet allows providers to contribute treatment information.

Provider/Organization Shopping: "What changed my life was changing doctors." There were some striking instances where patients who felt they were not receiving optimal health care changed providers or health care agencies. These situations are examples of the ultimate decision-making power of patients; if patients feel they are not getting what they want from their provider or clinic, they simply switch to an alternative practice. For example, one patient reported, "I just want to say what changed my life was changing doctors because initially, I didn't have a very good relationship with the doctor that I had before." Another study participant, who had a number of problems with providers ignoring his questions, commented:

> I have had doctors who've had problems with me asking so many questions. Well, this is my body, you know? And if I have a doctor like that I have not hesitated at any time to ask for another doctor . . . because they need me just as much as I need them.

Besides changing providers, some respondents changed where they received their health care and treatment. One participant recommended attending HIV clinics over private doctors because one can get to know the provider better, "I hate private doctors so I'm trying to encourage all of my friends who go to these private doctors to leave them and go to an HIV clinic because they [can get to know] the doctors." On the other hand, another participant preferred private doctors over HIV clinics because the participant got to see multiple providers, "I went from being in a clinic where, every time I went there was a different doctor or a different nurse practitioner (they never knew me and I had a bad experience with that), to a private doctor where I'm feeling terrific and my life changed." These examples highlight the varied preferences patients have regarding their health care. Ultimately, what is important is that there be a good match between patients' expectations of care and the actual care provided by their providers and clinics.

Initial Passivity, Then Involvement: "I got on-board with them"

Some of the focus group participants relayed incidents where they were first passive about their treatment options (letting their health care providers make all the decisions), then became more involved over the course of time. These statements appeared to be associated with the initial shock associated with HIV diagnosis, including not knowing what to do once they were infected. For example, one participant who was recently diagnosed at the time of the study illustrated this confusion and initial passivity:

> And I was just recently diagnosed . . . this year, so kind of what you said, I haven't had any information on anything. I totally put my trust in [the provider] over here at the immunology clinic because I was diagnosed right here . . . so I just really put my trust in them and just said forget it.

Another participant had a similar response after being diagnosed, "I had no clue as to what was going on. There was not so much involvement. But as you live with this on a daily basis and you become more aware of what's going on, then I became more involved." Both of these cases suggest initial levels of confusion after diagnosis, with the second case noting greater involvement over time.

Other participants reported similar experiences, letting their health care providers first make all the decisions, then getting more involved. One participant reported, "I don't let the doctor make full decisions for me. I did in the very beginning, but once I started to learn about the medication and what it was doing to me, then I got on-board with them." Another participant reported that she started to learn more about treatments at conferences, which eventually made her more involved, "At first . . . I didn't really say too much. I just kind of went along with whatever the doctor said. But then I started going to conferences . . . and I started getting more . . . involved."

Patients as Knowledge Gatherers

Patients who want to be involved in their antiretroviral treatment decisions with their providers tend to have a strong desire for HIV-related information. Patients can gather HIV/AIDS-related information about drug treatments from a variety of sources, including HIV-positive peers, friends and/or family members, health-related professionals, and the media.

Talking to Others: "I just milk them." A number of participants reported that simply talking to others helped them acquire treatment information. For example, one participant noted seeking out others' experiences with treatment options, "Everybody's experience, listening to what people say, reading, a little of everything." Similarly, another participant said, "[I talk to people] whenever possible, whenever I can hook up with someone who has some opinions . . . you know, I will milk them. I will just corner them and milk them."

Other participants were more specific in discussing from whom they acquire information. Some participants noted that they interact directly with other HIV-infected individuals to learn about drug treatment regimens. One participant noted, "I discuss it with people who are further along with AIDS than me." Another person noted getting drug treatment information from her boyfriend's brother, "I told [my doctor] what to give me because my boyfriend's brother is infected and he has an excellent doctor. So [my boyfriend's brother] writes his bags of stuff down and I take his note into my doctor and he just writes a script." As these comments illustrate, the network of those infected with HIV functions to provide direct information about antiretroviral treatments.

Some participants also obtained knowledge from health care professionals. For example, one participant stated, "[I get] information from all sources I can find, but mostly from health care professionals." Another participant mentioned getting his information from a treatment advocate (a treatment advocate educates HIV-positive patients about the disease, medications and treatment regimens). He stated:

> I went to a treatment advocate . . . someone that's skilled in the different uses of HIV medications, they generally can tell you what some of the side effects are . . . a lot of places have treatment advocates now

> and the treatment advocate will say "Don't [do] what I say, I'm just saying that this is something you may want to ask your doctor about."

Although a minority of participants directly mentioned health care professionals (such as in the examples above), it may be inferred that study participants who were jointly involved with their health care providers in treatment decisions sought treatment information from their providers.

Media Resources: "I try to check-out the Web." Participants also noted getting information about antiretroviral therapy from the media, including newspapers, television, magazines, and the World Wide Web. One participant noted reading a number of HIV-related magazines to get information, "I'd read about Viracept in all of the ads in like POS magazine and other AIDS related magazines." Another person reported reading both HIV-related magazines and getting information from Web sites, "I've tried to get as many of the AIDS publications that I can, I try to check out the Web site." Television and newspapers were also noted as HIV/AIDS resources. For example, one participant reported that after being diagnosed, but before starting treatment, he actively prepared himself with a bounty of information, "Before I started taking medications . . . I found myself . . . [getting information from] television [and the] newest studies . . . involving all these different drugs. I would read voraciously in the newspaper anything that came out in the AIDS conferences that happened once a year." Finally, one individual stated, "They prescribed for me AZT by itself before I got into a study group. . . . I read a lot of papers and the briefs that come out every month about all the medications and everything that's out."

Discussion

HIV/AIDS patients reported various levels of involvement when interacting with their providers regarding antiretroviral treatment decisions. Joint decision making may be a function of the length of time patients have lived with HIV (including experience with antiretroviral treatments), with patients and providers becoming comfortable with each other over time. Although we did not collect information on length of treatment with a single provider, patients on average had been receiving antiretroviral treatments for over four years, with only a minority of participants reporting health care provider/organization changes in the past few years. This suggests our study participants generally had developed good working relationships with their providers or the agencies overseeing their treatment. For some of our study participants, the resulting affable relationship with their providers may be driven by the common goal of patient wellness, with both patients and providers working together to fight HIV. This camaraderie, with the common enemy of HIV, leads to a strong relationship between the individuals, one that instills trust, caring, and respect (Roberts, 1998).

Patients who reported making their own treatment decisions (through pushing providers to prescribe specific drug therapies, or who "doctor-shop" for providers or agencies that will suit their needs) reflect patient-provider interactions where trust may be lacking. It may be argued that these patients want to control their situations to the best of their abilities. Certainly, patients having an involved "say" in their treatment course can be positive for health outcomes (Greenfield et al., 1988; Kaplan et al., 1989; Roberts, 1999), especially if patients are up-to-date on current treatment regimens. However, sometimes information from peers or the media is incomplete or has not fully been evaluated, and this misinformation may actually be detrimental to the patients' health (Eisenberg et al., 1998; Heussner & Salmon, 1988). Although HIV/AIDS care (especially medications and regimens) is changing so rapidly that it is often hard for health care providers to keep up with emerging information, those who typically work with HIV/AIDS populations (e.g., HIV/AIDS specialists) usually have the most current treatment-related research (Stephenson, 1996). Patients should be reminded that their providers are working for them, not against them, and are often optimally informed about new treatments and guidelines for therapy.

Patient passivity (i.e., letting their providers make all treatment decisions for them) seems to occur only when patients are newly diagnosed, with increased involvement occurring over time. These results agree with the work of Strull et al. (1984), suggesting that as patients become more knowledgeable and experienced with their medications, they wish to be more involved in treatment decisions. However, three additional factors may play a role in initial patient involvement.

First, when initially diagnosed, it may be that patients are too sick to take a highly active role (Nease & Brooks, 1995). Some individuals may seek medical attention when they are feeling extremely ill, and by the time they are seen by a health care provider their goal is to simply alleviate their current negative health status. A second factor is that those newly diagnosed with HIV experience high levels of uncertainty with what to do and who to talk to. This "vu jà dé" feeling ("I've never been here before . . . I don't know who can help me") has been described by Weick (1993), and is typified by a breakdown in the normally played social roles of the individuals, and feeling lost and disconnected. Individuals then fall back into primitive or "base" states, which include the need to be taken care of. A third factor is that newly diagnosed patients may feel overwhelmed and depressed, and therefore be less active in their care. They may want the security of having an expert making the decisions—putting themselves in good hands may assist them in feeling less vulnerable and scared. As time progresses and they see that they can maintain their health, etc., the fear and anxiety are likely to abate to some extent, allowing them to become more active in treatment.

Patients who reported active involvement with their health care providers in treatment decisions were also vigorous knowledge gatherers. As noted in treatises on patient empowerment issues (e.g., Roberts, 1999), information is an important component to assist patients in their interactions with health care providers. Information seems to have been gleaned from a variety of sources, including other HIV-infected patients, peers, health care providers, and media sources. Given today's technological culture, with access to print media, television, radio, and newer communication outlets such as electronic mail and the World Wide Web, patients have a multitude of outlets to acquire information regarding their health, health care, and treatment options. As late as the 1970s, medical information had to be obtained through print media, libraries, or health care providers. Although patients could utilize these resources, often trudging off to a library or one's physician whenever questions came to mind was too much of a task for most patients. Now, access to a growing number of health information sites on the World Wide Web (Akatsu & Kuffner, 1998; Lindberg & Humphresy, 1998), and access electronically to medical journals, have made the information patients sometimes seek much more available. In addition, communication between patients, family members, friends, or even treatment advocates has become easier through electronic mail, chat rooms or special "on-line" subject interest groups.

Another possible reason for both active patient involvement and knowledge gathering concerns uncertainty of the care standards for those with HIV/AIDS. Marelich et al. (2000) noted a series of "fuzzy" care issues that can affect HIV health care provider decision making, including biomedical information, drug adherence considerations, and even organizational pressures. It is possible that if patients sense this uncertainty, they may wish to play a more active role. In addition, health care providers, also aware of this uncertainty, may be more open to jointly working with their patients to get the best health outcomes.

Overall, these results compare favorably to findings with other chronic disease types, yet differ with findings from nonchronic diseases. For example, Kaplan et al. (1989) studied individuals with ulcer disease, hypertension, diabetes or breast cancer and found that these patients preferred more control over their treatment options and showed increased levels of information seeking. Additional studies with cancer patients have shown that those newly diagnosed preferred their providers to make treatment decisions for them (Degner & Sloan, 1992), and that over two-thirds of these patients preferred involvement in their treatment decisions (Blanchard et al., 1988). Patients with nonchronic ailments, however, appear to take a more passive stance with decision involvement. For example, Nease and Brooks (1995) found that patients with benign prostatic hyperplasia, back pain, or mild hypertension showed little interest in being involved in their treatment decisions. Beisecker and Beisecker (1990), using a sample of both non-chronic and chronic disease types, also found that patients wanted their physicians to be the decision-making authority. These studies contrast with the current findings and with other studies that solely focus on chronic diseases. However, whether reliable differences exist between these two populations regarding decision-making involvement should be addressed in future research.

There are several caveats associated with this study that should be mentioned. First, the empowered nature of patients' involvement in their treatment decisions may be an artifact of the obtained sample. Those patients who volunteered to participate may have been more adherent to their medication regimen and/or more interested in their health and health outcomes than those who did not volunteer. Second, disease severity of the participants may have played a role in the reported outcomes. Those severely ill with HIV/AIDS did not participate in the study, and there is evidence to suggest that greater illness severity is associated with a more passive role in decision-making involvement (Benbassat et al., 1998; Nease & Brooks, 1995). Third, the majority of participants self-identified as African-American or White males, and therefore the findings may not be representative of other demographic categories. Further, although stratification on demographics would have been helpful in better understanding the qualitative findings, we were unable to make clear demographic identifications in the audiotapes.

In sum, study participants generally reported active involvement with their providers regarding antiretroviral treatment decisions. In some cases, patients reported "taking charge" of their treatments. Although there was an initial expectation that patients would report passivity in their treatment involvement based on past research (e.g., Degner & Sloan, 1992), our study participants appeared fairly empowered, seeking information from various sources and actively discussing treatment options with their health care providers. Whether these findings are unique to HIV/AIDS patients in general, or whether they are unique to our study participants, is unknown. More research is needed to validate these findings with other HIV-infected individuals. However, HIV/AIDS health care providers may want to prepare themselves for a growing number of empowered patients, to continue with "team" efforts with empowered patients, and realize that patient passivity may only be an initial state of affairs.

References

AKATSU, H. & KUFFNER, J. (1998). Medicine and the Internet. *Western Journal of Medicine, 169*(5), 311-317

BEISECKER, A.E. & BEISECKER, T.D. (1990). Patient information-seeking behaviors when communicating with doctors. *Medical Care, 28*(1), 19-28.

BENBASSAT, J., PILPEL, D. & TIDHAR, M. (1998). Patients' preferences for participation in clinical decision making: A review of published surveys. *Behavioral Medicine, 24*(2), 81-88.

BLANCHARD, C.G., LABRECQUE, M.S., RUCKDESCHEL, J.C. & BLANCHARD, E.G. (1988). Information and decision-making preferences of hospitalized adult cancer patients. *Social Science and Medicine, 27*(11), 1139-1145.

CARPENTER, C.C., FISCHL, M.A., HAMMER, S.M., HIRSH, M.S., JACOBSEN, D.M., KATSENSTEIN, D.A., MONTANER, J.S., RICHMAN, D.D., SAAG, M.S., SCHOOLEY, R.T., THOMPSON, M.A., VELLA, S., YENI, P.G. & VOLBERDING, P.A. (1997). Antiretroviral therapy for HIV infection in 1997: Updated recommendations of international AIDS society-USA panel. *Journal of the American Medical Association, 277*(24), 1962-1969.

COCKERHAM, W.C. (1982). *Medical sociology,* 2nd edition. Englewood Cliffs, NJ: Prentice Hall.

COULEHAN, J.L. & BLOCK, M.R. (1997). *The medical interview: Mastering skills for clinical practice,* 3rd edition. Philadelphia: F.A. Davis.

DAVIES, A.R., WARE, J.E. JR., BROOK, R.H., PETERSON, J.R. & NEWHOUSE, J.P. (1986). Consumer acceptance of prepaid and fee-for-service medical care: Results from a randomized controlled trial. *Health Services Research,* (3), 429-452.

DEGNER, L.F. & SLOAN, J.A. (1992). Decision making during serious illness: What role do patients really want to play? *Journal of Clinical Epidemiology, 45*(9), 941-950.

EISENBERG, D.M., DAVIS, R.B., ETTNER, S.L., APPEL, S., WILKEY, S., VAN ROMPAY, M. & KESSLER, R.C. (1998). Trends in alternative medicine use in the United States, 1990-1997: Results of a follow-up national survey. *Journal of the American Medical Association, 280*(18), 1569-1575.

ERGER, J., GRUSKY, O., MANN, T. & MARELICH, W. (2000). HIV health care provider/patient interaction: Observations on the process of providing antiretroviral treatment. *AIDS Patient Care and STDs, 14*(5), 259-268.

GERTH, J. & STOLBERG, S.G. (2000). Drug makers reap profits on tax-backed research. *The New York Times,* 23 April, pp. A1, A20, A21.

GREENFIELD, S., KAPLAN, S.H., WARE, J.E., YANO, E.M. & FRANK, H.J. (1988). Patient participation in medical care: Effects on blood sugar and quality of life in diabetes. *Journal of General Internal Medicine, 3*(5), 448-457.

HEUSSNER, R.C. & SALMON, M. (1988). *Warning: The media may be harmful to your health! A consumers guide to medical news and advertising.* Kansas City, MO: Andrews & McMeel.

KAPLAN, S.H., GREENFIELD, S. & WARE, J.E. (1989). Assessing the effects of physician-patient interactions on the outcomes of chronic disease. *Medical Care, 27*(3 Suppl.), S110-S127.

KASTELER, J., KANE, R.L., OLSEN, D.M. & THETFORD, C. (1976). Issues underlying prevalence of "doctor shopping" behavior. *Journal of Health and Social Behavior, 17*(4), 329-339.

LINDBERG, D.A. & HUMPHRESY, B.L. (1998). Medicine and health on the Internet: The good, the bad, and the ugly. *Journal of the American Medical Association, 280*(15), 1303-1304.

MARELICH, W.D., GRUSKY, O., MANN, T., ERGER, J. & ROBERTS, K. J. (2000). Medical markers, adherence myths, and organizational structure: A two-stage model of HIV health care provider decision making. In: J. KRONENFELD (Ed.), *Research in the sociology of health care,* Volume 17 (pp. 99-117). Stamford, Conn.: JAI.

MURPHY, D.A., ROBERTS, K.J., MARTIN, D.J., MARELICH, W. & HOFFMAN, D. (2000). Barriers to antiretroviral adherence among HIV-infected adults. *AIDS Patient Care and STDs, 14*(1), 47-58.

NEASE, R.F. & BROOKS, W.B. (1995). Patient desire for information and decision making in health care decisions: The autonomy preference index and the health opinion survey. *Journal of General Internal Medicine, 10*(11), 593-600.

PARSONS, T. (1964). *The social system.* New York: Free Press.

REISER, S.J. (1993). The era of the patient: Using the experience of illness in shaping the missions of health care. *Journal of the American Medical Association, 269*(8), 1012-1017.

ROBERTS, K.J. (1998). Adherence to antiretroviral treatment regimens: Physician and patient perspectives. Unpublished doctoral dissertation, University of California, San Francisco.

ROBERTS, K.J. (1999). Patient empowerment in the United States: A critical commentary. *Health Expectations, 2,* 93-104.

STARFIELD, B., WRAY, C., HESS, K., GROSS, R., BIRK, P.S. & D'LUGOFF, B.C. (1981). The influence of patient-practitioner agreement on outcome of care. *American Journal of Public Health, 71*(2), 127-131.

STEPHENSON, J. (1996). Survival of patients with AIDS depends on physicians' experience treating the disease. *Journal of the American Medical Association, 275*(10), 745-746.

STRAUSS, A. & CORBIN, J. (1990). *Basics of qualitative research: Grounded theory procedures and techniques.* Newbury Park, CA: Sage.

STRULL, W.M., LO, B. & CHARLES, G. (1984). Do patients want to participate in medical decision making? *Journal of the American Medical Association, 252*(21), 2990-2994.

WEICK, K.E. (1993). The collapse of sensemaking in organizations: The Mann Gulch disaster. *Administrative Science Quarterly, 38*(4), 628-652.

WEST, C. (1984). Routine complications: Troubles with talk between doctors and patients. Bloomington: Indiana University Press.

PART V

Health Policy and Future Paths

Essay: Health Policy, Future Paths, and Concerns

Jeff S. Erger and William D. Marelich

> You will find that the State is the kind of organization which, though it does big things badly, does small things badly, too.
>
> —John Kenneth Galbraith

Public policy, in general, includes the strategic goals governments promote within a certain type of society and the tactics they employ to achieve those goals. Health policy may be seen as a component of broader public policy, consisting of goals that will ultimately improve the society's health. The strategic health goals typically addressed by governments are often identified by balancing the issues such as the overall "good" of society, funding and personnel resources, various special interest groups, and competing public policy components that also require funding. In essence, simply working toward the goal of better societal health is fraught with so many twists and "politicking" that it is sometimes amazing that health policy makes any progress at all. Yet U.S. health policy has moved forward and is responsible for regulations regarding almost everything that surrounds us, including the air we breathe, the water we drink, and the homes we live in.

To put policy and strategic goals into perspective, think for a moment about one of your own strategic goals: deciding to pursue a college degree (designed to achieve a better life and contribute to the common good of society). To obtain this goal, you employ tactics such as choosing classes, studying, spending time and money in certain ways, and generally going about the day-to-day activities of getting educated. Have you noticed that the pursuit of this goal is not as simple as you thought prior to entering college? No doubt, you have felt at times that there are all sorts of people, departments, and government agencies working as barriers to keep you from doing the relatively simple thing of getting a degree. Financial aid might be hard to come by and requires all sorts of documentation and cooperation from others (like parents). University policies for required classes might slow you down, especially if the school does not offer enough sections of the class you need. Personnel changes might lead to courses you were counting on being canceled or force you to seek a new academic advisor with little notice. The sheer amount of paperwork you have to fill out to do something as simple as drop a class seems ridiculous. Changes in federal policies might affect the activities of the college in ways that increase tuition, which might require extra loans or delaying further classes to earn more money. Don't these people realize that you are doing good not only for yourself *but also for the larger society?* After all, you are becoming a productive citizen, right?

Now, consider the fact that in terms of educational policy, *everyone is on the same side.* You want an education, everyone in your family wants you to get an education, everyone in the college wants you to get an education, the government certainly wants you to get an education; so why is it so darned hard sometimes to do simple things? This is the way of complex systems. However, think of how much *harder* it would be to do simple things if there were powerful groups out there that did not want you to get an education and that opposed any change that would make getting an education easier.

This is the situation that crops up in health policy, or at least seems to at times. Someone or some group sees a problem with public health and wants to change the situation to make things better. There will be groups that oppose that change, for whatever reason. For example, having clean water to drink is a good mandate for a society. Some group might say increasing environmental funding would allow more money to be available to clean up groundwater, lakes, and rivers. Other groups might oppose this, but they do not oppose clean water; to do so would be political suicide, as everyone is for clean water. Instead of opposing increasing environmental funding, they might choose to oppose tax increases (after all, who wants higher taxes?). In the end, the government will decide whether "clean water" will receive additional attention and funding. Now, within the government, who makes the decisions? Elected officials. What does it take to get elected? Votes. What does it take to get votes? Money. Where does a great deal of money come from? Lobbyists. So, those that support increased environmental funding will lobby the elected officials, talking about all the benefits of cleaner water to benefit society. Those opposed will speak of the increased taxes to pay for the programs and emphasize the negative effects of higher taxes on society. Can you see how hard it must be to listen and appease these conflicting messages to set policy? What a balancing act.

Another thing to consider is that these debates, actions, and tactics are *long running;* public policy does not get created over the course of a day, or even weeks, but rather is a continually evolving process that never ends. Take the case of tobacco and public health policy. Tobacco has a long history intertwined with governmental policies that meander back and forth given the political climate. Consider that in 1603, physicians in England, upset that tobacco was being used by people without physician prescription, complained to King James I. The next year, King James, in his *Counterblaste to Tobacco,* said that smoking is a "custome lothesome to the eye, hateful to the nose, harmful to the brain, dangerous to the lungs, and in the black and stinking fume thereof, nearest resembling the horrible stygian smoke of the pit that is bottomless." He was the first to impose a heavy tax on tobacco. Even in the 17th century, lobbyists were working with the government to forward their interests.

During World War I, many governments included tobacco as part of the standard army rations. In 1930, researchers in Cologne, Germany, made a statistical association between cancer and smoking. Certainly, things would change after that, right? No. In World War II as part of the war effort, U.S. president Roosevelt made tobacco a protected crop. Cigarettes were included in soldiers' rations, and tobacco companies sent millions of free cigarettes to troops. So, it appears at least one government was encouraging smoking; free cigarettes certainly sends a positive message. However, to partially recoup costs after the war and increase available health care funds, England implemented a huge (43%) increase in cigarette tax, resulting in a 14% drop in cigarette consumption among British men and sending a discouraging message regarding smoking. Public policy, here in the form of taxes, changed behavior for the good of public health. Still, at this same time, movies continued to be filled with images of heroes smoking cigarettes, and smoking remained a common and accepted behavior.

In 1951, the first large-scale epidemiological study of the relationship between smoking and lung cancer was carried out by Richard Doll and Austin Bradford Hill and published in the *British Medical Journal.* Doll and Hill interviewed 5,000 patients in British hospitals and found that of the 1,357 men with lung cancer, 99.5% were smokers. A few years later, *Reader's Digest* published "Cancer by the Carton," documenting the evidence on the association between smoking and lung cancer. It wasn't until more than a decade later, however, that the U.S. Surgeon General produced his first report on *Smoking and Health.* The U.S. Surgeon General has produced annual reports since 1967 on the health consequences of smoking.

If the U.S. government found that smoking is unhealthy, what did they do about it? They did not outlaw it, but why? Could it be because tobacco is a huge crop, responsible for billions of dollars of sales a year? Does the massive tobacco lobby, with millions of dollars contributed to political candidates over the years, have something to do with it? This is not to say that nothing was done, for there were restrictions put on tobacco sales and on advertising, such as a ban on television advertisements. Still, the power of money can be seen long after these restrictions went into effect. In 1990, the United States realized a $4.2 billion trade surplus from tobacco products. Despite 2.5 million deaths worldwide due to smoking, Vice President Quayle remarked, "We ought to think about opening up markets." This, in effect, was a policy of exporting poison for profit.

Now, this might be ancient history—after all, aren't there huge restrictions on tobacco today? Indeed, lawsuits are being won against tobacco companies left and right! This was not always the case. For many years, suits were brought, but the plaintiffs never won; or if they won, they lost on appeal, or they died before the case went to trial. In any case, people assumed that those who smoked *knew* that smoking was dangerous and they took that risk. They, in effect, "got what they deserved." However, the lawsuits that have been won recently are different. In 1998, a settlement was reached in a Minnesota tobacco case. It involved a $6 billion payout to the state and Blue Cross and Blue Shield of Minnesota over 25 years. This was the first case filed by a state attorney general against the tobacco industry to go to trial. Several more states have sued the industry and have settled out of court.

What was different about these cases? The claim is not that smoking hurt the smoker, but rather that smoking hurt the government and thus the taxpayers who had to pay the medical costs for those who smoked and had no insurance! Also, consider the California smoking ban, passed in 1994 and fully enacted in 1998, banning smoking in all places of employment, including restaurants and bars. This legislation passed not to protect smokers, but rather to ensure a safe workplace. So, for years, the government failed to act in ways to protect those who smoked because that was seen as individual choice and money flowed into campaign coffers from tobacco money. The people would not support legislation to prevent people from smoking at all. However, when the issue was cast as a "recover taxpayer money" or "worker safety issue," then legislation did get passed.

Given the above, we would like you to ask yourself the following question, "Should we pass laws designed to limit fast food?" That's silly, you might be thinking. Jokes are made about people suing McDonald's and Burger King all the time. People choose to eat whatever they want, and if they overeat burgers and fries, supersized, it is their own fault and problem. John Banzhaf, a professor of law at George Washington University, who mounted some of the first lawsuits against tobacco companies in the 1960s, said in 1997 that tobacco was unique and other industries were in no danger of such lawsuits.

Now, consider the phrase "epidemic of obesity" that is thrown around by government agencies and the media (e.g., newspapers, television, radio) doing stories on the problem of overweight children and adults, and then consider what the government might do to stop an epidemic. The language of "epidemic" is that it is an out-of-control spread of a disease. Governments have acted in the past to stop the contagion of disease in a population. Consider that state and national governments pay considerable amounts of money for health care caused by people being overweight. The same logic that was applied to the states' tobacco-use lawsuits could be applied to fast food. It is, in fact, starting to be applied. In 2002, Banzhaf was involved with a movement of trial lawyers and public health activists to go after fast-food restaurants. He said that some of the same legislative and litigative tactics that worked so well against big tobacco could also work against the issue of obesity! His plan is to first go after changes in law (legislative), but if that fails, sue (litigative). Will this new campaign succeed? Will Big Macs and Whoppers be taxed heavily to lower consumption? Will companies be sued to recover government health care costs? Time will tell.

This section of readings, our final section, examines the many issues that surround public health policy and its implementation. Health policy is a complex issue, and we have tried to provide a series of readings that cover many of the players and pressures that influence health policy. Many of the policy recommendations noted can be viewed as "multileveled." In other words, for the good of public health, health policy should be evaluated in terms of the micro-, meso-, and macrolevels from *medical sociology* and include biological, psychological, ecological, and environmental perspectives in an effort to improve health outcomes and well-being. We end this set of readings with the emerging issue of bioterrorism threat and its effects on societal well-being, an unfortunate but current policy concern.

Health Policy and Activism

The first reading by Foreman examines the institutions involved in public health policy. We included this reading to underscore that health policy and implementation of such policies is a rather complicated process that is politically charged. State, local, and federal health officials; politicians, interest groups, and their constituents; and the media all act and interact in ways that affect public health. State and local health officials work in large bureaucracies with set procedures developed over the years, and they suffer from a degree of bureaucratic inertia that makes them respond slowly to new situations. Each office has specific mandated areas of concern, and when a problem falls squarely in that mandated area, action is simple. However, new situations often fall across these organization boundaries, and that makes actions difficult. Foreman shows how the complexities of coordinating action between the National Institutes of Health, the Centers for Disease Control and Prevention, the Food and Drug Administration, and local health agencies can delay appropriate action when an unprecedented health issue such as HIV/AIDS comes into being.

Overseeing and controlling these departments and agencies are politicians. Politicians usually ignore the day-to-day running of these agencies. However, when a crisis emerges, such as AIDS, Legionnaires' disease, Lyme disease, or SARS (sudden acute respiratory syndrome), then politicians will often use their power to effect changes. Politicians do face many constraints on their powers, not the least of which is resistance from health officials, who often see them as uninformed and inexpert actors trying to tell those who know what to do. Politicians are also engaged in a system where there may be other politicians in various levels of power supporting or opposing their actions. Throw into this mix the actions of interest groups and their lobbying powers and there is a situation in which many nonmedical personnel must be dealt with before medical personnel can make medical decisions. And the media are keeping an eye on all of this.

Sometimes, the press ignores public health issues, but when they act, they can exert great influence on other policy actors as well as altering the dynamics between those actors. When the mainstream press initially ignored AIDS, little happened, yet when stories were in the news every day, suddenly there was positive, albeit slow mobilization of resources. In a more recent example, take the outbreak of Norwalk virus on cruise ships. In late 2002, a series of stories about a strange viral illness erupted in the television news shows and newspapers across the country. Cruise ships are enclosed spaces where illness is common and the spread of illness is fast. How many outbreaks of illness have happened on cruise ships over the years and gone unreported? How many ill passengers attributed their symptoms to seasickness? How many queasy passengers will think first of an outbreak of Norwalk virus from now on? How likely is increased regulation of cruise ship health reporting and protective action in coming years?

The next reading looks in detail at one of the policy actors Forman discusses, that of interest groups and their constituents. In this article by Wachter, AIDS activism and its relation to political action are investigated. Note that this article was written over a decade after the discovery of the disease, and so it chronicles the relatively rapid rise of activist groups, especially ACT-UP. In fact, activism really crystallized 6 years after the outbreak. Wachter points out several factors that contributed to this. People in the gay community at first feared a backlash and increase in homophobia due to the disease, but that did not materialize. As they came to realize this, action increased. Also, during the first 6 years of the epidemic, a huge number of people became infected, and many died. By facing a rapidly growing problem and seeing the threat from inaction, people became willing to act.

Perhaps the largest factor was that with the advent of a viable test for HIV (the virus that causes AIDS), a large number of HIV-positive people learned of their infections before symptoms manifested. These people were still relatively healthy and very motivated to bring about change in terms of health care and research, given that they had often witnessed friends and lovers die from the disease. When news of effective treatments started to spread, the final piece of the puzzle was in place; if there are treatments, then there can be a cure, and fighting can bring that about. The movement soon created some tangible results, including increased funding, increased access to health care, lowered prices on medication, and faster approval processes for new medications.

With success come challenges. In 1987, those infected were mostly gay, white, and male. The homogeneity of those affected by the epidemic made for a relatively simple organization process, with the goals and tactics in the movement agreed upon by the vast majority. As the epidemic progressed, the affected population became more diverse, with more women, minorities, and intravenous drug users joining the ranks and attempting to bring about changes in public policy. Strategies that worked well in the close-knit gay community had to be adapted or even thrown out when used in other communities. The very goals of the movement had to be adapted. Goals of the early activists included social equality for homosexuals, but when large numbers of non-gay people became involved, they tended to seek medical treatment-based solutions and ignore calls for social change. All social movements see this type of evolution. Where small groups achieve consensus with ease, larger groups must struggle. As Wachter points out, there are other lessons that activist groups take from the example of AIDS activists (e.g., breast cancer activists have specifically used AIDS activists as an exemplar).

Behavior Change and Ethics

Given that we know how to change behavior, should we? When is it all right to do things to people "for their own good"? These are questions the next article in this section discusses, and we hope that you discuss these issues amongst yourselves when finished with this article. Kipnis looks at the ethics of employing interventions to alter people's behavior and health, the history of such interventions, and the power relationships in programs that have been implemented. The goal of early social psychologists was essentially a moral one, with the goal stated by the first president of the American Psychological Association Division of Personality and Social Psychology calling for the use of psychology to reduce people's inhumanity toward each other. The goal of "curing social ills" soon gave way to a new goal, that of advancing social psychological theories. This more abstract, less practical, and applied focus coincided with the development of powerful behavior control and behavioral change technologies and programs. This meant that those who developed the technologies no longer had a central goal of moral improvement of society, and when those from powerful social groups wished to promote their interests, there was no opposition from those who were directly involved with the technologies.

What does this mean in concrete terms? Consider the abstract theoretical problem of "job turnover," which is the leaving of jobs by employees. This is expensive for employers in terms of hiring, retraining, and loss of organization expertise. It makes sense that employers would want to limit such turnover. One place in which this turnover has been highly studied is the military. In a way, this means that social psychologists have helped the government control the behavior of military personnel, making them do something they would not otherwise have done: stay in the military. When such interventions and control of human action is taken, it is typically taken by those with the resources to act; the greater the resources, the more widespread the action can be. When change is sought on issues, such as changing sexual behavior, diet and exercise, or use of medications in a "proper" manner (to name a few), the easiest way to *change* behavior is to *control* behavior.

Looking to the Future of Health

While Kipnis is sending a message of caution to health researchers about the consequences of their actions, the next article by Kaplan addresses primary and secondary prevention and underscores the import of moving away from reactive health policy to a policy that is proactive. Primary prevention, being proactive, works to keep individuals from developing illness and to enhance well-being. Instead of focusing on early disease detection in a person and preventing its further spread, as is done through secondary prevention efforts, the focus with primary prevention is on "preventive maneuvers that reduce the chances that a health problem will ever develop."

From a health policy standpoint, primary prevention efforts fight an uphill economic battle, although in the long run, such efforts will actually save resources and money. For example, going back to the early days of the AIDS epidemic, individuals within the Centers for Disease Control called for primary prevention efforts to slow the spread of the disease, including recommendations for safe-sex education in at-risk populations regardless of disease status. The point was to educate uninfected individuals about how HIV spreads and to attempt to change their attitudes and behaviors toward practicing unsafe sex. Such recommendations, however, were viewed as much too costly to implement compared with secondary prevention efforts, which focused on keeping those already infected from spreading HIV. These secondary prevention efforts made some minimal impact, but the disease continued to spread at an alarming rate through naive at-risk populations, and today, morbidity and mortality costs have moved astronomically beyond the costs of the proposed primary prevention efforts.

Kaplan illustrates, first, the marginal effects of secondary prevention efforts with various health issues, including cholesterol, prostate, and breast cancer screening, and notes that health outcomes such as mortality generally have not been reduced with these efforts. Yes, the number of people identified with these screening procedures has increased, yet the mortality rates have remained flat. He next provides examples of primary prevention efforts that focus on issues such as tobacco use, physical activity, and safety. For these, benefits such as enhanced well-being and longer life have been noted, with the ultimate societal costs associated for such efforts being minimal. His article closes with a series of recommendations regarding primary prevention efforts and their movement into the public health forum.

Of Future Concern: Bioterrorism, Health, and Social Response

Finally, we turn to the last article, which focuses on the issue of biological weapons and terrorist attacks. Clearly, this is a current concern of public policymakers at all levels of the government, from local to federal and even international. It also involves many separate agencies, including law enforcement, medical care providers, customs agencies, emergency service workers, and even water treatment facilities; the list goes on and on.

This reading is from the *Journal of the American Medical Association* and was written in 1997 by Halloway, Norwood, Fullerton, Engel, and Ursano. Consider this article in light of its publication date, years before the hypothetical attack became a reality. This article is written as a "what if" or a "when it happens" article and so can be seen as making predictions about what was to come. These predictions involve both the medical implications of a biological attack and the psychosocial implications. Ask yourself how accurate these predictions were. Furthermore, several suggestions were made in terms of planning and preparations. To what extent were these suggestions followed?

Consider this last article in light of everything else you have read in this book. When unexpected things occur in terms of public health, there are clear problems in responding in a timely and effective manner. However, it seems that even when *expected* things occur, there are still problems!

A Final Note About Health Policy

Individual health seems a simple thing compared with public health. Eat well, exercise, deal with stress, and see the doctor. Public health involves no such simple formula. Eating well is good for people, so public policy should promote eating well. How? Through education? Taxation? Force? Even if you can do something, should you? Is it ethical? Maybe you have a great idea, one that will make people healthier, but you still will have to get those in power to join in promoting your idea. Policymakers and policy actors will be involved. There will be some who oppose your idea and fight with all their might to derail your proposal. Even if you succeed, there might be some unintended consequences. Sue the tobacco industry to recover health care costs and reduce smoking if you want; you might even win and reduce smoking. You might also cause a Big Mac to cost $10 down the road.

22

Institutions

Christopher H. Foreman

The involvement of multiple institutions complicates policymaking. Federal agencies must interact with several important external actors to cope with emergent public health hazards. The federal bureaucracy is itself diverse and may be hard to coordinate effectively, particularly against any large and multifaceted problem. No federal official or office controls more than a portion of the relevant machinery. Even the president of the United States lacks the ability, and usually the incentive, to play any active, ongoing role in hazard management.

Policy Actors

Four external actors play particularly significant roles in the shaping of public policy in response to an emergent hazard: state and local health officials, politicians, interest groups and their constituents, and the press.

State and Local Health Officials

State and local public health agencies are as noteworthy for their diversity of structure, procedure, and priorities as for their frontline position in the battle for public health.[1] This diversity is a familiar double-edged sword, allowing responsiveness to local interests and sensitivities while fostering unsettling inequalities across jurisdictions. An Institute of Medicine committee charged with a broad assessment of the American public health system observed:

In one state the committee visited, the state health department was a major provider of prenatal care for poor women; in other places, women who could not pay got no care. Some state health departments are active and well equipped, while others perform fewer functions and get by on relatively meager resources. Localities vary even more widely: in some places the local health departments are larger and more sophisticated technically than

EDITORS' NOTE: From *Plagues, Products, & Politics: Emergent Public Health Hazards and National Policymaking* (pp. 14-28). Reprinted with permission of The Brookings Institution.

many state health departments. But in too many localities, there is no health department. Perhaps the area is visited occasionally by a "circuit-riding" public health nurse—and perhaps not.[2]

Whatever the condition of state and local systems, the federal government has little choice but to work with and through them. Federal authorities rely on state and local agencies to collect data, to assist in identifying and investigating disease outbreaks, and to deliver goods and services pursuant to national health objectives. In the areas of immunization and control of tuberculosis and sexually transmitted diseases, the federal Centers for Disease Control and Prevention provides funds to the states. In fiscal year 1992, for example, the agency awarded more than $145 million in HIV/AIDS prevention project funds to facilitate state and local efforts, while sexually transmitted disease grants totaled $77.5 million.[3]

Because an emergent health hazard is often a localized or geographically skewed problem, the administrative and political burdens for particular state and local agencies, and their leaders, may be intense. Lyme disease has been a far higher priority for New York and Connecticut health agencies than for most other states or for the nation as a whole, despite the occasional surge of national publicity. Although a local or regional disease outbreak, such as the 1993 Washington state epidemic of bloody diarrhea caused by consumption of bacteria-contaminated hamburger, may have national public policy significance in the long run, its immediate burdens fall almost entirely on the jurisdictions of tangible victimization.[4] Even the HIV epidemic has remained a relatively modest problem in many places (notably the rural West and Midwest, where infection rates remain strikingly low), while overtaxing public health resources in such locales as New York, San Francisco, Miami, Houston, and other cities. Before AIDS, subnational public health agencies, even in big cities, performed tasks that tended to strike most politicians, and most of the public, as noncontroversial and routine. As one observer commented:

> [State and local] public health executives did not serve, or at least were not perceived to be serving, a particularly unattractive or unpopular clientele before the mid-1980's. If anything, public health executives were in the business of protecting the "public good," and their actions typically did not provoke either intense support or intense opposition. Activities such as the conduct of epidemiological surveillance, the regulation of food establishments, or even the enforcement of quality assurance in health facilities do not directly engage clients or constituencies that are highly stigmatized, nor are they activities that raise the questions of deservedness or moral hazard that are prevalent in the administration of social services or corrections agencies. . . .
>
> Public health officials, generally medical doctors with additional public health credentials, also have benefited from the sovereignty and authority of these professions. Most issues of public health are technically and scientifically complex, and administrators with specialized expertise (or access to that expertise) in fields such as epidemiology or toxicology have enjoyed considerable hegemony over their enterprise and received substantial deference from legislators, budget officers, and the executive branch.[5]

The advent of AIDS changed this political environment, thrusting many public health executives "into the eye of the storm."[6] The HIV epidemic would prompt more aggressive efforts by the CDC to influence local disease prevention through additional—and conditional—federal funding. But many controversies (such as whether to close gay bathhouses, distribute clean needles to injecting drug users, or promote condom use) would remain local issues as much as, or more than, federal ones. Federal officials could not single-handedly determine where a balance of urgency and restraint would be struck or keep AIDS from becoming an issue far beyond public health.

Politicians

Elected officials constitute the most directly important reservoir of demands, resources, rewards, and sanctions for public agencies in their respective jurisdictions. And in a federal system, politicians at one jurisdictional level may also make claims against resources, or otherwise try to shape governmental behavior, in another. Whether legislators or executives, politicians will perceive an imminent health hazard as a possible opportunity or potential threat, depending on at least a rough judgment of the chances for harvesting credit or blame. Each politician confronts a somewhat different universe of demands and needs, and embodies a distinctive set of basic competencies and stylistic attributes, from every other. Each will face much competition for his or her attention while having to nurture ongoing alliances and sources of support. Therefore the incentive and opportunity to become involved in an issue, and the nature of that involvement, can vary greatly among politicians. A legislator identified with health concerns, dependent upon health-focused constituencies, and possessing some formal claim to policy leadership (via committee or subcommittee chairmanship) will be best positioned to identify an emergent hazard as worthy of political attention, to scrutinize agency response, to offer credible assessments of official performance, and to promote favored policy reforms. Conspicuous in Congress have been such figures as Representatives Henry A. Waxman, Democrat of California, chairman of the Subcommittee on Health and the Environment of the House Committee on Energy and Commerce; John D. Dingell, Democrat of Michigan, chairman of the House Committee on Energy and Commerce and of its Subcommittee on Oversight and Investigations; Ted Weiss, Democrat of New York, chairman of a key subcommittee of the House Committee on Government Operations; and Senator Edward M. Kennedy, Democrat of Massachusetts, chairman of the Labor and Human Resources Committee. (Weiss died in 1992.)

Presidents tend to keep a low profile on emergent public health hazards. In one sense they are like the typical member of Congress, having little to gain and too much competition for their time. Exceptions occurred in 1976, when President Gerald R. Ford personally announced the swine flu program, and in 1987, when President Ronald Reagan ended years of official silence on the AIDS epidemic to deliver a speech on the eve of the third international conference on AIDS. In both cases, visible presidential involvement stemmed from a perception by the White House that the risks (political and otherwise) of inaction had become unacceptably high. Whatever his level of visibility, the president usually confines himself to statements of reassurance.

The presence of identifiable victims may either offer ammunition to the politician seeking to highlight a threat for peers and the public or create an obstacle to one with alternative priorities. During the early and mid-1980's congressional Democrats sought to pressure the Reagan administration toward greater funding for, and faster response to, both the AIDS epidemic and their health agenda more generally. For them, the availability of immediate victims offered leverage, a way to make these concerns concrete. For conservative lawmakers and the White House, the presence of the victims was an obstacle to efforts to spotlight alternative policy interests, to control spending, and to avoid caving in to organized homosexuals.

For many politicians, however, the presence of victims will be less the means to a preestablished set of policy goals than an open opportunity to become identified with a new issue—a threat raising fear among constituents and an expectation that the government will do whatever it can to manage the problem. An emergent hazard's primary impact is strongly reflected in the pattern of concern shown by politicians. Not surprisingly, the politicians with large and active gay constituencies were among the first to call for increased attention to the AIDS epidemic, and evidence of heterosexual transmission would prove crucial to galvanizing the attention and support of politicians without such constituencies. Pennsylvania politicians were understandably at the forefront during and after the deadly outbreak of Legionnaires' disease in Philadelphia in 1976. Similarly, politicians both in New York State and throughout the New England region have generally manifested the greatest awareness of and concern about Lyme disease.[7]

But politicians face powerful constraints. They want to avoid taking positions unpopular with constituents. They tend to be generalists lacking in the technical training and knowledge necessary for deep comprehension of many problems. Their second-guessing of professionals and government agencies may be ill-informed or superficial particularly when evaluated by experts. The separation between policy decisions and policy implementation means that members of Congress and their staffs must rely both on what they are told about agency performance and on trying to create incentives for effectiveness and truthfulness by agency officials. (It also means that legislators can generally avoid blame for implementation failures.) This separation and the prevalence of legal training among legislators combine with political incentives to give legislative oversight of the bureaucracy a strongly procedural, and sometimes prosecutorial, orientation. Procedural integrity, or lack of it, is easy for members of Congress to comprehend and to make comprehensible to others. Concern for procedural integrity and a finely tuned sensitivity to constituent anxieties (actual or potential) are hallmark themes of legislative oversight.[8] (The two themes can lead in contradictory directions. Politicians commonly preach procedural fidelity while urging exceptions or flexibility for favored interests.) When politicians can plausibly link faculty process to concrete victimization, they generate political blame and, possibly, a full-blown scandal. Agency officials are well aware of all these things and of the need to tread carefully to preserve political support and administrative autonomy. The technical nature of emergent hazards, combined with a perception of emergency, helps protect agencies, but only imperfectly.

Interest Groups and Their Constituents

The availability of victims can either serve as fodder for existing groups and their leaders or constitute the basis for entirely new organizations. In the former instance, the incentive will be much as it is for politicians, with whom group leaders often forge alliances. Victims capture attention and inspire sympathy, thus providing visibility for groups and their preferred causes. A group anxious to advance a more general criticism will seize on a problem that group leaders can employ to reinforce a broader agenda. Groups may use emergent hazards in this way. Public Citizen, the advocacy organization founded by Ralph Nader, did this with Reye's syndrome, toxic shock syndrome, and other episodes during the 1980's.[9] For advocacy organizations reliant on generating public alarm to counteract the inherently advantaged position of business interests in routine policymaking, a new hazard (or newly frightening information about an old one) may help capture the sympathetic attention of politicians, the press, and the public. Such an issue may also have implications for the internal life of the group, allowing leaders to mobilize followers, fend off challengers, and increase the resources available for enhancement of group activity. An irony visible throughout political life is that harm to a group's constituency can augment the power of the group itself.

Victims, their friends, and relatives may also organize to affect the agendas and political environments of decisionmakers. Dalkon Shield victims and parents of children claiming harm by the diphtheria-pertussis-tetanus (DPT) vaccine, infant formula, or aspirin-associated Reye's syndrome may lobby or litigate or employ other avenues in search of redress and policy change they believe will benefit them or prevent further victimization.[10] (The same phenomenon has occurred among families whose members have been killed in terrorist bombings or declared missing-in-action in war.) Moreover, grassroots organizations are more inclined to strong emotional appeals, and sometimes even militant antiestablishment protest, than are the more traditional health lobbies. Former Federal Trade Commission chairman Michael Pertschuk observed that "the organizational culture of [traditional] voluntary associations like the [American] Cancer Society is shaped by their dependence upon the support of business leaders. Much of the staff and many of the volunteer leaders are simply not comfortable taking an aggressive, adversarial stand against any segment of the business community, nor with any form of political advocacy other than support for research funding."[11] Organized persons with breast cancer, Alzheimer's disease, and, most conspicuously, AIDS have on occasion proved less restrained.[12]

Finally, a variety of organizations representing business and professional constituencies has become active in the politics of emergent hazards. Manufacturer participation arises on at least two fronts: the defense of established products and the availability of new ones. When products in general use come under attack, efforts are made to fend off adverse regulation. In recent years, business has faced demands to develop AIDS treatments and to make them available cheaply. Various health care providers (for example, physicians and hospitals) may also seek influence over policy. The Pharmaceutical Manufacturers Association (PMA) is a primary player on research and regulatory issues affecting the drug industry. The best-known lobby of professionals is the American Medical Association (AMA), a group with the reputation of being resourceful enough to eschew formal coalitions.

The political significance of interest groups lies largely in the rewards and sanctions they provide politicians (though the precise role of interest group money on the policy-relevant behavior of politicians is a matter of some dispute). While it would be misleading to think of politicians as mere empty vessels into which interest groups pour their assorted preferences, the drive for reelection is clearly important to how elected officials behave, and group evaluations can be crucial.[13] Politicians may hold relatively weak personal preferences on many issues, such as questions of administrative structure and procedure, which groups tend to perceive as vital to their interests. "To the extent this holds true [of politicians]," political scientist Terry M. Moe observed, "their positions on issues are not really their own but are induced by the position of others."[14] Groups and constituents (individuals, state governments and their agencies, business firms) also lobby agencies directly. When appealing to politicians seems too risky or otherwise unpromising, a group may have to make its position known before an agency without the oversight or casework that legislators provide. And where lobbies are divided or otherwise weak, their individual members may have strong incentives to proceed on their own.

Organized interests also go to court. The judicial role in emergent public health hazards stems from the incentives and resources of parties in judicial proceedings, the constraining influence of past decisions, and the power of judges to make law where statutes remain unclear. Aggrieved individuals and groups resort to the courts to defend claimed rights and to compel agencies to act or refrain from acting. Because judicial decisionmaking focuses so closely on rights and procedural correctness in particular cases, it is not a forum that should be expected to settle satisfactorily questions of urgency and restraint or of technical competence.[15]

The Press

A key aim of politicians and interest groups is obtaining favorable media attention. While points of tension exist among them, all three institutions function in tacit alliance out of mutual self-interest.[16] Reporters need groups and politicians as sources for stories and commentary. Groups and politicians seek public outlets to shape issues and perceptions of themselves. One commentator remarked that "the press plays an influential mediating role in the policy process by selecting, packaging . . . and passing on to the public risk assessments generated and framed by scientists, the government, industry, and advocacy groups, and by reflecting back to these groups the public's response."[17]

In health and science, reporters and editors are particularly drawn to four kinds of stories, which can be labeled fire alarms, breakthroughs, controversies, and human interest.

Fire alarm stories call attention to a hazard, such as a deadly meningitis outbreak on a college campus.[18] Press accounts may also highlight new scientific findings that attach risks to activities widely believed innocuous, such as coffee consumption. The untutored layperson getting brief, incomplete, and out-of-context accounts of scientific findings can be forgiven a fair amount of confusion about what to believe or take seriously, which is particularly distressing given the importance of the media as a source of important health information.[19] A National Cancer Institute (NCI) survey found that about 60 percent of respondents relied on newspapers, magazines, and television as their main sources of information about cancer prevention, while only 15 percent or less talked to physicians about it.[20]

Scientific breakthroughs attract press coverage, which usually offers little solace to disease victims because a new treatment is too limited or comes too late to help them or because the new knowledge reported is still a long way from usable technology. Most reports of AIDS discoveries are of this last sort, offering little or no immediate benefit to most people with AIDS.

Controversy also attracts journalists. It may involve allegations of misconduct, struggles over product labeling, or arguments over appropriate regulation. The more colorful the dynamics of attack, defense, and counterattack, the greater the coverage stimulated. Journalists also try to create controversy instead of merely reflecting it, and much investigative journalism is pursued with this in mind.[21]

Finally, victims allow reporters to inject human interest into an otherwise dry or abstract subject. The HIV epidemic and other emergent hazards have produced countless tales of personal suffering and resilience.

Not all emergent hazards will be carefully or comprehensively reported. Critics of media response to AIDS in the early years of the epidemic note that the mainstream press largely ignored what then was perceived as a "gay disease."[22] Even when reporters pay attention to a problem, biases rooted in standard operating procedures and dependence on particular technologies shape the treatment that stories receive.[23] Television news is notorious for relying on good visuals and on hooking viewers quickly to avoid defection to other broadcasts. The more accessible a story's location, the more likely it will be covered. Reporters and editors also have career ambitions and political preferences. And they may be constrained by community sensitivities and by their accountability to corporate management.

Coverage has both public health costs and benefits. As media coverage raises public awareness of a health hazard, additional persons, suddenly aware that they might be or once have been victims, may report to physicians and public health authorities, possibly skewing data collection and epidemiologic analysis in important ways.[24]

Whatever emotional investment they may have in a story, responsible journalists typically strive for at least the appearance of evenhandedness. Along with getting the facts, producing balanced coverage is highly valued and usually means getting all sides of a story (though considerable bias can creep in).[25] But emergent hazards may also raise a different sort of balancing responsibility akin to the urgency versus restraint dilemma that policymakers face. For example, having encouraged public fear with accounts that a five-month-old girl's death in late 1991 may have stemmed from tainted baby food, the New York media were then obliged to report the absence of a wider pattern of food tampering and, still later, that the infant had not died of food poisoning after all.[26] Also, reporting on a two-day meeting at the CDC devoted to the tuberculosis epidemic, *New York Times* medical writer Lawrence K. Altman produced successive accounts with contrasting headlines. The first was titled "Deadly Strain of Tuberculosis Is Spreading Fast," and the second, "For Most, Risk of Contracting Tuberculosis Is Seen as Small."[27]

Policy Mandates

The diverse policy actors interact with a federal Public Health Service (PHS) once limited to "sick or disabled seamen" and funded with a monthly tax of 20 cents extracted from a seafarer's wages.[28] When a devastating cholera epidemic struck the United States in 1832, the major federal "issue" was whether President Andrew Jackson should endorse a day of "fasting and humiliation" as an effective prophylaxis.[29] In that era, subnational jurisdictions fended for themselves. Decades of scientific and technological achievement, legislative activity, and institution-building have created a vastly larger and more complex role for government in public health. But the loose PHS umbrella that encompasses key federal agencies—including the National Institutes of Health (NIH), the Food and Drug Administration, and the Centers for Disease Control and Prevention—is far less significant for managing health hazards than the historic missions and approaches of individual agencies.

National Institutes of Health

The NIH includes twenty-five major administrative units—seventeen are institutes—which form the heart of federally sponsored biomedical research.[30] The intramural research program represents a relatively small, if prestigious, presence among the NIH's total commitments, accounting for perhaps 7 to 15 percent of spending in any given year and never more than about 30 percent in any institute. Extramural programs consume the vast majority of resources, making them, in political and substantive terms, the primary raison d'être of the agency. In fiscal year 1992, for example, Congress appropriated $10 billion for the NIH, of which $7.1 billion exited the agency as grants and contracts.[31]

Overall, the NIH is decentralized, and quick reaction to new public is largely the result of having to perform a technically complex task health hazards has not been its mission. The institutes have enjoyed substantial autonomy, organized largely around particular diseases and organs. This results from a political environment in which congressional advocates and disease lobbyists have tended to concentrate on specific ailments and to prefer the greater predictability, control, and symbolic payoff inherent in specialized research units.[32]

The existing state of affairs has proven reliable for assuring strong external support among scientists, policy advocates, and members of Congress, especially because it has appeared to facilitate scientific productivity. The NIH has thrived politically by deferring to outside scientists on review committees and in research labs regarding the paths most likely to enhance scientific knowledge, not by responding to sudden emergencies.

Food and Drug Administration

Keeping hazardous products off the market is largely the FDA's mission. Any public health hazard that stems from a food, food additive, drug, vaccine, or medical device will likely require FDA regulatory involvement. New drugs and devices require agency approval before marketing. The FDA's regulatory authority is also broader than its power to approve or disapprove products. The agency can attach precise conditions of approval by limiting drugs to particular ailments and requiring record-keeping and reporting. The FDA also exercises considerable regulatory authority over the information that manufacturers may or must make available to consumers, a responsibility directly relevant to emergent health hazards.

The FDA thus is in a critical position regarding many hazards, rendering it vulnerable to blame from politicians, interest groups, and the press. The FDA may either approve a substance that causes direct harm to some persons or fail to approve one for which an organized or organizable constituency exists. Vitriolic criticism by AIDS activists helped push the FDA to recast procedures to speed the review of drugs for life-threatening illnesses.[33]

The agency will find evading responsibility difficult, even though circumstances hard or impossible for it to control may contribute to the problem. Uncertainty goes with the territory, given the number of products, applications for approval, clinical trials, physicians, and individual patient outcomes the FDA must monitor. Ponderous process is largely the result of having to perform a technically complex task in a high-stakes political environment (including pharmaceutical and medical device manufacturers, farmers, health professionals, and consumer advocates), often with inadequate resources.[34] This can produce drawn-out policy battles, as with the interminable fight over six artificial food colors found to cause cancer in laboratory animals.[35] The environment of regulatory politics also accounts for why the FDA to date has lacked statutory authority to order product recalls. Many business lobbies oppose such authority as excessive and unnecessary.

Centers for Disease Control and Prevention

In contrast to the FDA, recommendations and technical assistance, not regulation, is the CDC's primary business. The agency, based in Atlanta, has cultivated a core identity and constituency as a provider of practical service to state and local public health bureaucracies, though some state and local officials complain that the CDC is insufficiently sensitive to their needs. Unlike the NIH, the CDC's research activities lean more strongly toward practical application and are almost entirely intramural.[36] Whether in immunization campaigns, epidemic investigations, laboratory analysis, or training, the CDC has been a source of funds, personnel, and advice at the state and local level.[37] Originating as an agency for malaria control in war areas during the Second World War, the CDC would be transformed into an institution with national responsibility for fighting infectious disease of all sorts. The CDC is the closest thing the nation has to an institutionalized national line of defense against sudden eruptions of disease, placing responsibility for emergent public health hazards at the heart of its mandate.

While such an agency might be expected to command virtually automatic support, the CDC's position is potentially precarious. State health agencies can be protective of their autonomy, and in its early years the CDC worked diligently to entice cooperation from state officials.[38] The agency's persistent difficulty in securing a consolidated permanent headquarters reflected its political weakness. While disease and organ constituencies (including highly motivated and attentive university-based research scientists) swelled the NIH coffers in the years after World War II, the Atlanta disease detectives labored in relative poverty. And even though the CDC is now solidly established, it remains vulnerable to the political and policy dilemmas of public health. Absent a visible health crisis, its mission has often tended to generate indifference. But when a crisis strikes, the country demands predictive and diagnostic certainty as quickly as possible. Because disease is inherently complex, its cause and course hard to foresee precisely, predictive and diagnostic failure (or, at least, delay) may occur. The resulting blame can be acute. The delicate and essential balance between urgency and restraint, difficult enough to strike in any field of policy under the best of conditions, is articulately troublesome when mass fear intrudes.

Surgeon General

The surgeon general occupies an ironic position in American public health: oldest and, formally at least, weakest.[39] The post predates much of the government—its first occupant was appointed in 1871—but its powers are today largely informal and hortatory. Despite a relatively recent loss of formal authority—until a mid-1960s reorganization, the surgeon general ran the PHS—the office retains considerable visibility as a national bully pulpit for public health.[40] During the late 1960's and early 1970's the position came under sharp attack by critics as a threat to political control by the president and the secretary of health, education, and welfare (HEW).[41] The position survived, albeit weakened. During the 1980's C. Everett Koop, a pediatric surgeon, displayed considerable energy and entrepreneurial skill handling such hot issues as cigarette smoking, abortion, and AIDS. The surgeon general remains a potentially powerful force in emergent problems (such as AIDS or RS) that are not quickly resolved by the other agencies. Politicians and interest groups recognize the latent importance of the surgeon general. That is why liberals, fearful of Koop's conservative credentials as an antiabortion crusader, opposed his nomination to the post and why conservatives, anxious about Joycelyn Elders's support for sex education and condom distribution, responded similarly in 1993.

Assistant Secretary for Health

At the apex of the Public Health Service stands the assistant secretary for health, who must bear the conflicting expectations inherent in such a position. As with similar posts, the initial appointment usually stirs little controversy.[42] But once confirmed, the assistant secretary must preside over such politically charged matters as abortion, fetal tissue research, food and pharmaceutical regulation, animal experimentation, scientific misconduct, and decisionmaking for epidemics. In the early 1980's Assistant Secretary Edward Brandt was caught between a largely Democratic Congress that wanted far more research money for AIDS and the Reagan administration's desire to hold the line on spending and fend off any identification with the political agenda of organized homosexuals.[43] During the Ford administration Assistant Secretary Theodore Cooper stood at the vortex of debate over and implementation of the ill-fated swine flu vaccine program that he strongly supported and that ultimately cost him his job.[44] Like the posts of CDC and NIH director and FDA commissioner, the position is demanding enough to have been dubbed one of the "100 toughest management and policymaking jobs in Washington."[45]

Conclusions

The organizational propensity to approach any new problem in a business-as-usual manner stems mainly from an attraction to routines, procedures, and orthodoxies anchored in experience, legitimated by specific organizational environments, and supported by formal authority or informal understanding. Such forces cannot be tuned around quickly. Neither the committed agency executive nor the angry activists can radically revise a large institution overnight. And expecting organizations that have long been applauded for a particular approach to routine matters instantly and dramatically to shift basic missions, decision processes, and internal reward structures is largely futile. Organizations do not easily accommodate new and unexpected problems (such as AIDS) posing complexities that lie well beyond anything in their experience. Not surprisingly, the FDA was slow to speed up drug approvals after decades of political reinforcement for keeping dangerous drugs off the market. The CDC, lacking regulatory authority and perceiving a need to nurture cooperative relationships with state and local agencies, is inclined to swim carefully in controversial waters. And if the NIH concentrates on a basic research agenda driven mostly by university-based scientists, it is because that is what the system was designed and maintained for.

Response to emergent public health hazards may be federalized, but it is not centralized. Although unburdened by deferral politics of the sort that bedevils much environmental policymaking, and despite enjoying a strong public presumption in favor of aggressive federal actions, emergent hazards arise, like most issues, in an institutional context wherein multiple actors may wield crucial direct or indirect influence. (This is not to deny or to understate the genuine cooperation routinely evident among public health officials at all levels.) Health hazards range from very difficult to relatively easy. Interaction between its technical peculiarities and its political-institutional context largely determines a hazard's place on the spectrum. Bureaucratic missions and procedures, the most significant of which not only resist change but are often quite defensible, complicate the search for effective and balanced policies to deal with emergent public health hazards.

Notes

1. See C. Arden Miller and Merry-K. Moos, *Local Health Departments: Fifteen Case Studies* (Washington: American Public Health Association, 1981); National Association of County Health Officials, *National Profile of Local Health Departments: An Overview of the Nation's Local Public Health System* (Washington: National Association of County Health Officials, 1990); Public Health Practice Program Office, *Profile of State and Territorial Public Health Systems: United States, 1990* (Atlanta, Ga.: Centers for Disease Control, December 1991).

2. Committee for the Study of the Future of Public Health, Institute of Medicine, *The Future of Public Health* (Washington: National Academy Press, 1988), p. 3. On this point, see also Edward F. Lawlor, "When a Possible Job Becomes Impossible: Politics, Public Health, and the Management of the AIDS Epidemic," in Erwin C. Hargrove and John C. Glidewell, eds., *Impossible Jobs in Public Management* (University Press of Kansas, 1990), p. 153.

3. Centers for Disease Control, Division of STD/HIV Prevention, *Annual Report—1992,* pp. 79-80.

4. On this epidemic, see Marcia Goldoft and John Kobayashi, "Scientific Work and Epidemiologic Vigilance Quickly Halt *E Coli* Epidemic," *Washington Public Health,* vol. 11 (Fall 1993), pp. 1-3.

5. Lawlor, "When a Possible Job Becomes Impossible," p. 154.

6. Ibid., p. 155.

7. Obviously the politician personally victimized by a hazard may manifest public concern about it regardless of the constituency he or she formally represents. Representatives Berkley Bedell, Democrat of Iowa, and Kenneth J. Gray, Democrat of Illinois, were forced into early retirement from Congress as a result of contracting Lyme disease. Though neither represented an area particularly associated with the disease, both later lobbied their former colleagues to sponsor legislation supporting Lyme disease research and education. See draft letter to members of Congress dated April 7, 1989, by Berkley Bedell and Kenneth J. Gray in support of the Comprehensive Lyme Disease Act of 1989.

8. Christopher H. Foreman, Jr., *Signals from the Hill: Congressional Oversight and the Challenge of Social Regulation* (Yale University Press, 1988).

9. See, for example, *Risking America's Health and Safety: George Bush and the Task Force on Regulatory Relief* (Washington: *Public Citizen*, October 1988), pp. 8-9, 14.

10. Health threats accorded public prominence and increased research funding partly as a result of this kind of mobilization include sudden infant death syndrome (SIDS) and Alzheimer's disease. See Abraham B. Bergman, *The "Discovery" of Sudden Infant Death Syndrome: Lessons in the Practice of Political Medicine*

(Praeger, 1986); and Patrick Fox, "From Senility to Alzheimer's Disease: The Rise of the Alzheimer's Disease Movement," *Milbank Quarterly,* vol. 67, no. I (1989), pp. 58-102.

11. Michael Pertschuk, *Giant Killers* (W. W. Norton, 1986), pp. 51-52.

12. Robert M. Wachter, "AIDS, Activism, and the Politics of Health," *New England Journal of Medicine,* January 9, 1992, pp. 128-33.

13. David R. Mayhew, *Congress: The Electoral Connection* (Yale University Press, 1974).

14. Terry M. Moe, "The Politics of Bureaucratic Structure," in John E. Chubb and Paul E. Peterson, eds., *Can the Government Govern?* (Brookings, 1989), p. 269.

15. Donald L. Horowitz, *The Courts and Social Policy* (Brookings, 1977).

16. A useful overview of the various forces at work in media treatment of the scientific and technological aspects of risk is a background paper by Dorothy Nelkin, *Science in the Streets: Report of the Twentieth Century Fund Task Force on the Communication of Scientific Risk* (Priority Press, 1984).

17. Stephen Klaidman, *Health in the Headlines: The Stories behind the Stories* (Oxford University Press, 1991), p. 9.

18. Lisa Leff, "U-Md. Takes Meningitis Precautions: 100 Get Antibiotics After Student Dies," *Washington Post,* April 10, 1992, p. A24.

19. Anthony Schmitz, "Food News Blues," *In Health,* vol. 5 (November 1991), pp. 40-45.

20. Dorothy Nelkin, *Selling Science: How the Press Covers Science and Technology* (W. H. Freeman, 1987), p. 77.

21. An example is the Pulitzer-Prize-winning reporting on the U.S. blood industry by Gilbert M. Gaul of the *Philadelphia Inquirer.* His work is reprinted in Kendall J. Wills, ed., *The Pulitzer Prizes*—1990 (Simon and Schuster, 1990), pp. 31-109.

22. See Randy Shilts, *And the Band Played On: Politics, People, and the AIDS Epidemic* (St. Martin's Press, 1987); and James Kinsella, *Covering the Plague: AIDS and the American Media* (Rutgers University Press, 1989).

23. Doris A. Graber, Mass *Media and American Politics,* 4th ed. (Washington: Congressional Quarterly Press, 1993), chap. 3. On the role of such factors in reporting on science and technology particularly, see Nelkin, *Selling Science.* See also Edward Jay Epstein, *News from Nowhere: Television and the News* (Random House, 1973).

24. Mary Harvey, Ralph I. Horwitz, and Alvan R. Feinstein, "Toxic Shock and Tampons: Evaluation of the Epidemiologic Evidence," *Journal of the American Medical Association,* August 20, 1982, pp. 840-46.

25. For example, research into the relationship between reporters and scientific experts discloses a strong journalistic predilection in favor of experts skeptical of both nuclear energy and intelligence testing—a skepticism sharply at odds with the majority of expert opinion in both fields. See Stanley Rothman, "Journalists, Broadcasters, Scientific Experts and Public Opinion," *Minerva,* vol. 28 (Summer 1990), pp. 117-33.

26. Robert D. McFadden, "Child in Tampering Scare Had Been Ill," *New York Times,* October 20, 1991, p. 25; and Calvin Sims, "Girl Not Killed by Baby Food, Examiner Says," *New York Times,* November 16, 1991, p. 22.

27. Lawrence K. Airman, "Deadly Strain of Tuberculosis Is Spreading Fast, U.S. Finds," *New York Times,* January 24, 1992, pp. Ai, B6; and Airman, "For Most, Risk of Contracting Tuberculosis Is Seen as Small," *New York Times,* January 25, 1992, pp. i, 9.

28. Fitzhugh Mullan, *Plagues and Politics: The Story of the United States Public Health Service* (Basic Books, 1989), p. 14.

29. Charles E. Rosenberg, *The Cholera Years: The United States in 1832, 1849, and 1866* (University of Chicago Press, 1987), pp. 47-53. See also Charles Warren, *Odd Byways in American History* (Harvard University Press, 1942), chap. 12.

30. National Institutes of Health, *NIH Data Book*—1993 (Bethesda, Md., 1993), p. ii.

31. Ibid., pp. 10, 20.

32. On the political environment of the NIH, see Stephen P. Strickland, *Politics, Science and Dread Disease: A Short History of United States Medical Research Policy* (Harvard University Press, 1972); Natalie Davis Spingarn, *Heartbeat: The Politics of Health Research* (Washington and New York: Robert B. Luce, 1976); and Rufus E. Miles, Jr., *The Department of Health, Education, and Welfare* (Praeger, 1974), pp. 168-90. Congress has also enacted legislation calling for special efforts within or among institutes for such ailments as sickle cell anemia and sudden infant death syndrome. See Thomas J. Kennedy, Jr., and Ivan L. Bennett, Jr., "The Planning of Research: The Role of the Federal Government," in Henry Wechsler, Ronald W. Lamont-Havers, and George F. Cahill, Jr., *The Social Context of Medical Research* (Ballinger, 1981), p. 47.

33. David Vogel, "AIDS and the Politics of Drug Lag," *Public Interest,* no. 96 (Summer 1989), pp. 73-85.

34. The implications of this for legislative oversight of FDA are discussed in Foreman, *Signals from the Hill,* pp. 45-55, and passim.

35. Marian Burros, "The Saga of a Food Regulation: After 25 Years, Still No Decision," *New York Times,* February 13, 1985, pp. C1, C8.

36. During an interview, one former NIH institute director highlighted the difference in institutional culture between the NIH and the CDC by observing that while his own organization included many members of the prestigious National Academy of Sciences, the CDC had none.

37. See generally Elizabeth W. Etheridge, *Sentinel for Health: A History of the Centers for Disease Control* (University of California Press, 1992).

38. On these difficulties, see Etheridge, *Sentinel for Health,* p. 58.

39. On the origins of the surgeon general, see Mullan, *Plagues and Politics,* chap. 1.

40. On the origins of the reorganization that abolished the surgeon general's authority to run the PHS, see Mullan, *Plagues and Politics,* pp. 154, 158, 162.

41. Mullan, *Plagues and Politics,* p. 173.

42. An exception in this regard was the 1969 effort by HEW secretary Robert Finch to persuade President Richard Nixon to appoint John H. Knowles, head of Boston's Massachusetts General Hospital, assistant secretary for health. Vigorous opposition by the American Medical Association and by a key congressional ally (Senate Minority Leader Everett McKinley Dirksen, Republican of Illinois), resulted in an unsuccessful five-month struggle by Finch to win the appointment for Knowles. See E. W. Kenworthy, "Finch Drops Fight to Give Knowles Top Health Post," *New York Times,* June 28, 1969, pp. 1, 16.

43. See Shilts, *And the Band Played On,* chap. 29.

44. Joseph A. Califano, Jr., *Governing America: An Insider's Report from the White House and the Cabinet* (Simon and Schuster, 1981), pp. 173-74.

45. John H. Trattner, *The Prune Book: The 100 Toughest Management and Policy-Making Jobs in Washington* (Lanham, Md.: Madison Books, 1988), pp. 274-78.

23

AIDS, Activism, and the Politics of Health

R. M. Wachter

The trends toward empowering patients and questioning scientific expertise antedated the epidemic of the acquired immunodeficiency syndrome (AIDS). As early as the late 1960s, observers noted an increase in the involvement of patients and their advocates in health care organization, provision, financing, and research (Strickland, 1979; Hamilton, 1982). Moreover, despite their traditional public emphasis on charitable activities, large health organizations like the American Cancer Society have long traditions of political advocacy (Bennett, 1990).

Nevertheless, the entry of AIDS activists into the health care scene has added a jarring new dimension to what was previously a genteel dialogue between patient advocates and clinicians, researchers, and policy makers. The activists' unprecedented modus operandi is a study in contrasts: street theater and intimidation on the one hand, detailed position papers and painstaking negotiation on the other. The effect has been to energize the fight against AIDS with an urgency that has translated into expedited drug approvals, lower prices for medications, and increased funding for AIDS research and care.

The increasing influence of AIDS activists on health care decision making has not been universally praised, however. The movement is under attack for using militant tactics (Dowd, 1991; Leo, 1990), alienating natural allies such as physicians and scientists, and inadequately embracing the viewpoints of the diverse groups at risk for human immunodeficiency virus (HIV) infection and AIDS. Recent articles in the *Journal* (Angell, 1991; Bayer, 1991b) have argued that partly because of the activists' clout, the United States has adopted a policy of "HIV exceptionalism" that has compromised the public health response to the epidemic.

Now, a decade into the epidemic and five years after the founding of the AIDS Coalition to Unleash Power (ACT UP), the best-known activist group, it is appropriate to examine AIDS activism and its

---

EDITORS' NOTE: Previously published in the *New England Journal of Medicine, 326,* pp. 128-133.

implications in the broad arena of health policy. In doing so, I will focus on four questions. First, what are the roots of AIDS activism, and why was the epidemic six years old before the movement crystallized? Second, why has AIDS activism been so successful in influencing policy? Third, what are the challenges faced by AIDS activists five years later? And finally, is this model of activism applicable to other diseases?

The Roots of AIDS Activism

To understand AIDS activism, one must examine the gay-rights movement, because after a tragic period of hesitation, the one evolved directly from the other. The modern gay-liberation movement began in 1969, when a police raid at the Stonewall Inn, a Greenwich Village bar, led to three days of rioting. During the 1970s the movement focused largely on sexual freedom, a focus that had two disastrous consequences when a new virus entered the gay community in the late 1970s. First, the promiscuity in the community facilitated the rapid spread of the new sexually transmitted pathogen. Second, when AIDS began to appear in the early 1980s, many members of the gay community resisted changes in sexual behavior and eschewed political militancy. Instead, groups such as the National Gay and Lesbian Task Force and the Gay Men's Health Crisis concentrated on caring for the ill and lobbying traditional targets (e.g., local officials) to oppose measures they saw as involving privacy issues, such as the closing of bathhouses and later, the notification of partners (Shilts, 1987; Bayer, 1991a). The reasons for this early resistance to more aggressive forms of political activism included denial, a fear of losing the hard-won sexual freedom gained during the 1970s, and concern that a vigorous gay response to the epidemic would unleash a surge of homophobia (Wachter, 1991).

It was not until 1987, six years after the first AIDS cases were reported, that AIDS activism began in earnest, with a speech by author Larry Kramer to a gay group in Greenwich Village. Kramer warned his audience that most of those present would die unless they pressed the biomedical establishment to expedite the search for new AIDS treatments: "If what you're hearing doesn't rouse you to anger, fury, rage and action, gay men will have no future here on earth" (Kramer, 1989). Soon after the speech, ACT UP chapters began to form in cities around the country and later, around the world.

Why did the AIDS activist movement finally coalesce in 1987? After all, some members of the gay community, including Kramer, had been arguing for increased militancy for years, arguments that had previously fallen on deaf ears (Shilts, 1987). What had changed? First, the gay community's fear that an active role in the epidemic would lead to an increase in homophobia had not materialized. In fact, polls showed an increase during the 1980s of nearly 50 percent in the percentage of adults who thought homosexual relations between consenting adults should be legal, a change that may have been fueled by sympathy for the gay community and respect born of its responsible handling of the epidemic (Salholz, 1990).

Second, the activist movement was stoked by the sheer dimensions of the epidemic. By 1987, more than 20,000 Americans, about three fourths of them gay, had died of the disease. It was now abundantly clear that the entire gay community was at risk; early hopes that the epidemic would be short-lived (like the outbreaks of Legionnaires' disease and toxic shock syndrome a decade earlier) had long since been dismissed.

Third, the discovery of HIV in 1984 and the widespread availability of testing for the virus a year later provided tens of thousands of homosexual men with evidence of their impending mortality. Previously, the only people with such an intensely personal stake in finding a cure had been those with full-blown AIDS, who were often unable to engage in political warfare because of infirmity. People with newly diagnosed HIV seropositivity, who were usually asymptomatic, were imbued with a passion that comes only from seeing oneself at proximate risk (Masterson-Allen & Brown, 1990).

Finally, the discovery of HIV led to research on antiviral agents, some of which were only partway through the pipeline of federal research by 1987. If the government bureaucracy remained unchallenged, activists thought, the testing and approval of effective drugs would take years—years they simply did not have.

The confluence of these factors explains the origins of ACT UP and a new style of AIDS activism in 1987. In its first five years, the activist movement—sometimes praised, sometimes vilified, but always noticed—has permanently altered American health policy.

The Impact of AIDS Activism

The pressures brought to bear by AIDS activists on researchers, health officials, and the pharmaceutical industry have led to important changes in the course of the epidemic. Lobbying by HIV-infected people and their advocates led the Public Health Service to approve an expanded-access program, designed to make drugs available before the Food and Drug Administration had completed its approval process (Kolata, 1990b). Similarly, pressure from activists led Burroughs Wellcome to lower the price of its antiretroviral drug zidovudine, or AZT (Chase, 1989). Finally, activists are at least partly responsible for pressuring Congress into allocating a large sum of money, currently $1.7 billion a year, for AIDS research.

Why has the activist movement succeeded in promoting its agenda? The answer lies in the movement's organization and group consciousness, prefigured in the gay-rights movement. Gay people were deeply skeptical of the commitment by government (and society) to ensuring their well-being, a skepticism that translated into grass-roots mobilization and a unified focus. It is no coincidence that many members of ACT UP have embraced the theme of Malcolm X: "By any means necessary" (Little, 1970).

The analogy to Malcolm X translates to strategy as well. Some civil-rights scholars attribute much of Dr. Martin Luther King, Jr.'s success to the radicalism of Malcolm X (Blumberg, 1984; Colaiaco, 1988). King, the argument goes, gained access to power brokers because they preferred to deal with him rather than with Malcolm X. The same argument explains some of the influence of radical AIDS groups, which has created room to operate not only for other, more temperate AIDS lobbying groups but also for more moderate elements of the activist movement itself, such as ACT UP's Treatment and Data committees.

Access to policy makers would have been of only limited usefulness had the activists not included persons who were articulate, knowledgeable about the media, and able to use the levers of power. The largely middle-class gay communities of urban America contained sizable numbers of young, well-educated professionals able to seize an opportunity to make their points. In cities like New York and San Francisco, gays also represented large and powerful voting blocs with considerable political clout.

Finally, the targets of the activists—often scientists or medical policy makers within the bureaucracy of the Public Health Service—were relatively easy marks. Many came from liberal traditions and were sympathetic to the plight of people with AIDS. Unused to being at the center of a political maelstrom, some policy makers were easily intimidated by the activists. Moreover, health researchers and their patients are mutually interdependent. Researchers had to take seriously the threats of AIDS activists to sabotage drug trials, since the researchers required the participation of patients to complete their projects.

Because of all these factors, AIDS activism has enjoyed unprecedented success in shaping health policy. So much success, in fact, that in the past few years some have begun to ask whether AIDS is now getting more than its fair share of resources and whether it is being handled in a way contrary to the best interests of the public health (Grossman, 1990; Thompson, 1990; Krauthammer, 1990).

Beginning in 1989, some criticized the level of AIDS funding as being too generous as compared with funding for other serious illnesses (Winkenwerder, Kessler, & Stolec, 1989; McIntosh, 1990). For example, federal spending for AIDS was $1.6 billion in 1990, a year after 40,000 Americans died of the disease. During the same year, federal spending for cancer, a disease that killed 500,000 in 1989, was $1.5 billion, and spending for heart disease, which killed 750,000, was less than $1 billion (Thompson, 1990). Although spokespersons for the AIDS community often noted that AIDS resources did not come at the expense of other health care needs, in fact overall spending for health care research remained essentially fixed; it was self evident that money spent on AIDS was money not spent on something else (Fuchs, 1974). Similarly, the more hours that were used to expedite trials of antiviral agents and PDA evaluations, the fewer were available for other worthwhile pursuits.

In defending the recent priority given to AIDS, AIDS advocates say that AIDS is different from other diseases because it is epidemic and infectious—prompt action could contain the spread of the causative agent. It tends to strike the young, whereas cancer and heart disease tend to strike people in their 50s and 60s. AIDS has been centered in a dozen cities around the country and has ravaged their public health systems. Finally, progress on cancer and heart disease is seen as slow and incremental, whereas there is hope that AIDS—like polio before it—will one day be eradicated by a major scientific advance (McIntosh, 1990). The point here is not that any particular allocation of resources is right or wrong, but rather that the success of AIDS activists demonstrated that decisions about the allocation of resources—even in health care—are inherently political and thus amenable to effective lobbying.

Before passing judgment on whether AIDS activists have indeed secured more than a fair share of resources for the HIV epidemic, we should ask whether activism would have been necessary had the initial response of government, the media, and the biomedical establishment been commensurate with the magnitude of the crisis (Shilts, 1987). Despite the activists' successes, the epidemic may still receive less money and attention than if it had struck mainstream American society with the same viciousness.

A second area cited by critics of AIDS advocacy involves the drug-approval process. AIDS activists, led by San Francisco's Project Inform, assert that they, not a federal agency, should be given the right to decide whether the benefits of an unproved but potentially effective new drug outweigh the risk for people suffering from fatal illnesses (Thompson, 1990). Activists challenged the FDA's regulatory authority directly by carrying out underground tests of new drugs, threatening to sabotage government-sponsored drug trials, and conducting massive demonstrations at FDA headquarters (Kolata, 1990a). These tactics prompted the FDA to approve an expedited drug-approval process (Delaney, 1989), hailed as lifesaving by AIDS advocates but criticized as dangerous and costly by some in the scientific community. What, some researchers ask, will prevent the FDA from approving another Laetrile under its new policy, or even worse, another thalidomide? (Annas, 1989) Moreover, why should society subsidize the cost of medications prescribed simply because they might work?

Third, critics of the AIDS lobby point to its emphasis on developing new drugs to treat those already infected with HIV, as opposed to creating programs to prevent the spread of the virus. Politically, this bias can be explained by the lobby's origins in the gay activism of the 1970s. Homosexual men constituted the majority of people initially infected by HIV, and this relatively well-educated population quickly learned to practice prevention. Despite some recent reports of recidivism (Stall, Ekstrand, Pollack, McKusick, & Coates, 1990), the low rate of new seroconversions among homosexual men has left that community concerned primarily with finding drugs to treat HIV infection and AIDS-related illnesses. Although AIDS activists have begun to pay more attention to prevention programs, such as needle exchange, their continued emphasis on cure over prevention has only limited relevance to other Americans, primarily heterosexual people of color in urban centers, who are still at high risk for HIV infection. This emphasis also troubles health care workers and policy makers in Africa and the rest of the developing world. In these countries, where the annual per capita health care budget is often less than $10, America's focus on determining the superiority of one antiviral agent over another seems cruelly wasteful and immaterial. Prevention is the only viable strategy.

Finally, critics of the activist movement, including many gay and HIV-infected people, condemn ACT UP's stridency and seeming willingness to deny free speech to such "enemies" as Dr. Louis Sullivan, secretary of the Department of Health and Human Services, who was shouted down at the Sixth International Conference on AIDS (Wachter, 1991). One gay editorialist expressed the community's misgivings as follows:

There is a fine line between, on the one hand, street theater, civil disobedience, and the right to demonstrate, and on the other, mob behavior and brownshirting. . . . Many fear that the politics of anger is causing the community to abandon its commitment to the freedom of expression and the right to privacy, the two ideas used most often to support gay rights (Vollmer, 1990a, 1990b).

AIDS activists defend their tactics, observing that their unprecedented access to medical decision makers—the opportunity to serve on advisory committees at the National Institutes of Health and the FDA and give major speeches at international AIDS conferences—was won largely because decision makers feared the disruption activists could create. Nevertheless, even supporters of the activist agenda are concerned that the tactics of harassment and intimidation may be generating an AIDS backlash, alienating members of mainstream society, and causing some researchers and pharmaceutical concerns to leave the choppy waters of AIDS politics in search of calmer seas.

Challenges to AIDS Activism

As the AIDS crisis enters its second decade, the biggest challenge to activists comes from this backlash from society, researchers, drug companies, and advocates for patients with other diseases (Garrison, 1989). But there are other challenges as well, products of the unique history and culture of the activist movement itself.

First, the movement and the epidemic are becoming increasingly diverse. When ACT UP was founded in 1987, homosexual men (most of them white) constituted 70 percent of Americans with AIDS and the vast majority of AIDS activists. Today, such men make up 55 percent of people with AIDS, and the percentage is shrinking (Garrison, 1991). The increasing numbers of drug users, people of color, and women at risk for HIV infection are greatly concerned about preventing the spread of HIV. This means that the strategies that were so effective in the gay community must be reevaluated and adapted to the particular cultures, languages, and institutions of the communities newly at risk.

Moreover, these communities are besieged with other overwhelming social maladies, many of them linked to the HIV epidemic. Effective AIDS strategies for these groups must address issues of poverty, racism, violence, drug abuse, teenage pregnancy, abortion, and access to health care—issues that were less important to the earlier gay, white AIDS activists.

A second type of diversity that divides the activist movement relates to the serologic status and agenda of the participants. The early activists were generally HIV-positive or had full-blown AIDS, which accounted for their devotion to the quest for effective drugs. Attracted by the success and high visibility of the activists, recent entrants into the AIDS movement, some of them seronegative, have more complex motivations. The primary goal of these people is often to eradicate the social ills of homophobia, racism, and sexism. The conflict between the "treatment" activists and the "social agenda" activists has led to infighting within the movement and even to the breakup of ACT UP into two distinct chapters in San Francisco (Krieger, 1990).

The activist movement has also been wrenched by disagreement over strategy. As would be expected of a movement whose tactics range from disrupting the New York Stock Exchange to publishing position papers that evaluate new reverse transcriptase inhibitors, activists disagree on whether confrontation or collaboration is the most effective strategy. Those primarily concerned with treatment have generally favored working with the system, because it is the biomedical establishment that must be counted on to develop, test, and approve new drugs. More radical factions argue for a more confrontational strategy (Spiers, 1989). Larry Kramer called for riots at the Sixth International Conference on AIDS (Kramer, 1990). Although this call was promptly repudiated by other activists (Wachter, 1991), the fact that it was made by ACT UP's founder exposed the wide range of opinions on strategy within the movement.

Perhaps the greatest challenge to AIDS activism is posed by the merciless nature of the disease itself. Although activists have succeeded in demanding that the world take note of the urgency of the epidemic, that very urgency is what robs the movement daily of its best soldiers through burnout, illness, and death.

Does the Model of AIDS Activism Apply to Other Diseases?

The successes of AIDS activism have not gone unnoticed by advocates for patients with other diseases. As Dr. Robert Young, president of the American Society of Clinical Oncology, lamented in 1990: "Why is it that we have such an effective AIDS lobby and we have such a relatively quiet cancer lobby in this country, despite the fact that we're going to lose 500,000 people this year from cancer deaths . . . ?" (McIntosh, 1990). The answer to this question is that the gay political movement, already organized, provided many of the ingredients of the emergent AIDS lobby. As a group, patients with cancer lack a previous political agenda, a sense of group consciousness, and a feeling of being marginalized and stigmatized. There is one striking exception—women with breast cancer, who now constitute an increasingly outspoken and militant lobby.

The rise in activism related to breast cancer has been fueled by a number of factors: the extraordinary incidence of the tumor, which strikes 1 in 10 women; the presence of a parallel move—pressing the American scientific establishment to pay more attention to women's issues in general (Healy, 1991); and the coming of age of the politically powerful baby-boom generation, in which the cancer is highly prevalent. But these influences might not have generated a potent lobby without the earlier development of the feminist movement, which had been urging women for years to take control of medical decisions affecting their bodies. Together, these factors have resulted in the appearance of dozens of breast cancer advocacy groups around the country, lobbying for increased research funding, expedited drug approvals, and better insurance coverage for mammography and experimental treatments (Fintor, 1991; Gross, 1991).

The role of AIDS activism in the genesis of the breast cancer lobby has been pivotal and complex. Advocates for women with breast cancer have advanced their cause by highlighting the disparity between federal funding for AIDS and that for breast cancer, which amounted to only $77 million in research money in 1990 (1/20 the AIDS allocation) for a disease that killed more than 43,000 Americans that year. Meanwhile, these advocates have clearly learned lessons from the AIDS activists. "They showed us how to get through to the Government," one breast cancer activist told the *New York Times* in January 1991. "They took on an archaic system and turned it around while we have been quietly dying" (Gross, 1991).

While the advocacy movement for patients with breast cancer was forming, a potent lobby for patients with Alzheimer's disease was being created in response to the issue of approving an experimental drug, tacrine. The roots of the Alzheimer's lobby can be found in the preexisting self-awareness and recent empowerment of the elderly as a group, a surge in biomedical research on the disease, and the overwhelming sense of frustration and hopelessness shared by patients with Alzheimer's disease and their families (Fox, 1989). In the case of tacrine, the recommendation of an PDA advisory committee in March 1991 not to approve the drug, because of limited evidence of benefit and substantial potential for liver toxicity, unleashed a firestorm of protest. Many argued that as with AIDS, the PDA's rules for drug approval should be relaxed when life-threatening diseases are at issue (Rothman & Edgar, 1990). "The time is long past for being polite and courteous and willing to wait while the PDA wastes the lives of five million victims," wrote the spouse of a patient with Alzheimer's disease to Dr. David Kessler, the PDA commissioner (Kolata, 1991a).

Nevertheless, in July 1991 an PDA committee again refused to approve the distribution of tacrine until better data on its efficacy became available. The decision was particularly troubling to Alzheimer's activists, since it was followed days later by the PDA's approval of didanosine, an anti-HIV agent, despite a similar paucity of data on efficacy (Kolata, 1991b). Kessler defended the tacrine decision but promised to expedite the drug's ongoing evaluation. "Therapies for Alzheimer's disease deserve the same focused energy and high priority that we now devote to AIDS and cancer," he said, highlighting the scrutiny his agency is under from the three advocacy groups (Kolata, 1991a).

What effect will these groups have on overall health policy? Advocates for patients with different diseases might form powerful coalitions of health consumers, since the groups' members have a number of issues of concern in common. For example, the lobbies for AIDS, breast cancer, and Alzheimer's disease may work in concert to improve access to health care for all Americans, expedite the approval process at the FDA for all drugs, and fight discrimination against victims of all diseases.

On the other hand, disease-specific activist groups may find themselves pitted against one another as they advocate their own interests. This possibility raises two matters of concern. First, it will render the players in the health policy arena increasingly fractious, making collaborative and multidisciplinary work more hazardous. Second, and perhaps more worrisome, if advocates for AIDS, breast cancer, and Alzheimer's disease succeed in garnering larger slices of the resource pie for their groups and the overall health budget remains static, smaller and smaller slices will be left for other groups that support equally deserving causes but that lack activists to argue on their behalf.

Dealing with Health Activism

Because AIDS activists have demonstrated the degree of influence that a well-organized, highly motivated advocacy group can have, we can be certain that the empowerment of patients will be a major part of the American social landscape of the 1990s. In this new order, some health professionals will view a powerful consumer movement as a direct threat to their competence and power. Without question, having our patients and research subjects ask—or demand—to have an active voice in what we do and how we do it will at times be difficult, laborious, and even unpleasant. It is also undeniably right (Wachter, 1991).

Rather than feel threatened, we as physicians and researchers should embrace this movement and, whenever possible, work with our patients and their advocates toward our many shared goals. Together, we form a coalition—albeit a fragile one—with immense power to shape health policy (Wachter, 1991). We have far more to gain from pooling our strengths than from emphasizing our differences.

Nevertheless, there are sure to be times when we ourselves will be the targets of the activists' ire. As we have seen from the first decade of the AIDS epidemic, we will often benefit by heeding the fresh perspective of our patients and their advocates. But we must not bow automatically to the winds of protest. Activists may try to push us to do things that we judge not to be in the best interest of the public health, or even in the best interest of those for whom they purport to speak. At such times, we must explain our position without arrogance or paternalism, remaining open to the possibility of change while carefully preserving our scientific credibility. Society empowers us with this responsibility, and it deserves no less.

References

Annas, G.J. (1989). Faith (healing), hope and charity at the FDA: The politics of AIDS drug trials. *Villanova Law Rev, 34*(77), 1-97.

Angell, M. (1991). A dual approach to the AIDS epidemic. *New England Journal of Medicine, 324,* 1498-500.

Bayer, R. (1991a). *Private acts, social consequences: AIDS and the politics of public health.* New Brunswick, N.J.: Rutgers University Press.

Bayer, R. (1991b). Public health policy and the AIDS epidemic—and to HIV "exceptionalism." *New England Journal of Medicine, 324,* 1500-4.

Bennett, J.T. (1990). *Health research charities: Image and reality.* Washington, DC: Capital Research Center.

Blumberg, R.L. (1984). *Civil rights: The 1960s freedom struggle.* Boston: Twayne.

Chase, M. (Sept. 19, 1989). Burroughs-Wellcome cuts price of AZT under pressure from AIDS activists. *Wall Street Journal:*A3.

Colaiaco, J.A. (1988). *Martin Luther King. Jr.: Apostle of militant nonviolence.* New York: St Martin's Press.

Delaney, M. (1989). The case for patient access to experimental therapy. *Journal of Infectious Diseases, 159,* 416-9.

Dowd, M. (Aug 17, 1991). Bush chides protesters on "excesses." *New York Times:*7.

Fintor, L. (1991). Patient activism: Cancer groups become vocal and politically active. *Journal of the National Cancer Institute, 83,* 528-9.

Fox, P. (1989). From senility to Alzheimer's disease: The rise of the Alzheimer's disease movement. *Milbank Quarterly, 67,* 58-102.

Fuchs, V.R. (1974). *Who shall live? Health, economics, and social choice.* New York. Basic Books.

Garrison, J. (Dec 17, 1989). The AIDS research backlash. *San Francisco Examiner:*A1.

Garrison, J. (1991). Update: Acquired immunodeficiency syndrome—United States, 1981-1990. *MMWR, 40,* 358-69.

Gross, J. (Jan 7, 1991). Turning disease into political cause: First AIDS, and now breast cancer. *New York Times:*A12.

Grossman, H. (Aug. 19, 1990). Keep politics out of scientific research. *New York Times:*111:13.

Hamilton, P.A. (1982). *Health care consumerism.* St. Louis: C.V. Mosby.

Healy, B. (1991). The Yentl syndrome. *New England Journal of Medicine, 325,* 274-6.

Kolata, G. (March 9, 1990a). Unorthodox trials of AIDS drugs are allowed by FDA to go on. *New York Times:*A1.

Kolata, G. (May 19, 1990b). U.S. to expand use of AIDS medicines. *New York Times:*A8.

Kolata, G. (July 16, 1991a). PDA panel approves test distribution of Alzheimer's drug. *New York Times:*B6.

Kolata, G. (July 28, 1991b). For new PDA drug policy, dismay and delight. *New York Times:*13.

Kramer, L. (1989). *Reports from the holocaust: The making of an AIDS activist.* New York: St. Martin's Press.

Kramer, L. (March 14, 1990). A call to riot. *Outweek Magazine:*6-8.

Krauthammer, C. (June 25, 1990). AIDS: getting more than its share. *Time:*80.

Krieger, L.M. (Oct 14, 1990). Ideology clash underlies split within ACT UP. *San Francisco Examiner:*B1.

Leo, J. (Feb 5, 1990). When activism becomes gangsterism. *U.S. News & World Report:*18.

Little, M. (1970). *By any means necessary.* New York: Pathfinder Press.

Masterson-Allen, S., & Brown, P. (1990). Public reaction to toxic waste contamination: Analysis of a social movement. *International Journal of Health Services, 20,* 485-500.

McIntosh, H. (1990). AIDS lobby earns respect from cancer leaders. *Journal of the National Cancer Institute, 82,* 730-732.

Public Health Service. (1990). Expanded availability of investigational new drugs through a parallel track mechanism for people with AIDS and HIV- related disease. *Federal Registry, 55,* 20856-60.

Rothman, D.J., & Edgar, H. (1990). Drug approval and AIDS: Benefits for the elderly. *Health Affairs (Millwood), 9,* 123-30.

Salholz, E. (March 12, 1990). The future of gay America. *Newsweek:*20-5.

Shilts, R. (1987). *And the band played on: Politics, people, and the AIDS epidemic.* New York: St. Martin's Press.

Spiers, H.R. (1989). AIDS and civil disobedience. *Hastings Center Report, 19,* 34-5.

Stall, R., Ekstrand, M., Pollack, L., McKusick, L., & Coates, T.J. (1990). Relapse from safer sex: The next challenge for AIDS prevention efforts. *Journal of Acquired Immune Deficiency Syndrome, 3,* 181-7.

Strickland, S.P. (1979). Medical research: Public policy and power politic. In D. Cater & P.R. Lee (Eds), *Politics in health* (pp. 75-97). Huntington. N.Y.: Robert Krieger Publishing.

Thompson, D. (Jan 22, 1990). The AIDS political machine. *Time:*24-5.

Vollmer, T. (June 28, 1990a). How far with the politics of anger? *San Francisco Sentinel:*9.

Vollmer, T. (Aug 2, 1990b). Three points for ACT-UP to consider. *San Francisco Sentinel:*9.

Wachter, R.M. (1991). *The fragile coalition: Scientists, activists, and AIDS.* New York: St. Martin's Press.

Winkenwerder, W., Kessler, A.R., & Stolec, R.M. (1989). Federal spending for illness caused by the human immunodeficiency virus. *New England Journal of Medicine, 320,* 1598-1603.

24

Accounting for the Use of Behavior Technologies in Social Psychology

David Kipnis

Considerable scholarly effort in social psychology is devoted to the development of techniques that change behavior. In this article, the social and political forces that have guided the development of these techniques are examined. Also, ethical and psychological issues associated with the use of behavior technologies are discussed. These issues arise from the fact that to change behavior, it must first be controlled.

Social psychology shares with all disciplines in the social sciences the task of describing and predicting behavior. Over the past five to six decades, social psychology has taken on the task of changing social behavior. Even in a cursory examination of present-day social psychological journals and textbooks, one finds considerable scholarly effort devoted to the development of systematic techniques for shaping how people think and behave toward each other—that is, the development of behavior technologies.

The purpose of this article is twofold. The first is to analyze the social and scientific reasons that promote the development of behavior technologies in social psychology. The second is to review social issues associated with the use of technology in society at large and to suggest that similar issues may arise in particular settings that use psychological knowledge for practical purposes. Although the article focuses on social psychology, the issues discussed apply, I believe, to all areas of psychology that have developed and use systematic techniques for solving practical problems of human behavior.

EDITORS' NOTE: From *American Psychologist, 49,* pp. 165-172.

Why Do We Want to Change Behavior?

We begin by asking why social psychology has taken on the task of developing systematic procedures to changing people's behavior. Other social science disciplines, such as political science, seem content to describe and predict events, not to change them.

Perhaps the simplest answer is that social psychology has available a methodology to change behavior. From the 1870s on, psychologists have offered as proof of their ideas the fact that they could experimentally change human activities in predictable ways. Recall, for instance, John B. Watson's boast about his ability to control people's lives using the methods of classical conditioning:

> Give me a dozen healthy infants, well formed, and my own specified world to bring them up in, and I will guarantee to take any one at random and train him to become any type of specialist I select—doctor, lawyer, artist, merchant, and yes, even beggar-man and thief, regardless of his talents, penchants, tendencies, abilities, vocation, and race of his ancestors. (Watson, 1925, p. 82)

Clinical psychology and organizational psychology also serve as models for social psychology. Unlike experimental psychology, however, in which people are changed to demonstrate an experimental principle, behavioral changes produced by clinical and organizational psychologists are designed to solve practical problems.

If one is not satisfied with methodology as an answer and want to pursue further the question of why social psychology has developed techniques for changing behavior, then one must look at the goals that are set for people by Western culture, not only in their roles as, say, parents or citizens but as scientists.

In this regard, the philosopher Raimundo Panikkar (1986) observed that in Western societies the goal of science is to make practical contributions. Scientists are not educated simply to contemplate knowledge but to use it. The first and foremost question asked about new knowledge is "how can it be used?" Discoveries in chemistry and physics are rapidly applied to engineering, and discoveries in biology and biochemistry to medicine. Similar instances of the wedding of basic research with application can be found in the behavioral sciences. Ideas about intelligence produced the IQ test, the social psychology of leadership produced contingency leadership training, and theories of learning produced programmed instruction, to name but a few of the ways in which social science knowledge is used to solve practical problems.

The Purpose of Change

Given that social psychologists can change behavior, are there particular end states toward which these changes are directed? Is it to make people more altruistic, less aggressive, and more loving? Or is it, as Herman and Chomsky (1988) suggested in *Manufacturing Consent,* to make people more compliant to authority? Perhaps, it is simply to demonstrate that social psychology's knowledge base has matured to the point at which it can, if it chooses, change behavior.

A survey of contemporary applications of social psychology would suggest no simple answer. Some social psychologists apply psychological knowledge to reduce racial prejudice, others to help win elections, and still others to attract consumers to particular products. In the 1940s and 1950s, however, the first and second generations of social psychologists were in agreement about the uses of behavior change techniques. These social psychologists wanted to use them to produce a better world.

Gordon W. Allport (1947), in his inaugural speech as first president of the newly formed Division of Personality and Social Psychology of the American Psychological Association (APA), urged that social psychological knowledge be used to solve the many social problems facing society.

> In forming this Division we are . . . announcing, in effect, that as a group of scientists we believe we have a contribution to make in interpreting and in remedying some of the serious social dislocations of today. . . . The test of our fitness to exist and to prosper will be our ability to contribute substantially in the near future to the diagnosis and treatment of the outstanding malady of our time . . . the fact that man's moral sense is not able to assimilate his technology. (p. 82)

Allport (1947) went on to say that the problems spawned by modern technology—unemployment, wars, and more—problems that were produced by the physical sciences and that have overwhelmed society were not being addressed by the mental and moral sciences (i.e., social psychology). "What public officials want from social psychology is instant help . . . in the improvement and enlargement of man's moral sense and betterment of human relationships on an international scale" (p. 183).

Allport's (1947) address also called attention to the fact that until the early 1900s, psychology was commonly classified as a moral science. The goals of psychology, he argued, should be "to devise means to redirect human actions to be consistent with these moral roots" (p. 184).

In essence, Allport was calling for the use of psychological knowledge to reduce people's inhumanity toward each other. Although Allport was not specific about how social psychologists were to cure the social woes created by technology, his use of terms such as treatment and means to redirect human actions suggest some kind of engineering of human behavior to solve these problems. These engineering treatments, based on social psychological knowledge, would solve the many social problems created by technologies based on knowledge from the physical sciences. In other words, social psychology would provide technological "fixes" to undo the problems created by a technology based on the physical sciences.

Allport's address is remarkable on several counts. First, it is optimistic about what social psychology could do to solve social problems. If by social dislocations, Allport meant that social psychologists should devise remedies for the modern social plagues of poverty, discrimination, delinquency, violence, and loss of hope, he was showing great faith in the theories of social psychology. Underlying this optimism was the commonly shared belief of most people that technology, if properly used, could solve common human problems and so create a Utopia.

Second, Allport showed great temerity in suggesting that social psychology should espouse what today would be labeled mildly liberal views. In the mid-1940s, the Cold War was just beginning, and conservative legislators in Congress perceived such action-oriented speeches as reflecting a Marxist or socialist ideology in psychology. As Johnson (1992) pointed out, congressional opinion in the late 1940s was that the social sciences were radical. This view helped block, for 10 years, psychologists' attempts to receive federal research support.

Finally, Allport's address is remarkable for its bland assumption that psychologists had the right to change social behavior without the consent of the people whose behavior was to be changed.[1] Like the physicians in Ivan Illich's (1976) *Medical Nemesis,* Allport assumed that psychologists know what is best for society. That is, they have the right to decide what constitutes social diseases and how best to eliminate them.

Curing Social Ills

From the 1930s through the 1950s, much of the important research in social psychology was consistent with Allport's call to help humankind regain its moral roots and use knowledge to solve social problems. Systematic techniques were designed that sought, in President Franklin Roosevelt's words, "to cultivate the ability of all people, of all kinds, to live together and work together, in the same world, at peace" (quoted in Allport, 1947, p. 183).

Thus, Krech and Crutchfield (1948), in their innovative social psychology text, reported on means for reducing prejudice through educational techniques. Sherif, Harvey, White, Hood, and Sherif (1961) described techniques for eliminating intergroup conflict by creating crises that required the cooperative actions of previously conflicted groups. Kurt Lewin (1948) demonstrated the value of democratic, rather than autocratic, leadership. He also provided a theoretical rationale and accompanying procedures for reducing resistance of people to change. Chein, Cook, and Harding (1948) were involved in the development of action research techniques that would allow social psychologists to actively intervene in social problems, while still using the methods of science.

These were but a few of the many attempts to "redirect human actions so as to be consistent with their moral roots." Deutsch and Collins (1951) studied interracial housing as a means of reducing racial prejudice. Social psychologists' testimony before the U.S. Supreme Court contributed to overturning the country's segregated school system. During this time, the Society for the Psychological Study of Social Issues was formed to encourage research on moral issues, ranging from poverty to studies of inequality and injustice.

To this day, many social psychologists define social psychological theory in terms of wrongs that need to be righted. This tradition is reflected in chapters in modern social psychological textbooks that address problems of conflict, sexism, prejudice, cultural diversity, and inequality. And, as I discuss in the following section, the failure to maintain this tradition is a source of continuous criticism and debate among psychologists (e.g., Kidder & Fine, 1986; Prilleltensky, 1989; Sampson, 1978).

Social Psychology Redefined

Beginning in the 1950s, one could also find an ever-increasing number of research studies in social psychology that were not directly concerned with the pursuit of Allport's moral goals. Theoretical rather than practical studies became the vogue. These studies were concerned with understanding the psychological basis for social behavior. Practical studies that were reported focused on helping persons who could already help themselves (e.g., advertisers, managers, psychotherapists, labor mediators). The only constant trend from the 1930s to the 1960s, and later, was that most persons whose behavior was changed were not consulted.

In essence, beginning in the 1950s, social psychologists developed a new agenda for social psychology, in which solving social ills played a lesser role. Although I have no certain explanation for this shift, several related events may have contributed. For one, social psychological knowledge is probably inadequate, by itself, to unravel the complex causes of social ills. Second, many psychologists identify with a general model of science that is objective and value free. Allport's call for social psychological research that had a moral basis appears inconsistent with this value-free model of science. Third, the hostility of federal funding agencies to social science research suspected of being "politically left," and not "methodologically rigorous, objective . . . and important for national welfare and defense" (Johnson, 1992, p. 146), no doubt, encouraged social psychologists to alter their research agendas and their strategies of research. Finally, it is probable that many social psychologists did not share Allport's views.

For these reasons, and perhaps others, the times were right for the exciting theoretical explanations of social behavior offered from the late 1930s through the 1950s by Kurt Lewin. Lewin's ideas about how people perceived their worlds was the point of departure for a "new look" in social psychology. Behavior was explained in Lewin's scheme by tension systems, valences, and other hypothetical constructs that guided social behavior. Although Lewin stressed the impact of the environment on these psychological systems, in practice, real-world events became less important than how these events were perceived and then acted on. In essence, Lewin helped move social psychology from what in philosophy can be labeled a materialistic view of the world to an idealistic view (Fromm, 1969).

Subsequently, students and colleagues of Lewin used these ideas, along with their own, to explain social behavior. Such psychological constructs as dissonance, balance theory, attributions, expectations, cognitions, and beliefs about inequity soon competed with or complemented Lewin's explanations. Today, social psychologists are even seeking explanations of social behavior in evolutionary processes (Buss, 1990) and physiology (i.e., brain functioning and hormonal activity).

Thus, from a discipline oriented by its early leaders toward the solution of social problems, social psychology transformed itself into a discipline oriented toward explaining the psychological causes of social behavior. With this new orientation, the real world and events in it took second stage. Explanations of changes in social behavior were now in terms of the individual's psychology, rather than in terms of changes in society. Events such as unemployment, city crowding, crime, environmental events, and technology were only important to the extent that individuals responded to these events. To be sure, there was and is an active group of environmental social psychologists (e.g., Altman, 1975) who take into account the interplay between world events and individual psychology, but this group remains a minority.

The Experimental Study of Social Behavior

Along with the emphasis on social theory, social psychologists developed a range of sophisticated methodologies for testing their theories. Of all the methods that were developed, the experiment was (and still is) given priority as the way to demonstrate the validity of social psychological ideas.

The successful use of the experiment in learning and perception, no doubt, served as a model for social psychology. Also, leaders of social psychology, such as Kurt Lewin and Leon Festinger, vigorously championed the experiment as the means to clarify and test ideas about social behavior (Deutsch, 1992). In the laboratory, complex social behaviors could be turned on and off at will. One could examine, for example, whether people become more or less aggressive as they experience cognitive dissonance or whether they become more or less altruistic when they are paired with people who are similar or dissimilar to themselves. In short, the use of laboratory techniques allowed social psychologists to progress from simply observing life to controlling it.

It is not surprising that the use of the laboratory study also complements and reinforces social psychology's focus on the perception of events, rather than on the events themselves. This occurs because performing laboratory research requires investigators to spend most of their time in activities such as developing scenarios that selectively mimic events in larger society; making sure that psychological feelings, presumed to mediate responses to these events, are created (e.g., dissonance, expectancies); observing the reactions of college students to these events; and writing articles that describe the findings of these studies. These research activities leave little time to study social behavior outside of the laboratory.

Developing Behavior Technologies

From the 1950s on, it was apparent that the findings of social psychology could be used to solve practical problems. In Laudan's (1977) and Panikkar's (1986) terms, social psychology had become a useful science. By 1971, applications of social psychological knowledge had increased to the point that Jacobo Varela could summarize these efforts in his book *Psychological Solutions to Social Problems: An Introduction to Social Technology.* The book taught people how to use laboratory-validated techniques to persuade others, to resolve conflicts, to control people by Skinnerian conditioning techniques, to become an effective leader, and more.

Although Varela's (1971) book promised to solve social problems, the problems discussed were not Allport's social problems of society. Rather, the focus was on social problems caused by one person refusing or being unable to do what a second person wanted.

The book was only the beginning. Since its publication, behavior technologies have been developed that cause people to change their attitudes, be more persuasive, learn how to make friends, be better salespersons, communicate persuasively, be more restrained and less impulsive, be effective leaders, win elections, obey, or work effectively. Other behavior technologies have been developed to help management decide whom to hire, whom to fire, whom to promote, and what people like or dislike about their business firms or their products. Still other technologies have been developed with a more sinister bent, as for example, helping government agencies break down the beliefs of hostile people by using esoteric, mind-altering drugs and sensory deprivation.

In short, in almost all realms of human activities, behavior technologies have been developed to change social behavior, either with or without people's consent. Although some of these techniques were developed by clinical or organizational psychologists rather than social psychologists, I have listed them because they are used to change social behavior.

Power and Behavior Technology

Robert Dahl (1957) included among the elements of a power act that Person A causes Person B to do something that B would ordinarily not do. Substitute for Person A the term behavior technology, and we have a description of what behavior technologies do. In essence, behavior technologies are simply influence tactics developed through science, which agents use to give new direction to people's behavior.

At the beginning of this article I suggested that there are problems associated with the use of technology in society at large that may also arise with the use of behavior technology. These problems arise because of the close relation between technologies of all kinds and social power. I will discuss three related problems. The first concerns who decides what technologies should be developed and what technologies should not be developed, the second concerns the relation between technology and individual autonomy, and the third concerns the ethical neutrality of technology.

Why Some Technologies But Not Others

Earlier, I listed many of the behavior technologies that are currently in use. In this section, the questions are why were these diverse technologies developed and why were other equally useful technologies, such as those that might have solved Allport's "serious dislocations of today," not developed.

One explanation is that technologies are ways of building order in our worlds. The particular order that technology builds depends on the distribution of power and the exercise of control in society (Dickson, 1974; Mumford, 1967). Before time, money, and effort are invested in developing a new technology, be it new life-sustaining drugs, new computers, or new weapons, someone must decide that this development is to their benefit—not to the advantage of people in general but to the advantage of some specific person or group of persons.

Quite simply, most technologies are developed to sustain and promote the interests of the dominant social groups. The water mill was developed to increase the capacity of millers, the steam loom to improve the profitability of English manufacturers, and new drugs to increase the profits of drug firms. In other words, technologies are developed because people with power are experiencing problems that they want to solve. Although these technologies may benefit everyone over the long run, it is incorrect to believe that they are developed to increase the good life for all people. The actual uses of pure knowledge mainly reflect the interests of people whose opinions count.

These observations about power can be applied to the development of behavior technologies. Most are developed to strengthen existing social institutions, not to change them. Behavior technologies in such core areas of social psychology as leadership, motivation, social influence, persuasion, conformity, and conflict negotiation are used to help schools, businesses, and government agencies guide individual behavior in ways acceptable to those sponsoring institutions. For example, since the 1950s, the military establishment, research foundations, and businesses have generously funded the study of leadership. The findings of this research have spawned numerous behavior technologies that provide managers and military leaders with guidelines for maintaining the productivity of subordinates.

To be sure, the application of social psychological knowledge is not completely one-sided. The tradition of using psychological knowledge to solve Allport's "serious dislocations of our times" by working for the powerless still lives. McGuire's (1964) attempts to teach soldiers to resist brainwashing; Cialdini's (1985) techniques to help individuals recognize and resist persuasion tactics; and Aronson, Blaney, Stephan, Sikes, and Snapp's (1978) use of systematic procedures to reduce prejudice in classrooms typify the genuine concern of social psychologists for the well-being of people. However, I would describe these efforts as modest compared with the widespread use of social psychological knowledge to support rather than change existing institutions. Moreover, many technologies designed to help the powerless eventually are used by persons with power.[2]

Foucault (1980) remarked that all societies suppress knowledge and sentiments that do not support the existing social order. He argued that what the underclass knows, values, believes, and wants threatens the stability of the existing society. Approaching this issue from a psychological perspective, Kidder and Fine (1986) also described the reluctance of social researchers to conduct research supportive of the views of persons "outside" the system. I believe it is fair to say that no foundation would support, for instance, the development of behavior technologies that could be used by homeless people to gain admittance to our homes as guests or that workers could use to give the appearance of work without actually working. In other words, the research that we do not do, the behavior technologies that we do not build, are concerned with Foucault's suppressed knowledge. For the most part, research applications that validate the existing social order are supported.

I have already listed several reasons for the failure of Allport's plea that social psychologists should use their knowledge to reduce social ills. I now add what is perhaps the most important: That is, Allport did not take into account the realities of power and politics. The belief that research is directed to areas in which the needs are strongest is in the same class as the belief that Santa Claus comes at Christmas time. Allport failed to take into account the social class of the people who were hurting. He failed to reckon that when the parties who are hurting are without power, money, status, and clout, there is limited interest in supporting research to find solutions for their problems.

The point that social power guides the development of social theory and practice is hardly new. In one form or another, critics have suggested that psychology is the guardian of the status quo (e.g., Prilleltensky 1989; Sampson 1978; Sarason, 1981). What may be annoying in my discussion is the implication that psychologists are simply servants of power, eager to trade knowledge for money, perks, and status. This is not my intent. As I have written elsewhere (Kipnis, 1976), most people in Western society lead comfortable lives. As a result, the goal of persons in society, including behavioral scientists, is to maintain and improve this state of affairs. Accordingly, our efforts are directed toward binding people to society, rather than tearing society apart.

My intent in this section has been to make explicit the social and political forces that guide the development of behavior technologies. This leads to the next item for discussion: the circumstances under which behavior technology restrains or enhances individual freedom.

The Issue of Control

The question of how much freedom and how much control is best for people has been debated by social philosophers, by politicians, by psychologists (e.g., Brehm, 1966; Deci, 1992; Fromm, 1941; Rogers & Skinner, 1956; Seligman, 1975), and by people in general. Are people happier when they are told what to do or when they can decide for themselves? Is society better off when people are told what to do?

When the issue of control is examined in relation to behavior technology, we find that it provides increased freedom and choice for some but takes freedom and choice away from others.

The Winners

It is not surprising that behavior technology enriches the lives of people with power. It provides its sponsors and users with the significant advantage of being able to cause behavior in other people. Argyris (1975) reached a similar conclusion in his analysis of the research and theory of major social psychologists. He concluded that research in areas such as conformity, persuasion, and interpersonal attraction is designed to reduce free choice. Similarly, Zimbardo (1969) observed, "Control. That's what current psychology is all about. . . . It has become the all-consuming task of most psychologists to learn how to bring behavior under stimulus control" (pp. 237-238).

Neither Argyris nor Zimbardo considered who benefits from psychology's focus, although it is perhaps obvious. Technologies, such as management by objectives, contingency leadership, psychological tests to select and promote employees, and self-managed work teams, provide managers with a range of techniques for producing satisfied and productive employees. The newer techniques of psychotherapy, such as flooding, desensitization, and cognitive restructuring, have increased the range of treatment options for therapists. By providing greater control of clients, these newer techniques allow therapists to treat more patients more effectively and in a shorter period of time than was possible using the earlier psychodynamic techniques of therapy.

Similar benefits are found in marketing, in which systematic techniques of persuasion and attitude change have facilitated the sale of products by advertisers and sales personnel. Politicians and government agencies also have benefited from the use of behavior technologies. In the political realm, systematic techniques have been used to persuade voters and to promote support for government policies.

In short, behavior technologies provide people in positions of power with the ability to solve problems involving the exercise of influence. Using these techniques, target persons can be influenced to vote, buy products, work harder, feel better about themselves, and be more compliant, to name but a few of the many behaviors controlled by technology.

The Losers

From Karl Marx in the 19th century to Jacques Ellul (1964) today, a consistent criticism of technology has been that it deprives the ordinary citizen of the ability to behave as he or she might want. Sometimes this loss of freedom is the direct goal of the technology; at other times, the loss of freedom is simply an inadvertent by-product of using the technology (Crabb, 1992).

The reason why the targets of behavior technology lose freedom is because the easiest way to change behavior is to control it. To illustrate: Attitude-change technology works by restricting the alternatives that are available for people to consider when forming opinions, programmed instructions control the numbers of incorrect responses that trainees can make, operant conditioning ties desired rewards to compliance, and leadership technology teaches leaders to select the influence tactics most likely to control their subordinates. In short, a target person's freedom of choice is diminished by such means as disguising the influence attempt, reducing the options available to him or her, manipulating his or her psychological state, or increasing the costs of refusal.

Unnoticed or Welcomed Restraint

Although controlling behavior is a necessary ingredient of behavior technologies, most people do not experience its influence as coercive. In most instances, people barely notice that their behavior has been altered. In other instances, such as in psychotherapy, the changes produced are welcomed by clients.

In his well-known analysis of how to produce changes in behavior, Kurt Lewin (1948) stated that techniques that "push" people to change are experienced as coercive because most people resent being told that their behavior must change. Techniques that reduce restraints against change—for example, showing that people you respect are supporting the change and showing that change will allow you to grow, prosper, and be respected—are not experienced as coercive. Lewin's group techniques for changing behavior relied on these principles. By manipulating group consensus, he reported, it was possible to induce people to voluntarily change their behavior in the desired direction. Not only was change voluntary but the desired new behavior was maintained for some time afterward.

Most behavior techniques, then, are based on reducing restraints against change, rather than on pushing people to change. The description offered by Petty and Cacioppo (1981) of peripheral routes to attitude change helps us understand the reason why behavior technologies can change behavior with little discomfort being experienced. The peripheral route to attitude change is accomplished by distracting the person, so that the issues involved are distorted or there is no active thinking about the issues. For instance, Leon Festinger's (1957) research on cognitive dissonance pioneered in developing techniques that use the peripheral route for changing behavior. Festinger found this could be done by placing people in situations that forced them to believe they were behaving inconsistently. The human desire to act consistently was, for Festinger, the lever to change behavior in the direction desired by an influencing agent.

Psychological Costs of Using Behavior Technology

So far, the discussion of psychological costs has focused on persons who are the targets of the technology. Users of behavior technologies also experience costs, although they are, perhaps, not as obvious. In particular, users have difficulty maintaining cordial relations with persons they influence and in satisfying their personal need to express competence. These difficulties occur because the use of behavior technologies routinizes the influence process. That is, the skills needed to change a target person's behavior are contained in the technology. The job of the user is simply to follow the script provided by the technology and speak the lines it provides. One consequence is that users are no longer able to take credit for changing the target person's behavior. Rather, changes are seen as being caused by the technology.

Another consequence is that users gain little satisfaction from causing behavior in others. The experience is reported as bland, mechanical, and requiring little skill (Bramblett & Kipnis, 1993; O'Neal, Kipnis, & Craig, in press). Readers may recognize that these reports parallel those of organizational studies, which also find a negative relation between task routinization and job satisfaction (Blauner, 1964; Chadwick-Jones, 1969; Gutek & Winter, 1990).

Still another consequence of attributing control to the technology is that users evaluate target persons unfavorably. Users of such diverse behavior technologies as scientific management, leadership technology, cognitive behavior psychotherapy, and attitude-change technology have been found to devalue persons whose behavior was changed (Kipnis, 1993; O'Neal et al., in press). These findings reflect a general principle of social power research: We devalue the worth of persons who are perceived as not in charge of their own behavior.

The Ethics of Behavior Technology

I do not believe that it is necessary to spell out in any detail the ethical issues involved in using psychological knowledge to change people's behavior. Peripheral-route behavior technologies short-circuit free choice and undermine the democratic process when people's behavior is changed without their consent or knowledge. A cornerstone of the APA's statement about ethical research is that of informed consent. That is, people must be informed in advance of the manipulations to which they will be exposed. People must also be informed of any potential harmful effects.

When the applications of behavior technology are examined, investigators find that the principle of informed consent is largely ignored. I have attended psychology meetings at which the papers presented had titles such as "When and How Message Effectiveness Can Be Increased by Matching Appeals to Recipients' Personalities" and "The Effects of Different Communications and Type of Authority on the Motivation to Volunteer for Officer Training." Presumably, the application of these studies—to make people believe persuasive communications or to increase the rate of volunteering—would not involve asking recipients for permission first. Permission would not have been sought, because the behavior technologies were developed for parties whose goals differed from those who were to be influenced. It is hard to imagine an advertising firm asking consumers for permission to influence them.

The principle of informed consent may also be needed to protect users of behavior techniques. Any procedure in psychology that systematically causes people to dislike other people and to feel dissatisfied for no therapeutic purposes and without their informed consent must be viewed with suspicion.

What is to be done? One answer is, nothing. After all, the eventual use of any discovery, for better or worse, is beyond any single person's control. Another possibility, suggested by Perry London (1969), is to eliminate on ethical grounds technologies that restrain individual autonomy. Of course, this kind of radical surgery does not solve the social and ethical problems generated by behavior technologies. It merely buries them. At best, the autonomous individual is an ideal, with many virtues and some hidden faults (Hare-Mustin & Marecek, 1986; Monsma, 1986; White, 1967). Even if behavior technologies were eliminated, one would find that individual autonomy was still eroded by inequalities in power, by laws, by society's focus on competition and individual achievement, by the day-to-day demands of other people, and by our own feelings of inadequacy.

I do not expect solutions to the issues of power and control raised in this article. What remains bothersome, however, is the absence of debate by social psychologists about these issues. Do we need ethical guidelines? Should we build technologies to order for anybody who has money? Is it okay to develop techniques that brainwash people? Does the use of behavior technologies strengthen anti-democratic forces, as the historian William Graebner (1986, 1987a, 1987b) suggested. Are there ethical limits to the use of psychological knowledge? These kinds of questions need airing. I do not believe that the problems of ethics and control will go away by ignoring them or by saying "I only build them, but don't use them." This argument is about as disingenuous as "guns don't kill people, people do." There are ethical issues associated with both the construction and the use of technologies.

Concluding Observations

The working assumptions of an earlier generation of social psychologists have conspired to create a science whose underlying text is the study of power. These assumptions include the belief that psychological constructs are sufficient to explain social behavior; that social behavior can be controlled, both in the laboratory and in natural settings; and that social psychology should use its science to resolve social ills. Although this last assumption has not been universally accepted, the idea of changing social behavior to solve practical problems has become woven firmly into the assumptions of social psychology.

In this article, I have described some of the ethical and psychological problems inherent in the use of psychological knowledge to change behavior. One might argue that these problems simply reflect the workings of a conservative social psychology; that is, these problems would not occur if the goals of social psychology were directed toward remedying Allport's "serious dislocations of society." I do not agree. The problems I have described are just as likely to occur in a social psychology committed to the elimination of injustice as in a social psychology committed to maintaining the status quo. In other words, political ideology is not the cause of these problems; rather, the exercise of power is the cause.

Perhaps it is time to broaden our perspectives about the significant problems of social psychology. The most insistent demand on social psychology today is to provide a scientific account of how humans adapt, not only to each other but to our ever-changing social environment. I believe that the Lewinian paradigm of studying the relation between psychological states and social behavior has run its course. What remains to be answered is the question of how transactions with society change psychological states (i.e., people's beliefs and feelings). How we should approach this question is a matter of debate (see, e.g., Altman, 1975; Buss, 1990; Lana, 1991; Prilleltensky, 1989; Sampson, 1978; Sarason, 1981). My preference would be to examine how changes in technology alter people's feelings, beliefs, and interactions with others (Kipnis, 1991).

Less debatable is the need to reexamine the assumptions of social psychology. Can we obtain deeper understanding by including societal events as well as conscious events in our studies? Is it necessary for the findings of our science to produce winners and losers? Should we examine the ethical implications of changing behavior? I believe that spending time and money developing behavior technologies takes us far from the vision of the Enlightenment: people basing their lives on reason and the ability to think and choose for themselves.

Notes

1. Morton Deutsch (1975) has discussed the ethical dilemmas involved in using social psychological knowledge to influence people.

2. For example, in a late 1960s civil rights trial, Richard Christie and colleagues (Schulman, Shaver, Colman, Emrick, & Christie, 1973) developed a technique for identifying jurors likely to acquit a defendant charged with murder. Since then, techniques to identify friendly jurors have mainly been used by lawyers whose clients can afford the costs of using the technology.

References

Allport, G. (1947). The emphasis on molar problems. *Psychological Review, 54,* 182-192.

Altman, I. (1975). *The environment and social behavior.* Monterey, CA: Brooks/Cole.

Argyris, C. (1975). Dangers in applying results from experimental social psychology. *American Psychologist, 30,* 469-475.

Aronson, E., Blaney, N., Stephan, C., Sikes, J., & Snapp, M. (1978). *The jigsaw classroom.* Beverly Hills, CA: Sage.

Blauner, R. (1964). *Alienation and freedom.* Chicago: University of Chicago Press.

Bramblett, D., & Kipnis, D. (1993). *Psychotherapy as behavioral technology: Evidence for reduced job satisfaction from performing "high tech" therapy.* Manuscript submitted for publication.

Brehm, J. W. (1966). *A theory of psychological reactance.* San Diego, CA: Academic Press.

Buss, D. M. (1990). Evolutionary social psychology: Prospects and pitfalls. *Motivation and Emotions, 14,* 265-286.

Chadwick-Jones, J. K. (1969). *Automation and behavior: A social psychological study.* London: Wiley-Interscience.

Chein, I., Cook, S. W., & Harding, J. (1948). The field of action research. *American Psychologist, 3,* 43-50.

Cialdini, R. B. (1985). *Influence: Science and practice.* Glenview, IL: Scott, Foresman.

Crabb, P. (1992). Effective control of energy-depleting behavior. *American Psychologist, 47,* 815-816.

Dahl, R. A. (1957). The concept of power. *Behavioral Science, 2,* 201-218.

Deci, E. L. (1992). On the nature and function of motivation theories. *Psychological Science, 3,* 167-171.

Deutsch, M. (1975). Introduction. In M. Deutsch & H. A. Hornstein (Eds.), *Applying social psychology* (pp. 1-27). Hillsdale, NJ: Erlbaum.

Deutsch, M. (1992). Kurt Lewin: The tough-minded and tender-hearted scholar. *Journal of Social Issues, 48,* 11-44.

Deutsch, M., & Collins, M. E. (1951). *Interracial housing: A psychological evaluation of a social experiment.* Minneapolis: University of Minnesota Press.

Dickson, D. (1974). *Alternative technology and the politics of technical change.* Glasgow, Scotland: Fontana/Collins.

Ellul, J. (1964). *The technological society.* New York: Knopf.

Festinger, L. (1957). *A theory of cognitive dissonance.* Stanford, CA: Stanford University Press.

Foucault, M. (1980). Two lectures. In C. Gordon (Ed. and Trans.), *Power/knowledge: Selected interviews and other writings* (pp. 78-101). New York: Pantheon Books.

Fromm, E. (1941). *Escape from freedom.* New York: Holt, Rinehart & Winston.

Fromm, E. (1969). *Marx's concept of man.* New York: Ungar.

Graebner, W. (1986). The small group and democratic social engineering, 1900-1950. *Journal of Social Issues, 42,* 137-154.

Graebner, W. E. (1987a). Confronting the democratic paradox: The ambivalent vision of Kurt Lewin. *Journal of Social Issues, 43,* 141-146.

Graebner, W. E. (1987b). *The engineering of consent: Democracy and authority in twentieth century America.* Madison: University of Wisconsin Press.

Gutek, B., & Winter, S. J. (1990). Computer use, control over computers, and job satisfaction. In S. Oskamp & S. Spacapan (Eds.), *People's reactions to technology* (pp. 121-144). Newbury Park, CA: Sage.

Hare-Mustin, R. T, & Marecek, J. (1986). Autonomy and gender: Some questions for therapists. *Psychotherapy, 23,* 205-212.

Herman, E., & Chomsky, N. (1988). *Manufacturing consent.* New York: Pantheon.

Illich, I. (1976). *Medical nemesis.* New York: Random House.

Johnson, D. (1992). Psychology in Washington: Next to nothingness and being at the National Science Foundation. *Psychological Science, 3,* 145-149.

Kidder, L., & Fine, M. (1986). Making sense of injustice. In E. Seidman & J. Rappaport (Eds.), *Redefining social problems* (pp. 49-64). New York: Plenum.

Kipnis, D. (1976). *The powerholders.* Chicago: University of Chicago Press.

Kipnis, D. (1991). The technological perspective. *Psychological Science, 2,* 62-69.

Kipnis, D. (1993). Unanticipated consequences of using behavior technology. *Leadership Quarterly, 4,* 149-171.

Krech, D., & Crutchfield, R. S. (1948). *Theory and problems of social psychology.* New York: McGraw-Hill.

Lana, R. E. (1991). *Assumptions of social psychology: A reexamination.* Hillsdale, NJ: Erlbaum.

Laudan, L. (1977). *Progress and its problems.* Berkeley: University of California Press.

Lewin, K. (1948). *Resolving social conflicts.* New York: Harpers.

London, P. (1969). *Behavior control.* New York: Harper & Row.

McGuire, W. J. (1964). Inducing resistance to persuasion. In L. Berkowitz (Ed.), *Advances in experimental social psychology* (Vol. 1, pp. 191-229). San Diego, CA: Academic Press.

Monsma, S. V. (1986). *Responsible technology.* Grand Rapids, MI: Eerdmans.

Mumford, L. (1967). *The myth of the machine.* London: Seeker & Warburg.

O'Neal, E. C., Kipnis, D., & Craig, K. M. (in press). Effects on the persuader of employing a coercive influence technique. *Basic and Applied Social Psychology.*

Panikkar, R. (1986). Some theses on technology. *Logos, 7,* 115-25.

Petty, R. E., & Cacioppo, J. T. (1981). *Attitudes and persuasion.* Dubuque, IA: Brown.

Prilleltensky, I. (1989). Psychology and the status quo. *American Psychologist, 44,* 795-802.

Rogers, C., & Skinner, B. F. (1956). Some issues concerning the control of human behavior. *Science, 124,* 1057-1066.

Sampson, E. E. (1978). Scientific paradigms and social values: Wanted a scientific revolution. *Journal of Personality and Social Psychology, 36,* 1332-1343.

Sarason, S. B. (1981). *Psychology misdirected.* New York: Free Press.

Schulman, J., Shaver, P., Colman, R., Emrick, B., & Christie, R. (1973, May). Recipe for a jury. *Psychology Today,* pp. 37-44.

Seligman, M. E. (1975). *Helplessness.* San Francisco: Freeman.

Sherif, M., Harvey, Q., White, B., Hood, W., & Sherif, C. (1961). *Intergroup conflict and cooperation: The Robber's Cove experiment.* Norman, OK: Institute of Group Relations.

Varela, J. A. (1971). *Psychological solutions to social problems: An introduction to social technology.* San Diego, CA: Academic Press.

Watson, J. B. (1925). *Behaviorism.* New York: Norton.

White, L., Jr. (1967). The historical roots of our ecological crisis. *Science, 155,* 1205-1207.

Zimbardo, P. G. (1969). The human choice: Individuation, reason, and order versus deindividuation, impulse, and chaos. In W. J. Arnold & D. Levine (Eds.), *Nebraska Symposium on Motivation* (Vol. 17, pp. 237-307). Lincoln: University of Nebraska Press.

C. Looking at the Future of Health

25

Two Pathways to Prevention

Robert M. Kaplan

In January of 1998, Medicare expanded its coverage of preventive services. President Clinton introduced these changes during his weekly radio address on December 27, 1997, stating,

> On New Year's Day, we'll introduce a series of changes in Medicare that will make screening, prevention and detection of cancer more affordable and frequent. . . . By detecting cancer early on we offer our loved ones one of the greatest gifts of all—the gifts of life, health and many holidays to come. (*Office of the Press Secretary, The White House, 1997*)

To initiate the program, President Clinton ordered Medicare to cover annual mammograms for all women 40 years of age and older. The new policy also called for Pap smear tests for cervical cancer and pelvic examinations every 3 years, with annual tests for women at higher risk. Further, the new policies covered regular colorectal cancer screening, which improved upon previous policies that had covered only patients with symptoms.

It might be argued that many of these changes are moot. Medicare already covered mammograms and Pap smears for older women. The new policy initiated the use of mammography for women age 40 and above, revising the guideline that mammograms should begin at age 50. With only a few exceptions, however, Medicare is a program for people age 65 and over. Changing the threshold for mammograms from age 50 to age 40 affected very few Medicare recipients.

Despite affecting only a few people, the policy change was symbolic for two reasons. First, it represented the growing recognition that preventive medicine is important and that preventive services must be reimbursed. Supporting prevention is politically wise because voters believe in it. Second, the policy reflected the endorsement of a specific model of prevention. In this article, I argue that there are at least two pathways to prevention. One pathway is medical prevention that typically involves identifying an existent disease at an early

EDITORS' NOTE: From *American Psychologist, 55,* pp. 382-396.

stage and eliminating the problem before it gets out of control. In the public health vernacular, medical prevention is known as secondary prevention. An alternative pathway is primary prevention. Primary approaches to prevention require preventive maneuvers that reduce the chances that a health problem will ever develop. Primary prevention almost always requires behavior change, therefore, successful primary prevention efforts must use behavioral theories and behavioral interventions.

PRIMARY AND SECONDARY PREVENTION

The terms primary and secondary prevention can be confusing because they are used inconsistently. In the mental health literature, the term primary prevention is usually used as defined above, although there have been serious debates about terminology.[1] The World Health Organization (Pan American Health Organization, 1996) defines primary prevention as the prevention of the onset of the initial episode of disease. The term primordial prevention is used to describe the prevention of a risk factor (Labarthe, 1998). Secondary prevention is defined as the prevention of further episodes of disease. These definitions make disease and diagnosable risk factors central to the discussion. For example, saving lives by designing safer highways might not fit any of these categories because it does not prevent a disease or modify an individual risk factor (Spielberger & Frank, 1992). The definition of primary prevention in this discussion groups primordial and primary prevention together and includes prevention of disability or death from nondisease causes.

Primary and secondary prevention are different in a variety of ways. Secondary prevention is typically based on a traditional biomedical model that requires the diagnosis and treatment of an existing condition and that usually involves one or more of the following: medical diagnosis, surgery, or use of medications. Primary prevention is usually based on a behavioral rather than a disease model. Diagnosis plays a lesser role because there is no disease to diagnose. Intervention is typically behavioral and might include exercise, dietary change, or the avoidance or reduction of tobacco use. Interventions might also include public policy changes (Winett, 1995), regarding issues such as water sanitation or highway improvements (Albee, 1996).

Secondary prevention is often recognized by health insurance companies. The United States and Canada have developed preventive services guidelines which, for the most part, instruct physicians on how to make and implement early identification and treatment of existent disease states or how to use vaccines (U.S. Preventive Services Task Force, 1996). In these guidelines, the United States and Canada reviewed 50 different screening tests but found insufficient evidence to recommend most of them. In contrast to these guidelines, there is relatively little formal guidance or public support for primary prevention programs.

The purpose of this article is to argue that the traditional secondary prevention approach may produce relatively little public health benefit. In contrast, a primary prevention approach has substantial potential to enhance public health. In this article I use new conceptual models to show the potential of behavioral primary prevention efforts. However, to achieve the potential of primary prevention, researchers must first provide evidence that behavioral intervention results in public health benefit.

The two pathways to prevention arise from two fundamentally different paradigms: one medical and one behavioral. In the next sections, I consider these different models. First, however, I discuss the linear thinking that gives rise to the secondary prevention model.

Secondary Prevention and Mechanistic Thinking

The secondary prevention medical model builds upon traditional linear thinking (Ackoff, 1994). If a prostate gland is too large, it must be surgically reduced. If blood pressure is too high, it must be lowered, and if a child is hyperactive, he or she must be made less active. Certainly, mechanistic thinking has produced some sensational successes (Checkland, 1994). Many patients benefit from hernia repairs, total joint replacement, and pharmaceutical control of blood pressure. However, repairing a problem in one part of the body often creates a new problem in another part of the system. For example, a surgery for severe lung disease might have a high chance of repairing the lung problem. However, the procedure might also cause problems with other organs and carries risk of death from surgical complications or adverse effects of the anesthesia. For example, patients disabled from emphysema may benefit from a new surgical technique; however, nearly 5% may die during or shortly after the surgery, and 15% may die within the first year (Brenner et al., 1999). Side effects from medications and complications from surgery are common.

An alternative view, known as the outcomes model, arises from a behavioral tradition. The outcomes model regards the human body as a system that cannot be divided into component parts. Although the outcomes model is similar to the traditional biomedical model, its objective is to treat the person rather than the disease. The goal of health care is to extend the duration of life or to improve the quality of life. Disease processes are of interest because pathology may either shorten life expectancy or make life less desirable. The same variables that predict disease process may also predict life expectancy or quality of life. However, in contrast to the traditional biomedical model, behaviors or biological events may affect life expectancy independently of disease process. Further, the measures of success in the outcomes model are different than those in the traditional biomedical model. The outcomes model emphasizes quality of life and life duration instead of clinical measures of disease process. Prevention can be secondary or primary, and attention is given to efforts that produce the longest life and highest life quality. Prevention can involve medical intervention, behavioral intervention, or changes in public policy. In contrast to the medical model that treats disease, the outcomes model treats the person or a population of people.

How the Outcomes Model Leads to Different Decisions Than the Traditional Biomedical Model

Although the traditional biomedical model and the behavioral outcomes model are similar in many ways, they lead to different decisions about the use of resources for prevention. In the following sections, several examples of these models are reviewed.

The secondary prevention model is based on medical diagnoses. A diagnosis defines the problems that have been found and gives direction concerning what needs to be fixed. The medical care system pays providers for using diagnostic tests to find problems and for using therapeutic interventions to fix the problems. Despite its importance, diagnosis often obscures or confuses the importance of some health problems. There are at least three reasons why focusing on diagnosis may have led the medical community in some wrong directions. First, diagnoses do not always lead to better health outcomes. Often, people are placed in categories, but identification of a condition does not necessarily mean that an effective treatment can be applied. Second, diagnoses are not always correct. Some individuals will be treated for conditions they do not have, and others will fail to be effectively treated because the correct diagnosis was missed. Third, in many cases, poor health outcomes result from risky behavior or from exposure to risk factors. Public health can be enhanced by removing the risk factor or by modifying behavior. The identification of a disease on the pathway between the risk factor and the outcome is interesting but not essential. Although investing more in the early identification and treatment of cancer might increase average life expectancy, the same benefits might also be achieved by investments to reduce cigarette use, to build safer roads, or to make firearm access difficult.

The secondary prevention model has appeal because it fits the linear thinking that predominates health care. However, in spite of this logical appeal, the public health benefits of secondary prevention have been limited, at least from an outcomes perspective. A few case studies are considered in this article.

Conceptualizing Benefits

Recently, the Institute of Medicine of the National Academy of Sciences (Field & Gold, 1998) reviewed measures of population health. The report suggested that policies designed to improve the health of populations have focused on death from diseases such as smallpox and cholera. Priorities for health care programs have traditionally been set in relation to the ability to limit deaths. However, most interventions in health care are designed to go further than the prevention of early death: Health care also involves preventing disability, improving functioning, relieving pain, addressing mental health concerns, and helping people cope with the symptoms of illness. To accurately compare primary and secondary prevention efforts, researchers must have models to conceptualize and measure health benefits. In contrast to the traditional medical model that quantifies cases of disease, the outcomes model evaluates health care according to how much health is produced. A disease or an environmental exposure is of concern if it reduces health. Treatments do not necessarily convey benefit, even if they eliminate a specific disease. By eradicating one disease, the treatment may create other problems, such that total health is reduced.

To understand health outcomes, it is necessary to build a comprehensive theoretical model of health status. The major aspects of the model include mortality (death) and morbidity (health-related quality of life). Diseases and disabilities are important for two reasons. First, illness may cause the life expectancy to be shortened. Second, illness may diminish the health-related quality of life, making life less desirable (Kaplan & Anderson, 1996; Kaplan, Sieber, & Ganiats, 1997). Environmental exposures or risky health behaviors might reduce life expectancy or quality of life, even if researchers do not understand their specific effects upon the disease process (Winett, 1995). Treatments may make life better or longer, even though researchers do not understand the mechanisms through which they influence a biological process. However, to understand health outcomes, it is necessary to quantify health using measures that do not necessarily depend upon medical diagnosis.

Some outcomes measurement models are refinements of generic survival analysis. In traditional survival analysis, those who are alive are statistically coded as 1.0, whereas those who are dead are statistically coded as 0.0. Mortality can result from any disease, and survival analysis allows comparison between different diseases. For example, the life expectancy for those who will eventually die of heart disease can be stated and compared with the life expectancy of those who will eventually die of cancer. Thus, there is an advantage over disease-specific measures, such as measures of blood output from the heart and tumor size. The difficulty with a survival measurement model is that everyone who remains alive is given the same score. A person confined to bed with an irreversible coma is alive and is counted the same as someone who is actively participating in athletics. Utility assessment allows the quantification of levels of wellness on the continuum anchored by death and optimum function.

Quality-adjusted life years (QALYs) are measures of life expectancy with adjustments for quality of life (Gold, Siegel, Russell, & Weinstein, 1996; Kaplan, Alcaraz, Anderson, & Weisman, 1996; Kaplan & Anderson, 1996). QALYs integrate mortality and morbidity to express health status in terms of equivalents of well years of life. If a woman dies of breast cancer at age 50 and one would have expected her to live to age 75, the disease was associated with 25 lost life years. If 100 women died at age 50 (and also had life expectancies of 75 years), 2,500 (100 × 25 years) life years would be lost.

Death is not the only outcome of concern in cancer. Many people suffer from disabling effects over long periods of time; although still alive, the quality of their lives diminishes. QALYs take into consideration the quality of life consequences of these illnesses and their treatments. For example, a disease that reduces quality of life by one half will take away 0.5 QALYs over the course of one year. If it affects two people, it will take away 1 QALY (2 × 0.5) over a one-year period. A pharmaceutical treatment that improves quality of life by 0.2 for each of five individuals will result in the equivalent of 1 QALY if the benefit is maintained over a one-year period. The basic assumption is that two years scored as 0.5 QALYs add up to the equivalent of one year of complete wellness. Similarly, four years scored as 0.25 QALYs are equivalent to one completely well year of life. A treatment that boosts a patient's health from 0.5 to 0.75 for one year produces the equivalent of 0.25 QALYs. If applied to four individuals and if the duration of the treatment effect is one year, the effect of the treatment would be equivalent to one completely well year of life (1 QALY). This system has the advantage of considering both benefits and side effects of programs in common terms: the common QALY units. Although QALYs are typically assessed for patients, they can also be measured for others, including caregivers who are placed at risk because they experience stressful life events.

Although treatment programs provide health benefits, they also have costs. Resources are limited, and good policy requires that their allocation maximize life expectancy and health-related quality of life. Methodologies for estimating costs have now become standardized (Gold et al., 1996). From an administrative perspective, cost estimates include all costs of treatment and any costs associated with caring for side effects of treatment. Typically, economic discounting is applied to adjust for using current assets to achieve a future benefit. From a social perspective, costs are broader and may include costs of family members taking time off of work to provide care. When comparing treatment programs for a given population with a given medical condition, cost-effectiveness is measured as the change in costs of care for the program compared with the existing therapy or program, relative to the change in health measured in a standardized unit such as the QALY. The difference in costs over the difference in effectiveness is the incremental cost/effectiveness and is usually expressed as the cost/QALY. Since the objective of all programs is to produce QALYs, the cost/QALY ratio can be used to show the relative health benefits from investing in different programs (Kaplan & Anderson, 1996).

There are several concerns about the way cost/effectiveness analysis has been applied to the analysis of prevention programs. Although it is widely proclaimed that preventive mental health services save money, few mental illness prevention programs have been evaluated using the same standards as those applied in other areas of preventive medicine. One of the difficulties is that many cost/benefit studies have failed to include the societal perspective (Russell, 1986). According to this strategy, cost accounting must consider all the costs and effects of the program, regardless of who pays for them and who benefits from them. It includes everyone the intervention affects. For example, if a prevention program saves money for Medicare because diseases are prevented but costs money for employers, both are counted. Similarly, if saving money by not paying for services makes Medicare costs go up, both savings and losses are considered. Some programs benefit one group of people but harm others because there is no money left to pay for their care. The societal perspective argues that both harms and benefits must be considered.

Some evaluations of health services have considered only the deferred costs of those who eventually get sick. However, it costs money to employ people to screen for health problems and to provide care. Extra care requires extra expenditures. For screening programs, it is important to consider all of the costs of screening and all of the costs of any additional care that is provided. For preventive programs, one must recognize that most of the people who are treated (with preventive measures) would never have developed a problem even if they were left alone. One interesting example concerns the prediction of violent behavior. Recent violent episodes in schools have increased the demands to identify and treat those at risk for such violent behavior. The problem is that predicting dangerousness is difficult. Early reviews of the literature (Monahan, 1981) suggested that psychiatrists and psychologists were only slightly better than chance in predicting violent behavior among institutionalized populations. Only about one in three of their predictions of violent behavior proved accurate (Monahan, 1981). In the past two decades, there have been significant improvements in predictions of dangerousness. Predictions are now significantly better than chance but still tend to be highly inaccurate (Borum, 1996; Monahan & Steadman, 1996). Although accuracy of predicting arrest or readmission to psychiatric hospitals for violent behavior has greatly improved (Steadman et al., 1998), risks for violent behavior in the general population remain relatively low. As a result, simple screening tests are likely to seriously overidentify potentially violent individuals. This has become a civil rights issue because of suggestions that those deemed at risk for violent behavior be required to receive treatment or even be restricted in their activities. Screening high school students for violence potential will identify many adolescents eligible for treatment. Whether or not the investment in screening and treatment will result in reduced violent behavior has never been demonstrated. The primary prevention model argues that the screening phase may be unnecessary and that the focus should instead be on the best use of resources. Alternatives (to screening) might include weapons detection and strict gun control legislation. Neither of these require a diagnosis. Although data are not currently available, the outcomes model would ask which approach achieved the greatest public benefit, given the available resources.

In the following sections, the outcomes model is used to evaluate three approaches to secondary prevention and three approaches to primary prevention.

Evaluation of Secondary Prevention

There are numerous secondary prevention procedures in contemporary health care. Three procedures were chosen for this discussion: screening for breast cancer, screening for prostate cancer, and screening for high cholesterol. These examples were chosen because each is widely accepted and commonly advocated as a component of preventive medicine. Before presenting evidence on the cost/effectiveness of each program, some general background on the controversies surrounding screening is offered.

Disease Reservoir Hypothesis

According to the American Cancer Society (1999), screening and early detection of cancers save lives. It is believed that there is a reservoir of undetected disease that might be eliminated through more aggressive intervention. Screening guidelines have been proposed, and those who fail to adhere to these guidelines are regarded as irresponsible.

For one to better understand the problem, it is necessary to understand the natural history of disease. Public health campaigns assume that disease is binary: either a person has the "diagnosis" or he or she does not. However, most diseases are processes. It is likely that chronic disease begins long before it is diagnosed. For example, autopsy studies consistently show that most young adults who died early in life from noncardiovascular causes have fatty streaks in their coronary arteries, indicating the initiation of coronary disease (Strong et al., 1999). Not all people who have a disease will ultimately suffer from the problem. With many diseases, most of those affected will never even know they are sick.

Among those who do have problems, some may not benefit from treatment. For example, if smokers are screened for lung cancer, many cases can be identified. However, clinical trials have shown that the course of the disease is likely to be the same for those who are screened and those not subjected to screening, even though screening leads to more diagnosis and treatment (Sanderson, 1986). There may be large reservoirs of disease that can be detected through screening: Very high proportions of elderly (older than age 75) women have ductile breast cancer in situ, and nearly 40% of elderly men may have prostate cancer (Coley, Barry, Fleming, & Mulley, 1997). The harder researchers look, the more likely it is that cases of disease will be found. However, only about 3% of elderly men will die of prostate cancer, and only about 3% of elderly women will die of breast cancer. A very sensitive test for prostate cancer may detect disease in 10 men for each 1 man who will eventually die of this condition. These problems are not limited to cancer. Advanced magnetic-resonance-imaging technology has revealed surprisingly high rates of undiagnosed stroke. One cross-sectional study of 3,502 men and women over age 65 found that 29% had evidence of mild strokes and that 75% had plaque in their carotid arteries (Manolio et al., 1999).

Black and Welch (1997) made the distinction between disease and pseudodisease. Pseudodisease is disease that will not affect life duration or quality of life at any point in a patient's lifetime. When the disease is found, it is often "fixed" with surgical treatment. However, the fix may have consequences, often leaving the patient with new symptoms or problems. The outcomes model considers the benefits of screening and treatment from the patient's perspective. Often, using information provided by patients, one can estimate the quality-adjusted life expectancy for a population and determine if that population is better off with or without screening and treatment (Kaplan, 1997).

There may be analogies between screening for disease and screening for mental health problems. For example, the current epidemic of depression may result from greater public sensitivity and more screening. The Medical Outcomes Study (Wells, 1997) found that the prevalence of minor depression in primary care clinics was nearly 25%, whereas the prevalence in mental health clinics was 60%. The reservoir of children who could be diagnosed with attention deficit hyperactivity disorder (ADHD) could be huge. In one county-wide screening program, half of the children in special education qualified for a diagnosis of ADHD (Bussing, Zima, Perwien, Belin, & Widawski, 1998). Evidence does not clearly demonstrate whether more aggressive screening and treatment of ADHD will result in improvements in population health status.

Prostate Cancer Screening

The disease reservoir hypothesis helps explain controversies surrounding several cancer screening tests. One example of the differences between the traditional secondary prevention (biomedical model) and the outcomes models concerns screening and treatment for prostate cancer. Most cancer prevention efforts follow a traditional "find it-fix it" secondary prevention model. The identification of cancer dictates treatment, which in turn is evaluated by changes in biological process or disease activity. In the case of prostate cancer, a digital rectal exam may identify an asymmetric prostate, leading to a biopsy and the identification of prostate cancer. Diagnosis of cancer often leads to a radical prostatectomy (surgical removal of the prostate gland). The success of the surgery would be confirmed by eradication of the tumor, reduced prostate-specific antigen (PSA), and patient survival.

In contrast to this traditional biomedical model, an outcomes perspective embraces public health notions of benefit. Instead of focusing on disease process, benefit is defined in terms of life duration and quality of life. Studies have demonstrated that serum PSA is elevated in men with clinically diagnosed prostate cancer (Hudson, Bahnson, & Catalona, 1989) and that high PSA levels have positive predictive value for prostate cancer. Despite the promise of PSA screening, there are also significant controversies. Prostate cancer is common for men age 70 years and older (Lu-Yao, Barry, Chang, Wasson, & Wennberg, 1994). Averaging data across eight autopsy studies, Coley, Barry, Fleming, Fahs, and Mulley (1997) estimated the prevalence of prostate cancer to be 39% in 70- to 79-year-old men. The treatment of this disease varies dramatically from country to country and within regions of the United States. For example, radical prostatectomy is done nearly twice as often in the Pacific Northwest as it is in New England. Yet, survival rates and deaths from prostate cancer are no different in the two regions (Fleming, Wasson, Albertsen, Barry, & Wennberg, 1993). PSA screening finds many cases. However, in the great majority of cases, the men would have died of another cause long before developing their first symptom of prostate cancer.

Several decision models have been developed to evaluate the value of screening and treatment of prostate cancer. One model considered three options for the treatment of prostate cancer: radical prostatectomy, external-beam-radiation therapy, and "watchful waiting." Both radical prostatectomy and radiation therapy carry high risks of complications that may reduce life satisfaction. For example, there are significant increases in the chances of becoming impotent, incontinent, or both (Flood et al., 1996; Fowler, Barry, Lu-Yao, Wasson, & Bin, 1996). Watchful waiting, on the other hand, does not require therapy but only evaluation and supervision by a physician. The watchful waiting option has been used least often because it does not treat the cancer.

Similar decision models have been used to evaluate screening for prostate cancer. When QALYs are used as an outcome measure, simulations suggest there are few benefits of screening. For example, Krahn et al. (1994) estimated the population benefit of programs to screen 70-year-old men for prostate cancer. They found that the benefits, on average, were improvements in the life expectancy from a few hours to two days. However, when they adjusted the life expectancy for quality of life, they discovered that screening programs actually reduced quality-adjusted life days. The reason for this negative impact is that screening identifies many men who would have died of other causes. These men, once identified with prostate cancer, are then likely to engage in a series of treatments that would significantly reduce their quality of life. For these men, the treatment causes harm without producing substantial benefits. Because the traditional model and the outcomes model focus on different outcome measures, they come to different conclusions about the value of screening.

Screening for Breast Cancer

The use of screening mammography for women 40-50 years of age is another secondary prevention controversy. Mammography has become the "poster child" of secondary prevention. In 1997, President Clinton used his endorsement of mammography for women 40 years of age and older as evidence supporting his commitment to preventive medicine (Office of the Press Secretary, The White House, 1997). Early in the Clinton administration, it was recommended that the age to initiate mammography be set at 50. As a result of this decision, Clinton was attacked for being against preventive medicine (Kaplan, 1998; Navarro & Kaplan, 1996). However, the public health benefit of promoting screening mammography for 40- to 50-year-old women may be somewhat limited. All clinical trials and meta-analyses have failed to show a population benefit of screening women in this age group (Fletcher, 1997; Kerlikowske, Grady, Rubin, Sandrock, & Ernster, 1995).

In January of 1997, the National Institutes of Health convened a panel to make recommendations about the use of screening mammography for women 40-50 years of age. In contrast to diagnostic testing used when a woman is in a high risk group or has felt a lump, screening mammography is used to evaluate asymptomatic women. The conclusion of the panel review shocked the American Cancer Society. The headline of *USA Today* (January 24, 1997) read, "Mammogram Panel Only Adds to Furor." Commentators on morning talk shows were outraged by the committee's decision. Richard Klausner, the director of the National Cancer Institute, decided to disregard the report of his own expert panel. Shortly thereafter, the American Cancer Society appointed a panel of experts chosen because each already believed that screening was valuable for 40- to 50-year-old women. To no one's surprise, this American Cancer Society panel recommended that 40- to 50-year-old women be screened (Fletcher, 1997).

The cost/effectiveness of mammography has been estimated in several analyses. These analyses are difficult because most meta-analyses fail to show that screening mammography has any benefit for 40- to 49-year-old women (there is little debate about the value of screening for women 50-69 years of age). Under the assumption of no benefit, the cost/QALY goes toward infinity because the model would require division by zero. Using studies suggesting some benefit of mammography for women 40-49 years of age, Eddy (1989) estimated the cost to produce a QALY as $240,000. Salzmann, Kerlikowske, and Phillips (1997) used newer data to evaluate the cost/effectiveness of guidelines requiring screening for women 40-49 years of age. They noted that screening women 50-64 years of age produces a QALY at about $21,400. By contrast, the expected benefit of screening women 40-49 years of age increases life expectancy by only 2.5 days at a cost of $676/woman, resulting in an incremental cost utility of $105,000/QALY.

Stable mortality rates appear to contradict the suggestion that survival from cancer is increasing and is attributable to better screening and treatment (American Cancer Society, 1999). Although there appeared to be a small increase in prostate cancer deaths in the 1980s, the mortality rate has since declined and may have been an artifact (Henkey et al., 1999). The disease reservoir hypothesis would argue that screening changes the point at which disease is detected (lead time) without necessarily changing the course of the illness. If the date of death is unchanged, earlier detection will make the interval between diagnosis and death appear longer. This is known as lead time bias.

Cholesterol Screening

There are many reasons why the public has become weary of recommendations offered by providers. For example, the National Cholesterol

Education Program (1994) developed detailed guidelines on screening for high cholesterol. A national campaign was developed that emphasized that all Americans should be screened for high cholesterol. The evidence supporting that campaign came from two sources. First, epidemiologic investigations have shown significant correlations between elevated serum cholesterol and deaths from coronary heart disease (Grundy et al., 1998). Second, clinical trials have demonstrated that reductions in total cholesterol and in the low-density lipoprotein subfraction of cholesterol resulted in reductions in deaths from coronary heart disease (Grundy, 1998). The national policy was based on the mechanistic thinking that high cholesterol is bad and lower cholesterol improves health status. Consumers were led to believe that those with elevated cholesterol were likely to die of heart disease whereas those with normal levels would survive.

Many difficulties in these analyses have now become apparent. First, the National Cholesterol Education Program recommended cholesterol screening tests for all Americans, independent of age, gender, or ethnicity ("Report of the National Cholesterol Education Expert Panel," 1988). However, the clinical trials supporting the policies were based exclusively on middle-aged men, and there was no specific evidence for children or for older adults (Kaplan, 1985; Russell, 1994). A second concern was that systematic clinical trials consistently failed to demonstrate improvements in life expectancy resulting from cholesterol lowering (Kaplan, 1984). In all clinical trials, reductions in deaths from heart disease were offset by increases in deaths from other causes (Muldoon, Manuck, & Matthews, 1990). For example, the Coronary Primary Prevention Trial showed that a drug effectively lowered cholesterol in comparison to placebo. Further, those taking the cholesterol-lowering medication were significantly less likely to die of heart disease than were those taking the placebo. However, over the time period these participants were followed, there were more deaths from other causes among those taking the drug, and the chances of being alive were comparable in the two groups (Lipid Research Clinics Program, 1984). More recent evidence also demonstrates systematic increases in deaths from other causes for those taking cholesterol-lowering agents. Biological mechanisms for these increases have been proposed (Golomb, 1998).

There have been several cost/utility analyses of cholesterol screening and treatment. Goldman, Weinstein, Goldman, & Williams (1991) modeled the value of screening for high cholesterol and treatment with the latest 3-hydroxy-3-methylglutaryl-coenzyme A (HMG CoA) reductase inhibitor (in this case, Lovastatin). Their model considered recurrent heart attack rates using data from the Framingham Heart Study. One simulation considered men with total cholesterol values in excess of 300 mg/dl but with no other risk factors for heart disease. For these men, the cost to produce a year of life was estimated to be between $71,000 and $135,000. For women, estimates ranged from $84,000 to $390,000 per life year. If the threshold for initiating treatment is lowered to 250 mg/dl, the cost to produce a year of life increases to between $105,000 and $270,000 for men. Recent campaigns have attempted to increase the number of adults undergoing treatment. Until recently, the threshold for a diagnosis of hypercholesterolemia was 240 mg/dl. Under that definition, about one in five adults qualified. In line with the more recent push toward defining high cholesterol as greater than 200 mg/dl, about half of all adults can be deemed abnormal (Fisher & Welch, 1999). However, as shown by the simulations, the lower the diagnostic threshold, the less cost/effectiveness screening and treatment will be.

Primary Prevention Approaches

In contrast to secondary prevention, several primary prevention approaches should also be considered. Three examples are reviewed: tobacco use, physical activity, and injury control. These were selected because, like the secondary prevention procedures, they have received considerable public attention. However, these primary prevention efforts require behavior change rather than medicine or surgery, and health care providers typically cannot be reimbursed for offering programs relevant to any of these problems.

Tobacco Control

In the late 1970s, two eminent British epidemiologists were retained by the National Cancer Institute to evaluate evidence on the causes of cancer. After detailed and extensive study, it was estimated that about 30% of cancer deaths in the United States were attributable to cigarette smoking. Health habits, including nutritional practices, accounted for most of the cases of cancer (Doll & Peto, 1981). Tobacco use not only causes cancer but also is a primary cause of emphysema and cardiovascular disease. There have been several attempts to compare investments in primary versus secondary prevention of cardiovascular disease. In one analysis, Taylor, Pass, Shepard, and Komaroff (1987) compared three different approaches: cholesterol reduction, blood pressure reduction, and smoking prevention. They found that both cholesterol reduction and blood pressure treatment, two well-established secondary prevention approaches, produce relatively little benefit in comparison with smoking prevention programs. Cholesterol reduction has very little impact on life expectancy, particularly if it begins at age 60. In fact, cholesterol reduction programs may add only about two months of life for a 60-year-old man. Smoking prevention programs may produce a full five years of life for those individuals prevented from smoking by age 20. The Taylor et al. analysis (1987) is informative but does not take into consideration the costs of interventions. In a more recent analysis, Brown and Garber (1998) also found the cost/effectiveness of brief behavioral interventions for smoking cessation to offer superior cost/effectiveness ratios than several approaches used in cholesterol lowering.

The Food and Drug Administration has evaluated the cost/effectiveness of restricting tobacco sales to minors. The study assumed that the restrictive policies might reduce tobacco use among minors by 25%. The analysis considered the cost of such a program to tobacco manufacturers, retailers, consumers, and federal agencies. Because reduced tobacco use would have substantial public health benefits, the analysis estimated that the cost/QALY would be less than $1,000 (Graham, Corso, Morris, Segui-Gomez, & Weinstein, 1998; U.S. Food and Drug Administration, 1996). Kaplan, Ake, Emery, and Navarro (1999) evaluated the impact of tobacco tax and found that tax increases result in significant increases in both QALYs and revenues.

In an analysis of the potential for smoking-cessation programs, the Agency for Health Care Policy and Research considered the impact of applying its "Smoking Cessation Clinical Practice Guideline" to the U.S. population (Fiore, 1997). The report identified 15 different smoking-cessation guidelines, ranging from minimal counseling to intensive counseling. Each intervention was considered with or without concomitant use of nicotine replacement in the form of gum or nicotine patches. The analysis assumed that the interventions would be available to 75% of adult smokers, which corresponds to the proportion that have made a previous attempt to quit. The model assumes that the program would yield 1.7 million new quitters, of whom 40% would have quit on their own and 60% may have been influenced in some way by the program to quit. Further, the model assumed that 9% of smokers would quit with no intervention, 11% would quit with minimal counseling, 12% would quit with brief counseling, and 19% would quit with counseling lasting more than 10 minutes. Use of a nicotine replacement would boost these effects further. The program would cost an estimated $6.3 billion, or about $32 per smoker. Cost per QALY was estimated at $1,915. Considering a variety of assumptions, the cost/QALY ranged from $1,108 to $4,542, placing it well below most programs that have been analyzed (Cromwell, Bartosch, Fiore, Hasselblad, & Baker, 1997).

Physical Activity

Research (e.g., Blair et al., 1989; Blair & Brodney, 1999) shows that people who are physically active live significantly longer than those who are sedentary. These studies have documented a relationship between physical activity and mortality from coronary heart disease, diabetes mellitus, cystic fibrosis, and all causes (Sallis & Owen, 1999). In addition to living longer, those who engage in regular physical activity may be better able to perform activities of daily living and enjoy many aspects of life. Further, those who exercise regularly have better insulin sensitivity and less abdominal obesity (Kahn, Tatham, & Heath, 1997; Manson et al., 1992). Regular exercise has been shown to improve psychological well-being for those with mood disorders (Morgan, 1994). Some evidence suggests that the costs of poor health outcomes associated with physical inactivity exceed those attributable to obesity, hypertension, and smoking (Francis, 1996). The Centers for Disease Control estimate that physical inactivity is the most common among risk factors for heart disease and carries a greater population-attributable risk than does high cholesterol or hypertension. Successful programs have been developed to promote exercise for the general population (Dunn et al., 1997). Further, specific interventions have been developed for those diagnosed with particular diseases (Sallis & Owen, 1999).

Despite the benefits of exercise, few people will start an exercise program, and many of those who start do not continue to exercise (Dishman & Buckworth, 1996). Some predictors of failure to exercise regularly include being overweight, low socioeconomic status, female gender, and smoking (Sallis, Zakarian, Hovell, & Hofstetter, 1996). However, the most commonly reported barriers to exercise are lack of time and inaccessibility of facilities. Studies show that exercise patterns change as people age. Physical activity begins to decline by the late teens and early twenties (Physical Activity and Cardiovascular Health, 1995). It appears that Americans are shifting toward less vigorous activity patterns, with walking becoming the most common form of exercise. Physical inactivity is increasing as Americans spend more time watching television, working with computers, or doing both (Sallis & Owen, 1999).

To estimate the cost/utility of exercise programs, Hatziandreu, Koplan, Weinstein, Caspersen, and Warner (1988) developed a computer simulation model. The computer model created two hypothetical cohorts of 35-year-old men and followed them for 30 years. The model was calculated for 1,000 men who were assumed to jog regularly and another 1,000 men who were assumed to be inactive. In addition to the health benefits of exercise, negative effects were subtracted from the benefits. These included injuries and low adherence. Costs included costs of running equipment, costs of treating injuries, and the value of the time spent exercising. The costs of treating heart disease for those estimated to be affected were also included. The analysis showed that jogging reduces heart disease, so money is saved for those who exercise regularly. The analysis suggested that regular exercise produces a QALY for about $11,313. In other words, the cost to produce a year of life is quite low relative to most medical and secondary prevention efforts.

Safety

A variety of analyses have considered the cost/effectiveness of primary prevention interventions that have nothing to do with the health care system (for a review, see Tengs et al., 1995). These make interesting comparisons because the programs share the common goal of extending the quality-adjusted life expectancy. However, the resources used to achieve this goal are not directly related to health care, and medical diagnosis has no role in program development. Williams and Lancaster (1995) evaluated the benefits of daytime use for running lights on automobiles. If drivers used these lights, it would cost less than $3 per vehicle, per year. The added costs occur because of greater fuel consumption. The authors assumed that daytime use of these lights would be associated with a 10% reduction in vehicle crashes. The analysis demonstrated that daytime use of running lights could produce a QALY at essentially no cost. Graham et al. (1998) evaluated a variety of other safety measures including laws requiring lap and shoulder belts in automobiles (with the assumption that they are used only 50% of the time) and compulsory use of helmets for motorcyclists. All of these programs produced a QALY at essentially no cost. There are some programs that may be quite expensive to produce a QALY. For example, the 55 mph speed limit in comparison with the 65 mph speed limit (for rural interstate highways) may cost about $82,000 to produce a QALY. Frontal air bags in comparison with seat belts would cost about $24,000 to produce a QALY.

What Does This Mean for Psychologists?

The preceding sections cover a broad range of topics relevant to outcomes of preventive programs, but what does this discussion mean for psychologists and other behavioral scientists? At least four separate messages can be found.

Message 1: Evaluations of prevention services often confuse primary and secondary programs. Methodologies comparing the cost/QALY are important for helping researchers understand the most appropriate way to use health care resources. Several primary prevention programs produce QALYs at very little cost. Many traditional secondary prevention programs have produced few, if any, measurable benefits. Yet, secondary prevention efforts form the core of current health care policy in prevention. This has led some authors to challenge the value of prevention. For example, Russell (1986) found in her book *Is Prevention Better Than Cure?* little evidence to support prevention programs. Later, Russell (1994) raised serious questions about prevention programs that use medical-screening tests. Yet nearly all of her analyses focused on prevention programs designed to detect and treat a disease that already exists. Russell's books have been very influential and are commonly cited as evidence that prevention does not work. However, the arguments are drawn principally from secondary prevention—primary prevention was not discussed or evaluated in any detail.

Message 2: Primary prevention must be recognized as distinct from health care. If primary prevention efforts produce health, scientists and researchers should find ways to support them. Some researchers have also suggested there is a need for greater focus on primary prevention. For example, Bailar and Gornik (1997) analyzed progress in the war on cancer that was initiated by President Richard Nixon in 1970. In considering changes in mortality since 1970, Bailar and Gornik concluded that cancer has not been defeated. The find it-fix it model has found and treated significantly more cancer, but the increased treatment has not produced clear public health benefits. Bailar and Gornik argued that it is time to reevaluate the dominant strategy of the past 40 years that placed most emphasis on improving treatments and secondary prevention and little emphasis on primary prevention. The major increases in cancer have been associated with cigarette smoking (Doll & Peto, 1981). Analysis of trends in U.S. cancer deaths suggests that over the 46 years between 1950 and 1996, changes in all deaths from cancer are attributable largely to variations in lung cancer. Lung cancer death rates are driven to a large extent by smoking rates and are not greatly affected by screening and treatment. Yet, few resources have been devoted to the eradication of tobacco products. Bailar and Gornik (1997) concluded, "A national commitment to prevention of cancer, largely replacing reliance on hopes for universal cures, is now the way to go" (p. 1574).

Message 3: More resources should be devoted to primary prevention research. The comparison between primary and secondary prevention is difficult because there have been few experimental trials that evaluate primary prevention interventions. The observational data suggest that behavioral factors, such as physical activity, have strong relationships to health outcome. However, some biological variables, such as high serum cholesterol, were also highly correlated with poor health outcomes. When experimental trials attempted to show that reducing cholesterol would increase life expectancy, the results were unimpressive. It is possible that intervention trials on large-scale behavior change will also fail to fulfill their promise. To date, results of community-wide intervention trials have often produced benefits that were less than expected (Luepker et al., 1996). On the other hand, there are few known risks of these interventions. Rose (1992), the noted British epidemiologist, suggested that controlled clinical trials must demonstrate that benefits exceed risks, except when the intervention restores people to a biological evolutionary norm. These norms include higher levels of physical activity and consumption of less saturated fat and more vegetables. Certainly, humans did not evolve to smoke cigarettes, and little harm would be done by returning to a more natural tobacco-free state.

One must recognize that prevention research is difficult. A committee of the Institute of Medicine of the National Academy of Sciences (1994) systematically reviewed research on prevention of mental disorders. Although optimistic about the value of preventive interventions, the committee concluded that significantly more research was necessary. The evidence base for the value of preventive interventions in mental health was even less well developed than the knowledge base for evaluating programs to prevent physical illness. To understand the value of preventive interventions, the committee strongly recommended the development of offices for the prevention of mental disorders at the state level. The committee also suggested increased funding for prevention research and more training of experts in the field. The committee proposed the development of more systematic experimental trials in which participants are randomly assigned to treatments and assessed at multiple points in time. The report recognized the need to consider preventive interventions that address the overlap between physical and mental health. Population studies that characterize the natural history of mental health problems were also advocated. Enacting this change will be challenging because prevention research is difficult. Quality research requires long-term follow-up, and the application of traditional experimental designs is usually not feasible. In many studies, substantial proportions of the original samples are lost to follow-up, and missing data are common. Nevertheless, methodologies for community-based prevention studies are advancing, and there are now many good examples (Israel, Schulz, Parker, & Becker, 1998; Sorensen, Emmons, Hunt, & Johnston, 1998).

The Centers for Disease Control and Prevention have shown considerable interest in behavioral intervention (Snider & Satcher, 1997), and funding is now available for some behavioral programs (Roberts, Banspach, & Peacock, 1997; Rugg, Levinson, DiClemente, & Fishbein, 1997). These efforts are among the first to break away from the disease-oriented model (Galavotti, Saltzman, Sauter, & Sumartojo, 1997). Nevertheless, many of the programs emphasize diagnosis rather than behavioral outcome. True primary prevention studies may take decades to complete and require the cooperation of large numbers of investigators as well as long-term funding. Documentation that interventions change risk factors is important but not sufficient. Truly effective interventions must affect long-term outcomes and must be shown to be safe. Treatments may show positive effects in the short run. However, long-term effects of treatments, particularly those requiring medications, must be carefully studied.

Message 4: Prevention must be recognized in public health policy. Using measures of combined life expectancy and quality of life, one can assess the global effects of different approaches to health care. On the basis of these methods, the productivity of secondary prevention in terms of QALYs has been quite limited. Although less formally evaluated, it appears that the potential benefit of primary prevention may be substantial. Another way to consider the benefit of preventive actions is to estimate the days of life they are expected to produce. For secondary prevention efforts, these estimates have been modest. For example, PSA screening for 70-year-old men extends the life expectancy by 0.2 days (less than five hours; Krahn et al., 1994). Mammography screening for 50-year-old women may extend the life expectancy by 24 days, but screening for women between 40 and 50 may yield only a few days (Lindfors & Rosenquist, 1995). Lowering cholesterol to 200 mg/dl for those at moderate risk for heart disease (200-240 mg/dl), according to low estimates, produces no life expectancy benefit (Golomb, 1998) and, according to high estimates, offers moderate benefits of 180 days (Tsevat, Weinstein, Williams, Tosteson, & Goldman, 1991). On the other hand, participation in regular exercise starting at age 35 offers benefits of 186 days (Hatziandreu et al., 1988). Smoking cessation, according to the lowest estimates, offers 300 days (Tsevat, 1992) and, according to high estimates, can extend life expectancy by 1,800 days (Taylor et al., 1987).

One recent review of the cost/effectiveness of strategies to prevent heart disease claimed to compare primary and secondary prevention strategies. The interventions included approaches to smoking, exercise, hormone replacement, hypertension, and high cholesterol. Smoking-cessation programs, particularly those using behavioral interventions without nicotine supplements, were the most cost-effective among the alternatives (Brown & Garber, 1998). Despite these analyses, public policy does not clearly recognize smoking-cessation programs because they do not fit the diagnosis and treatment model. For example, Medicare pays for medical and some surgical treatment for people with emphysema. However, it does not support modification of smoking behavior because tobacco use is not a disease. To change this policy, some have tried to convert tobacco use to the "disease" of nicotine addiction (Henningfield & Slade, 1998). Under its authorizing legislation, Medicare cannot pay for prevention services because there is no medical diagnosis. To even consider preventive services, Medicare requires evidence of cost neutrality, which means that the services will not add costs. When analyzed this way, very few services could meet the cost-neutral criterion. Yet, when analyzed as health return for the investment, the cost/QALY for smoking-cessation programs shows that such programs are a better use of resources than treating nearly any disease.

Conclusion

It is not known whether primary prevention programs will produce large public health benefit because few experimental trials have been completed. However, there are many reasons to believe that primary prevention will pay substantial dividends. Primary prevention is about the prevention of disease. Primary prevention does not necessarily follow the dictates of the traditional biomedical model. It does not depend on diagnosing problems, nor does it depend on therapy. Secondary prevention involves detecting and treating disease that already exists. Current policy favors secondary prevention in health care, even though the payoff from secondary prevention appears to be quite limited. Conversely, primary prevention still remains outside the core of health care and public policies to improve health. Although the traditional biomedical model emphasizes secondary prevention, there are at least two pathways to prevention. Although evidence is still incomplete, the primary prevention pathway may offer the most health at the lowest cost. There are two paths to prevention, and as a rich country, the United States can afford to follow both during the extended time it will take to evaluate the value of primary prevention.

Note

1. A 1994 report from the Institute of Medicine of the National Academy of Sciences (IOM) divided the spectrum of mental health into prevention, treatment, and maintenance. Prevention was further divided into (a) universal programs, (b) programs directed at selective subgroups of the population, and (c) programs directed at those who already had some diagnosis (Munoz, Mrazek, & Haggerty, 1996). Indicated preventive interventions were defined as those targeted at high risk people who had minimal but detectable symptoms of illness. The IOM report spurred some disagreement. Heller (1996) leaned toward supporting preventive programs targeted at high-risk individuals. However, Albee (1996) attacked the disease-oriented model that dominated most prevention sciences. Albee emphasized that the report had a "disorder orientation" (p. 1131). Recognizing the long history of primary prevention efforts, Albee argued that the most important prevention programs do not require a diagnosis. Quoting Senator Daniel Inouye, Albee cited the most important contributions of public health as not involving a diagnosis. These included water quality, improved sewer systems, better nutrition and food, and loving attention of infants and children. Perhaps because of these disagreements, the IOM classification system has rarely been used.

References

Ackoff, R. L. (1994). Systems thinking and thinking systems. *System Dynamics Review, 10,* 175-188.

Albee, G. W. (1996). Revolutions and counterrevolutions in prevention. *American Psychologist, 51,* 1130-1133.

American Cancer Society. (1999). *Cancer facts and figures—1999* [Brochure]. Atlanta, GA: Author.

Bailar, J. C. & Gornik, H. L. (1997). Cancer undefeated. *New England Journal of Medicine, 336,* 1569-1574.

Black, W. C. & Welch, H. G. (1997). Screening for disease. *American Journal of Roentgenol, 168,* 3-11.

Blair, S. N. & Brodney, S. (1999). Effects of physical inactivity and obesity on morbidity and mortality: Current evidence and research issues. *Medicine and Science in Sports and Exercise, 31,* Suppl. 11 S646-S662.

Blair, S. N., Kohl, H. W., Paffenbarger, R. S., Clark, D. G., Cooper, K. H. & Gibbons, L. W. (1989). Physical fitness and all-cause mortality: A prospective study of healthy men and women. *JAMA, 262,* 2395-2401.

Borum, R. (1996). Improving the clinical practice of violence risk assessment: Technology, guidelines, and training. *American Psychologist, 51,* 945-956.

Brenner, M., McKenna, R. J., Chen, J. C., Osann, K., Powell, L., Gelb, A. F., Fischel, R. J. & Wilson, A. F. (1999). Survival following bilateral staple lung volume reduction surgery for emphysema. *Chest, 115,* 390-396.

Brown, A. D. & Garber, A. M. (1998). Cost effectiveness of coronary heart disease prevention strategies in adults. *Pharmacoeconomics, 14,* 27-48.

Bussing, R., Zima, B. T., Perwien, A. R., Belin, T. R. & Widawski, M. (1998). Children in special education programs: Attention deficit hyperactivity disorder, use of services, and unmet needs. *American Journal of Public Health, 88,* 880-886.

Checkland, P. (1994). Systems theory and management thinking. *American Behavioral Scientist, 38,* 75-91.

Coley, C. M., Barry, M. J., Fleming, C., Fahs, M. C. & Mulley, A. G. (1997). Early detection of prostate cancer: Part II. Estimating the risks, benefits, and costs—American College of Physicians. *Annals of Internal Medicine, 126,* 468-479.

Coley, C. M., Barry, M. J., Fleming, C. & Mulley, A. G. (1997). Early detection of prostate cancer: Part I. Prior probability and effectiveness of tests—The American College of Physicians. *Annals of Internal Medicine, 126,* 394-406.

Cromwell, J., Bartosch, W. J., Fiore, M. C., Hasselblad, V. & Baker, T. (1997). Cost-effectiveness of the clinical practice recommendations in the AHCPR guideline for smoking cessation: Agency for Health Care Policy and Research. *JAMA, 278,* 1759-1766.

Dishman, R. K. & Buckworth, J. (1996). Increasing physical activity: A quantitative synthesis. *Medicine and Science in Sports and Exercise, 28,* 706-719.

Doll, R. & Peto, R. (1981). The causes of cancer: Quantitative estimates of avoidable risks of cancer in the United States today. *Journal of the National Cancer Institute, 66,* 1191-1308.

Dunn, A. L., Marcus, B. H., Kampert, J. B., Garcia, M. E., Kohl, H. W. & Blair, S. N. (1997). Reduction in cardiovascular disease risk factors: 6-month results from Project Active. *Preventive Medicine, 26,* 883-892.

Eddy, D. M. (1989). Screening for breast cancer. *Annals of Internal Medicine, 111,* 389-399.

Field, M. J. & Gold, M. R. (1998). *Summarizing population health.* (Washington, DC: Institute of Medicine).

Fiore, M. C. (1997). AHCPR smoking cessation guideline: A fundamental review. *Tobacco Control, 6,* 2, Suppl. 1 S4-S8.

Fisher, E. S. & Welch, H. G. (1999). Avoiding the unintended consequences of growth in medical care: How might more be worse? *JAMA, 281,* 446-453.

Fleming, C., Wasson, J. H., Albertsen, P. C., Barry, M. J. & Wennberg, J. E. (1993). A decision analysis of alternative treatment strategies for clinically localized prostate cancer: Prostate Patient Outcomes Research Team. *JAMA, 269,* 2650-2658.

Fletcher, S. W. (1997). Whither scientific deliberation in health policy recommendations? Alice in the Wonderland of breast-cancer screening. *New England Journal of Medicine, 336,* 1180-1183.

Flood, A. B., Wennberg, J. E., Nease, R. F., Fowler, F. J., Ding, J. & Hynes, L. M. (1996). The importance of patient preference in the decision to screen for prostate cancer: Prostate Patient Outcomes Research Team. *Journal of General Internal Medicine, 11,* 342-349.

Fowler, F. J., Barry, M. J., Lu-Yao, G., Wasson, J. H. & Bin, L. (1996). Outcomes of external-beam radiation therapy for prostate cancer: A study of Medicare beneficiaries in three surveillance, epidemiology, and end results areas. *Journal of Clinical Oncology, 14,* 2258-2265.

Francis, K. (1996). Physical activity in the prevention of cardiovascular disease. *Physical Therapy, 76,* 456-468.

Galavotti, C., Saltzman, L. E., Sauter, S. L. & Sumartojo, E. (1997). Behavioral science activities at the Centers for Disease Control and Prevention: A selected overview of exemplary programs. *American Psychologist, 52,* 154-156.

Gold, M. R., Siegel, J. E., Russell, L. B. & Weinstein, M. C. (1996). *Cost-effectiveness in health and medicine.* New York: Oxford University Press.

Goldman, L., Weinstein, M. C., Goldman, P. A. & Williams, L. W. (1991). Cost-effectiveness of HMG-CoA reductase inhibition for primary and secondary prevention of coronary heart disease. *JAMA, 265,* 1145-1151.

Golomb, B. A. (1998). Cholesterol and violence: Is there a connection? *Annals of Internal Medicine, 128,* 478-487.

Graham, J. D., Corso, P. S., Morris, J. M., Segui-Gomez, M. & Weinstein, M. C. (1998). Evaluating the cost-effectiveness of clinical and public health measures. *Annual Review of Public Health, 19,* 125-152.

Grundy, S. M. (1998). Hypertriglyceridemia, atherogenic dyslipidemia, and the metabolic syndrome. *American Journal of Cardiology, 81,* 18B-25B.

Grundy, S. M., Balady, G. J., Criqui, M. H., Fletcher, G., Greenland, P., Hiratzka, L. F., Houston-Miller, N., Kris-Etherton, P., Krumholz, H. M., LaRosa, J., Ockene, I. S., Pearson, T. A., Reed, J., Washington, R. & Smith, S. C. (1998). Primary prevention of coronary heart disease: Guidance from Framingham—A statement for healthcare professionals from the AHA Task Force on Risk Reduction–American Heart Association. *Circulation, 97,* 1876-1887.

Hatziandreu, E. I., Koplan, J. P., Weinstein, M. C., Caspersen, C. J. & Warner, K. E. (1988). A cost-effectiveness analysis of exercise as a health promotion activity. *American Journal of Public Health, 78,* 1417-1421.

Heller, K. (1996). Coming of age of prevention science: Comments on the 1994 National Institute of Mental Health—Institute of Medicine prevention reports. *American Psychologist, 51,* 1123-1127.

Henkey, B. F., Feuer, E. J., Clegg, L. X., Hayes, R. B., Legler, J. M., Prorok, P. C., Ries, L. A., Merrill, R. M. & Kaplan, R. S. (1999). Cancer surveillance series: Interpreting trends in prostate cancer—Part I. Evidence of the effects of screening in recent prostate cancer incidence, mortality, and survival rates. *Journal of the National Cancer Institute, 91,* 1017-1024.

Henningfield, J. E. & Slade, J. (1998). Tobacco-dependence medications: Public health and regulatory issues. *Food and Drug Law Journal, 53,* Suppl. 3 75-114.

Hudson, M. A., Bahnson, R. R. & Catalona, W. J. (1989). Clinical use of prostate specific antigen in patients with prostate cancer. *Journal of Urology, 142,* 1011-1017.

Institute of Medicine of the National Academy of Sciences. (1994). *Reducing risks for mental disorders: Frontiers for preventive intervention research* (P. J. Mrazek & R. J. Haggerty, Eds.). Washington, DC: National Academy Press.

Israel, B. A., Schulz, A. J., Parker, E. A. & Becker, A. B. (1998). Review of community-based research: Assessing partnership approaches to improve public health. *Annual Review of Public Health, 19,* 173-202.

Kahn, H. S., Tatham, L. M. & Heath, C. W. J. (1997). Contrasting factors associated with abdominal and peripheral weight gain among adult women. *International Journal of Obesity and Metabolic Disorders, 21,* 903-911.

Kaplan, R. M. (1984). The connection between clinical health promotion and health status. A critical overview. *American Psychologist, 39,* 755-765.

Kaplan, R. M. (1985). Behavioral epidemiology, health promotion, and health services. *Medical Care, 23,* 564-583.

Kaplan, R. M. (1997). Decisions about prostate cancer screening in managed care. *Current Opinion in Oncology, 9,* 480-486.

Kaplan, R. M. (1998). Breast cancer screening: When to begin? In E. A. Blechman & K. D. Brownell (Eds.), *Behavioral medicine and women: A comprehensive handbook* (pp. 213-220). New York: Guilford Press.

Kaplan, R. M. (1999). Shared medical decision making: A new paradigm for behavioral medicine. *Annals of Behavioral Medicine, 21,* 3-11.

Kaplan, R. M., Ake, C., Emery, S. & Navarro, A. M. (1999). *Simulation of tobacco tax variation upon population health in California.* (Manuscript submitted for publication)

Kaplan, R. M., Alcaraz, J. E., Anderson, J. P. & Weisman, M. (1996). Quality-adjusted life years lost to arthritis: Effects of gender, race, and social class. *Arthritis Care and Research, 9,* 473-482.

Kaplan, R. M. & Anderson, J. P. (1996). The general health policy model: An integrated approach. In B. Spilker (Ed.), *Quality of life and pharmacoeconomics in clinical trials* (pp. 309-322). New York: Raven.

Kaplan, R. M., Orleans, C. T., Perkins, K. A. & Pierce, J. P. (1995). Marshaling the evidence for greater regulation and control of tobacco products: *A call for action. Annals of Behavioral Medicine, 17,* 3-14.

Kaplan, R. M., Sieber, W. J. & Ganiats, T. G. (1997). The Quality of Well-Being Scale: Comparison of the interviewer-administered version with a self-administered questionnaire. *Psychology and Health, 12,* 783-791.

Kerlikowske, K., Grady, D., Rubin, S. M., Sandrock, C. & Ernster, V. L. (1995). Efficacy of screening mammography: A meta-analysis. *JAMA, 273,* 149-154.

Krahn, M. D., Mahoney, J. E., Eckman, M. H., Trachtenberg, J., Pauker, S. G. & Detsky, A. S. (1994). Screening for prostate cancer: A decision analytic view. *JAMA, 272,* 773-780.

Labarthe, D. (1998). *Epidemiology and prevention of cardiovascular diseases: A global challenge.* Gaithersburg, MD: Aspen.

Lindfors, K. K. & Rosenquist, C. J. (1995). The cost-effectiveness of mammographic screenings strategies. *JAMA, 274,* 881-884.

Lipid Research Clinics Program. (1984). The Lipid Research Clinics Coronary Primary Prevention Trial results: I. Reduction in incidence of coronary heart disease. *JAMA, 251,* 351-364.

Luepker, R. V., Råstam, L., Hannan, P. J., Murray, D. M., Gray, C., Baker, W. L., Crow, R., Jacobs, D. R., Pirie, P. L., Mascioli, S. R., Mittelmark, M. B. & Blackburn, H. (1996). Community education for cardiovascular disease prevention: Morbidity and mortality results from the Minnesota Heart Health Program. *American Journal of Epidemiology, 144,* 351-362.

Lu-Yao, G. L., Barry, M. J., Chang, C. H., Wasson, J. H. & Wennberg, J. E. (1994). Transurethral resection of the prostate among Medicare beneficiaries in the United States: Time trends and outcomes–Prostate Patient Outcomes Research Team (PORT). *Urology, 44,* 692-698.

Manolio, T. A., Burke, G. L., O'Leary, D. H., Evans, G., Beauchamp, N., Knepper, L. & Ward, B. (1999). Relationships of cerebral MRI findings to ultrasonographic carotid atherosclerosis in older adults: The Cardiovascular Health Study–CHS Collaborative Research Group. *Arteriosclerosis, Thrombosis, and Vascular Biology, 19,* 356-365.

Manson, J. E., Nathan, D. M., Krolewski, A. S., Stampfer, M. J., Willett, W. C. & Hennekens, C. H. (1992). A prospective study of exercise and incidence of diabetes among U.S. male physicians. *JAMA, 268,* 63-67.

Monahan, J. (1981). *The clinical prediction of violent behavior* (DHHS Publication No. ADM 81-921). Rockville, MD: U.S. Department of Health and Human Services.

Monahan, J. & Steadman, H. J. (1996). Violent storms and violent people: How meteorology can inform risk communication in mental health law. *American Psychologist, 51,* 931-938.

Morgan, W. P. (1994). Psychological components of effort sense. *Medicine and Science in Sports and Exercise, 26,* 1071-1077.

Muldoon, M. F., Manuck, S. B. & Matthews, K. A. (1990). Lowering cholesterol concentrations and mortality: A quantitative review of primary prevention trials. *British Medical Journal, 301,* 309-314.

Munoz, R. F., Mrazek, P. J. & Haggerty, R. J. (1996). Institute of Medicine report on prevention of mental disorders: Summary and commentary. *American Psychologist, 51,* 1116-1122.

National Cholesterol Education Program. (1994). Second report of the expert panel on detection, evaluation, and treatment of high blood cholesterol in adults. *Circulation, 89,* 1333-1445.

Navarro, A. M. & Kaplan, R. M. (1996). Mammography screening: Prospects and opportunity costs. *Women's Health: Research on Gender, Behavior, and Policy, 2,* 209-233.

Office of the Press Secretary, The White House. (1997, December 27). *Radio address of the president to the nation* [Press release]. Washington, DC: Author. Retrieved March 8, 2000, from the World Wide Web: http://www.pub.whitehouse.gov/urires/I2R?urn:pdi://oma.eop.gov.us/1997/12/27/1.text.

Pan American Health Organization. (1996). *Health promotion: An anthology* (PAHO Scientific Publication 557). Washington, DC: Author.

Physical activity and cardiovascular health: National Institutes of Health Consensus Development Conference statement (1995, December 18-20). [Statement]. Retrieved March 9, 2000, from the World Wide Web: http://text.nlm.nih.gov/nih/cdc/www/101.html

Report of the National Cholesterol Education Program Expert Panel on detection, evaluation, and treatment of high blood cholesterol in adults. (1988). *Archives of Internal Medicine, 148,* 36-39.

Roberts, G. W., Banspach, S. W. & Peacock, N. (1997). Behavioral scientists at the Centers for Disease Control and Prevention: Evolving and integrated roles. *American Psychologist, 52,* 143-146.

Rose, G. A. (1992). *The strategy of preventive medicine.* New York: Oxford University Press.

Rugg, D. L., Levinson, R., DiClemente, R. & Fishbein, M. (1997). Centers for Disease Control and Prevention partnerships with external behavioral and social scientists: Roles, extramural funding, and employment. *American Psychologist, 52,* 147-153.

Russell, L. B. (1986). *Is prevention better than cure?* Washington, DC: Brookings Institution Press.

Russell, L. B. (1994). *Educated guesses.* Berkeley, CA: University of California Press.

Sallis, J. F. & Owen, N. (1999). *Physical activity and behavioral medicine.* Thousand Oaks, CA: Sage.

Sallis, J. F., Zakarian, J. M., Hovell, M. F. & Hofstetter, C. R. (1996). Ethnic, socioeconomic, and sex differences in physical activity among adolescents. *Journal of Clinical Epidemiology, 49,* 125-134.

Salzmann, P., Kerlikowske, K. & Phillips, K. (1997). Cost-effectiveness of extending screening mammography guidelines to include women 40 to 49 years of age. *Annals of Internal Medicine, 127,* 955-965.

Sanderson, D. (1986). Lung cancer screening: The Mayo study. *Chest, 4,* Suppl. 324S.

Snider, D. E. & Satcher, D. (1997). Behavioral and social sciences at the Centers for Disease Control and

Prevention: Critical disciplines for public health. *American Psychologist, 52,* 140-142.

Sorensen, G., Emmons, K., Hunt, M. K. & Johnston, D. (1998). Implications of the results of community intervention trials. *Annual Review of Public Health, 19,* 379-416.

Spielberger, C. D. & Frank, R. G. (1992). Injury control: A promising field for psychologists. *American Psychologist, 47,* 1029-1030.

Steadman, H. J., Mulvey, E. P., Monahan, J., Robbins, P. C., Appelbaum, P. S., Grisso, T., Roth, L. H. & Silver, E. (1998). Violence by people discharged from acute psychiatric inpatient facilities and by others in the same neighborhoods. *Archives of General Psychiatry, 55,* 393-401.

Strong, J. P., Malcom, G. T., McMahan, C. A., Tracy, R. E., Newman, W. P., Herderick, E. E. & Cornhill, J. F. (1999). Prevalence and extent of atherosclerosis in adolescents and young adults: Implications for prevention from the Pathobiological Determinants of Atherosclerosis in Youth Study. *JAMA, 281,* 727-735.

Taylor, W. C., Pass, T. M., Shepard, D. S. & Komaroff, A. L. (1987). Cholesterol reduction and life expectancy: A model incorporating multiple risk factors. *Annals of Internal Medicine, 106,* 605-614.

Tengs, T. O., Adams, M. E., Pliskin, J. S., Safran, D. G., Siegel, J. E., Weinstein, M. C. & Graham, J. D. (1995). Five hundred life-saving interventions and their cost-effectiveness. *Risk Analysis, 15,* 369-390.

Tsevat, J. (1992). Impact and cost-effectiveness of smoking interventions. *American Journal of Medicine, 93,* 43S-47S.

Tsevat, J., Weinstein, M. C., Williams, L. W., Tosteson, A. N. & Goldman, L. (1991). Expected gains in life expectancy from various coronary heart disease risk factor modifications. *Circulation, 83,* 1194-1201.

U.S. Food and Drug Administration. (1996, August 15). *Regulations restricting the sale and distribution of cigarettes and smokeless tobacco to protect children and adolescents, Final Rule, 21 C.F.R.* (Pts. 801, 803, 807, 820, & 897, RIN 0910-AA48). Federal Register.

U.S. Preventive Services Task Force. (1996). *Guide to clinical preventive services: Report of the U.S. Preventive Services Task Force* (2nd ed.). Baltimore: Williams & Wilkins.

Wells, K. B. (1997). Caring for depression in primary care: Defining and illustrating the policy context. *Journal of Clinical Psychiatry, 58,* Suppl. 1 24-27.

Williams, A. F. & Lancaster, K. A. (1995). The prospects of daytime running lights for reducing vehicle crashes in the United States. *Public Health Reports, 110,* 233-239.

Winett, R. A. (1995). A framework for health promotion and disease prevention programs. *American Psychologist, 50,* 341-350.

26

The Threat of Biological Weapons

Prophylaxis and Mitigation of Psychological and Social Consequences

Harry C. Holloway, Ann E. Norwood, Carol S. Fullerton, Charles C. Engel Jr., and Robert J. Ursano

Biological weapons have emerged as a significant threat in the 1990s.[1-2] Other reports in this issue have established the potential likelihood of the use of biological weapons and the nature of the biological and toxic threats. Herein, we discuss the psychophysiological and social implications of such agents and propose recommendations for developing primary interventions and treatment.

Psychological Responses Following a Biological Attack

The idea of infection caused by invisible agents is frightening. It touches a deep human concern about the risk of being destroyed by a powerful, evil, imperceptible force. These beliefs activate emotions that are extremely difficult to direct with the tools of reason. The response of specialists in

EDITORS' NOTE: From the *Journal of the American Medical Association, 278,* 1997, pp. 425-427. Reprinted with permission.

medicine, epidemiology, infectious disease, molecular biology, nursing, and emergency medical services can bring some discipline and rationality to this situation. To be effective, the response must be well organized, and communication must be made in terms that the public understands. Multiple organizations with conflicting and overlapping goals and responsibilities (e.g., health care, law enforcement, and social welfare) may increase the confusion and anxiety for the individual and community. The novelty of biological weapons in combination with the activation of deeply rooted fears predict that strong psychological and physiological responses will occur.

The immediate stressors associated with a biological terrorist attack are the threat and the consequences of infection. The specific nature of these stressors will depend on the organism or toxin used. Characteristics such as the incubation period and the virulence and toxicity of the agent will contribute to the psychological impact. The process of seeking and receiving immunization or treatment is potentially stressful.

One can anticipate that there will be acute and chronic psychiatric casualties as in other disasters.[3-6] While the majority of people do not develop long-term psychiatric sequelae following disasters, certain groups are at higher risk (e.g., the previously traumatized, those without social supports, and first responders, such as police and emergency medical personnel). Biological agents may cause mental disorders due to toxins or infectious conditions such as viral encephalitis or bacterial meningitis. Illness and injury secondary to the attack increase the risk of the development of acute stress disorder and posttraumatic stress disorder, as well as depression and bereavement in survivors.[7-8] Psychiatric disability is a likely chronic outcome of biological attack. The incidence and prevalence of such problems remain a matter of speculation, although past occurrences can be used to anticipate consequences. Experiences with chemical weapons used by terrorists have demonstrated that psychiatric casualties are likely.[9]

The psychiatric sequelae will depend on the nature of and the response to the assault. In contrast to explosive or chemical weapons, biological weapons may not produce instantaneously horrifying results. (An exception to this might be the use of a biological toxin that kills quickly and with frightening manifestations, such as seizures or suffocation.)

As the attack is discovered and the media reports the news, exposed and unexposed individuals may experience acute autonomic arousal. Signs and symptoms of muscle tension, tachycardia, rapid breathing (perhaps hyperventilation), sweating, tremor, and a sense of foreboding are likely to generate health concerns. These signs and symptoms may be misattributed to infection or intoxication. The acutely stressed and symptomatic individuals will add complexity and additional patients for triage during the initial phase of the crisis. However, if initial triage and management are successful, the risk for the development of psychiatric problems can be minimized.

Forensic issues involved in the medical response influence psychological responses and treatment options. Preservation of evidence maximizes the possibility of the perpetrators' being punished. The perception that justice is ultimately served can have a very positive psychological impact on those exposed and society. Some survivors may be critical witnesses in future legal actions. This may have little consequence for immediate lifesaving care, but it might prompt the selection of psychotropic drugs that minimally interfere with recall or discourage the use of a technique, like hypnosis, that can potentially damage the future credibility of a witness report.

Acute Intervention Following a Biological Attack

Rapid, accurate triage and effective treatment (or immunization) will be the cornerstones of initial management. Distinguishing symptoms of hyperarousal from those of intoxication and infectious disease prodromes will be crucial. The type of exposure and any lack of complete information about the agent will increase uncertainty and the risk of psychiatric morbidity. The risk for secondary psychological trauma will increase if actions by leaders or helpers fail to provide a quick, accurate diagnosis, a sensitive process for communicating the nature of the risk, and a supportive environment for those exposed and their families.

An attitude of expectation that those with hyperarousal or demoralization will soon return to normal activities should be conveyed. Patients should be moved out of the patient role as quickly as possible. Diazepamlike anxiolytics may be helpful in reducing anxiety for patients who do not respond to reassurance. The assignment of simple work tasks that facilitate the care of other patients can help restore function to the psychological casualties. The recovery environment should be constructed to create a sense of safety and to counteract the helplessness induced by the terrorist act.[10]

A well-organized, effective medical response contributes to the creation of a supportive environment and accurate data for the at-risk population. Individuals can assess their risk and determine the actions that they can take to reduce the risk. Ideally, risk information should involve dialogue. Dialogue lets the at-risk population define the information that they need, and it enables the community leaders to assess their effectiveness in communicating the appropriate data. Failure to provide a public forum for information exchanges may actually increase anxiety and misunderstanding and amplify health concerns since individuals will tend to attribute autonomic symptoms to catastrophic illness. One consequence of appraisal error may be disabling somatic complaints offered in a setting where failure to find a medical or surgical disease is experienced as stigmatizing and sadistic by the patients. In this situation, the patient's life may become focused on an unending search for an "acceptable" diagnosis.[11-13]

Implications of Psychological Reactions for the Medical System

Following a biological terrorist attack, physical injury, disruption of daily communal routine, and increased use of public health facilities could place overwhelming demands on the medical systems.[14] Feelings of helplessness and hopelessness could be increased if the rescue and postdisaster medical efforts appear to be failing.[15] Angry, intense competition for available but limited resources can generate even more societal disruption and casualties. The belief that treatment will be provided to some but not to others will contribute to the possibility of social disruptions such as riot or panic. Panic will be a particular risk when biological agents are used to threaten or to attack a sizable civilian population.[16] Demoralization can also be a response to the predicaments presented by a biological attack. Demoralized individuals often lose their sense of social and group responsibilities and roles. If major community institutions fail to provide protection, citizens can lose faith in the ideological metaphors that bind the community together. In this way, demoralization can increase isolation and feelings of hopelessness. In this complex setting, some are likely to manifest psychiatric symptoms. Given the stigma attached to psychiatric illness and the fact that the individuals who manifest them are more likely to have been injured and to have been exposed to multiple infectious, environmental, and toxicological risks, the diagnostic and therapeutic dilemmas will be quite difficult.[17-18]

Quarantine requires the development of a specialized environment that will limit exposure to secondary infections. The creation of such an environment may disrupt social supports that reduce the postexposure risk of stress-induced disorders. It can create a situation characterized by separation from friends and family, isolation, and a sense of stigmatization. Prior planning can ensure that modern communication technology (telephone, television, and computer Internet connection) can be used to mitigate these untoward effects by providing ongoing contact with families and others in the community outside quarantine. The maintenance of contact between parents and children is particularly important for the children. This may result in putting unexposed adult caregivers in quarantine.

Additional stressors may arise from the mundane logistical demands associated with managing mass contamination and infection. One of the difficulties in the Japanese sarin attack was undressing patients and disposing of their clothing.[9] Obtaining the necessary shower facilities for a large number of exposed survivors may be problematic. The provision of privacy and assurance of conventional modesty may have to be sacrificed. It should not be forgotten that privacy and modesty are important to maintaining an individual's sense of control and autonomy. The imposition of special requirements such as public bathing should be accompanied by an explanation that attributes this undesirable demand to the terrorist attacker.

Disaster responders and medical personnel also will have to contend with their own psychological reactions. One of the terrorist's goals is to provoke intense emotions that interfere with the capacity of caregivers to react in a thoughtful, organized fashion. A biological attack using a highly infectious and virulent organism (e.g., anthrax), dispersed in a fine spray, poses special stressors. Medical responders may be required to work in protective clothing and masks ("moon suits"). This barrier protection will make the care of patients more difficult and increase the risk of heat, fatigue, and isolation stress for medical personnel.[19-20] It will be important to establish work-rest schedules and to limit the exposure of medical and rescue personnel to the grotesque and the dead.

Planning and Preparation

Disaster plans for managing a biological attack must be developed and realistic training provided to ensure effective response to an actual terrorist event. These plans must assume that emotional and psychiatric problems will occur in the unexposed population as well as the exposed. The exercises should be carried out with sufficient realism, so that the process of disrobing and showering is practiced in real time. Medical responders will need training to recognize the symptoms of anxiety, depression, and dissociation. It is critical that psychological responses be managed in ways that facilitate the triage, diagnosis, and treatment of those exposed or infected.[21] Such plans need to include strategies for prevention and mitigation of stress for survivors as well as for those responding to the crisis and its consequences. Debriefing, commonly used by emergency personnel following trauma, has been used to mitigate the effects of severe stress and can be helpful in identifying individuals who may need further assistance. Results from controlled studies of debriefing are only now beginning to become available.[22-23] These studies will help clarify the role of intervention in the alleviation of pain, prevention of disability, return to social involvement, and the prevention of disease. Ironically, should a highly infectious agent be used, bringing people together for a debriefing may be contraindicated. Perhaps "teledebriefing" (analogous to telemedicine) is a technology that could be developed for such situations.

Communicating Risk to the Public

The communication of the risk to individuals following a bacteriologic attack will critically affect how communities and individuals respond.[24-28] The media coverage and behavior of public officials can contribute to the stress and precipitate panic or demoralization, particularly if inaccurate, confusing, or contradictory information is provided to the public. Rumors must be anticipated, monitored, and corrected with accurate information.[17] Any damage to public trust at the beginning of the crisis ensures that distrust will continue throughout the crisis. There are psychological and physiological costs attendant to the loss of trust.

For example, the handling of information by officials and the media during the release of nuclear radiation at Three Mile Island became a major source of anxiety and stress for people living in the vicinity of the nuclear facility. At Three Mile Island, there were no casualties or severely injured individuals. The stress was fear and uncertainty about exposure to excess radioactivity, loss of faith in local authorities and those managing operations of the reactor, and financial uncertainties.[29] Baum followed individuals at the Three Mile Island site and at 3 control sites for 10 years.[29] He found evidence of chronic arousal as indicated by elevated norepinephrine and epinephrine in some individuals.

Conclusion

Governmental and private agencies should develop detailed strategies for responding to a biological terrorist attack that include consideration of the psychological and social impact of such an attack. Inattention to the phenomenon of terror and its consequences for individuals, institutions, and society jeopardizes the efficacy of disaster mitigation efforts. Leaders, scientists, and the media should develop protocols covering a broad range of scenarios that communicate accurate information about risk and diminish rumors. These primary prevention efforts will be critical in preventing panic and demoralization in the attacked community. The possible forensic responsibilities of first responders should receive appropriate consideration when collecting data and preparing for future action that will determine responsibility for the attack.

Realistic training for biological attacks should include the probability of large numbers of psychological casualties. Training exercises should be designed to test cooperation and coordination between organizations as well as test first responders and hospital staff. Hospital accrediting bodies should encourage medical facilities to incorporate biological scenarios into their annual training.

Planning and preparation for biological attacks and their attendant psychological consequences can diminish the terrorists' ability to achieve their overall goal—the induction of terror. Education of the public and institutional preparedness can mitigate the horror of terrorism. The media could play an active prevention role by realistically educating the public about the impact of terrorist attacks with biological weapons. Such preparation efforts should be given high priority.

References

1. US Congress, Office of Technology Assessment. *Technology Against Terrorism: The Federal Effort.* Washington, DC: Government Printing Office; 1991. Publication OTA-ISC-481.

2. Flanagin A, Lederberg J. The threat of biological weapons: prophylaxis and mitigation: call for papers. *JAMA.* 1996;276:419-420.

3. Ursano RJ, Fullerton CS, Norwood AE. Psychiatric dimensions of disaster: patient care, community consultation, and preventive medicine. *Ham Rev Psychiatry.* 1995;3:196-200.

4. Ursano RJ, Rundell JR. Psychological problems of prisoners of war: the trauma of a toxic and contained environment. In: Ursano RJ, ed. *Individual Response to Disaster.* Bethesda, Md: Uniformed Services University of the Health Sciences; 1988:79-112. Publication DTIC: A203310.

5. Ursano RJ, Fullerton CS, McCaughey BG. Trauma and disaster. In: Ursano RJ, McCaughey BG, Fullerton CS, eds. *Individual and Community Responses to Trauma and Disaster: The Structure of Human Chaos.* Cambridge, England: Cambridge University Press; 1994:3-27.

6. Weisaeth L. War-related psychopathology in Kuwait: an assessment of war-related mental health problems. In: Fullerton CS, Ursano RJ, eds. *Posttraumatic Stress Disorder: Acute and Long-Term Responses to Trauma and Disaster.* Washington, DC: American Psychiatric Press; 1997:91-122.

7. *American Psychiatric Association. Diagnostic and Statistical Manual of Mental Disorders,* Fourth Edition. Washington, DC: American Psychiatric Association; 1994.

8. Shalev A. Posttraumatic stress disorder among injured survivors of a terrorist attack: predictive value of early intrusion and avoidance symptoms. *Nero Ment Dis.* 1992;180:505-509.

9. Okumura T. Takasu N, Ishimatsu S, et al. Report on the 640 victims of the Tokyo subway sarin attack. *Ann Emerg Med.* 1996;28:129-135.

10. Raphael B, Wilson J, Meldrum L, McFarlane AC. Acute preventive interventions. In: van der Kolk B, McFarlane AC, Weisaeth L, eds. *Traumatic Stress: The Effects of Overwhelming Experience on Mind, Body, and Society.* New York, NY: Guilford Press; 1996:463-479.

11. Kassirer JP. Our stubborn quest for diagnostic certainty. *NEngUMed.* 1989;320:1489-1491.

12. Schwartz SP, White PE, Hughes RF. Environmental threats, communities, and hysteria. *J Public Health Policy.* 19S5;6:S8-T7.

13. Blackwell B, De Morgan NP. The primary care of patients who have bodily concerns. *Arch Fam Med.* 1996;5:457-463.

14. Relationship of mustard agent and lewisite exposure to psychological dysfunction. In: Pechura CM, Rail DP, eds. *Veterans at Risk.* Washington, DC: National Academy Press; 1993.

15. Ursano RJ, Fullerton CS, eds. *Performance and Operations in Toxic Environments.* Bethesda, Md: Uniformed Services University of the Health Sciences; 1988. Publication DTIC: A203162.

16. Russell PK. Biologic terrorism: responding to the threat. *Emerg Infect Dis* [serial online]. 1997; 3. Accessed June 26, 1997. Available at: http://www.cdc.gov/ncidod/E ID/eid.htm.

17. Ursano RJ, Fullerton CS, eds. *Individual and Group Behavior in Toxic and Contained Environments.* Bethesda, Md: Uniformed Services University of the Health Sciences; 1988. Publication DTIC: A203267.

18. Fullerton CS, Ursano RJ. Behavioral and psychological responses to toxic exposure. In: Ursano R J, ed. *Individual Response to Disaster.* Bethesda, Md:

Uniformed Services University of the Health Sciences; 1988:113-128. Publication DTIC: A203310.

19. Fullerton CS, Ursano RJ. Health care delivery in the high-stress environment of chemical and biological warfare. *Mil Med.* 1994;159:524-528.

20. Fullerton CS, Ursano RJ, Kao T, Bhartiya V. The chemical and biological warfare environment psychological responses and social support in a high-stress environment. *Appl Soc Psychol.* 1992;22:1608-1623.

21. Fullerton CS, Brandt GT, Ursano RJ. Chemical and biological weapons: silent agents of terror. In: Ursano RJ, Norwood AE, eds. *Emotional Aftermath of the Persian Gulf War: Veterans, Families, Communities, and Nations.* Washington, DC: American Psychiatric Press; 1996:111-142.

22. Kenardy JA, Webster RA, Lewin TJ, Carr VJ, Hazell PL, Carter GL. Stress debriefing and patterns of recovery following a natural disaster. *J Trauma Stress.* 1996;9:37-49.

23. Raphel B, Meldrum L, McFarlane AC. Does debriefing after psychological trauma work? *BMJ.* 1995;310:1479-1480.

24. National Research Council. *Health Risks of Radon and Otlier Internally Deposited Alpha-emitters (BEIR IV).* Washington, DC: National Academy Press; 1988.

25. National Research Council. *Improving Risk Communication.* Washington, DC: National Academy Press; 1989.

26. National Research Council. *Risk Assessment in the Federal Government: Managing the Process.* Washington, DC: National Academy Press; 1983.

27. National Research Council. *Understanding Risk: Informing Decisions in a Democratic Society.* Washington, DC: National Academy Press; 1996.

28. Presidential Advisory Committee on Gulf War Veterans' Illness. *Presidential Advisory Committee on Gulf War Veterans' Illness: Final Report.* Washington, DC: US Government Printing Office; 1996.

29. Baum A. Stress, intrusive imagery, and chronic distress. *Health Psychol.* 1990;9:653-675.

Author Index

Subject Index

About the Editors

Jeff S. Erger, Ph.D., is an assistant professor of sociology at the University of Wisconsin–Eau Claire. He teaches courses on social psychology and medical sociology, among others. His research looks at the links between identity, community, and health. He rides his bicycles a lot, which is healthy other than when he ends up crashing down a mountain trail. Once a year he makes chocolate truffles that enslave all who dare taste them.

William D. Marelich, Ph.D., is an assistant professor of psychology at California State University–Fullerton. In addition to his current position, he remains a lecturer at UCLA and a consulting statistician with Health Risk Reduction Projects (affiliated with UCLA's Department. of Psychiatry/Integrated Substance Abuse Programs). His research interests include decision-making strategies in health and organizational settings, patient/provider interactions, interpersonal relationships, and statistical/methodological approaches in experimental and applied research. He surfs as a hobby for health and peace of mind.